LATIN AMERICA, ITS PROBLEMS AND ITS PROMISE

The Western Hemisphere
Reprinted, with permission, from Margaret Daley Hayes, *Latin America and the U.S. National Interest: A Basis for U.S. Foreign Policy* (Boulder, Colo.: Westview Press, 1984).

Second Edition

LATIN AMERICA, ITS PROBLEMS AND ITS PROMISE

A MULTIDISCIPLINARY INTRODUCTION

edited by
Jan Knippers Black

MONTEREY INSTITUTE
OF INTERNATIONAL STUDIES

Westview Press
BOULDER • SAN FRANCISCO • OXFORD

Photo Credits: The photographs in Chapter 8 were taken by Mary Grizzard. The collages introducing each part were prepared from photographs taken by Jan Knippers Black.

Published in 1991 in the United States of America by Westview Press, Inc., 5500 Central Avenue, Boulder, Colorado 80301, and in the United Kingdom by Westview Press, 36 Lonsdale Road, Summertown, Oxford OX2 7EW

Library of Congress Cataloging-in-Publication Data
Latin America, its problems and its promise : a multidisciplinary
    introduction / edited by Jan Knippers Black. — 2. ed.
        p.   cm.
    Includes bibliographical references and index.
    ISBN 0-8133-0904-2 (hardcover). — ISBN 0-8133-0905-0 (paperback)
    1. Latin America.   I. Black, Jan Knippers, 1940–
F1406.7.L38   1991
980—dc20   90-44422
                                                                       CIP

Printed and bound in the United States of America

∞ The paper used in this publication meets the requirements
    of the American National Standard for Permanence of Paper
    for Printed Library Materials Z39.48-1984.

10   9   8   7   6   5   4   3   2   1

To my parents
JUDGE OTTIS J. KNIPPERS
and
OPAL MOODY KNIPPERS
of Lawrenceburg, Tennessee

CONTENTS

PART EIGHT
CENTRAL AMERICA AND PANAMA

PART NINE
CUBA AND THE CARIBBEAN

PART TEN
THE ANDES

PART ELEVEN
THE SOUTHERN CONE

PART TWELVE
BRAZIL

MAPS, TABLES, FIGURES, AND ILLUSTRATIONS

Maps

Tables

Figures

Illustrations

1

INTRODUCTION: APPROACHES TO THE STUDY OF LATIN AMERICA

JAN KNIPPERS BLACK

To the student who must launch his or her exploration of Latin America through the eyes and ears, the assumptions and perspectives, and the theoretical and ideological filters of others, it would be useful to know something of the intellectual paths that have been traveled by the specialists in the field. Those paths have circled, dead-ended, and U-turned, merged and diverged; they are now, as always, subject to turns in new directions. The attempt to understand social relations, especially in an area so diverse and complex as Latin America, can never be a simple matter of learning "the facts." There will always be many facts in dispute; answers depend on the nature of available data, on the interests of the sources consulted, and on how questions are asked. Confronted, as one must be in a multi-authored text, with differing points of view and, thus, differing interpretations of the same historical and social data, the student may find it worthwhile to begin the study of Latin America with a study of Latin Americanists.

It is to be expected that interests and interpretations of social phenomena will vary from one discipline to another. The geographer may find, for example, that soil quality, climate, and topography determine settlement patterns and socioeconomic relations, which in turn configure political systems. The anthropologist may find explanation for social harmony or social conflict in ethnic and cultural patterns. The economist may find that political trends derive from economic ones, while the political scientist may see power relationships as overriding. In the study of Latin America, however, there has always been a unifying theme.

From the perspectives of U.S.- and European-based scholars, as well as from those of Latin America's own creative and scholarly writers, the study of Latin America has been approached as the study of a problem, or set of problems. The problems might be capsulized as underdevelopment and political instability or, more simply, as poverty or inequality and the failure of democratic systems to take hold. The search for the roots, causes, and progenitors of these problems has generally led in one of three directions: to the Iberians—the conquistadores and the institutions, attitudes, and cultural traits they brought with them to the New World; to the Latin Americans themselves—the alleged greed of the elites, absence of entrepreneurship in the middle classes, or passivity of the masses; or to the United States and the international capitalist system it promotes and defends.

Long before U.S. scholars began to direct their attention to Latin America's problems, the area's own intellectuals were absorbed by the question of where to place the blame. Domingo Faustino Sarmiento and other nineteenth-century intellectual and political leaders of cosmopolitan Buenos Aires blamed the cycles of anarchy and tyranny their newly independent country was suffering on Hispanic influences.[1] Sarmiento in later life directed his scorn toward Latin America's own "melting pot." Influenced by social Darwinism, he diagnosed "the decadent state" of Argentine society as deriving from its racial components of Spanish, mestizo, Indian, and Negro.

Turning the tables at the turn of the twentieth century, José Enrique Rodó, Uruguay's foremost literary figure, urged the youth of his country—in his masterpiece, *Ariel*—to shun the materialism of the United States and to cling to the spiritual and intellectual values of their Spanish heritage. A strong current of Latin American social thought, reflected in art and music as well as literature, that gained momentum a few decades into the twentieth century has touted the strengths of native American cultures and blamed both Hispanic and North American influences for the prevailing instability and social injustice. Likewise, in the Caribbean, the Black Power movements of the sixties and seventies called Europe and Anglo-America to task for the region's underdevelopment.

Latin American studies as an interdisciplinary field in the United States and, by extension, the coming of age of analysis of Latin American social and political systems are clearly the illegitimate offspring of Fidel Castro. Prior to the Cuban Revolution, historians, anthropologists, and literary scholars had generally pursued their studies of Latin American subjects in disciplinary isolation. Political analysis had been largely limited to formal-legal studies highlighting the·fact that Latin American regimes rarely lived up to the standards, borrowed from France and the United States, embodied in their constitutions. Such studies generally drew their explanatory theses from the distinctive historical and cultural traditions of the United States of North America and the disunited states of Latin America and, in so doing, contributed to the mystification of the political process in both areas.[2] The Iberian heritage of feudalism, authoritarianism, and Catholicism was seen as the major obstacle to democratic and socioeconomic reforms.

The surge of interest in Latin America on the part of U.S. politicians and academics (encouraged by newly available government-funded fellowships and contracts) that accompanied the Cuban Revolution followed closely upon the expansion of attention to the Third World generally by the previously parochial disciplines of economics and political science. Thus, development and modernization theory, formulated to address change processes in other parts of the Third World, came to dominate the study of Latin America as well. Studies falling under these rubrics generally posited that either the economic and political systems of Latin America would increasingly approximate those of the United States and Western Europe or the area would be engulfed in violent revolution.

The invalidation of many of the assumptions of development and modernization theorists by the onrush of events—particularly by the fall of democratic regimes and their replacement by military dictatorships—resulted in a theoretical backlash as well as in long overdue attention to the work of Latin American theorists. The backlash was expressed in a reassertion of the tenacity of tradition, of the fundamentally conservative character of Latin American society. This perspective has been endowed with greater theoretical and conceptual sophistication in studies using the corporatist model. Corporatism stresses the hierarchical organization of modern institutions and the persistence of control from the top.

There existed a large body of literature by Latin Americans, dating back to "the black legend" of Spanish rule, to support the historical and cultural explanations for the failure of democracy. But the trends that had dominated the social sciences in the major Latin American countries were variations on the Marxist themes of class conflict and imperialism. One such body of thought, known as dependency theory, has come to rival development and modernization theory for predominance among U.S. specialists in Latin American studies. Dependency theory assumes that Latin American underdevelopment cannot be understood without reference to the international capitalist system.

These theoretical trends and approaches have permeated all aspects of Latin American studies, because—to a far greater extent than in Europe or the United States—philosophy, literature, the arts, and other pursuits of the intelligentsia in Latin America tend to reflect national or regional concerns. It could hardly be otherwise; the cataclysmic episodes of insurgency and repression, revolution and counterrevolution, leave no one untouched.

BLAMING THE IBERIANS:
CORPORATISM AND CULTURE

The historical-cultural approach to the study of Latin America and its problems draws attention to the persistence in contemporary Latin America of attitudes, institutions, and social relations that are said to have been characteristic of the Iberian peninsula in medieval times.[3] According to this view, the Spanish conquistadores, crown officials, and Roman Catholic missionaries transplanted in the New World a social system firmly based on elitism, authoritarianism, and militarism.

The Portuguese legacy differed from that of Spain in its greater tolerance of racial and cultural diversity, but, like the Spanish, the Portuguese inculcated in their New World offspring a rigid sense of social, political, and cultural hierarchy. The patriarchal view, deriving from Iberian monarchism, held that culture and personality were functions of education and that the uneducated man was incapable of participating in the dominant political culture. (That women, educated or otherwise, were to be seen but not heard was taken for granted.) The uneducated man was expected to accept his status in society as a function of a divinely ordered hierarchy. However, as the uneducated were not expected to be responsible for their own welfare, the dominant class was obligated to contribute to the amelioration of their suffering. Public morality was an integral part of the political culture, and the Catholic Church, also hierarchical in structure, absolutist in doctrine, and authoritarian in practice, shared with the institutions of government the responsibility for the maintenance of the political and moral order.

During the early colonial period, a great debate raged among intellectuals and governmental and spiritual leaders in Spain and its colonies as to whether native Americans were fully human. It was finally concluded that the Church's Christianizing mission implied recognition of the fundamental human attributes of the Indians. But in much of the empire, the slaughter or enslavement of the Indians proceeded nevertheless, and it is clear that many contemporary Latin Americans continue to see the Indians as belonging to a lesser order of humanity.

Corporatism

The corporatist model, drawn primarily from medieval Catholic thought and observed, to some degree, in Spain under Franco and Portugal under Salazar, has been found to "fit" contemporary Latin American politics to a greater degree than some of the models derived from development and modernization theory. The model, elaborated in works by Wiarda, Schmitter, Malloy, Erickson, and others, has called attention to the tendency to vertical, as opposed to horizontal, organization among politically active groups in Latin America.[4] Such groups, in corporatist systems, are controlled and manipulated by authoritarian governments so that communications and power flow from the top down rather than from the bottom up.

Corporatist forms of organization are easily identifiable in a number of Latin American countries, but they have been particularly well studied in Brazil. Under Brazil's Estado Novo (New State), a dictatorial system imposed by Getúlio Vargas in the late 1930s, institutions and interest groups were required to secure government "recognition." The government's power of recognition thus made all formal groups dependent. Such means of manipulation were retained and refined by the military government that ruled Brazil from 1964 to 1985.

Few Latin Americanists would dispute the observation that vestiges of medieval Iberia are still to be found in Latin America. Nor is the existence of corporatist tendencies a subject of great controversy. The point at which many Latin Americanists depart from the findings of some scholars pursuing historical-cultural or corporatist approaches is the supposition that contemporary manifestations of elitism and authoritarianism are due primarily to colonization by Spain and Portugal.

Critics note, for example, that some countries recently under fiercely authoritarian, military rule (Chile and Uruguay, for example) had enjoyed constitutional and more or less democratic rule throughout most of the twentieth century. Furthermore, the Southern Cone (Argentina, Uruguay, and Chile) was among the areas least influenced by colonial Spain. In Argentina, descendants of Italian immigrants, who arrived in great waves around the turn of the twentieth century, now outnumber the descendants of Spanish settlers. Surely some common denominators of vintage more recent than the colonial period are needed to explain the resurgence of authoritarianism in Latin America in the late twentieth century.

In addition, corporatism has tended to remain descriptive—a model rather than a body of theory—and its contribution to explanation of social and political change is limited. For those of its elaborators who attribute its workings to the institutions and experiences peculiar to the Iberian peninsula, the larger perspective afforded by models and theories applicable to all countries and regions is lost. The parallels, for example, between the co-optative practices of right-wing authoritarian regimes in Iberia and Ibero-America and the practices of authoritarian regimes elsewhere in countries with comparable levels of economic development have generally been over-looked. And the qualitative difference between traditional corporatism and the modern bureaucratic-technocratic variety has often been understated. By the end of the 1980s, the popularity of the corporatist paradigm appeared to be waning, and some of its former proponents, including Howard Wiarda, had turned to an emphasis on cultural causation.

Cultural Causation

The late 1980s saw a revival of interest in the explanatory power of culture as an independent variable. Samuel Huntington, noting that contemporary concepts of modernization and of Westernization are beginning to diverge, suggests that development and modernization may be distinctively Western goals. He alleges that aspirations to wealth, equity, democracy, stability, and autonomy emerge from Western, particularly Nordic, experience, and that other cultures may prefer simplicity, austerity, hierarchy, authoritarianism, discipline, and militarism.[5] This view represents a considerable retreat for a theorist who once believed Western-style modernization to be irresistible.

BLAMING THE LATIN AMERICANS: DEVELOPMENT AND MODERNIZATION THEORY

Whereas analyses of contemporary Latin America based on the traditional, or historical-cultural, approach tended to have a static quality, development and modernization theory introduced a new dynamism into the field. The new approach highlighted the facts that for better or worse, social change was indeed under way and that to a great extent, that change was in response or in reaction to the spread of the ideas and technologies of the more industrialized world, primarily the United States and Western Europe, to the Third World.

The body of thought that came to be known as development and/or modernization theory—terms often used interchangeably—was pioneered primarily by U.S. scholars in the late 1950s and the first half of the 1960s. In economics, development theory presumed that with the infusion of capital and the acquisition of business skills, and with the advantage of not having to reinvent the wheel, the nations that had yet to experience their industrial revolutions would pass at an accelerated pace along paths already broken by Western Europe and the United States. Walt W. Rostow further assumed that economic development, at least beyond a stage he called "take-off," was irreversible.[6]

From the perspective of anthropologists and sociologists, "modernization" generally meant the ingestion of the supposedly Western attitudinal traits of rationalism, instrumentalism, achievement orientation, and the like. Sociologist Daniel Lerner asserted in 1965 that social change everywhere was a function of the number of individuals who adopted the attitude and behavior patterns associated with modernity.[7]

This approach stressed the felicitous consequences of the spread of modern communications media, of education in science and the liberal arts, and of technology transfer. And it implied that Third World societies could (and should) become developed through the accelerated absorption of individuals into the middle class or the modern industrial sector.

Political scientists borrowed liberally from the other social sciences, often without seeming to notice that in their extreme formulations these theories amounted to a virtual denial of the stuff of their own discipline: power relationships. Political scientists did, however, add their own set of indices of development and/or modernization to those compiled by scholars of other disciplines. Gabriel Almond, for example, stressed structural differentiation (the elaboration of economic and political roles), whereas Samuel Huntington stressed the strengthening of political institutions.[8] Other scholars focused on participation, egalitarianism, and governmental capability. Some assumed that such attributes were mutually reinforcing. Huntington, however, seeing expanding participation in the absence of institutionalization as destabilizing, stressed the importance of stability.

These trends in the social sciences coincided with the Cuban Revolution and thus with the Alliance for Progress and the emergence of interdisciplinary programs in Latin American studies. Development came to be one of the major goals of the Alliance for Progress; the other was security—the prevention of "another Cuba." These goals were deemed to be interdependent; it was rarely imagined that they might be contradictory. The few critical voices, such as that of Albert O. Hirschman, who argued that popular pressure, sometimes assuming violent form, was essential to the achievement of reform, were generally ignored.[9] The prevailing view, that "unrest" was an impediment to progress and had to be contained by strengthened security forces, won out in academic as well as in governmental circles until a wave of military takeovers forced a reevaluation.

Critics of development and modernization theory have pointed out that its adherents often emitted an optimism bordering on euphoria. Huntington had said that "modernization is not only inevitable, it is also desirable."[10] Such positivistic assumptions, that what was good was inevitable and vice versa, had predictable consequences for analysis. Researchers were inclined either to see what they wanted to see or to label whatever they saw as progress. Economists, for example, measured development by using aggregate data on the growth of gross national product or per capita income, data that were blind to the skewed distribution of income. While U.S. economists lavished praise on Brazil's "economic miracle," Brazil's own dictator, General Emilio Garrastazú Médici, commented in 1970 that "the economy is doing fine, but the people aren't."[11]

Critics have also argued that many of the supposed attributes of modernism are not even characteristic of the industrialized countries, much less of what they project to or promote in the Third World. Nor do the undeniable influences of the so-called developed countries necessarily contribute to the kind of development desired by leaders and peoples of the so-called under-developed ones. Technology transfer, for example, has generally meant a transition from labor-intensive to capital-intensive industry in areas where labor markets are glutted and capital is scarce.

A tendency common to much of the work based on development and modernization theory was a peculiar sort of ethnocentricity based on an idealized and class-delimited national or North Atlantic self-image. The terminology employed in such work, for example, was often charged with unacknowledged value judgments. All cultures other than our own, from a sophisticated ancient civilization such as China's to a preliterate society of nomads, were lumped together under the single epithet "traditional." Such terms as "secularism" and "rationalism" were sometimes defined as openness to the scientific and technological, accompanied by rejection of the religious and ideological, but there was the thinly veiled implication that they referred to the thought processes of clear-headed folks like us. If Latin Americans and other peoples of the Third World had failed to achieve development or modernization, it was assumed to be because they lacked our industriousness and had failed to see their own problems as clearly as we saw them. In effect, the blame for poverty and powerlessness was placed squarely on the poor and powerless.

There were those, of course, who used some of the concepts and models of the developmentalists but rejected such ethnocentric assumptions. Scholars of the period were not necessarily in accord as to which of the indices of development and modernization were most relevant and useful. Nevertheless, distinctions between value-free and value-laden concepts were rarely well drawn. The behavioralist tendency in the social sciences, which was also coming into its own in the 1960s, sharpened the inclination of social scientists, attempting to be "scientific," to hold acknowledged bias in disdain. Most scholars felt constrained to assert that their work was value free ("rigorous" was often a euphemism for unbiased). Thus, those scholars who argued that economic growth and stability were the most important indices of development and those who challenged that redistribution of wealth and the expansion of political participation were more important tended to maintain the pretense that they were arguing over facts rather than over values.

Recognizing many of these problems, Martin C. Needler, one of the Latin Americanists who made important contributions to development theory, observed that there was nothing inevitable about political development, that such development was only one of many possible outcomes of ongoing political conflict. His own definition of political development in the democratic era had two dimensions: the maintenance of constitutional integrity and the maximization of participation on terms of equality. Yet the requirements of constitutionality and participation were in conflict with each other, a conflict that could only be resolved by steady economic growth. In the absence of such growth, Needler wrote, increasing "social mobilization" (popular awareness and organization) and participation have a destabilizing effect on democratic political systems, which results in the imposition of authoritarianism.[12]

Although the development approach is now out of vogue, most of the work done in the 1980s, including that of critics pursuing newer trends, such as dependency, was built in some ways on the ideas and the findings of a generation of development and modernization theorists. Meanwhile, some of the theorists once attracted to that paradigm have become persuaded by the arguments of dependency theory; others, more recently, have been drawn to the premise that the more important relationship between peoples of First and Third Worlds is one of interdependence.

BLAMING THE UNITED STATES: DEPENDENCY AND RELATED THEORIES

Brazilian political scientist Fernando Henrique Cardoso, one of the originators of dependency theory, once responded to the question, "What is dependency?" by saying, "It's what you call imperialism if you don't want to lose your Ford Foundation grant." More precisely, as Susanne Bodenheimer Jonas has noted, dependency refers to the perspective from "below," whereas the Marxist theory of imperialism provides the perspective from "above."[13] As the Marxist theory of imperialism seeks to explain why and how the dominant classes of the dominant capitalist powers expand their spheres of exploitation and political control, dependency theory examines what this relationship of unequal bargaining and multilayered exploitation means to the dominated classes in the dominated countries.

Like most of the other trends and perspectives that have been designated theory, dependency by no means refers to an integrated set of if-then propositions. Rather, it is a focus of inquiry and a body of thought built upon common assumptions. Unlike the behavioral approach that has held sway over most aspects of social science in the United States since the mid-1960s, dependency is unabashedly normative. Its impulse derives largely from the attempts of the United Nations Economic Commission for Latin America (ECLA), under the leadership of Argentine economist Raúl Prebisch, to understand and counteract such problems as the deterioration in the terms of trade for producers of primary (nonindustrial) products. A renewed awareness of economic exploitation and dependency followed upon disillusionment with industrialization through import substitution, Latin American economic integration, and other solutions proposed by ECLA. Thus, a number of Latin American political scientists and sociologists, including Brazilians Cardoso and Teotonio dos Santos and Chilean Osvaldo Sunkel, renewed their efforts to explain patterns of social class structure and predict the structural changes that are inherent in the process of capitalist development in a dependent state. This new focus derived in part from a recognition that the form of this exploitative relationship was constantly subject to change and that the consequences of the industrialization of the periphery—that is, the Third World—through the medium of multinational corporations had not been adequately addressed by previously prevalent theories.

Cardoso noted that "if these studies do in fact have any power of attraction at all, it is not merely because they propose a methodology to substitute for a previously existing paradigm or because they open up a new set of themes. It is principally because they do this from a radically critical viewpoint." He added, "In these analyses, therefore, there is no presumption of scientific 'neutrality.' "[14] In other words, although dependency theorists attempt to be scientific in method, they freely admit that their purposes in pursuing such studies are political: to promote fundamental change in the existing economic and political order.

Among the assumptions that underpin dependency theory are the following. First, the distribution of power and status in national and international arenas is ultimately determined by economic relationships. Second, the causes of underdevelopment are not to be found in national systems alone but must be sought in the pattern of economic relations between hegemonic, or dominant, powers and their client states. The perpetuation of the pattern of inequality within client states is managed by a clientele class, which might be seen as the modern functional equivalent of a formal colonial apparatus. Third, both within and among states, the unfettered forces of the marketplace tend to exacerbate rather than to mitigate existing inequalities. That is, the dominant foreign power benefits at the expense of its client states, and the clientele class benefits at the expense of other classes.

Implicit in these assumptions are the convictions that development will not take place through the "trickle-down" of wealth nor through the gradual diffusion of modern attitudes and modern technology; that the upward mobility of individuals expressed by their gradual absorption into the modern sector is no solution to the problem of the impoverishment of the masses; and that stability is no virtue in a system of pronounced inequality. In fact, most dependency theorists, or, in Spanish, *dependentistas,* believe that only by breaking out of the international capitalist system and establishing socialist regimes will Latin American nations gain control over their own decision making and expand the options available to them.[15]

Dependency theorists reject the notion that national industrialists could lead the process of capitalist development in the contemporary underdeveloped nations as they did in Europe and the United States and the notion that the dependent countries could be expected to experience the stages of development that characterized the process in the centers of capitalist expansion. Whereas modernization and development theorists see foreign investment and foreign aid as critical to development in the Third World, *dependentistas* see such investment and aid as means of extracting capital from client states. *Dependentistas* would probably agree with the observation of U.S. Congressman Dante Fascell (D-Florida) that aid is a means whereby the poor of the rich countries contribute to the rich of the poor countries. They might also add that aid is yet another means whereby the poor of the rich countries contribute to the rich of the *rich* countries.

Some dependency theorists have suggested that the expansion of capitalism in a dependent state can lead only to stagnation. Andre Gunder Frank, for example, comparing the experiences of the Latin American states during World War I and the depression of the 1930s with their experiences during periods when the links were stronger between those states and the industrialized West, hypothesized in 1970 that satellites, or client states, experience their greatest industrial development when their ties to the more developed states are weakest. Other scholars, noting, for example, the industrial expansion of Brazil in the late 1960s and early 1970s, maintain that rapid industrial growth may take place under conditions of dependency. There is general agreement, however, that to the extent that economic growth takes place under conditions of dependency, it is a distorted pattern of growth that exacerbates existing inequalities among both classes and regions within client states.

In general, however, although dependency has provided a very useful macrotheoretical perspective, Cardoso notes that it has generated relatively impoverished political analysis. Like development theory, dependency theory has been limited by an excessive reliance on aggregate data and a "black box" approach—which treats nations like black boxes, shedding no light on internal dynamics or relationships. Such an approach deals with the outcome of unequal relations between nations but fails to facilitate case-by-case studies of the political mechanisms whereby dependent relationships are perpetuated.

Furthermore, in assigning primacy to economic relationships, *dependentistas* tend to give short shrift to other factors, such as the pursuit of institutional, or bureaucratic, interests, which may have an important bearing upon relations between dominant powers and client states and upon relations among political actors within client states. And in focusing upon international capitalism as the cause of inequities within and among states, the approach contributes little to an understanding of the similarities in relationships, for example, between the United States and Latin American countries and, until the late 1980s, between the Soviet Union and its East European client states.

Penetration Theory and Bureaucratic Authoritarianism

Other approaches that share many of the assumptions of dependency theory but that serve to elaborate or refine our understanding of politics in dependent states include penetration theory and the model of bureaucratic authoritarianism. Penetration theory seeks to identify the means whereby a dominant foreign power influences policy in a client state not only directly, through diplomatic pressures, but also indirectly, through the manipulation of political competition within the client state.[16] Bureaucratic authoritarianism, according to Argentine political scientist Guillermo O'Donnell, who coined the phrase, is the likely outcome of social and economic modernization in the context of delayed, or dependent, development. Such impersonal, institutional dictatorship is not a vestige of the feudalistic rule imposed by Spain or Portugal but rather a response to a perceived threat to the capitalist system. According to O'Donnell, the levels of coercion and of economic orthodoxy that are imposed depend upon the level of perceived threat.[17]

The Center-Periphery Model

The relationships hypothesized or described by dependency theorists have been incorporated by Norwegian scholar Johan Galtung into a model of elegant simplicity.[18] According to the center-periphery model, elites of the center, or metropolis, draw bounty from the periphery of their own state system (through taxes, for example), which they devote to the nurture and support of co-opted elites of client or "peripheral" states. In turn, elites of those client states, dependent upon elites of the center for assistance in exploiting and suppressing their own peripheral, or nonelite, populations, have no choice but to allow center elites to participate in, or share in the product of, the exploitation of the peripheral peoples of the peripheral states.

World Systems Theory

World systems theory, pioneered by Immanuel Wallerstein, also views the world economy as segmented into core and periphery areas.[19] Rather than focusing on the interactions of governments, however, this approach calls attention to the transnational interactions of nonstate actors, particularly multinational corporations and banks. The international economy is said to be driven by the initiatives of economic elites, particularly of the developed capitalist states, whose governments normally do their bidding. The control centers of the world economy then are financial rather than political capitals. The farther one lives from such a center, the less the "trickle down" of its wealth will be experienced.

Wallerstein, who sees the ideas of *dependentistas* as falling within the world system perspective, takes issue with more traditional Marxists and liberals alike for what he calls a rigidly developmentalist approach. That is, both schools assume that each nation-state must pass through the same set of stages, or modes of extracting surplus, in the same order. As he sees it, the nation-state system, which came into being in part as a convenience to economic elites of an earlier era, has ceased to be the essential institutional base of the global economy. The contemporary struggle, then, is not between rich and poor states, but rather between rich and poor classes in a global society.

SEEKING COMMON GROUND

None of the approaches, models, and theories discussed in this chapter has a monopoly on "truth," and none wholly excludes the others. The differences among them are largely differences of perspective, emphasis, and value judgment. Adherents of development and modernization theory, like those of the historical-cultural approach, tend to focus on the attitudes of individuals and the behavior of institutions, though the former are more attuned to the indices of change whereas the latter more often stress continuity. Both pay tribute to the achievements of the modern West and deplore the antidemocratic influences of the Iberian tradition, but development and modernization theorists, more readily than historical-cultural analysts, see approximation to the Western model as a plausible solution.

Drawing explicitly on Marxist concepts, dependency theory looks to material interests and class conflict as well as to international patterns of trade, aid, and political control for explanations of political process at the national level. Thus, even when scholars of differing schools can agree as to what happened, they are likely to disagree as to why it happened. Whereas development and modernization theorists, for example, have generally viewed the public and private vehicles of U.S. influence as forces for democratic and social reform, dependency theorists have viewed them as antidemocratic and anti-egalitarian forces.

In the late 1980s, a number of scholars have sought to resolve the debate between development and dependency theorists by seeking common ground or to supercede the debate by asking a different set of questions. One consequence has been a new emphasis on "interdependence." Another has been a wide-angle focus, reaching across disciplines and deep into the history of industrialization to explore, in particular, relationships between the state and the private sector, domestic and foreign. That approach has been labeled the new international political economy.

Interdependence

Whereas scholars dealing with relations between developed states and the Third World tended to focus in the 1960s on the benefits of such relations for the Third World and, in the 1970s, on the detriment of such relations to the Third World, many scholars in the 1980s began to focus instead on complementary needs and common problems. Some have noted, for example, an increasing vulnerability on the part of the industrialized states to economic problems in the Third World. The high interest rates of the early 1980s in the First World, particularly the United States, were devastating to Latin American economies. The consequent debt crisis in Latin America has threatened the solvency of U.S. banks and closed markets for U.S. manufactured goods.

International Political Economy

The international political economy (IPE) agenda recaptures the scope of nineteenth-century social concerns for the purpose of addressing contemporary policy issues. Thus, the assumptions and findings of IPE theorists tend to cut across, and perhaps defuse, the development-dependency debates. In addressing Third World issues, IPE theorists, like dependency theorists, seek explanation for means and levels of development in class conflict rather than in assumptions about attitudes. Like modernization and development theorists, however, they generally find a positive relationship between development and democracy. They accept, to a point, the *dependentista* assertion that Third World countries have been disadvantaged by their participation in the global economy, but hold that positive results have on occasion been achieved where Third World governments had the capacity to negotiate the conditions of their participation.

International political economy shares with the world system school the conviction that development follows no preordained sequence of stages. IPE, however, faults the world system approach for underestimation of the role of the state in determining economic outcomes. Rejecting both the liberal preference for an unfettered market and the Marxist choice of state dominance of economic decision making, international political economy theorists contend that both state and market have important roles to play and that on occasion they are mutually reinforcing. Effective operation of the market may in fact be dependent upon the vigilance of a strong state, prepared to intervene where necessary.

Like dependency theorists, adherents of the IPE approach concern themselves with the contradiction between the geographic character of state power and the transnational character of economic power, but IPE theorists argue that the penetration of foreign capital does not necessarily shrink the economic role of the state. Studies of petrochemical and iron industries in Brazil by Peter Evans, of the oil industry in Venezuela by Franklin Tugwell, and of the copper industry in Chile by Theodore Moran have shown that foreign-owned extractive sectors may stimulate state entrepreneurial activity; that in itself, however, does not necessarily advance living standards or other indices of development.[20]

These approaches, which have dominated the field of Latin American studies for the past three decades, by no means exhaust the available theoretical frameworks, much less the possible ones, for interpretation of continuity and change and of the enduring problems that have plagued the lives of so many Latin Americans. It is to be hoped that some students will find in this book the information and inspiration from which to derive their own more useful theories.

NOTES

1. Sarmiento's best known work is *Facundo* (in English translation, *Civilization and Barbarism: The Life of Juan Facundo Quiroga* [New York: Collier Books, 1961]).

2. This author submits that one of the reasons that Latin American politics has been so poorly understood by North Americans is that North American politics is also poorly understood by them.

3. Among the Latin Americanists whose works have tended to be in this vein are Fredrick Pike, John Mander, Charles Wagley, Claudio Veliz, Ronald Newton, William S. Stokes, and William Lyle Schurz.

4. Works highlighting corporatism or employing corporatist models include Howard J. Wiarda, *Corporatism and Development: The Portuguese Experience* (Amherst: University of Massachusetts Press, 1977); Wiarda, ed., *Politics and Social Change in Latin America: The Distinct Tradition* (Amherst: University of Massachusetts Press, 1974); Philippe C. Schmitter, *Interest Conflict and Political Change in Brazil* (Stanford: Stanford University Press, 1971); James M. Malloy, ed., *Authoritarianism and Corporatism in Latin America* (Pittsburgh: University of Pittsburgh Press, 1977); and Kenneth Paul Erickson, *The Brazilian Corporative State: Working Class Politics* (Berkeley: University of California Press, 1977).

5. Samuel Huntington and Myron Weiner, eds., *Understanding Political Development* (Boston: Little, Brown and Co., 1987), pp. 21–28.

6. Walt W. Rostow, *The Stages of Economic Growth* (London: Cambridge University Press, 1960).

7. Daniel Lerner, *The Passing of Traditional Society: Modernizing in the Middle East* (New York: Free Press, 1965), p. 83.

8. Gabriel Almond and G. Bingham Powell, *Comparative Politics: A Developmental Approach* (Boston: Little, Brown and Co., 1966); and Samuel Huntington, *Political Order in Changing Societies* (New Haven: Yale University Press, 1968).

9. Albert O. Hirschman, *Journeys Toward Progress: Studies of Economic Policymaking in Latin America* (New York: Twentieth Century Fund, 1963).

10. Samuel Huntington, "The Change to Change," *Comparative Politics* 3 (April 1971), p. 290.

11. Cited in Dan Griffin, "The Boom in Brazil: An Awful Lot of Everything," *Washington Post*, May 27, 1973.

12. Martin C. Needler, *Political Development in Latin America: Instability, Violence, and Evolutionary Change* (New York: Random House, 1968). Other applications of development theory to the study of Latin America have included Charles W. Anderson, *Politics and Economic Change in Latin America* (Princeton: Van Nostrand, 1967), and Edward J. Williams and Freeman Wright, *Latin American Politics: A Developmental Approach* (Palo Alto, Calif.: Mayfield, 1975).

13. Susanne Bodenheimer Jonas, "Dependency and Imperialism: The Roots of Latin American Development," *Politics and Society* 1:3 (May 1977), pp. 327–357.

14. Fernando Henrique Cardoso, "The Consumption of Dependency Theory in the United States," *Latin American Research Review* 12:3 (1977), p. 16.

15. Richard Fagen, "Studying Latin American Politics: Some Implications of a Dependency Approach," *Latin American Research Review* 12:2 (1977), pp. 3–26.

16. For an elaboration and application of penetration theory, see Jan Knippers Black, *United States Penetration of Brazil* (Philadelphia: University of Pennsylvania Press, 1977).

17. Guillermo O'Donnell, *Modernization and Bureaucratic-Authoritarianism: Studies in South American Politics,* Politics of Modernization Series, no. 9 (Berkeley: Institute of International Studies, University of California, 1973).

18. Johan Galtung, "A Structural Theory of Imperialism," *Journal of Peace Research,* 8:2 (1972), pp. 81–117.

19. Immanuel Wallerstein, *The Modern World-System: Capitalist Agriculture and the Origins of the European World-Economy in the Sixteenth Century* (New York and London: Academic Press, 1974).

20. See Peter Evans, *Dependent Development: The Alliance of Multinational, State, and Local Capital in Brazil* (Princeton: Princeton University Press, 1979); Franklin Tugwell, *The Politics of Oil in Venezuela* (Stanford, Calif.: Stanford University Press, 1975); and Theodore H. Moran, *Multinational Corporations and the Politics of Dependence: Copper in Chile* (Princeton: Princeton University Press, 1975).

PART ONE
THE LAND AND THE PEOPLE

Photographs in part-page collages were taken by Jan Black

2

PHYSICAL LANDSCAPE AND SETTLEMENT PATTERNS

ALFONSO GONZALEZ

Latin America is among the largest world culture regions with an area of 20.5 million sq km (7.9 million sq mi), more than double the size of the United States. It has the greatest latitudinal range of any world region, extending from 32° north latitude to 56° south latitude. The airline distance from northwestern Mexico to northern South America is nearly 5,000 km (+3,000 mi),* and from there to Cape Horn, following the general curvature of the continent, is an additional 7,500 km (+4,600 mi). As a consequence, the region has a highly diversified ecology. Although it is primarily tropical, it encompasses some midlatitude environments, and there is great variation in the physiography, climate, vegetation, soil types, and minerals that are encountered in the region.

OUTSTANDING PHYSICAL CHARACTERISTICS

There are some outstanding physical characteristics in Latin America that combine to render a uniqueness to the region. The Andes, for example, comprise the highest continuous mountain barrier on earth with a lineal extent of +7,000 km (4,400 mi). The chain includes the highest summits outside of central Asia with at least three dozen peaks higher than Mt. McKinley (6,194 m [20,320 ft]), the highest summit in North America. Virtually every maximum or near-maximum elevation for most of the world's features (except summits) occurs in the Andes—the highest settlement, capital city, railroad, highway, mining activities, commercial airport, volcanoes, navigable lake, snowline, etc. Furthermore, the steepest coastal gradient anywhere occurs in Colombia.

---

*+ before a number means "more than"; − means "less than."

The Amazon is physically the world's greatest river. Although second to the Nile in length, it has by far the greatest discharge volume, drainage basin, and length of navigable waterways of any river on earth. The highest and most voluminous waterfalls are located in South America. Two or three of the world's highest falls occur in the Guiana Highlands, and five of the seven greatest waterfalls in the world in volume of flow are in the Brazilian Highlands. Although the waterpower potential of Latin America is somewhat less than that of Asia or Africa, one-fifth of the world's potential hydroelectric power is found in Latin America.

Latin America is a unique faunal region, the Neotropical Zoogeographical Realm, which covers all of Latin America except northern and central highland Mexico and the Bahamas. Although the diversity of mammalian animal life is somewhat greater in the African region, no world region has so many unique mammalian families. Furthermore, Latin America also has the most diverse bird life and a highly varied and complex collection of lower animal forms.

Latin America has the highest proportion of any world region (approximately one-half) of its area in forests, and the regions of Amazonia and the Guiana Highlands represent the largest continuous tropical rain-forest area on earth. Latin America also contains the greatest absolute area in forest, one-quarter of the world total, and the highest per capita forested area of any world region. Unfortunately, perhaps only one-third of this forested area is both economically productive and accessible, so that Latin America, in reality, is a net importer of forest-based products. Currently, the reduction of the forests is occurring at an unprecedented rate: +250,000 sq km (100,000 sq mi) of forested area were cleared for other uses in the first half of the 1980s.

There are a number of extremes that distinguish the climate of Latin America. Some of the coastal lowlands and island stations approach the world record of only approximately 13° C (23° F) between the highest and lowest temperatures ever recorded. Probably the driest region on earth is the Peruvian-Atacama Desert, especially in northern Chile. Nevertheless, southern Chile is one of the rainiest places on earth, receiving measurable precipitation for as many as 325 days a year. The wettest place in the Western Hemisphere is located in the western Colombian Andes, which receive more than 8.5 m (335 inches) of rainfall annually.

Latin America is periodically beset by major natural disasters that are destructive of both lives and property. In this regard, the area is second only to the Orient in major natural disasters. Earthquakes occur with great frequency along the western highland margin of the region. Two of the greatest quakes outside the Orient occurred in 1868 and in 1970 in highland Peru, each causing the loss of 50,000 to 70,000 lives. Recently, devastating quakes occurred in 1972 at Managua, Nicaragua, in 1975 in central Guatemala, and in 1985 in Mexico City. There are fifty or more active volcanoes in the region (approximately one-quarter of the world total). The eruptions of Mt. Pelee (Martinique) in 1902, which resulted in the deaths of at least 30,000 people, and Nevado del Ruiz (Colombia) in 1985, with more than 22,000 killed, rank among the greatest volcanic eruptions of modern times. Hurricanes occur regularly within the Caribbean Basin and with less frequency on the Pacific coast of Mexico, often causing thousands of deaths. Perhaps the greatest avalanche ever recorded occurred in the Andean region of Peru.

OUTSTANDING POPULATION AND SETTLEMENT CHARACTERISTICS

The population and settlement pattern of Latin America is also distinctive. The population in mid-1989 was nearly 438 million (see Table 2.1). Approximately 8 percent of the world's population now resides in Latin America compared to less than 2 percent during the colonial period. It is the only world region that has consistently increased in population faster than the world average since the mid-eighteenth century. Latin America became the fastest growing region in the early post–World War I period and continued to be so for half a century until it was equaled or surpassed by the Middle East and sub-Saharan Africa during the 1970s or even earlier.

Latin America's rate of population growth has been gradually decreasing since the early 1960s although very recently the decline has been more significant. Nevertheless, the region's population continues to increase by nearly 9 million annually. During the early post–World War II period, the average rate of growth was 2.7 to 2.9 percent per year. It is currently expanding at 2.3 percent or less annually. The greatest rates of growth occur in northern Central America and in Andean South America. Traditionally, the slowest growth has occurred in Argentina and Uruguay, although more recently these countries have been joined by Chile and most of the Antilles. The potential for further population growth remains in those countries in which the death rate remains relatively high, notably in northern Central America, Haiti, and the central Andean countries. Family planning programs in the region became generally significant only in the late 1960s.

The age structure of the population is characteristic of underdeveloped regions generally—a high proportion of the younger ages (40 percent or more younger than 15) and a low proportion of older people (fewer than 5 percent 65 years or older). Dependency ratios (proportions of the very young and very old in relation to the productive ages, 15–64) are generally high in the region, placing an additional burden on the economy. Partially related to this situation is the fact that only approximately one-third of the population is economically active (compared with two-fifths in developed regions). With reduced mortality, increasingly large numbers will be entering the labor force, currently more than 3 million annually, which will result in heavy demands on employment opportunities as well as on educational and health facilities and housing.

In Latin America, infant mortality rates are the lowest of any underdeveloped region, and life expectancy is the longest. A subregion of the Orient, East Asia, however, now has rates that are an improvement over the Latin

Table 2.1
Latin America: Population Characteristics

	Area (thousand km²) 1958	Population (million) 1989	Density (per km²) 1988	Percent Annual Population Increase 1980s	Birth Rate[a]	Death Rate[b]	Infant Mortality Rate[c]	Composition of Population by Age (percent)		Percent Population	
								-15	65+	Urban	Agricultural
Mexico	1958	86.7	42	2.2	30	6	50	42	4	66	33
Guatemala	109	8.9	80	2.9	40	9	59	46	3	40	53
El Salvador	21	5.1	242	1.5	35	9	62	46	4	43	40
Honduras	112	5.0	43	3.4	40	8	69	47	3	41	59
Nicaragua	130	3.5	28	3.5	43	8	69	47	3	57	41
Costa Rica	51	3.0	52	2.5	29	4	17	37	5	45	27
Panama	77	2.4	30	2.2	27	5	25	37	5	52	27
Belize	23	.2	8	2.6	36	6	36	45	5	50	—
Cuba	111	10.5	94	1.0	17	6	13	25	8	72	21
Dominican Republic	49	7.0	141	2.4	31	7	65	39	3	56	40
Haiti	28	6.4	199	1.2	35	13	117	40	5	26	63
Puerto Rico	9	3.3	363	.2	19	7	15	28	10	67	4
Jamaica	11	2.5	219	1.5	22	5	20	37	6	49	31
Trinidad/Tobago	5	1.2	246	1.9	27	7	14	34	6	64	8
Guyana	215	.8	4	1.9	26	7	44	38	4	32	24
Surinam	163	.4	3	2.7	27	7	33	37	4	66	18

Venezuela	912	19.1	21	2.8	28	4	36	39	4	83	12
Colombia	1139	31.2	27	1.9	28	7	46	36	4	67	30
Ecuador	284	10.5	38	2.9	33	8	63	42	4	54	34
Peru	1285	21.4	17	2.6	29	8	69	41	4	69	39
Bolivia	1099	7.1	6	2.7	40	14	110	43	3	49	43
Paraguay	407	4.2	10	3.1	36	7	45	41	4	43	49
Chile	757	13.0	17	1.7	22	6	19	31	6	83	14
Argentina	2767	31.9	12	1.6	22	9	30	31	9	85	11
Uruguay	177	3.0	17	.5	18	10	28	26	11	84	14
Brazil	8512	147.4	17	2.2	28	8	63	36	4	71	27
Latin America	20535	438	21	2.3	29	7	55	38	5	68	29
Canada	9976	26.3	3	1.0	15	7	8	21	11	77	4
United States	9373	248.8	26	1.0	16	9	10	21	12	74	3
Underdeveloped Countries	80754	4028.0	50	2.0	31	10	84	37	4	32	59
WORLD TOTAL	135793	5234	38	1.7	28	10	75	33	6	41	47

[a]Number of births annually per 1,000 population.
[b]Number of deaths annually per 1,000 population.
[c]Number of deaths of infants (less than 1 year of age) annually per 1,000 live births.

Sources: Population Reference Bureau, Inc., *1989 World Population Data Sheet;* United Nations, *Demographic Yearbook 1986; Britannica Book of the Year 1989;* Britannica World Data; Food and Agriculture Organization, *Production Yearbook 1986.*

American average. Mortality aside, there is still a significant gap between the levels of living in Latin America and in the more developed regions.

The population density of Latin America averages approximately 21 inhabitants per sq km (+54 per sq mi), which is only slightly more than half the world average and is comparable to a number of other world regions. Most of the countries of Latin America are, therefore, below the world average in density; exceptions include the Antilles, El Salvador, Guatemala, Costa Rica, and more recently, Honduras, Mexico, and Ecuador. Partly as a consequence of relatively low crop yields, population pressure on available cropland is greater in Latin America than in any developed world region, but such pressure is less than in any other underdeveloped area.

The pattern of population distribution in Latin America includes a concentration on the periphery, especially in South America and on the Pacific margins of Central America. Population is also concentrated in the highlands within the tropics, with one-half to three-quarters of the national populations in the upland areas. Exceptions are the Antilles, Nicaragua, Panama, Belize, and the Guianas. Latin America has a larger population in the highlands than any other world region.

The region has a nucleated pattern of settlement, with semi-isolated population clusters and national population cores. Population clusters are detached, although this is diminishing with increased population and improved transportation. Generally 10 to 25 percent of the national area of a Latin American country contains one-half or more of the national population. As a result, in most countries there are large areas that are very sparsely settled— half of the area of Latin America contains only about 5 percent of the region's total population. The population pattern demonstrates that the effective area of settlement in most countries is still a small segment of the total national territory.

A rapid process of urbanization has characterized Latin America, especially since World War II. It is, by far, the most highly urbanized underdeveloped region. Its population was one-half urban by 1965 and is now nearly two-thirds urban, the result of both natural increase (excess of births over deaths) and internal migration, with probably 3 to 4 million migrants moving into the urban centers annually. The causes of rapid urbanization include rural poverty (the "push" factors—expulsion from the countryside); the fast rate of natural increase in the rural areas; the scarcity of available arable land, especially in the traditional areas of settlement; the land tenure system (*latifundia,* the predominance of large estates, and *minifundia,* the prevalence of many very small landholdings); limited rural employment opportunities; and low wages; restricted social services provide an undesirable rural habitat over most of the region. Also, the attractions of the city (the "pull" factors)— the possibility of employment, higher wages, and improved social services— make the cities, especially the capitals, appealing to impoverished rural residents.

The largest city of each country (the capital except in Brazil, Ecuador, and Belize) tends to dominate the life of the country and is generally several times larger than the second largest city. This degree of primacy is more accentuated in Latin America than in any other world region. Some countries are highly urbanized, notably Venezuela and the Southern Cone countries of South America, while the most rural areas are Central America, Haiti, and some of the smaller countries of South America.

NATURAL REGIONS

Although there is a great variety of physical habitat in Latin America, it is possible to subdivide the area into thirteen natural regions (see Figure 2.1). These regions, although based fundamentally on physiographic characteristics, also possess some unifying characteristics of climate, natural vegetation, and soils. Therefore, since these natural regions present differing sets of problems for human settlement and economic development, the human patterns are often in large measure a response to the prevalent locational and physical factors. Crude approximations of the areas, populations, and densities for the natural regions of Latin America are presented in Table 2.2.

Gulf-Caribbean Coastal Lowlands

The Gulf-Caribbean Coastal Lowlands are a continuation of the Atlantic-Gulf Coastal Lowlands of the United States, but south of the Rio Grande (Rio Bravo to the Mexicans) the coastal plain is narrower and interrupted. In the northernmost section, in the Mexican state of Tamaulipas, the climate is mostly subhumid (low-altitude steppe). This section is relatively sparsely settled, although the lower Rio Grande Valley has dense settlement because of agriculture and the newly developed gas fields. South of Tamaulipas, the coastal lowland is tropical in climate, vegetation, and soils.

The coastal plain becomes very restricted in portions of Veracruz and along sections of Central America; it becomes broadset in Yucatán and is fairly broad in Nicaragua and adjoining sections of Honduras and Costa Rica. Many portions of the coastal plain are characterized by poor drainage, resulting in swamps and marshes. Precipitation occurs throughout the year, but it is concentrated in the warmer months and is often twice as great as on the Pacific littoral. Many parts of the coastal lowlands are subject to violent tropical storms, especially from August through November. These hurricanes sometimes cause losses of thousands of lives and very extensive property damage.

The soils generally are not highly productive under continuous tillage. These lowland areas have traditionally had only scattered areas of settlement, frequently associated with commercial plantation agriculture, especially bananas, and with fishing and logging. However, in recent decades, there has been an influx of migrants into the lowlands.

The Yucatán peninsula, a platform of coral rock with limestone beds, is characterized by shallow, dry rendzina soil, with many sinkholes (*cenotes*) and few surface streams. The eastern and southern sections of the Mexican

LATIN AMERICA:
NATURAL REGIONS

1 Gulf-Caribbean Coastal Lowlands
2 Antilles (West Indies)
3 Pacific Littoral:
   Coastal Plains & Valleys
4 Cordilleran Ranges,
   Intermontane Basins &Plateaus
5 Llanos
6 Guiana Highlands (& associated
   coastal lowlands)
7 Amazonia
8 Brazilian Highlands (& associated
   coastal lowlands)
9 Peruvian-Atacama Desert
10 Middle Chile
11 South Chile
12 Patagonia & Northwest Argentina
13 La Plata -Parana Basin

Kilometres
0 200 400 600 800

Compiled by Dr. Gonzalez and M. Styk, U of Calgary

Figure 2.1. Latin America: Natural Regions

Table 2.2
Natural Regions of Latin America

	Area (thousand km²)	Population (thousand) 1988	Percent Annual Growth 1980–88	Density (per km²)	Percent of Total Area	Percent of Total Population 1988
Gulf-Caribbean Coastal Lowlands	730	25285	2.6	34.6	3.6	5.9
Pacific Littoral	467	18734	2.6	40.1	2.3	4.4
Cordilleran Highlands	3270	137016	2.5	41.9	15.9	32.1
Antilles	234	31847	.9	135.8	1.1	7.5
Llanos (Orinoco)	641	3644	2.4	5.7	3.1	.9
Guiana Highlands	1109	2287	1.7	2.1	5.4	.5
Amazonia	5125	10432	4.1	2.0	25.0	2.4
Brazilian Highlands	4493	136161	1.9	30.3	21.9	31.9
Peruvian-Atacama Desert	402	10258	2.4	25.5	2.0	2.4
Middle Chile	255	11611	1.8	45.6	1.2	2.7
South Chile	241	224	a	.9	1.2	.1
La Plata-Paraná Basin	2025	33027	1.7	16.3	9.9	7.7
Northwest Argentina-Patagonia	1536	6504	4.0	4.2	7.5	1.5
TOTAL	20529	427028	2.2	20.8	100.0	100.0

Note: Figures are estimates and totals may not coincide with above data or with other data for Latin America because of rounding.

aPolitical subdivisions were modified in the 1980s so that an estimate is not possible.

portion of the peninsula, Belize, and the northern third of Guatemala (the Petén) comprise the most sparsely settled area of the coastal lowlands. Nevertheless, in pre-Columbian times, this area was the cultural hearth of the Mayan civilization, with population densities significantly above current levels.

The older petroleum fields of Mexico were centered in northern Veracruz. Reduced production continues from fields near Tampico, Tuxpan, and Poza Rica, but the great petroleum and natural gas fields were opened in the 1970s in southern Veracruz, Tabasco, adjacent Campeche, and on the offshore banks. Agricultural expansion in this region predates the development of the petroleum and natural gas industries.

The Gulf-Caribbean Coastal Lowlands extend into neighboring Colombia and Venezuela in South America. There they mainly comprise the Atrato and Magdalena valleys of Colombia and the Maracaibo Basin of Venezuela, which contains Latin America's largest lake. These areas have been attracting migration from the more traditional highland centers of settlement because of the production of bananas and other tropical crops in Colombia and the great petroleum production in the Maracaibo district of Venezuela.

Antilles (West Indies)

The Antilles comprise one of the world's most important archipelagoes. The total area of the islands is only about 238,000 sq km (92,000 sq mi), approximately the size of Oregon. Cuba alone embraces one-half of the area; most of the remainder consists of the other Greater Antilles: Hispaniola, Jamaica, and Puerto Rico. The islands enclose one of the world's largest seas, the Caribbean, on the north and east.

The Greater Antilles are a complex folded and block-faulted mountain system that is mostly submerged. They consist of two ridges, separated by a deep trough. The Lesser Antilles, extending from east of Puerto Rico to the Netherlands Antilles off the coast of South America, consist of a great number of much smaller islands with an arcuate shape, convex toward the Atlantic Ocean, and structurally connected with the highlands of Venezuela. The northern section, the Leeward Islands, extend from the Virgin Islands to north of Guadeloupe, or possibly as far south as Martinique. The southern islands are the Windwards. The total area of the Lesser Antilles is less than 13,000 sq km (5,019 sq mi), about the size of Connecticut. The Antilles region, like the northern mainland of Central America and most of Mexico, is regularly exposed to hurricanes. The climate throughout the Antilles gives rise to either tropical rain-forest or tropical savanna.

The Antilles, except for the Bahamas and the Turks and Caicos, are far more densely settled than any other area of Latin America. Their populations are predominantly of African descent. The geographic location, combined with an equable climate and productive soils, gave rise to the earliest plantation economies of the New World. These were based primarily on sugar, although later bananas, coffee, and other crops were added.

The plantation agricultural economy has declined recently, especially on the smaller islands. Other economic activities, including tourism, subsistence agriculture, and commerce, have generally proved inadequate to support the dense populations. Mineral wealth in this region overall is minor but is of importance in eastern Cuba, Jamaica, and Trinidad. Recent relatively rapid population growth without compensating socioeconomic development has caused a large exodus of emigrants to the United States, the United Kingdom, France, the Netherlands, and Canada.

Pacific Littoral: Coastal Plains and Valleys

The Pacific margins of Middle America and the northern section of South America represent a narrow zone of diverse physical landscapes. The peninsula of Baja (Lower) California, in Mexico, represents the southern extension of the Pacific mountain system of North America and consists of a long series of blocks tilted toward the Pacific Ocean with a steep fault scarp on the Gulf of California side. This essentially desert, shrub-covered region has been, with parts of Yucatán, the most sparsely settled and isolated area of Mexico. However, in 1972 a paved highway was opened, and it runs the length of the peninsula, nearly 1,900 km (1,180 mi).

Across the Gulf of California lies the almost equally arid Sonoran Desert, the southward extension of the basin-and-range topography of the United States. Although the population is greater toward the more humid south, many of the river valleys of southern Sonora and northern Sinaloa are densely settled and intensively utilized due to the irrigation projects developed since the Revolution.

From approximately Mazatlán southward, the remainder of the coastal margin of Mexico, Central America, Colombia, and Ecuador is generally narrow; in places it disappears completely as the highlands reach the shore. The population along the Mexican section of this coastal zone is relatively sparse but increasing. The Pacific coastal margins of Central America tend to have greater population settlements than the Caribbean coasts, except in Honduras, but the coastal lowlands on both sides of the isthmus are undergoing a rapid increase in settlement. The great majority of the population of Panama is located in the Pacific lowlands, whereas that of Nicaragua is in the lake district lowlands close to the Pacific.

The extremely humid Pacific coastal margins of Colombia are sparsely settled and relatively isolated from the country's national settlement core. However, the growing commercial importance of the port of Buenaventura has stimulated population migration into this heavily forested area. The coastal margins and Guayas lowlands of Ecuador contain approximately half of that country's population and constitute a very rapidly expanding area of development. The cultivation of a number of tropical products, especially bananas, since World War II has encouraged settlement in this region where the ports and the largest city (Guayaquil) of the country are located.

Cordilleran Ranges: Intermontane Basins and Plateaus

The highland spine of the American Cordillera extends the length of Latin America near the Pacific margin of the region. Clearly, this is the most extensive of all the natural regions, with an airline distance of more than 12,000 km (7,458 mi); it is also one of the most populous, with more than 100 million inhabitants. From Mexico to Bolivia, this highland zone contains from about half to more than three-quarters of the populations of every country except Belize, Nicaragua, and Panama.

The Cordillera is a young, complex mountain system with a considerable diversity of features, rock types, and geologic structures. Peaks attain elevations of nearly 7,000 m (22,966 ft). Aconcagua, rising 6,960 m (22,835 ft) on the Chilean-Argentine border just north of Santiago, is the highest summit in the world outside of central Asia. The passes are extremely high in the Andes, and throughout most of the Cordillera the high elevations, steep slopes, and extremely rugged terrain present very serious obstacles to transportation. Glacier and ice fields occur throughout much of the mountain system, even at the equator, and reach sea level in southern Chile. There are snowcapped peaks in the highland zones of Mexico and every country of South America within the Cordilleran system.

Within Latin America, the Cordillera attains its greatest width in northern Mexico (1,000 km [+600 mi]) and Bolivia (800 m [500 mi]). It becomes very narrow in portions of southern Central America and again in Chile. There are only four major topographic breaks in this formidable barrier: (1) the Isthmus of Tehuantepec in Mexico; (2) the Nicaraguan graben lowlands, which run from the San Juan River in the Caribbean coastal zone through the lake district northwest to the Gulf of Fonseca (part of this route was considered an alternate for a canal during the last century); (3) the Panamanian isthmus, where the canal is located; and (4) the Atrato–San Juan river valleys across northwestern Colombia.

The mountain system also contains numerous intermontane basins and plateaus, the largest being those of northern and central Mexico and the Altiplano of Peru and Bolivia. These plateaus are the major population zones of Mexico and Bolivia. The system contains some fifty active volcanoes—the greatest concentration in the world outside the Orient—concentrated in five zones: (1) the volcanic axis of Mexico, along the southern margin of the Mexican Plateau; (2) the Central American Pacific volcanic belt, extending from just inside the Mexican border to Costa Rica; (3) southern Colombia and Ecuador, including the Galápagos Islands; (4) central and southern Peru; and (5) Chile, where the two highest active volcanoes in the world are found. The only volcanic activity in Latin America outside the Cordilleran system occurs on three of the lesser Antilles. Throughout its length, except in northern Mexico, the Cordilleran region is one of the most earthquake-prone regions on earth. Very strong quakes occur regularly and cause considerable loss of life.

Most of the population in the western Cordilleran highlands of Latin America is found in the tropical zone or just on its margins where there is a considerable range of climate. Climates and vegetation vary in accordance with variations in altitude and temperature. The altitudinal boundaries of the climatic zones vary among localities because of latitude, windward/ leeward location, exposure, precipitation, and humidity. In the highlands, although the seasonal range of temperature is comparable to that in the adjacent lowlands, the diurnal range is usually considerably greater, especially during the dry season. Table 2.3 gives a general overview of the major altitudinal zones in Latin America.

Throughout the Cordilleran highlands, the more productive basins have numerous urban communities and high rural densities. Increasing population pressure and the land-tenure system have stimulated a massive rural to urban migration, and, to a lesser degree, agricultural colonization of the more sparsely settled lowlands. The region has a great diversity of mineral wealth, but it is concentrated in northern and central Mexico and in Peru and Bolivia.

The higher zones have a very high proportion of Amerindians, especially in Guatemala and the central Andean counties. The *tierra caliente* zone, especially the Caribbean lowlands of Central America, the lowlands of Colombia, and to a lesser degree, the coastal zones of Venezuela and Ecuador, has the greatest concentration of blacks.

Orinoco Llanos

The Llanos ("plains") lie between the Venezuelan-Colombian Andes and the Guiana Highlands and are drained by the Orinoco River system. This basin, nearly evenly divided between Venezuela and Colombia, is the third largest in Latin America, accommodating the third greatest river discharge of the region. In size, the Llanos region approximates the state of Texas; it is one of the five very sparsely settled natural regions of Latin America.

Petroleum and iron ore have been exploited for some time in the eastern Llanos of Venezuela, but the most widespread activity, by far, is cattle ranching. In recent decades, there has been migration in both countries from the densely settled highlands to the forested margins and the open grassland districts of these lowlands. The settlers have reportedly encountered resistance from a few nomadic Amerindian tribes in the area.

Guiana Highlands

The Guiana Highlands, and the associated coastal lowlands, are perhaps two-thirds larger than the Llanos but contain even less population, making the Guiana region, Amazonia, and South Chile the most sparsely settled regions in Latin America. There is a narrow coastal lowland along the Guianas, which contains approximately nine-tenths of the population of those countries. There is also a narrow riverine lowland between the Guiana Highlands and the Orinoco River, which contains the greater part of the population and economic activity of the Guiana Highlands of Venezuela, nearly one-half the area of that country.

Table 2.3
Altitudinal Zonation of Climates in Latin America

Altitude	Zone	Average Monthly Temperature	Major Agricultural Commodities
4,500 m (14,000–21,000 ft)	permanent snow fields (nevados)	<0°C (<32°F)	
3,000–3,500 m (10,000–11,500 ft)	alpine meadows (tierra helada, páramos)	6°–10°C (43°–54°F)	livestock grazing (especially sheep and goats, with llamas and alpacas in the central Andes (above tree line and general crop cultivation)
2,000 m (6,000–6,500 ft)	temperate (tierra fría)	10°–17°C (54°–65°F)	midlatitude crops: wheat, barley, white potatoes, apples, and other deciduous fruits
600–1,000 m (2,000–3,000 ft)	subtropical (tierra templada)	17°–24°C (65°–75°F)	coffee, maize, cotton, rice, citrus, sugarcane
0–600 m (0–2,000 ft)	tropical (tierra caliente)	24°–28°C (75°–83°F)	bananas, cacao, rubber, palms (coconut, oil), pineapples, mangoes (crops of subtropical zone also, except for coffee)

Note: Metric and English measure figures are rounded so conversion is not exact.

Much of the upland surface has been dissected by streams, and the world's highest waterfalls are located near the Venezuelan-Guyanan border. This highland massif and the Brazilian Highlands are composed of remnants of the oldest rocks on the continent—primarily a granitic base partially capped by a resistant sedimentary layer. Bauxite, iron ore, and manganese are the most important mineral deposits of the area, but gold and diamonds are also found there.

Amazonia

The Amazon Basin is the largest natural region of Latin America and one of the most homogeneous. Although nearly three-quarters of the basin lies within Brazil, portions of the region extend into Peru, Bolivia, Colombia, and Ecuador. Despite the basin's immense area, its population is extremely sparse: Only about 2 percent of the population of Latin America resides in this largest river basin on earth.

The Amazon River is, in volume, the greatest river on earth, although it is slightly shorter than the longest river, the Nile. The Amazon accounts for nearly one-fifth of the total world river discharge into the oceans. The outlet of the river is more than 300 km (186 mi) wide and contains an island the size of southern New England. It is the most navigable river system on earth. There is no bridge across the Amazon in its entire lowland traverse of the continent. Despite the river's immense silt discharge, the delta has undergone little development because of coastal subsidence and coastal currents. Few places on earth can match Amazonia with regard to the diversity of life forms that are encountered.

The Amazon Basin can be generally divided into two major parts: the low-lying, level alluvial lowlands, or floodplain, and the upland plains. The floodplain is of varying width and comprises approximately one-tenth of the basin's area. This zone consists of a series of broad, disconnected swamps with natural levees. Much of the area is inundated at various times of the year. The most fertile soils, replenished by river silt, constitute the best agricultural land, and by far the greater part of the settlements lie within this zone. The upland plains are generally above the periodic river floodings and contain the highly leached and laterized soils typical of many tropical environments. The population in this zone is extremely sparse. Recently deforestation has accelerated to alarming proportions. Increasing areas are being devoted to crop cultivation and cattle ranching. Since the 1970s an extensive highway network is being constructed along with hydroelectric dam projects. Considerable mineral wealth has been discovered and is being exploited, especially iron, ferro-alloys, bauxite, gold, and petroleum. The destruction of the habitat is of serious concern for the aboriginal Amerinds; soil erosion, the loss of wildlife and plant species, and the alteration of regional and global climates are also sources of global concern.

Brazilian Highlands

The dissected Brazilian Plateau and its associated coastal lowlands make up the second largest natural region of Latin America and, with the Cordilleran

Highlands, have the largest population of the entire region. Nearly one-third of Latin America's population is in this natural region, which accounts for half of Brazil's area and almost all of that country's population.

The diverse Brazilian Highlands consist of (a) a prominent seaward escarpment, the Serra do Mar of the southern section, which acted as a transportation handicap and barrier to early penetration of the interior; (b) the rolling, dissected plateau of the interior of this highland zone, which is inclined away from the ocean so that drainage is generally toward the interior before it eventually reaches the ocean; and (c) the old, eroded and rounded mountain ranges that are found in different sections of the uplands. The east-central section of this Brazilian shield, notably in the state of Minas Gerais (General Mines), is highly mineralized with significant deposits of iron, ferro-alloys, diamonds, and gold.

The narrow and discontinuous coastal plain accounts for only 5 to 10 percent of the area of Brazil but at least a third of the population, including four of the half-dozen largest cities—Rio de Janeiro, Recife, Salvador, and Porto Alegre. The coastal lowlands have a tropical rain-forest, or monsoon, climate and broadleaf evergreen forests. Tropical savanna occurs along much of the northeastern coast and the northern and central portions of the interior highlands. However, the interior northeasten section is a comparatively subhumid region. Its periodic droughts have had devastating effects on the 30 percent of the national population residing in the poverty-stricken nine states of this section. This has been a zone of out-migration, primarily to the coastal plantation zone and the industrial and commercial centers in the south and southeast.

The southern highland section has a humid subtropical climate and, on the Parana Plateau, soil hospitable to coffee. Population growth is faster in São Paulo and the three southern states—which, combined, contain two-fifths of the national population—than in the other eastern sections of the country. The interior plateau is also undergoing in-migration and rapid growth and development, although the state of Goiás and the Mato Grosso are still sparsely settled.

Peruvian-Atacama Desert

The Peruvian-Atacama Desert region consists of a narrow coastal zone that extends 3,000 to 3,500 km (+1,800 to +2,000 mi) from near the Ecuadoran-Peruvian border to Coquimbo, Chile. The coastal plain is extremely narrow or absent, and the coastline generally lacks enclosed, protected harbors. Isolated blocks and low coastal hills also characterize parts of the zone, and in places, there are low, but steep, escarpments behind the shore. There are few perennial streams, especially toward the south.

The combination of the Pacific anticyclone, the cool Humboldt current, and winds that parallel the coast makes this coastal zone perhaps the driest on earth. Arica, Chile, near the border of Peru, has the lowest average annual precipitation (0.5 mm [0.02 in]) of any weather station on earth. Another station, Iquique, less than 200 km (+100 mi) to the south, has experienced a period of fourteen years without measurable precipitation. However, the El Nino phenomenon occurs occasionally and brings heavy rains and floodings. Atmospheric and oceanic disturbances displace the cool Humboldt (or Peru) current farther offshore, permitting warmer water from the equatorial region to move southward off the coast of Ecuador and Peru. The loss of fisheries and marine birds can also be catastrophic.

The great mineral wealth in what is now Chile, first of nitrates and later of copper, opened sections of the arid north of that country to development. However, this one-third of the country contains only 7 percent of the national population. Significant iron ore is exploited in southern Peru and the extreme south of the Atacama in Chile. In Peru, as in Chile, many stretches are barren both of vegetation and habitation, but fairly dense settlement occurs in the irrigated narrow coastal valleys, especially from Lima north.

Middle Chile

The relatively small Middle Chile region, lying between Coquimbo and Puerto Montt, comprises only one-third of the national area but contains slightly more than nine-tenths of the country's population, most of the agricultural land and industrial production, and much of the mineral wealth.

The northernmost section of this region is desert/steppe, a transition to the very arid region of the Atacama. Most of northern Middle Chile, however, has essentially a Mediterranean climate. In this sector, the summers remain dry; the mild winter is the season of precipitation. In some places, irrigation is necessary during the summer. This sector, which includes the capital, Santiago, contains more than 70 percent of Chile's population. The remainder of Middle Chile, south of Concepción, is less densely settled. Precipitation is greater in this area and occurs throughout the year. Southern Middle Chile is the most important forest-producing region of the country. The major mineral wealth is copper.

South Chile

South Chile, another small natural region, has a very sparse population. The coastal range is now partially submerged to form an archipelago, and much of the longitudinal valley is drowned. Andean glaciers reach sea level in this region, which is one of the four major fjorded coasts on earth. The region is rugged and isolated, cold, rainy, and dreary. There are no road or rail extensions south of Puerto Montt.

Only 3 percent of Chile's population resides in this third of the country. Most of those people are concentrated in the northern sector, on Chiloé Island—where forest quality and soils are relatively good—and in the Atlantic portion of Chile. There, in the rain shadow of the low Andean chain along the Strait of Magellan, the main economic activities are sheep raising, forestry, and the production of coal and petroleum.

Northwest Argentina and Patagonia

Patagonia and Northwest Argentina compose one of the larger of the natural regions of Latin America and lie entirely within Argentina. The Northwest is larger and more populous than Patagonia, yet the two subregions contain less than a fifth of the country's population in more than half the national territory. In addition to sparse settlement, aridity and uplands characterize this natural region.

Northwest Argentina is characterized by a series of pre-Cordilleran and Pampan ranges that attain their greatest breadth at 30°–35° south latitude and extend into the provinces of San Luis and western Cordoba. Most of the settlement and irrigated agriculture occur in the basin oases of the foothills.

The desert and steppe area of Patagonia is unique in that it is the only midlatitude arid climate in the Southern Hemisphere and the only major arid region on the east coast of a continent. The soils of Patagonia and part of Tierra del Fuego, like those of arid northern Mexico, are typical desert soils—productive when irrigated—and important agricultural output, especially of fruits and sugarcane, is obtained from the densely settled and intensively cultivated oases. There are some mining communities in Northwest Argentina. Petroleum is produced in both coastal Patagonia and in the Andean foothills of the Northwest. Much of the region, however, is sparsely settled and devoted to livestock ranching.

La Plata–Paraná Basin

The La Plata–Paraná Basin, the third largest in the Western Hemisphere after the Amazon and the Mississippi, encompasses the La Plata estuary, the master stream—the Paraná—and its tributaries, notably the Paraguay and Uruguay rivers. The basin lies mostly within northeastern Argentina but also includes all of Uruguay and Paraguay and a portion of southeastern Bolivia. (A significant portion of Brazil is also drained by this river system, but that region of Brazil is included in the Brazilian Highlands natural region.) The La Plata–Paraná Basin is also one of the most populous of the natural regions and contains the Argentine nucleus of settlement.

This natural region has several subregions: the Gran Chaco (west of the Paraná and Paraguay rivers from 29°–30° south latitude northward to Bolivia), eastern Paraguay (east of the Paraguay River), Mesopotamia (Argentina between the Paraná–Alto Paraná and Uruguay rivers), the Pampas (grasslands radiating outward from Buenos Aires for +600 km [400 mi]), and Uruguay. The soils over much of the area are mollisols, deep and dark with organic matter and minerals, that develop near the humid-dry climatic boundary in the midlatitudes. These are the richest soils in Latin America and among the best in the world. The Pampa is the major food-surplus-producing region of Latin America. However, soil quality deteriorates toward the drier Northwest and Patagonia and, especially, northward into the humid tropics. The prevailing climate over most of the region is humid subtropical, comparable to the southeastern United States, with hot, rainy summers and mild winters.

SUMMARY AND CONCLUSION

The natural environments of Latin America are diverse and display varying degrees of settlement and development. The three largest regions—Amazonia, the Brazilian Highlands, and the Cordilleran system—comprise nearly two-thirds of the total area of Latin America. The Cordilleran highlands are very rugged, presenting enormous problems for cultivation and transport, but this has been the traditional area of settlement since pre-Columbian times for most of the countries that lie within the region. The Cordilleran and Brazilian highlands contain nearly two-thirds of Latin America's population. At the other extreme, five regions—Amazonia, Guiana Highlands, Northwest Argentina and Patagonia, Llanos, and South Chile—compose almost half of Latin America but contain about 5 percent of the population. Rates of population growth in these sparsely settled areas, however, are rapid, as pressures on land and resources in the traditional settlement areas stimulate internal migration. Despite this significant movement, the great migration within Latin America is into the major urban centers. This rural-urban migration is many times greater than the migration into sparsely settled regions.

SUGGESTED READINGS

Physical Geography

Handbook of Middle American Indians. Vol. 1, *Natural Environment and Early Cultures,* ed. Robert C. West. Austin: University of Texas Press, 1964. 570 pp. Eight of the chapters provide a good detailed study of the different aspects of the physical environment of Middle America. Probably the best overview of the physical geography of this part of Latin America.

Handbook of South American Indians. Vol. 6, *Physical Anthropology, Linguistics, and Cultural Geography of South American Indians.* U.S. Bureau of American Ethnology, ca. 1948/1949; reprinted New York: Cooper Square, 1963. 715 pp. The section by Carl O. Sauer, "Geography of South America" (pp. 319–344), pertains to the physical landscape of the continent and can serve as a companion piece (although not as detailed) to the *Handbook of Middle American Indians* to complete the coverage of all of Latin America.

Kendrew, Wilfrid George. *The Climates of the Continents.* 5th ed. Oxford: Clarendon Press, 1961. 608 pp. Part 6, "South America, Central America, Mexico, the West Indies" (pp. 464–527). Probably one of the best accounts, although perhaps too detailed, of meteorological and climatic conditions in Latin America.

Martinson, Tom L. "Physical Environments of Latin America," in Blouet, Brian W., and Blouet, Olwyn M. (eds), *Latin America: An Introductory Survey.* New York: John Wiley & Sons, 1982. Chapter 1.

Robinson, H. *Latin America.* 4th ed. London: MacDonald and Evans, 1977. Chapter 1.

Verdoorn, Frans, ed. *Plants and Plant Science in Latin America.* Waltham, Mass.: Ronald Press, 1945. 381 pp. Despite this work's age, it is still an informative source, not only for the phytogeography and agriculture of the region, but also for other aspects of the physical environment.

Population

Blouet, Brian W. "Population: Distribution, Growth, and Migration," in Blouet, Brian W., and Blouet, Olwyn M. (eds), *Latin America: An Introductory Survey.* New York: John Wiley & Sons, 1982. Chapter 5.

Gonzalez, Alfonso. "Latin America—Population and Settlement," in Boehm, Richard G., and Visser, Sent (eds), *Latin America: Case Studies*. Dubuque, Iowa: Kendall Hunt Publishing Co., 1984. Chapter 6.

Merrick, Thos. W. et al. "Population Pressures in Latin America." *Population Bulletin* 41:3 (1986).

Sánchez-Albornoz, Nicholás. *Population of Latin America: A History*. Berkeley and Los Angeles: University of California Press, 1974. 299 pp. A very good and thorough study of the growth and development of Latin America's population (Chapters 1–4) but also contains chapters (6–8) that deal with recent trends and prospects.

3

THE INDIAN POPULATIONS
OF LATIN AMERICA

KARL H. SCHWERIN

In order to understand the contemporary character and distribution of Indian populations in Latin America, it is necessary to know something about the nature of indigenous societies at the time of European discovery. The native inhabitants of the New World represented a great range of cultural development, from simple hunting and gathering bands to complex and literate civilizations. Within the area of present-day Latin America, the great majority of the peoples had reached levels of significant cultural achievement. Most societies were food producers, and in many respects, the region from central Mexico southward was far more advanced than the area lying to the north in what is today northern Mexico, the United States, and Canada. In fact, North America is the only major world region where the majority of the aboriginal peoples relied on gathering, hunting, and fishing for their subsistence. By contrast, South America was inhabited by predominantly agricultural societies.[1]

Nonetheless, a full range of cultural variability also existed in the Latin American region. Although specialists might want to differentiate a great number of categories, it is more instructive for our purposes to treat the early Indian societies as belonging to one of three major types. Marginal hunters and gatherers were restricted for the most part to Argentina, Uruguay, and parts of coastal Brazil. They were also predominant on the northern frontier of the Spanish Empire, the arid deserts of northern Mexico. Lowland extensive agriculturists were much more widespread, ranging from central Chile throughout most of interior Brazil to the whole of the Amazon Basin, including those portions now within the territorial borders of Bolivia, Peru, Ecuador, Colombia, Venezuela, and the Guianas. They also occupied the rest of Colombia and Venezuela and ranged northward through the whole of Central America and the Antilles. The third principal type was the highland intensive agriculturists, many of whom achieved state-level societies in the mountains and plateaus of Mexico, Guatemala, Ecuador, Peru, and Bolivia.

During the past generation, a vigorous debate has raged among historical demographers concerning the aboriginal population of the Americas at the time of European discovery. Estimates range from 13 million to more than 100 million. For the Latin American region, however, an estimate of 80 million seems likely. Sixty million of these people belonged to the civilized states of Middle America and the central Andes. Most of the remaining, numbering about 18 million, were lowland agriculturists in the interior of South America, the northern coastal region, the Caribbean, and Central America. Hunting and gathering peoples accounted for no more than 2 million persons, and the figure was probably closer to 1 million.

European conquest radically disturbed the aboriginal societies. Perhaps the most drastic effect was a rapid and massive population decline, characterized by modern investigators as a "demographic disaster." The principal cause of the disaster was the introduction of several new diseases that decimated the native populations through repeated epidemic outbreaks. The wars of conquest also took their toll, as did slavery and other abuses of Indian labor, and there were ecological repercussions because of interference with the seasonal rhythm of native agriculture (by removing native labor for Spanish needs at critical periods in the agricultural calendar) and the introduction of livestock (which competed with natives for land and invaded their planted fields).

Estimates of the rate of depopulation differ, but the best calculations suggest an average decline of 95 percent in 130 years, leaving only about 4 million Indians south of what is now the United States in 1650. It must be remembered, however, that an unknown portion of this decline is represented by the mestizo offspring of European or African fathers and Indian mothers, who were treated as a class or caste apart from their parents and who often sought to "pass" into the higher-status European category.

The Caribbean population, which was conquered first, was wiped out in less than fifty years. African slaves were introduced to replace the Caribbean Indians as a labor force. Most of the continental hunters and gatherers have also become extinct. The lowland agriculturists declined drastically, with many groups becoming extinct (some continue to disappear today); others, however, have survived and are today increasing in number. In the areas of highland civilization, there was also a drastic population decline, but the population reached its low of perhaps 3 million to 5 million around 1650. Thereafter it grew slowly until around the beginning of the nineteenth century. Since that time, the Indian population of Middle America and the central Andes has been growing at an increasingly rapid rate.

PRECONQUEST SOCIETIES

A moment's reflection about the areas occupied by these three major culture types helps one realize that these regions are still characterized by distinctive populations today. Elman Service has dubbed these areas Euro-America, Mestizo-America, and Indo-America, respectively.[2] Why are such differences of aboriginal culture type reflected in differences among the modern populations? Commonly, this is explained as resulting from differences in administrative policies of the European colonial powers. Not only did such policies differ among Spain, Portugal, and Great Britain, but there were differences in the way the policies were implemented in various parts of the colonial empires. Thus, it is frequently maintained that colonial policies were enforced more rigorously in the Antilles, Mexico, and Peru and that greater control was exerted over the colonists in those areas, both because these colonies were more valuable and because they contained greater numbers of colonists. In contrast, there was less interest in colonies like Venezuela and Buenos Aires, and consequently, crown control was much more lax in those areas.

There is, however, another way of looking at the question of contemporary differences. This approach begins by looking at the diversity of aboriginal cultures encountered by the white man and recognizing that the Europeans were forced to adjust differently in accordance with the basic differences in native cultures.[3]

The object of European conquest was to profit from these newly discovered areas. The preferred ways of doing so were to assess tribute from the native populations (by means of the *encomienda* and the *corregimiento*) or to exploit native labor in profit-making enterprises (through forced labor projects, or the *repartimiento*) such as construction, mining, ranching, and later, textiles.

In the highland areas of Mexico and Guatemala and in the central Andes, native societies had achieved a high level of cultural development, with complex state organization. The native peoples were integrally involved with complex economic, social, and political institutions and depended upon them to maintain their traditional way of life. It would not have been easy to survive on their own if they had been cut off from these state-level institutions. In addition, most of them had no easily accessible refuge areas to which they could flee from Spanish domination. Given the existence of well-defined state institutions, within which the native populations were accustomed to function, it was relatively easy for the European conquistadores to take these institutions over from the top and continue to control the population in much the same way as had the native elite. Such control was particularly effective because of the system of indirect administration that was worked out. Only minor modifications were made in most native institutions (except for religious ones), especially on the lower levels where native intermediaries continued to be employed in governing the mass of the population.[4]

Throughout the colonial period, there was a fair amount of racial mixture, and the native elites were gradually absorbed into the dominant Spanish ruling class. Among Indian commoners, local community and familial institutions retained strength in spite of racial mixture with the Spanish overlords and their African slaves. To this day, many Indian languages continue to be spoken throughout these areas, many rural communities have maintained their identification as Indian, and many aboriginal and/or ethnically distinct customs have been retained as central features of the local cultures. These are the areas Service characterizes as Indo-America.[5]

Lowland areas were occupied mostly by extensive agriculturists who were organized principally as independent localized tribes or villages.[6] Here there were no large organized communities or state-level institutions. It was much more difficult to control these small independent tribes, for conquest of one did not give the victor authority over its neighbor. The European strategy was to capture single families and individuals and force them to become household servants or to work as agricultural slaves. The intimacy that existed between masters and household slaves or small numbers of agricultural slaves led to a rapid mestization of the native groups. Mestizos tended to identify with the dominant European population and to be absorbed into its lower levels. Thus, there was a continuing need to acquire additional slaves from the native groups. The Paulistas of Brazil are the best-known example of this type of exploitation. Their periodic expeditions ranged far and wide throughout the interior to capture Indian slaves. This type of exploitative relationship between the European colonists and native societies led to a breakdown of the more accessible Indian communities and the flight of many more to remote refuge areas where they might avoid the depredations of slavers. In some of these isolated locations, the Indians have been able to survive to the present day, particularly in southern Chile, parts of Amazonia, the interior of Venezuela, parts of Central America, and the extremely rugged and isolated regions of northern Mexico. These are the areas that Service identifies as Mestizo America.[7]

Where plantation agriculture developed, there was need for large numbers of laborers. Because of the social and physical separation between owners and field laborers, the latter, which existed in large numbers, were treated impersonally. Under the rigors of the plantation system, Indian slaves often fled to the interior, which they could easily do because they were familiar with the environment and knew how to survive there. Even when they were unable to return to their own community, other native communities and social systems were similar enough that they were usually able to plug into them with relatively little difficulty. The very serious problem, for plantation owners, of runaway Indian slaves led to the introduction of African slaves who were much easier to control. The Africans were in a wholly unfamiliar environment—an alien terrain filled with unknown plants and animals. They could not speak the native languages, and they did not know how to behave or participate in the aboriginal social systems. Consequently, African slaves were much more inhibited from fleeing the slave situation. These plantation areas developed principally in coastal Brazil, the Caribbean, and coastal Peru. In most of these areas, the African racial type remains predominant today, and I would therefore characterize them as Afro-America.

Where the European intruders found it impossible to control the native population, even as slaves over the short term, their only recourse was to exterminate the natives or to drive them from the areas of settlement. Hunters and gatherers lived a simple life, unburdened with abundant possessions or a complex technology. They were more or less nomadic and thus could readily flee areas of control. They could survive quite well away from European control. In some cases, they found it possible to survive on the margins of European settlement. And in some instances, they actually developed a new and highly successful adaptive strategy of attacking and living off the European settlements. Among such groups we may count the Tehuelche and Puelche of Argentina; the Pehuenche of Chile; the Argentine Araucanians; the Abipón, Mbayá, and other Guaicuruan tribes of the Gran Chaco in Paraguay; and the Charrúa of Uruguay. At the northern limits of the Spanish colonies, in northern Mexico and New Mexico, similar groups developed; Apache, Ute, and Comanche raiders preyed on Spanish settlements for several hundred years. The result in most of these cases of active raiding by native groups was chronic warfare between them and the Spanish colonists. The Spanish settlements grew gradually over time and eventually reached the point at which the Spanish were able to carry on intensive warfare against the native raiders, usually exterminating them completely. These areas, where the native populations have been wholly eliminated, are what Service calls Euro-America,[8] and they include Argentina, Uruguay, and Costa Rica.

One other point is worth emphasizing in this analysis of differential relations between the conquering Europeans and native societies. European culture was structurally complex, representing a state level of organization. In this sense, it was most like the cultures of the highland state-organized peoples, less like those of the lowland agriculturists, and most distinct from the cultures of the marginal hunters and gatherers. It is clear that there was a more or less direct correlation between the cultural complexity of a native society and its survival after European conquest. It thus appears that the more alike the conquerors and the conquered, the more simple and easy the adjustment to conquest; the less difficult and disruptive the adjustment, the more likely the survival of the conquered people and the preservation of at least the local basis of their native social organization and cultural forms.

CONTEMPORARY LATIN AMERICA

Euro-America and Afro-America

Table 3.1 gives the current distribution of the Amerindian population in Latin America according to the latest more or less complete data readily available, which are for the year 1980. It will be noted that in Euro-America and Afro-America, the indigenous population generally accounts for less than 2 percent of the total population. In Euro-America, it is close to 1 percent, and in Afro-America it actually averages much less than that. The principal exception is to be found in the three Guianas, where population is sparse and total population numbers are low. There, because of the limited population and the concentration of intrusive groups along the coast, the indigenous groups that occupy the interior of these countries have not previously been faced with as much direct competition as in Brazil or the Antilles. This situation is now changing, because since independence, the Guianas have increasingly looked to development of the interior as integral to their goals of national economic development. In the case of Guyana, development of

Table 3.1
Amerindian Population of Latin America, 1980

Country	Total Population	Indian Population	Indian Percent of Total
Euro-America	36,502,000	353,638	1.0
(<2 percent)			
Argentina, Uruguay, Costa Rica			
Afro-America	139,620,198	236,764	0.2
(mostly <2 percent)			
Coastal Brazil	103,012,578	34,165	—
Guianas	1,183,619	60,767	5.1
Northern Colombia	5,678,001	139,596	2.5
Antilles	29,746,000	2,236	—
Mestizo America	101,530,496	1,577,276	1.6
(>1 percent, <6 percent)			
Northern Mexico	20,413,622	387,704	1.9
Central America (excl. Costa Rica)	12,144,599	376,981	3.1
Southern and Eastern Colombia	22,189,325	182,547	0.8
Venezuela	14,516,735	140,040	1.0
Amazonia	17,867,995	185,835	1.0
Paraguay	3,068,484	24,025	0.8
Chile	11,329,736	657,125	5.8
Indo-America	83,287,634	17,239,437	20.7
(>10 percent)			
Central and Southern Mexico	46,433,211	4,793,334	10.3
Belize	145,350	13,850	9.5
Guatemala	6,043,559	2,536,523	42.0
Ecuador	8,060,712	2,656,000	34.1
Peru	17,005,210	6,020,000	35.4
Bolivia	5,599,592	1,220,000	21.8

Source: National census data and various issues of *American Indígena* (Mexico City).

the interior is also a means of assertion and consolidation of rights to territory claimed also by neighboring Venezuela.[9]

Mestizo America

The surviving indigenous populations of this region are mostly of the tribal Indian type. For the most part, they retain their aboriginal cultures and their identity as members of a tribal community. They are not integrated into national society but continue to function as members of distinct cultures within the national boundaries of the modern state. It should be noted, however, that numerous native groups in this region are currently in the process of acculturating to the dominant national cultures, including significant numbers that are migrating to the cities. There are slightly more than 1.5 million Indians out of a total population of more than 100 million. On a country-by-country basis, the Indians make up more than 1 percent but less than 6 percent of the total population, for an overall average of 1.6 percent (see Table 3.1).

In northern Mexico, the principal group is the Tarahumara, whose numbers exist mostly as isolated subsistence farmers. Increasing numbers are, however, emigrating from their rugged mountain homeland to work in the cities. In Central America, interior Venezuela, and the vast Amazon Basin, the aboriginal populations were relatively sparse at the time of European contact. Disease, slavery, and European warfare against these highly divided groups led to their decimation and extinction in many localities. Nonetheless, a number of tribal groups persist in more isolated localities or on reserves protected by missionaries or national governments. Most of these populations are found in the lowland, tropical areas.

The economy of these lowland tribes is based on subsistence slash-and-burn farming of tropical crops. The most important staples are manioc, bananas, and yams, but these are supplemented by a variety of other crops. Some tribes, like the Karinya of Venezuela, cultivate nearly a hundred. Fishing is also an important subsistence activity, providing the principal source of dietary protein. Hunting is generally less important, and even this activity is often oriented toward riverine and aquatic species (turtle, caiman, ducks, manatee, etc.). In some groups, which lack ready access to the rivers—such as the Jivaro and the Yanomamö—hunting assumes greater importance. By exploiting the diverse resources of agriculture, fishing, and hunting, most of these groups have maintained a nutritionally balanced diet. Their crafts are generally simple, although many tribes make excellent baskets and some like the Jivaro are known for their fine pottery.

Villages are politically independent, and tribal identity is recognized only as a consequence of sharing a common language, common customs, and a mutual ethnic consciousness. Settlements generally number fewer than 300 inhabitants, although they may occasionally range up to as many as 1,000 to 2,000. Traditional residence was in communal houses, with one or more located in each settlement. Sociopolitical organization is based on kinship ties. Marriage tends to be endogamous within the local group. The headman or chief has limited authority over the group; he usually enjoys few, if any, special privileges. His influence is based on personal prestige and does not extend beyond the local village. The division of labor is based strictly on age and sex. With the exception of the shaman, there is no full-time specialization.

Warfare is frequent and often bitter, but it is never pursued for purposes of conquering territory or exacting tribute. Usually it is justified in terms of revenge, or sometimes to gain prestige or to acquire trophies that are supernaturally powerful. Many anthropologists subscribe to an ecological explanation for warfare among these tribes—seeing it as a mechanism for acquiring and maintaining access to scarce resources, such as rivers, with their abundance of fish and game; good farmland, also mostly along the rivers; and, among the Yanomamö, women. Warfare may also serve to keep populations dispersed so as not to overexploit the limited resources of the tropical environment.

Except for marriage, which tends to be treated in a matter-of-fact way, life crisis rites are particularly emphasized among these peoples. Shamanism is also important and highly developed. The shaman works to cure illness, to affect the weather, and to ensure success in warfare. Often he organizes magical-religious festivals and dances as well. He is generally the guardian of tribal religious tradition. The shaman may also practice witchcraft and sorcery, though he rarely admits to doing so unless it is directed against tribal enemies. A wide variety of narcotics are used by the shamans, and sometimes by all adult men, in curing and other religious ceremonies. Although the concept of a high god may exist, it is relatively unimportant in religious belief and ritual. Instead, religion centers on culture heroes, who made the world as it is today, and on nature spirits who are closely associated with subsistence concerns, particularly fishing and hunting.

The Mapuche of southern Chile are somewhat distinct from the other groups being discussed here, since they have adopted European crops and farming techniques and participate, to a certain extent, in the national society. Crop surpluses are sold in the regional market, children receive formal schooling, and the Mapuche participate, at least marginally, in national political, legal, and judicial institutions. Under the Pinochet regime, however, they suffered severe discrimination and many communities lost their land.

All of the groups in Mestizo America are under increasing pressure from national societies because the isolated areas they have occupied up to now are being opened up by the construction of highways, spontaneous colonization by peasant farmers, national development programs, and projects for the exploitation of natural resources by numerous multinational corporations. In Central America, the native groups seem to be holding their own so far, although there are concerns for the future. In Nicaragua the revolutionary Sandinista government was startled to find the 120,000 Miskito Indians living in the Caribbean lowlands resisting efforts to absorb them into national society. After several years of tense relations, the Mosquitia region has been formally recognized as an autonomous region within the Nicaraguan state. In Venezuela, the government has been attempting to protect Indian lands through legal action. This protection was recently called into question, however, when the Karinya were denied legal rights to the lands they have occupied for generations, rights confirmed by royal decree during the colonial period. Authorities in Colombia, Bolivia, and Paraguay have generally ignored the problems of the natives, but in Colombia, special interest organizations formed by knowledgeable Indian leaders have been accused of aiding terrorist groups. Efforts in Colombia to legislate a more rigorous paternalistic control over indigenous groups have so far been defeated. Brazil has vacillated between looking the other way while natives are pushed out or exterminated and attempting to resettle them on reserves such as the Xingú National Park. However, when faced with pressures from development interests, responsible officials have generally allowed these reserves to be fragmented or whittled down. For example, in spite of a vociferous international outcry, Brazil has made no concerted effort to keep thousands of prospectors, miners, and traders from intruding on Yanomamö territory.

Although most of these Indians have remained in distinct, small-scale tribal communities, increasing numbers have also followed the general demographic trend in Latin America of rural to urban migration. While it has often been recognized that there are significant numbers of Indians in Latin American cities, it has been nearly impossible to get any reliable estimate of their numbers. To judge from the available figures, at least 200,000 Indians are probably urban dwellers in Mestizo America.

These tribal peoples cannot be ignored as human beings. Certainly, they are equal in importance to any other identifiable group in the nations of Mestizo America. Many of their current difficulties arise from the fact that in terms of their gross numbers and the economic or political impact that they exercise within those nations, they represent a very small segment of the modern population.

Indo-America

By far the most significant indigenous populations, in terms both of numbers and of their place in national society, are the modern Indian types found in Indo-America, comprising most of Mexico, Guatemala, and the central Andean countries of Ecuador, Peru, and Bolivia. These Indians, who mostly live in the highland regions of those countries, must be included in any consideration of modern Latin America. Although their way of life differs strikingly from that of the non-Indians in the countries in which they live, they share many patterns and institutions, mainly of European origin, with the other citizens. Numerically, they are an important segment of the population, constituting more than 10 percent in almost all of these countries, and in some countries, such as Guatemala and the Andean nations, representing more than one-third the total population. Taking Indo-America as a whole, the indigenous population amounts to more than 17 million, or 21 percent of the total population (see Table 3.1).

During the colonial period, the Indians of these countries were taught Catholicism and often were concentrated into Spanish-type villages, where European forms of community organization were forced upon them. They borrowed freely from the European culture of the sixteenth and seventeenth centuries—a culture that in many respects contained as many "folk features" as their own. By at least the beginning of the eighteenth century, the fusion of the aboriginal and colonial Spanish patterns had formed a new culture among these peoples. This culture persists today, unchanged in its main outlines, and constitutes an important variant of *national* patterns in these highland countries. Because this culture is relatively unchanged from colonial times, it contrasts markedly with modern cultural patterns and is sometimes erroneously believed to represent a survival of aboriginal cultural practices.

Modern Indians in these countries generally speak an aboriginal language, although they frequently speak Spanish as well. Community cohesion tends to persist at a high level despite the encroaching power of the national states. The Indians of each community generally think of themselves as ethnic units, separate from other Indian groups and from non-Indian nationals of the country in which they reside. They are people of the village or town rather than Mexicans, Guatemalans, or Peruvians. Frequently, they wear a distinctive costume that identifies them as members of a particular pueblo.

Community structure is characteristically of the type known as the closed corporate peasant community. It is an organized communal structure with clearly defined social boundaries; in other words, it is very clear who does and who does not belong to the community. The community generally does not identify with the nation; its members find their personal and social satisfactions within the community by adhering to its traditional value system. The corporate peasant community is held together not by ties of kinship but by co-ownership of a landholding corporation. Members are not allowed to sell or rent land to outsiders, and this taboo severely limits the degree to which factors outside the community can affect the structure of private property or the development of class differences within the community. This is one of the most important ways of promoting and maintaining community integration.

Another common pattern, especially in the central Andes, is for the Indians to be clustered as peons on large hacienda estates. These Indians have no secure rights to property; instead, they provide labor to work the land belonging to a non-Indian owner. In exchange, they receive a plot of land on which to build a house and grow subsistence crops. Although a small wage may be paid, the plot of land serves in lieu of most wage income. The hacienda owner discourages community organization and tries to establish personal ties between himself and each laborer, thereby exercising greater control over his labor force. At the same time, by encouraging maintenance of the peons' native language and distinctive ethnic identity, with its own traditional customs, he ensures that the peonage community will remain isolated from the larger society.

These peasant communities depend on agriculture as their principal means of subsistence. Most of the land that the peasants receive for their own use is of marginal productivity. It is exploited by means of traditional technology, which involves continuous physical effort and much manual labor. Peasants rely on both the hoe and the plow drawn by draft animals, but there is little use of modern machinery. Their staple crops include the principal cereal grains (corn, wheat, barley), a variety of legumes (beans, broad beans, lentils, garbanzos, peas), chile peppers, and in the Andes, a variety of root crops, including potatoes. Most agriculture follows a short fallow cycle, with fields being rested for one year after several years of cropping. There is little use of fertilizers, although insecticides have become popular in recent years. In some areas irrigation is important.

Crafts are highly developed. The great variety of objects being manufactured includes textiles, pottery, baskets, wood carvings, jewelry, and toys, which often achieve a high degree of aesthetic creativity. The economy of the closed corporate community is closely linked to a peculiar sort of regional marketing system. Different villages specialize in different commodities, and these are brought together and exchanged in the market. For the same reason, the market brings together a much larger supply of articles than merchants in any one community could afford to keep continuously in their stores. Thus, there is much wider access to the products of each community. A shortage of money requires that sales and purchases in the market be small. The producer typically offers his or her goods for sale in order to obtain small amounts of cash, which can be used to purchase other needed goods. In recent years, increasing quantities of cheap manufactured goods have also been introduced into the regional market system and in some cases, they have provided stiff competition for locally produced handicrafts. Another source of cash income is seasonal migration to work on plantations and *fincas* that produce sugar, coffee, or other goods for export. Typically, this migration involves movement from highland peasant communities to lowland areas.

The basic social unit of these communities is the nuclear family. Households average about six persons. Marriage may be consecrated through formal religious ceremonies, but there is also a high incidence of marriages that are the result of elopement or abduction. Marriage is usually with an unrelated person, but it is preferentially endogamous within the village. This preference serves as another mechanism for local community integration. Fertility is high among these people, and although the rate of infant mortality has also been high, the mortality rate has been declining over the past several decades, leading to a rapid growth of population. The institution of *compadrazgo,* which establishes a special relationship between the parents and godparents of a child, is another important mechanism for social integration and mutual support.

Settlement patterns vary considerably. In some areas, such as central Mexico, residence is concentrated in a compact village. In others, such as southern Mexico or highland Ecuador, the preference is to scatter residences throughout the community's territory. In the organization of the local community, traditional native officials are often maintained alongside representatives of the national bureaucracy. The community's system of power embraces the male members of the community and makes achievement of power a matter of community decision rather than one of individually achieved status. This system of power is tied into a religious system or a series of interlocking religious systems. The politico-religious system as a whole tends to define the boundaries of the community and acts as a symbol of collective unity. Prestige within the community is largely related to rising from office to office within this system. Conspicuous consumption, principally by putting on elaborate fiesta celebrations, is geared to this communally approved system of power and religion, and it serves to level differences of wealth within the community. The system thus avoids the development of class divisions that might undermine the corporate structure of the community. Various psychic mechanisms of control, such as institutionalized envy and the concept of "limited good," serve as additional conservative factors that help in maintaining the traditional values and way of life.[10]

The modern Indian is nominally Catholic, but his religious beliefs and practices have incorporated a considerable amount of aboriginal belief as well. In addition, Catholic saints are endowed with local characteristics and powers. Fiestas are held to honor the patron saint and other locally important saints, and *cargos,* or magical practices, are assumed to preserve and promote these saint cults. Maintenance of traditional fiestas and associated ceremonies and celebrations is an important part of the traditional culture, and it serves as one more way of preserving a distinctive local identity. Some communities maintain folk priests—cantors, for example—who have contributed to the survival of the folk beliefs and practices in the absence (sometimes for several generations) of Catholic priests.

Illness and disease are explained as resulting from an imbalance in the hot and cold humors that occur in the body, in the foods consumed, and in other objects with which the individual comes into contact. Certain psychological disorders are also explained as a result of *susto* or *espanto* ("fright"), in which the individual is frightened by an encounter with a supernatural entity, sometimes resulting in loss of the soul. The curing of these disorders is usually in the hands of local *curanderos* ("folk doctors") who may attempt to restore the hot-cold imbalance, call upon aboriginal supernaturals or Christian saints, apply herbal remedies, etc. Ethnographic reports suggest that many of the empirical remedies of these *curanderos* are effective and that their treatments are largely successful. If the family members of the sick person can afford it, however, they may try to hedge the probabilities of a successful cure by also consulting a modern physician.

Adherence to the traditional culture validates membership in an existing society and acts as a passport to participation in the life of the community. The amount of wealth that can be gained by a typical peasant is enough to gain the prestige symbols of the Indian system, and thus, the individual is encouraged to maintain his identification with that system. The particular traits held by an Indian help him remain within the equilibrium of relationships that maintain the community. On the other hand, the non-Indian individual is attempting to gain wealth within the national system, where it is impossible to accumulate enough wealth through hard work to permit access to the prestige symbols of the upper sector. The non-Indian peasant is thus perpetually frustrated in his attempt to achieve meaningful goals.

These modern Indian populations are important elements of the national societies. Numerically, they represent a significant proportion of the total population. They participate, if only marginally, in the economic, political, and religious institutions of the nation, and they represent a large, inexpensive pool of labor that can be recruited whenever unskilled labor is required. There is also a slow but constant interchange of ideas between the Indian subcultures on the one hand and the national culture on the other.

With modernization, education, improved communication, etc., such interaction is increasing all the time. Continuing population growth and the resultant pressures on the land have led to a large-scale migration to the cities. Today, there are probably 4 million Indians or more living in the towns and cities of Indo-America. Once they have arrived in the cities, there is a rapid acculturation to urban life. But at the same time, they maintain their ties to and identification with the home community. Urban residents frequently return to visit their relatives or to attend major fiestas. There is also evidence that with increased incomes and greater sophistication, traditional customs and practices are being revived and even intensified in many of these communities.[11] Thus, in spite of modernizing influences, there are indications that for the foreseeable future, many of these modern Indian communities will retain their ethnically distinctive subcultures.

NOTES

1. Herbert Barry III, "Regional and Worldwide Variations in Culture," *Ethnology* 7:2 (1968), pp. 207–217, and George Peter Murdock, "Ethnographic Atlas," *Ethnology* 6:2 (1967).
2. Elman R. Service, "Indian-European Relations in Colonial Latin America," *American Anthropologist* 57 (1955), pp. 411–412.
3. Ibid., p. 411.
4. Ibid., p. 418.
5. Ibid., pp. 411–412.
6. Some lowland societies were organized as chiefdoms—small, weakly centralized societies that were transitional between independent villages and strongly centralized states; in fact, they generally integrated a number of dependent villages. Chiefdoms were typically unstable, and with European conquest, removal of the ruler usually resulted in social disintegration. The constituent villages then reverted to the level of independent communities (Karl H. Schwerin, "The Anthropological Antecedents: Caciques, Cacicazgos, and Caciquismo," in *The Caciques: Oligarchical Politics and the System of Caciquismo in the Luso-Hispano World,* ed. Robert Kern and Ronald Dolkart, pp. 5–17 [Albuquerque: University of New Mexico Press, 1973]).
7. Service, "Indian-European Relations," pp. 411–412, 418.
8. Ibid., pp. 411–412, 420.
9. William Heningsgaard and Jason Clay, "The Upper Mazaruni Dam," *Cultural Survival Newsletter* 4:3 (1980), p. 103.
10. George M. Foster, *Tzintzuntzan: Mexican Peasants in a Changing World,* rev. ed. (New York: Elsevier, 1979), pp. 122–166.
11. See, for example, Hugo Nutini, *San Bernardino Contla: Marriage and Family Structure in a Tlaxcalan Municipio* (Pittsburgh: University of Pittsburgh Press, 1968), and Frank Cancian, *Economics and Prestige in a Maya Community: The Religios* cargo *System in Zinacantan* (Stanford: Stanford University Press, 1965).

SUGGESTED READINGS

Barry, Herbert, III. "Regional and Worldwide Variations in Culture." *Ethnology* 7:2 (1968), pp. 207–217. A cross-cultural statistical analysis, based on the *Ethnographic Atlas* (see

Murdock 1967), of the distribution worldwide, and by continents, of the major types of subsistence economy, family customs, and social structure.

Buechler, Hans C., and Judith-Maria Buechler. *The Bolivian Aymara.* Case Studies in Cultural Anthropology. New York: Holt, Rinehart and Winston, 1971. One of the few complete ethnographic descriptions of an Andean community and the best short study available.

Cancian, Frank. *Economics and Prestige in a Maya Community: The Religious* cargo *System in Zinacantan.* Stanford: Stanford University Press, 1965. Offers a thorough analysis of a typical religious *cargo* system and shows how traditional practices have been modified and elaborated in response to population growth and increasing wealth differentiation within the community.

Chagnon, Napoleon A. *Yanomamö: The Fierce People.* Case Studies in Cultural Anthropology. New York: Holt, Rinehart and Winston, 1968. The classic study of an extremely warlike people who inhabit an isolated area in the northern Amazon Basin.

Cultural Survival. "Nicaragua." *Cultural Survival Newsletter* 4:4 (1980), pp. 8–9. Cultural Survival is an international organization of anthropologists and other concerned individuals who seek to document cases of injustice, exploitation, and ethnocide suffered by indigenous peoples and, where possible, to bring pressure to bear or to intervene to protect the interests of the native groups.

Davis, Shelton H. *Victims of the Miracle: Development and the Indians of Brazil.* Cambridge: Cambridge University Press, 1977. Attempts to document the disruptive impact on the native peoples of the tropical forest of programs to develop the Amazon in Brazil.

Denevan, William M., ed. *The Native Population of the Americas in 1492.* Madison: University of Wisconsin, 1976. A collection of papers that treats the historical demography of the Americas. Each paper considers some aspect of the basic disagreement about the relative size of the aboriginal population of the New World.

Faron, Louis C. *The Mapuche Indians of Chile.* Case Studies in Cultural Anthropology. New York: Holt, Rinehart and Winston, 1968. An excellent summary of contemporary culture among the peasant Araucanian farmers of southern Chile.

Foster, George M. *Tzintzuntzan: Mexican Peasants in a Changing World.* Rev. ed. New York: Elsevier, 1979. The best general account of peasant society and world view in Latin America. Although most inhabitants of Tzintzuntzan are mestizo, they share many characteristics with the modern Indian, or the closed corporate peasant communities of Indo-America.

Gregor, Thomas. *Mehinaku: The Drama of Daily Life in a Brazilian Indian Village.* Chicago: University of Chicago Press, 1977. The peaceful Mehinaku, who live in the southern Amazon Basin, contrast strikingly with the warlike Yanomamö (see Chagnon 1968).

Heningsgaard, William, and Jason Clay. "The Upper Mazaruni Dam." *Cultural Survival Newsletter* 4:3 (1980), p. 103. A brief account of the economic and political factors behind the construction of the dam and why this project means the Akawaio are being deprived of their land.

Isbell, Billie Jean. *To Defend Ourselves. Ecology and Ritual in an Andean Village.* Austin: University of Texas, 1978. Good analysis of a typical Andean community that treats both traditional culture and the processes of accommodating to a changing nation.

Lewis, Oscar. *Tepoztlán: Village in Mexico.* Case Studies in Cultural Anthropology. New York: Holt, Rinehart and Winston, 1960. Perhaps because of its proximity to the highway connecting Mexico City, Cuernavaca, and Acapulco, Tepoztlán is the most studied village in Mexico. Lewis's work there is particularly notable because he questions the findings of his famous predecessor Robert Redfield.

Mayer, Enrique, and Elio Masferrer. "La población indígena de América en 1978." *América indígena* 39 (1979), pp. 217–337. The most recent effort at a comprehensive calculation of the indigenous population of Latin America and the United States. Users of this study should check the figures carefully, however, for I have encountered numerous errors of computation.

Murdock, George Peter. "Ethnographic Atlas." *Ethnology* 6:2 (1967). The culmination of Murdock's lifelong interest in tabulating the occurrence of cultural traits on a worldwide basis.

Murphy, Yolanda, and Robert F. Murphy. *Women of the Forest.* New York: Columbia University Press, 1974. An excellent account of a typical Amazonian society with an emphasis on the role of women and the woman's point of view.

Nutini, Hugo. *San Bernardino Contla: Marriage and Family Structure in a Tlaxcalan Municipio.* Pittsburgh: University of Pittsburgh Press, 1968. A good account of a typical central Mexican community.

Schwerin, Karl H. *Oil and Steel: Processes of Karinya Culture Change in Response to Industrial Development.* Latin American Studies, 4. Los Angeles: UCLA, 1966. A comparison of social and cultural characteristics in two Venezuelan Indian communities with a theoretical analysis of the processes of culture change that have occurred there during the present century.

————. "The Anthropological Antecedents: Caciques, Cacicazgos, and Caciquismo." In *The Caciques: Oligarchical Politics and the System of Caciquismo in the Luso-Hispano World,* ed. Robert Kern and Ronald Dolkart, pp. 5–17. Albuquerque: University of New Mexico Press, 1973. A summary statement on the general nature of chiefdoms, or *cacicazgos,* in pre-Columbian Latin America with discussion of their distribution and principal social and cultural characteristics.

Service, Elman R. "Indian-European Relations in Colonial Latin America." *American Anthropologist* 57 (1955), pp. 411–425. Presents the thesis that major differences in the character of modern Latin American states can be traced to European responses to differences in aboriginal cultural patterns, especially in relation to subsistence and sociopolitical complexity.

Stein, William W. *Hualcan: Life in the Highlands of Peru.* Cornell Studies in Anthropology. Ithaca: Cornell University Press, 1961. An excellent study of a representative Quechuan community. It is instructive to compare this work with the Buechlers' account of an Aymaran community in Bolivia (Buechler and Buechler, 1971).

Steward, Julian H., ed. *Handbook of South American Indians.* 7 vols. Bureau of American Ethnology Bulletin 143. Washington, D.C.: Smithsonian Institution, 1946–1959. This monumental survey of the native peoples of South America (including Central America and the Caribbean) represents the first attempt to collect all the available anthropological knowledge for any single continent.

Steward, Julian H., and Louis C. Faron. *Native Peoples of South America.* New York: McGraw-Hill Book Company, 1959. An attempt to distill the massive amount of data published in the *Handbook of South American Indians* into a single textbook volume.

Vogt, Evon Z. *The Zinacantecos of Mexico: A Modern Maya Way of Life.* Case Studies in Cultural Anthropology. New York: Holt, Rinehart and Winston, 1970. Since 1960, Vogt has directed the Harvard Chiapas Project in the *municipio* of Zinacantan in southern Mexico. This project has been dedicated to twenty years or more of continuous observation and study in the same community in order to gain a better understanding of the types of directional processes that are at work in social and cultural systems.

PART TWO
HISTORICAL SETTING

4

COLONIAL LATIN AMERICA

PETER BAKEWELL

The colonial period in Latin America lasted just over 300 years. That is an impossible amount of history to describe even broadly in a few pages. So this chapter does not try to give a summary of events in colonial times. Rather, its aim is to examine two broad themes: What, in a quite practical way, is meant by "colonialism" in Latin America in the 1500s, 1600s, and 1700s? and What features and influences of colonial times have carried over into, and helped to form, the Latin America of today?

CONQUEST AND SETTLEMENT

We begin with some basic dates and geographical data. The colonial period of Latin America began when Columbus sailed across the Atlantic from Spain in 1492 and claimed the lands he touched on for Spain. They were, on that first voyage of 1492–1493, the islands of Cuba and, as the Spaniards came to call it, Hispaniola (now divided between the Dominican Republic and Haiti). It is illogical to say that Columbus "discovered" the Americas, because, obviously, the true discoverers were the people who first entered and settled them. And people from Asia had done those things many tens of thousands of years before Columbus arrived, becoming in the course of time what are now referred to as "native Americans." From the point of view of Spain and Europe in general, however, Columbus did find the Americas, and more important, his "discovery" led to the establishment of a permanent link between the two sides of the Atlantic—something that the Norse expeditions to North America from Greenland, around A.D. 1000, had failed to do.

As soon as Columbus reported the existence of Cuba and Hispaniola to the Spanish crown, Spain claimed the right to settle and govern those islands and other lands that might be found in the same direction. The pope of the day, Alexander VI, who was a Spaniard, confirmed the claim. His confirmation was sought because, as the chief representative of God on earth, he was the highest authority in the world known to Christian rulers. In any case, no other European state, with the possible exception of Portugal, was strong enough to challenge Spain's claim to possess and govern the lands Columbus had found.

The Portuguese had themselves been exploring westward and southward in the Atlantic for many decades before 1492 and were understandably disturbed by Spain's claim to all land on the west side of the Atlantic. Conflict was averted, however, by an agreement (the Treaty of Tordesillas), drawn up in 1494, that divided the tasks of exploring and settling the world between the two countries. To the west of an imaginary north-south line in the Atlantic, Spain should explore and settle, and to the east of that line, Portugal should do so. Although it was not realized at the time, that agreement was to give to Portugal a large section of eastern South America since, as defined in the treaty, the line passed down through the mouth of the Amazon, leaving the coastline again at about 30° south latitude. Hence, the eastern "bulge" of South America, once it was discovered in 1500, became Portuguese territory, forming the basis of modern Brazil.

The colonial history of Spanish America, having begun in 1492 with Columbus, ended in the years 1810–1825. This was the period in which the various Spanish colonies in the Americas, with two small exceptions, fought for and gained their independence. The exceptions were Cuba and Puerto Rico, which did not become free of Spain, for various reasons, until 1898. Brazil broke from Portugal in 1822. So, in both the Spanish and Portuguese cases, the colonial period was long—almost twice as long, in fact, as the time that has elapsed between independence and the present.

Colonial Spanish America was much larger than Portuguese America. Even though the Portuguese did gradually push westward beyond the Tordesillas line, still Spanish America covered a greater area, extending ultimately from the southern tip of South America to well within the present limits of the United States. In the 1700s, Spain had settlements as far north as San Francisco in California, southern Arizona, most of New Mexico, and much of Texas—as well as in a substantial part of Florida. And all territory, with a few exceptions—by far the most notable being Brazil—between that northern frontier and the far tip of South America was Spanish. Spain also held the larger Caribbean islands and some of the smaller ones. The empire in the Americas—Las Indias (the Indies), as the Spanish called their possessions—was truly vast: some 9,000 mi (almost 14,500 km) from north to south.

COLONIAL GOVERNMENTS AND ECONOMIES

What is meant by saying that these great areas explored and settled by Spain and Portugal were colonies? First, certainly, is the fact that the two home countries governed them. One of the remarkable features of Latin American colonial history is that governments were set up and actually worked. The difficulties of accomplishing this task were forbidding. For one thing, distances were enormous, not only within the Americas, but also between the Americas and Europe. The whole colonial period was, of course, a time of sailing ships, which were slow and unreliable. (Ships improved technically with time, but not until the 1700s were they good enough to allow regular sailings around Cape Horn to the colonies on the west coast of South America. Before then, communication between Spain and the west coast was by Atlantic shipping to the Isthmus of Panama, barge and mule across the isthmus, and Pacific ships to the various west coast ports.) Travel in the colonies themselves was difficult in most cases because of mountains, deserts, forests, and extremes of temperature. One basic necessity of effective government—communication—was therefore difficult to achieve from the start. Nevertheless, governments were installed, and their authority was extended into remarkably remote areas. A brief explanation of how this task was accomplished is necessary.

The Spanish had the greater problems because of the size and the distance from Spain of their colonies. (Brazil was quite easily reached by sea from Portugal.) The Spanish home government saw, once the size of the Americas began to be appreciated, that it would have to delegate a great deal of responsibility to administrators in the colonies, because it would be simply impossible to make all the necessary decisions in Spain. So two very powerful positions were created—those of viceroys who would live in Mexico City and Lima. The holders of these offices were usually Spanish noblemen of much experience, who were to act in their areas in place of the king (which is precisely the meaning of the word "viceroy"). They had authority to make all but the largest of decisions, and each was ultimately responsible for everything that happened in the area under his command. The first viceroy appointed to Mexico City arrived there in 1535. As the area of Spanish exploration expanded, this viceroy came to have control of the whole of Mexico, the Spanish islands of the Caribbean, and all of Central America except Panama. This area of authority, or jurisdiction, was known as the viceroyalty of New Spain. The first viceroy in South America reached Lima in 1544. The territory of this official eventually came to include everything from Panama in the north to Tierra del Fuego in the south, excluding, of course, Portuguese America. The jurisdiction centered on Lima was known as the viceroyalty of Peru. In the 1700s, for closer control, two further viceroyalties were created in South America: New Granada (corresponding roughly to modern Colombia) in 1739, and River Plate (roughly speaking, modern Argentina) in 1776.

It was obviously impossible for individuals to run these vast viceroyalties unassisted. So the Spanish government at home quickly created, in the 1500s, a series of councils to assist the viceroys and to carry their authority far from the two viceregal capitals of that time. These councils were called *audiencias.* Besides having the task of advising the viceroys and in many matters making executive decisions themselves, these councils also functioned as regional courts of appeal. By 1570, there were ten *audiencias,* each with authority over a large sub-area. At a lower administrative level than the *audiencias* were local governors, some of them in charge of large frontier regions and others, of lesser rank, administering towns and villages.

There was much wrong with this system. By modern administrative standards, it was certainly clumsy and corrupt. Many officials, for example, paid more attention to preventing other officials from intruding on their powers than they did to implementing the king's law. And nearly all officials, in the general manner of the times in Europe, saw their positions as means of enriching themselves far beyond the rewards of their salaries, which were often low. Nonetheless, in view of the difficulties, it is a near miracle that the system worked at all. Also very surprising was the speed with which the system was constructed. Generally speaking, within a few years of the conquest of a given region, there were royal administrators in place to enforce laws, collect taxes, and send reports home. Although Spanish America was a vast and rough place, the king's men made their presence felt throughout most of it, and they commanded respect.

The Portuguese set up a rather similar system in Brazil, centered on Bahia (until the mid-1700s when Rio de Janerio became the capital). They never, however, succeeded in achieving quite such a powerful grip on their colony as Spain did. There were various reasons for this difference. Two important ones were that Portugal, being a smaller and poorer country than Spain, simply did not have the resources of cash and men to create such a powerful administrative machine as Spain built in the Americas and that for many decades after locating Brazil, Portugal was far more attentive to its spice-yielding colonies in the Far East than it was to the apparently rather poorly endowed coast of Brazil.

The first outstanding feature of colonization, therefore, was government. The second was the extraction of wealth from the Americas—the Spanish themselves freely admitted that they had gone to and conquered the Americas for the sake of gold and God. One of the main tasks of the colonial governments was certainly to ensure that Spain and Portugal received as large an income as possible from the colonies. The main type of wealth that Spain received from its colonies was silver. We tend to think of Spanish gold, sunk perhaps in galleons off the coast of Florida, and the conquerors did seek, and find, large amounts of gold. But the more plentiful precious metal proved, in the long run, to be silver. One of the main reasons for Spain's very rapid exploration and settlement of the Americas (and hence, for the quick expansion of government) was that the conquerors ranged far and wide in search of mines. In a surprisingly large number of places, they found them, especially in the highlands of Mexico and what is now Bolivia. These mines were the greatest sources of silver in the world throughout the Latin American colonial period, and they made Spain the envy of its neighbors in Europe. Other profitable goods that Spain took from the Americas were red and blue dyes, chocolate beans, hides, sugar, and some spices.

The Portuguese also did well from their colony in Brazil. Before 1560 or so, the main export was a wood that yielded a red dye. From then until about 1700, a far more profitable export predominated: sugar, which the colonists produced on large plantations. For fifty years thereafter, gold and diamonds were the most spectacular products of the Brazilian economy, stimulating substantial population of the interior for the first time and an increase in immigration from Portugal. Finally, in the last half-century or so of colonial times, there was a recovery of the sugar trade and an increase in the cultivation of other crops, such as chocolate and rice.

The term "exploitation" is often applied to the extraction of wealth by Spain and Portugal from their American colonies. It is a term of criticism, signifying an unjust and a greedy grasping by the colonizing powers of the natural riches of Latin America—a process that had the result, among others, of leaving the states of Latin America considerably poorer than they otherwise would have been after independence. But an unqualified charge of exploitation against the Spanish and Portuguese is too crude to be convincing. In some cases, the valuable export product was something that the colonizers had introduced into the Americas: sugar, for instance, in the case of Brazil, or hides from cattle introduced into Mexico by the Spanish. And even where the exported wealth was something already existing in the Americas, such as silver, that wealth was not merely lying on the ground waiting to be picked up and sent back to Europe. In all cases, and especially in that of mining, successful extraction of the product was the result of the application of new techniques, investment of capital, and use of freighting methods not known in the Americas before the Spanish and Portuguese arrived. The wealth of the Americas was great, but it did not come for nothing, even to the greatest of the conquerors or the most fortunate of settlers.

EXPLOITATION OF LABOR

That said, it cannot be denied that the term "exploitation" is a just description of the use made of the native Americans by Spaniards and Portuguese for labor. Within a very few years of the conquest, the idea became firmly rooted among settlers, and even among some theologians and government officials, that the native Americans were by nature inferior to Europeans. It seemed, therefore, quite natural to both sets of colonists and both governments that the natives, once conquered, should work for their conquerors. Some enlightened Spaniards and Portuguese opposed this reasoning, but their views were far outweighed by Iberian public opinion. So the American native peoples were forced in one way or another to work for the colonists. Sometimes they were enslaved. This was particularly common in both Spanish and Portuguese America between the conquest and the mid-1500s. Also in the 1500s, many natives were distributed among Spanish settlers in a system called *encomienda* ("entrustment"). According to this system, the people who had been "entrusted" were to work for the settler, or to supply a tribute in goods or cash, in return for being taught Christianity and the Spanish way of life in general. Settlers were also charged with protecting the people entrusted to them from any enemies who might appear. On paper, this *encomienda* arrangement had strengths. The natives were not legally slaves of the settler in question, but free people. In return for services rendered, they were at least to receive physical security and what was for the Spanish, at least, the highest spiritual gift imaginable: Christianity. In fact, however, few Spaniards fulfilled their part of the bargain, and the *encomienda* often became an oppressive means of making the native people work for the settlers.

Because of its damaging effects and because it tended to direct disproportionate amounts of native tribute and labor toward the conquerors and early settlers at the expense of later Spanish immigrants, the *encomienda* soon ceased to be the home government's preferred arrangement for the supply of native labor to the colonists. Indeed, from the 1540s on, the home government actively opposed the *encomienda* and tried to take native people away from those settlers to whom they had been entrusted—much to the settlers' anger. Another system for obtaining native labor then became needed, and draft labor was introduced in many places from the 1550s on. Rather elaborate arrangements were made according to which a small proportion of the adult men from each Indian town would be assigned each year for a period of time—between a week and a month, generally—to a Spanish employer. The assignments were made by a Spanish official, and, at least in principle, workers were directed to tasks that were of public utility: agriculture, road and bridge building, and mining (because it was so central an economic activity).

When the system began, draft labor was probably less of a burden on the natives than *encomienda* had been. It also probably made more effective use of native labor than *encomienda* had, because the draft spread the available workers more evenly among Spanish employers. During the second half of the 1500s, however, the number of settlers wanting workers increased while the native population decreased, with the result that draft work also soon became a very great burden for the native people. Their solution to this problem was to offer themselves for hire to individual Spanish settlers, evading the draft as best they could. Since many employers were in great need of workers, the native volunteers could obtain much higher wages than they were paid under the draft system. Wage labor by volunteer workers naturally appeared first in situations in which the settlers were both very short of labor and able to pay high wages. Silver mining was one of these. By 1600, for example, three-quarters of all mining workers in Mexico were native people who had been drawn to that sort of labor by the high pay. After 1600, wage labor became increasingly common in many occupations in Spanish America. Broadly speaking, it gave the workers more freedom and better conditions than the previous labor arrangements had done. So it is generally true that the years of harshest exploitation of native workers by the Spanish were the 1500s.

Where, for one reason or another, there were not enough native people to do the Europeans' work, black slaves were imported from Africa. Exactly how many slaves were brought across the Atlantic in colonial times to Latin America is not known, but the number was certainly in excess of 3 million, with the main importing regions being Brazil and the Spanish Caribbean. Demand for black slaves was high in both of these regions because both produced sugar on plantations—a strenuous sort of labor that blacks proved more able to tolerate than native Americans. In the Spanish Caribbean, there was, in any case, little choice in the matter. Nearly all the native populations of the large islands were destroyed in the sixteenth century by maltreatment, enslavement, and above all, disease. In Brazil, the natives survived in larger numbers, but they proved too primitive to be easily adapted to plantation labor. The importation of blacks into Brazil was, furthermore, simplified and cheapened by the proximity of Brazil to the West African coast, which was the source of most slaves in colonial times, and by the fact that Portugal had several small colonies and bases on that coast in which slaves were traded.

The need for the labor of black slaves was greatly increased after the Spanish and Portuguese conquests in the Americas by the drastic decline in the native populations. There were several reasons for this decline. The battles of the conquest killed some natives. More serious, however, were the aftereffects of conquest: the seizure of good agricultural land by the Europeans; the disruption of families resulting from the imposition of labor burdens on the natives; and the fall of the birthrate of the native peoples as a result of poorer nutrition, dislocation of society, and above all, discouragement at finding themselves, their beliefs, and their gods so easily overcome.

Even more damaging to the native populations, however, were the diseases that the Europeans, quite unintentionally, brought with them. Many diseases common in Europe, Africa, and Asia were unknown in the Americas because of the geographical separation of the continents. Consequently, the American native peoples suffered very severely from diseases that today seem minor: the common cold and measles, for example. Other diseases that are still considered dangerous were also transmitted to the Americas by the conquest: plague and most damaging of all, smallpox. These sicknesses cut great swaths through the natives in conquered areas in the 1500s. In most regions settled by the Spanish, native populations had fallen, by the end of the 1500s, to one-tenth or less of what they had been just before the conquest. In Brazil, the drop may have been smaller. It is hard to tell because many native people there fled into the inland forests so it is not clear how many fled and how many died.

This terrible destruction of the native populations is one of the striking features of the social history of colonial Latin America, and its effects were equally striking. It made necessary a far larger importation of black slaves than would otherwise have taken place. It made the fate of the surviving Indians considerably harder since they were forced to do the work of those who had died (although some survivors at least received higher wages for their work if they chose to become wage laborers), and it reduced the difference in numbers between the native population and the white population, thus accelerating the rate of racial mixing between whites and natives. As a result, the present-day populations of Latin America are notably whiter and more European in culture than they would have been if the natives had survived in their original numbers.

ROMAN CATHOLIC EVANGELISM

In view of the work burden placed on the native Americans by the conquerors and the many very clear cases of harsh treatment, it might seem contradictory to say that Roman Catholic evangelism was one of the two main motives for the conquest and settlement of Latin America. But it was indeed so, especially for the Spanish. Spain was the most powerful Christian country in the world when Columbus crossed the Atlantic, and it continued to be strong for a century thereafter. The Spaniards were sure, for a variety of reasons, that it was not a matter of chance that their expedition, led by Columbus, had established the link between Europe and the Americas. They felt that Spain, as the leading Christian nation of the time, had been singled out by God to conquer and settle the Americas and to carry the Christian faith (for them, of course, the only true faith) to the native peoples of that region. Some Spaniards held an even more extreme belief. These were the believers in certain biblical prophecies that stated that once the whole world had been converted to Christianity, Christ would return and rule in justice and peace for a thousand years (the millennium). Clearly, the Americas made up a very large piece of the world, and until Christians knew of it and converted its peoples, the millennium could not begin. God, therefore, in apparently entrusting the Christianization of the Americas to Spaniards, had given Spain a central part to play in the history of the world. Spain's work in spreading the true faith was to be a large and direct contribution to the second coming of Christ. Only a small minority of Spaniards, mainly some rather mystically inclined Franciscan friars, truly believed in this prophecy, but the fact that even a few priests could see Spain's mission in the Americas as having such cosmic importance is some indication of the religious zeal of the Spanish as a whole.

That zeal resulted in great efforts to convert American native peoples during the first fifty years or so after the conquest in various regions of the Americas. Many remarkably tough and intelligent missionaries—drawn mainly from the Franciscan, Dominican, and Augustinian orders—set to work in Spain's expanding colonies. Their efforts were especially vigorous in Mexico, as manifested by the many church buildings that have survived from the 1500s. Millions of native people were baptized. Most of them did not understand Christianity very well and ended up with a faith consisting of elements of their preconquest religion mixed with elements of Christianity. The friars, however, generally took the view that it was better to convert many people partially than a few thoroughly.

After the mid-1500s, Spain's missionary zeal wore off considerably for many reasons. One was an understandable fatigue among the missionaries after many years of effort and after the newness of the challenge had gone. Another reason was that by then, many native people in the central areas of Spanish settlement had been converted up to a point and could be entrusted to the more humdrum care of parish priests. There were always missionaries active in some parts of the colonies, however—mainly in remote frontier areas where there were new peoples to convert. Among the best-known and longest-lasting of these later missionary enterprises were those of the Franciscans in New Mexico and the Jesuits in Paraguay.

The Portuguese were, on the whole, rather less concerned than the Spanish with making natives into Christians. From the start, the Portuguese had less religious zeal than the Spaniards, and their possession of colonies in Africa and Asia, as well as in the Americas, meant that the effort they made was spread rather thin. Precisely because of this lack of effort by the state, however, the Jesuits found in Brazil, from about 1550 onward, an open field for mission activity. The Jesuits, indeed, dominated the religious history of colonial Brazil as no single order managed to do in Spanish America. The spread of Jesuit missionary villages into the interior became, in fact, one of the means by which Portuguese America advanced westward beyond the Tordesillas line in the 1600s and 1700s.

CONCLUSION

Those, then, are some of the main features of colonization by Spain and Portugal in the Americas: rapid exploration and settlement (particularly by the Spanish), rapid installation of government (again more noticeable in the case of the Spanish than the Portuguese), economic employment of the settled lands for the profit of individual colonists as well as the home governments, exploitation of native labor, importation of black slaves, and the spreading of Christianity. Some of the processes, of course, took place only in the 1500s, though their influence persisted long after that time. Others—the utilization of land and other resources and the exploitation of native and black workers—continued through colonial times. They continued, though, in changing forms, as illustrated, for example, by the progression from slavery and *encomienda* to draft labor and finally to wage labor.

Similarly, there were changes, as time passed, in the strength of colonial governments. The initial, rapid formation of an administrative apparatus in Spanish America in the 1500s was a strenuous business, and there was a natural tendency toward a relaxation in the system once it had been built. This tendency was increased by the growth of Spain's problems in Europe in the late 1500s, which distracted the home government's attention from the colonies. As a result of these and other influences, colonial governments were less effective and disciplined in the 1600s than in the previous century. In the 1700s, Spain attempted, with some success, to remedy this weakness. The creation of the two new viceroyalties already mentioned was part of this effort (New Granada in 1739 and River Plate in 1776). Many other administrative reforms were introduced. The results were that the force of Spanish government was felt by the colonists in areas where it had never been strongly present before and that Spain's income from taxes on the colonies increased several times over. These were gains that Spain enjoyed only briefly, however, for the increasing pressure of government and taxation that the colonies felt in the late 1700s was resented by many colonists. Such pressures helped turn their thoughts toward greater self-determination and, in the end, toward outright independence from Spain.

SUGGESTED READINGS

Chevalier, Francois. *Land and Society in Colonial Mexico*. Berkeley: University of California Press, 1963.

Gibson, Charles. *The Aztecs Under Spanish Rule: A History of the Indians of the Valley of Mexico*. Stanford: Stanford University Press, 1964.

Haring, Clarence H. *The Spanish Empire in America*. New York: Oxford University Press, 1947.

Hemming, John. *The Conquest of the Incas*. New York: Harcourt, Brace, Jovanovich, 1970.

Lockhart, James, and Enrique Otte, eds. *Letters and People of the Spanish Indies: The Sixteenth Century*. Cambridge: Cambridge University Press, 1976.

Lockhart, James, and Stuart B. Schwartz. *Early Latin America. A History of Colonial Spanish America and Brazil*. Cambridge: Cambridge University Press, 1983.

Lynch, John. *Spain Under the Hapsburgs*. 2 vols. Oxford: Oxford University Press, 1964–1969.

———. *The Spanish-American Revolutions, 1808–1826*. New York: Norton, 1973.

Maclachlan, Colin M., and Jaime E. Rodriguez. *The Forging of the Cosmic Race: A Reinterpretation of Colonial Mexico*. Berkeley: University of California Press, 1980.

Parry, John H. *The Spanish Seaborne Empire*. New York: Knopf, 1966.

Phelan, John L. *The Kingdom of Quito in the Seventeenth Century: Bureaucratic Politics in the Spanish Empire*. Madison: University of Wisconsin Press, 1967.

Schwartz, Stuart B. *Sovereignty and Society in Colonial Brazil: The High Court of Bahia and Its Judges, 1609–1745*. Berkeley: University of California Press, 1973.

5

THE CONTINUITY OF THE NATIONAL PERIOD

E. BRADFORD BURNS

Interpreting the Latin American past from the period of independence to the present challenges the imagination of any historian. A wide range of peoples descended from Europeans, Africans, and Indians inhabits diverse lands. No one can doubt the great variety of human experiences, nor underestimate the individuality of the numerous regions. Yet, on another level, there exists a certain similarity of experiences that allows us to consider also broad and common themes pervading the past of all—or most—of Latin America. At any rate, for the purposes of a short introduction to the topic, I will have to dwell on broad themes to the exclusion of details.

One prominent theme emerges to provide a sobering interpretation of the past, to give meaning, to impart understanding of Latin America's national period. It emerges in the form of an enigma: Poor people inhabit rich lands. Most Latin Americans are poor, yet Latin America boasts an impressive array of natural resources. Most Latin Americans are malnourished, yet only a small fraction of the arable land has ever been cultivated.

Efforts to explain the enigma have been numerous but less than satisfactory. Many experts point to the population increase as the cause of persistent poverty. Latin America's population grew from approximately 15 million in 1820 to over 425 million in 1990. The increase sounds impressive, of course, but we must remember that these 425 million people are dispersed over almost 8 million sq mi (20,566,000 sq km). That area is over twice the size of Europe but contains only one-third of Europe's population. To put it in yet another perspective, Latin America occupies 19 percent of the world's land but contains only 7 percent of the world's population. It is, in short, underpopulated. Food experts estimate Latin America could feed many, many times its present population. At any rate, a century ago, when Latin America had but a fraction of its present population, it nevertheless suffered a proportionate amount of poverty. Population pressures, which exist in El Salvador and a few small Caribbean islands, do not offer a rational explanation for Latin America's persistent poverty.

Other specialists have blamed the region's geography. They term it "stingy." However, Latin America boasts of natural resources, including fertile lands, proportionate to any other comparable area in the world. There are rugged mountains, trackless swamps, and bone-dry deserts but no more so proportionately than in the United States and Canada. Furthermore, Latin America has supplied the world for five centuries with an impressive catalogue of mineral and agricultural products. The argument has been persuasively made more than once that the gold and silver flowing from Latin America financed much of Europe's industrial revolution. Further, Latin America has become a major supplier of food to the world's markets. In fact, Latin America probably has been dispossessed of more natural wealth over a longer period of time than any other part of the Third World. A harsh or stingy geography cannot be accepted as an explanation of the enigma.

Although now disguised by polite language and an impressive arsenal of euphemisms, the charge persists that Latin Americans, for one reason or another, lack the skill, intelligence, drive, ability, or will to enrich themselves. It is—it always has been—an insidious argument. The Latin Americans certainly have been capable of enriching others: Spain in the sixteenth century, Portugal in the eighteenth, England in the nineteenth, and—some might argue—the United States in the twentieth. Considering that their diets are minimal to inadequate, their education rudimentary, and their limited health facilities concentrated in the capital cities, the Latin Americans excel at work.

Other experts argue the lack of technology as a major contributor to the enigma. They counsel that only as the technology transfer accelerates will poverty diminish. This explanation puzzles because Latin America has been importing the most up-to-date technology from abroad for at least the past century. Perhaps it has been the wrong kind of technology, or perhaps it has been put to the wrong use, but a very persuasive case can be made that as "modernization" increased, both poverty and dependency in Latin America deepened. Recent transfers of technology seem to aggravate unemployment and to multiply the stockpiling of industrial goods a poor population is unable to buy. Technology contributes disproportionately to the export sector. It seems only to have helped foreigners exploit Latin America's resources. It has contributed minimally—if at all—to raising the standard of living of the average Latin American.

A more profound explanation of the persistent poverty in the midst of potential wealth is needed. History, I think, will provide a better explanation if we examine the institutional structures of Latin America from the time of independence to the present. We will find not only an astonishing similarity of institutions between otherwise diverse regions but an impressive uniformity of consequences resulting from those institutions as well as of reactions to them.

INSTITUTIONAL CONTINUITY AND
INCOMPLETE INDEPENDENCE

Iberian institutions, which is to say those institutions developed by Spain and Portugal, embodied a curious mixture of feudalism and capitalism at the time of the discovery and conquest of the New World. The Iberians transferred their institutions to the New World, imposing them on the Indians and on the black slaves imported from Africa. The presence of both feudalism and capitalism (highly modified forms to be sure) can be seen and contrasted in the hacienda and plantation, both key rural institutions. Both were immense estates. The hacienda was the more self-sufficient of the two, a world almost unto itself, governed by the family patriarch with minimal outside contacts. It produced almost secondarily for an international marketplace. It resembled the fief of the late Middle Ages. The plantation, in contrast, produced in quantity for the international market. It shipped its products away from the plantation; it catered to and became involved in rather complex commercial systems, a part of the expanding capitalist system. The sugar plantations of Brazil in the sixteenth and seventeenth centuries, of the Caribbean in the eighteenth century, and particularly of Cuba in the nineteenth century offer some excellent examples of the New World plantation producing profitably for foreign trade. Other examples would be cacao, coffee, bananas, and wheat. By the late nineteenth century, ranches—the equal in size and purpose to the plantations—supplied beef, mutton, hides, and wool. All these great capitalist enterprises linked Latin America ever more tightly with the interests and markets first of Western Europe and then of the United States.

Both Madrid and Lisbon devised mercantile policies to ensure their own benefits in the lucrative export trade of the New World. The mother countries reaped profits from agriculture but also from mining, particularly of gold and silver. Spain and Portugal considered the New World their "milch cow." Clearly, the colonies existed to benefit the two mother countries, but through them, much of Western Europe profited, especially England. The dynamic part of the Latin American economy—the part that grew and prospered— was both capitalistic and export oriented. The neofeudal heritage, however, imparted a peculiar pattern to local social, economic, and political life. The great landowners ruled like the lords of the manor, which, indeed, they were.

During the long colonial period, the psychology of the Latin Americans, particularly the elite, a majority of whom were Europeans born in the New World—called Creoles in Spanish-speaking regions, *mazombos* in Brazil— changed significantly. A feeling of inferiority before the Iberian-born gave way to a feeling of equality and then of superiority. At the same time, nativism, a devotion to one's locality, matured into feelings of nationalism, a group consciousness attributing supreme value to the land of one's birth and pledging unswerving dedication to it. Such changes of attitude also resulted from a fuller understanding on the part of the local elites that their own interests could be better served if they, not distant Iberian monarchs, made the fundamental economic and political decisions. Inspired by the example of the United States and encouraged by the changes wrought in Napoleonic Europe, they declared the independence of the new Latin American nations. The elites took command of those new nations, exercising the powers once reserved for the Iberian masters.

The independence of the new nations proved to be nominal. The ruling elites depended spiritually on their Iberian past, culturally on France, and economically on Great Britain. They tended to confuse their own well-being and desires with those of the nation at large, a fallacious identification since they represented considerably less than 5 percent of the total population. Nonetheless, that minority set the course upon which Latin America has continued to the present. Since the elites had benefited handsomely from the colonial institutions, they were loath to tamper with them. As one newspaper editor of the period put it: "Let us have no excesses. We want a constitution not a revolution." In sum, they sought to institutionalize the past, not to challenge or change it.

The elites first faced the questions of what type of government they would institute and who would rule. These problems have never been satisfactorily resolved. Brazil and Chile were the most successful in establishing and maintaining order. It took Argentina and Mexico, for example, more than half a century to do so. With the notable exception of Brazil, the nations eventually chose a republican form of government that centralized almost all power in the presidency. A handful of men selected and supported the presidents, who, with some interesting exceptions, did not even pretend to represent the majority of the citizenry. A powerful emperor ruled Brazil for most of the nineteenth century.

Independence provided no panacea for Latin America's economic ills. A Chilean intellectual asked at the end of the colonial period, "Who would imagine that in the midst of the lavishness and splendor of nature the population would be so scanty and that most of it would be groaning under the oppressive yoke of poverty, misery, and the vices which are their inevitable consequences?" He blamed the unhappy economic condition of Chile on the unequal distribution of the land that favored a few large landowners but condemned most of the population to the role of overworked, underpaid, and landless peons. His diagnosis of Chile's economic ills applied equally to the rest of Latin America as it entered the national period.

The economy after 1825 remained as subordinate to the economic needs of Europe as it had throughout the long colonial period. In fact, it became increasingly integrated into the widening network of international capitalism, in which the Latin Americans were a junior partner, subordinate or dependent. The very institutions that the elite preserved from the Iberian past perpetuated dependency, a situation in which Latin America's economy was subordinate to the development or expansion of the mother countries. Such economic dependency presupposes a political subordination, encourages cultural imitation, and perpetuates social iniquity.

During the first half of the nineteenth century, Europe and the United States entered an active period of population growth and accelerated industrialization and urbanization. They demanded raw products: food for their urban centers and materials for their factories. In turn, they sought markets in which to sell their growing industrial surpluses. The newly independent Latin American nations, with their abundant natural resources but limited industries, were pressed into a working relationship with the burgeoning capitalist centers: They exported the raw materials required in Europe and the United States and imported the manufactured goods pouring from the factories. Latin America's exports depended upon and responded to the requirements of Europe and the United States. In catering to the caprices of an unpredictable market, the Latin Americans encouraged the growth of the reflexive economy, little different, except perhaps more hazardous, than the previous colonial economy. External factors, over which the Latin Americans had little or no influence, determined whether the economies prospered or vegetated. The economic cycles of boom and collapse repeatedly occurred in all regions of Latin America. Responding to the needs and requirements of Europe and the United States condemned most of the area to remain on the periphery of international capitalism.

The governing elites, always closely related to the great landowners and merchants, had selected by default policies that favored growth over development. Of all the elements of society, the governing elites profited most from growth, and the immediate advantage they reaped wed them to their policies. Furthermore, development would have required changing some basic institutions—those governing land and labor, for example—from which the elites drew immediate benefits. From their own point of view, then, the elites favored growth, simple numerical accumulation, over development, the maximum use of a nation's potential for the greatest benefit of the largest number of inhabitants. That particularly helps to explain why the new governments tampered very little with the well-established colonial institutions that had maintained rigidly the precedence of growth over development.

A remarkable continuity existed between the colonial period and the decades following independence. Economic changes were few. Agriculture and the large estate retained their prominence, and the new nations became as subservient to British economic policies as they once had been to those of Spain and Portugal. The wars of independence had shaken and weakened some of the foundation stones of society, but the edifice stood pretty much intact. A small, privileged elite ruled over the muted masses. Fewer than one in ten could read, and fewer than one in twenty earned enough to live in even modest comfort. Land remained the principal source of wealth, prestige, and power, and only a few owned the land.

THE MODERNIZATION OF INEQUALITY

The continuity, however, was not perfect. Two major political changes marked the early national period. The first and most obvious was the transmission of power from the Iberians to the Creole and *mazombo* elites.

Political power no longer emanated from Europe; it had a local source. The second was the emergence of the military in Spanish America as an important political institution destined to play a decisive role in history. It did not emerge as a powerful institution in Brazil until the late nineteenth century. The military forces were the elite's only guarantee of order; initially, the officer class provided prestigious employment for the sons of the wealthy as well as one means of upward mobility for talented and ambitious plebians. Early in the national period, the liberals challenged the status of the military, thus alienating them and driving them into the welcoming embrace of the conservatives. The elites, intent upon conserving the past—tantamount to preserving their privileges—found useful allies in the military and the Roman Catholic hierarchy, both powerful institutions in their own right. The remarkable early stability of both Chile and Brazil can be partially explained by the close identification and harmony between the Church, the conservatives, and the military.

By mid-nineteenth century, it was possible to see that some of the nations were achieving political stability and enjoying greater economic prosperity. Foreign threats had diminished. Stronger centralized governments exerted greater authority over larger areas. Nationalism became a better defined force as more and more Latin Americans expressed greater pride in their homelands, appreciated their uniqueness, and pursued their visions of progress.

In the second half of the century, Positivist ideology dominated in many governmental circles. The "scientific laws" of society codified by Positivism seemed to promise the Latin American elite and emerging middle class the progress they sought, primarily a material progress. Outward manifestations of progress—railroads and industrialization were prime examples—assumed great importance in Positivism, emphatically so among Latin Americans. With an emphasis on material growth and well-being, Positivism favored a capitalist mentality, quite different from the communal spirit pervasive among the indigenous peoples of Latin America. Indeed, private accumulation of wealth was viewed as a sign of progress as well as an instrument for progress. Because of the weakness of domestic, private institutions, the state had to assume the role of directing progress, which, in turn, required the maintenance of order and guarantee of stability. With its special emphasis on political order and material progress, Positivism reached the height of its influence between 1880 and 1900. It became almost an official doctrine of the regime of President Porfirio Díaz in Mexico (1876–1911). Some of his principal ministers were known as *científicos* as they offered "scientific" solutions to the problems confronting the nation.

As their warm embrace of the ideas associated with Positivism might indicate, the elite and middle class customarily adopted the latest ideas from abroad, even if they ill suited the local scene. They ordered the capital cities to be rebuilt to resemble Paris as much as possible. Not all of them understood that anything more than "cosmetic" modernization was impossible in nations whose basic institutions retained the neofeudalistic, neocapitalist orientation of the colonial past. Still they persisted.

The progress or modernization pursued by the Latin American governments required increasing sums of money to import the machinery, railroads, luxuries, and technology that would be used to try to transform their nations into replicas of the European nations the elites and middle class so much admired. To earn that money, the Latin Americans increased their exports, the foods or minerals they traditionally had sold abroad. The export sector of their economies received the most attention. In that sector, they increasingly concentrated investments, technology, and labor, leaving the domestic economy weak and increasingly inadequate. The number of those exports was limited. Usually each nation or region depended on the sale of one or two, possibly three, such exports: for Brazil, it was coffee; for Chile, nitrates and copper; for Bolivia, tin; for Argentina, beef and wheat; for Peru, guano. The highly prized railroads, built at staggering expense, opened new lands for exploitation but always were linked to the export sector, rushing the material products of the interior to the coastal ports where ships waited to transport them to Europe and the United States. Most of the modernization concentrated in the export sector. It contributed to some impressive growth but did little to develop Latin America. In fact, modernization contributed to deepening dependency.

Most significantly, the nineteenth century witnessed the growth in size, importance, and power of the latifundia, those huge estates that produced all too often for the export market. The latifundia grew at the expense of the Indian communities, peasants, and small landowners. Inefficiency characterized most of the large estates. The owners used only a fraction of their extensive lands. They kept large acreages under their domination in order to control labor, always in scarce supply. By denying access to land, they assured themselves of a ready supply of workers who otherwise would have been independent peasants.

The growth of large and inefficient estates raised serious social and economic questions. An editorial in the Buenos Aires newspaper *El Río de la Plata,* September 1, 1869, lamented: "The huge fortunes have the unhappy tendency to grow even larger, and their owners possess vast tracts of land that lie fallow and abandoned. Their greed for land does not equal their ability to use it intelligently and actively." Similar complaints were voiced everywhere. It became all too obvious that the expansion of cultivation for export was accompanied by a decline in food production for local consumption. The province of Rio de Janeiro, undergoing a coffee boom at mid-century, provided the perfect example. The landowners quickly converted their land to coffee plantations. Foods that had been grown in such abundance in 1850 that they were sold outside the province had to be imported a decade later. The price of basic foodstuffs—beans, corn, and flour—rose accordingly.

For the majority of the Latin Americans, progress resulted in an increased concentration of lands in the hands of ever-fewer owners; falling per capita food production, with corollary rising food imports; greater impoverishment; less to eat; more vulnerability to the whims of an impersonal market; uneven growth; increased unemployment and underemployment; social, economic, and political marginalization; and greater power in the hands of the privileged few. In fact, the more the majority of Latin Americans were forced to integrate into world commerce, the fewer the material benefits they reaped. But poverty through progress must be understood in more than the material terms of declining wages, purchasing power, or nutritional levels. A tragic spiritual and cultural impoverishment debased the majority, forced by circumstances to abandon previously more satisfactory ways of life and to accept alien ones that provided them little or no psychic benefits.

The impoverished majority both bore the burden of the inequitable institutional structures and paid for the modernization enjoyed by the privileged. The deprivation, repression, and deculturalization of the majority by the minority created tensions that frequently gave rise to violence in the nineteenth century. The poor protested their increasing misfortunes as modernization increased. For their part, the privileged were determined to modernize and to maintain the order required to do so. They freely used whatever force was necessary to accomplish both. Consequently, the imposition of progress stirred social disorder that took the form of Indian and peasant rebellions, slave uprisings, banditry, and millenarian movements. Those popular protests tended to be local and uncoordinated. Thus, despite the frequency of such protests, the elites using the military forces at their disposal imposed their will and brand of progress. The triumph of that progress set the course for the twentieth-century history of Latin America: It bequeathed a legacy of mass poverty and continued conflict.

Although the overwhelming majority of the Latin Americans lived in the countryside during the nineteenth century, the population began to shift toward the cities during the last quarter of the century. Argentina's urban population doubled between 1869 and 1914, so that in the latter year, the urban sector represented 53 percent of the population. Chile, too, witnessed an impressive urban surge. In 1875, approximately 27 percent of the population could be classified as urban dwellers, but a quarter of a century later, the figure reached 43 percent. During the three decades after 1890, the population of Rio de Janeiro—Brazil's primary city and port as well as capital—doubled while São Paulo increased eightfold in size. A few cities played increasingly important roles in each nation. The government and administrative apparatus, commerce, and industry were located in those cities. Increasingly, they served as hubs of complex transportation and communication networks. Further, they provided important recreational, cultural, and educational services. Urban growth resulted from the arrival of greater numbers of foreign immigrants, a constantly increasing population (Latin America had 61 million inhabitants in 1900), and the rising tide of rural migrants who arrived attracted by the promise of the city or propelled by the grinding poverty of the countryside.

Unfortunately, the cities did not contribute to national development. The urban facade of modernization deceived. Dependency shaped the cities just as it molded other aspects of life. The high concentration of land in few hands weakened the urban network throughout Latin America. The large estates, combined agrarian-industrial units, demonstrated little need for the intermediary services that support small trading, servicing, and processing towns. A national economy whose most dynamic sector was export oriented encouraged the rapid growth of maritime ports, a transportation system focusing on the ports, foreign investment in or connected to export products to the neglect of the rest of the economy, the spending of export wealth to beautify and service the capital city, and the concentration of landowners in the capital to be near the center of power. The capital and the ports (in the cases of Argentina and Uruguay, for example, the capitals are also the principal ports) served the dynamic export sector of the economy. They shared in the growth and prosperity while other cities and towns played secondary roles, stunted in both growth and development, just as overreliance on the export sector restricted national growth and development on yet another level. Dependency helps to explain why there were only one, two, or three major and "modern" cities in each Latin American nation and even further why that modernity remained more a facade than a reality.

THE NEW URBAN CLASSES AND THE RISE OF NATIONALISM

As Latin America approached its independence centennial, two trends, one of external origin and the other internal, emerged with greater clarity. Together they would have a mighty impact on events in the twentieth century. The first was the emergence of the United States as a major world power preoccupied with its security in the Western Hemisphere and with a strong drive to invest in and trade with Latin America. The other was the emergence of a more clearly defined middle class within Latin America. The two trends intertwined, reinforcing and supporting each other. The growing middle class looked for its own sources of inspiration, its own example to emulate. The industrializing and progressing United States attracted the attention of that class. Members of the Latin American middle class visited New York before Paris; they learned English rather than French. Above all else, they admired the new technology associated with the United States. They saw in industrialization their key to advancement, and no country industrialized more rapidly and more thoroughly than the United States. They may have feared the expansion of their mentor and ridiculed its materialism, but nonetheless, they were drawn toward it, and the lifestyle of the Latin American middle sectors increasingly reflected that of the United States.

Commerce, business, and industry contributed heavily to the ranks of the middle class, and foreign immigrants continued to compose a disproportionately large percentage of its members. Certain characteristics of that class became increasingly evident. The majority lived in the cities and boasted an above-average education. Their income level placed them between the wealthy few and the impoverished many. Although the varied groups within that class never unified, on occasion a majority of them might agree on certain goals—such as improved or expanded education, increased industrialization, or more rapid modernization—and on certain methods—such as the formation of political parties or the exaltation of nationalism. They consented to the use of the government to foment change (a change that, following their perceptions, most closely resembled growth), and with minimal dissention, they welcomed the government's participation in—even direction of—the economy. Still, political preferences within their ranks varied from far right to far left.

As urbanization and industrialization grew, a larger, more cohesive, and more militant proletariat appeared. Slowly becoming aware of their common problems and goals, these workers unionized despite relentless government repression. By 1914, about half a dozen nations boasted well-organized unions, and at least some attempt had been made in the rest to institute them. The economic dislocation caused by World War I and the financial collapse of 1929 sparked labor unrest, militancy, and strikes. A working-class consciousness took shape as labor thought in terms of changing the national institutions to suit its own needs.

In their periods of formation and expansion, the unions could and did cooperate with other urban elements, specifically the middle class. Both groups sought change, however modest, and realized they had to challenge the traditional elites to foment it. The privileged oligarchy resented and opposed that alliance. Once the middle class achieved its more limited goals and began to participate in the national institutions, it broke that alliance to align itself with the elites.

The Brazilian middle class was the first to exercise power. It allied with the military to overthrow the monarchy in 1889 and for five years governed through an uneasy or uncertain cooperation with the generals. The coffee elite nudged both from the government in 1894, and the Brazilian middle class did not get its second taste of power until 1930. In Argentina, the middle class entered power through the election of President Hipólito Irigoyen in 1916, and shortly thereafter, in 1920, the Chileans elected a middle-class president, Arturo Alessandri. But it was in Uruguay that the Latin American middle class won its greatest victory in the early twentieth century. Uruguay changed dramatically under the government of the middle class, providing one of the best examples of peaceful change in Latin America. José Batlle, the outstanding political representative of the middle class, served twice as president (1903–1907 and 1911–1915), but his influence over the government lasted until his death in 1929. During those decades, he sought to expand education, encourage industrialization, restrict foreign control, enact a broad welfare program, and unify the republic. Succeeding brilliantly in each instance, he transformed Uruguay into a model bourgeois nation. In the long run, however, the middle class throughout Latin America proved to be cautious, if not conservative. Its members came to fear that too much reform might harm rather than benefit their interests. As they began to participate in the major institutions of their nations, they saw less reason to challenge or to reform them.

Forces favoring basic institutional change continued to grow, and mounting pressure on the static institutions ranks as one of the major historical trends of the twentieth century. Ambitious new groups—organized labor, nationalists, intellectuals, and students, for example—in an increasingly complex society opposed the rigid institutions that impeded their rise or stunted national development as they perceived it. They demanded a more fluid society, and they sought to alter the old one. They sought national development rather than simply the unsatisfactory growth of the past. They repudiated the dependency that they rightly identified as a restriction on development. At the same time, under skillful direction, nationalism emerged as a potent force favoring change and development.

The Fate of Revolutions

Five nations have attempted change by revolution in the twentieth century: Mexico, 1910–1940; Guatemala, 1944–1954; Bolivia, 1952–1964; Cuba, 1959 to the present; and Nicaragua, 1979 to the present. Revolution is a very specific—and widely abused—term. It denotes the sudden, forceful, even violent overturn of a previously stable society and the substitution of new institutions for those discredited. Similarities characterize the five Latin American revolutions (although notable differences also distinguish one from the other). All five of the revolutions had in common a desire to modify or eradicate traditional institutions considered incompatible with the drive for meaningful modernization and greater social equity. All recognized the importance of land reform in the restructuring of society and set about to radically change the ownership patterns. All were manifestations of intense nationalism. All involved the participation of the masses. All accelerated efforts to educate the masses. All favored one or another form of socialism. All hoped to increase the economic viability and the independence of action of their nations. All favored greater industrialization. All removed from power—at least temporarily—representatives of the old oligarchy.

The fates of the five revolutions have varied. The Mexican Revolution seemed to be succeeding until it grew rigid and conservative after 1940. The Guatemalan Revolution was first halted and then reversed. The Bolivian Revolution accomplished much in its first years, grew increasingly timid after 1956, and expired with the military coup d'etat in 1964. The Cuban and Nicaraguan revolutions continue.

Since the Cuban and Nicaraguan experiments continue, any judgment of their success or failure would be premature. The Cuban experiment with change is the most radical to date. For the first time in the Western Hemisphere, a revolution has been put through in the name of socialism. Scarcely any of the prerevolutionary institutions remain, and much of the prerevolutionary privileged class is gone and without ready access to power. Cuba thus provides an example of socialist solutions to the old problems that have beset Latin America.

The United States reacted hostilely to four of the five revolutions. It took nearly three decades for Washington to reconcile itself to the new turn of events in Mexico. Washington has steadfastly opposed the Guatemalan, Cuban, and Nicaraguan revolutions. In alliance with Guatemalan dissidents, the U.S. Central Intelligence Agency (CIA) succeeded in ending the Guatemalan experiment, and in cooperation with Cuban exiles, the CIA later tried to remove Fidel Castro and blunt the Cuban Revolution. Thus far, its efforts have failed. From 1979 to 1989, the CIA armed, financed, and trained Nicaraguan exiles who repeatedly invaded Nicaragua from Honduras. Only the Bolivian Revolution received support from the United States, and that aid went to the moderate wing that eventually came to dominate the revolutionary process. Such a record doubtless reflects a nervous metropolis fearful of any change in or challenge from its client states.

The Backlash Against Democratic Reform

Reform, the gradual change or modification of institutions, has had no greater success in changing old and iniquitous institutions than revolution. (Once again, I make the exception of the ongoing revolutions in Cuba and Nicaragua.) The two longest experiments with democratic reform, those in Uruguay and Chile, collapsed in dismal failure in 1973, to be replaced with brutal military dictatorships that held sway in Uruguay until 1984 and Chile until 1990.

Uruguay long had been judged the Latin American bastion of reform and democracy, a kind of middle-class paradise, thanks largely to the changes brought about by José Batlle. Commendable as his reforms were, they did not adjust the mainsprings of the economy: land monopoly and overdependence on the export sector. When events after the mid-1950s shook and crumbled the foundations of the economy, the edifice of democracy came crashing down.

Between 1955 and 1970, Uruguay witnessed the worst inflation and the poorest economic performance in Latin America. The complex causation of this disaster had its roots in the countryside. The land provided Uruguay's wealth, but it was used inefficiently. Uruguayan prosperity depended on wool and beef exports, but Uruguayan producers made a poor international showing, their productivity barely half that of some of their major world competitors. As the population of the small nation increased in the twentieth century, agricultural production declined proportionately. The weakening agrarian sector undermined industrialization. Those who suffered most called for reforms: land reform, socialization of industry, and the expropriation of foreign-owned banks, businesses, and industries. As the economy continued to deteriorate, demands for change escalated and intensified, the level of violence rose, the frightened middle class swung more to favor order and the status quo than reform, the government proved its ineffectiveness, the military intervened in 1973 at the insistence of the wealthy and middle class to overthrow the government. Uruguay, for half a century the model of democracy and reform in Latin America, was reduced to a shameless military dictatorship devoid of any freedom, reform, or hope. The military officers were unable to revive the economy because they were unwilling to challenge the institutions that perpetuate its inefficiency.

At the same time, events in another "model democracy," Chile, followed an all-too-familiar course. There, too, the middle class demonstrated an equal distaste for democracy and a fear of reform in late 1973. A combination of increased political participation of the lower classes, the declining economic position of the poor, and the inability of unimaginative governments to bring about reform had brought Salvador Allende to the presidency in the hotly contested elections of 1970. The aims of his Popular Unity government were to transform Chile from a capitalist and dependent society into a socialist and independent one and to do so gradually within the democratic and constitutional framework of the nation.

Once in office, President Allende nationalized the foreign-owned copper industry, the source of three-quarters of the value of all Chile's exports. He accelerated agrarian reform, distributing during his first year in office more land than his predecessor had in six. The government bought control of most of the banks, thus controlling the use of credit in order to favor development over mere growth. Allende paid considerable attention to improving the living conditions of the poor. Salaries rose, and real buying power increased. Unemployment dropped sharply. The government rechanneled distribution to favor the underprivileged. Those changes took place within a democratic framework; all liberties were respected.

The shifting balance of political and economic power frightened the middle class, unaccustomed to sharing the nation's political decision making or its limited resources with the poor. Allying with the traditional elite, the middle class refused any cooperation with the Allende government. Hostile to the socialization process, the international banks and the U.S. government cut loans and aid to the Allende government to a trickle. A process of economic destabilization was planned and carried out by the still economically powerful middle and upper classes. The United States contributed to that destabilization. The resulting economic chaos generated a class conflict. The middle and upper classes called on the military to intervene. It did on September 11, 1973, imposing a barbaric military dictatorship.

Democracy, freedom, and reform in Latin America suffered a staggering blow in Chile. Events there, coupled with those in other key nations, indicated that the middle class has no commitment to either democracy or change. Indeed, the arguments for democracy in Latin America now seem hopelessly idealistic, as does the case for reform. They simply have no historical support.

The Bitter Fruit of Military Governments

Military governments have a poor record of economic and political performance. They are authoritarian, some exceedingly barbarous; they permit little or very limited popular participation. They sometimes facilitate economic growth for limited periods but never encourage development. Development would necessitate reform of basic institutions, most notably landowning and land use, anathema to the middle class and elites and—with the exception of Peru in the early 1970s—to their military allies as well.

Brazil offers a splendid recent example of military governments wed to growth but hostile to development. When the Brazilian middle class and elite summoned the soldiers from their barracks in 1964 to overthrow a democratic government that promised reforms, the soldiers repressed every form of freedom and liberty. Economically, they concentrated on controlling inflation and accelerating the growth rate. The phenomenal growth rate during the years 1969–1974, averaging 10 percent a year, attracted considerable envy throughout Latin America. That economic record emphasized a rising gross national product (GNP). Pursuit of an ever-higher GNP is never, however, a search for social objectives but rather, a blind chase of numbers that can be expanded to infinity without much social value resulting. Brazil, in fact, provides the perfect example of an upwardly spiraling GNP without much development or resultant social benefit. As a matter of fact, the gap between the rich and the poor widened during those years. Instead of solving any basic problems, the military government intensified them. Inflation surpassed the 100 percent rate in 1980, higher than it had ever been in 1964 or before. Foreign debt reached alarming proportions. By 1990 the government had run up an international debt of over $110 billion, for which the annual carrying charges consumed half of the country's export earnings. At least by the end of 1990, no sign had appeared that economic growth, which had declined to a 4 percent average after 1975, might promote development. Thus, in the short run, the military governments fostered growth, but in the long run, they not only were unable to sustain their earlier growth but they accelerated inflation and drove the economy to the brink of bankruptcy. The Brazilian military provided no solutions to old problems; they did not speak to the tragic enigma besetting their nation. The army assured order; it prolonged the status quo, but the officers merely postponed for the middle class and the elites the day of reckoning.

In the past decades, the aspirations of larger and larger numbers of the Latin American population for change and development have vastly outpaced actual change. Too few enjoyed the benefits of whatever growth took place, and too many of the age-old political, economic, and social structures and patterns remained to permit any real development. As the rate and extent of change and development have failed to meet expectations, frustrations have mounted. Further, the failure of change and development has created a widespread feeling of disillusion with democracy and capitalism and has contributed to mounting violence in contemporary Latin America, well exemplified by the present civil war in El Salvador. Violence, disillusionment, the failure of democracy, the propensity for economic growth at the expense of development, and continuing dependency are characteristics of contemporary Latin America.

ECONOMIC GROWTH WITHOUT DEVELOPMENT

From the vantage point of the present, we survey the Latin American past and contemplate its future. There is much to admire: the blending of races and cultures to create unique civilizations; the beauty of the lands; the talents of the peoples; intellectual achievements such as the brilliant twentieth-century literature of Jorge Amado, Carlos Fuentes, Gabriel García Márquez, and Jorge Luis Borges; the enviable ability to settle international disputes peacefully; magnificent examples of contemporary architecture such as Brasília; among other things. Yet, the grim reality of social, economic, and political inequity remains. Injustice seems to predominate. A series of challenging questions confront us in our effort to better understand Latin America. Why does dependency tend to deepen rather than recede? How can the quality of life for the majority be improved? What is the best role for the United States to play in Latin America, and how does a knowledge of the past help us prepare for it?

In considering these difficult questions, it is useful to recall a challenging historical judgment made by Will and Ariel Durant, authors of the widely acclaimed, multivolume historical survey, *The Story of Civilization*. They capped their survey with a slender volume based upon their observations of the past. Entitled *The Lessons of History,* it observed, "When the group or a civilization declines, it is through no mystic limitations of a corporate life, but through the failure of its political or intellectual leaders to meet the challenges of change." The ability—or lack of it—of Latin America's leadership to meet these tough challenges of change will determine the course of the future.

Change always occurs. Change has taken place in Latin America. Latin America in the 1990s differs considerably from Latin America in the 1890s. Perhaps most noticeable among the changes is the presence of a significant middle class exercising a dominant role in the social, economic, and political life of each nation. Many of the most vigorous political parties spring from that class. Some leaders from that class direct the potent force of nationalism, encourage industrialization and progress, and contribute to the vitality of the cities. Urban unionized laborers constitute a relatively new and important group as well. Some of them enjoy a reasonable wage and impressive social benefits. On occasion, they have exerted political influence. Transportation and communication networks now cover large parts of most of the nations, giving them a greater cohesion than ever before. Increasingly, Latin Americans use their own natural resources to promote national growth—Mexico's use of its own oil to propel local industrialization illustrates that trend. But to balance this assessment of change we must return to a familiar theme: Despite pockets of change, a veneer of progress, and apparent modernity, much of Latin America retains the flavor of a distant past. In short, the change and modernization that have occurred in the last century have had little positive effect, particularly on the quality of life of the majority.

A major reason for this constancy is that one characteristic still dominates—and enervates—Latin America: The economies grow but do not develop. The most dynamic part of each economy remains linked to exports. The economic policies and performance strengthen institutions nurturing dependency. It is those institutional structures, minimally altered by time, that create the ever-present enigma of widespread poverty amid potential wealth.

As Latin America moves through the decade of the 1990s, the problems created by the remarkable continuity of those institutions weigh heavily, perhaps more heavily than ever. They beg for a solution. No reason exists to believe that time alone will solve these problems. On the contrary, the passage of time has only compounded them. The level of frustration felt by the majority certainly seems higher than ever. It will require some imaginative restructuring of institutions to solve the problems and to relieve the frustration.

The human dimension of these problems staggers the mind. The terrifying reality is that most of the population is hungry, malnourished, and sick. In 1990, nearly three-quarters of a population of 425 million, which was increasing at a rate of nearly 2.5 percent a year, were physically undernourished in one form or another. The social problems assume yet other directions. The overall illiteracy rates still hover at about 40 percent. The work forces grow at a faster rate than the creation of new jobs. The annual per capita income remains low, about one-tenth that of the United States. However, in reality, even that income is highly unbalanced, with a few receiving most of it. In Mexico, for example, about 1 percent of the gainfully employed population receives 66 percent of the national income, while most of the workers receive an income insufficient to satisfy minimal needs. There, as elsewhere in Latin America, the actual purchasing power of the worker has been declining since the early 1960s. In sum, the quality of life for the majority remains abysmally low.

In analyzing the institutional causes for these many problems, one should look first at the utilization of the land. It continues to be used inefficiently, not by the small farmer and peasant, but by the owners of the large estates. Roughly 90 percent of the land belongs to 10 percent of the owners, a degree of concentration far greater than that in any other world region of comparable size. The agrarian sector of Latin America is less and less able to satisfy the needs of the population. Although it has been estimated that in the 1970s population increase and agricultural production kept pace with each other, the statistics deceive. Large amounts of agriculture went into export. A growing proportion of the cereal crop became cattle feed. In other words, the amount of grain available to feed people decreased. At the same time, one must remember that beef feeds the wealthy only, so that the majority benefited in no way from increased cattle feeding. The distressing reality is that Latin Americans do not feed themselves. Latin America expended 60 percent more for the importation of food in 1978 ($6.4 billion) than it had in 1971 ($4 billion). Under present conditions in Latin America, there is no justification for predicting a decline or even a stabilization of mounting food imports. The tragedy of hunger remains a dominant characteristic of Latin America at the end of the twentieth century. After a visit to El Salvador in 1977, Father Timothy S. Healy, president of Georgetown University, noted the arresting contradiction: "An agricultural people . . . starve to death on rich land while they farm it."

It is a measure of Latin America's underdevelopment—its traditional propensity to grow rather than to develop—that this vast region, which must spend its hard-earned international currencies to import food to feed the population, is in reality a net exporter of foods, the primary exports. Latin America continues to export grains, meats, sugar, bananas, coffee, cacao, and soybeans because the large landowners, foreign as well as domestic, earn handsome profits from such exports, more than they might earn selling food in the domestic market. It is a further measure of Latin America's underdevelopment that most of the arable land lies unused or underused: Only about 10 percent is in use.

Latin America is fully capable not only of feeding its own population well but of contributing significantly to world food supplies. One must recall, as a point of comparison, that the vast and relatively populous Incan Empire fed its inhabitants well and maintained large food surpluses to compensate for lean years and natural disasters. That same area has been unable to do so since the Spanish conquest. In this particular case, we are challenged to understand why Incan technology, efficiency, and productivity surpassed Western technology, efficiency, and productivity. The Incan Empire in the fifteenth century was more developed than Peru or Ecuador or Bolivia in the twentieth century.

One probable solution to the staggering agrarian problems of contemporary Latin America is to put the unused and underused lands into the hands of the unemployed and underemployed. The newly created peasant class could feed itself and provide surpluses for the local marketplaces. Furthermore, access to land might reduce the flow of migrants from the countryside into already overcrowded cities. The answer sounds easy; its implementation would be extremely difficult. The middle class, and particularly the elite, owning the land partly for speculative and investment purposes, partly for profit, and partly to control the labor supply, have no intention of divesting themselves of their lands for the benefit of the impoverished masses, for national development, or for any other reason. It would take all the force of a strong government to alter the landholding structure in Latin America and then to sustain the new peasants with the agrarian reforms they would need. But until that agrarian reform takes place, no amount of investment, certainly no amount of rhetoric, will fundamentally alter the unjust institutions inherited from the past.

THE BURDEN OF THE PAST

There was little evidence, in the twilight of the twentieth century, of an emergence of greater agricultural efficiency, and where the efficiency does manifest itself, it usually produces for export rather than for national consumption. Those oases of efficiency are capital intensive, supplanting people with machinery. Besides forcing hundreds of thousands of would-be peasants to trek to the cities, that machinery consumes gasoline, the price of which has skyrocketed in all but a few privileged regions. The high cost of oil imports already has burdened Latin America with an unprecedented debt that threatens some nations with bankruptcy. Thus, mechanized agriculture is a risky, and possibly even a negative, answer to rural deficiencies of production.

In a few regions of Latin America—Peru and Bolivia, for example—land reform has taken place in recent times. But a land reform that does not give people access to water, credit, and/or services is not the correct answer either. It becomes increasingly clear that land reform and agrarian reform are not synonymous. The former constitutes changes in ownership; the latter includes changes in production and service structures as well, a much deeper institutional change.

Current patterns of land ownership and use exemplify perfectly the prevalence of the institutions of the past. Furthermore, they illustrate a basic theme that runs through Latin American history: The historical institutions contribute significantly to the creation and perpetuation of mass poverty. There seems little doubt that so long as those historical institutions predominate, poverty will remain a major characteristic of Latin America. To bring about development, basic institutional changes will be needed, although, it must be emphasized, basic institutional changes legislated but not enforced, in law but without spirit, will not produce development.

Solution to the prevalent poverty in the midst of potential plenty lies not in exotic formulas eagerly imported into or imposed upon Latin America by the left or the right or any political hue in between. Unfaltering loyalty to imported solutions for domestic problems has reaped few rewards for Latin Americans. That a solution might lie within Latin America itself, within the pragmatic communal approach of the majority, is a possibility governments shun. Yet, solutions to old problems might well be found in local values and experiences. Given access to land, seeds, tools, water, and credit, the rural masses conceivably could make Latin America flourish. They could feed themselves, supply the local marketplace, and minimize dependency. Such a solution entails the restructuring of power because it would remove land from the monopoly of the few and distribute it to the many, thereby diminishing the former's wealth, prestige, and power while enhancing the latter's position; the luxuries and privileges of the few might diminish as the basic welfare of the many improved.

Accompanying that fundamental shift in land ownership and productivity, there must be a centrally administered national plan for development. Massive public works projects would alleviate urban unemployment and underemployment while providing needed housing, schools, and hospitals. Industry would be directed to meet the basic needs of the many, not the exotic tastes of the few. A rational manufacturing plan would produce trucks to transport food, not sports cars for the privileged; pasteurized milk for schoolchildren, not carbonated soft drinks; sturdy sandals for the barefooted, not expensive leather shoes for export. Such a government would have to respond to the desires of the majority; it would have to lean upon and be supported by the majority. Identification between the people and the government would have to be complete. Through that identification, the local culture would triumph. The challenge for change would have been met.

Well-defined institutions from the past, enshrined by the elites and middle classes and relying on the strength of the military and the support of foreign allies, still prevail. Brazil, Uruguay, Chile, Nicaragua, and El Salvador have given us proof in the last two decades that those who enjoy privileges and benefits from society will not freely give up their position. If history does in fact suggest "lessons" on which we can draw, then it teaches that change of any fundamental nature will not be achieved easily. Eventually, change will probably result from the dialectic of violence so long a characteristic of Latin America—the violence expressed by those who feel oppressed, who desire to share in the benefits of society, and who seek change and the violence imposed by those who enjoy power, who benefit from the status quo, and who desire to perpetuate their domination. As we have seen, it is much easier to maintain an existing system than to bring about authentic change. In the late 1980s, Latin America entered another phase of formal democracy. The new leaders offer no innovative ideas to spur development. They raise the haunting questions of whether democracy in its present form is capable of addressing the challenges of change.

The Latin American experience indicates that change will require that strong, determined, and well-led governments break with the past and pursue an innovative course. Until such governments appear, Latin American countries, with the exceptions of Cuba and Nicaragua, manifest all the signs of being underdeveloped: low per capita income, unequal distribution of wealth, economic dependency, high birth and death rates, endemic diseases, undernourishment, and illiteracy. The enigma remains: Poor people inhabit rich lands.

SUGGESTED READINGS

Burns, E. Bradford. *Latin America: A Concise, Interpretive History.* Englewood Cliffs, N.J.: Prentice-Hall, 1982. This text sweeps through history from pre-Columbian times to the present and emphasizes those forces that shaped and are reshaping Latin America.

Conde, Roberto Cortés. *The First Stages of Modernization in Spanish America.* New York: Harper and Row, 1974. The author concentrates on the growing export economies of Latin America in the last half of the nineteenth century and details the consequences of those exports and the accompanying modernization for Latin America.

Lindquist, Sven. *Land and Power in South America.* New York: Penguin Books, 1979. With an incisive understanding of South American problems, Lindquist grasps the fundamental significance of land ownership patterns. The book first treats the need for agrarian reform and then proceeds to study the efforts to make such reforms.

Mariátegui, José Carlos. *Seven Interpretive Essays on Peruvian Reality.* Austin: University of Texas Press, 1971. In the mid-1920s, Mariátegui isolated and discussed the major issues in Peruvian society—and by extension, in most of Latin America. Most discussions in the last half century of Latin America's past have only expanded on the sharp insights of Mariátegui.

Morner, Magnus. *Race Mixture in the History of Latin America.* Boston: Little, Brown and Company, 1967. Discusses the mixing of the races on a scale unprecedented in world history and the resultant emergence of new cultures, which constitute some of the most dramatic chapters in Latin American history.

Reed, Nelson. *The Caste War in Yucatán.* Stanford: Stanford University Press, 1964. Using the example of nineteenth-century Yucatán, Reed offers a splendidly thought-provoking study of the rejection of Europeanization and modernization in favor of a folk society.

Stein, Stanley J., and Barbara H. Stein. *The Colonial Heritage of Latin America: Essays on Economic Dependence in Perspective.* New York: Oxford University Press, 1970. This succinct and sophisticated book is the classic statement on the imposition and growth of Latin America's dependency.

Wolf, Eric R., and Edward C. Hansen. *The Human Condition in Latin America.* New York: Oxford University Press, 1972. These two anthropologists indicate how both the dominant and the popular institutions of Latin America have affected large groups of people.

PART THREE
CULTURAL EXPRESSION

6
PHILOSOPHY AND THE INTELLECTUAL TRADITION

FRED GILLETTE STURM

From the early years of colonization to the contemporary period, philosophical speculation and analysis have played important roles in the development of Latin American culture. Indeed, it might be argued that whether one's concern is with literature and the arts, or with history and the social sciences, a full and adequate comprehension of the Latin American scene can be achieved only if the philosophical dimension is included in the study.

Until recently, the educational systems in Spanish America and Brazil have followed a classical tradition as far as the curriculum of secondary schools is concerned, philosophy being included as a compulsory subject during the last year or two of studies. In this way, all secondary school graduates have been exposed to the European philosophical tradition—its history, major movements, and principal problems—however cursory the survey may have been. In many instances, the textbooks used have included an appendix that introduces the reader to the philosophical history of the particular country itself, so that the student understands that philosophy is not confined to Europe but is practiced in the Americas as well.

On the university level, philosophy has been closely linked to the human and cultural sciences. Until recently, no sharp distinctions have been drawn between psychology and philosophical anthropology, sociology and social philosophy, political science and political philosophy, or jurisprudence and the philosophy of law. Earlier in the history of Latin American education, the same was true of the natural sciences. Physics had been an integral part of the philosophy curriculum in Spanish and Portuguese universities during the centuries of colonization, so that concern with physical, chemical, and biological phenomena was considered to be a branch of philosophical investigation termed "natural philosophy." Although this close relationship between philosophy and the sciences was not peculiar to university studies and research in Latin America and Iberia—the same was the case in the

United States and the countries of northern and Western Europe well into the nineteenth century—the tradition tended to remain in effect longer, only recently falling victim to the fragmentation of learning and research into increasingly self-contained specializations.

If philosophy has had a close relationship with the sciences in Latin America, it has been even more closely linked to the literary arts: poetry, the novel, theater, and especially the essay form. Any study of Latin American intellectual or philosophical history must take into account the history of literature in order to understand the philosophical ideas that were being considered and debated at any given period. Today, philosophy continues to have a close link with literature and theatrical expression. Many philosophers use, to good advantage, the essay form for the transmission of their thought, and Sunday newspapers often feature such essays in their supplements of art and culture.

The close connection between philosophy and the arts and sciences can be noted in many cultures, but it is especially true in Latin American culture, a fact that is often overlooked by U.S. students of Latin America to the impoverishment of many of their analyses, whether in the area of the social sciences, literary criticism, or history.

INTELLECTUAL DEPENDENCY AND THE "NEW WORLD" CONCEPT

It has become fashionable to use the word "dependency" to describe the Latin American situation, whether one is referring to economics or to the world of culture in general. Political independence from Spain and Portugal did not bring with it either economic independence or intellectual independence. Instead, there was a clear transference of dependency. Economically, the relationship of dependency was shifted from the Iberian colonial powers to the industrial and commercial establishments of northwestern Europe, Britain, and "the colossus of the North" and has largely remained in that state to the present. Intellectually, a similar transference of dependency occurred earlier, during the latter half of the eighteenth century, as ideas from France and Britain, and to a lesser extent the United States, began to gain dominance in those circles that were calling for reform and eventually, independence. To a large degree, it is accurate to refer to Latin American culture as being one of dependency, an extension of the Western European and Anglo-American worlds. In this respect, Latin America does not differ from many other regions of the world that are equally dependent, culturally as well as economically.

The profound interrelationship between ideas and institutions, or philosophy and culture, can be studied more easily, perhaps, in the case of societies that are classified as being culturally and intellectually dependent. The dominant ideas come from outside the culture and are adapted to specific historical situations, making it easier for the analyst to identify the components and the relations involved. Although the originating process of ideation emerging directly out of a cultural problematic is lacking, the mutual interaction of idea and sociohistorical situation can be observed under circumstances in which the two are readily identifiable.

There is an important sense, however, in which Latin America differs from all other regions of cultural and intellectual dependency in the world. This difference has its center in the notion of "new world," a concept born in Europe in the early decades of the sixteenth century when attention was directed to the Western Hemisphere, which hitherto had been ignored, if not largely unknown. What "new world" signifies has varied from period to period, but it has been a persistent idea throughout the history of Latin America from the time of European discovery, conquest, and colonization. This concept of a "new reality" was especially evident at the time of Spanish American independence. Suddenly, new nations were born, seemingly ex nihilo, whose previous history was solely that of politico-juridical units within a larger colonial administrative entity. There was a consciousness not only of having constituted a new national identity but of having become a new social entity that needed to address the problems of forging institutions suited to its peculiar needs and of creating a cultural tradition expressive of its own concerns and values.

PHILOSOPHY: "PERMANENT ACTIVITY OF THE HUMAN SPIRIT"

Before proceeding, it is necessary to indicate what is to be included in a study of "philosophy," a controversial topic in professional philosophical circles. This chapter is concerned with more than just academic philosophy, however, and in it, the word shall be used in its broadest possible meaning.

In common linguistic usage, there are three ways in which the word is employed. First, we talk about a person's "philosophy of" something. It could be a general philosophy of life or a more specific philosophy of art. In this sense, "philosophy" translates into "attitude toward" or "way of understanding." This use can be generalized to make reference to an entire society's "philosophy of . . . ," so we can refer to "the ancient Egyptian philosophy of death" or "the Japanese philosophy of beauty." In this use of the term, philosophy refers to a basic comprehension and means of approaching a given dimension of experience or existence. Considered in its broadest dimension, philosophy in this sense is equivalent to what the Germans have called *Weltanschauung* and *Lebensanschauung*: a particular way of "looking at the world" and "looking at life," a world view and a life view. More often than not, an individual's "philosophy of *x*" has never been thought through carefully, unless some situation has arisen that posed a serious challenge to it, and almost always the *Welt- und Lebensanschauung* of a society is inarticulate, a matter of taking for granted a certain set of attitudes and values and a system of acceptable behavior. Employed in this sense, it can be said that every human being and every society has a philosophy, even though the task of philosophizing is not "being done."

Second, we refer to the philosophy of a given social movement or institution. It is possible to discuss the philosophy of Marxism, or of a given Marxist political party, for example; the philosophy of a given society's educational system, or the philosophy of higher education held by the board of regents and administration of a particular university; or the philosophy of artistic creativity held by a group of artists who have banded together to achieve certain common goals in the creative use of a particular medium or set of media. The positions taken are almost always clearly articulated and published in party platforms, charters, manifestos, constitutions, legislation, and the like. Here philosophy of x is equivalent to ideology, in the broad sense of referring to a set of agreed-upon perspectives and goals that can serve as the basis for determining directions of common action.

Third, we use philosophy to refer to a specialized intellectual activity, often, but not necessarily, associated with institutions of higher learning. In this instance, people who have received training in effective techniques engage in critical analysis of the various dimensions of experience and existence, as well as in a continual reassessment of the techniques of critical analysis itself. The dimensions of critical philosophy are many and include such disciplines as the philosophy of science, the philosophy of art, ethics, and political philosophy as well as the technical fields of logic, epistemology, and ontology. Histories of philosophy usually confine themselves to activity corresponding to this third usage of the term "philosophy."

That there are three major ways in which "philosophy" is used does not mean that we are dealing with a case of simple ambiguity—the same word being employed to designate separate meanings because of some vague associations, often lost in linguistic history. The three ways of using the term are, in fact, interrelated. The task of the critical philosopher often involves undertaking the articulation of a position that has been taken for granted. On the other hand, critically articulated positions often filter down into common usage and become assumed world views after a generation or two. Marxism is a good example of the appropriation of a critically articulated philosophical system for the purpose of creating a political and social ideology. Indeed, it could be argued that critical analysis and ideological articulation have advanced in conscious interaction within the history of Marxism. An excellent example of the interrelationship of all three usages of the word is to be found in the philosophy of the Quechua-speaking Amerindians of the Andes. They share, of course, an unarticulated (except in the case of nonverbal religious ritual and artistic expression) *Weltanschauung*, the result of many generations dwelling in, and interacting meaningfully with, a common environment. Several attempts have been made during this century to articulate some of this outlook verbally and transform it into an ideology, one of the most notable being that of the sociopolitical movement associated with the charismatic Peruvian figure, Victor Raúl Haya de la Torre. More recently, a concerted effort has been undertaken in the University of Cuzco's department of philosophy to provide a complete articulation of the Quechuan world view on the basis of linguistic and behavioral analysis for the purposes of critical analysis and restatement. Because the university serves the predominantly Quechua-speaking highlands of Peru, students who enroll in the philosophy program are required to take courses in the scientific study of the Quechuan language so they will be prepared to deal critically with Quechuan philosophy.

Keeping these three interrelated usages of the word in mind, we may define philosophy as being the effort to comprehend human existence and experience coupled with a continuing effort on the part of certain intellectuals to evaluate critically the articulation of such comprehension. This is undertaken, not only for the sake of a better understanding of the human situation, but in order to designate directions for action toward the achievement of desired goals, involving the discovery of values and the imposition of norms.

THE PROBLEM OF PERIODIZATION
IN LATIN AMERICAN PHILOSOPHY

A fundamental problem in the writing of any history is that of periodization, a determination of the meaningful temporal units that permit an adequate comprehension of the development of that which is being studied. Periodization is especially important when attempting an intellectual history of a given culture in which the development of ideas must be correlated with the wider history of the society in which those ideas were articulated. When more than one society is being considered, as in the case when dealing with Latin American intellectual history, the question becomes even more acute. Can the problem of periodization be resolved uniformly for all Latin American societies?

Efforts at writing overall histories of Latin American philosophy have been divided, in general, into six periods.

1. Colonial thought during the sixteenth and seventeenth centuries
2. The impact of the European Enlightenment on Latin American intellectual circles during the eighteenth century
3. The search during the first decades after independence from Spain and Portugal (and in the case of Haiti, from France) for adequate and appropriate philosophical bases to serve the task of constructing new national states and "peoples"
4. The dominance of Positivism throughout almost every aspect of social and cultural life during the final decades of the nineteenth century
5. The reaction against nineteenth-century Positivism in the early decades of the twentieth century, with the search for national cultural identity
6. The contemporary period

Although this periodization is very rough and needs much modification, it will serve as an introduction to the subject of the history of Latin American philosophy.

The first two centuries of colonial rule in Spanish America witnessed a remarkable richness in intellectual life. Universities that often rivaled those of Europe were founded throughout the viceroyalties and attracted outstanding European professors as teachers. Such universities later produced competent scholars who not only served their own institutions but found employment on European university faculties as well. Philosophical works published by scholars in Spanish America were read and discussed in European university circles, and there was a healthy interchange of ideas between American and European intellectuals. Only recently has serious work been undertaken to uncover and analyze this rich body of sixteenth- and seventeenth-century Spanish American philosophical literature. The very thorough bibliography of that literature prepared by Walter Redmond indicates the work that is yet to be done before we can appreciate it to the fullest extent.

The great bulk of this academic philosophy in Spanish American universities falls within the movement known as the Second Scholasticism; this movement involved the renaissance and reinterpretation of the great medieval philosophical traditions that occurred within Catholic university circles, especially in Spain and Portugal, as the intellectual phase of the Counter-Reformation as well as the effort to stem the tide of "new thought" that was sweeping across northwestern Europe. There were examples in the sixteenth century, however, of Latin American followers of such Renaissance figures as Erasmus and Thomas More and later, in the seventeenth century, of Latin American intellectuals who were influenced by the new ideas of such European philosophers as Descartes, Gassendi, and Malebranche.

What was most exciting, perhaps, about this first period in Latin American intellectual history was the appearance of a new set of problems that were debated not only in the Americas, where they originated, but in European circles as well. The central focus had to do with the indigenous populations of the New World. Were they fully human? If not, then they could not be said to enjoy the rights that humans enjoy under natural law, including the rights to hold property and to lay claim to sovereignty. They could be employed as beasts of burden. On the other hand, missionaries were sent along with the conquistadores and colonists to proclaim the gospel and save the souls of the indigenous populations, a mission that implied the fundamental human nature of the Amerindians. Two names loom large in the articulation and discussion of this issue: Bartolomé de las Casas in Spanish America and Manuel da Nóbrega in Brazil. The repercussions were strong and led, among other things, to the development of the discipline of international law in European legal circles as well as to laying the groundwork for a new articulation of the notion of fundamental human rights during the Enlightenment.

During the second period, Latin American intellectual circles were increasingly influenced by contemporary developments in England and France, a phenomenon that occurred also in the mother countries of Spain and Portugal but to a much lesser degree. There was a proliferation of intellectual activity outside the universities. In Brazil, where all requests for establishment of a university had been denied, this was of special import. Academies flourished in the form of literary and debating societies in which new ideas were expounded and discussed through the reading of learned papers and poetry. The "new thought" from Europe, including developments in the natural sciences and French *enciclopedismo,* made its way into the Latin

American mind largely by way of these academies. An important influence at this time was the new approach to economics being taken by Adam Smith, whose ideas became a rallying cry for the nascent Latin American bourgeoisie.

It was not merely the scientific and technically philosophical ideas from French Encyclopedism that were promulgated in the academies but the political concepts as well, which, along with an acquaintance with John Locke's social contract theory and certain revolutionary ideas from the Anglo-American colonies, helped to forge the ideologies that were adopted by the various groups that began to speak of independence. Alongside the academies there emerged Masonic lodges, centers of the new rationalism of the Enlightenment and seedbeds for revolutionary discussion and activity.

With independence came the problem of defining the newly emerged national identities. It was not only necessary to articulate political and economic ideologies but to lay the foundations for a new cultural tradition as well. These were confusing decades in the history of most of the new republics, and the intellectual scene mirrored this turmoil. One movement does seem to predominate in the philosophical literature of the time, however, viz., the Eclecticism of Victor Cousin. Philosophically, Cousin had insisted on the harmonization of what at first sight were conflicting doctrines. This stress on pluralistic harmonization was welcomed by many Latin American intellectuals, although by no means all, in a time of emergent nationhood with all its attendant instability and strife. Eclecticism especially influenced the Brazilian mentality of the period, which had important political consequences, notably in the "moderative power" granted to the emperor and the eventual coalition formed between the Liberal and Conservative parties.

The concern for the inauguration of a new cultural tradition, growing out of the consciousness of having become suddenly a new entity—the awareness of being Argentinian, Chilean, Mexican, etc., and thereby constituting a new "peoplehood" as well as "nationhood"—led to a great debate in several of the Spanish American republics concerning the desirability, and feasibility, of severing all linguistic and literary ties with Spain. Closely allied with this was Sarmiento's well-known plea for large-scale, non-Hispanic European immigration in order to create the new Argentine nation and culture.

Perhaps the most important figure in Latin American philosophical circles during this third period was Andrés Bello, the Venezuelan native who spent years in London in the service of Simón Bolívar and the cause of Spanish American independence. He later accepted the invitation of the Chilean government to provide important services in educational and juridical reform. Thoroughly versed in Lockeanism, Utilitarianism, and the Scottish school of "common sense philosophy," and with an impressive knowledge of Roman law as well as international law, Bello made a profound contribution toward the establishment of Chile as a nation state with a distinguished cultural tradition, not only through a life of practical administrative activity, but especially through his prolific literary production.

By the middle of the nineteenth century, it is clear that if any generalizations are to be made concerning Latin American developments, they must be made in a highly tentative fashion and accompanied with many qualifications as the situations in the individual countries were markedly diverse. Despite this diversity, there was a common thread, linked somewhat to an awareness of the highly successful northern European phenomenon known as the industrial revolution along with a strong desire for stability in many of the societies. This common thread was the prevalence of the movement to which reference was made earlier, viz., Latin American Positivism. It was not a monolithic movement by any means, and it was marked by much internal controversy, but the component elements can be identified as Comtean Positivism, Spencerian Evolutionary Naturalism, and the Utilitarianism and inductive logic of John Stuart Mill.

There are three studies of this period, focusing upon developments in individual societies, that have become classics in their own right. The earliest, which includes a careful analysis of the preceding intellectual period as well, is by one of Argentina's own Positivists, José Ingenieros. Leopoldo Zea, in several works, has traced the introduction, ascendancy, and fall of the doctrines of Positivism within the fabric of Mexican history. João Cruz Costa has done much the same with reference to Positivism in Brazil. If and when a general analysis of Positivism in Latin American culture is undertaken, it will reveal a very deep imprint made by these rather heterogeneous ideas upon a wide spectrum of social life, including the political, economic, religious, educational, and literary sectors.

The reaction against Positivism was as vocal as Positivism's impact had been profound. In Mexico, it was first articulated through the Ateneo de La Juventud (Atheneum of Youth), which provided the intellectual base for the Mexican Revolution that toppled the old Porfirian establishment. Francisco Romero, who belonged to the second generation of anti-Positivists in Argentina, referred to such figures as José Vasconcelos and Antonio Caso in Mexico, Alejandro Korn in Argentina, Raimundo de Farias Brito in Brazil, Alejandro Deústua in Peru, and Carlos Vaz Ferreira in Uruguay as *Los Fundadores* (the Founders), intellectuals who were striving to create a new philosophical stance that would be authentically Latin American. Ironically, these philosophers were greatly influenced by similar work being done in European circles at the time in the sense of reacting to Positivism and Evolutionary Naturalism, the greatest influence coming from the French philosopher, Henri Bergson. Strong emphasis was given in their writings to aesthetics, which had been downplayed during the reign of Positivism, and metaphysics, which had been eliminated, along with a concern for the study of the spiritual dimension of human life.

Contemporary periods are always difficult to characterize because one lacks the necessary historical perspective to evaluate them adequately, but four features seem to stand out over the past half century. First, there has been a continuation of the work of *Los Fundadores* through a second, as well as a third, generation in several of the countries. This is evident especially in Mexico, where first Samuel Ramos and then Leopoldo Zea were seen as standing in the tradition of Vasconcelos and Caso. Ramos is remembered for his work in philosophical anthropology, through which he attempted to clarify the uniqueness of the Mexican personality. Zea is known for the impetus that he has given to the study of Mexican intellectual history as it relates to the development of national institutions.

Second, there has been the forging of what has become a dominant ideology for much of Latin America, a concern for liberation from a status of dependency of national political economies and for the liberation of the underprivileged classes within those economies. On the one hand, this ideology has been expressed through heterodox Marxist positions, perhaps most clearly in the writings of the Peruvian, José Mariátegui. On the other hand, it has found its roots in Catholic tradition, where the new Liberation Theology has arisen to make its revolutionary impact felt far beyond the Latin American geographical area. This new theology has spawned in Latin America philosophies of liberation and pedagogies of liberation as well.

What may be designated as the golden age of Latin American philosophy of law falls within this half century, and it is exemplified by important works by Luís Racaséns-Siches and Eduardo García-Maynez from Mexico, Juan Llambías de Azevedo of Uruguay, Carlos Cossio of Argentina, and the Brazilian, Miguel Reale. Within academic philosophy, the present period has witnessed a new maturity that recalls the situation described in the discussion of the sixteenth and seventeenth centuries in Spanish American universities: Work being done by philosophers in the Americas has paralleled that being accomplished by European faculties. Important contributions have been made in the methodologies both of phenomenology and of linguistic analysis, as well as in the disciplines of philosophy of science, philosophy of mathematics, epistemology, ethics, and the history of philosophy. Mario Bunge, whose father was an important figure in Argentinian philosophy earlier in the century, can be considered representative of this new philosophical maturity, although he has left his native Argentina to teach in the United States and Canada. His ambitious multivolume system of philosophy has been well received by critics and has made a decided contribution to contemporary philosophical dialogue in Europe and Anglo-America as well as in Latin America.

When we turn from Latin American philosophy in general and focus our attention upon the histories of thought in individual countries, we confront the problem of a much more finely tuned periodization. José Ortega y Gasset, the Spanish philosopher who has had a profound influence throughout Latin America, partially because several of his former students moved there during the Franco years in Spain, developed the concept of "historical generations" as a means of approaching intellectual and cultural history. The concept has been refined by his close disciple, Julian Marias, and promises to be a fruitful approach to the problem. My own article "Philosophical Ambiance of Brazilian Independence" is an effort to illuminate the various cross-currents of thought that were operative during a significant "generation" in the life of one nation.

Everything written thus far about the problem of the periodization of Latin American intellectual history refers exclusively to Euro-America, of course. Satisfactory periodizations for Indo-American and Afro-American histories remain to be done. The task is formidable, especially because the sources are largely nonwritten and the investigator must rely heavily on work done by ethnologists, cultural anthropologists, art historians, folklorists, and linguists who, because of the nature of their respective disciplines, are not concerned with the philosophical dimensions of the mythology, ritual, art, linguistic usage, and behavioral patterns that they analyze; nor are they generally concerned about unraveling the historical strands that are woven therein. A much more difficult problem will remain even if, and when, a successful periodization is worked out for the Indo-American and Afro-American dimensions of the cultures of Latin American nations; namely, the effort to correlate the histories of Indo-, Afro-, and Euro-America so that an adequate periodization can be formulated that would serve as a framework for the writing of a history of Latin American philosophy that will faithfully reflect and report the pluralistic nature of the subject matter. The question raised at the outset of this section must, then, be restated this way: Can the problem of periodization be resolved uniformly for Latin American societies that are culturally and intellectually pluridimensional?

REPRESENTATIVE PROBLEMS IN THE STUDY OF LATIN AMERICAN PHILOSOPHY AND INTELLECTUAL TRADITION

It is necessary to develop more adequate techniques for uncovering and studying Indo-American and Afro-American philosophical thought. Some primary sources of a written nature are available, but they are highly limited. Leon-Portilla has done pioneering work in analyzing Nahuatl and Mayan codices, which date from the century before European conquest and the early years of the colonization of New Spain, in order to reveal their philosophical content. I have already referred to the work being done at the University of Cuzco to clarify the philosophical presuppositions embedded in Quechuan grammar and linguistic usage. A few studies have appeared in Brazil that analyze Tupí-Guaraní mythology in an effort to uncover its implicit *Weltanschauung*. The Afro-Brazilian cult communities have begun to produce a substantial literature of their own, in which there is a tendency toward critical philosophical discourse and which provides a rich source for the student of Afro-American cultural and intellectual history.

Much of the source material is not written, of course. Required for the task of analyzing it are scholars who are trained both as philosophers and historians of ideas on the one hand and as anthropologists, linguists, or art historians on the other. A multidisciplinary effort will be necessary to work fruitfully in the areas of Indo-American and Afro-American intellectual history.

A perennially controversial question is: Can a genuinely Latin American philosophy be identified and distinguished from European philosophy in the Americas? A parallel problem is whether a genuinely Afro-American mentality can be identified and distinguished from the philosophies of traditional African societies.

The question of what is distinctively Latin American about intellectual activity in the Americas is related to a third set of problems: How have certain words, concepts, and themes, which have their origins in European thought, been modified through use in the context of Latin American realities? Three configurations of terms come to mind immediately:

1. The terms *libertad* (Port.: *liberdade*) and *liberación* (Port.: *libertação*) have been used throughout most of the intellectual history of Latin America with varying meanings in each of the periods. There has been a cumulative effect in this history of usage so that it might be argued that there has come to be a peculiarly Latin American range of connotative significance attached to them.

2. *Independencia, dependencia,* and *interdependencia* are used in more than a political and economic sense to encompass the cultural and intellectual as well. The relationship between Latin American populations and the powers that have exercised political and economic colonial domination is not the same as the relationship that characterizes other colonial and former colonial situations in the world. This difference gives a special nuance of meaning to the notion of cultural dependence and independence that deserves to be carefully delineated.

3. The associated terms of "sovereignty," "international law," and "human rights" have been important throughout Latin American history. We have already noted that the discipline of international law owes its origin to the controversy over Amerindian nature and rights and what should be the correct political and juridical relations between the European colonizing powers and the Amerindian societies they had to deal with. The question of human rights, with reference to certain segments of the population, has been a perennial issue in Latin American history, from the days of Bartolomé de las Casas and Manuel da Nóbrega to the present-day concern of liberationists and freedom fighters. An analysis of the contributions made by Latin American intellectuals who have been dealing with these issues to world understanding would help to reveal the creative edge of the Latin American intellectual tradition.

The analysis of Latin American philosophy and intellectual history is an important dimension of Latin American studies and constitutes a fascinating field for the student who has an interest in the life of the mind and the close interaction of ideas and social institutions. It is an area that has been relatively neglected in the past and therefore offers an especially challenging opportunity for fresh and innovative research and interpretation.

SUGGESTED READINGS

General Works

Davis, Harold Eugene. *Latin American Thought: Historical Introduction.* New York: Free Press, 1974. A brief, informative survey from pre-Columbian times to the present.
Encyclopedia of Philosophy. 8 vols. New York: Macmillan, 1967. In addition to a general article on Latin American philosophy, there are separate articles about several of the leading figures. A listing of periodicals is given in the article "Philosophical Journals."

Pan American Union. *Revista interamericana de bibliografía/Interamerican Review of Bibliography*. A quarterly publication of the Pan-American Union (OAS), which includes articles about Latin American intellectual history.

Amerindian Thought

Leon-Portilla, Miguel. *Aztec Thought and Culture*. Norman: University of Oklahoma Press, 1963. Reconstruction of Nahuatl thought during the period before the Spanish conquest of New Spain based on a careful analysis of the available codices.

————. *Time and Reality in the Thought of the Maya*. Boston: Beacon Press, 1968. Reconstruction of Mayan thought prior to the Spanish conquest based on studies by leading investigators of available sources.

Afro-American Thought

Bastide, Roger. *The African Religions of Brazil*. Baltimore: Johns Hopkins University Press, 1978. A thorough and sympathetic analysis of the Afro-Brazilian religious communities by a leading French sociologist who, as a convert, has a unique perspective.

Herskovits, Melville J. *The New World Negro: Selected Papers in Afroamerican Studies*. Bloomington: Indiana University Press, 1966. A variety of essays including studies of cult life in Brazil, the world view of blacks in Paramaribo, Trinidad "Shouters," "Voodoo," and Afro-Catholic syncretism.

Philosophy During the Colonial Period

Redmond, Walter. *Bibliography of the Philosophy in the Iberian Colonies of America*. Hague: Nijhoff, 1972. A listing of books and articles written and published by philosophers in Spanish America and Brazil during the centuries of colonial rule that reveals the breadth and richness of philosophical production during the period.

Eighteenth-Century Enlightenment

Whitaker, Arthur P., ed. *Latin America and the Enlightenment*. 2d ed. Ithaca: Cornell University Press, 1961. A collection of short essays about various aspects of Enlightenment thought throughout Latin America.

Intellectual Developments During the Nineteenth Century

Crawford, William Rex. *A Century of Latin-American Thought*. Rev. ed. Cambridge: Harvard University Press, 1963. A survey of social and political thought in Latin America during the nineteenth century with brief summaries of the positions of individual writers.

Davis, Harold Eugene, ed. *Latin American Social Thought: The History of Its Development Since Independence, with Selected Readings*. Washington, D.C.: University Press of Washington, 1961. An anthology of selections from the writings of leading social and political thinkers of Spanish America and Brazil during the nineteenth century.

Zea, Leopoldo. *The Latin American Mind*. Norman: University of Oklahoma Press, 1963. An analysis of Liberalism during the first half of the nineteenth century, and Positivism during the second half, throughout Spanish America.

Intellectual Developments During the Twentieth Century

Boff, Leonardo, and Boff, Clodovis. *Introducing Liberation Theology*. Maryknoll, N.Y.: Orbis Books, 1987. A good, brief introduction to the historical development and basic tenets of Liberation Theology by one of the best-known Brazilian leaders in the movement and his brother.

Chavarría, Jesus. *José Carlos Mariátegui and the Rise of Modern Peru, 1890–1930.* Albuquerque: University of New Mexico Press, 1979. A study of the intellectual development of one of Peru's best-known political ideologists.

Freire, Paulo. *Pedagogy of the Oppressed.* New York: Seabury Press, 1970. The "bible" of the Pedagogy of Liberation Movement in Brazil, Spanish America, and the Third World.

García, Jorge J. E., ed. *Latin American Philosophy in the Twentieth Century: Man, Values, and the Search for Philosophical Identity.* Buffalo: Prometheus Books, 1986. An anthology of leading Spanish-American and Brazilian philosophers that supplements the Sanchez-Reulet volume with some overlapping.

García, Jorge J. E., et al., eds. *Philosophical Analysis in Latin America.* Dordrecht: Reidel, 1984. A study of the impact of Anglo-American analytic philosophy in Spanish America and Brazil.

Gutiérrez, Gustavo. *A Theology of Liberation: History, Politics, and Salvation.* Maryknoll, N.Y.: Orbis Books, 1973. One of the germinal works of the Latin American Theology of Liberation Movement.

Handbook of Latin American Studies. Gainesville: University Presses of Florida, 1935–. An annual report of publications in which the section on philosophy provides a yearly overview of philosophical activities in Latin America.

Himelblau, Jack. *Alejandro O. Deustua: Philosophy in Defense of Man.* Gainesville: University Presses of Florida, 1979. Analyzes the thought of Peru's great philosopher of art.

Ireland, Gordon, trans. *Latin American Legal Philosophy.* Cambridge: Harvard University Press, 1948. English translations of works by Luís Recaséns-Siches, Eduardo García-Maynez, Juan Llambías de Azevedo, and Carlos Cossio.

Kunz, Josef L. *Latin-American Philosophy of Law in the Twentieth Century.* New York: New York University School of Law, 1950. A brief survey of the golden age of Latin American legal philosophy, placing it within the broader context of European philosophy of law and dealing with several minor figures as well as the major ones.

Sanchez-Reulet, Aníbal, ed. *Contemporary Latin-American Philosophy.* Albuquerque: University of New Mexico Press, 1954. An anthology of selections from writings of late nineteenth-century and early twentieth-century philosophers from various Spanish American countries and Brazil. Although a few Positivists are included, the majority of writings belong to *Los Fundadores.*

7
LATIN AMERICAN LITERATURE

TAMARA HOLZAPFEL

More than a century before the Pilgrims reached the shores of North America, Spanish and Portuguese explorers were busy discovering, conquering, and colonizing the vast territory to the south. It was at this time of feverish activity that Latin American literature came into existence. The discovery of a strange new continent inhabited by hitherto unknown peoples with exotic customs had the greatest impact imaginable on the European mentality. The conquerors and colonizers took on the additional task of describing and interpreting this amazing discovery to the European world. They recorded living history in chronicles and heroic deeds in epic poems. These two genres begin the history of Latin American literature.

During the three-century colonial period, Latin American literature followed the literary models of the mother countries. The coming of independence in the first quarter of the nineteenth century brought forth a large number of separate nations, and literature in Latin America acquired national characteristics. To the original complexity of the two languages dividing Latin American literature into two distinct literatures, Spanish American and Luso-Brazilian, was now added the difficulty of distinguishing among the literatures of nineteen Spanish-speaking countries. If it is obvious that Luso-Brazilian literature is unique in Latin America, it is quite another matter to define the characteristics that separate Argentine from Nicaraguan or Colombian from Mexican literature.

Nevertheless, similar historical circumstances—from conquest, colonialism, and independence to the political turmoil of the present—provide a common denominator for scrutinizing Latin American literature. Another unifying characteristic of this literature is a persistent concern with social issues. In contrast to European literary tradition, always preoccupied with the discovery of new literary techniques, Latin American literature has had to deal with a myriad of extraliterary factors. From the beginning, it was the strangeness and the diversity of a new reality that asserted itself over a mere concern with literary form. History and politics, geography and sociology, have always been an integral part of Latin American literary expression.

Although Latin American literature has been in existence for nearly half a millennium, it is only since the mid-1960s that it has broken through the barrier of silence that has surrounded it. At this recent point in time, an unprecedented interest in the literary productions of Latin America developed simultaneously in Europe and North America. This became known as "the boom" of Latin American literature. Critics everywhere agreed that Latin American literature had finally emerged from obscurity and that Latin American writers could now stand comparison with the best of Europe and North America.

Latin Americans are proud of such names on their literary roster as Pablo Neruda, Jorge Luis Borges, João Guimaraes Rosa, Miguel Angel Asturias, Gabriel García Márquez, and a score more. Their books, readily available in good translations in all major languages, are read, discussed, and admired throughout the world. But with the discovery of a "new" literature, it is easy to overlook the fact that Latin American literature did not develop out of nowhere. Let us now look at the highlights of the literary tradition that helped forge a new and significant literature in the twentieth century.

THE COLONIAL PERIOD

The entire literary expression of the sixteenth century was devoted to the description of the American experience. The conquerors, the colonizers, and the missionaries were the authors. They found a vast land of untamed nature that they proceeded to explore and subjugate. At the time of the conquest, novels of chivalry were at the height of their popularity in Europe. These stimulated the imagination of the early explorers, and they came to the Americas with their minds filled with legends of the Fountain of Youth, the Seven Enchanted Cities, and the myth of El Dorado. In many instances, even the style of the chronicles is taken from the novels of chivalry. The Americas, from the beginning, became lands of "magical realism" to the European imagination. Magical realism denotes the fusion of two planes, the real and the fantastic, or marvelous. The term has been used extensively in the critical literature of the fictional writings of contemporary authors who have readily acknowledged the chronicles as a source of inspiration.

These historical accounts begin with the log book of Christopher Columbus (1492) and include the famous dispatches, *Five Letters* (1519–1526), Hernán Cortés sent from Mexico to Charles V of Spain as well as histories of every stage of colonization. The most vivid of these first-person narratives is *The True History of the Conquest of New Spain* (1552) by Bernal Díaz del Castillo. Bernal Díaz was a simple soldier who accompanied Cortés in the conquest of Mexico. He took part in 119 battles and skirmishes and at the conclusion of the conquest, was rewarded with an *encomienda* in Guatemala where he spent the rest of his long life. Although he wrote his book when he was eighty-four, he seems to have had phenomenal powers of recall, remembering the names and the colors of horses in the expedition. The book stands out because of the author's individuality of character and his personalized point of view, both traits much appreciated in contemporary writing. Bernal Díaz relates in great detail and in a natural, colloquial language the events in which he took part. He does it with much bragging about himself and praise for the 400 soldiers who achieved the conquest rather than for their commander, Cortés.

The second generation of chroniclers was born in the Americas. Creoles, mestizos, and even Indians contributed a number of significant narratives during the second half of the sixteenth century. By far superior are the *Royal Commentaries* (1609–1617) by Inca Garcilaso de la Vega of Cuzco, Peru. Son of a conquistador (who was a cousin of the gifted Castilian poet of the same name) and an Incan princess, Garcilaso wrote a historicist account of the Incan Empire and its conquest, stressing the parallels between the civilizations of the New World and the Old. Much of the information he gleaned from oral tradition and the memories his relatives had of preconquest times. He was a gifted scholar who established his reputation as a humanist in Spain. But what attracts the modern readers is Garcilaso's imaginative bent. Legendary and fantastic episodes enliven the narrative. He and Bernal Díaz represent authentic Americanism in colonial letters, their works being typical of the contribution made by the chronicles.

Epic poetry was the other genre cultivated in the sixteenth century. Two works in particular stand out, one in Spanish, the other in Portuguese. The Spanish nobleman Alonso de Ercilla participated in the struggle to subdue the hardy and warlike Araucanians of Chile. He was so impressed by their bravery and their stoic composure that he dedicated his epic poem *La Araucana* (1569–1589) to them. Although he could not help but extol the prowess and valor of his countrymen, he was not blind to their greed and cruelty. Yet he admired unquestioningly the fortitude and patriotism of the Indian chieftains. Caupolicán, Lautaro, Colocolo, and Rengo have truly Homeric stature and their names have retained resonance to this day.

The first colonial poet in the Portuguese language was Bento Texeira Pinto who is remembered for his epic *Prosopopéa* (1601). Here, as in Ercilla's *Araucana,* American man and American nature play the principal roles. Both works may be considered truly American even if their authors were not born in the New World.

The seventeenth century in Latin America was dominated in life and in art by a Spanish import: the baroque style. Characterized by excessive ornamentation in the plastic arts and sumptuousness and artificiality in dress and manners, it appeared in literature as *culteranismo,* a complicated stylistic obscurity, and as *conceptismo,* which refers to the complexity of concepts and sharpness of wit. *Culteranismo,* especially, also known as *gongorismo* after the Spanish poet Luis de Góngora y Argote, caught on as a literary style in the cultural centers of Latin America: Mexico City; Lima, Peru; and Bahia, Brazil. Colonial society was rigidly stratified, and this stylistically sophisticated literature was produced exclusively by and for an aristocratic class. The baroque has been persistent in Latin American literature. It reappeared with a new face in the contemporary novel in which it creates tension and paradox in imagery and translates into a rich, hedonistic use of language.

The greatest literary figure of the baroque was Sor Juana Inés de la Cruz. She was Mexican by birth and a woman of rare beauty and intelligence. She learned to read at the age of three, when she stopped eating cheese because she had heard it made people stupid. She learned Latin in twenty lessons. Because of her beauty, she was invited to live at the court of the viceroy, the Marquis de Mancera. Much impressed with her intelligence, the marquis brought forty great scholars to the court to question her on their particular subjects. Sor Juana answered all questions to everyone's satisfaction and amazement. At the age of sixteen, she entered a convent to pursue her genuine and considerable intellectual interests. Her literary achievement earned her great fame in colonial society, and she became known throughout the Spanish-speaking world as "the tenth muse." But Sor Juana had also considerable talent for empirical observation, and had she lived in a more propitious environment, she might have become the world's first woman scientist.

Sor Juana's literary production is varied, representing all the different genres cultivated in colonial Latin America: lyric and metaphysical poetry, comedies and religious plays, satirical and theological writings. Her poetry is technically skillful and reveals a personality beset by intellectual problems. It shows that she was torn not only between religious obedience and her passion for learning but also between following the *autoridades* ("authorities") or turning to the new pragmatic methods.

Among her prose writings, *The Critique of a Sermon* (1690) provoked a sensation in the Church because she had daringly criticized a sermon by the celebrated Jesuit, Father Antonio Vieira. This resulted in an exchange of letters between the nun and the bishop of Puebla, who had published her critique. Her most famous piece of prose forms part of this correspondence. *Answer to Sor Philotea* (1691) is autobiographical and explains her lifelong pursuit of learning. She defends her intellectual inclination as a God-given gift, but modern readers consider this candid self-analysis an important forerunner of feminist expression.

One great literary figure of colonial times is usually classified as a Spanish author. He was the Mexican Juan Ruíz de Alarcón, gifted as a dramatist, who became, together with Lope de Vega, Tirso de Molina, and Calderón de la Barca, an original contributor to the creation of a national theater in Spain. Today, Alarcón's comedies—he wrote twenty-five of them—are considered more modern than those of his colleagues, for he gave more importance to construction, restraint, and psychology. His masterpiece, *The Liar* (1630), was rewritten by Pierre Corneille for the French theater and became the model for Molière's comedies of manners. That this talented Creole writer had to seek his fortune in Spain is an indication of cultural domination by the mother country over its colonies. By the seventeenth century, the excitement over the conquest had subsided, and the robust Americanism that had developed earlier in Spanish America had almost disappeared.

In Brazil, on the contrary, the heroic spirit of the conquest was prolonged into the eighteenth century by the *bandeirantes,* or explorers of the hinterland, the Brazilian *sertões.* They were adventurers of the first order who audaciously and brutally fought against Indians and nature in their search for lodes of precious metals and stones. In the second half of the seventeenth century, the inland mining center of Minas Gerais became the home of the *mineira* "miner" school of Brazilian poetry. José Basilio de Gama was its greatest representative, and his masterpiece, *The Uruguay* (1769), of lasting literary merit, describes the war of Spain and Portugal against the Paraguayan Indians in 1756. Santa Rita Durão, a contemporary of da Gama, was another important poet inspired by native elements. His *Caramurú* (1781) is the epic of Brazil. It tells the story of the discovery of Bahia by Diogo Alvares Correa about the middle of the sixteenth century.

The eighteenth century was in every way a sterile period for Spain. The country was spent as a world power, and its two-century-long golden age had come to an abrupt end when the last great poet and dramatist of the age, Calderón de la Barca, died in 1681. The cultural decadence was still more pronounced in the colonies; it was only toward the end of the colonial period that a few writers, influenced by the French *philosophes,* Voltaire, Rousseau, Diderot, and Montesquieu, took up the struggle for literary emancipation. But they did not form a cohesive group. Scattered all over the huge continent, they only shared in the hardships imposed by censorship and persecution.

THE MODERN PERIOD

Literary activity almost came to a halt during the years of the struggle for independence. Instead of imaginative literature, the first quarter of the nineteenth century produced war reports and descriptions of battles. But one work, published in 1816, made a unique contribution to Latin American letters. *The Itching Parrot,* a picaresque novel by the Mexican journalist José Joaquín Fernández de Lizardi, was the first novel to appear in the Americas. Lizardi had managed to become well acquainted with the ideas of the French *philosophes,* and when Father Hidalgo initiated the revolutionary movement in 1810, Lizardi became an eager supporter of the struggle for independence. He founded a journal, *The Mexican Thinker,* in 1812 and became famous as a propagandist and pamphleteer. His novel was the result of censorship rather than artistic vocation. Lizardi wrote *The Itching Parrot* to express opinions that were unpublishable in the journals of the time.

The novel satirizes Mexican middle-class life on the eve of independence. The hero Periquillo (Little Parrot) is an all-around rogue who goes through every imaginable adventure in late colonial Mexico City. The novel's faithful portrayal of social life and its racy and popular language made it the most readable work of the period.

Romanticism

During the turbulent and chaotic independence years, there was a pronounced antagonism toward everything Spanish and Portuguese, and the cultures of France, England, and Germany began to exert a strong influence on the new nations. Literary groups were founded with the express purpose of encouraging a national literature. These circles were often political as well as literary and were exceedingly important in the nineteenth-century history of Latin America.

The most pressingly discussed topic in these literary circles was Romanticism, a movement encompassing political, social, and philosophical concerns as well as changes in sensibility and literary form. Romanticism was identified above all with individual freedom and nationalism. In Cuba and Argentina, literature and politics were linked through the novel. In those two countries, the genre served as a vehicle to promote a national cause. In Uruguay, the historical novel was to provide a sense of national identity. A new genre, *tradiciones* ("traditions"), based on national themes, appeared in Peru. Its creator, Ricardo Palma, combined legendary material with historical anecdotes taken from every period of Peruvian history, from preconquest times to his own. The pure-blooded Aztec, Ignacio Altamirano, pursued in his writings and teachings the cause of a national literature in Mexico. By precept and example, he showed the younger generation of writers the value of using local customs, village types, and the dramatic events of their times as literary material. Brazil's concern with national themes is notable in novels dealing with the Indian and the hinterland.

The most significant body of Romantic literature in Latin America is associated with the Rosas reign of terror in Argentina. Juan Manuel Rosas, dictator of the eastern La Plata provinces, persecuted Argentine intellectuals as his natural enemies. The writers fought back through revolutionary societies and by recording his infamies in a variety of literary genres.

First among the writers was Esteban Echeverría, who introduced Romanticism into Argentina. He had espoused the new movement while in France, and he hoped to bring about a cultural revolution upon his return to his country in 1830. But the romantic conventions he learned in Europe conflicted with American reality. In an Argentina where Rosas had established a bloodthirsty tyranny with the aid of gaucho troops, it was difficult to idealize the common people and the noble savage. Thus, in Echeverría's important works, *The Slaughter House,* a long short story, and *The Captive,* a narrative poem, he depicts the conflict between the forces of primitive barbarism and the civilized, Europeanized individual. *The Slaughter House* is an allegory of the Rosas dictatorship: Under his rule, Argentina has been turned into a veritable slaughterhouse in which the civilized person is destroyed by the forces of barbarism.

Another important Argentine writer of this time was Domingo Faustino Sarmiento, who became one of Argentina's presidents after the fall of Rosas. His *Civilization and Barbarism: The Life of Juan Facundo Quiroga* (1845) has become a classic of Latin American literature. It is first of all a biography of a gaucho *caudillo* ("strongman") who duplicated Rosas's terror in the western provinces. He was eventually assassinated by the more powerful tyrant. The book is also a study of the influence of the physical environment in shaping the gaucho mentality. A seminomadic people, the gauchos roamed the vast Pampa, fiercely independent and antisocial. Sarmiento ultimately blames the rise of strongmen like Quiroga and Rosas on the gauchos who opposed civilized life because they could not understand it. With this work, Sarmiento captured the lasting conflict in Latin American society, between civilization and barbarism, between the law and order imposed by the city versus the lawlessness of the frontier. He was the first writer to articulate this dichotomy, one that has remained a constant in Latin American literature.

But the most original contribution of Latin American Romanticism was the gauchesque genre that derived from the songs of the gaucho minstrels who roamed the pampas of southern Brazil, Uruguay, and Argentina. The masterpiece is a narrative poem, *Martín Fierro* (1872) by José Hernández, who opposed his citified countryman Sarmiento and actively conspired against him. In politics and in literature, Hernández took the side of the gaucho *caudillo* against the city.

The protagonist of his narrative poem is a gaucho persecuted by the authorities because he represents a different view of life. Martín Fierro does not believe in the right of private property and takes justice into his own hands. His moral enemies are judges, mayors, army officers, and the police— all of them corrupt. They have destroyed his way of life. They have taken him away from his loved ones and sent him to the frontier to fight the Indians. But despite his great suffering, he retains his sense of dignity and achieves heroic stature as a champion of liberty.

Hernández imitated the speech and the manner of thought of unlettered country people and was the first writer to break down the barrier that divided the cultural elite and the masses. The poem was a huge popular success, and in time, attained the status of a thoroughly American epic independent of European norms and influences.

Many of the nineteenth-century Romantic novels were written as a result of the support writers received from literary circles formed to promote the publication of literary works and to offer encouragement and criticism. The best Romantic novel of Latin America, *María* (1867) by Jorge Isaacs, was published with financial help from the Colombian literary group El Mosaico. Jorge Isaacs was the son of an English Jew who had settled on an estate called El Paraíso in the beautiful Cauca Valley. Unsuccessful business ventures and the civil war of El Cauca ruined the family financially. Between 1864 and the year of his death, 1873, Isaacs made every effort to win back his fortune in order to own again the home of his childhood. He never succeeded, but in his novel he charmingly re-creates his patriarchal country home. *María* is an elegiac love story of two young people who enjoy an enchanting moment of happiness under the protective care of their parents and faithful servants. But María is fatally ill and dies while Efraín is in London where he has gone to complete his studies. This sentimental story, with its combination of realistic detail and delicate romantic melancholy, has enjoyed continuing success and has been more widely read than any other Spanish American novel of the time.

Realism and Naturalism

During the latter part of the nineteenth century, Romanticism began giving way to Realism and Naturalism in fiction and in drama. In Chile, Alberto Blest Gana wrote *Martín Rivas* (1862), a novel that is a social document of the times. He was one of the first writers to describe social change in Latin America. The novel portrays a poor young man from the country and parasitic lower-class city people trying to improve their situation by marrying into upper- and middle-class families. The young provincial succeeds because of his admirable qualities. Clorinda Matto de Turner became the author of the first novel of social protest on behalf of Peruvian Indians. *Birds Without a Nest* (1889) strongly denounces the exploitation of the Indians by a village priest but does not offer a viable solution to their problem. The more sordid aspects of life in Buenos Aires were the subject of the novels of Eugenio Cambaceres. *Aimless* (1885) reflects the helplessness of people in a period of rapid social change. The protagonist of the novel, having lost his traditional faith, comes to the pessimistic conclusion that "knowing is suffering: knowing nothing, eating, sleeping and not thinking of the exact solution of the problem is the only happiness in living."

Throughout the nineteenth century, and everywhere in Latin America, native dramatists amused audiences with plays depicting local types and customs. But it was only in the Río de la Plata region that a realistic drama of originality based on rustic gaucho themes began to develop in the early 1880s. This theater, featuring gaucho heroes such as Juan Moreira and Santos Vega, grew from pantomime and crude melodrama and ranged from improvised representation without scripts to written drama of an original type. The earliest and best playwright of this period was Florencio Sánchez of Uruguay, who wrote his many plays on both rural and urban themes in Argentina. He brought to the stage typical problems of the Río de la Plata region: conflicts between original settlers and new immigrants, the individual and conventional social institutions, parents and children, city and countryside. His use of Argentine dialect and native characters accounts for his great success in Buenos Aires. *Downhill* (1905), his best play, dramatizes the decline and death of an old-fashioned Creole farmer. His downfall and suicide are brought about by social change and opposition to his ways, even by members of his family. Swindled of his land and surrounded by hostility, he loses all hope and self-respect and hangs himself. The play has been interpreted as the swan song of rural Argentina.

A mixture of Realism and Naturalism was used by many novelists and short-story writers at the turn of the century. On the whole, the quality of the writing is not impressive. An important exception, however, was the work of Brazil's Machado de Assis, author of *Dom Casmurro* (1900) and a number of other highly original works of fiction. A truly sophisticated novelist, Machado was profound in his treatment of character and was a forerunner, along with Henry James, in the use of an unreliable narrator as the central figure of a novel. Dom Casmurro (whose nickname means Sir Grumpy) is an aging widower who recounts his life story since the day he fell in love, at the age of fifteen, with the girl next door. He describes his long but successful campaign to avoid the priesthood and marry his true love, a captivating girl/woman named Capitu. Once married to her, he becomes jealously possessive and ultimately destroys their marriage and his love for their son. Thus, the novel becomes an old man's justification for having exiled his wife and son forever. Because the reader has only Dom Casmurro's version and because Machado made him exceedingly convincing by endowing him not only with intelligence but with Machado's own erudition and firsthand experience of jealous imaginings, Dom Casmurro's unreliability is not usually fully comprehended. Another reason why the reader tends to accept his account is that Machado diverts attention by creating a mystery that teases the reader's curiosity: Was Capitu innocent or guilty of adultery and can the reader figure out the truth? But the mystery is insoluble because the narrator's subtle and often undetected unreliability taints all the "evidence." Rarely has an unreliable narrator been so believable in presenting not just his side of the story but a view of life that seems convincing.

Modernism in Spanish American Poetry

In poetry, the move was not so much a departure from Romanticism as a rebellion against its excesses and an assimilation of new techniques from French Parnassianism and Symbolism. This gave rise to Spanish America's most important literary innovation. *Modernismo* (Modernism) revolutionized the Spanish language and the form of poetry. It derived its greatest impetus from the publication of *Azul* (1888) by the Nicaraguan poet Rubén Darío. It was Darío who gave the movement its name and definition. Although *modernista* poets were a disparate group of individual writers, Darío saw three essential strands that bound them together: (1) the rejection of any overt message, (2) emphasis on beauty as the highest goal, and (3) the need to free verse from traditional forms. Darío became the central personality of the whole movement because of his creative example and his extensive travels in Spanish-speaking countries. His presence helped link poets of different places and gave them a sense of solidarity. He participated in the founding of many literary magazines that spread the message of Modernism all over the continent. These magazines, or *revistas,* significantly influenced the literary climate throughout the Spanish-speaking world and did much to increase the importance of literature in Latin America.

Modernismo was guided in its literary innovation principally by models from France. Spain was too traditional, but France had undergone a literary revolution represented by Romanticism, Parnassianism, and Symbolism, three schools that offered the greatest variety imaginable of techniques and poetic resources. The *modernistas* learned from these models everything they could, but their poems were far from being mechanical imitations. Their search for new poetic methods and themes led them still further into foreign literatures: English, German, Italian, Scandinavian, and Russian. From all these multifarious elements, Spanish American poets created a poetry all their own, one that was entirely new in form, vocabulary, subject matter, and feeling.

Initially characterized as an art for art's sake movement, by a cosmopolitan outlook, and as a cult of the exotic, Modernism in its later years became increasingly concerned with American themes and thus was a forerunner of what was to follow: a period of literary rediscovery of the New World. The force of the Modernists' renovation of poetry also spread to prose and has extended in contemporary times to the writers of both Spanish America and Spain. *Modernismo* was Spanish America's first original contribution to world literature and was eminently representative of the cultural life of the times.

During the same period, poets in Brazil were classified as Romantics, Parnassians, and Symbolists, although at least one poet, Joaquín María Machado de Assis, transcends these categories. His poetry resembles that of Rubén Darío, and Machado, like the Nicaraguan poet, was a writer of refined temperament who modernized Brazilian poetry.

One of the last consequences of Modernism was the emergence of feminine literature. The movement had been decidedly masculine in character. Most of the women who participated were either too conservative or too timid in assimilating the essentially innovative and revolutionary manner. But one woman, Delmira Agustini of Uruguay, can truly be called a Modernist. She carried furthest the sensuality and eroticism expressed in the poetry of Rubén Darío. In her poems, she yearns for a higher kind of love, one that would more nearly satisfy both her carnal and her spiritual needs. Her poetry has been defined as the "first spectacle in the open of a woman's heart." Delmira had many followers, the most famous among them being the Chilean Gabriela Mistral, who became known everywhere as a great humanitarian and poet. Gabriela Mistral was the first Latin American writer to receive the Nobel Prize for literature (1945).

Brazilian Modernism and Spanish American Vanguard Poetry

Brazilian *modernismo* (not to be confused with the Spanish American movement of the same name) dates from 1922, when a new poetic era was ushered in, one that broke completely with the past. It proclaimed the destruction of the old and the idea that modernity was more important than beauty itself. The extremists among these modern poets founded *The Cannibalistic Review,* which proclaimed reversion to cannibalism and destruction of everything foreign in Brazilian literature. Yet this school also produced such outstanding contemporary poets as Jorge de Lima (Negro poetry), Mario de Andrade (futuristic poetry), and Carlos Drummond (revolutionary poetry).

A new, radical poetry also came into existence in Spanish America in the years following World War I. Early practitioners of this avant-garde poetry were the now internationally famous Jorge Luis Borges (Argentina), Pablo Neruda (Chile), and César Vallejo (Peru). Vanguard poets sought their inspiration in the new isms of the day, principal among them being Surrealism. But the best of these poets eventually found their own original expression. Brazilian and Spanish American poets of our day, like contemporary poets everywhere, seek their own inner voice to faithfully and aesthetically interpret their experience in the world.

Pablo Neruda, the most prolific and widely known of the major Latin American poets, won the Nobel Prize for literature in 1971. His most ambitious work, *Canto general* (1950), is a vast and diverse epic of the American continent, a poem of patriotism and propaganda. It has also been described as a poetic version of Latin American history. Neruda begins his history in primeval times in order to trace the tellurian nature of man. Poems on the flora and fauna, on rivers and minerals, constitute the first section. Following is a meditation on the Inca ruin of Machu Picchu and sections on the conquerors, on the geographical panorama of the continent, on Chile with its workers and peasants. The poem concludes with an address to the United States, invoking the spirit of Lincoln and condemning imperialism, and a final Whitmanesque affirmation of his life and an expression of gratitude to the Communist party. *Canto general* was Neruda's attempt to reach the common man, to express his concern for social problems, and to proclaim his faith in communism.

Perhaps the most notable development in the literary panorama of the twentieth century has taken place in fiction. Novelists moved in the right direction when they chose to take a closer look at American nature and man. At first, they concentrated on the semisavage areas of the continent, the vast hinterlands of mountains, plains, and jungles, thus bringing the regions largely overlooked since conquest times to the attention of the reading public. With this renewed interest in the regional peculiarity of Latin America, the novelists discovered a genuine American theme.

One result was the novel of the *selva* ("jungle"), which was cultivated in all countries with tropical forests, from Brazil to Bolivia. *The Vortex* (1924) by the Colombian José Eustasio Rivera became a forerunner of many novels that recognized the importance of the natural environment. Rivera, as a member of the Venezuela-Colombia Boundary Commission, had traveled along the great jungle rivers, lived among the Indians there, and experienced the horrors of the jungle—in which he had become lost. He wrote his only novel at the journey's end. Against the background of the vast tropical forest, which comes alive in all its beauty and savagery, Rivera deals with a sociological theme: the plight of Colombian rubber gatherers in the upper Amazon region. The setting dominates. Nature represents primeval chaos, and the men who inhabit this green hell—be they the enslaved extractors of rubber or their more "civilized" exploiters—all degenerate to the extent that they lose their human feelings and social control. The jungle is a tentacular force, attacking the mind and the body, incubating fevers that bring on hallucinations and insanity. It drives men to kill each other or to commit suicide, and those who try to escape are devoured by the forest.

The novel par excellence of the llanos, or tropical plains, is *Doña Bárbara* (1929) by Rómulo Gallegos of Venezuela. Its focus is the exposition of the traditional theme of civilization versus barbarism. Doña Bárbara is an incarnation of the lawlessness and primitivism of the llanos. She is strongwilled and dominates a band of ruthless men whom she uses to enlarge her estate. Her opponent is Santos Luzardo, a city-educated lawyer, who has to resort to violent means to defeat her. Although the novel is as powerful as *The Vortex* in its natural setting and in the violent passions nature engenders in the characters, it provides us with a view that is less pessimistic. As the ending of the novel suggests, violence can be overcome by education. Santos Luzardo educates Doña Bárbara's daughter and marries her.

The greatest of the novels in this series is *Don Segundo Sombra* (1926) by Ricardo Güiraldes. The Argentine Pampa forms the background for the adventures of a boy on the threshold of manhood. He becomes a cattle driver and reaches maturity under the expert guidance of Don Segundo Sombra, a gaucho of mythical stature. Nature is portrayed here as a blind force, and without man, it is chaotic and malevolent. To mature as a man is to learn to control nature and to control one's own nature.

The treatment accorded nature in these novels was opposite to the European concept of nature as civilized by art and literature. For the first time, Europeans found something stimulating in Latin American literature. Many novels of this type were translated into the major European languages and were influential in bringing about a change in European attitudes toward non-European cultures.

At the same time, Latin American novelists also discovered a new protagonist, rural man, who appears not as an individual but as a mass protagonist: the Indian, the mestizo, the Negro, the miner, the fisherman, the peasant— in other words, the little, forgotten people of Latin America. The outstanding example of the novel of the mass protagonist is *The Underdogs* (1915). Written during the Mexican Revolution, the novel went unnoticed until after the Revolution had triumphed. Its author, Mariano Azuela, was a physician who had participated in the fighting. He chose his hero from the anonymous mass of Mexican illiterate peasants. Demetrio Macías and each member of the band he leads in the Revolution, including the women who follow the camp, represent some aspect of Mexican society, so that characters and history form an inseparable whole. Azuela's view of the Revolution is a pessimistic one. He presents the self-interested element in society as the winner, while the peasants, because they are ignorant, fail to bring about a change in their position as underdogs.

Through the 1930s and 1940s, Azuela's numerous followers in Mexico shared his concern for the plight of Indians and peasants whose condition had hardly improved after the Revolution. Elsewhere in Latin America the picture was similar. In the Andean countries, writers exposed the exploitation of Indians and mine workers. In Chile, fishermen, dockworkers, and the lumpen proletariat received sympathetic treatment in fiction. In Brazil, novelists showed the misery of the sugar plantation workers in the poverty-stricken northeast and the helplessness and wretchedness of slum dwellers, street urchins, and blacks.

Fantasy and Magical Realism; Experimental Theater

Although fiction writing during the first half of the twentieth century was dominated by an overwhelming interest in social and national problems that were best expressed in a realistic style, there were also some early adventures in innovation. These included the aesthetic novels and short stories of Modernism and the avant-garde period as well as experimentation with psychological, philosophical, and fantastic fiction. A masterful early innovator was the Argentine short-fiction writer Jorge Luis Borges, who has become an international cult figure. Borges began his literary activities in the 1920s as an avant-garde poet. In the 1930s, he wrote his first stories, called *ficciones* ("fictions"). He achieved literary maturity in the following decade when he published his best collections, *Ficciones* (1944) and *El Aleph* (1949).

Borges's stories have no message, no social or psychological concerns. They are rather in the nature of computer programs, patterned analogously on the way the human mind works. A common theme, for instance, is that of a man caught in a trap he has unwittingly created for himself. "Death and the Compass" (1942), one of Borges's most widely read stories, illustrates this situation. The detective Lönnrot, in his effort to solve three mysterious murders, quickly discovers a pattern that shows clearly the place and time of each crime. With the help of this pattern, it is possible for him to establish where and when a fourth murder will occur. He thinks he can now trap the murderer, but when he meets him, he finds himself face to face with an old enemy who tells him that he has invented the scheme to trap and kill Lönnrot.

This story gives us a nightmarish view of man's understanding of the universe, showing how the human intellect, bent on seeking meaningful patterns and solutions, is its own worst obstacle. Most of Borges's fictions present us with such a view of the universe and with man's consistent failure to decipher it or make sense out of it. Yet his universe is not entirely nihilistic, for man has the ability to dream and to use his imagination creatively. This Borges proves with his own puzzlelike creations, which absorb our attention and thoroughly entertain us.

In the 1940s, writers everywhere in Latin America began to experiment widely with new narrative techniques. They concerned themselves with authenticity and experimented with languages and literary devices. The "new" novel, or the novel since the mid-1940s, like its predecessor, is largely the result of the writers' confrontation with national problems—including the struggle between man and hostile nature—but the technique is no longer realism. Fantasy and what has been called "magical realism" (an offshoot of European Surrealism) have become weapons against dictatorship and a variety of other social ills.

The first novelist to abandon conventional realism was Miguel Angel Asturias of Guatemala, winner of the 1967 Nobel Prize for literature. His novel *El Señor Presidente* (1946), although inspired by the Guatemalan dictatorship of Estrada Cabrera, takes place mostly in the subconscious of the characters living in the nightmare of dictatorship. They express their true feelings through dreams, memories, and imaginings rather than through straightforward language that the ever-present ear of a spy might intercept. Reality is further distorted through the grotesque and the way language is used. It is thus that the novel convinces us that dictatorship is a distortion of social function.

Asturias was alone in his creative enterprise to transform objective reality in 1922 when he started writing *El Señor Presidente.* But by the time of its publication in 1946, he had been joined by a substantial group of writers. Alejo Carpentier (Cuba), Juan Rulfo and Agustín Yáñez (Mexico), Eduardo Mallea and Ernesto Sábato (Argentina), and Carlos Onetti (Uruguay) all published novels in the 1940s that incorporated a large variety of new techniques and used fantasy or magical realism. From this moment on, we can speak of "the new novel" in Latin America.

Ever since Florencio Sánchez had signaled a more serious approach to the theater by probing into the social problems of the Río de la Plata region, more and more dramatists contributed to a growing repertoire of thesis plays that "dissected" a variety of conflicts and social ills. On the whole, however, they initially failed to achieve an interpretation of Latin American life in universal terms. The change came after World War I when experimental groups, either on their own or with support from the government, began to search for new approaches and techniques, discovering in the process such important European and North American innovators as Shaw, Pirandello, O'Neill—in the 1920s and 1930s—and Sartre, Camus, Miller, Brecht, and Beckett—in the 1940s and 1950s.

Rodolfo Usigli (1905–1979), dramatist and critic, was the leading figure of the Mexican theater during three decades. In the 1930s, 1940s, and 1950s, he wrote for and about the theater and virtually singlehandedly created a generation of new dramatists, among them Emilio Carballido and Luisa Josefina Hernández. The 1950s and 1960s saw an unprecedented development of the theater craft everywhere in Latin America. Such well-known dramatists as René Marqués (Puerto Rico), Egon Wolff and Jorge Díaz (Chile), Virgilio Piñera and José Triana (Cuba), and Osvaldo Dragún and Griselda Gambaro (Argentina), among others, were instrumental in revitalizing the professional stage, producing plays of universal appeal and based on sound aesthetic principles. This experimental theater has increased its ranks in recent decades with new talent, including such major novelists turned playwrights as Carlos Fuentes and Mario Vargas Llosa. The theater continues to be a vital force in Latin American culture today.

The Boom in Latin American Fiction

There has been some confusion in the use of the terms "new novel" and "the boom." The latter is part of the new novel, but it refers to a different period. "The boom" began in the mid-1960s and refers to the international recognition of the quality of Latin American fiction. Many of the writers who began publishing novels and short stories in the 1940s are prominent figures of "the boom."

The first book of literary criticism that called attention to the maturing of Latin American fiction was published in 1966. *Los Nuestros* by Luis Harss—the English version, *Into the Mainstream* by Luis Harss and Barbara Dohmann (1967)—discusses the ten most important authors of the new fiction. This selection is representative of the variety and geographical distribution as well as indicative of the time it took for this fiction to develop. The ten authors are from seven Spanish-speaking countries and Brazil. The oldest members of the group were born at the turn of the century, 1899 and 1900, and the youngest was born in 1936, a generation later. Two are cosmopolitan writers, four are regionalists, and the remaining four fall somewhere in between the regional and the urban, categories that are not necessarily incompatible. What all these writers have in common is that they invented a literary form that could encompass the uniqueness of their experience. By combining linguistic virtuosity with fantasy and temporal and spatial superimposition, they created a verisimilitude that the earlier realistic novelists had failed to achieve.

The cosmopolitan writers are Jorge Luis Borges and Julio Cortázar, both Argentines. Argentina, as Borges himself has stated, can only follow European tradition since it has nothing comparable to the indigenous heritage of Mexico or Peru. Cortázar, who lived for many years in France, can be considered an expatriate writer, unlike Borges who lived and wrote in Buenos Aires. Cortázar's major work is *Hopscotch* (1963), its title referring to the idea of reading as play, to the structure of the novel, and to the protagonist's search for fulfillment. The game element is apparent from the start when readers find an "Instruction Chart" telling them that *Hopscotch* is many books but principally two. One is to be read in the traditional manner and consists of chapters 1–56; the other, to be read in a hopscotch manner, consists of all chapters in an order indicated in the "Instruction Chart" (73–1–2–166 and so on). The first 56 chapters tell the story of an uprooted Argentine student, Horacio Oliveira, who lives first in Paris and later in Buenos Aires. These two sections are titled "About That Side" and "About This Side," respectively. A third section, "About Other Sides" and subtitled "Expendable Chapters," serves primarily to bring about an awareness in readers of the act of creating. Readers wishing to read the entire book will most likely choose the hopscotch manner. In this reading, they will get only patterns and events instead of a plot. Readers may even lose sight of Horacio, whose search never ends, and they will certainly never know whether Horacio has gone completely mad or whether he will finally commit suicide. The book itself has no end because the next to last chapter sends readers to the last chapter, but the last chapter sends them back to the next to last chapter, a process than can go on forever.

Miguel Angel Asturias was the first Latin American writer to transcend regionalism in the novel, to go beyond the photographic and the picturesque in order to probe deeply into the experience of the region. João Guimarães Rosa, Juan Rulfo, and Gabriel García Márquez are the other authors included in Harss's book who have contributed to the new regionalism.

The Brazilian *sertão,* the vast desert hinterland of Minas Gerais, is the setting of Guimarães Rosa's *Grande sertão: veredas* (1956). The novel contains factual information, accurate in the smallest detail, as well as insight into the psychology of the inhabitants of the *sertão* derived from observation of life and from legends and songs. The narrator and protagonist is Riobaldo, whose nickname Tatarana means firefly but is a euphemism for sharpshooter. Now settled on his estate, Riobaldo tells of his early adventures as a *jagunco.* The *jaguncos* were a mixed lot of individuals—outlaws, mercenaries, homeless peasants, even idealists—who fought under different political chieftains and local warlords. They were mostly violent and destructive, but when led by a man with vision, they could be a civilizing force. Riobaldo embodies this duality. He has lived life both physically and spiritually, and his memoir is replete with experience and wisdom.

Juan Rulfo's *Pedro Paramo* (1955) imaginatively transposes the deep-rooted Mexican belief in the life of the dead. The reader soon discovers that in the story of a landowner turned into a powerful *cacique* ("boss"), all the characters are dead. The story is about the Mexican's inner solitude and inability to communicate, but it also explores several Mexican myths such as the two facets of the macho myth through the characters Pedro Paramo and his son Miguel.

In *One Hundred Years of Solitude* (1967), García Márquez tells the story of the rise and fall of a town in the tropical lowlands of Colombia and of a family. Macondo, founded by the Buendía family, has its beginning in primal innocence. But though isolated, it does not remain immune to outside influences. Gypsies, civil war, the railroad, and North Americans bring the world to Macondo. In the long run, however, no real progress is made. Macondo is destroyed by a deluge that lasts four years, and the family dies out, as prophesied, when a child is born with a pig's tail, the fruit of an incestuous union. The novel depends for most of its effects on magical realism and on comic exaggeration. It brings to mind the facts that Latin America was conquered by men who had read the novels of chivalry and believed in the myths of the Fountain of Youth and El Dorado, and that on the new continent, nature was the great adversary of man.

Alejo Carpentier, Juan Carlos Onetti, Carlos Fuentes, and Mario Vargas Llosa deal with the confrontation of civilization and primitive life in Latin America and life in Latin American cities in contemporary times. Carpentier made an original contribution when his novels broached the theme of the coexistence of primeval jungle and European civilization in the tropical countries of Latin America. *The Lost Steps* (1955) has as its protagonist a sophisticated musician who, overwrought by civilized life, is given a chance to escape it. He is sent from New York on an expedition into the Venezuelan jungle in search of primitive musical instruments. He and a band of adventurers he meets on the way discover a Garden of Eden, a spot unspoiled by man's presence, on the upper reaches of the Orinoco River. Here is an opportunity for them to start anew, to found a life based on living in harmony with the environment. But the musician abandons the experiment. Despite his alienation from the modern world, he is not able to give it up. Carpentier traces the conflict between marvelous nature and overordered society, between spontaneity and intellect, and between creative activity and everyday routine— a conflict that ultimately remains unresolved.

Juan Carlos Onetti gives us a sordid vision of Uruguayan city life. In his masterpiece, *The Shipyard* (1961), a city of his own invention, Santa María, provides the setting. The protagonist is the old and worn-out Junta Larsen, who has spent his life dealing in dubious businesses. His attempt to resurrect the defunct shipyard of Santa María is his last effort to gain for himself a measure of security. To achieve his purpose, he courts the idiot daughter of the shipyard owner, and, upon becoming the manager of the shipyard, he studies old records and supposedly oversees the work of two clerks. They had stopped doing any meaningful work a long time before. They make their living by selling off old machinery and machinery parts. In the end, Larsen must face defeat, and he leaves the shipyard only to die within a week of pneumonia. The novel expresses, as few other Latin American works do, a complete sense of futility, decay, and bitterness.

Carlos Fuentes analyzes in his works different aspects of contemporary Mexico. His first novel, *Where the Air Is Clear* (1958), has Mexico City as its central locale. A character, Ixta Cienfuegos, symbolizes the dynamism and human suffering of the metropolis and incarnates the values and myths of Indian Mexico. There is no main protagonist in the novel. Many characters' lives are woven into the texture of its narrative, and most of them are significant as prototypes, not as individuals. The novel shows the confrontation of a cosmopolitan mind with a semiprimitive country that has a whole range of institutionalized myths hiding reality and stifling authentic life. The theme is that of the Revolution betrayed. Fuentes deals even more effectively with this theme in *The Death of Artemio Cruz* (1962). Artemio, who began life as an illegitimate outcast, was able to rise to the top of Mexican society because of the Revolution and a series of successful schemes. The novel is set in the last months of Artemio's life as he lies dying in a Mexico City hospital, and the story is told from three different points of view: in the first person, stream-of-consciousness of the dying man; in the second person, Artemio's alter ego, in the future tense; and in the third person, omniscient, in the past tense. This technique allows the reader to penetrate deeply into the human psyche. In the course of the novel Artemio emerges a fully rounded figure, revealed in all his strengths and weaknesses. In both of these novels, Fuentes projects the view that man is not the maker of history, but rather, that he is caught up in it with little opportunity for movement or freedom of choice.

The youngest of the authors included in Harss's book is the Peruvian Mario Vargas Llosa, who won the prestigious Seix Barral Prize for his first novel, *Time and the Hero,* in 1962. The work is based on the author's personal experience of life in a Lima military school. Here boys are encouraged to develop the false value of machismo, all-pervasive in Peruvian society. A far more difficult novel is *The Green House* (1966). It is composed of several interlocking stories and is set in the town of Piura in the northwestern part of Peru and in the *selva* in the department of Amazonas. The lives of many characters—nuns, military men, adventurers, underdogs—intersect in a non-sequential order so that the reader cannot establish a clear pattern of development or the identity of the characters. The theme of this novel, however, is similar to that of *Time and the Hero*: Civilization corrupts. The central figure, Bonifacia—also known as La Selvática, or Jungle Woman—is exploited by the Church, by the army, and by modern commercialism as symbolized by the brothel called the Green House. Vargas Llosa's novel, *The War of the End of the World* (1981), is curiously not about Peru but about Brazil. The novel is based on a historical event, a popular insurrection that was both revolutionary and reactionary, which took place in northeastern Brazil at the end of the nineteenth century. Through the striking intermingling of Portuguese words with the Spanish of the narrative, the novel takes us beyond the limitations set by national borders and becomes a moral and political parable of the Latin American continent.

The ten writers included in Luis Harss's *Into the Mainstream* by no means exhaust the list of authors associated with "the boom" of Latin American literature. But this number suffices to show that though Latin America remains socially and politically backward, it is no longer underdeveloped culturally. Most of the younger writers discussed in this chapter and those who have joined their ranks since 1967 are politically committed to the left, but they understand that writing a novel is not as simple as making a political pronouncement. They have learned from the older generation of successful writers that politics is just one component of a complex field of reference and that what matters is to relate their intimate experience of life in Latin America with authenticity, imagination, and the skill they now possess.

SUGGESTED READINGS

Brushwood, John S. *The Spanish American Novel: A Twentieth-Century Survey.* Austin: University of Texas Press, 1975. Traces the development of the Spanish American novel during the twentieth century. Emphasis is on works, not on authors. The novel is viewed as a cultural organism; therefore, consideration is given to the cultural milieu that created a work.

Castro-Klaren, Sara, Sylvia Molloy, and Beatriz Sarlo. *Women's Writing in Latin America.* Boulder, Colo.: Westview Press, forthcoming.

Englekirk, John E., et al. *Outline History of Spanish American Literature.* New York: Appleton-Century-Crofts, 1965. Literature is divided into three major periods in the history of Latin America. Further sectioning is made along literary-cultural lines, each section being devoted to the three principal genres of poetry, prose, and drama. The introductory summaries to these sections are fairly detailed and complete, and the author entries are essentially bibliographical.

Foster, David William. *Currents in the Contemporary Argentine Novel.* Columbia: University of Missouri Press, 1975. A study of the contemporary Argentine novel focusing on the major work of four major novelists—Roberto Arlt, *The Seven Madmen*; Eduardo Mallea, *The Bay of Silence*; Ernesto Sábato, *On Heroes and Tombs*; and Julio Cortázar, *Hopscotch*. The introductory chapter surveys the contributions of the principal novelists of the nineteenth and early twentieth centuries. The final chapter deals with future trends.

Franco, Jean. *An Introduction to Spanish American Literature*. London: Cambridge University Press, 1969. A most readable history of Spanish American literature from the conquest to the mid-sixties. Emphasis is on general tendencies, but there are references to a national context. This work can be read as a gloss of the principal literary texts.

———. *The Modern Culture of Latin America: Society and the Artist*. Rev. ed. London: Penguin Books, 1970. Although this work deals with modern culture in general, a great deal of attention is given to literature. All modern periods are discussed in detail with a special view toward the problematic nature of Latin American artistic endeavor.

Gallagher, D. P. *Modern Latin American Literature*. London: Oxford University Press, 1973. The core of this book consists of seven monographic essays on major contemporary Spanish American writers—César Vallejo, Guillermo Cabrera Infante, Jorge Luis Borges, Gabriel García Márquez, Mario Vargas Llosa, Pablo Neruda, and Octavio Paz. The introduction surveys the literature of the nineteenth century. Two additional chapters give an overview of poetry between 1880 and 1925 and of regionalist fiction.

Guibert, Rita. *Seven Voices*. New York: Knopf, 1973. The author interviews a group of notable Latin American writers—Pablo Neruda, Jorge Luis Borges, Miguel Angel Asturias, Octavio Paz, Gabriel García Márquez, and Guillermo Cabrera Infante. The discussion ranges over a wide variety of topics of concern to Latin American writers, from Che Guevara to technology as well as literature.

Harss, Luis, and Barbara Dohmann. *Into the Mainstream*. New York: Harper and Row, 1967. Based on interviews with ten representative Latin American writers identified with "the boom." The question-answer format of the interview is replaced with a narrative description of the authors and a literary analysis of their works. The introductory chapter reviews the strengths and weaknesses of traditional Latin American fiction.

Schwartz, Kessel. *A New History of Spanish American Fiction*. 2 vols. Miami: University of Miami Press, 1972. The most detailed history of Spanish American fiction from colonial times to the late 1960s. Organized according to traditionally recognized literary movements, the book contains plot synopses, critical judgment, and analytical commentary.

Sommers, Joseph. *After the Storm: Landmarks of the Modern Mexican Novel*. Albuquerque: University of New Mexico Press, 1968. An operating premise of this study is that the Mexican novel reached a new level of maturity with the publication in 1947 of *The Edge of the Storm* by Agustín Yáñez. An introductory discussion of the Mexican novel of the Revolution is followed by four monographic chapters on the novel by Yáñez, Juan Rulfo's *Pedro Páramo,* and Carlos Fuentes's *Where the Air Is Clear* and *The Death of Artemio Cruz*. Several emerging younger writers are dealt with more summarily in the last chapter.

Spell, Jefferson Rea. *Contemporary Spanish American Fiction*. Chapel Hill: University of North Carolina Press, 1944. A collection of essays on authors who are considered to be the big names of the first forty years of this century. The book provides detailed plot summaries and critical evaluations.

Torres-Ríoseco, Arturo. *The Epic of Latin American Literature*. Berkeley: University of California Press, 1961. When originally published in 1943, this literary history was the most complete work to appear on the subject in English. Covering Latin American literature from the colonial period to 1940, most of the volume is devoted to Spanish American literature; only the final chapter deals with Brazilian letters. Written with enthusiasm and an emphasis on the exotic nature of Latin American literature, the work nonetheless provides a scholarly treatment of the significant authors and the main currents and movements.

8

NATIONALISM AND MODERN LATIN AMERICAN ART

MARY GRIZZARD

Today there is often a basic disagreement about what art is and what it should do. This point is very evident if one visits art galleries in any one of the major cities of the world. There are exhibits that represent every new twist and turn of modern art. Probably the most startling thing about twentieth-century art has been its tendency to swing back and forth from one extreme to another. We are no sooner comfortable with one style or movement than a new one erupts on the scene. Thus, in the United States, the pendulum has swung from turn-of-the-century neoclassism to impressionism, the ashcan school, the synchromists and other modern movements of the 1910s and 1920s, the regionalist and American schools of painting, abstract expressionism, pop art, minimalism and conceptualism, photorealism, new-imagism, and now to whatever is new in the galleries of New York or the West Coast.

It is therefore with something of a sense of relief that one looks at twentieth-century Latin American art and finds some consistency of purpose and focus, although still a great diversity of styles. Although one certainly finds representatives of most of the modern-art isms, or movements, in the galleries of Latin America, there is an identifiably nationalistic current in Latin American art that reflects aspects of Latin American culture—its color, its folk traditions, its history, its heroes, even its social problems.

Art in twentieth-century Latin America tends to be an extension of society—it does not exist of and for itself. Latin American artists seem never to have lost sight of the simplest and most obvious fact of all: Art is the product of a person in society, and society, therefore, is intrinsic to art's identity and purpose. A painting without some echo of humanity is a thing. It is not art. The artist does not create more objects with which to litter this globe. He or she creates symbolic projections of human realities and human ideals—or, at the very least, clues to what people want, are, or dream about.

121

International modernism, and art that is totally abstract, subjective, and intuitive, are foreign to the Latin American experience. From pre-Columbian to Spanish colonial times, and through the nineteenth century to the present, Latin American art has manifested a variety of styles, but it has traditionally been a narrative, representational art. The most characteristic feature of modern Latin American art is its tendency to focus on social and political issues. This feature, which tends to criticize society's ills in an effort to reform them, is called "social realism." This term refers to content rather than style. It is quite different from Soviet socialist realism, a term coined by Maxim Gorky at the Soviet Writer's Congress in 1934. Soviet socialist realism does not embrace a variety of styles and tends to result in Zdanovism, a rigidly controlled program of positive, nationalistic images done in an idealized, dry, neoclassical style.

MEXICO

The modern muralist movement was largely responsible for the momentum given to modern Mexican social realism. The muralist movement was the product of artists who viewed art in its sociopolitical context. This was almost inevitable, for they first became active artists during the immediate aftermath of the 1910 Revolution, a time of national consolidation and class realignment.

Postrevolutionary Mexican social realism, also variously known as the Mexican school or the muralist movement, consisted primarily of gigantic murals and popular graphic art. It was the primary manifestation of Mexican nationalist painting from the 1920s through the 1960s. Although the participants in this movement did not completely eschew easel painting, commercial galleries, museums, and other cultural paraphernalia of the middle and upper classes, they did generally strive to direct their explicit, didactic art to the people. Each of the participants knew that art is potentially more than a thing of beauty, that it is also a very powerful means of communicating ideas in an effort to reshape society.

Not only had the Revolution in Mexico changed the economic and political status of a great many people, it had also unleashed a tide of nationalism in reaction to the European-influenced culture of the Porfirio Díaz era. Under government patronage, muralism became a key part of the plan to reeducate the masses according to the ideals of the Revolution.

Although mass communication had also been one of the primary objectives of Spanish colonial art, the 1910 Revolution thoroughly changed the context of art in Mexican society. In the colonial period, art had been patronized and preserved primarily by the Church. This patron had imposed the most severe standards of style and content, resulting in an art that served as an educational tool. Examples of extreme originality in style or content were rare, since a standard format was expected for the purpose of providing a consistent model for teaching. With independence and the later Reform period of the nineteenth century, the state urgently needed new types of artists who could communicate its ideological program. The Academy of

San Carlos, the official school for artists in Mexico City, did not produce an identifiably Mexican art in the nineteenth century. However, one does find a vigorous style, very much reflecting the sociopolitical ambience in the popular art forms, specifically among the printmakers.

A very important root of the modern, Mexican social realist movement is the country's strong tradition in graphic art, which often appeared in the poorly funded opposition newspaper, *Gaceta callejera* ("pennyrag"). The best-known newspaper illustrator of the late nineteenth century was José Guadalupe Posada, who worked for the publisher Vanegas Arroyo in Mexico City. Posada's anti-Díaz cartoons, as well as those that chronicled the rise of such revolutionary protagonists as Madero, Zapata, and Villa, are especially well known today. In Posada's engravings for the newspapers, figures were often represented as *calaveras,* or dressed skeletons, acting out parts. A famous example from 1910 (Illus. 1) shows Francisco Madero as a *calavera,* recognizable by the mustache and beard as well as by the brandy bottle he carries, for the distillery business was the source of his family fortune. The use of penny newspapers and broadsides by Mexico's prominent graphic artists as a forum for communicating socially oriented issues to the people established an important precedent that was continued by artists of the postrevolutionary period.

According to the muralist David Alfaro Siqueiros, the modern Mexican school began during 1911–1913. At that time, when Siqueiros was an art student at the Academy of San Carlos in Mexico City, students revolted against the remaining "Porfirian faculty." In place of the traditional, academic training, which included drawing the casts of antique statues, the new director, Ramos Martínez, installed in 1913, started "open-air schools" that sent artists into the communities to depict the Mexican people and to reflect their artistic traditions.

When Alvaro Obregón was inaugurated as president of Mexico in November 1920, the country entered a new era of improving the general quality of education. Government patronage of mural art became part of the program to educate the masses. Only the title and general description of the painting were specified by the government patron; the artists all employed different styles and were free to design their own compositions. Most of the credit for the Obregón administration's encouragement of muralism belongs to the secretary of education, José Vasconcelos. It was because of this patronage that Diego Rivera returned from Europe in 1921 and later painted a series of murals depicting the triumph and struggle of the Revolution on the walls of the Department of Education.

Mexican nationalistic painting flourished with this new freedom, and in 1922, artists organized the Syndicate of Revolutionary Painters, Sculptors, and Engravers. The executive committee included Siqueiros as general secretary, Rivera as secretary of the interior, and Xavier Guerrero as treasurer. José Luis Orozco also belonged to the syndicate, although he was not an officer. The painters' syndicate, only one of several peasants' and workers' organizations formed in the 1920s, had two major objectives: to abandon easel painting and to recognize that subject matter is as important as style in painting.[1]

The climate of social and economic reform during the Lázaro Cárdenas presidency fostered some of the finest products by the Mexican muralists, such as Orozco's and Rivera's paintings (both of 1934) in the Palace of Fine Arts in Mexico City. Lithography, linoleum prints, and woodcuts were also employed to defend the agrarian reform and the nationalization of the oil fields in 1938 and to combat the international threat of fascism.

The graphic artists used flyers, posters, and pamphlets and illustrated them with caricatures, *calaveras,* and representation of historic events. Theirs was not a commercial art, but an art directed to the people, to the streets. They used direct symbols, but also drew from the sentimental and the picturesque, in order to lend familiarity and recognition to their social and political satire. As seen in José Chávez Morado's lithograph, *Clergy and Press* (1939) (Illus. 2), artists were vigilant against any aspect of Mexican society that threatened the objectives of social reform fostered by the revolution. But Chávez Morado did not shrink from showing some of the weaknesses of Mexican society that the people inflicted on themselves. In one of his best-known prints, Calaveras *Against the People* (1950) (Illus. 3), he showed the Mexican people fleeing from *calaveras* that bear such labels as Black Market and Bribes.

Murals had shown man's place among the priests and the gods of pre-Columbian society; they had also been used in the Spanish colonial period to teach the stories of the saints and the Spanish social and religious order to the New World. The postrevolutionary Mexican muralists used a medium familiar in history, but they depicted subjects that were in keeping with the sociopolitical focus that Mexico's graphic artists had already achieved.

The dominant members of the muralist movement were Siqueiros (1898–1975), Orozco (1883–1949), and Rivera (1886–1957), or *los tres grandes* ("the big three") as they were sometimes called. Although each emphasized different aspects, they agreed on the need to represent certain didactic themes. These included the exposition of the historic struggle to achieve liberty and independence and the teaching of the ideals of the 1910 Revolution. Among the legacies of the Revolution were the glorification of the indigenous heritage of Mexico and the celebration of the modern mestizo civilization, that which resulted from a blend of Indian and Spanish peoples. In addition, several members of the muralist movement, including the big three, espoused socialist, antimilitarist, and anti-imperial views. Within this broad spectrum of agreement, Siqueiros emphasized the struggle of the working class; Orozco, the Revolution and the formation of the nation; Rivera, the Revolution and the indigenous culture.

Each of *los tres grandes* painted in a distinctive style. For instance, Siqueiros's figures in the Polyforum Cultural in Mexico City (1961) show a strong illusion of movement (Illus. 4). The telescoped positions suggest the rapid movement of sequential frames in a film. Siqueiros's images are also shown from many points of view at once. These polyangular compositions are comparable to the achievements of cubist painters, such as Picasso, in the first decade of the twentieth century. Although Siqueiros's methods of achieving the illusion of space were not new, he did combine different surface textures and materials to achieve bold, startling effects. The combination of sculpture and painting on one surface resulted in a three-dimensionality that contributed greatly to the power of his representation. The Polyforum murals, encircling an entire large room, present a complex picture of the progress of humanity through history and evolving technology toward a hopeful future.

Orozco was an expressionist who conveyed emotion by using vivid colors, vigorous lines, active composition, and when necessary, distorted figures. The results were very exciting paintings, similar in many respects to the style of German expressionists such as Max Beckmann after World War I. Orozco tended to emphasize good versus evil as universals, as in the transcendent, positive figure of the *Man of Fire* (1938–1939), Hospice of Cabañas, Guadalajara (Illus. 5). This figure in flames ascends with humanity's aspirations toward the heavens. In other sections of the vast fresco cycle in the Hospice of Cabañas, it is apparent that humanity has had much to overcome. There are unidealized representations of the pre-Hispanic culture, including sacrifices to Huitzilopochtli. Cortés is shown as a terrifying hybrid man/horse, as he must have appeared to the Indians of Mexico. Later episodes of history that are depicted include phalanxes of fascist troops and dictators wielding whips.

Rivera drew from a wide variety of sources, including the murals of proto-Renaissance Italy, cubism (particularly Picasso), Mexican folk murals (especially those of the *pulquerías*),[2] and pre-Columbian artifacts. His technique was conservative, with bold outlines containing largely flat, even colors. Among his best-known frescoes are those in the National Palace in Mexico City (1945). As in the portion of the fresco shown in Illus. 6, which depicts a preconquest view of life in the Valley of Mexico, Rivera tended to idealize indigenous culture, depicting an idyllic, ancient utopia in which no class or intertribal strife occurred. The problem with celebrating such a mythical view of the past, however well intentioned its nationalistic aims, is that the modern, native people can no longer identify with such a remote, alien culture. Also, the portrayal of exotic Indian costumes and artifacts tends to become a picturesque cliché by its frequent repetition.

By the 1950s, expository nationalistic murals were an established post-revolutionary tradition, and Mexican architects designed buildings with the anticipated need for mural space in mind. In response to the growth of a middle-class market, however, easel painting and a newer group of nonpolitical and even formalist artists developed alongside the continuing muralist tradition. Although second- and even third-generation muralists have emerged since the days of Orozco and Rivera, the majority of Mexican artists today are independents who produce easel paintings. Their work may be sometimes theoretical in concept, but they react to the times in their own ways and have never divorced themselves from their environment.

Rufino Tamayo (1899–) is an example of a Mexicanist who rejects the muralistic tradition and who himself does not fit exactly into any modern art movement. The shape of the animal in his howling-dog series (Illus. 7) draws as much from the pre-Hispanic ceramic Colima dogs as it does from Picasso's fragmented forms in *Guernica*. Vivid colors, a dry meridional light, and the frequent depiction of masked figures, native musicians, dancers, fruit vendors, and tropical still lifes all indicate that Mexican culture dominates his memories. On the other hand, modernity constantly thrusts its emblems into this dream: wheels, clocks, workers' tools. From this collision between mythical time and measured time, an extraordinary poignancy arises, and the best of Tamayo's works have not become dated.

Surrealism has long had a strong role in Mexican art, beginning in the 1930s with artists such as Frida Kahlo and the photographer Manuel Alvarez Bravo. Quite often the Mexican Surrealists' work contained a bitter social commentary. As an example of this, there is a Manuel Alvarez Bravo photograph entitled *Striking Worker Murdered* (1934). It is a disturbing close-up of a dead worker's body, lying at an angle on the pavement, with blood streaming from his nose and mouth. As grisly as it is, it has not lost that special visual quality of art—and belongs in a line with Mantegna's *Dead Christ* (fifteenth-century Italian) and Manet's *Dead Toreador* (nineteenth-century French). Other important Mexican Surrealists include European immigrants to Mexico, such as Leonora Carrington and Remedios Varo. Surrealism in their work especially illustrated fantasy, dreams, and imagination, as celebrated by the French Surrealist theorist André Breton in his attack on the "reign of logic" in the first *Surrealist Manifesto*. In a Mexico full of myths, *brujos,* and legendary animal-human gods, Surrealism found a receptive home. At times, a retreat to these traditions may have provided some comfort, given the bewildering reality of social and political events enveloping Mexico through the Depression, World War II, and the post-war period of rapid but unequal economic growth.

While Kahlo, Alvarez Bravo, and others never saw themselves as Surrealists, likewise there are several artists still producing in this vein today who express the same denial. Alfredo Castañeda, for example, creates beautiful, meticulously painted, hallucinatory images of persons with extra or even oddly formed body parts, set on an empty terrain. These compositions coincide with his own dream-like poetry. One cannot help but be reminded of the singular reality that myth and illusory dreams appear to have as phenomena in Mexico's cultural tradition.

The major creations of José Luis Cuevas, Francisco Corzas, Rafael Coronel, and Emilio Ortiz—those fantastic and even macabre paintings, drawings, and prints, at times viciously sardonic and farcical, which they produced between 1960 and the present—have been troublesome to many spectators, critics, and art historians since their appearance. In Francisco Corzas's painting *My Mother's Visitors* (1963), there are violent contrasts of light and dark with great dislocations and exaggerations in the shape and expression of the faces (Illus. 8). The figures in this painting, as in others by Corzas, are often received as memories of disagreeable actual situations. They recall the lonely vendors of newspapers, *chicles* ("chewing gum"), and lottery tickets— the hungry, the sad, and the despairing faces of Mexico's poor.

These and other artists with similar objectives exhibited together for a short period of time during the 1960s, when their artistic movement was known as Los Interioristas. They echo many of the themes emphasizing loneliness and the sense of tragedy in the Mexican personality that are found in Octavio Paz's *The Labyrinth of Solitude,* popular in the 1950s. Above all, these artists were shaped by contemporary social and historical forces, especially the witnessing of major urbanization, concentrated in Mexico City, which, in turn, emphasizes the growing gap between the cultural and economic lives of rural and urban areas.

Perhaps it is therefore ironic that one of Mexico's urban abstract artists, Mathias Goeritz, is acclaimed for the strong Mexican quality of his works. He came from Germany in 1949 and found his eclectic body of abstract work rejected by Rivera and Siqueiros. Goeritz created in Mexico of the 1950s and 1960s an architecture-sculpture of an imposing gigantism, which presaged the work of North American minimalists. The sculpture by which he is best known is a piece called *The Five Towers* (1957–1985), a group of sharply angled concrete slabs in Satellite City, Mexico City. These seem to celebrate the promise of progress in Mexico's modern city centers and in its industry. Yet, significantly, the heroic scale of the buildings poignantly dwarfs and dehumanizes any human being in the vicinity.

The modern independent Mexican artists are sensitive to popular feeling, social and intellectual issues, and the function of art in their society. They have reaffirmed the Mexican tradition of a socially oriented art—a thread that has continued from the nineteenth-century Reform period's graphic art through the politically didactic muralists of the postrevolutionary period to the present day.

PERU, BOLIVIA, ECUADOR

The art of Peru, Bolivia, and Ecuador has been greatly influenced by the indigenous heritage of the large Indian populations in those countries. Peru, the former center of the Incan Empire, retains a panorama of indigenous culture, including imposing ancient ruins, "native" agricultural methods, music, costumes, dances, festivals, etc. (though often mixed with European elements). After the disastrous defeat of Peru by Chile in the War of the Pacific (1879–1883), there began a long, often politically charged, search for the "reality" of Peru. Many historians, politicians, and artists found this Peruvian reality in indigenous life and customs. At first, during the early years of the twentieth century, there was a glorification of the picturesque aspects of the native culture, as found in Riva Aguero's *Paisajes peruanos* [Peruvian landscapes] (1912–1915). As the level of poverty and suffering of the modern heirs of the Incas became more apparent, more radical studies ensued, such as *Siete ensayos de interpretación de la realidad peruana* [Seven interpretive essays on Peruvian reality] by José Mariátegui. This study, published in 1928, combined Marxism with nativism, a stance that became increasingly influential. There have also been several strong, nationalistic movements in Peruvian painting since the 1920s. Especially during the 1930s and 1940s, Peruvian art shared many of the objectives of Mexican art, including nativism, nationalism, and a tendency toward Marxism.

José Sabogal (1888–1956), born in Cajabamba in northern Peru, was the founder and first leader of the *indigenista* ("indigenous," or "native") movement in Peruvian painting. Cajabamba is a region in which Indian traditions persist, but Sabogal was also influenced by the picturesque costumbrism of the Spanish artist Ignacio Zuloaga and the nationalism of the Mexican muralists. He became director of the National School of Fine Arts in Lima between 1933 and 1943, during which time his influence on Peruvian art greatly increased; he gained many followers, including Julia Codesido, Camilo Blas, and Enrique Camino Brent. The painters who were the closest followers of Sabogal have been called *indigenistas sabogalinos* to distinguish them from the independent nativists.

Among the most interesting independent nativists is Juan Manuel Ugarte Elésperu, who was at one time much influenced by the Mexican muralists, especially Rivera. Although there has never been much demand for mural painting in Peru and most modern Peruvian works are easel paintings, Ugarte Elésperu's early masterpiece was a large fresco in the Santo Tomás School in Lima. The fresco strives to represent in a detailed, ambitious composition the past, present, and future of Peru. Ugarte Elésperu taught at the National School of Fine Arts in Lima between 1946 and 1953 and was its director from 1956 to 1973.

There is also a form of indigenism in Peruvian painting called "abstract nativism," founded by the Limeñan artist Fernando de Szyszlo. He represented in abstract form the geometric designs found in pre-Columbian textiles, ceramics, and architectural sculpture. In 1963, Szyszlo exhibited at the Institute of Contemporary Art in Lima a series of paintings inspired by a Quechuan elegy on the death of the last ruling Inca, Atahualpa. Each of the paintings in the series was named after a line from the anonymous Quechuan poem, *Apu Inca Atawallpaman*. The "search for Peruvian reality" proclaimed by writers and artists in the early twentieth century continues even in the art influenced by international stylistic trends some sixty years later.

Bolivian art was also affected by the example of *indigenismo* in Peru. The leader of Bolivian indigenism was Cecilio Guzmán de Rojas, who returned from Spain in the early 1930s under the art deco influence of Romero de Torres. This influence accounts for Guzmán de Rojas's use of hard, curvilinear outlines on human forms set in geometric, stylized landscapes (Illus. 9). His subjects were usually Indians, mountains, Lake Titicaca, and the towns of the Altiplano. Between 1935 and his death in 1950, there was little else depicted in Bolivian painting.

By 1950, the tide of Bolivian nationalism had given rise to a group of followers of Guzmán de Rojas who were also influenced by the Mexican muralists. Miguel Alandia Pantoja headed this group of artists who were particularly interested in depicting the plight of miners and agricultural workers. In Sucre, a politically motivated group of artists formed an organization called ANTEO, led by Solón Romero. Inspired by the example of Diego Rivera, the group painted murals on the telephone building and at the San Francisco Xavier University.

The beginning of the 1950s also saw the disappearance of traditional liberal and conservative parties and the emergence of Marxist and other worker movements. The accompanying strong surge of nationalism resulted in agrarian reform and nationalization of the mines. Realizing that state promotion of the arts could further the cause of Bolivian nationalism, the government sponsored the first Salon Pedro Domingo Murillo in 1952 as a national forum for Bolivian artists.

As might be expected, Ecuadoran art also has many similarities with that of Peru, since both countries have large indigenous populations and have experienced a long, polemical search for national identity. Several Ecuadoran *indigenistas* especially well known, not only in Latin America but in Europe and North America as well, are Camilo Egas, Bolívar Mena, Diógenes Paredes, Eduardo Kingman, and Oswaldo Guayasamín.

Camilo Egas began as an academic painter, but early in his search for national expression he was influenced by the example of the Mexican muralists. He was for a time also influenced by surrealism, as is seen in his painting *Dream of Ecuador* (1939). The ground is barren, scattered with shabby huts, populated by emaciated peasants. Egas's paintings, which are often allegories of despair, are credited with popularizing the indigenist movement in Ecuadoran art.

Eduardo Kingman was long the leader of the indigenist movement in Ecuador, especially during the 1940s and 1950s. His first important recognition came in 1936 when he won the Mariano Aguilera Prize, the country's highest artistic award. He was later the founder and director of the Caspicara Art Gallery in Quito, director of the National Museum of Art, and director of the National Artistic Patrimony. He was influenced by the Ecuadoran *indigenista* novelists, such as Jorge Icaza, and by the example of nationalism and nativism in the work of the Mexican muralists. In Kingman's painting *Los Guandos* (1941), the tyranny of unjust labor practices is apparent, as the foreman cracks a whip over the backs of the Indians who are already bent double under the weight of an enormous cargo (Illus. 10).

Eduardo Kingman continued the *indigenista* theme through his later works, but adopted a very powerful form of expressionism that uses dark, angular lines and vivid colors to convey the force of its feeling. A recent work of his (1983) (Illus. 11) celebrates the victory of the Battle of Pichincha (24 May 1822). It is a huge outdoor mural that covers the entire side of El Templo de la Patria, located on the side of Mount Pichincha, overlooking Quito. The mural may be seen from the city, and highlights Atahualpa, Eugenio Espejo, and the 1809–1810 Junta of Quito, which ultimately proclaimed independence. Spread magnificently below the above figures is a massive pair of indigenous, copper-colored hands, which break apart heavy chains.

Oswaldo Guayasamín, eight years younger than Eduardo Kingman, became well known in the United States during a State Department–sponsored tour during 1942–1943. He won the Mariano Aguilera Prize the same year and also traveled to Mexico where he met Orozco, with whom he worked for three months. After 1942, Guayasamín's style evolved into the synthesis of influences from Orozco and Picasso by which we recognize his work today. After a tour of several countries in South America in 1944–1945, he produced the series of paintings entitled *Path of Tears* (1952), which laments the difficult life of the underprivileged throughout the world. An extension of this series is represented in his set of paintings *Age of Anger,* which was exhibited in Mexico and several cities of Europe during the 1960s. Among his most recent works are two murals in government buildings in Quito. One is a large mural entitled *El mural Ecuador* (1980), sponsored by the Provincial Council of Pichincha. It is composed of several separate panels representing the stoic faces of Ecuador's national heroes, such as the Inca Atahualpa, and the eighteenth-century nationalist leader Eugenio Espejo. Other panels depict geometricized, anonymous faces and torsos wrenched into expressions of agony. Near the center are a jack-booted, military dictator (Illus. 12) and a bearded, helmeted Spanish *conquistador.* The subject is an amplification of an earlier theme by Guayasamín: the suffering of the indigenous Ecuadorean people throughout history. In a more recent mural (1988) in the Ecuadorean Congress of Quito, there is a similar montage of the social and political history of Ecuador.

COLOMBIA AND VENEZUELA

Although abstract art is not unimportant in Colombia—the work of Eduardo Ramírez Villamizar in painting and of Edgar Negret in sculpture would prove otherwise—the two most influential artists in Colombia today are neofigurative painters. The influence and fame of Alejandro Obregón and Fernando Botero have emphasized the importance of representational painting in Colombia.

Obregón, the older of the two artists, was born in Barcelona in 1920. He continues to live in the Colombian town where he grew up, the seaport of Barranquilla, and his paintings are rich in anecdotes from that environment. There are repeated images of Colombian flora and fauna, condors and cocks, bulls and iguanas. Some of his work has strong sociopolitical overtones, such as the *Mourning for a Dead Student* (1956). Despite the seriousness of the theme, the painting contains semiabstract representations of several of Obregón's favorite Colombian emblems: a bird, flowers, and tropical fruit.

Fernando Botero, born in Medellín, Colombia, produces paintings that have much in common with the work of Latin American writers of the magic realism movement. As the Argentine critic Enrique Anderson has said, "magic realism does not show magic as if it were real, but reality as if it were magic." Botero paints the parochial Colombian middle class, a class composed of businessmen, professionals, generals, and politicians. In this class, there are no extravagant luxuries or terrible tragedies, but time to enjoy family gatherings and long, relaxed dinners. It is a calm, peaceful world, which none of its inhabitants would think of disturbing. His paintings of activities in this placid world may be considered social criticism, but Botero's gaze never trivializes or demeans his subjects to the point of vulgarity. In Botero's painting *Junta militar* (1971), which is more real, the monumental personages or, wheeling above them, the tiny, astonishingly veristic flies? Which is the president's family, the two generals and the clergyman or the diminished figures of the wife and child? Who is playing the game, the father in military uniform or the child, also in uniform, who believes in the reality of his own game?

Although Latin American art is often mistakenly perceived as an undifferentiated whole, it is, in fact, a complex amalgam of different styles, approaches, and concerns. The art of Venezuela demonstrates a wide variety of styles and objectives, but a vital form of expression that has undergone a revival in recent years is realism. Venezuelan realism, however, is more lyrical than that of many other Latin American countries and often displays the spirit of fantasy.

The first internationally acclaimed Venezuelan realist of this century was Armando Reverón (d. 1954), an eccentric recluse who lived in the coastal town of Macuto. His studio was populated with large rag dolls, for which the artist made clothes, furniture, and musical instruments. His paintings often depicted the surrounding Venezuelan landscape, as well as these rag dolls, in a style influenced by the French impressionists.

The neofigurative movement in Venezuelan art continues to draw many followers. It is perhaps surprising that the currently best-known artist, who depicts contemporary Venezuelan racial types, local urban and rural scenes, as well as religious subjects, emigrated to Venezuela from Czechoslovakia in 1949. Guillermo Heiter combines expressionism and cubism to depict the faces and colors of the Caribbean. Although he has depicted people and communities of all social classes, his most acclaimed works are industrial urban scenes such as *Cranes,* a semiabstract composition of verticals and horizontals. Such paintings express the rapid commercial and urban development associated with Venezuela's petroleum industry.

HAITI AND CUBA

There was no national movement of painting in Haiti until the Center of Art opened in Port-au-Prince in 1944. Before the existence of this art center, there was no encouragement or recognition of artists, no systematic training, and no outlet for Haitian art. A North American painter, Dewitt Peters, filled this void by establishing the Center of Art in a large old building in the capital.

Since that time, Haiti's popular art movement has gained momentum and has become one of the richest national expressions in Latin America. It is much influenced by Haiti's rich folklore and the vital African element of voodoo. The strongly geometrized, blocky figures that populate the canvases of Haitian painting stem in part from the *vêver,* a voodoo geometric design traced on the ground. The *vêver* is essential to the voodoo ceremonial rites and is used to invoke particular divinities. Many of the subjects in Haitian painting are identical to those in the *vêver*, but one also sees its influence in the flat, symmetrical compositions and the linear, simplified outlines of the figures. All of these are characteristics of folk art in general, but certainly not to the degree of development that one finds in Haitian art.

Most prominent in Haiti's popular national art movement are the so-called primitive, or naif, painters, whose style is described above. Of these, the late Hector Hyppolite is probably the most famous, in part because he was also a voodoo *hougan* ("priest") whose art depicted supernatural aspects of his religion. Before his death in 1948, his paintings were praised in a UNESCO exhibit in Paris. Other primitive painters, such as Philomé Obin, are popular realists who draw their inspiration from their native rural backgrounds.

The accepted masterpiece of Haitian primitive art is the mural cycle at the Episcopal cathedral of St. Trinité in Port-au-Prince. Among the artists who contributed to these murals were Philomé Obin, Castera Bazille, and Wilson Bigaud. Bigaud (Illus. 13), who won recognition at the Center of Art, is a self-taught artist whose *Miracle at Cana* covers 528 sq ft (49 sq m) in the St. Trinité mural cycle. The cycle is especially noteworthy for the depth of spirituality that it conveys, a characteristic that is also the heart and soul of Haitian music and dancing.

In 1950, a group of painters broke away from the primitive-style national Haitian art movement associated with the Center of Art and founded the Plastic Arts Gallery (Foyer des Arts Plastiques). The chief encouragement and inspiration for the nonprimitives came from Europe. It is significant that three of the leading semiabstract and abstract "international" artists— Luce Turner, Roland Dorcely, and Max Pinchinat—have lived in France for several years. Proof of the vitality of Haitian art is the fact that primitive, popular art continues to flourish amid the many modern art movements represented in the Plastic Arts Gallery.

The strains of patriotism and indigenous identity that began in the representation of folklore, social classes, and political caricature in such countries as Ecuador and Mexico found their continuation in the most pronounced nationalistic medium of Cuba, the poster. Previously, Cuban commercial posters, especially those advertising beverages, cosmetics, and the cinema, were imported from the United States and bore the imprimatur of the northern culture. Since the Revolution, Cuban artists and designers have produced posters for domestic use as well as for export to other Latin American countries. In Cuba, the poster industry is under the supervision of the revolutionary government, which seeks to diffuse its cultural viewpoint by using a medium that is readily accessible to all levels of society. A study of the Cuban poster is, in effect, a study of a contemporary living chronicle of the views of the Revolution. Although few of the posters are signed, the most unified, collective group has been done by members of the Cuban Institute of Art and Cinematographic Industry (Instituto Cubano de Arte e Industria Cinematográfica), who have produced many of the archetypal Cuban iconographic forms. In this institute are two of the most important producers of popular Cuban imagery, the graphic artist Alfredo Rostgaard and the painter Raul Martínez. The latter has developed a very successful and unusual style, based on colonial reminiscences as well as on modern imagery, which draws heavily on the influence of the Mexican muralists. Two main themes emerge in Cuban poster art: portraits of Cuban heroes such as José Martí, Fidel Castro, and Che Guevara and the images of unidentified people who represent the aspirations of the masses.

This chapter is but a brief introduction to the iconography and style of the art of Mexico and some of the countries of South America and the Caribbean. It is the strong appeal to nationalism, to indigenous identity, or to the potential for massive social reform that links the twentieth-century Latin American art movements.

NOTES

1. For a statement of their objectives in the manifesto see Bernard Meyers, *Mexican Painting in Our Time* (New York: 1956), p. 25.
2. Rural beer halls.

SUGGESTED READINGS

Arguin, Florence. *Diego Rivera: The Shaping of an Artist.* 1971. A general biography and artistic history of Rivera.

Art in Latin America. The Modern Era, 1820–1980. Exhibition catalogue by Dawn Ades. The Hayward Gallery, London. 18 May to 6 August, 1989. The South Bank Center.

Atl, Dr. *Como Nace y Crece un Volcan.* 1950. A profile of the early days of the muralists and Mexican revolutionary politics by Gerardo Murillo (Dr. Atl), one of ideologues of the group.

Charlot, Jean. *Mexican Art and the Academy of San Carlos, 1785–1915.* 1962. The role of the primary school for Mexican artists during the crucial pre- and postrevolutionary years.

———. *Mexican Mural Renaissance.* Primarily a history of the early period of the muralists in the 1920s.

Fondo de Cultura Económica. *La pintura mural de la revolución mexicana.* 1967. Especially valuable for the plates.

Helm, Mackinley. *Man of Fire: J. C. Orozco.* 1971. A general biography and artistic history of Orozco.

Mérida, Carlos. *Modern Mexican Artists.* 1968. Contains short biographical sketches of twenty-five Mexican artists.

Murillo, Gerardo. *See* Atl, Dr.

Reed, Alma. *The Mexican Muralists.* 1960. A general survey of the muralists and their political objectives.

Rodríguez, Antonio. *A History of Mexican Mural Painting.* 1969. A general survey of the muralists; good plates.

Schmeckebier, Laurence. *Modern Mexican Art.* 1971. A brief general survey.

Siqueiros, José David Alfaro. *Alfaro Siqueiros.* 1968. Autobiography of Siqueiros; especially interesting for the views of artists on politics.

Illustration 1 *(left)*. *Madero as a Calavera* (1910), José Guadalupe Posada.

Illustration 2 *(above)*. *Clergy and Press* (1939), José Chávez Morado.

Illustration 3 *(below)*. *Calaveras Against the People* (1950), José Chávez Morado.

Illustration 4 *(above)*. Mural in the Polyforum Cultural (1961), David Alfaro Siqueiros.

Illustration 5 *(right)*. *Man of Fire* (Hospice of Cabañas) (1938–1939), José Luis Orozco.

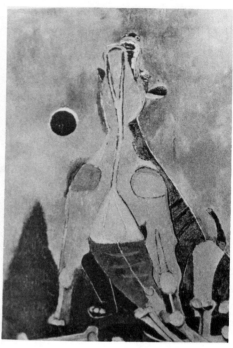

Illustration 6 *(above left)*. *Tenochtitlan* (National Palace) (1945), Diego Rivera.
Illustration 7 *(above right)*. *Howling Dog* (1942), Rufino Tamayo.
Illustration 8 *(below left)*. *My Mother's Visitors* (1963), Francisco Corzas.
Illustration 9 *(below right)*. *Mujeres Indias en Llojera* (1946), Cecilio Guzmán
   de Rojas.

Illustration 10 *(above)*. *Los Guandos* (1941), Eduardo Kingman.

Illustration 11 *(left)*. Mural on El Templo de la Patria, Quito, Ecuador (detail) (1983), Eduardo Kingman.

Illustration 12 *(right)*. Military dictator (detail) in *El Mural Ecuador* (1980), Oswaldo Guayasamín.

Illustration 13 *(below)*. *Papa Zaca* (1949), Wilson Bigaud.

PART FOUR
ECONOMIC AND
SOCIAL STRUCTURES

9
ECONOMIC ASPECTS OF LATIN AMERICA

WILLIAM P. GLADE

The heterogeneity of Latin America is notorious, grounded first of all in the varied geographical features of the region.[1] Further, the great diversity displayed in the economic and social characteristics of the several countries has tended to grow with the passage of time: The region's economic and social systems are today far more differentiated than they were, say, when the republics gained their independence from European rule.

Adding complications to study of the area is a tangled skein of political developments in which, over the past decades, the ebb and flow of events has exhibited a bewildering complexity. One is almost tempted to conclude that Latin America has pioneered the field of political-ideological conservation: i.e., a continual recycling of issues and politicians first typified, perhaps, by a remarkably durable Santa Anna in Mexico and more lately exemplified by Perón in Argentina. To be sure, new ingredients are from time to time added to the political stew, but on much of the continent the impression is not unlike that of a political museum.

Under these circumstances, it should be helpful, for understanding the economic prospects for the 1990s and thereafter, to stand back and take a longer-term perspective—to discern shared experiences and characteristics besides those of language and culture—to try to grasp how the experiences of this region, one of the most rapidly growing in the world, evolve from trends and relationships that have been operating for some time.

This longer-term perspective, incidentally, may also prove helpful in clarifying what happens elsewhere in the Third World, for Latin America has clearly been in the vanguard of those regions belatedly experiencing changes produced by the development process. Its policy innovations[2] have been echoed elsewhere, while Latin Americans have furnished the leadership in such international forums as the UNCTAD and the UNCSTD and in hammering out the outlines of the New International Economic Order.

Additionally, Latin American conceptualizations and social theorizing[3] have been widely borrowed by other Third World countries, intellectual development in Latin America having, in fact, produced a number of generative conceptions that have considerable utility for interpreting contemporary features of the Third World: e.g., the center-periphery view of unequal exchanges, the concepts of *dependencia* and internal colonialism, the interpretations of inflation and of regimes described as bureaucratic authoritarian,[4] the current rethinking of the systemic roles of the peasant sector and dualism, and so on.[5] Like the current boom in Latin American literature, this intellectual flowering in Latin America has enabled Latin American scholars to participate increasingly in writing the research agenda of our day. Both the policy community and the business community, for that matter, have much to learn from a study of Latin American developments. In dealing with such a complex reality, one is well advised to ground the discussion in a historical analytical framework that harks back to the fundamental constraints on political processes: namely, the forces of production, as they have been evolving in the twentieth century, and the social formations associated therewith.[6]

THE FORMATIVE YEARS OF MODERN LATIN AMERICA

Passing over the stately, cadenced tempo of economic and social life in the colonial age, a chief legacy of which was land concentration, and leaving aside the extraordinary dislocations that ensued after independence, one can identify the 1850–1930 period as the formative phase of modern Latin America, the time in which a basic institutional framework was devised to accommodate the dominant economic forces of that era.[7] This central economic experience was the rise of satellite economies drawn increasingly, if in different degrees, into the orbit of world capitalism. Although the eight decades in question were anything but tranquil, an overarching economic order gradually took shape and consolidated itself as the dominant system that constrained the possibilities for development in Latin America as well as elsewhere.

The twin engines of the substantial economic expansion that took place in 1850–1930 were export growth and the inflow of foreign capital, chiefly from the United Kingdom with lesser amounts from other European sources, and a gradual increase from around the turn of the century in U.S. investments in the region. Thanks to this influx of foreign capital (to both the public and private sectors) and foreign skills, most of the more populous regions of Latin America acquired a basic physical and organizational infrastructure consisting of railways, power companies, telecommunications, improved port facilities served by modern shipping lines, banks, foreign trade firms, insurance companies, and assorted municipal amenities. New product lines, mainly primary commodities, were developed to meet a growing and ever-more-diversified overseas demand, but an incipient industrial growth began to take hold as well in Mexico, Argentina, Brazil, Colombia, and elsewhere.

This long period of economic growth was occasionally punctuated by business crises and was placed in jeopardy by World War I, while the uneven or segmented development it produced was often characterized as dualistic or of an enclave nature.[8] For the most part, governments were formally democratic but de facto, largely autocratic—save for the Mexican Revolution that began in 1910 and the progressive regime that came to power in early twentieth-century Uruguay. Nevertheless, the economic leadership provided by some of the oligarchic groups was clearly superior to that supplied by others. At one level, the eighty years in question were full of policy disputes and irregular changes of government, but on the whole, Latin American society appeared reasonably well ordered in its new institutional framework— the devastating war that crushed Paraguay and the somewhat less destructive War of the Pacific constituting the major exceptions to the international peace of the era.[9] It is also worth noting that no Latin American country, before the Mexican Revolution picked up steam, experienced the kind of sanguinary internal conflict that the United States went through in the 1860s or the civil violence that swept much of Europe in the 1800s and thereafter.

THE ERA OF TRANSFORMATION

Starting around 1930, however, Latin America entered an extended period of stress from which it has not yet emerged.[10] Understanding the elements of this chronic crisis, of which political instability is symptomatic, is essential if we are to make sense of Latin America today. To this end, several factors have interacted to produce the problems the region has been wrestling with, but to generate more positive possibilities as well.[11]

Industrialization and Integration

Fundamental to the crisis has been the massive transformation of the economic structure that got under way when the global economic system of 1850–1930 was dislodged by the Great Depression, on the heels of which came further dislocations born of World War II. Since, in consequence, Latin American countries could no longer rely on the customary twin engines of growth, because of the loss of export markets and the drying up of foreign capital supply sources, policymakers were forced to embrace more inward-looking policies to keep their economies moving.[12] First as a pragmatic response to prevailing conditions and later as a more systematically elaborated policy rationale (thanks largely to the work of the United Nations Economic Commission for Latin America), various countries adopted an industrial policy designed to accelerate the growth of a manufacturing sector intended to serve national markets—using all kinds of expedients in furtherance of this goal. Light industry was pushed as the logical first wave of this deliberate industrialization, but in the larger countries, heavy industry also received attention. A secondary, but related, policy objective since 1930 has been that of integrating the different components of national economic structures so as to overcome the dichotomy between modern and traditional sectors that characterized the preceding period.

State-operated financial and industrial enterprises, joined in some instances by state-owned commercial firms, proliferated—along with regional development commissions, official crop institutes, and other types of parastatal undertakings. Fiscal incentives and loans at concessionary interest rates came to be widely employed; tariff protection was commonplace; and exchange controls, multiple exchange rates, import quotas, and licensing all had a role in the new policy packages associated with state-led development programs. The pricing of output produced by state enterprises was still another means of stimulating new patterns of growth. Some foreign operations were nationalized to wrest control of key productive assets from external decision makers and to harness them to local ends, while others were subjected to a variety of regulations with such policy aims as increasing the employment of nationals, purchasing more inputs locally, and sharing ownership with nationals. To a striking degree, foreign capital was shifted from the traditional extractive fields and utilities and channeled more into the burgeoning manufacturing sector. Altogether, then, there was a considerable expansion of state activity as a substitute for the market in allocating resources, and an enlarged public sector came to be a permanent feature of most Latin American economies. Economic planning was widely introduced, but in general, it was much more effective in improving and mobilizing economically relevant information than in actually guiding resource use in any prescriptive form.

As the fear grew that national markets might soon be saturated, and that, in any case, they were too small to support heavy industry on an economic scale, the import-substitution process was given a new lease on life. This came about through the establishment of various regional integration schemes: the Central American Common Market (CACM), the Latin American Free Trade Association (LAFTA), the Caribbean Integrated Free Trade Area (CARIFTA), and the Andean Common Market (ANCOM).

For the most part, such schemes have largely stalled, at least in terms of their original designs, but there has nevertheless been partial progress. LAFTA implemented a number of industrial complementation agreements to harmonize industrial investment plans across national borders, certain sectorial plans were carried out by the ANCOM countries, joint binational projects were moved along in transport systems and hydroelectric energy projects, and trade among the Central American countries, in particular, rose substantially. Altogether, intraregional exports as a percentage of total Latin American exports of goods and services rose from 6.5 percent in 1960 to 23 percent in 1970. In part, this growth helps explain how the manufacturing share of the gross regional product grew from 23.2 percent in 1960–1964 to 26.6 percent in 1970–1974.[13]

Meanwhile, there has been a notable deepening or elaboration of the industrial structure in such key countries as Brazil, Argentina, and Mexico, although Mexico has moved somewhat more slowly in this respect than the other two countries. In time, Colombia, Chile, Venezuela, and Peru also undertook to deepen their industrial structures. Indeed, from the 1940s and 1950s onward, the development of more-sophisticated industries, together with larger populations and rising incomes, has laid a stronger base than ever before for eventual resumption of regional integration in new guises over the years ahead. What is especially significant, though, is the fact that so many of the industrial efforts long criticized by orthodox foreign economists as "uneconomic" and as an extravagant departure from comparative advantage have enabled a number of the countries to return to export expansion policies during the 1970s on the basis of nontraditional (i.e., more diversified) exports. Thanks, in other words, to upgraded (by experience and training) managerial and labor skills; to generally improved physical and organizational infra-structures; to an expanded natural resource base in several instances; to a greater supply of technical specialists and support systems such as universities, research institutes, laboratories, and consulting firms; and to a vastly enriched information base, Latin American countries have come to possess an impressively increased industrial capability and versatility so that import-substitution policies can now be meaningfully supplemented by export-substitution policies.[14] Manufactures, for example, represented only 3.4 percent of Latin American exports in 1960; by 1978, the figure was 19.1 percent.

Brazil stands out sharply as the major new industrial power of the region, exporting a variety of products besides coffee and sugar: e.g., shoes, textiles, furniture, appliances, tractors and other motor vehicles, steel pipe, aircraft, and armaments. By 1979, in fact, the export value of automobiles and auto parts had even surpassed that of coffee.[15] Brazilian banking institutions have also reached abroad, including the acquisition of a chain of banks in Africa to facilitate the penetration of that market. Further, Brazilian engineering and construction firms have engaged in such projects as hydroelectric installations in Venezuela, Paraguay, and Bolivia; road building in Bolivia and Nigeria; the construction of universities and railway lines in Algeria; and oil-well drilling in Algeria and Iraq.

From a different vantage point, the case of Chile is no less instructive. Sheltered for years behind all types of protection and subsidy, Chilean manufacturers were abruptly subjected—right on the heels of the exceptional administrative and economic disorder of the Allende regime—to strong import competition, a competition intensified by the perverse determination of the new government to stick to a fixed exchange rate that overvalued the Chilean monetary unit. Under the circumstances, it would have been reasonable to anticipate the demise of very nearly all of the manufacturing sector. Yet, although bankruptcies occurred and unemployment rose, it is relevant to note that the industrial share of Chile's gross domestic product (GDP) in 1980 was only a small fraction below what it was in 1960. It is worth noting that the policy reforms of the 1970s, improved in the early 1980s, set the stage for a very strong surge in output and rapid gains in employment during the last half of the 1980s when most of Latin America was trapped in economic stagnation.

Naturally, progress in industrialization and the growth rates of GDPs have been uneven in recent years, the latter ranging in 1977–1980 from over 5 percent per year in Brazil, Mexico, Colombia, Chile, Ecuador, Paraguay, and several others to 3 percent or below in Argentina, Barbados, Nicaragua, and Jamaica. But of all the major world regions, up to the onset of the crisis in 1982, Latin America was industrializing and urbanizing the most rapidly, and its population was growing at the fastest clip. Unfortunately environmental modification (too often, deterioration) has also been occurring at a pace that is breathtaking. The present difficulties, precipitated by the global crisis, should not be allowed to becloud the underlying record of accomplishment.

It helps in keeping a clear perspective to note that in a relatively short period, Latin America has had to absorb all of the stresses and strains that in the United States produced a bloody civil war and in Europe occasioned more than a century of unrest and strife. Further, Latin America has had to accommodate all these changes and tensions without the cushion of the extra resources the more advanced countries captured through territorial conquest (e.g., the Mexican-American War, the partitioning of Africa, and so on) and the operations of the world market, resources with which they were able to finance their social democratic reforms and cope with internal contradictions.[16]

Population Growth and Urbanization

A second major change in the past fifty years, one that has already been mentioned in passing, is the rapidity of population growth and urbanization—detectable after 1930 but accelerating after 1950. While demographic growth rates have generally turned downward now, urbanization continues at a very fast pace. In India, China, and Indonesia, for example, only 11 percent of the population lives in cities of more than 100,000; for sub-Saharan Africa, the corresponding figure is 12 percent. By way of contrast, in Central America, the least developed portion of Latin America, some 20 percent of the population lives in cities of 100,000 or more, and in Argentina, Brazil, Chile, Mexico, Colombia, Venezuela, and Peru, the equivalent figure ranges between 35 percent and 55 percent. Moreover, an increasing number of Latin Americans live in very large cities. As late as 1950, one in every ten Latin Americans resided in a city of 1 million or more; in the early 1980s, with a total population more than double that of 1950, one out of four Latin Americans lived in a city of that size. Indeed, in 1980, Caracas had a population of over 3 million; Lima, almost 5 million; Rio de Janeiro, around 10 million; and Buenos Aires, São Paulo, and Mexico City ranged from 11 million to 14 million. Projections for the year 2000 for these largest cities are truly astonishing.

Although there is, as mentioned, evidence that Latin American population growth is now decelerating, by the end of the century a reasonable estimate for the total region is 600 million, in the course of which growth many secondary cities will expand as well—as, in fact, they have already. In Central America and Panama, for example, in 1950 there were twenty-six cities of 10,000–50,000; by 1980, ninety-five were in that size range. In 1960, Mexico and Brazil each had eight cities of 250,000 or more (excluding Mexico City,

Rio de Janeiro, and São Paulo); by 1980, the number had grown to twenty-seven in Mexico and twenty-five in Brazil.

From the standpoint of economic growth, this urbanization and deconcentration into secondary cities (sometimes fostered by public policy) carry a number of favorable implications: a growth in the market for manufactures, an upgrading of human resources (there have been giant strides forward in education), a wider range of choices for industrial location, and an increased (and geographically more dispersed) stimulus to agricultural development. Only a couple of decades ago it was feared that increased urbanization would radicalize the slum population, but the upward mobility out of rural poverty seems, more often than not, to have had a stabilizing influence.[17] No doubt the resilience of the growing informal sector has a lot to do with this, for it has been able to provide a livelihood for newcomers from the countryside as well as for much of the natural increase in the urban labor force and for those leaving (voluntarily or involuntarily) the formal sector.

Indirectly, though, these demographic trends may prove destabilizing as the growing number of participants in Latin America's urban-based political systems will influence the scale and composition of public investment programs. Just as urban demands outweigh effective rural demand in the market, the increased claims, both economic and political, of the cities on the available resources of the system will almost certainly continue to divert resources from rural activities, where they are much needed for sectorial advance.[18] On the one hand, then, urbanization has generated a market stimulus for agricultural modernization, but on the other, it has been a factor in undermining the capacity of the agricultural sector to respond to this stimulus. (Chile has, since the mid-1970s, been a major exception to this general entrapment of agriculture, and Brazil, too, was able to promote agricultural growth in significant measure.) For that matter, it must be recognized as well that various social expenditures associated with rapid urbanization are to some extent competing with directly productive capital investments in any sector for the available supply of resources.

More Workers, Fewer Jobs

A third development implied by the two trends already discussed has been the growth of an industrial labor force. Heretofore, conditions have tended to favor this group. The rapid growth of manufacturing, in a context of limited supplies of skills, has tended to push real wages up for important segments of the organized labor force. In the recent booms in some Latin American countries, there have even been shortages of skills—a problem to be sure, but one that attests to the success of the region's development in generating such a large demand for industrial skills. What is more, the close ties and frequent subordination of labor organizations to political parties (few have been as autonomously strong as the General Confederation of Labor [CGT] in Argentina or the Union of Colombian Workers [UTC] in Colombia) have produced a process of political bargaining alongside the collective bargaining process, which has also tended to work to the benefit of labor since mandated higher benefits could, in a protected industrial system, be passed along to captive consumers.

There are two factors, however, that may eventually tend to upset the relatively comfortable arrangements just sketched out. As the development of industry has moved into more capital-intensive and advanced-technology lines, the number of new jobs being created has tended to drop with the passage of time, and the capital investment required to create each new manufacturing job has risen. Simultaneously, the growing participation of the Latin American manufacturing sector in exports has placed a new constraint on the benefits that can be awarded organized labor. In consequence of both developments, Latin America will likely experience increasing difficulty in absorbing its growing labor force into the relatively high wage sector of manufacturing employment, so that the changing nature of the industrial-ization process may have opened up a contradiction for which there is no easy solution in sight.

Still worse has been the impact of the debt-induced crisis of the 1980s on labor market conditions. By severely reducing domestic capital accumulation and curtailing aggregate output, the problem has caused unemployment to soar in the formal sector and created a pool of job seekers that will require several years of vigorous growth to absorb.

Agricultural Retardation

A fourth element in the picture, again alluded to earlier, is agricultural retardation. In every Latin American country, there are examples of agricultural progress, and in general terms, agricultural organization is often quite modern in southern Brazil, northwestern Mexico, and much of the Southern Cone. There are scattered islands of modernity elsewhere, especially in export agriculture. Yet, for the most part, post-Allende Chile being the most notable exception, agricultural investment has been shortchanged, and in consequence, agricultural productivity has lagged behind industrial productivity. (Even in Brazil, where total agricultural output has risen notably, the increase has come at least as much from expansion along the extensive margin as from growth along the intensive margin.)

Rural incomes have remained generally quite low, and population growth has tended to lead to land fragmentation, overcrowding, land degradation, and widespread rural underemployment. And since aggregate agricultural output in many countries has had a hard time keeping up with population growth, especially given the high income-elasticity of demand for foodstuffs, governments have had to use scarce supplies of foreign exchange to make up through imports for the agricultural shortfall or, worse yet, have held staple prices down to appease the urban electorate while intensifying the disincentives for farmers.[19]

Efforts to reform the agricultural sector have been much talked about, but other than the Mexican and the Bolivian reforms—the latter instituted in 1953–1954—significant reform programs have been limited to Peru, Nicaragua, El Salvador, Cuba, and Chile. Although agribusiness development might seem to be an advantageous way to boost rural output in many cases, there is considerable fear that the labor-displacement effects of modernization might aggravate the income-distribution problem, flood the cities with still more difficult-to-absorb migrants, and exacerbate social and political tensions. Although the growing urban character of Latin American society has tended, in recent years, to reduce the salience of agricultural reform issues, the relative weakness of the agricultural sector remains the Achilles' heel of most national development programs and a potential source of political discontent in the future.

The Rise of the Middle Class

The main change in class structure associated with the twentieth-century evolution of Latin American economies has been the rise of the middle class, a fifth factor of reckoning. Whereas the seedbed of the middle classes in Europe and the United States was the commercial and industrial revolution that spawned capitalism, and whereas there has usually been an important rural component in the middle class in those parts of the world, the support system in Latin America has been based to a much greater extent on the growth of professions associated with urbanization and on state intervention. Only partly the outgrowth of commercial and industrial expansion, and without a significant rural base in most cases, the Latin American middle class has come into being chiefly as a professional and service-sector class— and as a bureaucratic class based on state expansion.

Nested strategically, in both an institutional (state apparatus) and a geographical (urban area) sense, the Latin American middle class is typically a politicized group tied closely to the exercise of state power—and well positioned, it must be remarked, to enforce its rising consumption claims on the economic surplus.[20] Besides generally complicating the task of the state in accumulating capital, such class relationships have been a major factor in generating severe frictions during economic restructuring and stabilization programs, whether induced by the International Monetary Fund or otherwise. This was surely a large factor in explaining the inability of the Alfonsín government of Argentina to devise a satisfactory growth policy, and part of the explanation for the economically ineffectual Sarney government in Brazil and the even more inept policies of the García government in Peru—to say nothing of the disaffection that sundered the PRI hegemony in Mexico in the 1980s.

In this connection, it is sobering to reflect briefly on the assumptions of the Alliance for Progress of the early 1960s. At the time, it was, of course, widely expected that the rise of a literate, urban, and reasonably prosperous middle class in Latin America would function as a bastion of democracy. What was sought, in other words, was a social structure most closely approximated in Latin America by Argentina, Uruguay, and Chile—in all of which the political system decayed dramatically and in the 1970s broke down almost totally. The contradiction between consumption and accumulation, indeed, raises considerable doubt about the viability of liberalization programs in a number of countries. Generally, the vast expansion of state activity over the past half-century, with the state regulating key relationships, has heated up the political contest as each group in society seeks to increase its relative share of the total product.[21]

Chronic Inflation

The sixth factor needed for understanding contemporary Latin American economies is the problem of chronic inflation, which has now seemingly engulfed even Mexico and Peru, two countries that formerly had relatively stable price levels. By the close of the 1980s, hyperinflation was threatening Argentina, Brazil, and Peru, having finally been brought to heel in Bolivia by an especially rigorous stabilization program. Partly attributable to the rising prices of energy and key imports as well as to domestic shortages of food and agricultural raw materials (and occasionally, human skills), the inflation rates that are rampant in most of Latin America owe much to continuing pressures to step up public spending from a weak fiscal base and a relatively low level of voluntary saving as well as, more profoundly, to the persistent struggle over income distribution. To no small degree, the inflation process appeared at one time to spring from various internal contradictions facing the new national security states in the region: e.g., the claims on resources to nourish the military apparatus, the basic claims on resources to accelerate capital formation, and the claims of various constituencies, organized and articulated in the urban political arena, for higher consumption of goods and services. The retreat of the military in the 1980s, however, showed that the dynamics of civilian rule were quite sufficient to produce macroeconomic instability.

What has happened in general can be illustrated by two sets of figures for several countries: the first being the average annual inflation rate for 1960–1970 and the second, the equivalent figure for 1970–1980. Among the major countries, the record runs as follows: Argentina 21.2, 119.5; Brazil 44.5, 35.3; Colombia 11.2, 21.0; Chile 27.2, 130.3; Mexico 2.5, 16.5; Peru 9.3, 30.2; and Venezuela 1.0, 2.0. For some of the smaller economies, the figures are Bolivia 5.5, 18.8; Costa Rica 2.3, 10.8; Ecuador 4.3, 12.6; El Salvador 0.6, 10.8; Paraguay 3.2, 13.1; and Uruguay 44.0, 62.7. Rates for the 1980s were higher still, far higher in most cases.

As is only too well known these days, the fiscal and monetary policies associated with these inflation rates often built up huge external debts—for the big three (Brazil, Mexico, and Argentina) certainly, but for smaller economies as well (e.g., Chile, Peru, and Costa Rica). Although to some extent global inflation scaled down the real burden of these debts, heavy service requirements eventually began to produce reschedulings and suspensions of payments with all the dislocations these entailed. Further developments of this nature are most assuredly in the offing, despite the help provided in the Baker and subsequent Brady plans.

Nevertheless, difficult though these external burdens are, in some ways they demonstrate the success of the development process by attesting to

Latin America's growing capacity to generate apparently bankable projects. Such a situation stands in contrast to, say, two or three decades ago when the amount of funding potentially available from international institutions for loans to Latin America generally tended to exceed the region's absorptive capacity and few private banks would have been willing to lend to Latin America anyhow.[22] Economies as feeble and limited as most of those in Latin America were some three or four decades ago could never have run up the debt levels that prevail today. Had not energy markets behaved as they have and had not the advanced countries entered a severe recession and interest rates risen so much, it is doubtful that the level of external indebtedness would have become quite the acute problem it has for much of the region (albeit for different reasons from country to country). Some countries have had to borrow to cover the sharply higher costs of fuel imports while others— especially Mexico but to some extent, Venezuela and Ecuador—simply started living beyond their means when petroleum prices rose in the 1970s. Other factors, too, have been involved, particularly in cases such as those of Chile, Argentina, and Peru, and in virtually all instances, the debt-servicing problem has been aggravated by a drop in export earnings occasioned by the world recession and by the prevailing high interest rates on international lending.

What is important, however, is to round out the picture by looking beyond the current financial travail to the underlying strength of the real assets that most Latin American economies have been building up over the past several decades.[23] Further, key economic policies are much better designed nowadays than they have ever been, at least in Mexico, Chile, Colombia, Venezuela, and, fleetingly, in Argentina and Brazil. Conditions are, therefore, far more propitious today than they were in the early 1960s for an efficacious use of external economic and technical assistance and for continued success in institution building as part of an economic recovery program, if a significant portion of the external debt were, as realism would call for, written off. Furthermore, it is virtually certain that given the rising per capita income levels of Latin American countries and their increasingly complex economic structures, the volume and variety of items traded among North and Middle and South America are destined to rise significantly over the long haul.[24]

Thanks to the concatenation of trends and problems mentioned thus far, a whole series of policy issues came to the forefront of concern in the 1980s: the viability of stabilization programs, the nature of relations between the state and the multinational corporations, issues of denationalization and privatization, performance criteria for the operations of the parastatal sector, basic provisioning programs, employment programs, energy development programs, and export diversification efforts. Real headway was made in realigning policies in a more productive way, particularly in respect of the parastatal and public sectors, and in a greater appreciation of the role of macroeconomic stability, exports, foreign investment, and domestic capital formation. It is too soon to draw firm conclusions about a general retreat from statism, but at the very least, there is growing skepticism about the efficacy of interventionism and a dawning appreciation of what the market contributes to a mixed economy. Regional integration and agrarian reform, in contrast, appear to have receded somewhat in importance as items on policy agendas.

THE CONTEXT OF POLICY DEBATE

A very problematic political picture emerges from the interplay of the forces described in the foregoing section. Some of the traditional actors on the political stage have changed their roles, especially the Church and the military, but not always in favor of the same set of policy preferences.[25] Some positions have varied from country to country and from time to time. Others have been superseded by the changes in social structure; for example, the landed oligarchy remains influential in several of the small states, but in the larger, more complex societies, it is greatly overshadowed by urban-based commercial, financial, and industrial interests. Meanwhile, urban labor and the bureaucratic-professional, or administrative, middle class also figure prominently in the policy process of a number of countries, generally favoring policies that diminish foreign control over local decision processes.

Even the dynamics of the policy process have been changing, for, as suggested earlier, the old-fashioned dictatorships and the authoritarian oligarchies of yesteryear have tended to fall by the wayside, along with such populist authoritarian systems as those led by Cárdenas, Vargas, Perón, Rojas Pinilla, Velasco, and Torrijos. In their stead, and replacing also some of the fragile liberal democracies of the region, arose a variety of more or less authoritarian regimes of a rather more bureaucratic nature, but which differed significantly: Argentina, Brazil, Mexico, Chile, Uruguay, and so on. Some were repressive; others, much more moderate. In all of them, however, technocratic civilian and/or military bureaucracies interacted with political bureaucracies in ways not fully apprehended by those outside the process to formulate public policy, and by the close of the 1980s, those military regimes, too, were toppled. In two cases, Cuba and, possibly more debatably, Nicaragua, a system closer to those of Eastern Europe was either installed or on the verge of installation, under leadership that seemed sadly out of touch with the developments that by the end of the 1980s were leading to a substantial abandonment in Europe of the shopworn formulae of Leninist central planning.

In a number of instances, one has the impression that incumbent groups remain in power more through a lack of robust options than through their own legitimacy or any demonstrable merit. In country after country, the old-time conservative parties have gone into near-total eclipse, many centrist parties seem to have lost their political creativity and ability to build a broad consensus, while in most cases, the left is highly fragmented. Redemocratization, where undertaken, could conceivably be as fleeting as it has been in the past, and political realignments are certain to take unexpected guises in the years ahead.

Under these circumstances, there is a certain element of unpredictability about the course economic policies will take and how each regime will define its national project. The political sphere, in other words, displays a character that is markedly at variance with the economic strength most of the Latin American countries have built up but that has been badly eroded by the protracted debt crisis of the 1980s. Perhaps the only safe generalization is that in Latin America, on the whole, political science has come to replace economics as "the dismal science."

NOTES

1. Today, it has become increasingly customary to speak of "Latin America and the Caribbean," adding, among others, the small English-speaking island states with their very different political tradition and ethnic composition. Obviously very few, if any, generalizations can be made that would fit both these ministates at one end of the spectrum and the enormous country of Brazil at the other.

2. Especially prominent have been relatively new forms of state intervention to promote import-substituting industrial development, new policies to regulate multinational corporations and encourage technology and science transfers, special-purpose government banks, and domestication policies for foreign enterprises in recognition that *il capitale è mobile* ("capital is fickle")—and not just women as the aria in *Rigoletto* tells us. A more self-reliant rather than purely autarkic development has been the aim of many of these policy instruments.

3. If one could categorize the mainstream of Latin American economic thought, it would be a kind of institutionalism or structuralism that represents a synthesis of neoclassical analytical techniques with the systemic dynamics of neo-Marxian approaches.

4. From the Latin American experience, for example, comes the distinction among traditional oligarchic authoritarianism (whether headed by military or civilian *caudillos*), populist authoritarianism, and bureaucratic authoritarianism—all of which have impinged differently on the configuration of development policies.

5. Among other phenomena, the explications of which have been enhanced by Latin American scholarship, are *caudillismo,* militarism, middle sectors, corporatism, populism, third positionism, peripheral capitalism, and the urban informal sector. The rise of the Latin American NICs (newly industrialized countries) out of the LDCs (less developed countries) is also instructive in regard to the problems of rearticulating changed national economies with the world system on the basis of new comparative advantages.

6. Put this way, of course, the framework identifies the locus of the exceptional heterogeneity of the Latin American social complex: Coexisting modes and relations of production have spawned a variety of social formations, abetted by the incomplete spread of national communications systems and the incomplete integration of the social structure and accentuated by geographical regional disparities in development. In these respects, Latin America contrasts sharply with Europe and the United States.

7. This periodization differs from the common practice of considering that World War I was the end of the formative era. Yet although the war temporarily interrupted the flow of events, its aftermath saw a resumption of business as usual over most of the region until the prevailing order collapsed with the Great Depression.

8. The incomplete transformation of the economic structure that took place during this period has led a number of Latin American and other scholars to argue that exports failed to fuel growth, or at least failed to instigate a genuine process of development. Indeed, this allegation has become the key thematic line in the school of Latin American social thought known as *dependencia,* and *dependencia,* in turn, has emerged as the favorite tune in the hymnody of the festive left throughout the region. Be that as it may, it cannot be gainsaid that the economic map of Latin America in 1930 was profoundly different from what it was in 1850.

9. Popular accounts have sometimes faulted Latin American countries for their militarism, attributing the area's relative economic backwardness to this phenomenon. Wars and weaponry there were, but they were picayune in comparison with those in Europe. Moreover, although

conspicuous consumption—another factor posited as an element of backwardness—was certainly in evidence, Latin American attainments in this quarter were much inferior to the conspicuous display that was characteristic of both Europe and the United States during the period.

10. The chief exceptions are Mexico after around 1930, Costa Rica from the late 1940s onward, and Venezuela after the late 1950s. Each, for different reasons, has enjoyed more political continuity in carrying out development policy than have their sister republics.

11. Since at least the late 1950s, it has become almost traditional to bewail and bemoan Latin America's present condition and its prospects. Seemingly intractable problems abound, sinister oligarchs (or guerrillas, if one prefers) populate the stage, and always there is an air of impending doom—a waiting for *Götterdämmerung*, as it were. Now there is no particular virtue in denying that Latin America, like most other parts of the world, still faces considerable difficulty in pulling itself together and getting on with the business of economic and social progress. It is no more immune to the global tides of prosperity and recession than are the United States or Europe. In spite of the obstacles, however, growth rates in Latin America have been generally quite respectable in terms of the historical record, the population explosion seems now to be moderating, and various indicators (e.g., infant mortality, life expectancy, etc.) indicate that social improvement is taking place as well.

12. For the most part, the larger countries had more options along this line than did the small ones, which necessarily had to remain more structurally open.

13. The relationship between gross investment and GDP went from 13.3 percent in 1961 to 17.1 percent in 1969, the average growth of regional GDP having risen from 4.5 percent in the 1950s to 5.6 percent in the 1960s. (*Integración latinoamericana* 4:39 [September 1979]). National policy was, of course, paramount, but it was helped along by the stimulus of regional integration. It could also be noted here that Latin American steel production grew at an average annual rate of approximately 10 percent from 1960 to 1978.

14. There is still a great distance to go, however, in becoming more self-reliant in science and technology, and the foreign relations aspects of technological transfer have come under increased scrutiny and regulation. In a rough sense, many Latin American social scientists see the early trade dependency of the continent as having given way (during 1850–1930) to an investment capital dependency, which, in recent years, has increasingly given way to a technological dependency. At the same time, however, this technological dependency is a benchmark of progress since it springs from Latin America's steady movement into ever more technically complex and sophisticated fields.

15. Over 350 firms, for example, had run up export sales aggregating over $300 million in military hardware in 1979.

16. It must also be kept in mind that in both Western Europe and the United States topography was more favorable, key resources were more accessible, and cheap river transport systems were available early to facilitate long-distance trade.

17. Although the first-generation migrants to the cities seem to have experienced significant improvement, the second generation of new urban dwellers will likely expect even more rewards and, becoming increasingly frustrated, may conceivably turn in a more radical direction. The experiences of long-urbanized Argentina and Uruguay, however, do not suggest such a likelihood.

18. Either more responsive or more repressive governments will be required to manage the social conflict inherent in this situation. Some have suggested that increasing urbanization facilitates social control and the containment of conflict, but the Latin American experience is not altogether clear on this point.

19. There has also been a fear that the strengthening of export agriculture may have adverse effects on the supply of basic foodstuffs for the domestic market.

20. Whether we take "the state" to refer to a set of institutions of governance or to a set of political relationships that serves to maintain the social relations of domination, the middle class functions in a way that is critical to the operation of the system. Not surprisingly, there is growing reference today in Latin America to a "state bourgeoisie." In part, this "class" grows out of the widespread insertion of public enterprise into the

patterned interaction of rudimentary national capitalist modes of production with the hegemonic one of international capital. The rise in the 1960s and 1970s of military-bureaucratic regimes, usually in close alliance with international capital, has tended to lead to a discarding of many (if not necessarily most) of the populistic trappings of the previous two or three decades.

21. Social critics in Latin America have tended to depict the outcome of this struggle as a "national security state," in which an authoritarian regime is relied on to deal with the disequilibrating forces that would upset the restructuring of the world economy being carried out by multinational or transnational enterprises. The interpenetration of multinational corporations (MNCs) and the state is, according to this reading of contemporary experience, conducive to corporatism, to an eventual depoliticization of the working and middle classes, and to the installation of measures to contain demands for radical change. Just as the state depends on the MNCs for foreign financing and technical inputs, so the MNCs depend on the state to provide a technocratic, authoritarian rule (a type of rule the old-fashioned, personalistic *caudillo* style could not provide).

22. Since private-sector banking has figured so prominently in the present crisis, it seems lopsided to say, as some commentators have, that the debt problem reflects a high level of economic mismanagement in Latin America. Clearly, since the transactions were voluntary, the misjudgment of the lenders is also revealed.

23. At the same time, one must keep in mind that the accumulation of assets and their productivity have varied widely from country to country. The average annual rate of increase in real GDP from 1970 to 1980, for instance, was as follows: Argentina 2.3, Bolivia 4.4, Brazil 8.8, Colombia 5.9, Ecuador 7.5, Guatemala 5.6, Mexico 4.5, Paraguay 8.6, Chile 2.9, El Salvador 3.2, Honduras 3.8, Nicaragua 1.2, and Peru 3.0.

24. For that matter, such developments could well occur even if more Latin American countries should, by embracing socialism, attempt to effect a divorce between aggregate demand and unemployment and to deploy their resources in new ways to meet basic human needs more fully.

25. In some instances (Guatemala in the 1950s, 1960s, and 1970s comes to mind), the military has been mainly reactionary (through the suppression of alternative viewpoints held by some factions). In Peru after 1968, the military was quite revolutionary in its political program; in Brazil, it proved highly adept in running the country. In Argentina, its ineptitude in power almost suggests that there is no such process as learning by doing.

SUGGESTED READINGS

Farley, Rawle. *The Economics of Latin America.* New York: Harper and Row, 1972. Similar in aim to the books by Hunter/Foley (1975) and Gordon (1965).

Glade, William. *The Latin American Economies: A Study of Their Institutional Evolution.* New York: American Book Company, 1969. A survey of the public sector–private sector relationship from colonial times to 1966.

Gordon, Wendell C. *The Political Economy of Latin America.* New York: Columbia University Press, 1965. An updated version of one of the earliest texts on Latin American development.

Griffin, Keith. *Underdevelopment in Latin America.* London: Allen and Unwin, 1969. One of the more sophisticated statements of the "development of underdevelopment" point of view.

Hunter, John M., and James W. Foley. *Economic Problems of Latin America.* Boston: Houghton-Mifflin, 1975. A textbook on the problems of contemporary development.

Inter-American Development Bank. *Socio-Economic Progress in Latin America.* Annual report, formerly called *Economic and Social Progress in Latin America,* on countries and topics, issued since 1971; superseded the *Social Progress Trust Fund Annual Reports,* which were published during most of the 1960s.

Prebisch, Raul. *Change and Development: Latin America's Great Task.* New York: Praeger, 1971. A rethinking of the Latin American predicament by a man who, more than any other individual, shaped Latin American economic analysis and policy in the decades following World War II.

Swift, Jeannine. *Economic Development in Latin America.* New York: St. Martin's Press, 1978. A good, short survey of trends and problems.

United Nations, Economic Commission for Latin America (ECLA). *CEPAL Review.* A useful periodical, begun in 1976, for monitoring important trends in development analysis in Latin America.

———— . *Notas sobre la economía y el desarrollo de America Latina.* Monthly publication of the ECLA Information Service. Contains valuable current statistics on various aspects of the Latin American economic scene.

University of California Los Angeles, Latin American Center. *Statistical Abstract on Latin America.* An annual publication presenting a wealth of statistical information on social, economic, and political matters.

10

SOCIAL STRUCTURE AND SOCIAL CHANGE IN TWENTIETH-CENTURY LATIN AMERICA

GILBERT W. MERKX

The term "Latin America" traditionally refers to the eighteen Spanish-speaking republics of the Western Hemisphere, together with Brazil and Haiti. These nations are remarkably diverse in size, social and economic structure, and historical tradition. Recognition of the differences among Latin American countries need not preclude, however, an awareness of their commonalities. Each participates in the world market but has little influence on world prices. The region as a whole is characterized by comparatively high inequality of income and wealth and large proportions of poor people. Although the economic growth of the region has been impressive in overall terms during the twentieth century, that growth has been uneven through time and uneven also in terms of its local and regional impact.

As a region, Latin America has clearly been peripheral to the great events of the century, neither causing those events nor determining their outcomes; just as clearly, it has been affected by those events and has responded to them. External economic factors have had significant consequences on the immediate situation of Latin America, and they have also played a major role in determining the nature of social and economic change over the long term. The inherent differences among Latin American nations are so great, however, that their interactions with the world at large have led to a fascinating variety of social outcomes.

The purpose of this chapter will be to characterize the shared peculiarities of social change, review the important differences among Latin American nations, comment on the class structures and conflicts that have resulted, and speculate briefly on the decade to come.

157

STRUCTURAL CHARACTERISTICS OF
LATIN AMERICAN DEVELOPMENT

Not long ago, it was commonly argued that developing nations would follow the same path as those nations that industrialized during the predepression era. Recent studies have demonstrated, however, that patterns of economic development and social change in Latin America are quite divergent from earlier cases. The newer pattern is termed "delayed development" or "dependent development," reflecting the international context of economic development in the postdepression period and related social changes that differ from the predepression experiences of industrial nations.

The basic divergence between European and Latin American development patterns can be clearly specified. One important feature is the extremely high rate of population growth in Latin America, which is up to twenty-five times higher than that of the industrial nations during the predepression era. Only the population growth rate of the United States during the 1875–1928 period, thanks to massive immigration from Europe, even approaches that of contemporary Latin America. Yet even the U.S. growth rate over that fifty-three-year period was 86 percent lower than that of Latin America during a comparable period ending in 1973 (during which time Latin America did not experience massive immigration).

Because the relative stagnation of rural employment meant that the rural sectors of Latin America were unable to absorb this massive population increase, an unprecedented influx of population into the cities took place. In 1925, the population of Latin America was only 30 percent urban, but by 1980, it had become 66 percent urban. This rate of urbanization took place in spite of the fact that the absolute size of the rural population also grew.

The human tidal wave overwhelmed Latin America's capacity to provide services, space, and housing, leading to the formation of vast slum areas, known by such names as *callampas, favelas, ranchos, barriadas,* or *villas miserias.* These areas, established at the initiative of the inhabitants, often showed a surprising degree of internal organization. Their very existence led to pressure on the urban labor market that tended to put established working- and middle-class groups on the defensive.

Latin American urbanization bears little relationship to the pattern of urbanization in the industrial nations, which was closely linked to economic changes. The sequence of change in the industrial nations involved the commercialization of agriculture, which led to urbanization and industrialization, and the accompanying and partially subsequent rise of urban middle classes. In Latin America, the first commercialization of agriculture was primarily focused on the export sector. The rise of urban middle classes based on this export sector actually preceded industrialization in most of Latin America. Industrialization, when it came, failed to absorb large quantities of labor; but, in spite of this, urbanization accelerated with a speed far exceeding European patterns.

Table 10.1
Occupational Structure of Three Latin American Nations Compared to Other
Nations at Time of Industrialization in Percentages

	Year	Primary Sector	Secondary Sector	Tertiary Sector
Brazil	1960	52	13	35
Mexico	1960	53	17	30
Peru	1960	54	15	31
Australia	1880	50	28	22
France	1886	52	29	20
Ireland	1841	51	34	15
Italy	1871	52	34	14
United States	1880	50	25	25

Source: Simposio Latinoamericano de Industrialización, *El Proceso de Industrialización en America Latina* (Santiago, Chile: United Nations Economic Commission for Latin America, 1966), pp. 11–13.

A characteristic feature of Latin America's delayed development pattern was the inability of the industrial sector to absorb a large share of the urban labor force. This reflects both the capital-intensive rather than labor-intensive character of modern manufacturing and the sheer volume of urban population growth. Again, the contrast with previous experience is instructive. If the occupational structure of selected Latin American nations at a time when about half of their populations had left the primary sector (basically agriculture) is compared with the occupational structure of industrial nations at the same point of change, the much smaller share of secondary-sector (manufacturing) employment in Latin America is striking (Table 10.1).

If the occupational structure of four Latin American nations with very small primary-sector employment (Argentina, Chile, Venezuela, and Uruguay) is compared with that of four industrialized nations at a later stage of development, the differences are equally noteworthy (Table 10.2). These data show that the urbanization process in Latin America is associated with the ballooning of the tertiary, or service, sector rather than with manufacturing employment. The inflated size of the service sector probably masks the underemployment of urban poor surviving on the margins of the modern economy.

If employment by sector is examined through time for Latin America as a whole, the same picture emerges. As shown in Table 10.3, the share of employment generated by the secondary sector increased by only 1.1 percent between 1925 and 1970, whereas the share of the tertiary, or service, sector grew by almost 20 percent. Despite the growth of industry in Latin America during the period, manufacturing employment failed to keep pace with the expansion of the labor force, much less to absorb the millions of workers leaving the agricultural sector.

Table 10.2
Occupational Structure of Four Latin American Nations with Low Employment
in the Primary Sector Compared to Selected Nations in Percentages

	Year	*Primary Sector*	*Secondary Sector*	*Tertiary Sector*
Argentina	1960	18	31	51
Chile	1971	21	32	47
Venezuela	1971	22	25	53
Uruguay	1963	18	26	56
France	1954	28	37	35
Germany	1929	30	41	29
Greece	1940	29	36	35
United States	1900	38	27	35

Sources: Figures for Latin American Nations from *Statistical Abstract for Latin America,* op. cit., pp. 110–111. Figures for other nations from Simposio Latinoamericano de Industrialización, *El Proceso de Industrialización en America Latina* (Santiago, Chile: United Nations Economic Commission for Latin America, 1966), pp. 11–13.

Table 10.3
Distribution of Latin American Labor Force by Economic Sectors, 1925–1970, in Percentages

	1925	*1950*	*1960*	*1970*
Primary sector	62.4	54.1	50.1	42.2
Secondary sector	13.7	18.6	20.0	14.8
Tertiary sector	23.9	27.3	30.0	43.0

Sources: Erik Thorbecke, "Unemployment and Underemployment in Latin America" (Document prepared for the Inter-American Development Bank, Washington, D.C., 1971); International Labour Organization, *Yearbook of Labor Statistics* (Geneva, 1960–1975); Pan-American Union, *America en cirfras* (Washington, D.C., 1960–1975).

The contrast with the experience of the industrial nations is again instructive. Historical data show that once the industrial nations reached a certain level of development, manufacturing employment was able to keep pace with other forms of urban employment. In fact, over long periods of time, the share of manufacturing employment in total urban employment remained almost unchanged in nations such as Great Britain, Italy, Australia, and France. For Latin America, on the other hand, the share of manufacturing employment has never been very high, and it actually declined from 35.4 percent to only 27.1 percent of total urban employment between 1925 and 1960 (Table 10.4).

The structural peculiarities of Latin America's "delayed development" in the period since the Great Depression are such that European-type societies are not likely to emerge. The main features of Latin American social change—

Table 10.4
Manufacturing Employment as a Percentage of Urban Employment in Selected Nations and Latin America

Nation or Region	Year	Manufacturing Employment	Other Urban Employment
Great Britain	1901	51.5	48.9
	1951	51.9	48.1
Italy	1901	59.5	40.5
	1954	53.5	46.5
Australia	1911	45.8	54.2
	1947	45.5	54.5
France	1881	51.4	48.6
	1954	51.3	48.7
Latin America	1925	35.4	64.6
	1960	27.1	72.9

Source: United Nations Economic Commission for Latin America, *The Process of Industrial Development in Latin America* (New York, 1966), pp. 36–38.

such as massive population growth, unprecedented rates of urbanization, stagnation of industrial employment, and the burgeoning of the labor force in the service sector—preclude the formation of social structures and of change processes such as those previously found in the industrialized nations.

In Europe, population growth, industrialization, and urbanization were relatively gradual, proceeding over the course of centuries. Higher rates of labor-force absorption into manufacturing employment, and lower rates of population growth, meant that European nations were able, for the most part, to incorporate the bulk of their populations into their evolving economic and political institutions, distributing to them some of the material benefits of economic modernization.

In Latin America, change is far more rapid and less controllable. The expansion of the modern sector is associated with an increase in the size of marginal groups and has resulted in increasing, rather than decreasing, social and economic inequalities. In consequence, social and political conflict in most Latin American nations has intensified in recent years. The form that such conflicts take depends upon the specific configuration of change in each nation, but all Latin American nations face the problems of coping with the difficulties of late development in a world economy dominated by the industrialized nations.

DIFFERENCES AMONG LATIN AMERICAN NATIONS

As noted, the development process in Latin America has led to great differences in the way Latin American nations are linked to the world market, in the size of their internal markets, and in the extent to which they have industrialized. A useful method, suggested by Guillermo O'Donnell (1973), of approaching the differences among Latin American nations is to compare them with respect to (1) the absolute size of the modern sector—that is, the sector that comprises a market for manufactured goods and urban services—and (2) the size of the modern sector relative to that of the marginal sector—the sector that has *not* been incorporated into the market for such goods and services. The latter comparison provides information about the extent of social cleavages and income gaps within a nation and the degree to which the population is integrated into the dominant economic system. The former indicates the extent to which an economy can sustain industrialization, generate capital, support a multiclass center, and provide the instruments of national power, such as a large military apparatus.

The general trend of Latin American development in the last fifty years has been for the modern sector to expand in relation to the marginal sector, although in most of the region, the marginal sectors have still grown in absolute terms because of the rapid population growth. In a few countries, such as Uruguay and Argentina, the marginal sector is now fairly small relative to the modern sector; in others, such as Haiti and Paraguay, the marginal sector is relatively large. In most countries of the region, however, a fairly large marginal sector coexists with a modern sector of equal or greater size, as in Mexico, Peru, and Ecuador. Needless to say, the relative size of the modern and marginal sectors has considerable impact on the political system and the behavior of different social groups in each country, as well as upon the course of economic change.

The absolute size of the modern sector is probably even more significant in economic terms, however, because it sets the limit on the size of the market for the internal economy. Argentina, Brazil, and Mexico are the "giants" of Latin America in this respect, even if they are less impressive when compared with the industrialized nations. Chile, Colombia, Cuba, Peru, and Venezuela form a clearly defined middle group of nations that have economies of moderate size. The remaining nations all suffer from the small size of their internal economies. With only one or two exceptions, the degree of industrialization is closely correlated with the absolute size of the modern sector in Latin American nations but not well correlated to the relative size of the modern sector.

The countries with large modern sectors in absolute terms can support the sophisticated activities found in industrialized nations, such as film and television production, book publishing, large universities, symphony orchestras, and other appurtenances of "high" culture. These countries have labor unions and political movements that are thoroughly modern in tactics and ideology, military establishments that have the latest in professional training and computerized intelligence operations, and urban environments that are as cosmopolitan as those of London, Paris, and New York.

In the smallest and least modern countries, traditional patterns of political and social control, based on kinship and patronage, remain paramount. The gadgets of civilization function sporadically or seem alien to an environment that is sometimes one step removed from the basic necessities of human survival. Rural issues, not urban questions, are paramount: Who owns the land, who farms the land, and who markets the produce. Relations between city and countryside are fraught with tension and marked by the great social distance that separates "modern" urban elites from rural populations, a distance often accentuated by ethnic and racial differences.

The opportunities for mass social mobilization through political parties and interest-group associations, such as labor unions, that are available in the countries with large modern sectors have proved threatening to the interests of local upper classes and international business alike. These countries also are characterized by large and relatively efficient governmental institutions—in particular, military establishments—and their recent social histories have been characterized by political polarization, military intervention, and repression. The exceptions are Mexico, which has remained under the domination of a single ruling party, and Venezuela, in which oil wealth has made possible a two-party system that has responded effectively to consumer demands.

The two countries having modern sectors that are small in absolute terms but large in relative terms, Uruguay and Costa Rica, are also exceptions to the small-country pattern. In the case of Uruguay, the cycle of import substitution and mass mobilization has led to authoritarian military rule. In Costa Rica, characterized by considerable income equality, the absence of a strong military, and well-developed welfare institutions, the institutions of parliamentary democracy survive.

CLASS STRUCTURE AND CLASS CONFLICT

Given the range of variation found in Latin American societies as a result of the development process, generalizations about class structure must be treated with caution. One means of approaching this matter is to distinguish between class issues in groups of countries that can be categorized as small, medium, or large in terms of the absolute size of their modern sector, while taking into account the relative size of that sector.

Comparing the three countries with large modern sectors (Argentina, Brazil, and Mexico) with the developed countries of Europe and North America is instructive. The success with which democratic political systems in the developed countries mitigated class conflict is generally attributed to the establishment of relatively stable class coalitions that permit the middle class and industrial working class to maintain effective popular majorities. The role of the middle class in these coalitions is viewed as particularly important because of its moderating influence and its commitment to the institutions of democratic politics, which were the vehicle for middle-class gains in relation to traditional and modern upper classes. The middle classes provided the leadership for political movements that counted on substantial support from the industrial working classes, and the demands of the working class moderated as their standard of living improved.

This pattern seemed to be developing in the more advanced Latin American countries before the onset of the Great Depression. Structural developments since that time, however, have made the European pattern less and less applicable to the Latin American context. The pricing and protective discriminations that supported import-substitution industrialization in Latin America hurt efforts to mediate among different sectors of economic activity, because the interests of the industrial sector required continued discrimination against other sectors of employment (through tariffs, exchange control, import and export restrictions, pricing controls, and other means).

Perhaps an even more fundamental problem was the relatively low level of industrial employment in Latin America—even in Argentina, which achieved a significant degree of industrialization. Moreover, the middle classes in Latin America failed to reach the size or influence of their Anglo-American or European counterparts. The proportion of families capable of achieving living standards comparable to middle classes elsewhere (as opposed to merely occupying the middle ranks of the income distribution) is a small and insecure minority of Latin American populations. In short, a coalition of industrial workers and middle-class groups, even if achieved, would represent a far smaller proportion of overall population in Latin America than in the developed nations.

The limitations of middle-class development in Mexico, Brazil, and Argentina are reflected in the fact that a major share of the upper third of the income distribution in these countries is composed of industrial workers rather than of persons in the entrepreneurial or bureaucratic occupations associated with middle-class status. Although such data are notoriously difficult to obtain, a suggestive study in Mexico, based on a 1963 household survey, found that of the top 5 percent of the income distribution, fully 9 percent were manual laborers (*obreros*) rather than white-collar workers (*empleados*) or self-employed workers; of the next highest 15 percent of the income distribution, 23 percent were manual laborers.

Because of the relatively small size of the middle class and the industrial working class in Latin America, the proportion of the population engaged in agricultural and service-sector employment is high. In the countries that still have large marginal sectors alongside their modern sectors—such as Brazil, Mexico, and the middle-ranking countries—the prototypes of the people engaged in agricultural and service-sector employment are peasants and slum dwellers, respectively. Both groups have tended to be apolitical or to be the targets of elite manipulation. When the frustration of these lower-class marginal groups leads to political action, that action, more often than not, has taken the form of rebellions or riots that are outside the confines of institutionalized political behavior (e.g., voting). This is not to say that peasants and slum dwellers cannot be organized politically (which occurred in Chile), but rather that for the most part, such organization has been prevented or manipulated in a manner not conducive to maintaining stable popular majorities.

The frustrations of middle-class political actors in Latin America also have played a role in the development of class alliances that differ from the European pattern. The failure of middle-class political parties to mobilize marginal groups on behalf of middle-class interests has led some elements to react to lower-class demands by supporting military intervention. Ironically, other middle-class elements have rejected democracy for opposite motives and have begun to play a leading role in fomenting revolutionary activity. The urban guerrilla activity that emerged in Argentina, Uruguay, and Brazil was primarily staffed by middle-class students and professionals and further contributed to divisions in middle-class responses to social change. A factor in the predominantly conservative response of middle-class actors probably has been the importance of public-sector bureaucratic employment (a greater source of middle-class status in Latin America than in the developed nations at comparable stages), which implies dependency on existing political authorities.

In the middle-ranking countries of Latin America (Chile, Colombia, Cuba, Peru, and Venezuela), the existence of sizable marginal populations alongside modern sectors has led to a considerable range of class alliances and political outcomes. The ability of upper-class interests in Chile, Colombia, and Peru to dominate and manipulate marginal populations allowed those countries to sustain the fiction of popular democracy for long periods, without threatening upper-class control. Only in Colombia, however, has this approach continued to be viable. In Peru and Chile, the threat of lower-class mobilization by radical groups led to preemptive military takeovers. In Venezuela, as noted, oil wealth has made democratic institutions viable, and in the Cuban case, a series of unique factors resulted in a revolutionary outcome.

The social process in the small countries with relatively small modern sectors (Dominican Republic, Ecuador, Guatemala, Nicaragua, Panama, Bolivia, El Salvador, Haiti, Honduras, and Paraguay) likewise reflects considerable variation, depending on the dynamism of local development and the structure of traditional social controls. The potential for agrarian revolutions in these countries exists if traditional social controls weaken. Such revolutions have occurred in Bolivia and Nicaragua, and one is under way in El Salvador. These upheavals reflect local conditions more than international influences, but too often they are interpreted as being Communist-inspired by officials in the United States and other countries. This interpretation, in turn, can lead and has led to outside intervention that significantly alters local dynamics, usually in the direction of increased violence and a widening of social conflict.

The outcome of rapid social change, high levels of marginality, and shifting class alliances in which no stable majority of social groups can predominate presages continued social conflict and political instability for Latin America. Latin American societies remain, with a few exceptions, confronted by a systemic crisis. The mechanisms of conciliation and coalition that can lead to civil, consensual societies are more distant, after nearly a century of rapid economic and social change, than they seemed to be at the start of the twentieth century.

THE CRISIS OF THE LATIN AMERICAN STATE

The nature of future social change in Latin America will depend in large measure upon the performance of the region's economies, which in turn are highly dependent upon world market conditions. Past economic growth has been remarkable, if uneven through time, and held up surprisingly well during the problematic years of the 1970s. During the 1980s, however, the economies of the region, confronted with mushrooming foreign debts, were plunged into deep crisis.

It can be reasonably assumed that the level of external indebtedness for most Latin American nations is now so high that past rates of borrowing cannot be sustained. Given the size of current account balance-of-payments deficits, a good many Latin American countries are facing severe austerity measures as part of the stabilization programs that international agencies and lenders require of countries that cannot meet their external obligations. Such programs slow investment, cause sharp contractions in economic activity, and lead to a greater degree of orthodoxy in the economic policies of affected nations. The prospects for economic growth in the region are therefore poor for the immediate future, and any recovery will still have to contend with a large overhang of past indebtedness. This posits, of course, that logrolling operations will refinance existing debts to prevent defaults.

Furthermore, world market trends do not seem encouraging for a recovery of prices or demand for Latin America's traditional commodity exports, other than oil, or for the nontraditional exports that have played an important role in recent development policies. Trends toward neoprotectionism are apparent in the OECD countries, and, since the economies of other non-OECD nations are, in general, even worse than those of Latin America, a substantial growth of future Latin American exports to such nations cannot be expected. In summary, it can be concluded that the growth of Latin America's export earnings is likely to be modest at best and that given the region's high debt-service requirements and negative balance-of-payments on current account, the years of rapid economic growth that have characterized Latin America are over at least for the short term and possibly the medium term.

This situation will have the impact of further increasing the income and wealth inequalities that have been such a prominent feature of Latin American development to the present. Although the exact nature of distributional trends in the region is the subject of considerable debate, there is general agreement that the income share of the top 5 percent of Latin Americans is very high in comparison to the experience of other nations, even though in some cases, such as Mexico, the next 15 percent had achieved significant gains by the 1960s. When economic hard times occur, the top 5 percent is generally more efficient in defense of its income share than other groups, as the experience of Argentina indicates. When the state sector in countries like Mexico is economically weakened, middle sectors that have benefited from public policies lose ground. Rising unemployment in consumer-goods and export-manufacturing industries also increases income inequality and exerts downward pressure on the wages of those who remain employed.

If revolutionary and counterrevolutionary approaches to such problems have been discredited, it should be noted also that faith in the efficacy of the institutions of parliamentary or liberal democracy is not high in Latin America. Even if parliamentary democracy is viewed in most quarters as preferable to military dictatorship, the disastrous economic legacy left by departing military regimes is such that newly emerging parliamentary governments are likely to lose much of their initial support once their inability to resume growth and reward popular sectors is discovered.

The exhaustion of such options suggests that the crisis of the Latin American state, which has been so widely predicted for so long, has finally arrived. Although Latin America as a region was able to exhibit impressive economic dynamism earlier in the century, its superstructural institutions were weak from the start and have grown weaker with time. Conflicts between classes, ethnic groups, and sectoral interests—which have been mitigated in developed nations by a rise of popular faith in, or at least popular acceptance of, political institutions and mechanisms of public order—have been exacerbated in Latin America through abuse and abolishment of such institutions.

The search for normative order and civil authority in such a situation can take one of two forms in the absence of a revolutionary alternative, which given the weakness of the industrial working class, the dependency of middle sectors, the fragmentation of the peasantry, and past failures, is not to be found in the larger Latin American nations. The first form is a continued alternation between civilian and military regimes of more or less ad hoc and transitory character until the prospects of world recovery generate renewed growth in Latin America.

The second outcome is suggested by Max Weber's famous analysis of types of authority, which points to charisma as the form of authority that emerges after the demise of traditional and "rational-legal" authority and the failure of repression. Examples of such leadership can be drawn from European experiences in the interwar period. The emergence of charismatic, or Bonapartist, leadership in response to the collapse of other forms of authority also has been common in a variety of Third World and European settings.

This impressionistic assessment of Latin America's situation is premised upon pessimistic assumptions about the economic future of Latin America and its impact upon class relations in the region. Assuming the worst, a disturbing element in the future is likely to be the role played by U.S. foreign policy in response to increased Latin American instability. The ability of the United States to structure the course of Latin American history is limited, but the myth of U.S. hegemony in Latin America seems hardly threatened by a century of policy failures and historical surprises. This myth continues to induce high officials to undertake Quixotic ventures that merely raise the level of conflict.

Real dangers are presented if the United States identifies too closely with any Latin American regime during a period likely to be filled with regime changes, some of which may directly threaten U.S. interests. The foreign policy process in the United States is poorly equipped to confront major problems in Latin America. Among the developed democracies, only in the

United States can heads of state and high cabinet officials enter office ignorant of foreign social and political contingencies. The sheer size of the higher-education establishment in the United States means that no nation boasts as many foreign policy experts, but in few developed countries are such experts as excluded from the policy formation process. Presidents and secretaries of state are tempted to play to the least-common denominator of public opinion or to implement the ideological priorities of a national security apparatus until recently preoccupied with the Soviet threat.

If U.S. policies continue to be premised on an attempt to maintain the status quo in Latin America, they run the risk of undermining popular respect in the United States for institutions of government that implement policies unacceptable to the public. Equally worrisome, such attempts to control the destiny of foreign peoples can predispose U.S. officials to techniques that undercut the consensual bases of American democracy. In short, the crisis of political institutions in Latin America may be met by inappropriate U.S. responses that could result in a crisis of political institutions in the United States.

SUGGESTED READINGS

Collier, David, ed. *The New Authoritarianism in Latin America.* Princeton: Princeton University Press, 1979. This is an excellent group of critical essays devoted to issues raised by the work of Guillermo O'Donnell on the rise of bureaucratic authoritarianism in Latin America.

Ferber, Robert, ed. *Consumption and Income Distribution in Latin America.* Washington, D.C.: Organization of American States, ECIEL Program, 1980. A state-of-the-art collection on social and economic inequalities in Latin America.

Fishlow, Albert. *The Mature Neighbor Policy: A New United States Economic Policy for Latin America.* Berkeley: University of California, Institute of International Studies, n.d. A distinguished economist reviews the history of U.S.–Latin American economic relations and suggests future policies.

Hewlitt, Sylvia Ann, and Richard S. Weinert, eds. *Brazil and Mexico: Patterns in Late Development.* Philadelphia: Institute for the Study of Human Issues, 1982. The essays in this book examine the special characteristics of Brazilian and Mexican development in useful detail.

Malloy, James, ed. *Authoritarianism and Corporatism in Latin America.* Pittsburgh: University of Pittsburgh Press, 1977. Leading specialists examine the roots and modern causes of Latin American dictatorships.

O'Donnell, Guillermo. *Modernization and Bureaucratic-Authoritarianism: Studies in South American Politics.* Politics of Modernization Series no. 9. Berkeley: University of California, Institute of International Studies, 1973. A path-breaking study of the political consequences of social and economic modernization under conditions of delayed development.

Schoultz, Lars. *Human Rights and United States Policy Trends Toward Latin America.* Princeton: Princeton University Press, 1981. This is the definitive study of U.S. policy toward Latin American human rights issues and contains valuable and well-researched information.

Simposio Latinoamericano de industrialización. *El Proceso de industrialización en America Latina.* Santiago, Chile: United Nations Economic Commission for Latin America, 1966. This classic monograph represents the influential perspective of the Economic Commission for Latin America and contains useful comparative and historical information.

PART FIVE
POLITICAL PROCESSES AND TRENDS

11
PARTICIPATION AND POLITICAL PROCESS: THE COLLAPSIBLE PYRAMID

JAN KNIPPERS BLACK

All political systems are systems of limited participation. Even the societies we might call primitive—societies in which essential tasks and rewards are shared more or less equally among families—generally limit participation on the basis of sex and age; that is, women and minors are excluded. Such systems of exclusion may enjoy "legitimacy," or acceptance, even by the excluded, but they are ultimately based on physical prowess. Exclusion in more-complex societies, like the modern nation state, typically follows the lines of class, often reinforced by racial or ethnic divisions. Exclusion may also be based on political ideology.

In the United States, for example, the franchise was generally limited to property-holding white males until the 1830s, when the populist movement headed by Andrew Jackson led to the elimination of property-holding requirements. The franchise was extended to women in 1920 only after years of struggle on the part of the suffragettes. Suffrage for blacks in the South did not become effective until the issue was forced by the civil rights movement, led by Dr. Martin Luther King, in the early 1960s. It was only after university students were mobilized in opposition to the Vietnam War that the voting age was lowered from twenty-one to eighteen. In parts of the country, poor blacks or Hispanics are still turned away from the polls by one device or another.

Furthermore, as suffrage has been extended, the vote, which is only one of many forms of political participation, has become devalued as a consequence of the preponderant role of money in the U.S. electoral system. As campaigns have become outrageously costly media events, the candidate or elected official has become far more attentive to the wishes of major campaign contributors than to those of an amorphous electorate. The low level of voter turnout in the United States suggests, among other things, that a great many eligible voters see campaign promises as hollow and electoral choices as meaningless.

Likewise in Latin America, participation takes many forms, and effective participation is by no means automatic. For all but the wealthiest it must be earned or won, often through protracted struggle and great sacrifice.

INEQUALITY AND
THE BID FOR PARTICIPATION

Most complex, highly stratified social and political systems can be traced to armed conquest, and the national systems of Latin America as we know them today are no exception. The subjugation upon which contemporary social inequality in Latin America is based included not only the conquest and enslavement by Spaniards, Portuguese, and other Europeans of native American populations, but also the kidnapping, by European merchants of flesh, of Africans and their subsequent enslavement in the New World.

The preponderance of brute force thus led to wealth, as the conquistadores acquired land and slaves or serfs and passed them on to their legitimate offspring. Over time, this system of exploitation acquired a measure of legitimacy, as it was moderated and condoned by the religious system imposed by the conquerors. In Latin America as elsewhere, the violent roots of such systems of inequality have been progressively obscured from subsequent generations of the conquered populations, and the myth has been established that differential reward and punishment and limitations of access to wealth and power rest somehow on divine purpose or merit. Those who would challenge that interpretation of the social reality are branded subversive and dealt with accordingly.

Through miscegenation, immigration, and an increase in the categories of tasks to be performed, classes of intermediate social and economic rank— that is, between the masters and the "slaves"—have come into being. It is quite possible, as social and political systems become more complex, for individuals, through accepting the social myth and incorporating the values of the conquering class, to rise above the status of their birth. The masters, however, do not voluntarily relinquish a share of their authority to a lower stratum on the social pyramid. Such a sharing of power across class lines comes about only when organization and the potential for the use of force on the part of a lower social stratum are such that the masters conclude that they must share their wealth and power or risk losing it all.

The concepts of social class and of class struggle bequeathed to us by Karl Marx are crucial to an understanding of the political process in its broadest implications, as the power system and the distribution of wealth and opportunity are interdependent. These concepts are, however, abstractions. Social classes do not compete as such. Individual competitors for political power act through or on behalf of groups, which, in turn, represent more or less limited sectors of society. Such groups may represent one or more social classes, or a sector within a single class. They may act on behalf of one class at one time and on behalf of another at a later date. They may act on behalf of very narrowly construed organizational or institutional interests, which only indirectly impinge upon the class struggle. They may represent interests fundamentally alien to their own societies. Or they may represent a combination of national and foreign, class and institutional interests.

Political parties constitute only one of many categories of group actors in politics. The alignment of groups that participate or seek to participate in political competition in a particular national system depends to a large extent on the level of differentiation, or complexity, of the socioeconomic system. In any system based on marked inequality, those in power will maintain armed bodies (vigilante squads, police, and/or military units) to keep the "have-nots" from going after what the "haves" have and to ensure that the labor force fulfills the role to which it has been assigned.

A ruling class cannot perpetually maintain its position through the use or threat of brute force alone, however. Thus, it will seek to fortify itself by propagating a religion or ideology that sanctions the existing order. The groups or institutions that provide force (e.g., the military) and legitimacy (e.g., the Church), since they are essential to the maintenance of the power position of the ruling class, will soon acquire a measure of power in their own right.

In an international system characterized by colonialism or hegemony (dominance by a foreign power), the ruling class of a colony or client state may be highly dependent on a foreign power. In most of Latin America, the conquering class remained Spanish or Portuguese, protected and legitimized by Spanish or Portuguese troops and clergymen for some 300 years.

Typically, in Latin America, participants in the political system at the time independence was achieved were the *hacendados,* or members of the landowning class; the military; and the Roman Catholic Church. The hegemony that had been exercised by Spain and Portugal during the colonial period was soon assumed by the United States in Mexico, Central America, and the Caribbean and by Great Britain (with lesser participation by other European powers) in South America. The United States gave strong competition to the British and other European powers in South America during the first half of the twentieth century and, by the end of World War II, had consolidated its position of dominance over the whole of Latin America.

The pace and order of the admission of new groups and classes to political participation have varied from country to country, having proceeded most rapidly in the Southern Cone countries and most slowly in the Andean and Central American highlands. In general, a commercial sector, associated with export-import operations, was admitted during the last half of the nineteenth century, and industrial elites and middle classes began participating in the first decades of the twentieth century. By the 1920s and 1930s, labor was organizing and making its bid, but in few countries was it admitted to participation before the 1940s and 1950s. The admission of peasants, by nonrevolutionary means, was scarcely even at issue until the 1960s, and it was not until 1979 in Ecuador and 1980 in Peru that new constitutions gave illiterates—that is, the Indian peasants—the vote for the first time in those countries. Peasant participation has been rare and tenuous, and the peasants' gains, like those of organized labor, were reversed in several countries in the 1960s and 1970s through counterrevolution. In politics, there is no "final analysis"; as far as we know, participation and its perquisites may be won and lost and won again ad infinitum.

POLITICAL ACTORS AND ARENAS

The means of seeking entry into, or control of, a political system depends upon the strengths of the particular group, or political actor, and the openness of the system. In general, however, elections and other processes associated with the democratic system become available to groups previously excluded only *after* they have become organized and have demonstrated, through illegal or extralegal means, their ability to disrupt the system and to threaten seriously the interests of the power elite. Furthermore, as Charles Anderson has noted, election results are by no means considered sacred by all participants; elections are but one of the many means of garnering and demonstrating power.[1]

Anderson has pointed out that there are certain resources, or "power capabilities," without which governments would find it difficult or even impossible to function. These resources include, for example, a cooperative labor force, agricultural or industrial production, control over the use of armed force, moral sanction, popular support, and the support of a dominant foreign power. In order to secure participation in or control over the political process, political groups, or "power contenders," must demonstrate control of a power capability.

In most contemporary Latin American countries, these power contenders would include landowners, industrial and commercial elites, religious leaders, military factions, labor unions, political parties, students and intellectual leaders, foreign corporations, and agencies of foreign governments. In distinguishing between power contenders and power capabilities, Anderson notes that within the military establishment, the business community, the labor movement, or even the Catholic Church, there are generally various factions seeking to speak for the institution or the community. (One might add that even agencies of the U.S. government have been seen marching to different drummers. Civilian politicians in several countries have found, to their dismay, that the support of the U.S. ambassador did not assure the support of the Pentagon and the CIA as well.) In order to be "taken into account" by those groups that are already participants in the system, a new power contender must flex its muscles. A military faction might demonstrate control of a power capability without firing a shot by establishing a credible claim to the loyalty of a few important garrisons. A labor federation might demonstrate such control by calling a successful general strike; a peasant group, by seizing a significant amount of land; a student group, by amassing a large turnout for a march; a political party, by receiving a sizable vote. Traditional participants, feeling threatened, might in turn demonstrate their own capabilities; disinvestment and capital flight are among the many ways economic elites may respond to threat.

When a new power contender demonstrates its capabilities, the power elite must decide whether the greater risk lies in admitting the new group to participation in the system or in attempting to suppress it. The new group may be admitted if the risk of suppression appears to be as great as the risk of recognition, and if groups that are already participating believe that the new group will be willing to abide by the rules of the game—that is, to respect the perquisites of the other players. Thus, what Anderson calls the normal rule of Latin American political change, and what we shall call the defining principle of the evolutionary process, is that new power contenders may be added to the system but old ones may not be eliminated.

Political conflict, as Martin C. Needler notes, takes place simultaneously in various "arenas," differing in accessibility to social groups, in methods or "weapons" of competition, and in visibility to the public.[2] In the least-developed political systems, the dominant arena is the private one, where family pressures, personal contacts, bribery, blackmail, and graft determine the outcome of political conflict. In the most highly developed polities, decisions are reached through popular election, parliamentary debate, and judicial review. Between the development levels of court intrigue and constitutional mediation of conflict is a level in which conflict takes place in the streets—in which demonstrations, strikes, and riots determine the outcome of the conflict.

Merging the models of Needler and Anderson, we might say that the "street arena" holds sway while the political elite is unwilling to admit new participants to the system but unable to repress them fully. It might be added that the street arena is employed not only by nonelites on the way up but by elites who fear that they are on the way down. When elites in a more highly developed constitutional system begin to feel that their interests are threatened by electoral and other constitutional processes, they will use the street arena—the provocation of highly visible "instability"—along with other arenas in preparing the way for counterrevolution.

SOCIAL CHANGE AND POLITICAL PROCESS

What factors, then, determine when and how participation will be won or lost by various groups and classes of Latin American societies? Many of the factors that contribute to pressure for social change fall into the category Karl Deutsch has labeled "social mobilization"—that is, urbanization, education, and mass communication and the consequent "revolution of rising expectations."[3] The transistor radio has been called the greatest force for change in the twentieth century.

The circulation of new ideas or ideologies imported from other societies (Liberalism at the turn of the nineteenth century, Marxism at the turn of the twentieth) or revived from earlier eras of preconquest or national experience (Mexican and Andean *indigenismo* or "nativism," Nicaraguan *sandinismo*) may give momentum and a sense of direction to otherwise sporadic or

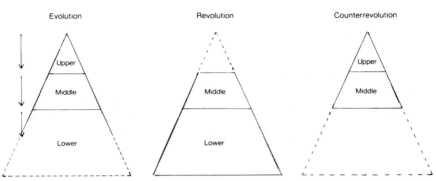

Figure 11.1. Political Participation by Social Strata: The Collapsible Pyramid Model

unfocused social unrest. Likewise, hope may be aroused and organization promoted by the appearance of agents of change. These agents may be foreigners who literally "appear" with new ideas and ambitions, such as labor leaders who immigrated from Europe at the turn of the century or representatives of foreign or international development agencies who have descended on Latin America since the 1960s. Or they may be Latin Americans associated with new institutions or with old institutions that are assuming new roles. Students, for example, became agents of change after national universities came into being in the early twentieth century, and Catholic clergymen and nuns, inspired by Liberation Theology, became powerful agents of change in the 1970s and 1980s. Pressure for change may also be generated by natural or man-made disasters, such as earthquakes or wars, by an abrupt downturn in the economy, or by a particularly greedy or brutal move on the part of the ruling classes—a paranoid overreaction, for example, to some minor incident of protest or insubordination.

The factors that contribute to pressure for social change do not, however, in themselves predetermine what the nature of that change will be. The nature of the change that comes in response to social mobilization is a product of the interaction of the forces of change and the forces of resistance. If the political elite is willing and able to share power, incorporating new groups into the polity, change will follow the evolutionary pattern. If the elite is unwilling to share, determined instead to repress would-be participants, change may take the form of revolution, of counterrevolution, or of a holding operation (indecisive cycles of insurrection and repression) we shall call "boundary maintenance." The outcome will depend largely upon the relative strength, unity, and determination of the opposing forces.

Thus, the major political processes that may flow from social change or pressure for additional social change will be labeled, for the purposes of a model that we shall call "the collapsible pyramid," as evolution, revolution, and counterrevolution (Figure 11.1). Political evolution implies the incorporation of new political actors, representing previously unrepresented social strata, without the displacement of previous participants in the system. Revolution is defined as the displacement or disestablishment of groups representing one or more strata from the upper reaches of the social pyramid. Our definition of counterrevolution is implied in that of revolution. It is the displacement, or elimination from effective participation, of groups representing strata from the base of the social pyramid.

EVOLUTION

The experiences of Latin American countries suggest that limitations on a client state's links to the dominant foreign power and racial or ethnic homogeneity are among the factors that make it more likely that change will follow the evolutionary pattern. Each of these two factors has independent explanatory power, but in Latin America, the two are also related historically.

Limitations on colonial or neocolonial control may be a consequence of, among other things, physical distance, competition among prospective hegemonic powers, or the relative absence of strategic or material assets. The political significance of such limitations is that, unable to rely on the backing of the dominant foreign power, the political elite may find it necessary to come to terms with new groups seeking participation. The first Latin American states in which the middle class, and to a lesser extent the working class, gained access to political power were those of the Southern Cone—Argentina, Uruguay, and, somewhat later, Chile. This area, which offered neither the gold and silver nor the exploitable Indian civilizations of the Andean and Middle American highlands, was of little interest to the Spanish crown. The Rio de la Plata Basin was among the last areas of the New World to be settled by Europeans and among the first to declare and win independence.

Relative to the rigid hierarchical systems of Mexico, Peru, and other early centers of royal domination, the social systems of the Southern Cone were loosely stratified, and their political systems were fluid. The nomadic Indians of the pampas were gradually exterminated, while those across the Andes in Chile—fewer than 100,000 in the late nineteenth century—were confined on reservations. Most of the African captives who were delivered to the Rio de la Plata Basin were subsequently transshipped north to zones where plantations were dominant. Argentina and Uruguay, predominantly mestizo at the time of independence, became overwhelmingly European as a consequence of large-scale immigration in the late nineteenth century. Chile's predominantly mestizo population was also relatively homogeneous. Thus, the social distance to be bridged in those countries in the incorporation of new groups into the polity was not nearly so great as in the countries of predominant Indian population, presided over by a tiny Hispanic elite.

From the late colonial period until the end of World War II, the Southern Cone countries were subjects of competition among hegemonic powers. Great Britain had competed very successfully with Spain for dominance in matters of trade even before the struggle for independence was undertaken. Britain then remained the dominant, though not unchallenged, foreign power in the area until World War II. The rise of the middle classes and the beginnings of labor organization occurred long before the United States acquired dominance over the area.

Other areas that have experienced evolutionary change have displayed some of the same characteristics. Venezuela and Costa Rica, for example, had sparse native American populations and were of little interest to the Spanish. Both have relatively homogeneous populations. Both were among the last areas to be settled by Europeans, and Venezuela, along with Argentina, was one of the first settlement areas to develop important trade ties with Britain and to rise in revolt against Spain. Political participation in Venezuela since 1958 has also been facilitated by oil wealth. Representative government has been the rule rather than the exception in Costa Rica since the 1880s. In abolishing its army in 1948, Costa Rica eliminated a major threat to participation.[4]

The bid of the middle classes for participation has generally come about in conjunction with urbanization and the expansion of national institutions and government services. Spearheaded by merchants, bureaucrats, or students and intellectuals, middle-class movements have often led to the organization of new parties advocating social reform and appealing to incipient labor organizations. Victory at the ballot box, however, has generally been the confirmation, rather than the means, of middle-class ascent. The strength of the movement or party has had to be demonstrated first in the street arena, and its initial assumption of power has often been assisted by "young Turks" within the military.

As middle-class parties have generally needed the support of organized labor, and to a lesser extent of peasants, in order to confront the traditional political elite, the assumption of power by such parties has meant at least limited participation for the working classes as well—participation expressed, for example, in the right of collective bargaining as well as in the vote. Working-class groups may also be admitted prematurely to the political system, before their capabilities for disruption are fully developed, through the initiatives of one sector of the political elite that is seeking to enhance its position over another or by power holders seeking to maintain some degree of control over the development of labor's capabilities. Brazilian *caudillo* Getúlio Vargas cultivated labor as a counterpoise to the economic elite, but he kept it under the firm control of the labor ministry. In Colombia, the preemptive admission of organized labor and its incorporation into the pyramidal structures of the traditional parties delayed labor organization along horizontal lines of class interest.

The redistribution of power implied in the evolutionary process should be reflected in the long term in a redistribution of goods and services toward the newly participant groups. But this does not necessarily imply a redistribution toward all disadvantaged classes. For example, the economic position of a participating organized labor force may be enhanced while that of unorganized peasants or of unemployed and underemployed urban workers deteriorates. In the case of Venezuela, the middle-class parties gained admittance to the system by incorporating the strength of organized labor into their own. Nevertheless, while organized labor has reaped the benefits of political participation, there is a large and growing class of unorganized poor in Venezuela for whom the resultant inflation has only made things worse.

Effective working-class participation and thoroughgoing redistribution have been known to come about, even in Latin America, through the evolutionary process. In the early twentieth century, Uruguay, without suffering the devastation of social revolution, came to enjoy one of the most fully democratic systems and most highly developed welfare states in the world. In 1973, however, Uruguay's social and political advantages were erased by a brutal counterrevolution that brought the military to power until 1984.

While economies were expanding (in Uruguay, for example, from early to mid-twentieth century), the demands of newly participant social strata, such as urban labor, could be met without undue threat to the perquisites of traditional elites and middle classes; a concession to one pressure group was not necessarily at the expense of another. Moreover, the illusion of economic expansion could be maintained for a while by artificial means such as inflation or foreign borrowing. But when economies began to decline, the upper and middle classes came to fear that the gains of labor could only be at their expense. Moreover, in highly dependent economies, like those of Latin America, foreign businesses that feel threatened may appeal to their home governments and to public and private lending institutions to initiate measures, such as credit freezes and trade embargoes, that damage all economic interests in the client state.

Thus, the economic elites, both foreign and domestic, with substantial middle-class support, backed by the dominant foreign power and fronted for by the armed forces, move to silence lower-class demands and to regain control of the processes whereby wealth and power are allocated. Such has been the fate of Brazil and the Southern Cone.

Costa Rica and Venezuela, the countries that most successfully maintained their evolutionary systems through the 1970s, were blessed with relatively healthy economies. But Costa Rica's economy, disabled by a drop in coffee prices, took a nose dive in the early 1980s. That country's democratic system was made more vulnerable by the efforts of the Reagan administration to transform its nonprofessional civil guard into a professional military establishment. After an interlude of nationalistic assertiveness under the presidency of Oscar Arias Sanchez (1986–1990) of the National Liberation Party (PLN), Costa Rica, on February 3, 1990, elected an opposition candidate, Rafael Calderon Fournier of the conservative Social Christian Unity coalition; his campaign was funded in part by the U.S. government.

Petrodollars have freed the Venezuelan government to meet the most urgent demands of lower and middle classes without seriously taxing the rich. But petroleum wealth has not been converted into agricultural development and industrial diversification fast enough to alleviate the effects of oil-induced inflation and to bridge the gap between rich and poor. Rather, the oil bonanza has served, for the most part, to bloat the bureaucracy. The experiences of Brazil and the Southern Cone countries suggest that a large middle class with acquired tastes, dependent on government itself, can swiftly turn reactionary when the economic pie begins to shrink. The global oil glut of the 1980s, coupled with the foreign debt and the austerity measures imposed by creditors have brought social tensions closer to the surface. Those tensions erupted in early 1989 in a popular rampage that left more than 300 dead and demonstrated the fragility of Venezuela's democracy.

REVOLUTION

The displacement of a social stratum through revolution does not necessarily mean the physical elimination of individuals or the blocking of their participation, as individuals, in the political system. Rather, it means the removal of the resources (material or institutional) that have enabled them to exercise power as a class.

The revolutionary process is likely to involve violence both in the initial phase of insurgency and repression and in the secondary phase of struggle among insurgent groups. If the redistributional phase is delayed, renewed violence is likely to accompany that phase as well. But politics is the process whereby power relationships are established, so violence—or the threat of it—is implicit in all political processes. The violence accompanying revolution is not necessarily greater than that which accompanies other political processes.

The Cuban Revolution claimed several thousand lives, but considerably fewer than the Chilean counterrevolution, which claimed some 10,000 to 30,000. About 50,000 people were killed in the course of the Nicaraguan Revolution, and another 30,000 or so have been killed in postrevolutionary struggles against the U.S.-sponsored "Contras," or counterrevolutionary forces, but an even greater number of Guatemalans have been killed, mainly by vigilantes and official security forces, in the "boundary-maintenance" effort— the effort, essentially, to keep the Indians "in their place"—that has characterized Guatemalan politics since 1954. The Colombian *violencia,* suggestive of the pattern whereby elites maintain their position while nonelites fight only among themselves, claimed more than 200,000 lives over more than a decade (mainly 1948–1958) of sporadic, nonpurposeful fighting. Revolution is only one—and perhaps the least likely—of many possible outcomes of violent confrontation.

The term "revolution" has been used very loosely, especially since the success of the Cuban Revolution in 1959 spread hope or fear, depending on one's point of view, throughout the Americas. It has been used as a synonym for violence, for social change or for regime change; it has even been appropriated by rightist military rulers, like those who seized the Brazilian government in 1964, in vain attempts to legitimize their own counterrevolutions. In fact, however, successful revolutions are most rare.

In the Western Hemisphere, the only society to dismantle an entire ruling class (the French planters) in the process of ousting the colonial power was in Haiti. Haiti was not only the first Latin American country to gain independence (1804) and to undergo a successful revolution, but the first state in the modern world to be born of a slave revolt.

The other Latin American countries that have experienced successful revolutions are Mexico (1911), Bolivia (1952), Cuba (1959), and Nicaragua (1979). Insurrectionary forces showed great strength in El Salvador in the 1980s and remarkable tenacity, at least, in Guatemala, but counterrevolutionary forces, backed by the United States, also remained strong, as conflict surged and ebbed and surged again without resolution (see Chapter 19).

Facilitating Factors

Reams have been written on the causes of revolution in Latin America. Most of the causal factors cited fall into the category we have labeled "social mobilization." Such factors may rightly be viewed as causing pressure for political change, but they do not in themselves cause violent revolution. A necessary, though not sufficient, cause of violent revolution is the violent arrest of the nonviolent pursuit of change—that is, the blocking of the evolutionary process.

Factors that have facilitated or contributed to the perpetual blockage of the evolutionary process, and thus to the maintenance of a very low level of political participation, have included great social distance between elites and masses and proximity to the hegemonic power. The importance of the social distance factor lies in part in paranoia. The small elites of European origin who preside over a different racial group with an alien culture tend to feel exceedingly vulnerable and to fear that the slightest break in the traditional system of authority will unleash the contained wrath of centuries. Rather than welcoming the development of an incipient middle class that might serve a brokerage role and accepting the marginal political changes that might allow "things to go on as they are," the elites systematically eradicate would-be political brokers and strive to maintain a vacuum in the political center. This pattern has been particularly clear in recent decades in El Salvador and Guatemala.

The significance of close ties between dominant and client states has several facets. The most obvious is that, bulwarked by the might of the colonial or hegemonic power, colonial or client-state oligarchies are under little pressure to offer incremental concessions to middle or lower classes. But, as previously noted, there is also a historical connection between the factors of social distance and external control. European civilization in the New World was built quite literally on the ruins of Indian ones, and figuratively on the backs of Indians and transplanted Africans; so it is not coincidental that the areas of earliest and deepest penetration by the colonial powers are also the areas of least racial homogeneity and greatest social distance. Those are also the areas in which landed aristocracies, with the long-term backing of colonial military, religious, and bureaucratic authority, became most firmly entrenched.

Furthermore, even after routing the Spanish, the supposedly free states of Middle America and the Caribbean had little respite from foreign domination. After seizing half of Mexico's territory, the United States, devastated by its own Civil War, had to suffer competition from the French in Mexico and from the British in Central America in the latter half of the nineteenth century—but by the turn of the twentieth century, U.S. control over that area was virtually complete. In the Dominican Republic, Hispanic elites, frightened by Haiti's successful slave revolt and a subsequent period of Haitian occupation of their end of the island, scrambled to exchange national sovereignty for security under the flag of some stronger country. They succeeded in persuading the Spanish to return for a brief sojourn. Cuba, after the Spanish American War, merely exchanged one foreign master for another.

Thus, there was rarely a time when middle-class pretenders, sporting reformist ideas, could pose a credible threat to ruling aristocracies. As major U.S. corporations became an integral part of the power elite of those countries, the U.S. government made it clear that it would intervene militarily, if necessary, to protect the economic order from the greed and depredations of hungry natives. In fact, the United States did intervene extensively in the area and established constabularies in several countries that, in time, replaced the original landholding oligarchy at the pinnacle of power.

Finally, the greater the economic and political dominance or penetration of a foreign power, the fewer will be the nationals with a major stake in the old order. By the mid-twentieth century, the extent of U.S. economic holdings in much of Middle America and the Caribbean, and the fact that ruling constabularies answered to the United States rather than to any sector of local society, meant that relatively few families had extensive economic interests to protect and fewer still had a stake in the political order. Furthermore, the crudeness of U.S. power plays enhanced the importance of nationalism as a unifying theme. All of these factors facilitated the construction of a multiclass alliance in opposition to the ruling groups, particularly in Cuba and Nicaragua and to varying extents in Mexico, Guatemala, and the Dominican Republic. In the last two countries, reformist, potentially revolutionary, movements were crushed in 1954 and 1965, respectively, by U.S. military intervention.

Another social phenomenon that has correlated with insurgency and, in some cases, with successful revolution in Latin America has been the physical uprooting of subject populations. In the case of the Chaco War between Bolivia and Paraguay (1932–1935), peasants on both sides of the border, mobilized for the war, were not prepared to be demobilized when the fighting was over. In Paraguay, they contributed to the rise of a new party, which seized power in 1936. In Bolivia, they organized other Indian peasants, who ultimately seized the land and disestablished the Hispanic landholding aristocracy.

Throughout Middle America in the late nineteenth and early twentieth centuries, Indians were driven from their traditional communally held lands by Hispanic planters or U.S. corporations intent upon cashing in on the expanding market for export crops, particularly coffee. Many of the peasant uprisings of the period, including that led by Zapata in Mexico, represented efforts to take back land that had been seized.

In Central America, the cycle of planter encroachment, peasant uprising, and government reprisal that gave rise, for example, to El Salvador's notorious *matanza* of 1932—the massacre of some 30,000 Indian peasants—has continued up to the present. The creeping uprootedness of Salvadorans was exacerbated suddenly in 1969 when the Soccer War, fought against Honduras, resulted in the displacement of some 300,000 Salvadoran peasants who had settled on uncrowded land across the Honduran border. These peasants were thrust back upon a rural society in which a majority of the peasants were already landless migrants in desperate competition for seasonal labor at meager wages. In northern Guatemala, the pace of seizure of Indian land by non-Indians was accelerated in the 1970s as a consequence of the discovery of oil in the region.

The Phases of Revolution

The phases of a successful revolution that runs its full course—that is, without falling prey to counterrevolution—might be described as (1) power transfer, (2) redistribution, (3) institutionalization, and (4) reconcentration.

Power Transfer. The political, or power transfer, phase is a twofold one, comprising the toppling of the offending regime and the consolidation of the new power structure. The first step of a revolution, the displacement of the old regime, calls for the launching of insurrectionary movements on different social levels, either independently or in coalition. Intra-elite political conflict is not, in itself, revolutionary. On the other hand, uprisings of workers or peasants stand little chance of success unless there are important pockets of alienation in the middle class as well or unless the ruling class is sharply divided.

The dethroning, however, is only the beginning of the reallocation of political power. The affluent and the indigent, who might agree on the kind of government they do not want, cannot be expected to agree on the kind they want in its place. The struggle then continues within the coalition itself. As has often been noted, revolutions consume many of their authors.

In Mexico, after the demise of the dictatorship of Porfirio Díaz in 1911, armed struggle continued intermittently for another ten years; yet another decade was to pass before power was consolidated in a predominantly middle-class party representing predominantly middle-class interests. In Bolivia, the middle-class party, the National Revolutionary Movement (MNR), which took power in 1952, chose to embrace the rampaging Indian peasants rather than to attempt to suppress them. Nevertheless, the brevity of the tenure of the Bolivian Revolution may be attributed in part to the facts that the competing interests of the three elements of the revolutionary triad—the MNR, the miners, and the peasants—were never reconciled and that no element of the triad was able to gain control over the others.

In the Cuban case, the consolidation of power in the hands of Castro and his rebel army, who favored, in particular, the rural poor, was facilitated by the mass exodus of middle- and upper-class Cubans to the United States. In Nicaragua, the multiclass coalition that strained to project unity when Somoza fled with the national treasury in 1979 began to unravel within the year. Anti-Somoza businessmen, overwhelmed in their bid for power by the workers and peasants mobilized in support of the Sandinistas, turned to subversion in league with exiled National Guardsmen and the U.S. government.

Class Demolition and Redistribution. The fate of the various upper-level social strata, and the organizations and institutions representing them in political competition, in the aftermath of revolution has varied greatly from country to country. In general, however, a successful revolution requires the displacement of the colonial or hegemonic power that has backed the ruling elite and underwritten the old order. Such displacement does not imply that the external power is stripped of influence over the client state; rather, it means that that power is deprived of some of its prerevolutionary points of access or of its means of participating directly and overtly in domestic power struggles and policymaking. (It is not uncommon, for example, in Latin American countries that have not undergone revolution, for U.S. officials to exercise a veto over presidential candidacies or cabinet appointments.)

In the case of Haiti, the colonial power and the landowning aristocracy were one and the same. French officials and planters were expelled (or killed) in the course of the fighting, along with the military and religious institutions that protected and legitimized the rejected social order. Fifty years were to pass before Catholic priests again appeared on the scene.

In the Mexican case, the Revolution disestablished the landowning aristocracy and the Church, which, until the reforms of the late 1860s, had itself been a major landowner. The Revolution also displaced that sector of the business elite whose wealth and power were based on export-import operations and other external ties and weakened the role of the United States in the manipulation of domestic power relationships. The national industrial sector was not a casualty of the Revolution, but rather a product of it; that sector was nurtured by the strengthened postrevolutionary state while the state itself began to fill the vacuum left by the displacement of foreign business interests from infrastructure (e.g., transportation and utilities) and the primary production sector.

Bolivia's landowning aristocracy was displaced in 1952 along with the private interests controlling the country's major industry, the tin mines. The Church, which had never been strong in Bolivia, was relatively unaffected, but the military officer corps was purged of the protectors of the prerevolutionary order. Although the United States had previously sought to suppress the MNR, that country had little visibility in Bolivia and thus was not a major target of the revolutionary process. Consequently, the new MNR government accepted U.S. economic and military assistance under conditions that contributed to the disintegration of the revolutionary coalition, the nurturing of a new military elite, and, ultimately, to counterrevolution. Hernán Siles Suazo, president from 1956 to 1960, commenting later on the strings attached to U.S. assistance, said that the United States had given him just enough rope to hang himself.

Prerevolutionary Cuba was so thoroughly penetrated by U.S. businesses that its patriarchal landholding elite and its nationally oriented industrialist class were relatively small and weak. Thus, the most important displacements of the revolution were those of the hegemonic power (the United States) and the military establishment that served it and of the businesses based in or linked to the United States. Ultimately, however, almost all owners of income-producing property were deprived, as the economy was thoroughly socialized.

The initial targets of the Nicaraguan Revolution were the Somocistas—that is, the dictator, his relatives and cronies, and the National Guard that propped up the Somoza dynasty on the local level—and the United States, which had been the ultimate benefactor and protector of the dynasty. The removal of the Somocistas provided the first fruits of victory for the purpose of redistribution. The economic squeeze imposed by the United States and the counterrevolutionary stance adopted by much of the remaining commercial elite led to some additional nationalizations. Nevertheless, some 60 percent of the economy remained in private hands.

The role of the Catholic Church in the Nicaraguan Revolution represents a first. Whereas in revolutions past the stance of the Church had ranged from moderate opposition to outright hostility to insurrectionary groups and revolutionary goals, the Nicaraguan Church was among the most potent and committed elements of the revolutionary coalition. In the aftermath of the Revolution, however, while most parish-level priests and nuns continued to support the Sandinista leadership, the bishops withdrew their support or made it highly conditional.

Just as there has been considerable variation in the extent of displacement and deprivation suffered by the upper classes in the aftermath of revolution, there has been great variation in the extent of redistribution of wealth and power and in the actual benefits reaped by lower social strata. The revolutionary process may be a protracted one. In the case of the Mexican Revolution, the constitution that set forth the principles of the new social order did not appear until six years after the overthrow of Porfirio Díaz in 1911, and the participation of workers and peasants was not reflected in significant redistribution until the 1920s, under the presidency of Alvaro Obregón. It was not until the administration of Lázaro Cárdenas (1934–1940) that the most far-reaching redistribution was undertaken. During that period, some 20 million hectares (49 million acres) of land were distributed to peasant communities (*ejidos*), workers' rights were expanded and wages raised, and the very important petroleum industry was nationalized.

The extent of redistribution, and thus the success of a revolution, depends, in large part, on how much wealth there is to redistribute. Cuba, at the time of its Revolution, was a relatively prosperous country as measured in GDP or per capita income. Redistribution took the form, primarily, of the extension of services, and within a few years, Cuba's public health and educational systems were among the most comprehensive in the hemisphere. In Bolivia and Nicaragua, by contrast, there was relatively little wealth to redistribute. Haiti, where prerevolutionary wealth evaporated with the abolition of slavery, presents the starkest proof that successful revolution does not necessarily mean living happily ever after.

Institutionalization. The process of institutionalizing a revolution includes the creation of an entirely new set of political support groups as well as new constitutions, laws, and behavior patterns. The process is complete when a mechanism for regulating succession to power is functioning more or less smoothly. The most important umbrella organization for the new support groups is usually a political party. The Mexican revolutionary party took shape in 1929. It was reorganized in the 1930s and again in the 1940s, when it was renamed the Institutional Revolutionary Party (PRI) and acquired its current configuration, comprising agrarian, labor, and popular sectors. The popular sector, by far the strongest, is a catchall, dominated by bureaucrats and other middle-class elements. Presidential elections take place every six years, and the revolutionary party has never acknowledged defeat, though the 1988 margin was the closest ever.

The institutionalizing vehicle of the Bolivian Revolution was to have been the MNR. The MNR's first president, Victor Paz Estenssoro, attributed the survival of the Revolution in its early years to the creation of armed peasant militias.[5] But the party did not succeed in fully incorporating or co-opting the miners or in institutionalizing succession by prohibiting reelection; thus, the uninstitutionalized Revolution succumbed, within twelve years, to counterrevolution.

In the Cuban case, the dominant vehicles of institutionalization on the national level have been the Communist Party and the Revolutionary Armed Forces. However, the levers of power in both organizations have remained in the hands of Castro and his rebels of the Sierra Maestra campaign. The national political superstructure is built upon an extensive base of popular organizations. Although the mechanisms for succession at the pinnacle of power remain untested, local representation has been regulated by direct election since 1975. Most administrative posts have been filled since the mid-1970s by individuals noted less for their vision than for their training and experience.

In Nicaragua, the Sandinista National Liberation Front (FSLN), which began in 1959 as a tiny insurrectionary group composed largely of university students, was already in a clearly dominant position at the time of the triumph of the revolution. Groups mobilized for fighting Somoza and his National Guard were quickly expanded and converted into vehicles for reconstruction and political support. Prerevolutionary political parties continued to operate after the Revolution, but without numerical significance. The Sandinista leadership enjoyed a strong base of support in the several hundred thousand members of popular organizations representing workers, peasants, women, youth, and other categories of loyalists.

In the first elections of the postrevolutionary period, in November 1984, the Sandinistas won 67 percent of the vote. Under pressure from the United States, a coalition of prerevolutionary parties and factions withdrew from the race; but several other small parties participated and claimed seats in the National Assembly. Elections were held again in February 1990. This time, after a decade of suffering economic strangulation and proxy war mounted by the United States, the Sandinistas succumbed to defeat. The National Opposition Union (UNO), a U.S.-funded coalition of fourteen organizations, won about 55 percent of the vote. The Sandinistas, nevertheless, remained by far the largest party in the National Assembly, and if constitutional procedure prevails, they should be able to block any all-out assault on revolutionary institutions and policies.

Reconcentration. Thomas Jefferson once quipped that every country needs a revolution every twenty years. There is no "happily ever after" in politics. Revolutions, like other secular readjustments of power relationships, are impermanent. Wealth and power tend to reconcentrate.

Reconcentration is akin to evolution in reverse. It refers to a gradual weakening of the power and income positions of political participants from the lower echelons of the social pyramid. If a revolution is not subsequently undermined by counterrevolution, a period of reconcentration may be expected to follow the institutionalization of the revolution.

Revolutionary leaders may themselves become a "new class"—an economic as well as a power elite, as happened in Mexico. Or the new class may derive from the bureaucrats who inherit power when the revolutionary generation passes from the scene. In the Cuban case, although Castro and his rebel cohorts have conspicuously avoided the material trappings of elite status, rank differentiation, with accompanying privileges, has already crept into what was once a "people's" army.

Nevertheless, countries that have undergone successful revolutions tend to be far more stable than those in which progressive movements have been thwarted. And countries in which revolutions have been aborted, or reversed by counterrevolution, are the least stable of all. The redistribution that generally takes place within the first few years following the consolidation of a revolution gives most citizens a stake in the new government. That loyalty is likely to last at least for a couple of decades, until the passing of the revolutionary generation, and may, in fact, last long after the redistributional phase has given way to the reconcentration of wealth and power in a new class. On the other hand, where reform has been thwarted or revolution aborted, a vicious cycle of insurgency and repression generally sets in, a cycle that likewise may last for several decades.

COUNTERREVOLUTION

Counterrevolution has been defined, for the purposes of this model, as the displacement of one or more strata of political participants from the base of the social pyramid. It may take place in response to an incomplete revolution or to rational or irrational fear of revolution. But it may reflect simply the recognition by economic elites that the logical long-term consequence of a political process that allows for the effective participation of nonelites will be redistribution of wealth as well as of power. In fact, since counterrevolution requires a military and paramilitary establishment at the service of an elite and/or of foreign interests, it is more likely to take place in countries in which political development has been evolutionary than in countries that have undergone successful revolution. It is precisely because the power bases of the economic elites and the connections of those elites with the military and the dominant foreign power have remained intact that a minority is able to override the apparent will of the majority—as imperfectly expressed, for example, in elections—and reverse the tide of redistribution. (The crushing of a political order through direct foreign occupation is not encompassed in this concept of counterrevolution.)

Although dictatorship has been the rule rather than the exception in the history of most Latin American countries, counterrevolution, as such, is largely a phenomenon of the latter half of the twentieth century; in earlier eras, there were rarely "participant" lower classes to be displaced. Among the first clear cases of counterrevolution was the overthrow of Guatemala's President Jacobo Arbenz in 1954, followed by the withdrawal of rights recently won by labor and the recovery by non-Indian *hacendados* of land that had been distributed to Indian peasants. Both Brazil and Bolivia underwent counterrevolution beginning in 1964, as did Chile and Uruguay in 1973. Argentina has experienced counterrevolutionary episodes periodically since 1930, the most dramatic having been those accompanying the military coups of 1966 and 1976.

Facilitating Factors

Deterioration of an economy, expressed particularly by runaway inflation, is among the most obvious factors that contribute to counterrevolution. In the face of a shrinking economic pie, middle-class elements, generally dependent and insecure, begin to see the demands of the working classes as a threat to their own precarious positions. Thus, a major portion of the middle class aligns itself with the upper classes in a bid to reverse the trend toward redistribution. If economic decline is accompanied by considerable popular agitation and/or scare propaganda, upper and middle classes may become convinced that revolution is in the offing or that "communism" is somehow responsible for national problems and social unrest.

Since the proponents of counterrevolution are a minority element of the population (were they not in a minority, their interests would not be threatened by democratic processes), counterrevolution can only be successful if that minority can rely upon military and paramilitary forces that are alienated from the majority of the population. Furthermore, as the military role is central, the ultimate provocation leading to the overthrow of a reformist president and his replacement by a military government—typically, the first overt step of a counterrevolution—is often a threat to the military itself: rank and file insubordination, a military budget cut, or a threat of suspension of foreign military aid.

Even so, national economic elites and military establishments are not likely to undertake counterrevolution unless they can rely upon the help, or, at the very least, the benign neutrality, of the dominant foreign power. With the possible exception of some of Argentina's counterrevolutionary episodes, all successful counterrevolutions in Latin America since the middle of the twentieth century have had the direct or indirect support of the United States. In some cases, economic deterioration, military alienation, middle-class fear, and other facilitating factors have been intentionally exacerbated by the actions of U.S. government agencies. The complicity of the United States was particularly apparent in the Guatemalan, Brazilian, and Chilean cases.

The Phases of Counterrevolution

The initial phases of counterrevolution are related to those of revolution in that the struggle between proponents and opponents of counterrevolution is immediately followed by struggle among the counterrevolutionary conspirators themselves. Counterrevolution, like revolution, calls for a multiclass alliance—in this case, of upper and middle classes. It also requires a coalition of military and civilian elements. Even within the military, there are various factions with differing perspectives and objectives. In the Chilean case, the counterrevolution began with a bloody purge of the military itself.

The initial agreement among military conspirators to topple the incumbent president and to assume power in the name of the armed forces by no means assures agreement on longer-term objectives. Thus, simultaneously with the process of demobilizing the nonelites—the disarming of opponents in the street and constitutional arenas—the conspirators engage in fierce competition among themselves in the private arena. In general, power is first consolidated in the hands of the military faction favored by the dominant foreign power, though rivalry within the military is perpetual and the balance of power among factions may shift over time. Meanwhile, civilian parties and political leaders who expected to profit from the demise of their civilian opponents soon find themselves stripped of their power bases and vulnerable to the whims of the new military authorities.

Political Demobilization. The most immediate and dramatic manifestations of counterrevolution are political. The street arena is the first to be closed down. Labor, peasants, and student leaders, for example, are killed or arrested, and their organizations are dissolved or "intervened" (taken over) by the new government. The constitutional arena is the next victim. Congress is dissolved or its less malleable members are purged. Courts and local governments are purged of uncooperative individuals. Some or all political parties are dissolved, and government ministries, university faculties, and communications media that might be obstructive or critical are purged and brought under government control. The political process moves back into the private arena, which is now centered in the military establishment but continues to embrace economic elites and representatives of the dominant foreign power.

The extent of violence involved and of government control required is dependent, of course, upon the country's level of political development: The greater the proportion of the population that had come to participate in the political system, the greater the violence required, at least initially, to demobilize it. In the cases of Argentina, Uruguay, Chile, and to a lesser extent, of Brazil and Bolivia, counterrevolution called for overt executions; disappearances (usually unacknowledged executions); the establishment of concentration camps; and systematic, highly modern, and sophisticated techniques of torture. In the case of less-developed Guatemala, counterrevolution was manifested in a reversion, so to speak, to the campaign of conquest and the Indian wars.

Although the Catholic Church, like most middle-class or nonclass national institutions, is subject to marked factionalism in the face of either revolution or counterrevolution, the severity of the violation of human rights in the course of modern counterrevolution has made the Church the primary bastion against the excesses of counterrevolutionary regimes. As the only national institution that cannot be crushed outright by military authorities, the Church becomes the refuge of last resort for the dissident and the devastated. It is not coincidental that the role of the Church in the face of Poland's Soviet-backed, military-administered counterrevolution of the early 1980s was parallel to its role in a number of Latin American countries.

Once power has been consolidated in a dominant military faction and effective opposition to counterrevolution has been crushed, authorities are free to move ahead with the transformation of the economy.

Economic Transformation. Counterrevolutions do not merely freeze socioeconomic relationships or maintain the status quo. The expulsion of lower social strata, e.g., workers and peasants, from the political arena results in redistribution of wealth from the bottom up. This may be accomplished through a combination of tax, tariff, budget, wage, and land tenure policies. Land reform measures may be revoked, or squatters may be expelled. Graduated personal and corporate income taxes may be diminished or abandoned in favor of regressive taxes. Social services may be cut, and wages may be frozen in the face of inflation.

The central role of the military and paramilitary forces dictates that their budgets will be expanded. The involvement of the hegemonic power and/ or the requirement of external aid and investment dictate acceleration of the denationalization of resources and the adoption of policies that favor foreign enterprises over national ones. Thus, the national industrialist class, which supported counterrevolution as a means of containing the demands of labor, finds itself crippled by tariff and credit policies and foreign competition. And the middle class, having lost free expression and political participation, suffers also the shrinkage of its economic mainstay—government employment.

Institutionalization. Institutionalization does not come easily to counterrevolutionary regimes, partly because of the difficulty of achieving legitimacy. Establishing procedures to routinize policymaking and the succession to power in a manner that does not threaten the power position of the ruling faction or of the counterrevolutionary elite also proves difficult.

Counterrevolutionary regimes have often sought the support, or at least the acceptance, of certain sectors or institutions by labeling themselves "revolutionary" or "Christian." Such regimes in Bolivia were able to court, or at least to neutralize, most peasant groups for the better part of the decade by waving the revolutionary banner while crushing the miners and other elements of organized labor. The revolutionary label adopted by Brazil's military rulers in 1964, however, did not appear to impress anyone.

Regimes claiming to be bastions of "Western Christian values confronting atheistic communism" often succeed initially in attracting support from some element of the Church hierarchy. But as the oppressed tend to cast their lot with any institution that dares to speak for them, the weight of the Church's influence has shifted to those members of the hierarchy who have defied the government. In defending the poor and other victims of government oppression, the Church itself becomes liable to government reprisal. Once clergymen and nuns have been added to the ranks of those subjected to imprisonment, torture, and execution, it becomes more difficult for any element of the Church hierarchy to continue to serve as apologist for the regime. Thus, appeals to the pious soon lose their credibility, and counterrevolutionary regimes fall back upon the slogans of "national security" and "free enterprise" that appeal to their own limited constituencies.

Counterrevolutionary regimes, like other ruling elites, have sometimes attempted to co-opt or to establish political movements or parties on the supposition that such movements or parties could be controlled from the top and grass-roots initiatives could be blocked. But, regardless of motive, attempts to organize nonelites fly in the face of the larger objective of political demobilization. Such attempts also tend to divide the military and other pillars of the counterrevolutionary regime. Thus, such regimes have generally found that organizational initiatives carry unwarranted risks and may prove counterproductive.

Military governments are not necessarily counterrevolutionary, but counterrevolutionary governments are necessarily military, generally with considerable paramilitary support (police, vigilantes, "death squads," etc.) as well, because the abrupt reconcentration of wealth and power can be carried out only by armed force. Such regimes have begun their tenure as institutional ones, or what we shall call "militocracies." Power is seized and exercised in the name of the armed forces, as such, rather than by a *caudillo,* and the military establishment as a whole becomes the first-line political base of the government. The nominal president may be civilian, as was the case in Uruguay from 1973 to 1981, and a congress may be allowed to convene, as was usually the case in Brazil between 1964 and 1985, but such officials hold their posts for the convenience and at the sufferance of the military. Elections and plebiscites, held with varying degrees of regularity and under varying degrees and techniques of control, are the rule rather than the exception.

The failure of such regimes to achieve legitimacy may be compensated for by the maintenance of a high level of repression and coercion, but the failure to routinize succession to power means continual instability and vulnerability. The process whereby the most powerful position, be it the presidency or the highest military or army post, changes hands among individuals and factions is generally one or another form of palace coup, although it may be bloodless and may be sanctified by "elections."

In the Brazilian case, probably the most successful institutionalization of a counterrevolutionary regime, the succession process generally involved an "election" or polling process carried out among the highest-ranking officers— e.g., four-star generals. The victor of that process was then "nominated" by the official party and duly elected by an electoral college including members of the national congress and representatives of state legislative assemblies. Military elections—formal or informal polling among upper-echelon officers— are not simulations of democratic process; rather, they are simulated battles, as votes are weighted in accordance with command of firepower.

Decompression. Decompression (in Portuguese, *distensão*) is one of the terms that has been used by Brazilians in reference to the process that got under way in their country about 1978. The term will be used here in the same sense, but to refer to the process in other countries as well—a process of attenuation of the power and control of the military and other counterrevolutionary forces, resulting in a lessening of repression and an increase in political participation, particularly by the middle class.

The factors that tend to weaken the grip of a counterrevolutionary elite are not unlike those that undermine other elites and other systems. They include division within the ruling group or between that group and its constituencies, economic stress, and external pressure. Commonly, all of these factors come into play simultaneously and reinforce each other.

The headiness of power and the spoils of office, not to mention the occasionally genuine conflicts of ideologies, are just as conducive to competition within a military caste as within a ruling civilian elite. If power becomes highly concentrated in the hands of an individual or a clique, other factions that have ceased to profit adequately from military rule may garner support from civilian groups in order to unseat the offending individual or clique. The price of civilian support will be a commitment to some degree of political opening.

Economic stress is likely to exacerbate divisions within the military as well as to alienate some elements of its constituency. The support of the dominant foreign power may be weakened or even withdrawn as a consequence of the regime's economic mismanagement. Also the level of repression may reach such proportions as to embarrass the hegemonic power. Such was the case in the mid-1970s when human rights policies adopted by the U.S. Congress and highlighted briefly by the Carter administration served to weaken, at least temporarily, some of Latin America's counterrevolutionary regimes.

In the Brazilian case, all of these factors were apparent in the 1970s. But Brazil's decompression gained additional impetus as the facade of democracy— the apparatus of parties, elections, and representative bodies that had served the regime well in the process of institutionalization—blossomed into a reality beyond the facile control of the still-dominant military. In Bolivia,

neither revolution nor counterrevolution has gained any semblance of institutionalization; instability has reigned supreme. When the military abandoned
power in 1982 to the government of Hernán Siles Suazo—elected, but
suppressed, in 1980—it was primarily because the economy had collapsed
under the weight of military corruption. Economic collapse was also a major
factor in the disintegration of the Argentine regime that occurred in early
1983, but the disintegration had been accelerated by humiliating defeat in
the Falklands/Malvinas War of 1982.

FROM ARISTOCRACY TO MILITOCRACY

In general, the constitutional and legal systems of Latin American countries
were borrowed from France and the United States and, at least until the
twentieth century, served merely to legitimize political arrangements that
had been reached in private—in the smoke-filled rooms of men's clubs and
other gathering places of the wealthy. In such arenas, competition among
landholding families, and later between landholders and representatives of
new wealth based on international commerce and industry, could be regulated.
Such competition was not necessarily peaceful; it often led to clashes among
armed hirelings of families or sectors of the economic elite. But electoral
and parliamentary systems were little more than a ritualistic adjunct to a
process based on wealth, force, and interpersonal intrigue.

It was only with the successful bid for participation by the middle classes
that electoral and parliamentary systems came to have a serious function.
In general, however, Latin America's middle classes have not constituted an
intermediate level of property holders. Nor have they represented other
independent sources of wealth. Rather, they have been a salaried class, derived
from and dependent upon the expansion of commerce and government.
Their bid for effective participation, beginning in the late nineteenth century
in Argentina and continuing into the late twentieth century in Central
America and the Andean highlands, could not (and cannot) rest upon their
own numbers and resources alone. They found it necessary to incorporate
the numbers and the potential disruptiveness of lower social strata, particularly
the incipient labor movement, into their power bases. Middle-class bids for
political power have generally been spearheaded by university students and
intellectuals and carried to fruition by political parties, but they have rarely
been successful unless they were believed to have the backing of organized
labor. Thus, the effectiveness of the ballot box has been preceded by an
effective demonstration of power on the streets and in the factories.

Where, for reasons of social distance based on racial and ethnic difference,
the original postconquest aristocracy has concluded that it *dare* not expand
political participation, and/or, for reasons of powerful external support, the
economic elite has concluded that it *need* not expand political participation,
the upshot has been either revolution or "boundary maintenance" depending
on the relative strengths of contending forces.

Where aristocracies have felt constrained to give in to middle-class demands
for effective political participation, democratic processes have acquired sub-

stance—for a time and to a point. But middle-class leaders have generally proved unable or unwilling to extend fully effective participation, through the electoral system, to urban workers and peasants, particularly when economic decline has sharpened competition between middle and lower classes.

Uruguay's felicitous early experience with the evolutionary process does not seem likely to be repeated in Latin America in the near future. Although a middle class may rise to the full exercise of political power through the evolutionary process, recent developments in Latin America suggest that, at least for the time being, there is a high threshold of participation that manual workers and peasants will not be allowed to cross.

Once middle-class parties and labor organizations have been incorporated into the system, political conflict may come to be centered in the constitutional arena. But, at least in Latin America and perhaps in most dependent states, limited participatory democracy contains the seeds of its own destruction. The greater the level of effective participation and the longer the unbroken tenure of constitutional rule, the more policy will incline toward nationalism, nonalignment, and egalitarianism. Unlike U.S. voters, Latin American voters tend to turn out in very high proportions when elections are expected to be free of fraud, and in the more developed countries, nonelites, as well as elites, tend to vote their economic interests. Thus, the middle class, dependent upon salaries from the government or the property-holding upper class and insecure in its status, begins to align itself with the upper class. These classes, seeing their power slipping away and their economic interests threatened, abandon the constitutional arena. They enlist the military establishment and the United States in their defense against what is portrayed as "the menace of communism." Thus, counterrevolution is most likely and most violent precisely in those systems that have achieved the highest levels of political development through the evolutionary process.

The destabilized constitutional system is then replaced by a militocracy— a system in which the military establishment as a whole serves as a ruling elite. Competition for power within this system assumes the form of simulated battles, as command of firepower confers political power. Civilian instigators and supporters of counterrevolution soon find that military rulers are not content to become their pawns. Although economic policy initially reflects the interests of the counterrevolutionary coalition, over time it increasingly reflects the institutional and personal interests of military officers themselves.

Counterrevolutionary systems, like evolutionary and revolutionary ones, and the political and economic gains and losses they represent, are impermanent. But the praetorianism, or militarism, that facilitates counterrevolution and is, in turn, strengthened by it appears more durable. Even more than civilian elites, the military, in power, generates enemies, and the more brutal the military government, the more numerous and intransigent those enemies are likely to be.

The Argentine military has often withdrawn in the period since the overthrow of Perón in 1955, but never to a safe enough distance to allow labor a free rein. Even though the military establishments of Chile and Uruguay have withdrawn in the 1980s from the direct exercise of power, it is most unlikely that those countries will return by the end of the century to the free-wheeling democracies that flourished before the counterrevolutions of the 1970s. Even if elections are unfettered, it will remain clear that full powers are not vested in the electorate. The experiences of Latin American countries suggest that nothing short of revolution would be likely to bring those military establishments under civilian control. And, as Bolivia can attest, even revolution offers no long-term guarantees against militarism. At any rate, in countries having acquired a large middle class, revolution is no longer an option.

NOTES

1. Charles W. Anderson, *Politics and Economic Change in Latin America* (Princeton, N.J: Van Nostrand, 1967).

2. Martin C. Needler, *An Introduction to Latin American Politics: The Structure of Conflict* (Englewood Cliffs, N.J.: Prentice-Hall, 1977).

3. Karl Deutsch, "Social Mobilization and Political Development," *American Political Science Review* 55:4 (September 1961).

4. Some scholars have viewed the outcome of Costa Rica's civil strife of 1948 as revolutionary. Others have viewed it as counterrevolutionary. The outcome, in this author's view, was a mixed one, with gains and losses for elements of both upper and lower social strata, but one that did not fundamentally alter the evolutionary course of change.

5. Conversations with Paz Estenssoro, Albuquerque, Spring 1978. Paz told of a visit during his presidency by a delegation of peasants from a village on the Altiplano. They had come to plead for a telephone for the village and for a bridge to connect the village with a road leading to La Paz. Paz Estenssoro responded that the demands on his administration were enormous and the treasury was bare. Thereupon, the spokesman of the delegation said: "Mr. President, I'm sure you remember that an angry mob hanged former President Villarroel from a lamp post. When the counterrevolutionaries come for you, you can call us on our telephone and we'll come running across our bridge and save you!" Paz said they got their telephone and their bridge.

SUGGESTED READINGS

From the perspective of development theory, Charles W. Anderson, *Politics and Economic Change in Latin America* (Princeton, N.J.: Van Nostrand, 1967), has provided a useful model of political actors—who they are, and how they go about seeking participation and power. Martin C. Needler, *Political Development in Latin America: Instability, Violence, and Evolutionary Change* (New York: Random House, 1968), foreshadowed more recent work on the relationships between economic and political development.

The paradigm that has had greatest currency for dealing with the counterrevolutionary trends of the 1970s was provided by Guillermo O'Donnell in *Modernization and Bureaucratic-Authoritarianism: Studies in South American Politics* (Berkeley: Institute of International Studies, University of California, 1973). Penny Lernoux, *Cry of the People* (New York: Doubleday, 1980), depicts the changing role of the Church in the face of revolution and counterrevolution. The roles of Latin America's modern military establishments are treated in Philippe C. Schmitter, ed., *Military Rule in Latin America: Function, Consequences, and Perspectives* (Beverly Hills, Calif.: Sage Publications, 1973). Military withdrawal and the trend to "redemocratization" during the 1980s are covered in James M. Malloy and Mitchell A. Seligson, eds., *Authoritarians and Democrats: Regime Transition in Latin America* (Pittsburgh: University of Pittsburgh Press, 1987); Larry Diamond, Juan J. Linz, and

Seymour Martin Lipset, eds., *Democracy in Developing Countries, Vol. IV: Latin America* (Boulder, Colo.: Lynne Reinner Publishers, 1989); and Robert A. Pastor, ed. (with a foreword by Jimmy Carter and Raul Alfonsin), *Democracy in the Americas: Stopping the Pendulum* (New York: Holmes and Meier, 1989).

Cole Blasier, *The Hovering Giant: U.S. Responses to Revolutionary Change in Latin America* (Pittsburgh: University of Pittsburgh Press, 1976), deals with the U.S. stance vis-à-vis revolution, and Jan Knippers Black, *United States Penetration of Brazil* (Philadelphia: University of Pennsylvania Press, 1977), outlines the U.S. role in destabilizing democratic governments and promoting counterrevolution. More-general coverage of U.S. involvement in the politics of Latin American and other Third World countries is found in Noam Chomsky and Edward S. Herman, *The Political Economy of Human Rights,* Vol. 1, *The Washington Connection and Third World Fascism* (Boston: South End Press, 1979).

Among the many noteworthy recent books on mature and fledgling revolutionary regimes are Martin C. Needler, *Mexican Politics: The Containment of Conflict* (New York: Praeger, 1982); Jorge Domínguez, *Cuba* (New Haven: Yale University Press, 1979); and Thomas W. Walker, *Nicaragua: The Land of Sandino* (Boulder, Colo.: Westview Press, 1981). Late-developing Andean countries receive good coverage in David Scott Palmer, *Peru: The Authoritarian Tradition* (New York: Praeger, 1981), and Osvaldo Hurtado, *Political Power in Ecuador,* trans. Nick Mills (Albuquerque: University of New Mexico Press, 1980).

Roots and branches of counterrevolutionary regimes are covered in Alfred Stepan, ed., *Authoritarian Brazil: Origins, Policies, and Future* (New Haven: Yale University Press, 1973); Arturo Valenzuela, *The Breakdown of Democracy in Chile* (Baltimore: Johns Hopkins University Press, 1978); and Peter G. Snow, *Political Forces in Argentina* (New York: Praeger, 1979). Recent trends in individual countries throughout the hemisphere are addressed in James D. Cockcroft, *Neighbors in Turmoil: Latin America* (New York: Harper & Row, 1989).

Among the many outstanding books on tumultuous Central America are Stephen Schlesinger and Stephen Kinzer, *Bitter Fruit: The Untold Story of the American Coup in Guatemala* (New York: Doubleday, 1982); Cynthia Arnson, *El Salvador: A Revolution Confronts the United States* (Washington, D.C.: Institute for Policy Studies, 1982); Jenny Pearce, *Under the Eagle* (London: Latin American Bureau, 1982); and Peter Calvert, ed., *The Central American Security System: North-South or East-West?* (Cambridge: Cambridge University Press, 1988).

12

"NORMALIZATION," POPULAR STRUGGLES, AND THE RECEIVER STATE

JORGE NEF

Latin America often defies academic vogues and linear predictions. Any discussion of its politics has to start by recognizing that assessing trends involves more than the objective analysis of general empirical tendencies (descriptive facts). Ideology, culture-bound constructions, and projections reflecting the observer's values and preferences are also part of interpreting such trends. This circumstance is particularly important for understanding the various fallacies about Latin America that have dominated official and academic discourses in the United States.[1] Enduring myths about Manifest Destiny, communism, revolution, and overall "otherness" extant in the "American ideology" color public and private, lay and scholarly attitudes toward the Latin American problem and its possible solutions. Underpinning this set of attitudes and beliefs is a Manichean and reactive logic. In the 1960s, especially during the Kennedy era, the common perception about the politics of the region was that of an ongoing struggle between two models of development. The preferred strategy from the U.S. perspective was evolutionary reform. Its undesirable alternative was revolution. Following the fall of several traditional dictatorships in the late 1950s (Manuel Odría in Peru, Rojas Pinilla in Colombia, Pérez Jiménez in Venezuela) and the Cuban Revolution, middle-class populism appeared to provide the alternative to Fidel Castro's brand of emerging national communism. The Alliance for Progress (1961) viewed modernization essentially as a counterinsurgency strategy. Planned development, along national-capitalist lines and under the leadership of a technocratic middle class allied with the modern entrepreneurial sector, was seen as the answer to leftist insurgency. Mass mobilization carried out by broad-based parties (either of the Democratic left or the Christian Democrats) was considered a condition both for governmental legitimacy and for developmental effectiveness.

In the late 1960s, these alternatives were increasingly perceived by U.S. political, economic, and military circles—and by their official intelligentsia— as elusive, frustrating, and even counterproductive. Under the spell of the Rockefeller "doctrine"[2] and the development-as-order model, the liberal utopia burst. By the late 1970s, the trend—and the preferred outcome— was neither reform nor revolution. Repression, forceful demobilization, and bureaucratic authoritarianism would substitute not only for the much-feared socialism but also for elections and other paraphernalia of democracy. Such drastic change in the role of the Latin American state from promoting development to maintaining national security, however, could not be explained solely as the outcome of Washington's shifting its containment paradigm vis-à-vis the Third World. A profound economic and political crisis of capital accumulation, legitimacy, and sovereignty rooted in the region's historical pattern of development set the stage for the emergence of national security regimes.[3] In a broader sense, the crisis was brought about by the exhaustion of import-substitution policies and the restructuring of global political and economic relations. Although the ensuing turmoil and repression were generalized traits in all of Latin America, the specific manifestations varied according to national and regional circumstances.

In most of South America, where the levels of economic and social modernity and of political institutionalization and bureaucratization were high, the overall trend in the 1970s was a crisis of legitimation and a movement toward "authoritarian capitalism."[4] In most of Central America, which ranked well below South America in terms of its levels of modernity and institutionalization, the trend was, by contrast, toward popularly based national revolutions. Such a crisis of domination resulted from the elite's growing inability to exercise effective physical coercion. The contradiction in Latin American politics in the early 1980s appeared to be one between the antidemocratic economic liberalism offered by the national security regimes of the Southern Cone and the antiliberal socialism through popular revolution exemplified by Cuba, the Sandinistas, and the Farabundo Martí National Liberation Front (FMLN).

Conservative intellectuals such as Jeane Kirkpatrick and Henry Kissinger attempted to trivialize the repressive-revolutionary dichotomy by building semantic distinctions between authoritarian and totalitarian options for Latin America. Authoritarian regimes, in their view, were those in which the Western capitalist model had been maintained, albeit by repressive methods, and could in theory at least evolve into liberal democracies.[5] Examples included fascist regimes in Europe like Portugal, Spain, and Greece. Totalitarian regimes, on the other hand, were those in which a simultaneous change of the socioeconomic, cultural, and political orders had taken place. According to conservative intellectuals, radical-revolutionary transformations made a transition to liberal democracy theoretically impossible. Therefore, authoritarianism was presented as a preventive and more tolerable alternative than totalitarianism (the latter label was solely applied to Nicaragua, Cuba, and other Marxist or pro-Marxist regimes). This reasoning not only justified military dictatorship but also masked a strong antidemocratic strain in American realpolitik. The lesser evil had become *the* optimal choice. However, such a fallacious dichotomy became increasingly meaningless, embarrassing, and divisive in the Western camp. It was also a poor predictor of new trends. Thus, the need for a new intellectual construction for U.S. policy options emerged. Transition theory[6] filled the void. With a dramatic debt crisis spreading throughout Latin America, both national security and revolutionary alternatives gave way to new coexisting but opposite modalities of conflict-management. On the one hand, there were debt-crisis strategies with recivilianization. Between 1975 and 1989 the number of countries under direct military rule decreased from fifteen to three, with processes of "normalization" leading to limited, semicompetitive polities under way in even the most recalcitrant militocracies such as Chile and Paraguay.

On the other hand, the 1980s saw the emergence of radically new forms of popular struggle running the whole gamut from mere survivalist to resistance to maximalist strategies. Examples have included base Christian communities in Brazil and Central America, self-managed urban communities in Peru, grassroots communal movements in Colombia, and popular economic organizations in Chile; revamped united leftist fronts in Peru, El Salvador, Colombia, Ecuador, Uruguay, and Chile; and more extreme social and ethnic irredentism such as Peru's Sendero Luminoso.[7]

Parallel to the aforementioned insurgent tendencies, new forms of violence became intertwined with endemic conflicts, creating an extremely volatile, polarized, and fragmented political environment. In many countries, such as Colombia, Guatemala, El Salvador, Peru, and Honduras, underneath the flimsy civilian facade, the security forces are engaged in "dirty wars" and semi-private death squads remain prominent. The U.S.-supported Contra war against Nicaragua has spread conflict throughout the isthmus. Likewise, the ascent of narco-traffickers in Bolivia, Peru, Paraguay, Panama, Mexico, and, especially, Colombia has had a profound impact on the present domestic and international alignment of political forces. Violence, however, is not limited to the political and the criminal. The generalized economic recession, combined with "structural adjustment," has increased income concentration, unemployment, poverty, and marginalization.[8] In most countries, the state has become the receiver and debt-collector of a bankrupt economy on behalf of transnational creditors.

The purpose of this chapter is to offer a general interpretation of these trends and to assess a number of possible scenarios that can be derived from such an interpretation. My central thesis is that the "politics of repression," and subsequently the "politics of exclusion" of the receiver state that characterize today's Latin America, cannot be seen as an aberration. They should be understood as a mutation of one continuous social project to secure the existing socioeconomic system and its related forms of political control, both domestically and internationally. Despite political turmoil and persistent violence, the underlying social, economic, and international forces that have enjoyed "metapower" in most of the region still prevail. Concurrently, this chapter challenges four widely held assumptions of pluralistic theories of politics. One is that profound class conflict can be arbitrated by the mechanisms of liberal, participatory democracy in the context of a dependent capitalist society. The second is that the liberal-democratic state is a neutral mechanism in which conflicting demands can be accommodated and equity-producing policies can be formulated and implemented. The third belief is that the socioeconomic status quo can be changed "from within" without violently altering the role of the state as an enforcer of the status quo. Last, but not least, is the belief that the peripheral state is indeed a national state, rather than a structure functioning to maintain precisely the dependent and under-developed nature of the society.

TRANSNATIONALIZATION AND THE LEGITIMATION CRISIS

Conventional treatments of the problems governments face in acquiring legitimation, or acceptance and popular support, following the state-centric model of political analysis have assumed that constituencies and coalitions are national. This assumption is unrealistic for most of the dependent, peripheral, or neocolonial societies of the Third World. Indeed, one central characteristic of the Latin American countries is their penetrability and internationalization. Support for specific policies, and even for a whole regime, depends upon an often contradictory interplay between domestic and foreign constituencies.[9]

This situation poses a severe constraint upon the degree of choice in policy formulation and implementation. The effectiveness—and at times the very existence—of a regime depends more on external than on internal constituencies. Conversely, broad acceptance by the domestic population is generally limited unless a government is able to continuously raise the level of goods and services it can provide.

Such growth is rare in economies characterized by chronic underdevelopment. A normal consequence of limited growth in societies unable to extricate their own poverty is an increased marginalization, if not outright alienation, of vast sectors of their populations. Accumulation of wealth in the hands of a small elite at home and its transnational associates raises the intensity of support among a very limited social base. This concentration of wealth, in turn, reduces the popular legitimacy of the regimes. A higher intensity of support (from the elite and its constituencies) may not suffice to offset a growing alienation resulting from the poverty and powerlessness of most of the populace. If alienation leads to mobilization by existing or emerging power brokers, the legitimacy of the political structure may be brought into question. Here, an ostensible discrepancy between the rhetoric of legitimation (or ideology) and the actual implementation of the elite's program emerges. Confronted with a devaluation of its own political myth and faced with opposition from below, the ruling elite normally chooses to resort to naked enforcement of the status quo through repression. This pattern represents, in a simplified manner, the relationship between socioeconomic stability and political instability in Latin America.[10] The pattern suggests that political and socioeconomic democratization cannot be reconciled with the existing mode of dependent development, which dominates the entire region. Nor can it be reconciled with the current trend toward the transnationalization of the state.

A HISTORICAL PERSPECTIVE

The Persistence of Underdevelopment

One fundamental fact in the analysis of Latin American underdevelopment is that the structures and patterns of production in the region are the outgrowth of a center-periphery mode of international division of labor. Several theses of dependency theory are mentioned in Chapter 1, but three important observations about Latin American dependent development should be stressed. First, since the conquest, Latin America has been economically subordinated to one or another more highly developed part of the world. Second, economic modernization by colonial and neocolonial powers has often been antidevelopmental, as genuine national initiatives have been undermined by decapitalization and marginalization. Third, nearly two centuries after formal independence, structural underdevelopment persists. It should be remembered, however, that the influence of international economic relations can be understood only through its reflection in the domestic political economy and its related social conflicts. Therefore, Latin America's dependent development has to be seen as being linked to the dynamics of class—or mass-elite—relations that occur in the domestic setting, not as a cause of underdevelopment but rather as a reinforcer of domestic inequality.[11]

The social structures resting upon international economic patterns have also tended to endure. The ranch, the hacienda, the mining town, or the Central American plantation created conditions for the emergence and perpetuation of a *comprador* (export-import or international commerce) elite, outward looking in orientation and parasitic in function.[12] This elite has owed its very existence to being a linkage, or intermediary, between the national society and the dominant foreign power, setting the conditions for a type of rentier economy and state.

Formal political independence in the 1800s did not significantly alter the function of the elite or the peripheral role of the Latin American economies in the international division of labor. It only moved the center of domination, first from Spain and Portugal to the British Empire and, at the turn of the century but more so after World War I, to the United States. Neocolonialism— economic, social, cultural, and political—ushered in with political independence was modernized, but structural underdevelopment and vulnerability continued as in the days of mercantile colonialism.

The expansion of the export economy in the late nineteenth century laid the foundations for the emergence of a "modern" labor sector. The transformation of peasants into a propertyless wage-earning class was accelerated by war (as in Chile), by "liberal" reforms in the countryside (as in Mexico, Guatemala, and El Salvador), or by export-oriented commercialization (as in Argentina, Brazil, and Uruguay). The poor lost either their communal lands or the paternalistic cushion of the *latifundio* system or both. Peons, tenant farmers, and tillers of communal lands who moved to the mines, plantations, docks, or slaughterhouses became an "instant proletariat" working under appalling conditions. As a consequence, relations between the relatively cohesive elites and the fragmented masses rapidly changed from the quiescence of latent class conflict to a manifest and specifically political confrontation between classes.

In the Southern Cone countries, as well as in Brazil, Costa Rica, and in postrevolutionary Mexico, the emergence of middle-class reformism defused a political powder keg by rerouting working-class frustrations through institutional and electoral channels. It also brought about an earlier bureaucratization and relative autonomy of the state. Changes in the political upper decks, however, did not mean a drastic alteration in the elite-controlled socioeconomic order. A symbiosis with the oligarchy meant a form of power sharing: The middle classes, acting both as a buffer and as guardians of the status quo, created a first line of physical and ideological defense to protect the establishment.

Conditions in most of Central America were very different. The overall level of surplus was lower. The middle classes were much smaller and weaker—appendages of the landed elites that enjoyed little autonomy—and foreign intervention was more pervasive. The role of the largely patrimonial state vis-à-vis the majority of the population was simply one of enforcement. With the spread of popular mobilization resulting from the commercialization of agriculture, a pattern of repression and resistance was established. Although rural rebellions were frequently bloody and certainly persistent—especially in El Salvador, Nicaragua, and Guatemala—they were also intermittent, localized, and disorganized. Nevertheless, in the course of ongoing struggles and with the steady progression of landlessness, certain manifestations of class consciousness began to appear.

With the Great Depression, a profound crisis of fiscal solvency set in throughout Latin America. The implementation of middle-class reformist policies, like those that had been attempted in the Southern Cone countries, became largely untenable. Military force became the political currency of the crisis. In most of South America, after an earlier conservative reaction, a mixture of import-substitution industrialization and political populism became the dominant mold. Populism was also the trend in Mexico. In Central America (with the exception of Costa Rica) and the Caribbean, however, this alternative was blocked.

Where populism prevailed, the role of the state was greatly expanded, thus securing employment for the middle strata whose status had been threatened by the drastic decline of the export economy. This expanded role permitted the maintenance of mechanisms for co-optation of would-be resentful members of the educated classes.

Until the beginning of World War II, import substitution went through the first of its two main phases. During this early stage, import substitution constituted an attempt at state intervention to prevent social and political catastrophe. With exports falling precipitously and without an import capacity, governments undertook the role of activators of the national economy. De facto Keynesianism was a matter of political expedience and survival. With the outbreak of the war and the relative recovery of Western economies, demand for Latin American raw materials increased dramatically. This increase gave impetus to a new policy of economic planning and management: import substitution *with* export expansion. Throughout this period, no serious emphasis was placed on shifting traditional exports or on diversification, the development of the peasant economy, and much less on self-sufficiency. Thus, import substitution had severe built-in constraints. True, the economies grew; but despite the myth held by Latin American economic nationalists, it is doubtful that the economies would have "taken off" on their own even if sustained growth had continued into the 1960s. The continuity of structural underdevelopment and the parasitic nature of the elites placed insurmountable constraints on any incrementalist economic strategy.

Import-substitution manufacturing, based on export expansion, in the Southern Cone countries, Brazil, and Mexico made it possible to strengthen and expand the populist programs of the prerecession years. The difference was that a large state machinery, under firm middle-class control, was already in place. Moreover, a noticeable recovery in the export economies had occurred because of the war demand. International conditions also facilitated alliances between blue-collar unions and the bureaucratic middle strata. Since lower-class mobilization had been physically and functionally limited, an alliance of the middle sectors with the unionized working classes did not pose any real threat to the economic and social positions of the traditional rural and commercial elites. On the contrary, the alliance broadened the basis of legitimation of the existing political structure.

This legitimation rested upon improvements in working conditions, wages, and union rights for urban workers. The widening of middle-class welfare programs, which had existed since the 1920s, extended the sources of employment to the middle classes charged with their administration. Moreover, state involvement in planning, financing, and implementing industrial recovery policies brought about qualitative changes in the role of the state in the economy.[13] The state bureaucracy constituted an important means of integrating emerging strata into the preexisting elite-controlled social structure. Thus, despite its populist appearance, the system on the higher levels remained elitist in structure and corporatist in style of decision making.

Once demand for raw materials stabilized and subsequently fell shortly after the implementation of the Marshall Plan in Europe, external financing for development schemes declined. Furthermore, import substitution did not alter the rentier nature of the export economy; it only responded pragmatically to a crisis of imports for the conspicuous consumption of the elites. The heightened demand of the war and postwar period made diversification and self-reliance a mere academic question. In the area of internal financing of development schemes, the commercial and landed elites were not about to accept the burdens of the state resting upon their shoulders. Government social security and development schemes were chronically underfinanced and depended for the most part on increases in the money supply, on unpredictable export earnings, and ultimately on U.S. foreign aid.

The most severe limitations on import-substitution industrialization, however, were social and political in nature. A full extension of the logic of import substitution into the realm of self-sustained national development required a dramatic expansion of an otherwise extremely limited market. In economic terms, such expansion meant the transformation of the bulk of the population subsisting outside the official economy into a mass consumer market with the capacity to buy nationally produced goods. To create such broad national markets would have required a drastic modification of the social structure, especially the lowering of class barriers and, in particular, a true revolution in the agrarian order. Thus, while the completion of a nationalistic development program required expansion of the domestic market, the maintenance of the elite-dominated socioeconomic order required just the opposite: the continuity of a narrow market, oriented toward conspicuous consumption. By the mid-1950s, import-substitution strategies had outlived their original purpose—system maintenance. The economies of Latin America rapidly returned to the traditional mold of export and outward-oriented development of the pre-Depression era.

The international system of the 1950s, however, bore little resemblance to the prewar picture. The emergence of U.S. power, the Cold War, rigid bipolarism, the Bretton Woods patterns of global economics, and the upsurge of the transnational conglomerate were among the new complexities and constraints facing the traditionally export-oriented Latin American economies. Furthermore, severe crises in the export sector, combined with deteriorating terms of trade for primary products, had a devastating impact on the financing of government projects.

Crises of Legitimacy and Domination

Once import-substitution strategies for economic growth had become exhausted, by the early and mid-1950s, inflationary politics substituted for the uneasy social contract between otherwise antagonistic social groups.[14] Wage and price spirals soon became a muted and protracted form of civil strife. The state mechanisms produced and accelerated "the pushup effect" of the institutionalized class conflict. In this context, the political issues of democracy, stability, and legitimation became inextricably linked to economic questions of growth and distribution. As labor militancy increased, the middle strata sought to reconstitute the ruling coalitions by shifting their political stance further to the right.

Although this type of stalemate politics was an inherent trait of the institutionalized class conflict, the exhaustion of import substitution introduced a new element: a crisis of accumulation in the midst of accelerated mass mobilization. The consequence of cumulative and multiple dysfunctions was a breakdown of the state. The timing and velocity of this process varied from country to country, but it became manifest by the 1960s.

In Central America and the Caribbean in general, where, with the exception of post-1948 Costa Rica, the state as an entity based on a constitutional order never really emerged, the crisis was more crudely one of domination: the inability of the existing repressive states and their foreign constituencies to control by military force. The Cuban Revolution was the first of a wave of national revolutionary movements backed by a political coalition very different from those of the past. Indeed, that Revolution, the most important development in contemporary Latin America since independence, highlights the growing internationalization of domestic conflicts in Latin America. This is not to say that there have not been external factors influencing domestic developments in Latin America in the past. There have been many U.S. Marine landings (e.g., in the Dominican Republic), invasions (e.g., of Nicaragua), and foreign-inspired coups (e.g., in Guatemala). Cuba is unique in that its conflict moved from the domestic scene of individual countries to the regional and global scene. Twenty years later, the Nicaraguan Revolution occurred, and similar revolutions appeared quite likely in El Salvador and even in Guatemala.

In the countries that were more highly developed politically and institutionally, the crisis of the state manifested itself mainly as a legitimacy crisis. In these countries, the existing socioeconomic order, both domestic and international, was maintained by resorting to naked, albeit highly bureaucratized, repression and by creating a new, but not necessarily legitimate, political coalition. Such a coalition basically entailed an alliance between the *comprador* bourgeoisie—or the externally linked economic elite that gives content to government programs—and the military institution, which is also externally linked. The latter provides the force required to keep the population at bay.

The bureaucratic-authoritarian "states of exception" that emerged in South America—a forerunner of which was the Brazilian "Liberating Revolution" of 1964—were in fact attempts at capitalist modernizations from the top (as well as from the outside). The benefits of this new authoritarian capitalist order accrued to a small elite of domestic entrepreneurs, speculators supported by a technocratic-military middle class and their respective business and military constituencies in the United States. The social cost for the majorities was always high, as overall living conditions declined and the gap between elites and masses widened. Nor did all these regimes succeed in unleashing thorough counterrevolutions; at best they acted as repressive brakes against social mobilization, economic nationalism, and incipient socialism.

The new transnationalized formula emphasized economic growth as a function of a reinsertion of the countries' economies into the international division of labor as exporters of raw materials. With the exception of Brazil in the late 1960s and the 1970s, economic modernization, far from "deepening industrialization," meant increased investment in the resource sector. It also involved the creation of favorable conditions, through deregulation, denationalization, and a dismantling of labor organizations, for transnational corporations to invest and increase profits. This model required large amounts of international financing, which was facilitated by massive deposits of recycled petrodollars in Western private banks. A deepening of indebtedness, fueled by the illusion of "economic miracles," ensued. As both the governments and the private sector in the region increased their financial obligations, the failure of production and exports to keep pace with borrowing and, most important, with swelling interest rates finally resulted in economic crises.

Although the experiments with authoritarian capitalism proved to be dismal failures as far as development was concerned, the radical restructuring of the economies along neoliberal lines was profound enough to prevent a return to economic nationalism. Likewise, the restructuring and transnationalization of the security establishment made utterly impossible the pursuit of nationalist foreign policies. In this sense, the political arrangements to emerge in Latin America as a result of "redemocratization," although possessing the formal trappings of sovereignty and democracy, are neither truly democratic nor sovereign. They are weak civilian regimes, with limited political agendas and narrow support, with significant exclusion of popular sectors from the political arenas, and with external constituencies, both economic and military, enjoying de facto veto power and holding the key to regime maintenance. In addition, the central role of the state has changed from that of promoting, at least symbolically, development and services to the public to that of ostensibly facilitating the service of the debt and implementing structural adjustments. The ultimate effects of this receiver state, as far as the society is concerned, are to perpetuate dependence and underdevelopment as well as chronic vulnerability, requiring ever-increasing doses of external supports.

A STRUCTURAL PERSPECTIVE: POLITICAL CRISIS AND THE LATIN AMERICAN STATE

In retrospect, the breakdown of the populist formula, with its neo-Keynesian economics, its import-substitution industrialization, and its emphasis upon big government, appears an almost inevitable consequence of the inherent contradictions in such a policy. Growing participation could coexist with dependent capitalism only under conditions of economic expansion. The loss of legitimacy at the national level was compensated for by broadening the class alliance to the international level and by forcefully demobilizing the bulk of the population. Repression in this instance is a fundamental component of economic freedom. As the late Orlando Letelier put it, "They are both sides of the coin."[15] In a sense it is ironic that the end of the cycle of the national security regime—the authoritarian component of "authoritarian capitalism"—in the 1980s was also a consequence of its internal unsustainability as a mode of conflict-management combined with its extreme vulnerability to external forces.

National Security and Trilateralism

As semiconsensual, pluralist political systems were displaced in the 1970s by a "corporate-technocratic" order, national security and antidevelopment policies substituted for the old developmentalist rhetoric. Characteristic of this order was the transfer of the systems-maintenance and planning functions from an elite civil service to a body of bureaucrats in uniform. Mobilization, participation, and national integration were displaced by order and antipolitics (an official attitude of contempt for open political competition). Development planning was thus replaced by social control as the key role for government administration.

Substantively, the national security model performed essentially the same containment function and maintained the same socioeconomic forces that the developmental reformism of the Alliance for Progress was supposed to maintain. The difference is that national security, with its antidemocratic and procapitalist biases, emphasized stability, often at the expense of development, the satisfaction of social needs, and democracy itself. Here, rather than "development administration," the predominant technology of conflict-management involved a package of openly terroristic state practices: harassment, intimidation, torture, disappearances, and other forms of dirty wars. Paradoxically, while the degree of social control increased in depth, the scope of government activity usually became quite restrained in the areas of economic management and social welfare. In this context, the modernization of the military, technocratic, and bureaucratic apparatus (administrative development) ended up in direct opposition to the neoliberal notion of development administration. The key function of the state became the creation of favorable conditions for private foreign investment and transnationalization through the repression of the civil society. Brazil in the 1960s and early 1970s, Argentina from 1976 to 1984, Uruguay between 1973 and 1985, and Chile from 1973 to 1990 are examples of this pattern.

Two parallel trends that set the ideological parameters of the U.S. government have greatly influenced the development of authoritarian capitalism in Latin America. One is "Pentagonism," particularly the ideology of counterinsurgency, "civic action," and low-intensity operations. The other is "trilateralism," the global business ideology espoused by transnational corporations. These two projects, with their respective wide-ranging sociopolitical alliances as well as contradictions, constitute the leading forces behind the logic of transitions to and from "bureaucratic-authoritarian regimes."

Pentagonism is a bureaucratic phenomenon that evolved almost simultaneously with the modern (i.e., New Deal) administrative state and has its roots in the consolidation of a relatively autonomous military-industrial complex in the United States with the onset of the Cold War. The policy orientation of Pentagonism is neo-Keynesian (demand-side economics), ultranationalist (U.S. Manifest Destiny), and rabidly anticommunist. In the last analysis, the objective of the state is highly specialized: the provision of security through the administration of violence. This policy runs an entire range of strategic doctrines, from nuclear massive retaliation to flexible response to counterinsurgency. The latter has become the hegemonic discourse in the U.S. Southern Command (SOUTHCOM), based in the Panama Canal Zone. SOUTHCOM's mission involves not only the coordination of the defense of the region under the provisions of the Rio Treaty but also, most important, the training—through the School of the Americas and multiple other training centers—of its Latin American clients. Since military structures, objectives, doctrines, and techniques—not to mention hardware—are among the most easily transferred technologies in the contemporary world, with rigid bipolarism and entangling alliances dominating the interplay between Latin America and the United States, continental military professionalism has become the most homogenizing bureaucratic trait. Such institutional modernization also serves as a link between U.S. and Latin American military establishments. In this sense, military modernization, especially along counterinsurgency lines and the concept of the "internal enemy," has meant the transnationalization and denationalization of the officer class. This development in itself is a fundamental limitation to the sovereignty of the Latin American nation-state.

Likewise, the spread of transnational corporations has meant a substantial transfer of organizational technology as well as a free-trading, antiprotectionist, supply-side, and monetarist ideology. It has also provided a vehicle for the transnationalization of a corporate and managerial elite. These two organizational developments are at times functionally, or symbiotically, related. Their impact upon traditional conceptions of the state and especially the role of the public sector in Latin America is quite significant. The technocratic-corporate state of the 1970s in part represents a marriage between the highly specialized and efficient exercise of violence by the public sector and the management of the economy by the private sector, controlled by large corporations. However, the two developments are quite distinct and correspond to different coalitions within the United States.

Trilateralism found political expression in the Democratic Party during the Carter administration through prominent "globalist" figures such as Cyrus Vance, George Ball, Sol Linowitz, and Zbigniew Brzezinski.[16] Pentagonism, as presented to U.S. constituencies, is a more patriotic and even "populist" Cold War perspective à la Jeane Kirkpatrick, Alexander Haig, or Vernon Walters, with constant appeals to patriotism, the flag, and military superiority. Symbolically at least, this nationalist imagery constituted the theme of the Reagan platform, while trilateralists remained an ostensible part of that administration's power block. After long-drawn power struggles within the outgoing administration, trilateralists appeared to have gained the upper hand within the inner circles in the Bush administration, with the nationalists in a relatively weaker position, at least for the time being.

A similar power play between a transnationalized "hard-line" officer corps (*duros*) and an equally transnationalized "soft-line" commercial and financial elite (*blandos*) occurs within the supporting coalitions in most Latin American states. Domestic manufacturers, traditional landowners, and the various factions of the petite bourgeoisie generally take a back seat, often shifting alliances within the power block. The drive toward further civilianization combined with the drastic economic orthodoxy of the Baker formula and the Brady Report can be explained by the above developments in the correlation of forces.

The antecedents of the present policy are to be found in the Linowitz Report[17] of 1975, a most articulate expression of the trilateral doctrine. It attempted to remove the nastier overtones of the Nixon legacy and called for a "new political order," including a peaceful end to military rule and a number of replacement formulas. In fact, it constituted the Trilateral Commission's position and blueprint for a revised North-South dialogue in the context of the entire Latin American region. It postulated that the national security regime was not the most effective system to generate the kind of development that could adequately serve the economic interests of the industrialized countries. Thus, "From positively favoring military governments and subverting democratic ones under Nixon and Kissinger, the U.S. government came out demonstratively in favor of the transition from authoritarian to democratic rule."[18] Fundamentally, however, despite emphasis on military withdrawal and a return to democracy, the approach advocated a type of restricted or limited democracy, restricted both in terms of the provision of government services and in terms of popular participation. In essence, the formula is not only conservative in socioeconomic terms, but it is also antidemocratic, even by comparison to the kind of populist reformism that existed in the 1930s in Latin America and the Western world. This formula has eventually unfolded throughout Latin America under the guise of "redemocratization."

Insurgency as Development

Contemporary Latin America is not a region undergoing a change toward increased democratization in the conventional sense. The concepts of "military withdrawal" and "limited democracy," as presented by the Carter administration, Reagan's "responsible right," and "friendly authoritarian regimes," or Bush's new open policies mask the consequences of a continuous pattern of dependence. The "dependent fascism" of the national security regimes proved to have severe limitations. Government by fear became ultimately untenable. Thus, the search for a new hegemonic formula reinserts the discourse of democracy—albeit limited—with neoconservative economies. While this imagery is quite appealing to North Americans and to Latin America's consumption-intensive middle classes, it also rests on flimsy and largely ideological assumptions. Trilateralism assumes a continuous expansion of the world capitalist system under the lead of transnationals, expansion that has failed to materialize thus far. Furthermore, trilateralism posits no serious contradiction between national interests in the peripheral state and the interests of transnational corporations. It relies heavily on a continuous use of selective and tactical repression as an effective deterrent against mass mobilization. Finally, it just entrenches under a legal facade the very same forces—economic, social, and political—that perpetrated the antidemocratic outrages of the past.

In the last analysis, the receiver state cannot be understood as simply a transitional phase in elite domination leading to a new genuine democracy: the return to "free" and participatory politics. Rather, the terrorist state of the 1970s and the receiver state of today are two different manifestations of the *same* cluster of interests. It represents the consensus of a largely transnationalized reactionary coalition. This consensus involves the prevention of (1) national self-determination and/or a nonaligned Latin America, (2) challenges to both the regional and national order and its internal and external constituencies, and (3) real economic, social, and even political democracy.

Keeping political participation down under conditions of constant social mobilization (e.g., migration, urbanization, and literacy) only compounded the long-run problems repression and exclusion were supposed to prevent. The present modality of conflict-management, while reducing the most blatant and uglier abuses of human rights, has left Latin America's most pressing and fundamental socioeconomic and political problems largely untouched. The combination of transnational integration of the Latin American elites (economic, military, and bureaucratic) into a U.S.-centered strategy of containment and the growing marginalization and alienation of the bulk of the internal Latin American constituencies has brought about a multisided crisis of both the state and the civil society. In the absence of tangible rewards to buy legitimacy, violence (insurgent, repressive, institutionalized, as well as criminal) becomes the most common political currency. Under the thin veneer of "normality," violence itself, including banditry, terrorism, repression, official abuses by security forces, and generalized lawlessness, becomes a distinct style of management of class conflict.

In this context, revolution—though muted in the current conjuncture—often evolves into a self-fulfilling prophecy either as the perceived alternative to oppression and hopelessness or as means for simple protection and survival (i.e., "liberated zones" during *La Violencia* in Colombia or *rondas campesinas* in contemporary Peru). The shrinkage of political spaces tends to reduce the generally multifaceted power intercourse into a simple first-degree military equation: Power equals force. The ongoing tragedies in El Salvador, Guatemala, Peru, and Colombia—where virtual civil wars prevail—are undoubtedly related to an accelerated reduction of any middle ground for compromise or negotiation. Cuba, Nicaragua, and Chile (1973–1990) illustrate, at opposite ends of the spectrum, the available models of stability. When national consensus fails and inflationary politics exhausts its bag of tricks, authoritarianism and revolution are always there. The question is, of course, one of social cost.

In the course of Latin American history, mass resistance has expressed itself through various forms and practices of social struggle. These include mere survival, resistance, insurrection, and revolution. In recent years, however, the call for radical changes in the existing social, economic, and political orders appears to be stymied by counterinsurgency, pseudo-democratization, and the debt burden. In the eyes of a superficial observer of the present, Nicaragua's could seem as the last possible—though problematic—revolution in the region. Nevertheless, from a long-range structural and historical (as opposed to conjunctural) perspective, revolutionary struggles and situations have not withered altogether, though their tactics and manifestations have changed. For many, revolution is still seen as an alternative to the perpetual cycle of poverty, repression, and dependency that has historically strangled the region's development. Where repressive and institutionalized violence have consistently blocked all channels for popular expression and participation, mass insurgency has posed as the sole opportunity for genuine change. This is not to say that all insurgency is necessarily revolutionary, nor that even if it were, fundamental, long-term progressive change would inevitably ensue. However, by opposing the prevailing order, popular movements are potentially developmental and revolutionary. What is noticeable in the last decade is that the focus of popular movements has shifted from the "triumphalist" center-stage of guerrilla warfare, leftist political parties, organized labor, and militant intellectuals, to the "chorus": shantytowns, grassroots organizations, and everyday life.[19] In this sense, new forms of control generate new forms of popular struggle and new manifestations of consciousness.

CONCLUSION

The analysis of contemporary Latin America over the last decade indicates that, despite formal redemocratization, there is a continuous reduction of real political spaces and alternative solutions for compromise. Consensus-building has become ever more unsustainable as the overall debt-ridden economies do not have the capabilities necessary for stable governance. Between the early 1970s and the early 1980s extreme political and social polarization, brutal repression, and exclusion became the regional trademarks of military rule. Side by side with political repression there was also rapid, yet inequitable, economic growth. The period between the mid-1980s and the present has been one of consolidation of basically the same exclusionary model, dressed now in civilian clothes. The substantial difference, however, is not the relative openness of the present formal political arrangements. They are not. The difference is that redemocratization is taking place in the midst of an economic debacle that makes political institutionalization nearly impossible.

Democratization and development in Latin America, if they were to occur, would remain largely meaningless unless their effects cease to be confined to the upper and middle classes. Profound social conflicts rooted in persistent inequities cannot be circumvented by the illusion of democratization. The possibilities of maintaining a minimal internal consensus by growth, as in Venezuela's and Mexico's oil-rich economies or in precrisis Costa Rica, seem to be exhausted. Venezuela's scarcely thirty-year-old democracy was shaken by the double impact of falling oil prices and International Monetary Fund–induced policies of draconian austerity, resulting in the death of about 500 people in the 1989 riots. Likewise, the attempt to consolidate democracy through an oil-based economic expansion in Ecuador lies in shambles. Mexico's crisis—the most serious since the 1910 Revolution—has not only affected the socioeconomic fabric of the nation but has also eroded the very institutional character of the regime.[20]

Argentina's liberal restoration under President Alfonsín crumbled. The country appears once again ungovernable, with an unmanageable foreign debt, economic recession, and open military rebellions. The prospects of a demogogic and ultimately repressive Peronista government, paving the road for another 1976-style coup, convey a sense of dejà vu. So it is also with Brazil's *democracia pactada*. The most appropriate description of Brazil's first experiment with civilian rule since 1964 is one of social chaos and governmental paralysis. Peru's social-democratic Aprista experiment, under Alan García, disintegrated in the throes of multisided civil war, coupled with economic collapse. The presidential election in 1990 did not resolve any of the country's profound crises. Colombia, though formally democratic since 1958, remains in a precarious balance. Most of the country is under martial law. A spiral of violent confrontation and association among security forces, right-wing death squads, narco-traffickers, and guerrilla groups has led to virtual free fire zones in many regions, with consequences similar to those of the post-1948 period.

The twilight of the continent's longest lasting (and most successful) dictatorships—those of Generals Pinochet in Chile and Stroessner in Paraguay—deserves to be mentioned. Transition theorists and practitioners point at these as examples of democratization. At close scrutiny, however, these "transitions" are hardly a "triumph for democracy." In Paraguay, the overthrow of General Stroessner in 1989 entailed the removal of the old tyrant by a close associate, General Rodriguez, while the nature of the regime was maintained. The largely internal feud has resulted, for all intents and purposes, in a strengthening of the socioeconomic order protected by the previous dictatorship and the preservation of military control over the state. In Chile, the Pinochet dictatorship suffered an unexpected setback in the 1988 plebiscite, and in the election of Christian Democrat Patricio Aylwin to the presidency in 1989.[21] But the logic of normalization is similar to other "openings," such as that of Uruguay. There, as in Chile, the military establishment has retained control over the tempo, limits, and direction of permissible change. Attempts to bring Uruguay's military under effective civilian control have been thwarted by the complex "safety devices" set by the national security regime before stepping down in 1985.

Despite the formal signing of the Central American Peace Accord in 1987, the real possibilities for internal peace, external nonintervention, development, and democratization in the region continue to be wishful thinking. The victory of ARENA in El Salvador—an extreme right-wing movement associated with the landowners, the army, and the infamous death squads— and the disintegration of the political center convey an image of catastrophic equilibrium, maintained by decisive U.S. military aid. The election of a civilian Christian Democratic government in Guatemala in 1985, after decades of almost uninterrupted military rule and brutal repression, has meant largely a figurehead government wherein civilians preside but do not govern. Repression by the security forces and death squads has in fact escalated in recent years, reaching the appalling levels of the past.

In Panama, the forms of democracy have been reintroduced under the presidency of Guillermo Endara, winner of the aborted May 1989 elections; but with the reconstituted Panamanian defense forces in place, the substance remains problematic. The U.S. invasion at the end of 1989 removed the drug-dealing rogue CIA asset General Manuel Noriega from power, but it also cast doubt upon the country's claim to sovereignty. Likewise, Washington's drives to strengthen and to re-create, respectively, the armed forces of Honduras and Costa Rica further militarized internal and regional conflicts.

In Nicaragua, strides toward social, economic, and political democratization—significant especially for a country without a pluralistic tradition— have, in turn, been weakened by the social polarization, the generalized scarcity of goods, and the state of emergency declared to cope with the U.S.-inspired aggression. The U.S.-sponsored Contra war has ravished an already crippled economy, leaving a legacy of natural and man-made calamities and contributing to the electoral defeat of the Sandinistas in February of 1990. Despite a smooth transition from the government of Daniel Ortega to that of Violeta Chamorro, which represents an opposition coalition, internal reconciliation will be almost impossible.

Washington's proclivity for seeing North-South issues and internal dynamics through East-West lenses has the potential for both the radicalization and the regionalization (and even continentalization) of conflict. Such oversimplification of indigenous and complex political and social problems into the equation of military force and communist aggression carries the seeds of self-fulfilling prophecies. It could even end up producing a 1970-style "Uruguayanization" and radicalization of the internal politics of Costa Rica, the only liberal democracy in Central America. Examples of contemporary U.S. intervention, openly and covertly subverting either established or potentially democratic governments in the region, abound: Guatemala in 1954, Cuba in 1961, Brazil in 1964, the Dominican Republic in 1965, Bolivia in 1967, Chile in 1973, Nicaragua, El Salvador, and Honduras since 1980. The consequences have been repeated entanglements in supporting "hard" but weak dictatorships, de-development, and lingering violence, eventually leading to militant, rigidly ideological, and uncompromising anti-American regimes.

Under these circumstances, the politics of normalization of the receiver state possesses built-in limitations as a project *for* and *by* Latin Americans to construct truly stable and democratic systems. As this alternative runs its course and the current crisis deepens, it is likely that these weak and limited civilian regimes will be replaced, once again by equally weak, yet violently repressive, military regimes. In such a context of power deflation, popular struggles in Latin America may in fact offer, by their very nature, the only possibility of drawing out the creative potentialities of the population: a Latin American attempt to redefine both nationalism and democracy. Indeed, it is this very mobilization and incorporation of growing numbers of former nonactors into the conscious practice of social transformation that increasingly allow people to conceive of alternatives to the existing structures. Radical social change in today's Latin America is thus simultaneously a liberating process and, in Paulo Freire's terms, an "educative" one.[22] It is a creative project stemming from the concrete practice of struggle, changing the course of history.

NOTES

1. See Rodolfo Stavenhagen, "Seven Fallacies About Latin America," in James Petras and Maurice Zeitlin, eds., *Latin America: Reform or Revolution? A Reader* (New York: Fawcett, 1968), pp. 13–31; also Suzanne Bodenheimer, "The Ideology of Developmentalism: American Political Science Paradigm-Surrogate for Latin American Studies," *Berkeley Journal of Sociology*, No. 15 (1970), pp. 95–137.

2. See Nelson Rockefeller, *The Rockefeller Report of a United States Presidential Mission for the Western Hemisphere*, New York Times edition (Chicago: Quadrangle Books, 1969).

3. See Arturo Siat and Gregorio Iriarte, "De la Seguridad Nacional al Tri-lateralismo," *Cuadernos de Cristianismo y Sociedad* (Buenos Aires, May 1978), pp. 17–30.

4. For an elaboration on the concept see Thomas C. Bruneau and Philippe Faucher, eds., *Authoritarian Capitalism: Brazil's Contemporary Economic and Political Development* (Boulder, Colo.: Westview Press, 1981), pp. 1–9.

5. See Henry Kissinger, quoted in *Trialogue*, No. 19 (Fall 1979), p. 3; also Jeane Kirkpatrick in "Human Rights in Latin America: A Symposium," *Commentary* 72:5 (November 1981), pp. 42–45.

6. See Guillermo O'Donnell, Philippe Schmitter, and Laurence Whitehead, eds., *Transitions from Authoritarian Rule: Prospects for Democracy* (Baltimore: Johns Hopkins University Press, 1986), passim; also J. Nef's critique, "The Trend Toward Democratization and Redemocratization in Latin America: Shadow and Substance," *Latin American Research Review* 22:3 (1988), pp. 131–153.

7. See Cynthia McClintock, "Sendero Luminoso—Peru's Maoist Guerrillas," *Problems of Communism* 23:4 (1983), pp. 19–34; also J. Nef's and J. Vanderkop's piece, "The Spiral of Violence: Insurgency and Counter-Insurgency in Peru," *North South, Canadian Journal of Latin American and Caribbean Studies* 13:26 (March 1990).

8. See David Crane, "Debt: Latin America's ticking time bomb," *Toronto Star,* Saturday, March 11, 1989, pp. D1, D6.

9. J. Nef, "Myths in the Study of Latin American Politics," in J. Nef, ed., *Canada and the Latin American Challenge* (Guelph, Canada: OCPLACS, 1978), pp. 20–22.

10. See Merle Kling, "A Theory of Power and Political Instability in Latin America," in Petras and Zeitlin, op. cit., pp. 76–93.

11. See Frederick Weaver, "Capitalist Development, Empire and Latin American Underdevelopment: An Interpretative Essay on Historical Change," *Latin American Perspectives* 3:4 (Fall 1976), p. 17.

12. Stanislav Andreski, *Parasitism and Subversion: The Case of Latin America* (New York: Pantheon, 1967), passim.

13. William P. Glade, *The Latin American Economies: A Study of Their Institutional Evolution* (New York: Van Nostrand, 1969), pp. 403–482. Also, for a perceptive analysis of import-substitution strategies, see Celso Furtado, *Economic Development of Latin America: Historical Background and Contemporary Problems,* 2d ed. (London: Cambridge University Press, 1976), pp. 107–117.

14. Albert Hirschman, "Alternative to Revolution," in Laura Randall, ed., *Economic Development: Evolution or Revolution?* (Boston: D.C. Heath and Company, 1964), p. 84.

15. Orlando Letelier, "The 'Chicago Boys' in Chile: Economic 'Freedom's Awful Toll,' " *Nation*, August 28, 1976, pp. 138, 142.

16. See "Trilateral Commission: How Influential," *U.S. News and World Report,* May 22, 1978, p. 74; Siat and Iriarte, loc. cit.; Alan Wolfe, "Capitalism Shows Its Face," *Nation,* November 29, 1975, pp. 557–563.

17. Commission on United States-Latin American Relations (Sol Linowitz, chair), *The Americas in a Changing World* (New York: Quadrangle Books, 1975); see also "A New Quest for Stability," *NACLA Report on the Americas* 12:2 (March–April 1979), p. 29.

18. Washington Office on Latin America, *Latin America Update* 5:5 (September–October 1980), p. 1.

19. See Fernando Leyva and James Petras, "Chile's Poor in the Struggle for Democracy," *Latin American Perspectives* 13:4 (Fall 1986), pp. 14–16; also J. Nef, "Alternatives to Development in Contemporary Latin America: An Interpretative Essay on Politics, Ideology and Social Change," *Cahiers GRAL* (Montréal: Université de Montréal, 1988), passim.

20. See Judith Teichman, *Policymaking in Mexico: From Boom to Crisis* (Boston: Allen and Unwin, 1988), pp. 111–149.

21. See J. Nef and R. Bensabat's "The Chilean Plebiscite of 1988: Exit Pinochet?" *International Perspectives* 18:1 (January–February 1989), pp. 18–21.

22. See Paulo Freire, *Pedagogy of the Oppressed* (New York: Seabury Press, 1970), pp. 75–186.

SUGGESTED READINGS

Alves, Marcio Moreira. "Urban Guerrillas and the Terrorist State." In H. Jon Rosenbaum and William G. Tyler, *Contemporary Brazil: Issues in Economic and Political Development,* pp. 51–67. New York: Praeger, 1972.

Andreski, Stanislav. *Parasitism and Subversion: The Case of Latin America.* New York: Pantheon, 1967.

Bodenheimer, Susanne. "The Ideology of Developmentalism: American Political Science Paradigm—Surrogate for Latin American Studies." *Berkeley Journal of Sociology* 15 (1970), pp. 95–137.

Bruneau, Thomas C., and Philippe Faucher, eds. *Authoritarian Capitalism: Brazil's Contemporary Economic and Political Development.* Boulder, Colo.: Westview Press, 1981.

Chalmers, Douglas. "Developing on the Periphery: External Factors in Latin American Politics." In Yale H. Ferguson, *Contemporary Inter-American Relations: A Reader in Theory and Issues,* pp. 11–34. Englewood Cliffs, N.J.: Prentice-Hall, 1972.

Furtado, Celso. *Economic Development of Latin America: Historical Background and Contemporary Problems.* 2d ed. London: Cambridge University Press, 1976.

Glade, William P. *The Latin American Economies: A Study of Their Institutional Evolution.* New York: Van Nostrand, 1969.

Jaguaribe, Helio. *Economic and Political Development: A Theoretical Approach and a Brazilian Case Study.* Cambridge: Harvard University Press, 1968.

Leyva, Fernando, and James Petras. "Chile's Poor in the Struggle for Democracy." *Latin American Perspectives* 13:4 (Fall 1986), pp. 5–25.

McClintock, Cynthia. "Sendero Luminoso—Peru's Maoist Guerrillas." *Problems of Communism* 24:4 (1983), pp. 19–34.

Nef, Jorge. "Alternatives to Development in Contemporary Latin America: An Interpretative Essay on Politics, Ideology and Social Change." *Cahiers GRAL* (Montréal: Université de Montréal, 1988).

Nef, Jorge. "Myths in the Study of Latin American Politics." In Jorge Nef, ed., *Canada and the Latin American Challenge.* Guelph, Canada: Ontario Co-operative Program in Caribbean and Latin American Studies, 1978.

Nef, Jorge. "The Politics of Repression: The Social Pathology of the Chilean Military." *Latin American Perspectives* 1:2 (Fall 1974), pp. 58–72.

Nef, Jorge. "The Trend Toward Democratization and Redemocratization in Latin America: Shadow and Substance." *Latin American Research Review* 22:3 (1988), pp. 131–153.

Nef, Jorge, and R. Bensabat. "The Chilean Plebiscite of 1988: Exit Pinochet?" *International Perspectives* 18:1 (January-February 1989), pp. 18–20.

Nef, Jorge, and J. Vanderkop. "The Spiral of Violence: Insurgency and Counter-Insurgency in Peru." North South, *Canadian Journal of Latin American and Caribbean Studies* 13:26 (March 1990).

Newton, Ronald C. "Natural Corporatism and the Passing of Populism in Spanish America." *Review of Politics* 36:1 (January 1974), pp. 34–51.

O'Donnell, Guillermo, Philippe Schmitter, and Laurence Whitehead, eds. *Transitions from Authoritarian Rule: Prospects for Democracy.* Baltimore: Johns Hopkins University Press, 1986.

Petras, James. *Political and Social Forces in Chilean Development.* Berkeley: University of California Press, 1969.

Petras, James, and Maurice Zeitlin. *Latin America: Reform or Revolution?* New York: Fawcett, 1968.

Stanley, Eugene. *The Future of Underdeveloped Countries: Political Implications of Economic Development.* New York: Praeger, 1961.

Sunkel, Osvaldo. "Transnational Capitalism and National Disintegration in Latin America." *Social and Economic Studies* 22:1 (March 1973), pp. 132–176.

Teichman, Judith. *Policymaking in Mexico: From Boom to Crisis.* Boston: Allen and Unwin, 1988.

Weaver, Frederick S. "Capitalist Development, Empire, and Latin American Underdevelopment: An Interpretative Essay on Historical Change." *Latin American Perspectives* 3:4 (Fall 1976), pp. 17–53.

PART SIX
EXTERNAL RELATIONS

13

INTERNATIONAL RELATIONS IN LATIN AMERICA: CONFLICT AND COOPERATION

JAMES LEE RAY

The battle of Ayacucho in 1824 traditionally marks the end of Spanish rule in South America; Brazil broke its ties with Portugal a couple of years earlier. This chapter will focus on the relationship among the states that emerged from the ruins of Spanish and Portuguese empires in Latin America. The United States has played an important role in those relationships, of course, but the foreign policy of the United States vis-à-vis its southern neighbors will be treated only tangentially (U.S. policy in Latin America is dealt with in Chapter 14). The United States will enter the discussion here, however, to the extent that it has presented challenges and problems with which Latin American states have tried to deal in their foreign policies and in their dealings with each other.

DREAMS OF UNITY, REALITIES OF STRIFE

The Early Years

The Spanish colonies achieved their independence in three more or less separate movements. The first movement originated in Mexico and was joined by Central America. Mexico emerged as an empire under Agustín de Iturbide, who annexed Central America. But that empire lasted only briefly. Central America went its own way in 1823, and by 1824, Iturbide had been kicked out of Mexico by General Antonio López de Santa Anna. Mexico, of course, evolved into a solitary independent nation, but the United Provinces of Central America had fallen apart by 1838, with Guatemala, Honduras, El Salvador, Nicaragua, and Costa Rica emerging as independent nations.

Simón Bolívar led the campaign for independence in the northern part of Spanish America while José de San Martín fought against the Spanish colonialists in the southern part of the continent. The two revolutionary leaders met in 1822 and discussed the possible coordination of their liberation efforts. For reasons that to this day are rather mysterious, they parted company without an agreement. So this early step toward the unification of Spanish America met the same fate as all the numerous succeeding ones to date. It failed.

When Buenos Aires revolted against Spain, the leaders of that movement tried to bring the territory that became known as Paraguay along with them. But a Paraguayan army defeated troops from Buenos Aires who aimed to persuade Paraguayan leaders of the wisdom of unity against the Spanish. Buenos Aires, of course, provided the core of what became Argentina. Chile and Argentina, one can reasonably surmise, were fated to emerge as two countries because of the Andes Mountains, which separate them.

If Simón Bolívar had had his way, the territory that obtained freedom under his leadership would have emerged as two large republics. But Upper Peru, led by Antonio José de Sucre, wanted freedom from both Spain and Peru, and the first great republic of Bolívar's dreams was split into the independent countries of Bolivia and Peru. Bolívar did manage to bring the republic of Gran Colombia into the world in 1819, but by 1830, this republic had also fallen prey to geographical barriers, regional antagonisms, and the ambitions of quarreling political leaders. Gran Colombia dissolved ultimately into the separate countries of Venezuela, Colombia, and Ecuador. Bolívar's death occurred soon after that of "his" republic. Shortly before he died, he mourned the demise of his dreams: "America is ungovernable. Those who have served the revolution have plowed the sea."

Nineteenth-Century Conflicts

Nineteenth-century relations among the newly independent countries in Latin America involved a series of important conflicts and wars, and the impact of those struggles has often been visible in the twentieth century. Conflicts between Brazil and Argentina, for example, evoked the mediation of Great Britain, which managed to arrange the creation of the buffer state of Uruguay in 1830. Peru and Colombia agreed to settle a dispute between them in a process that resulted in the birth of another buffer state at about the same time, i.e., Ecuador. By 1835, General Andrés de Santa Cruz in Bolivia established the Peru-Bolivia Confederation as part of an effort to enlarge his domain. Both Chile and Argentina objected to this confederation for the classical balance-of-power reason that it represented a concentration of power that was dangerous to their continued independence. Argentina declared war against the confederation, but it was the intervention of Chile that effectively brought about its dissolution in 1838.

The 1840s and 1850s were marked by subtle, more or less independent balance-of-power maneuverings among two sets of states: Chile and the other western states comprised the first set; Argentina, Uruguay, Paraguay, and

Brazil on the eastern half of the continent made up the second. Major warfare was avoided until a very bloody conflict occurred among the latter set of states beginning in 1864, with Uruguay serving as the pawn over which the other states fought. Both Brazil and Argentina had made repeated attempts to influence the frequently violent political conflict in Uruguay in ways that would benefit their interests. Left to their own devices, it seems likely that Brazil and Argentina might have become involved in a war against each other over Uruguay. But Paraguay managed to get all three of these states into a war against it.

Until the 1860s, Paraguay had been a rather isolated state, ruled by dictators since the days of liberation. The second of these, Carlos Antonio López, did modify this isolation somewhat, but perhaps his most fateful decision was to put his son, Francisco Solano López, in charge of Paraguay's army. In that role, the younger López traveled to England, France, Germany, Italy, and Spain in the early 1850s, picking up a large amount of arms and ammunition, ideas of grandeur from Napoleon III in France, and an Irish mistress, Elisa Lynch (whom he met in Paris), along the way.[1] Solano López became president of Paraguay upon the death of his father in 1862. In the ensuing years, he grew increasingly suspicious of the motives of both Brazilian and Argentine leaders with respect to Uruguay. In 1864, he became so certain of Brazil's imperialistic ambitions vis-à-vis Uruguay that he decided to thwart them forcefully. (This is not to deny that he had imperialistic ambitions of his own.) To do so, he requested permission for his troops to cross part of Argentina en route to Uruguay. Argentina refused to allow this. When Solano López sent his troops into Argentina anyway, he soon found himself at war with Brazil, Argentina, and Uruguay.

Whether little Paraguay had any chance of winning the war is an interesting historical question. What is not in much dispute is that Paraguay fought almost literally to the last man against its combined enemies. During the war, the provisions of a secret treaty signed by Brazil, Uruguay, and Argentina became known; it was obvious that Brazil and Argentina meant to destroy the government of Paraguay and to help themselves to ample slices of Paraguayan territory. Perhaps that is one reason that Paraguayans fought so desperately. In any case, almost half the population of Paraguay died in the war; something on the order of nine out of ten males perished. At the end of the war, women over fifteen outnumbered men by a ratio of more than four to one.[2]

Interestingly, both during and after the war, the nations of western Latin America objected to Brazilian and Argentine plans to dismember Paraguay and limit its sovereignty. This was an important step toward the integration of the two more or less independent balance-of-power systems on the continent.[3] That process was reinforced by rivalries among the western states that were to culminate in the War of the Pacific between Chile on one side and Bolivia and Peru on the other. They fought over the bleak Atacama Desert and the rich nitrates it contained. By 1870, Chileans, Peruvians, and Bolivians were all exploiting the mineral resources of the area. The Chileans were the most energetic and successful in these ventures. Unfortunately, from their point of view, many of their successes occurred in territories that belonged to Bolivia or Peru. When the Bolivians tried to increase taxes on Chilean operations in their territory and the Peruvians nationalized Chilean nitrate works in theirs, the Chilean government decided to resist these steps by military means.

Chile was eminently successful in this war, which began in February of 1879. By 1883, Chile had won, taking over Antofagasta from Bolivia and the provinces of Tarapacá, Tacna, and Arica from Peru. With the addition of that territory, "Chile entered . . . upon an era of unequaled prosperity from the sale of nitrates, copper and other minerals."[4] Bolivia and Peru, on the other hand, got nothing from the war but grievances, which survived for decades. Bolivia lost its only seaport, at Antofagasta, and despite consistent efforts for the last 100 years, has yet to regain it. Chile promised Peru that a plebiscite would be held ten years after the war in the provinces of Tacna and Arica to determine their permanent status, but that plebiscite was continually postponed. The dispute was finally resolved in 1929, with the help of the U.S. government; as a result of the Washington Protocol of that year, Chile retained Arica while Peru reclaimed Tacna.

THE CHANGING OF THE GUARD

The United States Edges Out Great Britain

The remainder of the nineteenth century in Latin America was most notable, perhaps, for the culmination of a long-term trend. The United States had issued its Monroe Doctrine in 1823, warning other states to refrain from colonizing efforts in the Western Hemisphere. It is widely agreed that the United States lacked the power to enforce the doctrine through most of the nineteenth century. Latin America was not, however, subjected to serious or sustained colonizing efforts for most of that century because Great Britain, in effect, enforced the Monroe Doctrine for the United States. (The most obvious exception to this rule occurred when France set up the empire of Maximilian in Mexico from 1864 to 1867.) Throughout most of the nineteenth century, Great Britain and the United States shared a common interest in keeping other powers out of Latin America. Long-range ambitions by the United States to replace Great Britain as the most influential power in the Western Hemisphere added a measure of conflict to the relationship, but it never became serious until the twentieth century approached.

In 1895, a crisis resulted from the culmination of a dispute between Great Britain and Venezuela over the boundary of British Guiana. President Grover Cleveland insisted on arbitration, and the British ultimately gave in, partly because they were more concerned at the time about the apparent inclination of the German kaiser to stir up trouble for them in South Africa.

Thus, the year 1895 marks the point at which British hegemony in South America began to be challenged seriously by the United States. Further indications of this "changing of the guard" were soon to follow. For example, in 1850, the United States and Great Britain had signed the Clayton-Bulwer Treaty, in which both agreed that neither would attempt to build or exclusively control any canal through Central America. But in 1901, the Clayton-Bulwer Treaty was superseded by the Hay-Pauncefote Treaty, which gave the United States exclusive rights to build and control such an interoceanic canal.

The Era of U.S. Military Interventions

In between the boundary dispute involving Great Britain and Venezuela and the Hay-Pauncefote Treaty, of course, the United States took on and defeated Spain in the Spanish American War of 1898, acquiring Cuba, Puerto Rico, and the Philippines. By 1903, the United States had helped arrange the independence of Panama from Colombia and had signed a treaty with the new Panamanian republic granting to the United States, in perpetuity, a zone in which a transisthmus canal was to be built. A year later, Theodore Roosevelt proclaimed his famous corollary to the Monroe Doctrine, in which he claimed the right to intervene in the internal affairs of other nations in the Western Hemisphere that through "flagrant . . . wrongdoing or impotence" give rise to a need for an "international police power." The United States used this corollary as a rationale for a lengthy series of armed interventions in the ensuing years. For example, the United States militarily occupied Haiti from 1915 to 1934, the Dominican Republic from 1916 to 1924, and Nicaragua from 1912 to 1925 and again from 1927 to 1932. Since these were only the most-prolonged examples among a longer list of interventions, it is not surprising that for the first decades of the twentieth century, one of the primary foreign policy concerns of the Latin American states was to find means of restraining "the colossus of the North."

It is, perhaps, a revealing indication of the desperate and vulnerable position in which the Latin American states found themselves vis-à-vis the United States that the first line of defense to which they resorted was international law. As early as 1868, the Argentine jurist Carlos Calvo had argued that intervention by foreign governments to enforce claims of their citizens residing abroad was illegal because it violated the principle of national sovereignty. In 1902, when Venezuela was the target of a blockade by Britain, Germany, and Italy, the Argentine foreign minister Luis Drago argued that it was also illegal for foreign governments to intervene in attempts to collect public debts (which is what Britain, Germany, and Italy were doing).

The Calvo Doctrine and the Drago Doctrine were originally designed to counter interventions by European states, but the "Roosevelt Corollary . . . and the subsequent U.S. interventions in the Caribbean area based on it, definitely shifted Latin American fears from Europe to the United States."[5] For the first three decades of the twentieth century, Latin American states tried repeatedly, and unsuccessfully, to get the United States to accept the international principle of nonintervention embodied in the doctrines espoused by Calvo and Drago.

Latin American states were only tangentially involved in World War I. Eight declared war, but only Brazil and Cuba played an active role in it. Five other states severed diplomatic relations with Germany, while such important states as Argentina, Chile, and Mexico remained neutral. Since the war cut Latin American countries off from their hitherto major trading partners in Europe, it dramatically reinforced the paramount role of the United States in the Western Hemisphere, and U.S. political pretensions were further reinforced by a burgeoning economic ascendancy. This made the Latin American states even more anxious, of course, to curb the interventionist tendencies of the U.S. government, and many thought they had found a useful instrument in the League of Nations. That organization emphasized the principle of nonintervention and might have provided allies for the Latin American states against any interventionist moves by the United States. It is not surprising, then, that most Latin American countries were disappointed when the United States refused to join the League, even though its covenant explicitly recognized the legitimacy of the Monroe Doctrine.

Since the Latin American states had not been successful in their efforts to restrain the United States within the framework of the League of Nations, they pressed even harder to construct such restraints within the inter-American system. The Pan-American movement had begun with a meeting in Washington in 1889. From that year to 1928, there were six international conferences of American states. Those meetings adhered to a definite pattern. The United States was primarily interested in measures that would facilitate international trade, while the Latin American states preferred to dwell on measures that would secure them against intervention by the United States.

The official attitude of the U.S. government began to change perceptibly in 1929. The new president, Herbert Hoover, ordered a study of the Monroe Doctrine in that year, and by 1930, he had publicly endorsed the results of that study in a move that amounted to a rejection of the Roosevelt Corollary. Franklin D. Roosevelt, of course, adopted the Good Neighbor Policy toward Latin America, the highlight of which was a nonintervention pledge made tentatively at the Seventh Inter-American Conference in Montevideo in 1933 and reaffirmed, with significantly smaller loopholes, at the Inter-American Conference for the Maintenance of Peace at Buenos Aires in 1936. The sincerity with which the Roosevelt administration adopted this new policy was given two significant tests when Bolivia nationalized foreign oil companies in that country in 1937 and Mexico nationalized its oil industry in 1938. Roosevelt resisted pressures to intervene in both cases.

TERRITORIAL CONFLICT IN SOUTH AMERICA

The Chaco War

As the Latin American states were in the midst of their successful effort (albeit only temporarily) to deal with U.S. interventions, two of the countries fought each other in the only really major war between Latin American states in this century. This war was fought between the two big losers of the most important South American wars in the nineteenth century, perhaps not coincidentally. After Bolivia lost its outlet to the sea during the War of the Pacific, some historians argue, its leaders began to look to the Rio de la Plata system and possible ports on the Atlantic. This meant that Bolivia needed access to the Paraguay River, and early in the twentieth century, Bolivia began building forts in the area of that river in order to ensure access to it. Paraguay, in the meantime, according to several accounts, was looking for some way to recover its national honor after its humiliating defeat in the war against Brazil, Uruguay, and Argentina. The emotions evoked in this manner soon focused on the Chaco Boreal, a desolate area near the border between Paraguay and Bolivia. Both countries had made claims to this area as early as the mid-1500s, during the colonial era, and border clashes between the two states occurred as early as 1927. Then rumors of vast oil deposits in the Chaco added fuel to the controversy, so to speak. War finally broke out in 1932.

Bolivia's population at the time was roughly three times that of Paraguay, but Bolivia suffered disadvantages that, in the end, turned out to be more important. Perhaps the most important was the composition of its army. Most Bolivian soldiers were Indians who had been drafted into the army off the 2-mi-high (3-km) plain known as the Altiplano. They were not accustomed to the tropical heat of the Chaco and had no understanding of the conflict (which is not to say that they would have been enthusiastic if they *had* understood the reasons for the war). Paraguayan soldiers, in contrast, were more comfortable in the climate of the area and felt they were defending their homeland.

Even so, the war dragged on for three years, with both sides suffering heavy losses. Estimates of these losses vary widely, of course: One apparently authoritative source concludes that 50,000 Paraguayan soldiers died in the conflict while 80,000 Bolivian soldiers met the same fate.[6] A truce was finally arranged in 1938. In the treaty, Paraguay was awarded most of the disputed Chaco area; Bolivia's reward was further frustration of its quest for an outlet to the sea.

Further Disputes

Two serious border disputes between Latin American states surfaced during the 1930s and 1940s. Both involved Peru. Peruvian troops seized the Amazon River town of Leticia in 1932. Since that town had been awarded to Colombia in 1930, the Colombian government sent troops to Leticia to make its objections known. There was some brief but bloody fighting. After a change of government in Peru, serious negotiations began. It took two years, but an amicable settlement was achieved, with Colombia retaining its hold on Leticia.

Peru was more successful in a dispute with Ecuador, which reached a crisis stage in 1941. Peruvian troops occupied territory claimed by Ecuador north of the Marañón River. That river is important because it allows access to the Amazon River. The dispute threatened to erupt into open warfare for several months, but peace in South America was saved, as it turned out, by the Japanese attack on Pearl Harbor in December 1941. In the wake of that catastrophe, the U.S. government was in no mood to allow neighbors in its "backyard" to fight among themselves. The United States imposed a solution, which gave Peru control over the disputed area. Naturally enough, Ecuador was not happy with this solution. The issue has never been resolved; it led to open border clashes between Ecuador and Peru in 1981.

WORLD WAR II AND ITS AFTERMATH

The Latin American countries played a minor role in World War II. With the onset of the conflict, the United States tried to get the Western Hemisphere organized, but this project met with more problems than might have been anticipated. Argentina was least enthusiastic about unification against the Axis powers. The government of Argentina, in fact, did not break relations with Germany until 1944 and did not declare war until 1945. Brazil, on the other hand, did send a significant number of troops to Italy, while Mexican troops served in the Pacific theater. Generally speaking, the effect of World War II on Inter-American relations was to reinforce trends set in motion by World War I. Once again, the Latin American states were cut off from the world outside the Western Hemisphere and became more closely tied to the United States. The United States, of course, emerged from World War II as the most powerful state in the world, regardless of how the controversial concept of power might be defined or measured.

In the years after the war, a controversy about the agenda of relations between the United States and Latin American countries surfaced in a shape that was to remain consistent in the postwar decades. For the United States, the primary issue was communist subversion; the Latin American states, on the other hand, were almost always more interested in policies and strategies that would foster their economic development.

One of the first indications of concern about international economic issues on the part of Latin American states was their proposal to form the Economic Commission for Latin America (ECLA) as a part of the new United Nations organization. The United States was opposed to the idea, but ECLA was created in 1948 in spite of that opposition. In the early 1950s, ECLA proposed the creation of a new inter-American bank and a Latin American common market (the Inter-American Development Bank was established in 1959). The United States was more interested in a collective defense treaty, i.e., the Inter-American Treaty of Reciprocal Assistance (Rio Treaty) signed on September 2, 1947, and the establishment of the Organization of American States (OAS) in 1948. Latin Americans preferred that economic issues be dealt with in ECLA, but "for years, the United States favored the OAS Inter-American Economic and Social Council and regarded the efforts of the competitor ECLA with political disapproval as well as deep distrust."[7]

REGIONAL APPROACHES TO DEVELOPMENT

Economic Integration as a Tool

One of the proposed solutions to the problems of underdevelopment seized on by ECLA and several Latin American economists was economic integration.[8] Integration might provide markets sufficiently large, for example, to make it feasible for Latin American states to manufacture their own capital goods, thus reducing their dependence on the imports of such heavy equipment. Large markets created by the elimination of intraregional tariff barriers, and the construction of common external tariffs that would be part of the economic integration processes, might also allow industries to benefit from economies of scale, which, in turn, could evoke efficiency at levels competitive on the world market.

With these ideas in mind, ECLA and national officials worked toward the creation of two regional integration organizations: the Central American Common Market (CACM) and the Latin American Free Trade Association (LAFTA). The former organization was launched in 1960 with Guatemala, El Salvador, Honduras, Nicaragua, and later, Costa Rica as its members. Ten South American countries, later joined by Mexico, formed LAFTA in the same year. Both organizations were inspired to some extent by the success enjoyed by the European Economic Community (EEC) at the time. Furthermore, both were based on a philosophy of economic integration similar to that utilized in Europe. That is, CACM and LAFTA both sought economic integration on the basis of the functional (or neofunctional) theory of integration. According to that theory, the benefits that accrue to the member states as a result of the activities of the central organization of the integration organization mean that the member states, little by little, become willing to allow that central organization much broader authority until some day (in theory), it is running virtually everything.[9]

Such ideas had seemed to work reasonably well in Europe, and they seemed to work for a time in Latin America. The CACM promoted a marked increase in intraregional trade, and the rate of economic growth of the Central American countries increased. Similarly, the members of LAFTA managed to negotiate numerous reductions of tariffs, and intraregional trade increased 100 percent from 1961 to 1968.[10] But the two organizations soon ran into problems, at least one of which plagued both.

That problem involved the distribution of the benefits of integration among the member states. The founders of both the CACM and LAFTA had anticipated this problem by initially giving special concessions to the poorer member states. In the CACM, for example, special incentives were adopted in order to lure new industries into the relatively poor states (i.e., Honduras and Nicaragua). Members of LAFTA divided themselves into three categories according to levels of development and size of domestic markets. The countries in the lower categories were given trade concessions and the right to protect some infant industries from competition with similar industries in such relatively developed countries as Brazil, Argentina, and Mexico. Nevertheless, by the end of the 1960s, both organizations were showing signs of strain resulting in part from suspicions by the less-developed members that they were receiving an unequal share of the benefits of integration.

Problems for CACM and LAFTA

In 1969, the CACM was plagued by an even more dramatic problem. Two of its member states, Honduras and El Salvador, fought a war against each other. El Salvador is densely populated, whereas Honduras is relatively underpopulated. Throughout the 1960s, unemployed workers from El Salvador poured into the empty fertile valleys in Honduras. By 1969, the military government of Honduras was faced with considerable internal unrest, and it decided to deal with that discontent with a land reform program that, not accidentally, deprived many Salvadoran squatters of their recently acquired property.

The government of El Salvador responded with a surprise attack in July 1969. The attack failed, and a bloody stalemate resulted. The OAS managed to arrange a truce, which was broken in January of 1970. A prolonged kind of "cold war" between Honduras and El Salvador ensued. Trade between them stopped, and Honduras put an embargo on trade between El Salvador on the one hand and Nicaragua and Costa Rica on the other. All in all, the war was a devastating blow to the CACM.

In the process of resolving the conflict between Honduras and El Salvador, CACM officials and government leaders discovered that other fissures in the organization threatened its existence. Honduras had been dissatisfied with the Common Market in any case, for the eminently predictable reason. Honduras, along with Nicaragua the least-developed country in that area, felt itself the victim of unfair competition. Relief from the burdens of such competition was difficult to arrange in the face of continued antagonism between El Salvador and Honduras. By the end of the 1970s, of course, the CACM faced a new set of problems. The overthrow of Somoza in Nicaragua and serious civil unrest elsewhere, especially in El Salvador, threatened to destroy what was left of the organization.

In the late 1960s, LAFTA also began to fall apart. Bolivia, Chile, Colombia, Ecuador, and Peru made plans to form a common market among themselves, excluding Argentina, Brazil, and Mexico. These five countries, later joined by Venezuela, formed what became known as the Andean Common Market (ANCOM). The members of ANCOM hoped to achieve sufficient economic progress to be able to compete successfully with the larger, more economically developed countries in LAFTA. Then, according to the plan, the ANCOM countries would rejoin LAFTA, able to share more equally in the benefits of economic integration provided by that organization.

ANCOM aroused a lot of interest in the Third World because of its approach toward foreign investment. By the late 1960s, the evidence arising out of the experience of the European Common Market made it obvious that multinational corporations (particularly U.S.-based ones) could benefit enormously from the new, enlarged, and protected markets resulting from the process of economic integration. There was fear that integration among Latin American states might make them even more vulnerable to penetration and domination by foreign investors than they had been in the past. It was this fear, in part, that led ANCOM to adopt regulations aimed at controlling foreign investment within the boundaries of its member states.

There were rules, for example, concerning which sectors of the economies were open to investors. There were limits on the amount of capital that could be repatriated. Parent companies were forbidden to restrict exports by their subsidiaries. Provisions were also made to ensure that subsidiaries of foreign corporations would become locally owned in time. "Foreign enterprises already established in the Andean region must within three years of the code's adoption work out gradual divestment plans that would give local investors . . . majority control (51%) of the total shares within 15 years. New foreign investors must adopt similar 15-year fade-out schedules two years after production begins."[11]

How well these rules aimed at controlling foreign investments have worked is a controversial question. Some corporations have managed to obtain exceptions to them in important cases. And there are ways in which these kinds of rules can be subverted even if they are ostensibly enforced.[12] Furthermore, there have been obvious differences in the manner in which the rules are enforced by the members. Chile has provided the most spectacular example of these differences. Under Allende, of course, the Chilean government was an enthusiastic supporter of strict controls on foreign investment. The post-Allende government, however, was so desperate to attract foreign investment that it pushed hard for a relaxation of those controls. Even though the other members of ANCOM gave Chile much of what it wanted in this regard, the Pinochet regime withdrew Chile from the organization in 1976.

Peru, in the meantime, underwent a political transformation of its own. The Peruvian "revolution" in 1968 served as an inspiration for many of the innovations adopted by ANCOM with respect to foreign investment. But the new regime experienced a series of economic disasters that helped bring about a change of government and a change of attitude about foreign investment. As a result of this transition, Peru became a less-enthusiastic supporter of some of the innovations adopted by ANCOM. This increased skepticism about the extent to which rules on paper were being enforced in fact. As the end of the 1970s approached, ANCOM could hardly be written off as a failure, but even sympathetic observers admitted that its future was uncertain.[13]

INTER-AMERICAN RELATIONS IN THE 1980s

The road to economic integration continued to be a rocky one as the 1970s turned into the 1980s. The Latin American Free Trade Association gave up the ghost entirely in August of 1980. It was replaced by the Latin American Integration Association (LAIA), but it is difficult not to be skeptical about the fate of this new organization. Its goals are even more vague and distant than those of LAFTA, and the members of LAFTA were forever postponing tough decisions. "The real question is not whether LAIA can promote new trade cooperation, but whether it can save the few tariff-cutting agreements reached under the auspices of LAFTA."[14] The Latin American Economic System, formed in 1975 at the initiative of President Luis Echeverría of Mexico, has accomplished little of note as of this writing. The Andean Common Market, with Chile's departure and movements toward democracy in Peru, Ecuador, and Bolivia, seemed at one point to be transforming itself into an organization of democratic states. But yet another interlude of military rule in Bolivia (1980–1982) derailed that trend. As verbal battles raged between the democratic members of ANCOM and Bolivia, two of ANCOM's ostensibly democratic members, Ecuador and Peru, once again engaged in real battles as a result of their perennial border dispute.

If economic integration did not, then, seem the road to the promised land, neither did any of the national approaches to economic development. Thanks largely to heavy borrowing in response to the twin "oil shocks" of the 1970s imposed by OPEC and the reactions by the industrialized world (especially the United States) to those shocks—which raised interest rates, created a serious recession in 1982, erected tariff barriers against Latin American exports, and contributed to a sharp decline in the prices of commodities that Latin American states depend on for exports—the international politics and economics of the 1980s in the Western Hemisphere were dominated by the international debt problem. Most Latin American countries during that decade had little or nothing left over to devote to economic growth and development once they had paid off the interest on their foreign debts, and paying off the principal seemed out of the question. In 1989, the World Bank designated seventeen countries as "highly indebted," and twelve of them were Latin American.[15] In part because of this problem, as Gert Rosenthal observed, "by now it has become a platitude to proclaim that, over the past decade, Latin America has experienced its deepest, most prolonged economic recession in modern history."[16]

Latin America's economic problems remained serious as the 1990s began, and while it is not at all clear whether they can be resolved anytime soon, it has become quite clear how most Latin American countries are going to go about *trying* to solve them. They are going to try, first, "neoclassical" or classical "liberal" economic strategies, stressing privatization, market-oriented reforms, and perhaps even foreign investment. This is true for President Salinas de Gortari in Mexico, newly elected President Fernando Collor de Mello in Brazil, and even for Peronist Carlos Menem in Argentina.[17] More surprisingly, even such socialists or radicals as Michael Manley in Jamaica, Carlos Andres Perez in Venezuela, and Jaime Paz Zamora in Bolivia *also* were talking (and acting) as if they believed in the "magic of the marketplace." It may have been this "free-market" mood in Latin America, in part, that accounted for the surprising electoral defeat of the Sandinistas in Nicaragua at the beginning of the 1990s.

Latin America is also going to try to solve its economic problems with "democratic" political approaches. No sooner had Latin Americanists in great numbers in the 1970s developed and largely adopted the notion that serious economic problems make "bureaucratic-authoritarianism" the "natural" form of government in Latin America[18] than the even more serious economic problems of the 1980s came along and *seemed* to provoke the broadest wave of democratization in Latin American history. South America is presently composed entirely of elected governments for the first time in its history. Manuel Noriega's ouster by means of a U.S. invasion in late 1989 was (to this writer) depressingly reminiscent of many similar events in inter-American history, but that event, along with the departure of Prosper Avril from Haiti in early 1990, brought Latin America very close to having nothing but elected, arguably "democratic" governments, except in Cuba. (Admittedly, the argument is much more difficult to make in some places, like Guatemala, El Salvador, and Paraguay, to name a few, than in other states.) Most Latin Americanists seem to feel that this wave of democratization is cyclical and bound to be replaced fairly soon by a new wave of dictatorships.[19] Perhaps they are underestimating the extent to which the movement toward democracy in Latin America is rooted in global forces?[20] In any case, what does seem safe to predict is that the liberalizing trend in Latin America in both economics and politics is not likely to survive the 1990s unless the recession of the 1980s is replaced by growth, stability, and (dare we even hope?) some measure of economic equity.

NOTES

1. Mention of the last acquisition might seem out of place in an otherwise somber and proper discussion, but Elisa Lynch reputedly had a significant impact on the policies of Solano López. Pelham H. Box, for example, asserts that "the nature of the influence that for sixteen years the 'lorette parisienne' expressed over the mind of Francisco Solano López has not been adequately investigated. That it was considerable admits of no doubt" (Box, *The Origins of the Paraguayan War* [Urbana: University of Illinois Press, 1927], pp. 181–182).

2. Charles J. Kolinski, *Independence or Death: The Story of the Paraguayan War* (Gainesville: University of Florida Press, 1965), p. 198.

3. Robert N. Burr, "The Balance of Power in Nineteenth-Century South America: An Exploratory Essay," *Hispanic American Historical Review* 25 (February 1955), pp. 40-41.

4. Hubert Herring, *A History of Latin America,* 3d ed. (New York: Alfred A. Knopf, 1972), p. 655.

5. G. Pope Atkins, *Latin America in the International Political System* (New York: Free Press, 1977), p. 323.

6. J. David Singer and Melvin Small, *The Wages of War 1816–1965: A Statistical Handbook* (New York: Wiley and Jones, 1972), p. 67.

7. Minerva M. Etzioni, *The Majority of One: Towards a Theory of Regional Compatibility* (Beverly Hills, Calif.: Sage Publications, 1970), pp. 118–119.

8. This section relies heavily on my earlier discussion of integration in Latin America in James L. Ray, *Global Politics,* 4th ed. (Boston: Houghton Mifflin, 1990), pp. 429–440.

9. David Mitrany, *A Working Peace System* (London: Royal Institute of International Affairs, 1943), and Ernst Haas, *The Uniting of Europe* (Stanford: Stanford University Press, 1958).

10. Joseph Grunwald, Miguel S. Wionczek, and Martin Carnoy, *Latin American Economic Integration and U.S. Policy* (Washington, D.C.: Brookings Institution, 1972), p. 51.

11. Roger W. Fontaine, *The Andean Pact: A Political Analysis* (Beverly Hills, Calif.: Sage Publications, 1977), p. 19.

12. Thomas J. Biersteker, "The Illusion of State Power: Transnational Corporations and the Neutralization of Host-Country Legislation," *Journal of Peace Research* 17 (1980), pp. 207–221.

13. Ricardo French-Davis, "The Andean Pact: A Model of Economic Integration for Developing Countries," in *Latin America and the World Economy*, ed. Joseph Grunwald (Beverly Hills, Calif.: Sage Publications, 1978), pp. 165–194.

14. "Latin America's Elusive Unity," *Economist*, November 8, 1980, p. 45.

15. World Bank, *World Development Report 1989* (New York: Oxford University Press, 1989), p. 154.

16. Gert Rosenthal, "Some Thoughts on Poverty and Recession in Latin America," *Journal of Interamerican History and World Affairs* 29 (Fall 1987), p. 63.

17. At this writing, Menem's reforms in Argentina are off to a rocky start indeed. Predictably, Collor de Mello in Brazil and free-market-oriented Mario Vargas Llosa in Peru argued that Menem's problems have arisen because he has not initiated neoclassical reforms with sufficient vigor.

18. Guillermo O'Donnell, *Modernization and Bureaucratic-Authoritarianism: Studies in Latin American Politics,* Politics of Modernization Series, No. 9 (Berkeley: Institute of International Studies, University of California, 1973).

19. See, for example, James M. Malloy and Mitchell A. Seligson, eds., *Authoritarians and Democrats: Regime Transition in Latin America* (Pittsburgh: University of Pittsburgh Press, 1987); Jorge Nef, "The Trend Toward Democratization and Redemocratization in Latin America," *Latin American Research Review* 23 (1988), pp. 131–153.

20. Francis Fukuyama, "The End of History?" *National Interest,* No. 16 (Summer 1989), pp. 3–18.

SUGGESTED READINGS

Atkins, G. Pope. *Latin America in the International Political System.* 2nd ed. New York: Free Press, 1989. A good broad and basic introduction to inter-American relations, as well as to the relationship of the Latin American region with the rest of the world.

Burr, Robert N. "The Balance of Power in Nineteenth-Century South America: An Exploratory Essay." *Hispanic American Historical Review* 25 (February 1955), pp. 37–60. An informative discussion of relations among the South American states in the nineteenth century, with a focus on the impact of the interstate wars in that time period.

Connell-Smith, Gordon. *The United States and Latin America.* New York: John Wiley and Sons, 1974. One of the liveliest historical accounts on U.S. foreign policy toward Latin America.

Davis, Harold Eugene, and Larman C. Wilson, eds. *Latin American Foreign Policies: An Analysis.* Baltimore: Johns Hopkins University Press, 1975. Concentrates on a country-by-country analysis of the foreign policies of Latin American states. Emphasizes recent foreign policy problems and approaches.

de Soto, Hernando. *The Other Path.* New York: Harper and Row, 1989. An English translation of this Peruvian work, which has apparently become a kind of "bible" of advocates of neoclassical reforms in Latin America. There is a rather lengthy introduction by Mario Vargas Llosa.

Dominguez, Jorge. "Consensus and Divergence: The State of the Literature in Interamerican Relations in the 1970s." *Latin American Research Review* 13:1 (1978), pp. 87–126. Interesting discussion of the current trends and competing viewpoints in the academic literature on inter-American relations.

Herring, Hubert. *A History of Latin America.* 3d ed. New York: Alfred A. Knopf, 1972. A very comprehensive, authoritative history of the region with each country discussed in some detail.

Levinson, Jerome, and Juan de Onis. *The Alliance That Lost Its Way.* Chicago: Quadrangle Books, 1970. A penetrating analysis of the Alliance for Progress. Especially good on the problems faced by the United States in its attempts to mold the internal political systems of Latin American states.

Malloy, James M., and Mitchell A. Seligson, eds. *Authoritarians and Democrats: Regime Transition in Latin America.* Pittsburgh: University of Pittsburgh Press, 1987. An analysis of the transition to democracy in several Latin American countries with a general, theoretical discussion of the phenomenon in both the introduction and a concluding chapter.

Sigmund, Paul E. "Latin America: Change or Continuity?" *Foreign Affairs* 60:3 (1982), pp. 629–657. An up-to-date analysis of the most recent events in Latin America.

────── . "Struggle in Central America: The Current Danger." *Foreign Policy* no. 43 (Summer 1981), pp. 70–93. A series of authors analyze the controversial events in Central America from several different points of view.

Szulc, Tad. *Fidel: A Critical Portrait.* New York: Avon, 1986. A very readable biography with lots of interesting tidbits about, for example, how the CIA helped Fidel financially in the 1950s, and how Fidel contacted and developed a close relationship with the traditional Communist party in Havana almost from the moment he came to town in 1959.

Walleri, R. D. "The Political Economy Literature on North-South Relations." *International Studies Quarterly* 22:4 (March 1978), pp. 587–624. This article does not focus specifically on Latin America, but it gives a useful overview of competing theoretical perspectives in the area of political economy that are certainly relevant to Latin America.

14

UNITED STATES POLICY IN LATIN AMERICA

JEROME SLATER AND JAN KNIPPERS BLACK

Ever since the early nineteenth century, the dominant objective of U.S. policy toward Latin America has been the preservation of the Western Hemisphere as a U.S. sphere of influence. The domination of Latin America has been sought, not primarily out of imperialist motivations or the desire for economic exploitation (though at times, imperialism and exploitation have indeed been a prominent part of U.S. policy), but rather because of the firm belief, dating from the founding fathers and remaining a critical part of today's U.S. political mythology, that U.S. security and prosperity are centrally dependent on the exclusion of "foreign" political ideologies and movements from the Western Hemisphere. Since independence, the major external threats have been seen to be European colonialism in the nineteenth and early twentieth centuries, fascism and nazism in the 1930s, and communism since the end of World War II.

There has also been an important ideological dimension to U.S. policy, the belief that the New World—dominated, led, and protected by the United States—was not only geographically but also politically, culturally, and morally separate from and superior to the rest of the world. It thus became the self-appointed mission of the United States to isolate and protect the entire Western Hemisphere from the corrupting influences of the rest of the world, particularly of Europe, or the Old World.

The classic formulation of U.S. policy toward Latin America is, of course, the Monroe Doctrine. This doctrine embodies both the strategic and ideological dimensions of U.S. policy, and it has created a powerful myth that to this day centrally affects U.S. policy. We will argue that this myth—the myth that the United States has both the moral right and the imperative national interest to continue to treat the Western Hemisphere as its sphere of influence—has been a pernicious one in that for nearly 200 years, it has blinded Americans to the nature of their real interests and behavior in this hemisphere.

In referring to the Monroe Doctrine and all the subsequent attitudes and policies that have essentially been reflections of that doctrine as "myth," it is *not* being implied that U.S. policymakers have consciously, deliberately, or cynically sought to use the Monroe Doctrine to mislead others about the true nature of U.S. policies and objectives. If that were the case, the doctrine would have had little importance in the political history of inter-American relations, for scarcely any Latin Americans have been deceived. On the contrary, what makes the Monroe Doctrine such a centrally important feature of the political mythology that underlies U.S. foreign policy is that it has functioned only too successfully to mislead and deceive U.S. citizens themselves, policymakers no less than the average citizen.

U.S. RELATIONS WITH LATIN AMERICA FROM INDEPENDENCE THROUGH WORLD WAR II

The Monroe Doctrine, promulgated in 1823, is a unilateral statement of U.S. policy and interests. On its face, the doctrine prohibits European interference in the domestic political affairs of Latin America; more generally, however, it was intended to exclude any foreign political influence from the Western Hemisphere and to stake out the entire New World as a U.S. sphere of influence. For most of the nineteenth century, the doctrine was largely bluff, for the United States had neither the military power nor the political will to enforce it. Thus, on numerous occasions the United States stood idly by while the major European colonial powers (mainly England, Spain, and France) continued to interfere in Latin America and to suppress independence movements. It was not until the end of the century, when U.S. military power, particularly naval power, became significant, that the Monroe Doctrine became an operational part of U.S. policy. However, the doctrine has been invoked far more often *against* the Latin Americans than for their protection, especially from the end of the 1890s through the early 1920s, when the doctrine served as an ideological cover for outright U.S. expansionism and imperialism. In effect, whereas in the nineteenth century the essential message of the Monroe Doctrine was "leave Latin America alone," with the rise of U.S. militarism and imperialism, the message shifted to "leave Latin America *to us*"—quite a different proposition.

U.S. imperialism in the Caribbean began with the Spanish American War when President McKinley sent U.S. troops into Cuba, ostensibly to aid a Cuban national independence revolt against Spanish colonialism. But once the marines had landed, it proved extremely difficult to get them out again, a pattern that was to be repeated frequently throughout the Caribbean and Central America during the first three decades of the twentieth century. Even though Spain quickly sued for peace and withdrew, a military occupation regime was established and Cuban resistance to such unwanted and unnecessary "assistance" was forcibly suppressed. The United States did not withdraw from Cuba until decades later, and then only after exacting a sweeping series of economic, political, and military concessions that reduced Cuba to a virtual semicolony of the United States.

The acquisition of the Canal Zone in Panama was the next major U.S. imperialist venture. Once the United States had embarked on becoming a global commercial and naval power, the perceived necessity for a canal across Central America as a means of shortening the route between the Atlantic and Pacific oceans became acute. The most feasible and economic route lay across the Isthmus of Panama, which was part of the country of Colombia. President Theodore Roosevelt offered to buy the land, but Colombia turned down Roosevelt's offer of some $10 million. Colombia's refusal to sell infuriated Roosevelt, so he fomented a phony "revolution" on the Isthmus of Panama, financed by the Panama Canal Company (a private construction company that stood to get the lucrative contract to build the canal if the Colombian problem could be disposed of) and spearheaded mostly by laborers under the corporation's employ. When Colombia sent a column of troops marching onto the isthmus to put down the revolt on its national territory, Roosevelt sent a U.S. naval task force to the area and threatened to intervene if the Colombian troops engaged the "rebels." Thus intimidated, the Colombian troops withdrew, whereupon the sovereign state of Panama declared its independence. The new Panamanian foreign minister, who happened also to be a stockholder in the Panama Canal Corporation, quickly negotiated a treaty that gave the United States the 10-mi-wide (16-km) Canal Zone "in perpetuity."

As the years passed, though, what began as the fictitious "republic of Panama" actually became a real nation, with real feelings of nationalism that came to focus on the quaint anomaly of the Canal Zone. Americans who failed to remember just how the United States came to control the Canal Zone were resentful of Panamanian demands for renegotiation of the treaty, particularly when those demands were accompanied by anti-American riots, as in 1964. At the turn of the century, however, there were few pious illusions. As Roosevelt himself put it, "I took Panama."

The taking of Panama in 1903 in turn intensified U.S. interventionist and imperialist activities throughout Central America and the Caribbean, for as the canal neared completion, the United States became increasingly sensitive to any disturbances in the area that might invite European intervention and pose a threat to the canal or the sea approaches to it. This concern for the maintenance of U.S. hegemony, best maintained in an atmosphere of political stability, combined with the desire to promote and protect growing U.S. commercial interests in the area and, especially under Woodrow Wilson, with the zeal to promote democracy for idealistic reasons and produced a series of U.S. military interventions.

The most important of these interventions, in terms of their long-term consequences, which still continue to centrally affect U.S. policy and attitudes, were in Nicaragua in 1912 and the Dominican Republic in 1916. In both cases, local violence, revolutions, and political instability that threatened U.S. economic interests posed a potential threat to the security of the Panama Canal and the sea approaches to it and offended U.S. political sensibilities. The United States intervened in both countries, and in both cases, harsh marine occupations were established and were terminated only years after the marines had created centralized local armies in their own image and installed at the head of these forces pro-American and "reliable" young officers. In Nicaragua, the legacy of the intervention and occupation was Anastasio Somoza, and in the Dominican Republic it was Rafael Trujillo; in each country, feudalistic family totalitarian regimes were established and remained in power for two generations, slaughtering their compatriots and bilking their countries.

Beginning in the 1920s, disenchantment with and political opposition to continued imperialism and military interventions in the Caribbean became increasingly powerful in the United States. European colonialism and intervention in the Western Hemisphere for all practical purposes had ended, threats to the Panama Canal were nonexistent, dictatorships were predominant in Latin America despite Wilson's impassioned but misguided efforts at "teaching the Latins to elect good men," and anti-Americanism was rampant throughout the hemisphere. The mood in the United States favored disengagement and fence-mending, particularly in light of the absence of direct threats to U.S. security or prosperity. As a result, beginning with the Hoover administration, interventionist rhetoric and behavior declined, and the withdrawal of marine occupation forces was begun.

Franklin Roosevelt then inaugurated the Good Neighbor Policy, the cornerstone of which was the formal renunciation of U.S. intervention in Latin America, including political and economic pressures as well as outright military intervention in the internal affairs of Latin American states. The Good Neighbor Policy was a dramatic success. Anti-Americanism declined, Roosevelt became a great hero throughout Latin America, and when World War II broke out, most Latin American states cooperated closely with the United States by making military bases available to U.S. forces, selling the United States strategic raw materials at very low prices while refusing to sell them to the Axis powers, and suppressing local Nazi and fascist movements.

U.S.–LATIN AMERICAN RELATIONS SINCE WORLD WAR II

With the end of World War II, the temporary political stability of Latin America and the period of goodwill between the United States and Latin America came to an end. Since 1945, Latin America has been in a state of political, economic, and social turmoil. The main lines of internal conflict have been between populist reform movements—sometimes radical, sometimes moderate, and occasionally (as in Peronist Argentina) even quasi-fascist—and the existing oligarchical social and economic structures, dominated by an alliance of landowners, big business, the Catholic Church (until recently), sectors of the new middle classes, and most important, the armed forces. Thus, populist mass movements, generally to the left, have confronted the conservative elites that have dominated the politics and economies of Latin America since the era of the Spanish conquest. The essential policy choice for the United States has been between support for the status quo in the name of order and stability and support for the forces of change, the aspirations of which have been closer to the professed values and purposes of the United States but which have also posed the danger of violence, chaos, and radicalism.

With the partial exceptions of the Kennedy and Carter administrations, policymakers in fact have had little difficulty in resolving this dilemma: They have opted for the status quo, regardless of the costs to supposed U.S. values of democracy and social justice. As in the past, the United States has sought to ensure that no Latin American government comes to power, or remains in power, if it represents a serious challenge to U.S. hegemony in the hemisphere. In the context of the Cold War, of course, that has meant the exclusion of Communist or even merely radical regimes.

As long as Latin American regimes have not been on the radical left, the United States has been indifferent as to how democratic, socially responsive, honest, and respectful of human rights they have been. Dictatorial and repressive regimes, as well as democracies, can and do cooperate with the United States; in fact, for both tactical and ideological reasons, the most repressive and reactionary regimes of Latin America have been generally among the most enthusiastic supporters of U.S. Cold War policies. So most U.S. governments have sought to shore up the status quo in Latin America, *any* status quo, so long as it is non-Communist.

A key weapon in the effort to bolster the status quo in Latin America has been the military assistance program. The Latin American armed forces, although occasionally siding with reformist forces, normally have acted as the major bulwark of the conservative ruling elites against economic, social, and political change. Furthermore, the military is normally the single most powerful political force in Latin America, whether ruling directly, utilizing a thinly disguised civilian front, or acting as a veto group to prevent specific actions. In this context, U.S. military assistance could, it was hoped, serve a number of purposes: gain the friendship of a key political group; strengthen Latin American military capabilities for the maintenance of "internal order"; and by preempting the military market, exclude nonhemispheric, and particularly Soviet-bloc, suppliers, thereby precluding a potential threat to U.S. hegemony in the hemisphere. To this end, large quantities of arms have been given or sold to Latin American military forces, thousands of military officers have been brought to the United States for courses in military education and training in combat schools, and joint training exercises have been held regularly.

When all else has failed, direct U.S. intervention to prevent radical, or even potentially radical, governments from coming to power has been resorted to. Prior to the Cuban Revolution and the Dominican intervention of 1965, the most direct use of U.S. power took place in Guatemala in 1954 when the Eisenhower administration used the CIA to organize, finance, arm, and direct a right-wing exile invasion that succeeded in overthrowing a radical, nationalist Guatemalan regime.

Throughout the Truman and Eisenhower administrations, then, the United States, as a result of its efforts to maintain the status quo in Latin America as part of its general policy of preserving the Western Hemisphere as a U.S. sphere of influence, was a major obstacle to economic, social, and political progress in Latin America. However, two events at the end of the 1950s precipitated major—though short-lived—changes in U.S. policy. In 1958, widespread anti-American rioting, directed specifically at Vice-President Richard Nixon during his tour of major South American states, came as a shock to the Eisenhower administration and the U.S. citizens generally. The riots dramatized the extent to which hatred of the United States had spread throughout Latin America.

By the end of the 1950s, Latin American grievances against the United States had destroyed any remnants of goodwill that had remained from Roosevelt's Good Neighbor Policy. The major grievances included close ties to such brutal dictatorships as those of Trujillo, Somoza, Pérez Jiménez in Venezuela, Rojas Pinilla in Colombia, and others; the relegation of Latin America to a peripheral part of U.S. global policies; the low amount of U.S. economic assistance; trade policies that discriminated against Latin America; and finally, the growing U.S. interventionism against alleged communist dangers, as in Guatemala and elsewhere.

The second major event was the revolution Castro led in Cuba in 1959. Although the extent of rising mass dissatisfaction with the status quo in Latin America had been well known to observers for years, its implications had escaped United States policymakers. But the revolt against Batista sharply dramatized this discontent, making it painfully obvious that rightist dictatorships, through their reactionary social and economic policies and repression of all political opposition, were creating an environment ripe for Communist or radical revolution. Kennedy's Latin American experts were convinced that die-hard resistance to change on the part of Latin America's conservative ruling elites would be futile and self-defeating and that continued U.S. support of those elites would alienate the new political leaders throughout Latin America. In order, then, to forestall the spread of "Castro-communism" and to align the United States with the newly emerging power groups, the incoming Kennedy administration decided to press actively for democracy and modernization in Latin America. Kennedy's policies still had political stability in Latin America as their *ultimate* objective, but they were based on the assumptions that the preservation of the status quo was a chimerical goal as well as an unworthy one and that the wisest course for the United States would be to help guide Latin American revolutionary forces into reasonably moderate, non-Communist channels. Thus, as the keystone to its anti-Communist strategy, the United States for a brief period became a powerful force for change in Latin America.

Kennedy's Alliance for Progress

The new program had both long-range and short-range dimensions. The Alliance for Progress represented the former. The Alliance was essentially an anti-Communist program in that it sought to remove the conditions in which communism was thought to flourish—low incomes, feudalistic landowning patterns, inequitable tax structures, poor housing, poor schooling, etc. The Alliance was squarely based on the assumptions that the political, economic, and social status quo in Latin America was doomed and that the only real choice lay between democratic, moderate reform and violent, radical revolution. According to the famous Kennedy formulation that introduced the Alliance, "Those who make peaceful revolution impossible make violent revolution inevitable."

In essence, the Alliance for Progress was to be a ten-year Marshall Plan for Latin America, according to which the United States would provide $20 billion to Latin American development programs that sought not only economic development but also the establishment of democracy, land reform, the redistribution of economic wealth, mass education programs, and other sweeping programs of political, economic, and social reform. If the plan had been fully implemented, the Alliance would have had a revolutionary effect on Latin America for it was a direct attack on the status quo, seeking to revise radically the nature of political power, economic organization, and social status in Latin America.

The other major, shorter-run component of Kennedy's program was the effort to create political conditions in Latin America that would facilitate the work of the Alliance. This effort required resistance to military coups against constitutional regimes and the favoring of moderate social democratic governments, such as the Betancourt regime in Venezuela, over traditionalist dictatorships. The use of diplomatic recognition as an instrument of policy was revived. The suspension of diplomatic relations, accompanied by a discontinuation of economic and military assistance, was employed against rightist governments or attempted military coups in Peru, Haiti, Honduras, and the Dominican Republic during the 1961–1962 period, with varying degrees of success.

The most dramatic application of the new policy was in the Dominican Republic. There is substantial evidence that the Kennedy administration encouraged and even provided arms for the successful assassination of Trujillo in 1961; following the assassination, the United States employed a wide range of diplomatic, economic, and even military pressures to prevent the reestablishment of Trujilloism and to pave the way for the holding of free elections. Once again, enlightened anti-communism, at least as much as democratic idealism, was at work, for the administration feared that chaos and resistance to change in the Dominican Republic would pave the way for a new, Dominican Castro. At one point, to avert a threatened Trujilloist military coup, U.S. aircraft carriers were moved to within sight of Santo Domingo, and coup leaders were bluntly warned that the United States would send in marines to prevent a coup. *This* brand of U.S. interventionism was greeted with popular jubilation in the Dominican Republic, the coup was called off, and free elections were held in 1962 under the aegis of U.S. support.

The Dominican situation, however, represented the high-water mark in the Kennedy administration's efforts on behalf of democracy and change in

Latin America. In the summer of 1963, an effort to undermine the Duvalier dictatorship in Haiti failed, and shortly after the assassination of Kennedy, the Johnson administration returned to the conservative stability-first posture of the Truman-Eisenhower period.

Reversion to the Hegemonic Tradition

Under Johnson, and continuing through the Nixon and Ford administrations, the emphasis once again was on preventing the spread of communism or Castroism elsewhere in the hemisphere by "subversion" or revolution. Not only were efforts to promote political and economic change deemed irrelevant to the overriding immediate exigencies of combating Cuban-supported radicalism in Latin America, but even worse, it was feared that such efforts would destabilize the continent and weaken the forces that were the most prone and best able to resist revolution. The Alliance for Progress was, in effect, abandoned, as was Kennedy's effort to promote democracy in the region. Instead, the emphasis was on propping up existing regimes and power groups in Latin America, particularly the armed forces, in order to forcibly suppress revolution.

The concern over Castroism, rooted in traditional attitudes about Latin America's being a rightful sphere of influence of the United States, manifested itself not only in political support, economic aid, and military assistance programs to the conservative political forces in Latin America, but in stepped-up, direct U.S. intervention. Even beginning during the Kennedy administration, for example, the CIA became heavily involved in British Guiana, backing a conservative political movement whose chief opposition was Marxist. The usual run of CIA activities was undertaken: financing friendly parties and politicians, supporting conservative newspapers and other mass media, backing conservative elements in the labor unions, spying on the left, and even supporting rightist goon-squad violence against the Marxists. The efforts proved successful, at least in the sense that the Marxists were denied political power, not only by revolution, but even through the use of the democratic process.

Of considerably greater importance was the extensive involvement of the United States in Brazil, supporting conservative forces against a moderately leftist, nationalist government that aroused U.S. apprehensions in the early 1960s. The details are still shrouded in some secrecy, but it is known that the CIA and other U.S. agencies were involved in conservative plotting against the Goulart government, and the United States immediately and enthusiastically supported the military coup in Brazil in 1964. For twenty years thereafter, Brazil was ruled by a succession of military dictators, some of them as repressive and murderous as the worst of similar regimes in Latin America in the last two decades.

By far the most critical event in U.S.–Latin American relations in the postwar period was the U.S. military intervention in the Dominican Republic in 1965. After the assassination of Trujillo and the elections of 1962, a freely elected reformist government headed by Juan Bosch came to office.

However, Bosch was in office only nine months when he was overthrown by a military coup backed by conservative forces angered by Bosch's economic and social reforms. In April 1965, a revolution designed to restore Bosch to power broke out. Initially led by reform-minded lower-ranking military officers and members of Bosch's political party, the movement attracted thousands of urban slum dwellers who acquired captured police and military arms. The mass uprising quickly overwhelmed the disorganized and divided police and military forces and was on the brink of victory when the United States intervened with a force of 40,000 marines and paratroopers that suppressed the revolution. The U.S. intervention was explained as a response to reports that several small Communist or Castroite groups had joined the revolution; Washington feared that they would soon outmaneuver the pro-Bosch forces, take control of the revolution, and install a second Communist government in the hemisphere. Few respectable analysts, at the time or in retrospect, have agreed with this assessment, and the intervention is best understood in the context of the anti-Castro hysteria that was a major force in U.S. domestic politics in the early 1960s. Because of the Cuban alliance with the Soviet Union and the Cuban missile crisis of 1962—which was ended in part through a commitment by the Kennedy administration not to invade Cuba—Castro himself was untouchable; however, the Johnson administration had adopted a firm no-second-Cuba policy.

Given the climate of public and congressional opinion, the Johnson administration was determined to err on the side of prudence, which was understood to mean a need to move hard and fast against any even potentially radical revolution. On the eve of his decision to intervene in the Dominican Republic, Johnson privately told a reporter, "When I do what I am about to do, there'll be a lot of people in this hemisphere I can't live with, but if I don't do it there'll be a lot of people in this country I can't live with." In effect, the United States had been trapped by its historical myths and outmoded policies, particularly the Monroe Doctrine in its various reincarnations through the years.

The U.S. forces remained to occupy and govern the Dominican Republic for the next eighteen months, withdrawing in September 1966 after generally free elections were won by Joaquín Balaguer, a conservative backed by the armed forces. Balaguer remained in office until 1978, running a semi-dictatorial government that was conservative and corrupt, though only moderately repressive by Caribbean and previous Dominican standards.

Elsewhere in Latin America, the no-second-Cuba policy was reflected in U.S. military assistance, including the direct presence of Green Beret forces in training and advisory roles as well as the provision of arms, to countries facing Cuban-supported insurgencies. By the early 1970s, Latin American armed forces, aided by the United States, had successfully suppressed such insurgencies in Peru, Venezuela, Bolivia, Colombia, Ecuador, and elsewhere.

At the same time, beginning with the Johnson administration and certainly culminating with Nixon, the Alliance for Progress, insofar as it sought to promote "peaceful revolution" in Latin America, was abandoned. However, the failure of the Alliance to bring about major change in Latin America was only partially the result of the shift in U.S. policies and the restoration of the traditional emphasis on short-range financial measures designed to restore stability and order instead of long-range projects designed to promote structural change. Of no doubt even greater importance was the successful resistance to the Alliance by the existing power structures in Latin America: the traditional political parties, the corporate interests, the landed oligarchies, the conservative wing of the Catholic Church, and, most critically, the military. Not surprisingly, the existing elites gave lip service to the Alliance and were happy to accept U.S. economic largess, but they were simply unwilling to reform themselves out of power and, especially after U.S. pressures for real change subsided, they were able to thwart substantial change. Thus, although the Alliance was an economic success in that the target figure of a Latin American per capita annual growth rate of 2.5 percent was met during the 1960s, it was a political and social failure. During the eight years the Alliance was officially in place, there were seventeen military coups in Latin America, highlighting a general drift toward authoritarianism and repression rather than toward democracy and human rights; land distribution patterns remained largely feudal; and the submerged masses of Latin America (peasants, Indians, unskilled laborers) are still largely illiterate, excluded from economic and political systems, and deprived of the fruits of economic growth.

The Nixon-Ford administrations completed the process begun by Johnson of returning to the policies of the 1940s and 1950s and downgrading Latin America to the lowest priority of U.S. foreign policy concerns. The major thrust of the Nixon-Kissinger policy appeared to be to deal with Latin America with the least possible expenditure of resources, time, and energy so that the United States could focus on such serious matters as Vietnam, China, the Middle East, and relations with the Soviet Union. To elaborate, the Nixon administration's policies seemed to rest on three major assumptions. First, the United States had a vital interest in a quiet and stable Latin America, free from radicalism, internal strife, and overseas penetration that might threaten U.S. economic and political predominance in the Western Hemisphere. But, second, there was no need to worry very much about Latin America, or to devote many resources to that region, since the situation there was generally favorable. The Soviet Union was staying clear of Latin America, Cuban revolutionary activities had been downgraded throughout the hemisphere, and Castroism had failed as an international movement; conservative regimes not only predominated at the moment but were likely to continue to do so, despite all the dire predictions about the coming demise of the status quo. Third, and conversely, attempts to promote moderate change, such as the early Alliance for Progress, might not stave off revolution at all but rather undermine existing power groups, who favored U.S. interests, and end by fomenting revolution.

Nixon's policies followed from these assumptions. The Latin American armed forces continued to be armed and cultivated, but otherwise Latin

America was largely ignored. Economic assistance was cut, and U.S. trade policies discriminated against Latin American products. In the absence of any overriding political or military concerns, the main emphases of the Nixon administration were on promoting U.S. private investment and on largely futile attempts to resist growing Latin American economic nationalism and the expropriation of U.S. corporate interests.

The major exception to the Nixon administration's policy of neglect took place in Chile. The United States had been heavily involved in Chilean internal politics at least since the early 1960s, after the Marxist Salvador Allende emerged as a major political leader in that country, seeking to come to power by free elections rather than by revolution. There is evidence that covert U.S. economic support to parties, politicians, and labor unions opposed to Allende began under Kennedy, and it has been definitely established that the CIA provided major financing and other forms of covert support to Eduardo Frei of the Christian Democratic Party, who defeated Allende in the 1964 presidential elections. Moreover, during the campaign, the CIA and U.S. corporations that had major interests in Chile worked together to finance and guide a massive anti-Communist and anti-Allende propaganda campaign through the Chilean media.

Despite continued U.S. covert involvement and another major financial and propaganda effort, Allende won a plurality in the 1970 presidential elections; he took office after the failure of a last-ditch CIA effort to bribe Chilean congressmen to vote against the installation of Allende as president. Even before Allende took office, Nixon and Kissinger decided to bring his government down by creating economic chaos in Chile and directly supporting a military coup. All U.S. nonmilitary aid was cut off; in addition, the U.S. government used its influence with U.S. private banks and corporations as well as with multilateral financial institutions like the World Bank and the Inter-American Development Bank in an effort to cut off other sources of investment, foreign exchange, and development assistance to the Allende government. This effort to destabilize the Allende regime through economic strangulation, however, was largely undercut by the Allende government's success in getting large amounts of economic assistance from the Soviet bloc and from a number of West European sources.

At the same time, though, large amounts of covert U.S. funds and political support flowed to groups that opposed Allende, ranging from the moderate Christian Democrats (led by Frei) to the extreme, terrorist right, which fomented mass marches, strikes, riots, and political assassinations, including the 1970 murder of the leader of the Chilean armed forces, General René Schneider, who had determined to prevent an anti-Allende military coup. Finally, Nixon directly ordered the CIA to use all possible means to organize a Chilean military coup against Allende, including the fomenting of military dissension, the organizing of plots, and the providing of arms to military plotters who wanted nontraceable weapons for a coup.

The central motivation for these shocking and brutal U.S. actions evidently was a fear of the domino effects of a successful Marxist government in

Chile, even one that had been freely elected in a democratic process. In 1970, Kissinger had privately told the press that an Allende electoral victory would undermine the anti-Communist governments of Argentina, Bolivia, and Peru and could even inspire Communist uprisings in Italy and France!

The combination of U.S. pressures, Allende's own serious political and economic mistakes, and the growing domestic opposition of large sectors of Chilean society shortly led to economic chaos, rampant inflation, and political turmoil. In 1973, a military coup (initially widely supported by Chile's upper and middle classes) overthrew Allende. Almost immediately, the new military regime established a full-fledged totalitarian government, based on terror and murder, which was enthusiastically supported by the Nixon administration. Only slightly moderated, that military regime remained in power in Chile until 1990.

The Carter Administration

Under Jimmy Carter, and for the second time in the postwar period, the U.S. government decided to use its power and influence in Latin America to promote peaceful change, support democracy, and help protect human rights. The general foreign policy record of the Carter administration was not notably successful, and, unlike the Kennedy administration nearly a generation earlier, the Carter effort to change traditional U.S. policies toward Latin America received little publicity or recognition; nonetheless, the judgment of history is likely to be kind.

One of the first steps of the new administration was to negotiate, and seek U.S. Senate ratification of, a new Panama Canal treaty. After a long and difficult struggle, the necessary two-thirds margin was obtained for a new treaty that relinquishes U.S. sovereignty over the Canal Zone and gradually turns over operation and control of the canal to Panama. The administration's success in getting the treaty through the Senate did much to restore U.S. prestige in Latin America, but domestically, it cost Jimmy Carter dearly.

Another shift in U.S. policy was reflected in Carter's early efforts to normalize relations with Cuba, although these efforts proved to be abortive. The Cuban missile crisis had stabilized U.S. relations with Cuba by removing the worst fears of each side: The crisis had been ended on the basis of an agreement under which Cuba would refrain from allowing Soviet missiles or other strategic weapons to be based in Cuba, in return for which the United States at least tacitly promised not to sponsor any future invasions of Cuba. After the crisis, Cuba made several tentative proposals for further reconciliation with the United States, whereby the United States would end its diplomatic and economic embargo against Cuba and cease supporting anti-Castro exiles, and Cuba would compensate U.S. corporations for the nationalization of their investments and would modify its anti-American rhetoric. However, Castro would not agree to sever his ties with the Soviet Union or end his support for overseas revolution.

The most promising period for a normalization of Cuban-U.S. relations was from about 1970 to 1978 when Castro sharply limited his support for revolutionary activities elsewhere in the Americas. Because of this situation, the Carter administration was seriously interested in seeing if any further progress could be made in improving relations with Cuba. Most specialists on Cuba supported the effort, arguing that Cuban ties with the Soviet Union did not threaten U.S. interests so long as Cuba did not become an offensive base for Soviet expansionism or seek to promote violent revolution. Indeed, it was frequently argued that Cuba's dependence on the Soviet Union might even be having the unanticipated side benefit of acting as a restraint on Cuban revolutionary militancy, for the Soviets appeared to be respecting the hemisphere as a U.S. sphere of influence. Moreover, the diplomatic and economic embargo had failed as increasing numbers of Latin American and European states restored normal diplomatic and economic relations with Cuba. Finally, it was commonly argued that if the primary U.S. concern was excessive Cuban links with the Soviet Union, the embargo was counterproductive for it left Castro little choice but continued dependence on the Soviets.

However sound those arguments might have been, they were cast aside after Cuba's direct military involvement in the Angolan and Ethiopian civil wars in 1978 and its provision of assistance to the Sandinista Revolution in Nicaragua in 1979. Under the circumstances, any further efforts by the Carter administration to normalize relations with Cuba would have been politically suicidal.

The most significant policy initiatives of the Carter administration were its active efforts to support democracy, human rights, and economic and social change in Latin America. As with the Kennedy administration's short-lived efforts along similar lines, the Carter administration was moved by both idealistic and political factors: The belief that the United States had a moral obligation to use its influence to help the Latin Americans was complemented by the belief that in the long run, U.S. interests would be best realized in a democratic and progressive Latin America. Among the steps taken to realize these objectives were the restoration of economic assistance to a socialist government in Jamaica (which had been cut off by the Ford administration); heavy pressures on the Dominican Republic's military to avert a threatened coup following the election of the democratic, reformist Antonio Guzmán as president in 1978; similar pressures to restore and preserve democratic processes in Peru, Bolivia, Brazil, and Ecuador; and coldness toward the harsh military dictatorships in Argentina, Uruguay, and Chile.

The most dramatic evidence of shifting U.S. policies came in Nicaragua, where the ending of all U.S. economic and military assistance to the Somoza regime during its civil war against its own society, accompanied by heavy pressures on Somoza to resign, helped bring an end to that regime and to that country's internal war. The United States had hoped to force Somoza out of power while there was still room for a moderate political solution, but by the time he fled, the only political alternative was the Sandinista junta, a broad coalition in which Marxists predominated. Even after the

Sandinista government took power in 1979, though, the Carter administration sought to aid Nicaragua and established a good working relationship with the junta, which, in turn, pursued moderate policies both at home and in the rest of Central America during its first year in power.

As Kennedy had reasoned following the Castro Revolution, the Carter administration decided in the wake of the Sandinista victory that hopes of averting further leftist takeovers in Central America rested on replacing the dictatorial rightist forces with the moderate left. As a result, the administration began a campaign for change in El Salvador, Honduras, and Guatemala, pressing ruling groups in those countries, especially the armed forces, for sweeping land reforms and free elections. At the same time, the administration made Latin America the main arena for its general policy of promoting human rights, and it ended military assistance to the worst violators, as in Guatemala, Brazil, Argentina, and Chile. Although some hard-line regimes refused to make any changes, it is generally agreed that Carter's human rights pressures vastly improved the U.S. image in Latin America and led to diminished repression and the release of significant numbers of political prisoners throughout the hemisphere.

As part of a general foreign policy shift to the right during its last year in office, the Carter administration drew back somewhat from its pressures for democratic change—for example, by restoring military assistance to the Salvadoran government of José Napoleon Duarte, despite Duarte's close links to and dependence upon the Salvadoran armed forces, and by suspending economic assistance to the Sandinista government in Nicaragua at a time when most observers still had hopes that the new regime would remain reasonably democratic. Nevertheless, the overall record of the Carter administration was quite good, especially by contrast to the dismal records of both its immediate predecessors and its immediate successor.

The Reagan Administration

By contrast to the Carter administration, the Reagan administration was nothing if not consistent, for it returned in unqualified fashion to traditional U.S. policies of asserting hegemony over the Caribbean and to aggressive support for the conservative forces throughout Latin America, regardless of considerations of democracy, human rights, or economic and social justice. Revolutionary unrest in Latin America was seen primarily as a matter of external Communist aggression, in which the Soviet Union, acting directly or through proxies in Cuba and Nicaragua, was threatening vital U.S. interests and seeking to undermine the Monroe Doctrine. To meet this perceived threat, the administration turned to its natural allies in Latin America, the military and the authoritarian right, actively wooing the more prominent military dictatorships in the hemisphere, notably those in Brazil, Chile, and (until the Falklands-Malvinas War) Argentina, with offers of normal diplomatic relations, increased bilateral aid, and the elimination of pressures to improve human rights.

The nature of the Reagan administration's policies and concerns was most clearly revealed in Central America. In El Salvador, the administration greatly increased U.S. economic and military assistance to the military-dominated regime, despite its inability or unwillingness to control the campaign of murder, torture, and massacre by the armed forces and extreme rightist groups. Moreover, the administration discouraged social and economic reforms and political negotiations with the revolutionary coalition, which, unable to defeat the U.S.-backed Salvadoran military, nevertheless proved able to hold its own against it.

In Nicaragua, from the outset the Reagan administration followed a policy of confrontation with the Sandinista government, seeking to overthrow or at least "destabilize" it with a program modeled on Eisenhower's destruction of the Arbenz government in Guatemala in 1954 and Nixon's subversion of the Allende regime in Chile in 1970–1973. The main features of this concerted policy were a steady drumbeat of hostile rhetoric against the Sandinistas; a refusal to respond to Nicaraguan overtures for discussions and a political settlement with the United States; an economic embargo against Nicaragua; efforts to mobilize other Latin American nations in support of the U.S. campaign; the arming and training on U.S. territory of pro-Somoza Nicaraguan exiles planning military attacks on Nicaragua (in direct defiance not only of international law but of U.S. domestic law as well); the provision of millions of dollars of covert financial assistance to opposition groups in Nicaragua; and a CIA-led campaign of military raids into Nicaragua by thousands of Honduran-based Nicaraguan exiles, dominated by remnants of Somoza's National Guard.

The Reagan administration also supported repressive military-dominated regimes in Guatemala and Honduras. Throughout Central America and Latin America as a whole, the Reagan administration piously decried revolutionary "terrorism," but the far more extensive, effective, and murderous *governmental* terrorism of the military and its reactionary allies was ignored, explained away, or in effect, actively supported.

It is in this context that the fall 1983 invasion of Grenada must be evaluated. There was no persuasive evidence that U.S. lives were endangered, and even if they had been, only a quick helicopter evacuation of U.S. citizens would have been justified, not an outright invasion followed by a political/ military occupation to overthrow the Grenadian government and establish a new one more nearly in keeping with the Reagan administration's ideological preference. Nor is there evidence that the Soviet Union and Cuba were planning a "takeover" of Grenada or establishing "bases" there; it is now clear that the U.S. administration greatly exaggerated the extent of Soviet-Cuban military assistance to the Grenadian government, the numbers and missions of the Cuban and other Communist-nation advisers in the country, and the inferences that could legitimately be drawn from the kind of external assistance that the Grenadian regime undeniably was receiving.

The real reasons for the administration's invasion of Grenada are hardly a mystery, despite the difficulty that the U.S. Congress and public had in discerning them: (1) to remove from power a Marxist government in the Caribbean, the mere existence of which was certain to mobilize the ideological anti-Communism and reach-for-the-gun reflexes that characterized the administration's overall foreign policy; (2) to make a "show of resolve" or to "send a message" to other Marxist governments or revolutionary movements in the Caribbean Basin; and (3) to test the waters of congressional and public opinion with a view toward more-serious military interventions in El Salvador or Nicaragua.

On several occasions during the course of his two presidential terms, Reagan appeared to be cultivating a climate of crisis in order to prepare public opinion for an invasion of Nicaragua. Opinion polls, however, consistently indicated that a majority of Americans opposed such belligerent undertakings in Central America. The U.S. armed forces, moreover, burned by an unpopular war in Vietnam, were not anxious to become more directly involved in the proxy war. Finally, the 1986–1987 Iran-Contra scandal revealed the administration's covert campaign to maintain support for the Contras. The revelation put a damper on such initiatives.

BUSH AND THE CHALLENGE OF THE 1990s

Over his initial protestations, George Bush found himself at the outset of his presidency presiding over the liquidation of the Cold War. The conflict was ending because both the Soviet Union and the United States had undermined their economies through the arms race, and each had lost the ability to determine events even in its own most jealously guarded spheres of influence. The Soviet government recognized that and called for a truce. The United States still refuses to face that reality.

Determined to cling to the vestiges of hegemonic control, the Bush administration was suddenly without an overarching rationale for its policies and actions, particularly the silencing of leftists (if there were any left to be found), the crushing of insurgencies, and the reinforcement of military and paramilitary organizations. To take up the slack, however, it soon seized upon the so-called War on Drugs. The most prominent early target was Panama's military *caudillo* Manuel Noriega, a drug trafficker and a life-long CIA asset who had refused to stay bought. The U.S. invasion of Panama, over the Christmas holidays in 1989, was ostensibly for the purpose of bringing Noriega to justice. But it had the fringe benefits of countering the "wimp" image that had always dogged Bush and of giving the U.S. government more reliable indirect control over the Canal, even as its administration passed to Panamanian hands (see Chapter 20).

Hegemony and "Redemocratization"

Meanwhile, by the beginning of the 1990s, most of the Latin American governments had acquired a facade, at least, of constitutionality. Responding in some measure to U.S. and European human rights policies of the late 1970s, but also to domestic circumstances, including economic crisis, military regimes in South America had begun to disintegrate, and democratic forces had been emboldened. After elections in Paraguay and Chile in 1989, military withdrawal from the presidential palaces of South America was complete; the withdrawal, however, was in no case to a safe enough distance to allow democracy to flourish.

The "redemocratization" of Central America responded to a somewhat different set of pressures and dynamics, including greater sensitivity to the peculiarities of foreign policy decision making in Washington. The U.S. Congress, under popular pressure to end support for human rights violators, had taken a firm stand on both sides of the fence; it had made the maintenance of a "democratic" civilian facade a condition for the ongoing provision of military aid, aid that served to underwrite the dominance of antidemocratic forces.

Except in Costa Rica, elected presidents were able to do little to promote democratic economic and political development. With firm support from the so-called Contadora and Support Group countries, however, they were able to launch and maintain a peace process that the U.S. government had sought to sabotage (see Chapter 19).

A peace plan drawn up in 1987 was followed in 1989 by a call to dissolve and repatriate contingents of the U.S.-sponsored Contra proxy army operating out of Honduras. Nicaragua, for its part, was to release its several thousand Guardsmen and Contra prisoners and move elections up to February 1990.

The incoming Bush administration and the "opposition" U.S. Congress responded with a much-ballyhooed bipartisan policy. The agreement called for extending some $50 million in nonmilitary aid to the Contras to allow them to maintain their organization until after the elections in Nicaragua. The Republicans thereby sought credit from their skeptical right wing for keeping the proxy war option alive, while Democrats sought to convince their constituency that this measure was somehow supportive of the peace plan drawn up by the Central American presidents.

At face value, the new "nonmilitary" aid was a direct affront to the Central American presidents, threatening to undermine yet another of the accords to which the United States was not a party. Even if the aid had served no military purpose—and the Contras in fact continued to attack military and civilian targets deep inside Nicaragua—it was designed to maintain a force the Central Americans sought to disband. And Nicaragua's pledges had been conditioned upon the disbanding of the Contras.

Nicaragua nevertheless went ahead, on February 25, with elections for the presidency, the national assembly, and municipal councils. The major challenger to the Sandinistas, a coalition known as the Unión Nacional Opositora (UNO), was heavily funded, both overtly and covertly, by the Bush administration. Even so, UNO's substantial victory appeared to come as a surprise to candidates, observers, pollsters, and voters alike. Most observers interpreted the outcome as reflecting exhaustion with the war and with economic deprivation. Whether voters blamed the Sandinistas or the United States for their misery, it seemed clear that relief lay only in a change of government.

Revelling in the UNO victory, the United States immediately lifted the trade embargo and pledged $300 million as a first installment of aid. U.S. aid to the Contras was to be continued as well but on the order of an entitlement program. The Contras had continued their attacks against military and civilian targets in various parts of the country throughout the electoral season. Through an accord reached at the end of March, several thousands of them were to be repatriated and settled in "security zones"; it was not clear, however, when they might actually be disarmed and demobilized.

Despite the lifting of the Cold War cover, it was clear that U.S. objectives in Central America would call for heavy military involvement for a long time to come. In South America, however, apart from antidrug and counterinsurgency campaigns in the Andes, U.S. interests were more straightforwardly economic.

The United States and the Economic Crisis

Until the global recession of the early 1980s that so deepened the debt crisis, Latin American economies had been growing at the rate of 6 percent annually since the late 1960s, and in the 1970s, Mexico, Venezuela, and Brazil emerged as major economic powers in the region. The growth and diversification of the Latin American economies have greatly reduced the dependence of the area on U.S. trade, foreign investment, and economic assistance. In the 1950s, 50 percent of Latin American exports went to the United States compared to about 30 percent in the 1980s; similarly, some 25 percent of Latin American imports come from the United States now compared to 50 percent a generation ago.

As for private U.S. investment, its importance in the Latin American economies declined drastically as a wave of economic nationalism swept Latin America in the 1960s and 1970s, resulting in the wholesale nationalization of U.S. investments and other measures designed to diminish both the economic and the political weight of U.S. corporations.

Moreover, bilateral economic assistance is no longer an important source of U.S. influence in Latin America. Countries seeking loans now rely primarily on multilateral institutions like the World Bank and the Inter-American Development Bank, on private banks, and on major non-U.S. donors like Venezuela, Mexico, Western European countries, and the Arab oil-producing countries.

Another vehicle of U.S. hegemony, the U.S. alliance with Latin American armed forces, has lost much of its effectiveness. Ninety percent of Latin American arms purchases are now from countries other than the United States (principally France, West Germany, Italy, Israel, Brazil, and Argentina), and some Latin American military regimes have lost interest in sending their officers to U.S. military schools or engaging in joint military training exercises with U.S. forces.

As the century slipped into its last decade, most Latin American economies were suffering from chronic inflation and unemployment, declining rates of production and productivity, shrinking wages, salaries, and services, and growing international debt. The antidote being promoted by the United States and the International Monetary Fund generally involved austerity measures primarily impacting the lower and middle classes, the privatization of state enterprises and services, and the denationalization of resources.

Thus stripped of economic sovereignty and unable to withstand the threatened cut-off of international credit, Latin American countries remain dependent on loans from U.S. and international banks and thus, to some extent, on the goodwill of the U.S. government. But these stop-gap loans extended to cover interest payments on previous loans are by no means viewed as "development assistance." Latin American nationalists may have little choice but to look to the United States for loans, but they no longer look to the United States for guidance.

A generation ago a sometimes generous, paternalistic U.S. government was telling its Latin American clients that the problem was underdevelopment and the solution was modernization. Modernization has indeed taken place, but at great cost. Today, Latin American leaders are likely to see the United States, identifying generally with creditors, as a part of the problem rather than of the solution.

It is also far from clear that the solution is to be found in the existing system. For the time being the very fragility of the international financial system gives the Latin American debtor countries a certain leverage of their own. The foreign banks are forced to continue to extend bad loans in order to maintain the facade of a system in good working order. But debtors and creditors alike know very well that the debts may never be paid. In the event of collective default, it is not clear that the United States, with all its military might, would be able to mount an impressive defense.

With the end of the Cold War, the rollback of U.S. hegemony in South America, and a new assertiveness on the part of some national leaders, it is likely that a new set of issues will come to the fore. Newly democratic governments have very real and pressing problems to deal with and no incentive to give credence to a "communist menace." Economic problems will have top priority, but that focus will not necessarily preclude the revival of old contentions and the emergence of new sources of friction.

Economic crisis, of course, makes more acute the need for new resources— resources in particular, like oil and gas, that are most likely to be found in remote, poorly demarcated, and contested border regions. The squeeze on imports, moreover, forcing retrenchment in industrial development, and the unreliability of prices and markets for traditional primary products, of late including even petroleum, have served to increase the importance of the area's only reliably lucrative cash crop: narcotic drugs.

Economic crises also often call for scapegoats, and if "communists" are no longer viable for that role the new scapegoats might be illegal aliens. In several areas the flood of would-be workers across national borders has accelerated in recent years. The final destination of a large portion of the uprooted from all over the hemisphere, and particularly from Central America and the Caribbean, is the United States. And the longer the United States seeks by force to contain political change in Central America, the greater will be the numbers displaced and ultimately seeking refuge in the United States.

Meanwhile, the debt trap that is undercutting Latin American economies is thereby destroying markets for U.S. manufacturers and wiping out jobs for U.S. workers. In fact, it is sadly ironic that even as the United States struggles against the encroachment of Japan, the European Economic Community, and the newly industrializing countries on traditional markets, it continues, through pressures for debt repayment, to weaken economies in the one area where it had the greatest trade advantages.

Though wiser policy might have delayed it, the passing of Pax Americana is not a matter of choice. The only choice the United States has at this point is whether to settle for a pattern of mutually beneficial trade and noncoercive diplomacy with politically and economically viable, independent states or to continue its hegemonial policies and practices of the past, perhaps doing grave damage to its own economic and political institutions as well.

SUGGESTED READINGS

History of U.S.–Latin American Relations from Independence to 1945

Dozer, Donald. *Are We Good Neighbors?* Gainesville: University of Florida Press, 1959. The best book on U.S.–Latin American relations from about 1925–1955.

Duggan, Laurence. *The Americas.* New York: Henry Holt and Company, 1949. Another excellent book focusing on inter-American relations in the first half of the twentieth century.

Mecham, J. Lloyd. *A Survey of United States–Latin American Relations.* Boston: Houghton Mifflin Company, 1965. A lengthy historical survey; useful for factual information but unanalytical.

Munro, Dana G. *Intervention and Dollar Diplomacy in the Caribbean, 1900–1921.* Princeton: Princeton University Press, 1964. The best historical analysis of the imperialist period in U.S. relations with Latin America.

Whitaker, Arthur P. *The Western Hemisphere Idea.* Ithaca: Cornell University Press, 1954. A classic work focusing on the origins and development of Pan-Americanism.

Wood, Bryce. *The Making of the Good Neighbor Policy.* New York: Columbia University Press, 1961. The definitive history and analysis of Franklin Roosevelt's Latin American Policy.

Political Histories of Latin America

Alba, Victor. *The Latin Americans.* New York: Praeger, 1969. A candid, brief history by a well-known Mexican analyst that is critical of both the United States and the Latin Americans for their political failings.

Dozer, Donald M. *Latin America: An Interpretive History.* New York: McGraw-Hill Book Company, 1962. An excellent overall political history of Latin America; thorough, analytical, and well written.

Mander, John. *The Unrevolutionary Society.* New York: Alfred Knopf, 1969. An excellently written, provocative book by a British journalist; argues that Latin America is a fundamentally unchanging society.

Rangel, Carlos. *The Latin Americans.* New York: Harcourt Brace Jovanovich, 1976. An excellent and biting survey of the contemporary Latin American scene: argues that the obstacles to progress in Latin America are inherent in Latin American attitudes and institutions, not in failures of the United States.

U.S.–Latin American Relations from World War II to 1970

Arevalo, Juan José, *The Shark and the Sardines.* New York: Lyle Stuart, 1961. A highly influential (in Latin America) and blistering critique of postwar U.S. policies in Latin America written by the leftist Guatemalan political leader.

Bonsal, Philip W. *Cuba, Castro, and the United States.* Pittsburgh: University of Pittsburgh Press, 1971. The best book on the first decade of the Cuban-U.S. crisis; written by a former U.S. ambassador to Cuba.

Connell-Smith, Gordon. *The United States and Latin America.* New York: John Wiley and Sons, 1974. A good objective survey of the postwar period by a British analyst.

Ferguson, Yale H., ed. *Contemporary Inter-American Relations.* Englewood Cliffs, N.J.: Prentice-Hall, 1972. A good collection of essays on various aspects of U.S.–Latin American relations.

Levinson, Jerome, and Juan de Onis. *The Alliance That Lost Its Way.* Chicago: Quadrangle Books, 1970. The best discussion of the failure of Kennedy's policies, particularly the Alliance for Progress.

Needler, Martin C. *The United States and the Latin American Revolution.* Boston: Allyn and Bacon, 1972. A good brief survey by a well-known U.S. political scientist; written from a liberal perspective.

Slater, Jerome. *Intervention and Negotiation: The United States and the Dominican Revolution.* New York: Harper and Row, 1970. An analysis of U.S. intervention in the Dominican Republic, 1965–1966.

―――. *The OAS and United States Foreign Policy.* Columbus: Ohio State University Press, 1967. A discussion of the uses of the inter-American system in U.S. foreign policy during the postwar period.

Williams, Edward L. *The Political Themes of Inter-American Relations.* Belmont, Calif.: Wadsworth, 1971. A good overall history of U.S.–Latin American relations in the twentieth century until the end of the 1960s.

Contemporary U.S. Policy Toward Latin America

Baily, Samuel L. *The United States and the Development of South America.* New York: New Viewpoints, 1976. A "revisionist" reexamination of contemporary inter-American relations; highly critical of the United States.

Black, Jan Knippers. "Central America: The Larger Scandal," *Cross Currents,* 37:2–3, Summer/Fall 1987.

Black, Jan Knippers. *Sentinels of Empire; the United States and Latin American Militarism.* N.Y.: Greenwood-Praeger, 1986.

Cotler, Julio, and Richard R. Fagen, eds. *Latin America and the United States.* Stanford: Stanford University Press, 1974. A radical, neo-Marxian collection focusing primarily on U.S. imperialism and Latin American dependence.

Gaspar, Edmund. *United States–Latin America: A Special Relationship?* Washington, D.C.: American Enterprise Institute, 1978. A relatively conservative treatment of the contemporary scene.

Landau, Saul. *The Dangerous Doctrine: National Security and U.S. Foreign Policy.* Boulder, Colo.: Westview Press (A PACCA Book), 1988.

Molineu, Harold. *U.S. Policy Toward Latin America: From Regionalism to Globalism.* Boulder, Colo.: Westview Press, 1986.

Morris, Michael A., ed. *Great Power Relations in Argentina, Chile, and Antarctica.* London: Macmillan Press, 1990.

Ronning, C. Neale, and Albert P. Vannucci, eds. *Ambassadors in Foreign Policy: The Influence of Individuals on U.S.–Latin American Policy.* New York: Praeger, 1987.

Schoultz, Lars. *National Security and United States Policy Toward Latin America.* Princeton: Princeton University Press, 1987.

Schraeder, Peter J., ed. *Intervention in the 1980s: U.S. Foreign Policy in the Third World.* Boulder, Colo.: Lynne Rienner Publishers, 1989.

Sigmund, Paul E. *The Overthrow of Allende and the Politics of Chile.* Pittsburgh: University of Pittsburgh Press, 1977. The best analysis of U.S. policies toward Chile since the rise of Salvador Allende.

Silvert, Kalman H., ed. *The Americas in a Changing World.* Chicago: Quadrangle Books, 1975. A series of essays by prominent U.S. liberals who had a major impact on Carter's policies; includes the influential Linowitz Report on U.S.–Latin American relations.

Slater, Jerome. "Dominos in Central America," *International Security,* 12:2, Fall 1987.

15

LATIN AMERICA IN THE WORLD

LARMAN C. WILSON

Latin America's role in the world has undergone extensive change in recent decades. Though progress was retarded in the 1980s by the oil and debt crises, the area's involvement in global affairs had been expanding in the 1970s. Among the several factors contributing to change and expansion have been U.S. policy toward Latin America and the response of the area, and of certain countries in particular, to that policy. In an attempt to reduce their dependence on the United States and thereby improve their bargaining positions, a number of Latin American countries have turned to the industrialized countries of Europe and Japan. Meanwhile, Japan and several Western European states have actively and successfully increased their trade with, investments in, and aid to Latin America. This has not only increased the influence of these countries in the region, but has assured the decline in relative terms of U.S. hegemony. Another reason for the redirection of economic relations has been the change in political and/or ideological orientations of certain Latin American governments, whether by military coup (Brazil in 1964, Peru in 1968, Chile in 1973, and Grenada in 1983), by revolution or insurrection (Cuba in 1959 and Nicaragua in 1979), or by election (Chile in 1970, Jamaica in 1972, and Peru in 1985). As a result of political changes, a few new governments joined the Nonaligned Movement and announced that they would pursue an independent foreign policy; Peru, for example, did so in 1968, although it backtracked to the U.S. fold after another coup in 1975. In addition, a few governments or presidents have aspired to Third World leadership via the Nonaligned Movement (e.g., Luis Echeverría of Mexico, 1970–1976, and Fidel Castro). Reflecting the Latin American preoccupation with economic development, a new approach was adopted in the United Nations Conference on Trade and Development

(UNCTAD) and the third UN Law of the Sea Conference (UNLOS III) for bringing about a New International Economic Order. Furthermore, the new states in the Caribbean, the former British territories, have views toward Latin America, and particularly toward Cuba, that diverge sharply from those of the United States. An additional factor contributing to change is the improving economic status of a few Latin American states—Brazil, Venezuela, and Mexico—which have become substantial exporters of manufactured goods and/or petroleum.

Brazil's new position in the world, particularly its major economic ties with the Federal Republic of Germany, illustrates a number of the above reasons for change. First, in 1975 Brazil turned to West Germany and signed a nuclear treaty with that country, which provided for the sale by West Germany of a complete nuclear fuel cycle. This arrangement was made because of U.S. restrictions on the export of technology and equipment for the enrichment of uranium and the separation of plutonium. The Carter administration applied diplomatic pressure on Brazil in an unsuccessful effort to secure annulment of the treaty. Brazil was antagonized by this pressure as well as by pressure exerted later when the United States announced that it was cutting off aid to Brazil on account of human rights violations. Brazil responded by rejecting U.S. military assistance, thus ending the long "special relationship" that had existed between that country and the United States. Although private U.S. capital in Brazil is still greater than capital from any other country, that of West Germany is substantial: in the early 1980s, 53 percent of West German private capital in Latin America was in Brazil.[1] In terms of trade, one-third of West Germany's Latin American imports came from Brazil, and one-third of its exports to Latin America went to Brazil.[2]

Latin America's changing role in the world highlights two triangular sets of relationships: an older Atlantic triangle linking Latin America with the United States and Western Europe,[3] and a newer Pacific triangle linking Latin America with the United States and Japan. As a result of recent changes, the side of the triangle joining Latin America with Western Europe is being strengthened while the one with the United States is being weakened in certain aspects. On the other side, the Pacific triangle is experiencing a strengthening of the side joining Latin America (particularly Brazil) and Japan and a concomitant weakening of the Latin American–U.S. linkage. The Japan–Latin American link is overshadowed, however, by the sizable trade between Japan and the United States.

Although focusing primarily on Latin American relations with Europe and Japan, this chapter will also consider Latin American relations with the Soviet bloc and China. The context for examination will be North-South— that is, developed or industrialized states vis-à-vis developing ones. There will be no consideration of the limited, but increasing, relations on the South-South axis.

RELATIONS WITH THE SOVIET UNION
AND THE COMMUNIST STATES

Cuba

Since Cuba's incorporation into the Soviet system, the Soviet Union has supported the Cuban economy not only through trade, but also through furnishing convertible currency for Cuba's trade with the Western states, financing trade deficits, buying Cuban sugar above the world price, providing military equipment, giving direct credit for economic development, and postponing credit repayment.

Cuba's dependency upon the Soviet bloc was well established by 1961, when the bloc accounted for 74 percent of Cuba's exports and 70 percent of its imports. The Soviet Union (USSR) itself accounted for 48.5 percent and 41 percent, respectively.[4] (Trade with the Soviet bloc declined in the late 1970s and early 1980s, but increased to 87 percent in 1987.[5]) While total USSR economic aid exceeded $8 billion by 1976, it has been between $4 and $5 billion per year since that time.[6] The sugar subsidy has been paid almost regularly, since the world price has usually been lower than the Cuban cost of production. In 1974–1975, however, Cuba had a bonanza because the world price was very high. Consequently, Cuba was credit worthy in convertible currency in its trade with the West and received credits in the early and mid-1970s from Canada, England, Japan, France, West Germany, Spain, and Sweden.[7] Soviet trade subsidies for 1961–1986 were at $35 billion, as follows: sugar—$27 billion; oil—$6 billion; and nickel—$555 million.[8] Soviet military aid has been considerable, estimated at $1.5 billion through 1969 and $875 million for the period 1975–1979 and $7.8 billion for the period 1982–1986 (see Table 15.1).[9] Military assistance from Eastern Europe has been in the form of loans, but such aid from the Soviet Union, since 1962, has been in the form of grants.

There is another side to Cuba's foreign policy stance, despite its economic dependency, its endorsement of the 1968 Soviet intervention in Czechoslovakia, and its membership, since 1972, in the Council for Mutual Economic Assistance (COMECON). Some Cuban autonomy in foreign policy has been demonstrated by its activism in the United Nations and the Nonaligned Movement, its support for revolutionary movements in both Latin America and Africa, and its strong support of Third World goals. Cuba was the first Latin American country to join the Nonaligned Movement when it was founded in Yugoslavia in 1961. (At various times in the 1970s, Argentina, Bolivia, Chile, Grenada, Guyana, Jamaica, Nicaragua, and Peru were members, although several of these countries have since withdrawn. Most of the Commonwealth Caribbean states joined when they became independent.) Castro has been very active in the organization and has tried to move it to the left, thus provoking great controversy, e.g., his endorsement of the 1979 Soviet invasion of Afghanistan. Nonetheless, Castro was elected president of the organization for a three-year term; he presided over the conference when it met in Cuba in 1979, the first meeting to be held in Latin America.

Table 15.1
Value of Arms Transfers, Cumulative 1982–1986, by Major Supplier and Recipient Country (million current dollars)

Supplier/ Recipient	Total	USSR	United States	France	United Kingdom	West Germany	Poland	Czecho- slovakia	Others
Latin America	17,160	8,120	1,695	790	100	2,370	135	405	3,545
Argentina	1,960	0	60	80	0	1,400	0	0	420
Barbados	0	0	0	0	0	0	0	0	0
Bolivia	20	0	5	5	0	0	0	0	10
Brazil	330	0	140	60	10	0	0	0	120
Chile	550	0	0	300	60	130	0	0	60
Colombia	900	0	110	0	5	675	0	0	110
Costa Rica	20	0	20	0	0	0	0	0	0
Cuba	7,830	6,400	0	0	0	0	130	400	900
Dominican Republic	30	0	10	20	0	0	0	0	0
Ecuador	630	0	50	70	20	0	0	0	490
El Salvador	345	0	310	0	0	0	0	0	35
Guatemala	85	0	5	0	0	0	0	0	80
Guyana	20	10	0	0	0	0	0	0	10
Haiti	20	0	5	0	0	0	0	0	15
Honduras	180	0	110	0	0	0	0	0	70
Jamaica	10	0	10	0	0	0	0	0	0
Mexico	345	0	140	20	0	10	0	0	175
Nicaragua	1,600	1,400	0	20	0	0	0	0	170
Panama	35	0	20	10	0	0	5	5	5
Paraguay	30	0	0	0	0	0	0	0	30
Peru	880	310	120	170	0	110	0	0	170
Surinam	35	0	0	0	5	0	0	0	30
Trinidad and Tobago	0	0	0	0	0	0	0	0	0
Uruguay	30	0	5	5	0	5	0	0	15
Venezuela	1,275	0	575	30	0	40	0	0	630

Source: U.S. Arms Control and Disarmament Agency, *World Military Expenditures and Arms Transfers, 1987* (Washington, D.C., 1988), p. 129.

Also in the 1960s, Cuba took a strong stand at the Tricontinental (1966) and Latin American Solidarity (1967) Conferences in favor of supporting revolutionary movements, a stance that was opposed by the Soviet Union. Cuba itself supported various guerrilla organizations both before and after these conferences and into the early 1970s. After a respite, Cuba resumed such support in the late 1970s, and along with several other Latin American states, including Costa Rica, Panama, and Venezuela, provided arms, training, and transport to the Sandinistas in their successful insurrection against Somoza in Nicaragua. In similar fashion, Cuba also helped the left in its rebellion against the government in El Salvador in 1981, an action the Reagan administration considered to be Soviet intervention via Cuba and Nicaragua. The United States thereby justified its increasing economic and military aid to El Salvador and covert activities against Nicaragua. These covert acts—prohibited by the Congress and which contradicted the Central American peace process—included the mining of Nicaraguan harbors and supporting (arming and provisioning) the Contras, a Nicaraguan exile army operating out of Honduras.[10] President Reagan's Cold War approach and his unilateral policies were opposed by most Latin American governments and members of the EEC and NATO.

What is more important for consideration here, however, is Cuba's support of revolutionary governments in Africa, particularly the sending of combat troops, which was unprecedented. There is great debate about whether Cuba became militarily involved in Africa, first in Angola in 1976, as a surrogate of the Soviet Union or for its own reasons. Whatever the motives, Cuban troops have been fighting to keep the revolutionary government in power in Angola, and they also have fought in Ethiopia against Somalia. It has been estimated that in the early 1980s, Cuba had almost 50,000 troops in seventeen African countries.[11] After many years of negotiations—mediated by the United States—to end the civil war in Angola as well as outside involvement by South Africa and the Southwest African People's Organization (SWAPO) in Namibia, agreement was reached and an accord signed in December 1988. The accord provides for the withdrawal of all foreign troops by July 1991: Angolan from Namibia, Cuban from Angola, and South African from Namibia.[12]

Relations between Cuba and the USSR have deteriorated since Mikhail Gorbachev became First Secretary of the Communist party in 1985. Although agreements have been signed providing new and increased credits of $3 billion for 1986–1990,[13] Gorbachev has announced that Soviet aid to Cuba will be cut (oil exports were cut back in 1985). His policies of *glasnost* (liberalization and openness) and *perestroika* (decentralization and modernization) have resulted in his criticism of Castro's policies. Castro had criticized Gorbachev's new approaches and the withdrawal from Afghanistan even before his visit to Cuba in April 1989.[14] Castro had also criticized the reforms in the People's Republic of China (PRC) that began in the early 1980s, but he approved the suppression that ended them the summer of 1989.

Other Latin American Countries

The various forms of relations between the Communist states and Latin America—economic and trade, diplomatic, military, and political—reflect common interests as well as the state of Latin American-U.S. and Soviet-U.S. relations. The Communist states, especially the Soviet Union, are striving to enhance their influence—economic, ideological, and political—as well as to improve their economic situation. They attempt to capitalize upon problems between the United States and individual Latin American republics, but in ways that do not involve running serious political risk. Soviet and Eastern European relations with Chile during the period of the Allende government, with Peru during the military governments of Generals Juan Velasco Alvarado (1968–1975) and Francisco Morales Bermudez (1975–1980), and with Nicaragua under the Daniel Ortega government (1980–1990) are examples. For their part, some Latin American governments have dealt with the Communist states as an offset to the United States—as a means of bargaining for better terms with the United States, to diversify their dependency, and/ or to demonstrate their independence from the United States. Argentina's large sale of wheat to the Soviet Union (1980–1982) in defiance of President Carter's embargo was a combination of an independent foreign policy, retaliation against the United States for its human rights policy, and the need for export income, which was exacerbated by Argentina's inability to sell wheat to EEC countries.

Trade began increasing between the Communist countries and Latin America, especially since the mid-1970s, but began decreasing in the mid-1980s. In general, however, this trade constitutes a relatively small percentage of total Latin American exports and imports. The Soviet-bloc countries, particularly the USSR and Poland, have a very unfavorable balance of trade with Latin America. In 1972, trade with the Communist states amounted to only 2 percent of Latin American trade ($669 million in Latin American exports and $312 million in imports).[15] By 1974, the total value of Latin American exports to and imports from the Communist countries exceeded $1 billion. While in 1981 the total value of exports was $3.8 billion (.045 percent of total exports), which was inflated by the large exports of wheat by Argentina to the USSR, and imports were valued at only $663 million (.005 percent),[16] in 1987, the totals were $2.4 billion and $943 million, respectively.[17] What is significant, however, is the much higher levels of Soviet trade with and economic aid (credits and loans) to certain Latin American countries for varying periods of time. Aside from the special cases of Cuba and Nicaragua, the experiences of a few other states are of interest.

During the presidency of Salvador Allende (1970–1973), Chile experienced an expansion of economic and diplomatic relations with the Communist states, including the People's Republic of China. The Allende government received a number of loans from the USSR and Eastern European countries, but not nearly enough to save the Chilean economy. The total value of loans received from these countries was $656 million: $260.5 million from the USSR and $395.5 million from the other Communist states ($276 million was provided by other Latin American countries, Western Europe, and Japan).[18] Following Allende's overthrow, the Communist states—with the exception of China and Romania—broke off or suspended relations with Chile. In 1977, however, the Pinochet government renegotiated the Allende-era debt, which resulted in a resurgence of trade with most of the Communist countries.

In the early 1970s, Argentina began establishing relations with Eastern European countries and permitting them to set up trade offices and/or consulates in Argentina. Thereafter, Argentine trade with the Soviet Union steadily increased, particularly Argentine exports of beef and wheat. Starting in 1978, the USSR began a sales drive to reduce its widening trade imbalance with Argentina. These efforts resulted in contracts for turbines for the Parana Medio Dam, a $2.5-billion project the Soviet Union had been awarded the contract to design. As already mentioned, Argentina refused to comply with the Carter administration's embargo on grain sales to the USSR and greatly increased its exports of wheat. In 1981, for example, Argentine exports to the Soviet Union were $1.8 billion, 78 percent of the Latin American export total to the USSR and 47 percent of total Latin American exports to all of the Communist states.[19]

Brazil's percentage of total Latin American exports to the Soviet Union increased from 4.6 percent in 1975 to 27 percent in 1979.[20] In 1981, it was 17 percent due to an increase in Soviet imports from Latin America, but the Soviet total decreased thereafter to $2.5 billion and remained there until the mid-1980s. Soviet imports dropped off in the late 1980s, which resulted in Brazil's portion—20 percent in the mid-1980s—increasing later in the decade. All the Communist states have trade imbalances with Brazil because of their heavy importation of food and raw materials. Consequently, they are providing credits to stimulate Brazilian importation of their equipment and machinery. In the late 1970s, Brazil accepted its largest single credit from Eastern Europe, $200 million from the German Democratic Republic, and signed trade agreements with Hungary and Poland.[21] China signed its first agreement with Brazil in 1978, which was followed by a contract for exchanging Brazilian iron ore for Chinese oil. In 1982, the Brazilian government proposed an industrial cooperation program with the USSR for manufacturing heavy equipment. At the time of the announcement, the secretary-general of the Brazilian Foreign Ministry stressed Brazil's commitment to increase its bilateral trade with the Soviet Union and thereby diversify its trade patterns. Its import package from the USSR cost $154 million in 1981; this increased to almost $200 million in 1982, but started declining and was below $100 million by 1985, where it remained through the 1980s.[22]

In 1967, Peru annulled a law forbidding imports from Communist states, and after the military took over in 1968, Peru reestablished relations with seven Communist countries. East European trade offices were established in Peru, and Peruvian consulates were set up in Eastern Europe. Even though the military government greatly increased its purchases of arms in 1972 (mainly from France), which constituted 10 percent of total imports in that year, even larger purchases were made in the mid-1970s from the USSR. For example, the USSR provided $650 million in arms between 1975 and 1979. These were the first major arms purchases from the USSR by a Latin American republic other than Cuba. Peru's turning to the Soviet Union as motivated by its arms race with Chile and the very favorable terms offered by the USSR, strained relations with the United States. In 1977, Peruvian arms purchases amounted to 21.7 percent of total imports (compared to 12.7 percent in 1967) and included Soviet artillery, jet aircraft, and tanks.[23] Peru has continued to buy arms from the USSR in the 1980s (see Table 15.1). (During the 1982 war over the Falklands, Peru offered Argentina a number of its Soviet MIGs, but no Argentine pilots were trained to fly them.) Since the late 1970s, the Communist nations have maintained their economic credits to Peru at constant levels while continuing to import about 15 percent of Peru's exports.

Nicaragua became a recipient of Soviet arms in the 1980s. Once the Sandinista-led insurrection toppled General Anastasio Somoza in 1979 and the Sandinistas came to power, Cuba became the first principal provider of aid. The USSR began making arms available and steadily increased them as the confrontation between Nicaragua and the United States mounted (see Table 15.1). The arms included artillery, helicopters, and tanks. In the 1980s, Nicaragua received $679 million and $1.6 billion in economic aid from Eastern Europe and the USSR, respectively.[24]

For the 1954–1987 period, economic aid to Latin America from the USSR and Eastern European countries amounted to almost $7 billion, with over 50 percent being furnished by the USSR. The principal recipients were (excluding Cuba and Nicaragua), in descending order, Brazil, Argentina, Peru, Bolivia, Colombia, and Peru with Argentina and Bolivia receiving more aid from the USSR than Eastern Europe[25] (if the cut-off year is 1979, Chile under Allende is in third place). Nevertheless, relations between the Soviet-bloc states and Latin America have been difficult at times; for example, several Latin American countries have expelled Soviet diplomats for meddling in their domestic affairs. There is also mounting tension between the USSR and Cuba and Nicaragua due to the critical and restrictive policies of Secretary Gorbachev.

LATIN AMERICA AND THIRD WORLD BARGAINING

Since the 1960s, Latin American initiatives to promote economic development have included the formation of bargaining blocs of developing states, operating on both the regional and the global levels. The contemporary struggle to alter their relations with the industrialized countries has resulted in a North-South confrontation. The main channels for bargaining and waging the struggle have been the United Nations, particularly two of its organs, the General Assembly and the Economic and Social Council (ECOSOC); certain conferences sponsored by the United Nations, e.g., UNCTAD and UNLOS III; the formation of commodity agreements patterned after those of the Organization of Petroleum Exporting Countries (OPEC); and the creation of the Latin American Economic System (SELA).

Certain long-run trends involving Latin America's changing place in the world have been clear for some time—although slowed in the 1980s by the debt crisis—and have been accelerated by Third World activism and bargaining. Two good examples concern trade and investment. The trend has been for Latin American exports of food and raw materials to decline, while exports of manufactures have increased, and for U.S. private investment to decline in relative terms in Latin America.[26] Although previously, the Latin American governments bargained on a regional basis with the United States for greater access for their exports to the U.S. market, for greater cooperation in support of commodity arrangements, and for the transfer of U.S. technology to Latin America, these states have now turned to Europe and Japan in seeking the same goals and have been bargaining more on an international basis. Interestingly, in recent years, many Latin American states have been stressing access to the industrial northern markets rather than higher export prices. Many have also changed their attitudes toward private investment and multinational corporations; now they want the former to increase and the latter to return, subject to local control. (The Reagan administration's 1983 Caribbean Basin Initiative, CBI, was a much-later partial response, even though its main goal was to isolate Nicaragua.)

Inspired by the ideas of ECLA, and disturbed by the serious economic problems of the late 1950s and early 1960s as well as by U.S. preoccupation with security, the Latin American republics began to work through certain regional caucusing groups, e.g., the Special Latin American Coordinating Committee (CECLA); the Special Committee for Consultation and Negotiation (CECON); the UN Latin American Group (LAG); and the Group of 77 (G-77, numbering about 120 members in the early 1980s), the caucus of developing states in the United Nations. The Latin Americans were successful in getting many of their regionally developed ideas and positions adopted by the UN General Assembly, by UNCTAD, and by UNLOS III. And the developed states accepted many of the demands and positions of the Third World.

The G-77 found UNCTAD to be a very useful forum in bargaining with the industrialized states (once the conference was organized, Raúl Prebisch of ECLA was appointed its executive secretary). At the first three meetings of UNCTAD—in 1964 (Switzerland), 1969 (India), and 1972 (Chile)—the G-77 put forward the following recommendations: that the industrialized countries provide 1 percent of their GNP in the form of aid to the Third World states; that an increased number of commodity agreements be concluded; that the developed countries grant concessions to the developing states without reciprocal concessions; that a compulsory code of conduct be drawn up for regulating transnational enterprises; and that a charter on the economic rights and duties of states be prepared as a major step toward creating the New International Economic Order.

In response, the northern states were willing to accept the 1 percent figure for aid to the Third World, but only on a voluntary basis. The formation of commodity agreements for the purpose of stabilizing prices, especially for food and mineral exports, was also supported, although some of the industrialized nations were opposed. (It is worth recalling that Venezuela initiated the formation of OPEC in 1960.) The developed states responded positively to the proposal of granting trade concessions on a nonreciprocal basis and committed themselves to the concept of granting preferences to the less developed countries (LDCs). This approach was accepted both by the General Agreement on Tariffs and Trade (GATT) and by the European Economic Community (EEC) in the Lomé accord, to be discussed below. The industrialized nations' response to a compulsory code to regulate the multinationals was mixed: They were not opposed to the drafting of such a code by the United Nations but believed that it should be applied on a voluntary basis. In 1974, the United Nations created a commission and a center on transnational corporations for the purpose of monitoring the conduct of such companies.

Latin America in general, and certain countries in particular, have made major contributions to changing the economic, legal, and political relations between North and South. These contributions are illustrated by Mexican leadership in the drafting of the 1974 economic charter and by Peruvian and Venezuelan leadership during the lengthy UNLOS III (1974–1982). At the 1972 UNCTAD meeting in Chile, Mexican president Luis Echeverría suggested that the United Nations draft a set of economic obligations on the rights and duties of states. His appeal resulted in the UN Charter on the Economic Rights and Duties of States, which was approved by the General Assembly in 1974 as a chapter in the Program of Action on the Establishment of a New Economic Order. Among other things, the charter stressed the right of expropriation of foreign assets, high and stable prices for Third World exports, and preferential treatment without reciprocity. (On a regional basis, the presidents of Mexico and Venezuela initiated the formation of SELA in 1975, a strictly Latin American bloc, including Cuba, to bargain over U.S. economic and trade policies.)

The Latin American contribution to UNLOS III began in the early 1950s when three states—Ecuador, Chile, and Peru—signed an accord in which they claimed a 200-mi (352-km) territorial waters limit for the purpose of regulating the catching of tuna off their coasts. They justified this extension of jurisdiction as a means of protecting an important resource and source of revenue for developing countries. This move was viewed by the United States, in particular, as contrary to international law. U.S. opposition and advice to private fishermen not to comply with the claim resulted in the so-called Tuna War, as Ecuador and Peru started seizing and fining U.S. fishing boats in the late 1960s and early 1970s. Starting in the 1960s, however, other Latin American governments followed suit in claiming a 200-mile limit. The claim became a regional approach or policy, and developing states in Africa and Asia soon joined Latin America in making such a claim. This was one of many issues that demonstrated the need to negotiate a series of new treaties on the law of the sea.

From the time the first session of UNLOS III began in Venezuela in 1974 until the final session ended in New York in 1982, the Third World countries employed a political bargaining strategy to achieve their goals. By means of bloc caucusing and bargaining, the G-77 was successful in having its positions adopted. One major goal was the acceptance of the 200-mile limit; this, in fact, became the 200-mile exclusive economic zone (EEZ). At the end of the long negotiation process, a few of the industrialized states, unfortunately, found the final draft unacceptable. In fact, the Reagan administration, which objected specifically to the deep seabed mining provisions, held up the signing of the convention by the entire conference for one year while it completed a review. The convention was voted on at the United Nations in 1982 and received overwhelming Third World support. Only four states voted against it—Israel, Turkey, the United States, and Venezuela—and seventeen abstained, including Belgium, the Netherlands, Luxembourg, West Germany, Britain, Italy, Spain, Thailand, the USSR, and most Eastern European states. (The convention needs sixty ratifications to make it effective. Although over 120 states have signed it, only around forty-five have ratified.)

RELATIONS WITH WESTERN EUROPE

The four Lomé accords (1975–1980, 1980–1985, 1985–1990, 1990–1995), which govern economic relations between the EEC and many Third World states, mainly in Africa but also some in the Caribbean and the Pacific, follow the model that resulted from the bargaining of the G-77 at UNCTAD. Lomé I was prompted by the 1973 entry into the EEC of Denmark, Great Britain, and Ireland and the decision of several former Commonwealth countries in Africa, the Caribbean, and the Pacific (ACP states) to join the eighteen African states already associated with the EEC via the 1963 Yaoundé Convention.[27] In 1975, there were fifty-seven ACP states associated with the EEC, six of them in the Caribbean (increased to eleven in 1981).

The European Development Fund contributes to financing the development of ACP projects, which are supplemented by loans from the European Investment Bank. The funds made available have been increased 72 percent by Lomé II. The EEC also has a small but expanding aid program to nonassociated states; four Central American states—Costa Rica, the Dominican Republic, Honduras, and Nicaragua—were added in the mid-1980s and Haiti was added via the 1987 "Comprex" plan to aid the world's least developed nations. In terms of development assistance, the European states—i.e., West Germany, England, France, Holland, and Sweden—have steadily increased their aid since the late 1970s, eclipsing that of the United States.[28]

Although the EEC entered into a trade agreement with the Andean Common Market in 1981, a number of the more developed countries in Latin America have encountered problems of access to the European market. The EEC also entered into a number of nonpreferential trade agreements in the 1970s for three- to five-year periods, subject to renewal, with Argentina, Brazil, Mexico, and Uruguay. Problems have developed, however, over agricultural imports from Latin America in view of the EEC's Common Agricultural Policy. This is one reason why Argentina has turned to the Soviet Union as a major buyer of Argentine grain exports, especially wheat. The Latin Americans hoped that the entry into the EEC by Portugal and Spain in 1986—the latter was seen as a "bridge"—would greatly improve the access of their exports. This has not resulted; in fact, increasing EEC restrictions favoring Africa have decreased Latin American exports.[29]

Another area of change is Latin America's increasing purchase of arms from Europe. The arms employed in the 1982 Falklands/Malvinas War between Argentina and Britain indicated the variety of arms sellers. Argentina had combat planes made in England, France, Israel, and the United States; its navy included vessels from England, West Germany, and the United States; and the infantry had weapons from England, Eastern Europe, Israel, and the United States. Until the late 1960s, the United States monopolized the sale of arms, particularly of planes, ships, and tanks, and the provision of military training to Latin America. Because of U.S. congressionally imposed restrictions, bureaucratic delays, and attractive terms offered by European countries, some of the Latin American governments, starting with Peru, turned to Europe. Despite the ending of the U.S. monopoly, the United States is still an important arms supplier (see Table 15.1). However, Argentina and Brazil are actively developing their own arms industries, and the latter is an ambitious arms exporter (mainly of armored vehicles so far) to its neighbors as well as to the other Third World countries.

RELATIONS WITH JAPAN

Becoming significant in a relatively short period, the influence of Japan has resulted in a balancing of commercial power among Japan, Europe, and the United States in Latin America. Japan's exports to Latin America began to mount in the late 1960s and moved from light manufactures to heavy-industrial and chemical products, reflecting the great development of heavy industry in Japan. The former exports were replaced by the latter categories, which increased threefold by 1970 and thereafter came to constitute 80 percent of Japan's total exports to Latin America in the 1970s and 1980s.[30] Although the composition of Japan's exports changed, the percentage of its total exports to Latin America has not fluctuated very much, remaining in the area of 4–7 percent.

On the other hand, Japan's imports from Latin America continued to increase in the 1970s and include, in descending order of importance, minerals, fuels, foodstuffs, and metal ores. More specifically, Japan imports copper from Chile and Peru; iron ore from Brazil, Chile, and Peru; cotton from Brazil and Mexico; and foodstuffs from Argentina and Brazil.[31] Imports started to decline after the second oil crisis in 1979 as Japan shifted to the Middle East for oil, and they have remained around 4.5 percent in the 1980s.[32] While Japanese exports greatly increased in the 1970s, especially to Argentina, Brazil, and Chile, in 1987, they were (plus imports): Panama—$3 billion ($89 million); Mexico—$1 billion ($1.4 billion); Brazil—$975 million ($1.8 billion); and Venezuela—$492 million ($330 million).[33] (Panama heads the list, receiving 33 percent of total exports, mainly because it buys Japanese ships that are used by third countries under Panama's flag of convenience.)

Concerning the flow of economic cooperation—a composite of aid, export credits, and private funds, according to the Organization for Economic Cooperation and Development (OECD)—Japan's flow to Latin America increased from almost 17 percent in 1971 to 46 percent only two years later, which then exceeded its flow to Asia (39 percent), the country's natural area of economic penetration. Japan's official development assistance (ODA) to Latin American countries amounted to about $118 million. Among the major beneficiaries were Brazil, Bolivia, and Paraguay.[34] What really has elevated the economic cooperation flow figure is direct private investment, for it has increased at a much faster rate than trade. During the period from 1969 until the mid-1970s, Japan's direct investment increased eightfold, thus placing Latin America in fourth place in terms of investment, right after the United States, Asia, and Europe, respectively. However, Latin America moved to third place in Japan's total accumulated foreign investment ($106 billion) by region for the period 1951–1986: North America—35 percent; Asia—21 percent; Latin America—19 percent ($20 billion); and Europe—14 percent.[35]

In the early 1970s, Japanese investment in Latin America bypassed that of France, and in the late 1970s, it bypassed that of England. Over one-half of Japan's direct investment is in Brazil, where it ranked sixth in 1973, following that of the United States, West Germany, Canada, England, Switzerland, and France, respectively. Since that time, however, Japan has surpassed the last four and is challenging West Germany, the most important European exporter of capital to Brazil. In the mid-1980s, Japan made an important change in its investment in Mexico (with 7 percent, it was in third place after the United States and Brazil): It began shifting out of its traditional fields of autos, electronics, and steel to Mexico's in-bond or *maquiladora* industry in order to compete in the U.S. market. Japan had twenty in-bond plants in operation in the late 1980s with twenty more being planned.[36] (It was announced during a summer 1989 visit by Prime Minister Toshiki Kaifu that Japan would give Mexico $1 billion for an air pollution project in its capital.[37])

CONCLUSION

This chapter has examined the changing role and place in the world of Latin America in general and of certain major Latin American countries in particular. Changing U.S. policies have prompted the Latin American countries to look elsewhere for trade and aid while Europeans and Japanese have actively and successfully promoted their trade with, aid to, and investments in Latin America. This promotion has increased their influence in the region and has diminished Latin America's dependence on the United States. Furthermore, occasional changes of political orientation in some Latin American countries have resulted in periods of participation in the Nonaligned Movement and/or attempts to pursue an independent foreign policy. A few governments, such as those of Mexico and Cuba, have aspired to Third World leadership. Latin America's preoccupation with economic development has also been expressed through a new collective approach and activism manifested in UNCTAD and in UNLOS III. A final factor in Latin America's changing global stature is the improving economic status of a few Latin American republics, despite the foreign debt setback of the 1980s, which have become exporters of manufactures and, in two cases—Argentina and Brazil—of armaments.

In their drive to become economically developed and to diversify their dependence, many of the more developed Latin American states appear to have come almost full circle. First they bargained for higher prices, for access to the U.S. market for their primary goods, and for more aid; they then placed restrictions upon private investment, nationalized some foreign companies, and demanded that international control be established over multinational corporations (MNCs). Now these states are bargaining for access for their industrial goods to the markets of the industrialized countries and are seeking more private investment and the reentry of the MNCs, although under effective local control.

Despite the enhanced role of Latin America in general, and of certain states in particular, in the international system and the changing patterns of dependence, it has become clear in the 1980s that one form of dependence increased in the early and mid-1980s: the dependence upon foreign lenders—governments, private banks, and multilateral lending institutions—as evidenced by the oppressive foreign debts and attendant problems suffered by most Latin American countries. (Fortunately, this dependency began abating in the late 1980s.) A very different form of dependency rapidly increased in the 1980s, which is continuing, one that is illegal and involves private individuals in Europe and the United States, primarily the latter. This is the dependence of millions of U.S. citizens upon cocaine, the major export of the drug traffickers in the Silver Triangle of Bolivia, Colombia, and Peru. The control of the supply side, which responds to the $100 billion per year demand side in the United States, has been assigned a higher and higher priority in U.S. relations with Latin America. In the summer of 1989, the Bush administration increased to $65 million aid to Colombia to help it gain control of the Medellin drug cartel.[38]

Latin American commerce is still dominated by the United States, Western Europe, and Japan, but there are emerging linkages with other Third World regions. These links will increase in the future, and they can be expected to attenuate somewhat the present and growing Latin American economic ties with the northern, industrialized states.

NOTES

1. Wolf Grabendorff, *West Germany and Brazil: A Showcase for the First World–Third World Relationship?* Occasional Papers Series no. 4 (Baltimore: Center of Brazilian Studies, School of Advanced International Studies, Johns Hopkins University, January 1980), p. 2.

2. Ibid. For Brazil's development and increasing status see Werner Baer and Carlos von Doellinger, "Determinants of Brazil's Economic Policy," in Joseph Grunwald, ed., *Latin America and World Economy: A Changing International Order* (Beverly Hills, Calif.: Sage Publications, 1978), pp. 147–161; Baer, *The Brazilian Economy: Growth and Development* (3d ed. New York: Praeger Publishers, 1989); and Wayne A. Selcher, ed., *Brazil in the International System* (Boulder, Colo.: Westview Press, 1981).

3. Wolf Grabendorff and Riordan Roett, eds., *Latin America, Western Europe and the United States: Reevaluating the Atlantic Triangle* (New York: Praeger Publishers, 1985); and Gustavo Lagos Matús, ed., *Las Relaciones entre América Latina, Estados Unidos y Europa Occidental* (Santiago: Editorial Universitaria, 1980).

4. Jorge I. Dominguez, *Cuba: Order and Revolution* (Cambridge: Harvard University Press, 1978), pp. 149–154.

5. Speech of Ernesto Betancourt, USIA, Radio Martí, at Cuban American National Foundation conference on "The Cuban Revolution at 30," January 10, 1989.

6. W. Raymond Duncan, *The Soviet Union and Cuba: Interests and Influence* (New York: Praeger Publishers, 1985), pp. 105, 178.

7. Jorge I. Dominguez, *Cuba: Order and Revolution* (Cambridge: Harvard University Press, 1978), pp. 149–154.

8. U.S. Central Intelligence Agency (CIA), Directorate of Intelligence, *Handbook of Economic Statistics 1988: A Reference Aid* (Washington, D.C.: CIA, 1988), p. 181.

9. U.S. Department of State, Bureau of Public Affairs, *Cuban Armed Forces and the Soviet Military Presence*, Special Report no. 103 (Washington, D.C., August 1982), pp. 3–5; and U.S. Arms Control and Disarmament Agency (ACDA), *World Military Expenditures and Arms Transfers, 1987* (Washington, D.C.: GPO, 1988), p. 129.

10. Larman C. Wilson, "Contra caper: a secret war on will of Congress," *Times of the Americas,* July 1, 1987.

11. William M. LeoGrande, *Cuba's Policy in Africa, 1959–1980* (Berkeley: Institute of International Studies, University of California, Policy Paper No. 13, 1984); and Carmelo Mesa-Lago and June S. Belkin, eds., *Cuba in Africa* (Pittsburgh: University of Pittsburgh Press, 1981).

12. David B. Ottawa, "The Peace Process in Southern Africa: How the U.S. Brokered a Political Settlement," *Washington Post,* December 23, 1988.

13. Richard J. Payne, *Opportunities and Dangers of Soviet-Cuban Expansion: Towards a Pragmatic U.S. Policy* (Albany: State University of New York Press, 1988), p. 9.

14. *Diario las Américas,* January 7, 1989; and *Washington Post,* July 27, 1988.

15. Harold E. Davis and Larman C. Wilson et al., *Latin American Foreign Policies: An Analysis* (Baltimore: Johns Hopkins University Press, 1975), p. 450.

16. International Monetary Fund (IMF), *Direction of Trade Statistics Year Book, 1982* (Washington, D.C.: IMF, 1982), pp. 44, 46.

17. IMF, *Direction of Trade Statistics Yearbook, 1988* (Washington, D.C.: IMF, 1988), pp. 46, 48.

18. Timothy F. Olsen, "What Caused the Downfall of the Allende Government?" (M.A. thesis, American University, Washington, D.C., 1979), p. 229.

19. IMF, *Direction of Trade Statistics,* 1982, pp. 46, 48, 66–67.

20. Augusto Varas, "The Soviet Union in the Foreign Relations of Latin America" (Paper presented at the 1982 annual meeting of the International Studies Association, Cincinnati, Ohio, March 24–27, 1982), p. 18.

21. U.S. Central Intelligence Agency (CIA), National Foreign Assessment Center, *Communist Aid Activities in Non-Communist Less Developed Countries 1978: A Research Paper,* ER 79–1041 2U (Washington, D.C.: CIA, September 1979), p. 29.

22. IMF, *Direction of Trade Statistics,* 1988, p. 400.

23. U.S. Arms Control and Disarmament Agency, *World Military Expenditures and Arms Transfers,* 1980, pp. 115, 132.

24. CIA, *Handbook of Economic Statistics, 1988,* pp. 178–179.

25. CIA, National Foreign Assessment Center, *Handbook of Economic Statistics 1980: A Research Aid* (Washington, D.C.: CIA, 1980), p. 108; and CIA, *Handbook of Economic Statistics, 1988,* pp. 178–179.

26. Obie G. Whichard, "Trends in the U.S. Direct Investment Position Abroad, 1950–1979," *Survey of Current Business* 56 (February 1981), pp. 39–56. Total U.S. investment in Latin America declined from 38 percent in 1950 to 20 percent in 1979, and its composition was changed by a decline in petroleum investment and a substantial increase in manufacturing investment (pp. 41, 44). These trends have continued in the 1980s. James W. Wilkie et al., eds., *Statistical Abstract of Latin America,* vol. 26 (Los Angeles: University of California, 1988), p. 711.

27. Lomé, where the two conventions were signed, is the capital of Togo; Yaoundé is the capital of Cameroon. For the leading works on the subject, see Glenn Mower, Jr., *The European Community and Latin America: A Case Study in Global Role Expansion* (Westport, Conn.: Greenwood Press, 1981), and Christopher Stevens, ed., *EEC and the Third World: A Survey, Renegotiating Lomé,* vol. 4 (New York: Holmes & Meier, 1985).

28. Over half of all development assistance to the Third World comes from Western Europe. In 1980, France gave over half the amount given by the United States, and the Federal Republic of Germany provided half the U.S. amount. Starting in 1970, the European states gave a higher percentage of their GNP than the United States did (Steven H. Arnold, *Implementing Development Assistance: European Approaches to Basic Needs* [Boulder, Colo.: Westview Press, 1982], pp. 2, 4). Interestingly, the Western European industrial states—plus the four Scandinavian states, Israel, Japan, Portugal, Spain, and Yugoslavia—have joined the Inter-American Development Bank.

29. Scott B. MacDonald and Albert L. Gastmann, "Grenada, the Caribbean Basin, and the European Economic Community," in Scott B. MacDonald et al., eds., *The Caribbean After Grenada: Revolution, Conflict and Democracy* (New York: Praeger Publishers, 1988), pp. 244–247.

30. Adalbert Krieger Vasena and Javier Pazos, *Latin America: A Broader World Role* (London: Ernest Benn, 1973), p. 119; and Akio Hosono, "Economic Relationship between Japan and Latin America," *Latin American Studies,* no. 6 (1983), p. 79.

31. Business International Corporation (BIC), *Business Latin America,* December 24, 1980, p. 414; and Wilkie, op. cit., vol. 21 (1981), p. 435.

32. IMF, op. cit., p. 245; and Hosono, op. cit., pp. 76–77.

33. BIC, op. cit., March 28, 1988, p. 99.

34. Hosono, op. cit., p. 82.

35. BIC, op. cit., p. 99.

36. BIC, op. cit., November 7, 1988, pp. 350–351.

37. *Washington Post,* August 30, 1989.

38. Foreign Policy Association, *Great Decisions 1989: Foreign Policy Issues Facing the Nation* (New York: FPA, 1989), pp. 80–83; and *Washington Post,* August 26, 1989.

SUGGESTED READINGS

Official Sources

There are several major sources of information and data on Latin American economic development, finances, and trade including:

Inter-American Development Bank. *Economic and Social Progress in Latin America.* Washington, D.C. Published annually.

International Monetary Fund. *Direction of World Trade.* Washington, D.C.

Organization of American States. *America en cifras.* Washington, D.C. Published annually.

United Nations, Economic Commission for Latin America. *Economic Survey of Latin America.* Santiago, Chile. Published annually.

———. *Statistical Yearbook for Latin America.* Santiago, Chile. Published annually.

Wilkie, James W., ed. *Statistical Abstract of Latin America.* Published biennially at the University of California, Los Angeles. An invaluable private publication.

Books

Atkins, G. Pope. *Latin America in the International Political System.* 2nd ed. Boulder, Colo.: Westview Press, 1989. This leading study in the field is by a political scientist who employs a systems approach in dealing with Latin America as a regional actor.

Davis, Harold E., and Larman C. Wilson et al. *Latin American Foreign Policies: An Analysis.* Baltimore: Johns Hopkins University Press, 1975. By a historian and political scientist and a group of country specialists who consider each country's relations with Europe, the Soviet bloc, and the Third World.

Ferris, Elizabeth, and Jennie K. Lincoln, eds. *Latin American Foreign Policies: Global and Regional Dimensions.* Boulder, Colo.: Westview Press, 1981. By a political scientist and a sociologist who have brought together an excellent set of articles. Part 2, "Latin American Global Foreign Policies," is especially relevant.

Fontaine, Roger W., and James D. Theberge, eds. *Latin America's New Internationalism: The End of Hemispheric Isolation.* New York: Praeger Publishers, 1976. By a political scientist and an economist who have included some very informative essays on Latin American relations with the Communist states, the Third World, Europe, and Japan.

Grabendorff, Wolf, and Riordan Roett, eds. *Latin America, Western Europe and the United States: Reevaluating the Atlantic Triangle.* New York: Praeger Publishers, 1985. By a West German and a U.S. scholar who have brought together the papers of leading experts in Europe, Latin America, and the United States presented at conferences held in each region.

Grunwald, Joseph, ed. *Latin America and World Economy: A Changing International Order.* Beverly Hills, Calif.: Sage Publications, 1978. Edited by an economist, and most chapters are by economists. Includes particularly factual and relevant essays in Part 1, "Economic Relations with Industrial Countries."

Hellman, Ronald G., and H. Jon Rosenbaum, eds. *Latin America: The Search for a New International Economic Role.* New York: John Wiley and Sons, 1975. By two political scientists who have integrated a series of important essays, mainly by other political scientists. Part 4, "Latin America and the World," is especially pertinent.

Jaguarabe, Hélio. *El Nuevo Escenario Internacional.* México: Fondo de Cultura Económica, 1985. A Brazilian scholar's analysis of Latin America's place in the new international scene.

Lagos Matús, Gustavo, ed. *Las Relaciones entre América Latina, Estados Unidos y Europa Occidental.* Santiago: Editorial Universitaria, 1980. An excellent collection of essays on many facets of relations by Latin American experts.

Munoz, Heraldo, and Joseph S. Tulchin, eds. *Latin American Nations in World Politics.* Boulder, Colo.: Westview Press, 1984. By a Chilean and a U.S. scholar who have assembled valuable essays by leading analysts in Latin America and the United States— and one West German.

Specialized Works

Blasier, Cole. *The Giant's Revival: The USSR and Latin America.* Rev. ed. Pittsburgh: University of Pittsburgh Press, 1987.

Domínguez, Jorge. *Cuba: Internal and International Affairs.* Beverly Hills: Sage, 1982.

Duncan, W. Raymond. *The Soviet Union and Cuba: Interests and Influence.* New York: Praeger Publishers, 1985.

Heine, Jorge, and Leslie Manigat, eds. *The Caribbean and World Politics: Cross Currents and Cleavages.* New York: Holmes & Meier, 1988.

Lowenthal, Abraham F. *Partners in Conflict: The United States and Latin America.* Baltimore: Johns Hopkins University Press, 1987.

Martz, John D., ed. *United States Policy in Latin America: A Quarter Century of Crisis and Challenge, 1961–1986.* Lincoln: University of Nebraska Press, 1989.

Maira, Luis, ed. *El Sistema Internacional y América Latina: Una Nueva Era de Hegemonía Norteamericano?* Buenos Aires: RIAL, Grupo Editor Latinoamericano, 1986.

Milenky, Edward S. *Argentina's Foreign Policies.* Boulder, Colo.: Westview Press, 1987.

Seara Vásquez, Modesto. *Política Exterior de México*. 3rd ed. México: Harper & Row Latinoamericana, 1985.

SELA, comp. *Relaciones Económicas Internacionales de América Latina*. Caracas: SELA, 1987.

Selcher, Wayne A., ed. *Brazil in the International System*. Boulder, Colo.: Westview Press, 1981.

Tomassini, Luciano, comp. *Relaciones internacionales de América Latina*. Mexico City: Fondo de Cultura Económica, 1981.

United Nations, Economic Commission for Latin America. *The Economic Relations of Latin America with Europe*. Santiago, Chile: ECLA, 1980.

Varas, Augusto, ed. *Soviet–Latin American Relations in the 1980s*. Boulder, Colo.: Westview Press, 1987.

Professional Journals

Two Latin American journals with frequent, relevant articles on the global role of certain countries and Latin America are *Estudios internacionales* (University of Santiago, Chile) and *Foro internacional* (College of Mexico).

Three journals published in the United States that have occasional articles on the subject are *Inter-American Economic Affairs, Journal of Inter-American and World Affairs,* and *Latin American Research Review*.

Newspapers

The three most useful newspapers in English are *New York Times, Washington Post,* and *Times of the Americas* (biweekly).

PART SEVEN
MEXICO

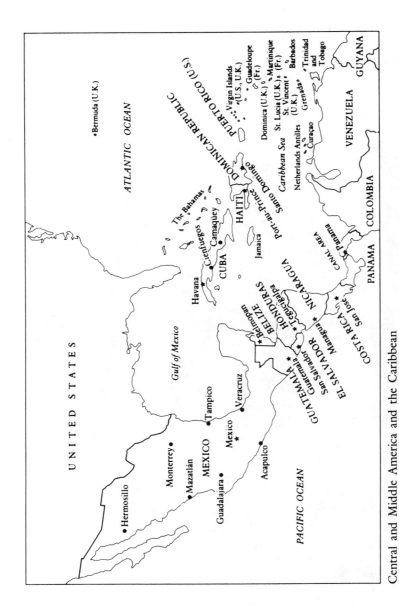

Central and Middle America and the Caribbean
Reprinted, with permission, from Howard J. Wiarda and Harvey F. Kline, eds., *Latin American Politics and Development*, Second Edition (Boulder, Colo.: Westview Press, 1985).

16
MEXICO:
HISTORICAL FOUNDATIONS

FRED R. HARRIS

All nations and peoples are, more or less, products of their own history. Mexico and Mexicans are more so than most. Mexican sociologist Raúl Béjar Navarro has shown that studies seeking to prove that there is a unique Mexican "character" are largely impressionistic and unscientific.[1] But there certainly is, in Mexico, such a thing as national experience, a shared history.

History is not only a chronological recording of past events but also an attempt to explain the events. In order to understand a country and a people, then, we must know not only what has happened to them but also what they choose to remember and what they choose to make of what they remember—what they teach.

"To say Benito Juárez is to say Mexico. To say Mexico is to say sovereign nation." Those were the beginning words of a patriotic speaker at the annual Mexico City ceremony on Benito Juárez Day, March 21, 1982—the 176th anniversary of the birth of the Zapotecan Indian who rose to be president of Mexico. Virtually every Mexican town and city has a monument to Juárez or a principal street named for him—this stern "man of law" who stripped the Catholic Church of its property and privileges; reformed Mexican politics; instituted public education; ended the rule of the Mexican dictator Santa Anna; and later, drove the French from Mexico.

Reform. Respect for law. Nationalism and resistance to foreign aggression. Civilian control of the government. The importance of "great leaders." Public morality. Separation of church and state. Pride in Indian history. These are some of the concepts that the memory of Benito Juárez evokes for Mexicans— and is used to evoke. To Mexicans, Juárez was an Indian who became a Mexican, as Mexico was an Indian nation that became a Mexican nation. But it was Indian first.

THE PRE-CORTÉS PERIOD

Within the great sweep of Middle America lies the Valley of Mexico (in which present-day Mexico City is situated). It is 7,000 ft (2,134 m) above sea level and encompasses some 5,000 sq mi (12,950 sq km). The valley is bounded on all sides by snowy volcano mountains. In prehistoric times, much of the valley floor was covered by large shallow lakes. By around 8000 B.C., people had begun farming in the valley. After 1500 B.C., population centers began to develop. Stratifications of power and wealth evolved. Trade flourished over wide areas. Agriculture became highly advanced.

Civilization was already ancient—great cities, like Teotihuacán and Tula, had already risen and then fallen—by the time the Aztecs came into the Valley of Mexico in the thirteenth century. They were an especially industrious, vigorous, and expansionist people. By 1425, they had subjugated, or made alliances with, all the other peoples of the valley. Eventually, their influence reached from the Mexican highlands to the coasts on either side and as far south as present Guatemala. Only the Tlaxcalans to the east, the Tarascans to the west, and some of the Mixtecs to the south remained apart.

By the time Moctezuma II became its principal lord in 1502, the capital city of the Aztecs, Tenochtitlán, was a clean, healthy, bustling metropolis, one of the largest cities of the world, with a population as high as 200,000 people. (By contrast, Seville, the Spanish city from which the conquistadores were later to sail, had a population of around 40,000, and only four European cities—Paris, Venice, Milan, and Naples—had populations of 100,000 or more.) There were some fifty other cities in the Valley of Mexico. Millions and millions of people lived in an area of one of the greatest population concentrations in the world.

THE SPANISH CONQUEST

When Hernán Cortés and the conquistadores came over the snowy pass to the east and first saw Tenochtitlán and the other cities in and around the lake, they could hardly believe their eyes. Bernal Díaz del Castillo, who was in the party, later wrote that "we were amazed and said that it was like the enchantment they tell of in the legend of Amadis, on account of the great towers and cues and buildings rising from the water, and all built of masonry." Within three years thereafter, Cortés was the ruler of all he had at first surveyed—except that, by then, the great city was in ruins.

Why did Moctezuma II, the Aztec ruler, let the Spaniards come freely into Tenochtitlán? Cortés's monstrous use of terrorism as a tactic must have been puzzlingly and terrifyingly different from any kind of war that Moctezuma II had known. Why destroy a huge tribute city like Cholula and the income one could derive from it, as Cortés did? Why kill such great numbers of people for no useful purpose? Moctezuma II must also have let the Spaniards come because he was certain that at any later moment when he wanted to, he could easily defeat and capture Cortés and his army. Moctezuma must have been influenced, too, by Cortés's continued and effusive expressions of friendly intention. And, philosopher and thinker that he was, intellectually curious, Moctezuma must have been intrigued by these strange white men and anxious to know more about their identity and their place of origin.

In any event, Cortés did indeed come in. Once inside Tenochtitlán, he seized Moctezuma and held him prisoner. But Cortés soon had to leave for the Gulf Coast to defeat a rival Spanish army sent by the governor of Cuba. While he was away, the Aztecs at last rose up and attacked the Spaniards. Moctezuma was killed in the bloody fighting. Cortés, with his Tlaxcalan allies, marched back to Tenochtitlán to relieve the embattled Spanish garrison there. But the Aztecs had had enough, and they drove Cortés and the Spaniards from the city.

Then came into play one of the most terrible factors in the success of the conquest—European disease, in this case, smallpox. The European plagues—smallpox, influenza, typhus, typhoid, diptheria, measles, whooping cough, and others—were unknown in the New World. The native peoples of the Western Hemisphere had built up no immunities to them. Time after time, then, with first contact, one or another of the European diseases decimated whole populations in the Americas. Such was now the fate of Tenochtitlán. Smallpox swept through the city with devastating effect, throwing social and political organization into disarray and shaking religious beliefs. Thousands upon thousands died within the span of a week. Bodies piled up and could not be disposed of rapidly enough. Cuitlahuac, the nephew of Moctezuma who succeeded him, was one of those who died. Cuauhtémoc assumed the leadership. As one historian has written, "Clearly, if smallpox had not come when it did, the Spanish victory could not have been achieved in Mexico."[2] Another historian concurs, writing that "the glorious victories attributed to Spanish arms would not have been possible without the devastation wrought by Spanish disease."[3] Cortés had time to regroup. When he attacked, he fought a weakened enemy. Still, Cuauhtémoc and the Aztecs resisted fiercely until, at last, they were defeated—and Cuauhtémoc captured— in the suburb of Tlatelolco on August 21, 1521. By that time, Tenochtitlán had been destroyed.

As Robert E. Quirk and others have written, one can tell a great deal about a country by the monuments it chooses to erect—and by the monuments it chooses *not* to erect. There are no monuments in Mexico to Cortés. Neither are there monuments to Malinche, the collaborating Indian woman who became mistress of and interpreter for Cortés (indeed, in Mexico today, *malinchismo* is the act of selling out one's country to foreigners). There are no monuments to Moctezuma. Cuauhtémoc is the Indian hero of Mexico history.

SPANISH COLONIALISM

Cortés had cut off the head of the Aztec Empire. In the next years, the body followed. The Spanish captain rewarded his men—and himself—as richly as he had promised. There were great quantities of gold. Cortés took for himself vast estates of rich land and huge *encomiendas* (entrustments or grants of Indians) to work them. He gave land and *encomiendas* to his followers, also.

The first year, Cortés began growing sugarcane. With this and other crops, the plow was also introduced. Soon, great herds of sheep and cattle were imported and set to graze. Slave labor built *ingenios,* or sugar mills. Forests were felled to provide fuel, lumber for building, and charcoal for cooking. Thus began, from the first year of Spanish colonialism, the overplowing, overgrazing, deforestation, and desertification that have continued to plague Mexico to this day.

Gold and silver mines were established, expanded, and worked, under incredibly brutal conditions, by Indian slave labor. *Obrajes,* or sweatshops, were everywhere set up to produce the coarse cloth and other products needed for domestic consumption. When the *encomienda* system and slavery were later made illegal, these monarchical edicts were often ignored, or were replaced by debt peonage, which was just as bad. Brutal treatment and European diseases wiped out more than two-thirds of the native population in the Valley of Mexico between 1519 and 1650!

Spanish colonialism, then, was characterized by exploitation of people and natural resources. It was also characterized by mercantilism—the crown's practice of keeping Mexico a producer of raw materials only and a purchaser of Spain's manufactured goods. Education was a privilege in colonial Mexico, not a right. The Roman Catholic Church was the established church. After a first period of missionary zeal, the Church fell, in many instances, into dissolution. The Church, itself, became a great landholder and exploiter of Indian labor. There were wholesale conversions to Catholicism, but the Indian converts still held on to much of their old religion. The Spaniards built churches on sacred Indian sites. The Virgin of Guadalupe appeared to an Indian convert, Juan Diego, at a site where there had previously been a shrine to an Aztec goddess.

After 1700, the Mexican and Spanish economies, both of which had been depressed, began to revive. The population in Mexico began to grow— mostly among the mestizos. The numbers of the *criollos* (Spaniards born in the New World) also grew, and they began to develop a pride in Mexicanness, which paralleled their increasing resentment of the privileged position of the *peninsulares,* who had been born in Spain.

Spain's wars in Europe meant more taxes in Mexico, more "forced loans" to the crown, and confiscation of Church charitable funds. Then, Napoleon Bonaparte imposed his brother on Spain as its ruler. At this, some *criollos* in Mexico attempted a revolt against the *peninsulares,* but this revolt was put down. Political dissatisfaction was soon joined by economic troubles.

INDEPENDENCE AND EMPIRE

Throughout Mexico, groups of dissidents began to meet in 1809, some to plot. One such group met regularly in Querétaro. Among its members were a young cavalry captain, Ignacio Allende, thirty-five, and a fifty-seven-year-old priest, Miguel Hidalgo y Costilla, whose parish was in the small nearby village of Dolores. Hidalgo, a *criollo,* had been investigated twice by the Inquisition for his political views. When word leaked out about the conspiracy in Querétaro, its members were warned by the wife of the local *corregidor,* or governor (she is celebrated in Mexican history as *la corregidora*). In Dolores, with Allende by his side, Father Hidalgo rang his church bell to summon his parishioners and issued what came to be called the *grito de Dolores,* a call to rebellion, on September 16, 1810. Many *criollos* were alarmed by the excesses of the mestizos and Indians who fought for Hidalgo and independence. Government forces rallied. Hidalgo and Allende were defeated, captured, and killed.

A mestizo priest, José María Morelos y Pavón, took up the sword of leadership, and in the Congress that he called in 1813, he made clear by his stirring speech to the delegates that the sword he carried was meant to cut the *criollo,* as well as the *peninsular,* bonds that had for so long held down the mestizos and Indians of Mexico. The constitution adopted by this Congress was a liberal document. Principles could not stand up to guns, however. *Criollos* and *peninsulares* joined together in opposition to this rebellion, and by 1815, Morelos, too, had been captured and killed. Still, the war—or wars—for independence sputtered on for another five years.

In Spain, Ferdinand VII had been restored to the throne in 1814, but the *criollos* of Mexico felt increasingly separate from Spain. In 1823, led by a conservative military man, Agustín de Iturbide, the *criollos,* backed by the Church, declared Mexican independence—a conservative independence, much different from that for which Morelos and Hidalgo had fought and died. Spain, after years of war, had no alternative but to agree to Mexican independence. The Mexican economy was in shambles. And after all the fighting, the lives of the great mass of the Mexican people had not changed. The identity of their oppressors had changed, but the nature of the oppression remained the same. Iturbide had himself declared emperor of Mexico—the first of its *caudillo,* or strongman, rulers. But the imperial grandeur in which Iturbide lived and ruled lasted only ten months.

Now, there rode onto the Mexican scene one of the most flamboyant and most enduring *caudillos* of Mexican history, the Veracruz military commander, a twenty-nine-year-old *criollo,* Antonio López de Santa Anna. Santa Anna had switched from the Spanish army to support Iturbide. After Iturbide dissolved the Mexican Congress, Santa Anna switched and led the forces that unseated Iturbide. He could be a monarchist or an antimonarchist. He could be a liberal or a conservative. He could be a defender of his country, or he could sell it out. For him, expediency and self-interest were the first principles. In February of 1823, Iturbide was driven into European exile, and his rule was replaced by that of a provisional government, run by a three-man military junta.

Needless to say, there are no statues in Mexico honoring Iturbide. By contrast, both Hidalgo and Morelos had states named after them, and there are many monuments to them. On each anniversary of the *grito de Dolores,* the president of the Mexican republic rings the old bell, now at the National Palace, in commemoration of that important event.

THE MEXICAN REPUBLIC

A new Mexican constitution was promulgated in 1824. It established the Estados Unidos Mexicanos, which consisted of nineteen states and four territories. Patterned after the constitution of the United States and influenced by the writings of the French philosopher, Montesquieu, the Mexican Constitution established a national government of three branches—executive, legislative, and judicial—a bicameral legislature, and a president to be elected by nationwide popular vote. Roman Catholicism was continued as the established religion. Military men and priests were guaranteed their special privilege of the *fuero*—that is, the right to be tried for any offense not by the civil courts but by military or Church courts.

After Manuel Félix Fernández Guadalupe Victoria was elected as the first president, poor Iturbide mistakenly thought he heard a call of the Mexican people—all the way over in Italy. He unwisely returned home, where he was arrested and executed. In 1827, Santa Anna put down another attempted revolt. In 1830, he was called on to defend the country and the government once more. When the second republican president had pushed through legislation expelling all Spaniards from Mexico, Spain had invaded Mexico at Tampico. Santa Anna laid siege to the Spanish forces and eventually forced their surrender. By then, he was easily the most popular figure in Mexico. The president of Mexico was then thrown out of office and executed by his vice-president. Santa Anna rose up and threw this usurper out of office. He was then elected president of Mexico in 1833.

It turned out that Santa Anna was not very much interested in governing. His vice-president, though, began to push through liberal reforms. So the army, the Church, and other conservatives banded together to overthrow the constitutional government and rescind the reforms. And who should lead this revolt but the president of the republic himself, Antonio López de Santa Anna. Now the foremost conservative, Santa Anna abolished the Constitution of 1824 and made the states into military districts. He required that he be addressed as Your Serene Highness. He was to occupy the presidency again and again, off and on, until 1855. During those years, the army became larger and larger, the bureaucracy became ever more bloated, taxes became higher and higher, the economy stagnated, bribery and corruption of officials became outrageous, and there were conflicts with foreign governments—first with the Republic of Texas, then with France, and finally, and disastrously, with the United States.

For years, Mexico had encouraged emigration from the United States to the sparsely settled, vast lands of Texas—provided only that the new emigrants were Catholics, would be loyal to the Mexican government, and would use Spanish as their official language. As the years passed, little was done to enforce these requirements. The flood of emigration swelled. Eventually, people from the United States greatly outnumbered Mexicans in Texas, and they became increasingly critical of the central government, until, at last, they rebelled and declared the establishment of the Lone Star republic in 1836. Santa Anna took personal command of the Mexican army and marched to San Antonio, where, at the Alamo on March 6, 1836, he defeated the Texas defenders there and killed them all. Another part of the Mexican army captured the small town of Goliad, taking 365 prisoners, all of whom Santa Anna had executed. Then, on April 21 of that same year, Santa Anna was himself defeated at the San Jacinto River and was taken captive.

To save himself, Santa Anna promised the Texans that Mexico would not again fight against Texas and that the Mexican cabinet would receive a formal mission from the Lone Star republic. When the cabinet heard of these agreements, they immediately repudiated them and sent Santa Anna back to his estate near Veracruz. Soon, however, the trumpets sounded again for Santa Anna. Provoked by Mexico's refusal—actually an inability—to pay its French debts, France ordered a shelling and invasion of Veracruz. Santa Anna led the Mexican forces that eventually drove the French away.

WAR WITH THE UNITED STATES

Then came the war between the United States and Mexico (1846–1848). U.S. attitudes toward Mexico and Mexicans were highly derogatory, even racist—especially after the war with Texas. Furthermore, the people and government of the United States felt that it was their Manifest Destiny to stretch their country's boundaries westward, all the way to the Pacific. The United States annexed Texas as a state of the Union in 1845. Mexican officials seethed, but were largely powerless to do anything else. Then, without any discoverable basis in law or fact, Texas claimed that its border went, not just to the Nueces River, but much past it to the Rio Grande (which the Mexicans call the Rio Bravo). Not only had Mexico suffered the loss of Texas, but it was now expected to accept the doubling of Texas territory— to include additionally, for example, San Antonio, Nacogdoches, and Galveston in Texas as well as Albuquerque, Santa Fe, and Taos in present New Mexico.

It is known from President James K. Polk's diary that he had made up his mind early to engage in a war with Mexico and was only waiting for a provocation. He sent U.S. troops into the area between the Nueces and the Rio Grande. When they skirmished with Mexican cavalry, Polk went before Congress, declared that he had made every effort at reconciliation, that the Mexicans had invaded U.S. territory and "shed American blood on American soil," and asked for a declaration of war. Congress complied.

The U.S. Army of the West was divided into three attack groups, which rapidly took New Mexico, California, and Chihuahua. The Army of the Center attacked Monterrey, where it was stopped by none other than Santa Anna. The main U.S. attack came from the Army of Occupation at Veracruz, which eventually marched all the way to Mexico City. The last battle there was on September 13 at Chapultepec Castle, the site of a military academy. Young Mexican cadets fought alongside the Mexican regulars, many preferring death to surrender. Mexico was defeated.

Peace was even more humiliating for Mexico than the war had been. According to the Treaty of Guadalupe Hidalgo, Mexico lost half of its territory in return for a payment of a little over $18 million dollars—all of California, some of present-day Colorado, and most of the present states of New Mexico and Arizona. More humiliation was to come. When Santa Anna again came to power in 1853, needing money, he sold the rest of present New Mexico and Arizona (in the so-called Gadsden Purchase) to the United States for $10 million.

Today, one of Mexico's principal national monuments is located in Chapultepec Park. It is dedicated to the *niños héroes* ("boy heroes") of the war with the United States. Similar national monuments commemorating the patriotism and courage of the young cadets have been erected in villages and towns throughout Mexico. There are no monuments to Santa Anna.

THE REFORM

By 1854, the liberals of Mexico had had enough of dictatorial government. Among them was Benito Juárez, the lawyer of Zapotec Indian origin who had been governor of his home state, Oaxaca. They rose up in arms behind the liberal Plan of Ayutla. Santa Anna was driven into exile in 1855. Thus began what is called La Reforma (the Reform). Benito Juárez, as secretary of justice in the new government, was instrumental in having promulgated three important new reform laws: *ley Juárez, ley Lerdo, and ley Iglesias.* The first law abolished the *fuero,* the right of priests and military men to be tried in their own courts. The second law prohibited the Church and public units (including *ejidos,* the communal landholdings of Indian villages) from owning more property than was necessary for Church or governmental functions. The extra lands were not divided among the people. They were put up for sale. The unfortunate result was that large landholdings went to those who had the money. The third law struck again at the Church—making registration of births, deaths, marriages, and adoptions a civil, not a Church, responsibility; giving control of cemeteries to civil authorities; and prohibiting priests from charging high fees for administering the sacraments.

The Constitution of 1857 incorporated these and other reforms. Pope Pius IX declared any who followed the constitution heretics. The lines were sharply and bitterly drawn between the liberals on one side and the conservatives and supporters of the Church on the other. The War of the Reform broke out in 1858. Conservative forces overran the capital. Benito Juárez, who had earlier been elected chief justice and was, therefore, next in line for succession to the presidency, took over that office when its occupant resigned. Juárez eventually made his capital in Veracruz.

The conservative government in Mexico City renounced the Reform laws and swore allegiance to the pope. The Juárez government, on the other hand, issued even stronger decrees against the Church. The Church and the state were formally separated. Monastic orders were outlawed. All Church properties and assets were nationalized. Taking advantage of dissension within conservative circles, the liberal forces began to win some battles. Finally, on January 1, 1861, Mexico City fell to them.

FRENCH INTERVENTION

Juárez entered Mexico triumphantly in March and was officially elected president. But before 1861 was over, foreign troops invaded. Mexico owed debts to France, Spain, and Great Britain, which it had not been able to pay. Napoleon III of France persuaded the other powers to join with him in an invasion of Mexico. The Spanish and British withdrew after they learned that Napoleon III was bent on conquest. The French troops were then reinforced, and they began to march toward Mexico City. On the *cinco de mayo* ("the fifth of May"), the French troops were defeated near Puebla by the Mexican army. After this victory, Juárez, incensed by the fact that many priests had urged their parishioners to support the French, issued a decree prohibiting priests and nuns from wearing distinguishing garments and from speaking against the government.

The *cinco de mayo* victory was short-lived. Juárez retreated northward, eventually all the way to El Paso del Norte (later to be renamed Ciudad Juárez). Now began one of the most bizarre and tragic episodes in Mexico's political history—the imposition in 1864 by Napoleon III of the Hapsburg prince from Austria, Ferdinand Maximilian, as emperor of Mexico. Poor Maximilian and his wife, Carlota, believed the Mexican conservative, monarchist, and pro-Church emissaries who came to urge Maximilian to accept the Mexican throne. They were told that the people would welcome them with warm enthusiasm. They also believed Napoleon III when he said he would finance Maximilian's rule and sustain him on the Mexican throne with French troops as long as necessary. They also believed their Mexican advisers who told them that Juárez was defeated and had fled to the United States. These things were not true.

When the U.S. Civil War ended, the United States again turned its attention to Mexico and began to pressure France to withdraw. At the same time, the U.S. government began to furnish munitions and other supplies to Juárez. In late 1865 and early 1866, the French troops were called home, and Napoleon III announced that he could no longer pay the costs of Maximilian's government. Carlota went to Rome to secure the pope's help; when this effort was unsuccessful, she lost her mind. Maximilian began a final and hopeless resistance to the republican army—being soundly defeated and captured in Querétaro on May 15, 1867. Despite a great number of petitions by numerous heads of state, Juárez denied clemency for Maximilian and had him executed. Juárez entered Mexico City once more, reinstituted the Constitution of 1857, and in December of 1867, was elected to a third term as president. During this "restored republic," Juárez reduced the size of the army, instituted economic and educational reforms, and began construction of a railroad system to pull Mexico together as one nation.

Mexico had developed a strong sense of nationalism—and significantly, this nationalism had flowered in struggles against foreign powers. There are, of course, no monuments in Mexico to Maximilian. There are many monuments dedicated to Juárez, and Mexico City's principal boulevard is named the Paseo de la Reforma.

THE PORFIRIATO

Perhaps Juárez stayed in office too long. There were complaints that he centralized too much authority in the presidency, manipulated and dominated the Congress, caused the alienation of *ejido* land, and increased the power of the national government, to the detriment of state and local governments. Nevertheless, Juárez announced for election to a fourth term in 1871. There was a three-way contest, and no candidate received a majority of the vote. The election was thrown into the Congress, which chose Juárez. One of the other candidates, a military hero of the battles with the French, Porfirio Díaz, attempted a revolt under the slogan of No Reelection. The attempt failed. The revolt was quashed. But, in July of 1872, before he could take office, Juárez died.

The chief justice, one of the other candidates, Sebastián Lerdo de Tejada, succeeded to the office and in special elections in October of that year, was elected president. Lerdo continued the basic policies of Juárez and then announced for reelection to a second term. Porfirio Díaz took to the field with his military supporters again. This time, his No Reelection slogan caught fire. By force of arms and general support among those who counted, Díaz took over the presidency in 1876. This Mexican *caudillo* was to rule Mexico for over a third of a century. True to his No Reelection theme, Díaz did not seek reelection in 1880. After the undistinguished administration of his successor, Díaz became president again in the election of 1884. Thereafter, he remained in office until he was forced out in 1911.

The Porfiriato, as the Díaz reign is called, was a time of stability, law and order, and overall economic growth. It was dominated by men whom detractors later came to call *científicos*—followers of French positivism (a belief in progress through scientific knowledge and the scientific method), pragmatism, and social Darwinism. Chief among the *científicos* was the son of a French emigrant, José Ives Limantour, who became secretary of the treasury. Porfirio Díaz and his backers believed, among other things, that Mexico needed a period of "administrative power"—a nice way to say dictatorship—if the country was to be transformed from a backward nation into a modern one.

Díaz created a powerful political machine, run from the top. He practiced a shrewd politics of conciliation and coalition. There were great political and economic benefits for those who joined up—jobs and positions, land, subsidies, concessions. Constitutional local government continued in theory, but real local power was vested in some 300 *jefes políticos* ("political chiefs"), named by Díaz. The military was also a part of the Díaz coalition. Key generals were allowed to dominate their states. Government policies encouraged bigness in agriculture, as in everything else. New laws allowed surveying companies to keep a portion of any idle, unclaimed, or public lands they surveyed. Great land grabs resulted. Four surveying companies, for example, were able to obtain two-thirds of all the land in the northern state of Sonora, territory equal to the size of England and Wales combined!

The *científicos* believed that Mexico's economic development depended upon attracting foreign capital through special subsidies and concessions. By 1910, U.S. interests controlled 75 percent of Mexican mines, 72 percent of the metal industry, 68 percent of the rubber business, and 58 percent of oil production. Other foreigners—mostly British, French, German, and Dutch—controlled 80 percent of the rest of Mexico's industry.

The theme of the Porfiriato was "peace, order, and progress." A modern railroad network was built. This helped to double cotton production. Mining flourished; so did industrialization. Some ports were modernized and others opened. Exports mushroomed—and Mexico became dependent upon them. Mexico's population doubled.

But the costs were exorbitant. The great majority of Mexicans lived in misery or in otherwise intolerable conditions. The Indians, who Limantour believed were biologically inferior, were considerably worse off by 1910 than they had been a hundred years earlier, prior to independence. The rural *peones,* or laborers, were also worse off. The *peones,* as well as the miners, were paid, not in money, but in scrip or special coins, which could only be spent at the *tienda de raya,* the company store, and they were perpetually behind in what they owed. *Rurales* ("rural police") hunted down and brought back anyone who tried to escape. Debts were passed on from one generation to another. Because Mexico's agriculture had increasingly been converted to cash crops and to the cattle and sheep business, especially for export, Mexico was producing less corn and beans in 1910 than it had produced in 1867— and was a large importer of food.

Railroad, mining, and industrial workers became increasingly hostile to the owners, to foreigners, and to their own government. Labor agitation and attempts at organization began in the 1880s—some of it encouraged by the Catholic Church following the issuance of a papal encyclical in 1891 that called for greater recognition of the rights of labor. Between 1881 and 1911, there were 250 strikes. In the worst of these, against French- and U.S.- owned companies, federal troops were used to break the strikes.

A growing Mexican middle class was also increasingly unhappy with the government. The economic policies and the educational programs of the Díaz regime had helped to create this middle class. But, as Porfirio Díaz and his administration aged, they turned more and more to a politics of exclusion. Liberal intellectuals began to speak out against the undemocratic practices of the government and the exploitation of Mexican labor. Two Flores Magón brothers, Jesus and Ricardo, started a liberal publication, *Regeneración,* to call for change. The publication was closed down by the government, and the Flores Magón brothers fled to the United States, where their writings and calls for action became increasingly radical.

On top of all this came bad economic times. The year 1907 was one of both severe drought in Mexico and severe economic problems in the world.

A financial panic in the United States cut off credit to Mexico. The worldwide economic problems deprived Mexico of its export market, upon which it had come to depend so heavily. Mines were shut down. The economy stagnated. The prices of food and clothing rose rapidly—the costs of flour, beans, wheat, corn, and chile nearly doubling.

Then, in an interview with a U.S. magazine in 1908, Porfirio Díaz announced—and this was widely publicized in Mexico—that he felt the time had come for Mexico to choose its own president in the elections of 1910. Díaz himself eventually became a candidate for reelection. In the meantime, Francisco Ignacio Madero, the son of a Coahuila *hacendado* who had studied for five years in France and eight months at the University of California in Berkeley, wrote a very important book, *The Presidential Succession of 1910,* in which he called for political reform (although he said virtually nothing in regard to land, labor, or other economic or social reforms). Madero formed an Anti-Reelection Party and began to expound his views in well-attended meetings around the country. Actually doubtful that Díaz would really allow a free election, Madero nevertheless announced as a candidate for president. Madero's doubts were well founded. He was arrested and jailed. Díaz was declared the winner in the 1910 elections; Madero went into exile in San Antonio, Texas.

THE REVOLUTION

With this latest usurpation of power by Porfirio Díaz, Madero's frustrations at last rose to a level that matched Mexico's. In October of 1910, he issued his Plan of San Luís Potosí, reiterating his call for political reform and asking Mexicans to rise up in arms against the Díaz regime on November 20. Rise up they did! This moderate man, with his moderate plan, became the lightning rod that attracted all of the dissident elements of the country. Some who joined him were more conservative than Madero; many were more radical. Some joined him to secure a share of the power and wealth, others to fight for social and economic, as well as political, reforms.

There was an uprising in Yucatán. The Flores Magón brothers led an uprising in Baja California. In Chihuahua, Pascual Orozco, Jr., a muleteer disgruntled by the political and economic stranglehold of the *hacendados,* raised an army and began to achieve significant victories over the federal forces. Among his lieutenants was a man who called himself Francisco "Pancho" Villa. Born Doroteo Arango into a poor family living on a hacienda, Villa had spent most of his life as a bandit and a cattle rustler.

In February of 1911, Madero returned to Mexico and took command of the revolutionary army. In the state of Morelos, Emiliano Zapata, a charismatic and dedicated leader for land reform, announced his support for the Madero revolution. It turned out that the federal army had become as debilitated by power and corruption as the government itself. It could not stop Zapata in the state of Morelos nor Orozco and Villa in the northern states. Zapata took Cuautla; Orozco and Villa captured Ciudad Juárez. It became clear to Díaz and those around him that after a third of a century, his government had lost its legitimacy and, with it, control of the country. Limantour went to Ciudad Juárez and negotiated a transfer of power. Díaz abdicated on May 25 and left for Europe, never to return. The Porfiriato had ended. Madero thought that the Revolution had also ended, but it had only begun.

The war was to continue for another decade. Countless Mexicans, including Madero himself, were to be killed by other Mexicans. The country was to be ravished, the economy devastated. The population of Mexico, which had been rapidly growing, was to suffer a decline of nearly 1 million people between 1910 and 1920. But all that was somewhere in the future when a triumphant Madero boarded the train for Mexico City. The troubles to come were presaged, though, by a harsh confrontation Madero had with Orozco and Villa just before he left Ciudad Juárez. In Mexico City, Madero made a strategic mistake. A stickler for legality, he allowed an interim president to serve until Madero could be formally elected in October of 1911. By then, perhaps, his moment had passed. Madero was to govern for only thirteen months. His meager and timid reforms did nothing to satisfy labor and land-reform demands. He continued the fiscal policies of Díaz and retained many of the Porfiriato's high officials.

Orozco took to the battlefield again. Zapata issued his Plan of Ayala, which demanded immediate land reform; denounced Madero; and recognized Orozco as the true leader of the Revolution. Now, Madero made another mistake, this one literally a fatal mistake. He called upon a Porfiriato general, Victoriano Huerta, a mestizo from the state of Jalisco, to head the federal army against Orozco and Zapata. Huerta was successful against Orozco (who later, opportunistically, joined forces with him), and he began to put pressure upon Zapata. Then came another challenge—from the right. Felix Díaz, a nephew of the former president, rose in arms in Veracruz against the Madero government. Again, Huerta was successful. This rebellion, too, was quashed, and Felix Díaz was brought to Mexico City and jailed. Soon, however, other conservative forces freed Díaz and threatened the government again. There then ensued what is called in Mexican history the *decena trágica* ("the ten tragic days"). The killing and destruction wrought by the Díaz and the Huerta forces, fighting against each other, were horrible. It appears now that Huerta might have been going through a sham in order, purposely, to cause the decimation of his own government army, because he was, at the same time, opening secret negotiations with Díaz. These negotiations culminated in an agreement, which was reached under the direction and guidance of the U.S. ambassador, Henry Lane Wilson. Huerta switched sides and the U.S. ambassador supported him. Herta immediately took over the government, arrested Madero, and had the president's brother killed. Madero was imprisoned. Despite the pleas for help by Madero's wife to Wilson, the ambassador did nothing, and Madero and his vice-president were taken out and cruelly murdered.

In the United States, President Woodrow Wilson refused to recognize the Huerta regime. But, in Mexico, most state governors did. Zapata, of course, did not recognize Huerta. Neither did Villa, and he was joined in arms by Alvaro Obregón, a former schoolteacher and *cacique* ("political boss") in Sonora, and a former revolutionary commander. The leadership of these constitutionalist forces was assumed by Venustiano Carranza, nearly sixty years old, the governor of Coahuila, and the patriarch of a distinguished *criollo* family there. Carranza took as his title, First Chief. He issued his Plan of Guadalupe, a moderate plan, promising, again, only political reforms. As the fighting worsened and widened, as villages were taken first by one side and then another, many people began to wonder what it was all about. Even the soldiers—in both the federal and constitutionalist armies—were not agreed among themselves on what they were fighting for.

Although, interestingly, Huerta probably achieved more in the way of reforms and in support of education than did Madero, he also severely suppressed the press, jailed opponents, countenanced the use of assassination as a political tool, and practiced harsh repression generally. Huerta also initiated forced conscription to supply his army with soldiers—producing an inferior army and depleting the Mexican work force, adding injury to the Mexican economy. President Wilson possessed a moralistic zeal for democracy. He replaced Henry Lane Wilson and, using the pretext of a Mexican affront to some U.S. sailors, sent an armed force to capture the port of Veracruz in 1914. This caused a new wave of severely anti-U.S. feeling in Mexico. The vigor and successes of the constitutionalist army, augmented by the facts that Huerta had to divert troops to Veracruz and that his outside sources of supply had been cut off by the U.S. occupation of that port, brought down the Huerta government in July of that same year. Huerta resigned, blaming the United States for his fall (he later died in a Texas jail in 1916, still plotting to return to Mexico).

The First Chief, Venustiano Carranza, took control of the Mexican government. Partisans of social and economic reform soon found out that he was not one of them. To consolidate his position, Carranza called a military convention in Aguascalientes in 1914. *Carrancistas, Villistas,* and *Zapatistas* met to pull the country together and to decide upon a provisional president until elections could be held. But the convention soon got out of hand. Led by the *Zapatistas,* a majority of the delegates, in a burst of revolutionary fervor, elected a provisional president who was opposed by Carranza. The First Chief disowned the convention and called for his representatives to withdraw from it. Fatefully, as time would show, one of those who decided to obey this order was Alvaro Obregón.

The troops of Villa and Zapata marched on Mexico City. Carranza withdrew his headquarters to Veracruz (from which, incidentally, the U.S. occupation forces were eventually evacuated). The provisional president chosen by the Aguascalientes Convention was installed in office. But Obregón was a student of the new tactics of war being used at the time in Europe. At Celaya, in April of 1915, he met an old-style massed cavalry charge with a deadly stationary defense. Thousands of Villa's men were killed and wounded, and Villa himself withdrew northward. Zapata thereafter confined himself and his forces to the state of Morelos.

Carranza returned to power in Mexico City. His government was recognized by President Woodrow Wilson. The First Chief then called another convention, this one a constitutional convention in Querétaro. To avoid his earlier mistake, he decreed that none of the delegates to be elected could include anyone who had fought with Huerta, Villa, or Zapata. But when the convention met, these restrictions proved unavailing. A majority of the delegates quickly rejected the moderate model constitution that Carranza had sent them. Instead, they wrote an organic law—still in effect in Mexico—which was a radical document for its day. It limited the president to one four-year term. Its Article 3 was vigorously anti-Church, incorporating all such earlier restrictions and prohibitions and, further, taking primary education away from the Church (making education purely secular as well as mandatory and free). Article 27 incorporated the basic philosophy and provisions of the Plan of Ayala in regard to land reform, made private ownership a privilege subject to the public interest as the government might define it, and restricted the right to exploit Mexico's water and mineral resources to Mexican nationals. Article 123 mandated extensive labor reforms—an eight-hour day, a six-day week, equal pay regardless of sex or nationality, and a minimum wage. The right of labor to organize and to strike was guaranteed.

Shocked as he was by the product of this second runaway convention, Carranza nevertheless accepted the constitution, although he made it clear that he had no intention of following it. He was elected president in March of 1917. Carranza distributed very little land. His labor reforms were also minor, although he did permit the organization of Mexico's first nationwide union, the Regional Confederation of Mexican Labor (CROM). In the north, Villa was relatively quiet—and wealthy—on his hacienda. But from Morelos, Zapata wrote a defiant open letter to Carranza, calling on him to resign and charging that Carranza and his friends had only fought in the Revolution for "riches, honors, businesses, banquets, sumptuous feasts, bacchanals, orgies." Carranza had tried direct military action against Zapata, to no avail. Now he decided upon treachery. On Carranza's orders, an officer of the federal army in Morelos, indicating that he wanted to defect to Zapata, led Zapata into a trap and killed him in 1919. Carranza rewarded the assassin with an army promotion and a generous cash prize.

But things were far from settled in Mexico, and the battered country had not seen the last of political violence—nor of political assassinations. General Obregón, the one-armed hero of the constitutionalist forces, had gone back to his native Sonora after Carranza's government had been firmly put in place. As a *hacendado*, a grower and "merchant of garbanzos," a cattleman and an exporter of beef and hides, and an all-around entrepreneur, Obregón had grown very wealthy. But power interested him as much as wealth. So, when he thought Carranza had passed over him in choosing the "approved" presidential candidate for 1920, Obregón led a military revolt against Carranza—a successful one. Sadly, Carranza was killed while retreating toward Veracruz. Obregón's subsequent election as president in 1920 was not the last time a presidential election would ratify a result earlier achieved by military means. But Obregón's revolt was the last successful revolt against the government.

The Mexican Revolution was over, and it was soon enshrined forever—with a capital *R*—in Mexican history. With time, the Mexican Constitution came to be regarded as a nearly sacred document—though it was a long way from actually being implemented. Time did not improve the image of Huerta, whom Mexican history remembers as "the bloody usurper." No Mexican monuments were erected in memory of Porfirio Díaz (although, ironically, a street in El Paso, Texas, still bears his name). But plenty of Mexican monuments and street names, today, pay homage to Madero, Carranza, and Zapata. Mexican history makes Madero "the apostle" of the Revolution and of Mexican democracy, Carranza "the father of the constitution," and Zapata the heroic fighter for the Mexican masses.

THE NORTHERN DYNASTY

Alvaro Obregón and his fellow Sonoran, Plutarco Elías Calles, who had fought with Obregón, apparently soon worked out an arrangement by which they agreed to pass the presidency back and forth between them in the years that were to follow. Obregón was elected president in 1920. He was a charismatic leader and a dynamic orator, and he gathered power into the presidency. Obregón was also a conciliator. He made a kind of peace with the Church and with his former foes. He had another rich hacienda bought for Pancho Villa, and the mellowing revolutionary of the North settled down (and was later assassinated in 1923). The economy recovered. Mexico became the world's third largest producer of oil. The first national system of education was established, and rural schools were built. Obregón allowed some cautious labor advances to be made and endorsed some cautious land reform. A sense of what came to be called revolutionary nationalism began to develop in the country—in its writings, in its music, and in its art. In the United States, Warren G. Harding, a friend of big oil, became president in 1921. He pressured Mexico to recognize the U.S. oil holdings there, and Obregón yielded.

Calles became president in 1924—after an attempted rightist rebellion was put down by military force. Taking office, Calles became the strongest—and, as it turned out, the longest-lived—president and *caudillo* since Díaz. He put down his enemies without mercy. He built up Mexico's economy, pushed health programs, expanded education, helped make labor more powerful, and established a cooperative relationship with CROM. He also vigorously enforced, as Obregón had not, the anti-Church provisions of the constitution. Militant Catholics rose up in a bloody rebellion, their cry being "Viva Cristo Rey!" ("Long live Christ, the King!"). Calles dealt very harshly with this *cristero* rebellion and, after much shedding of blood on both sides, eventually suppressed it.

Calles also confronted the United States in regard to oil. It was decreed that all interests that predated the Constitution of 1917 would have to be renegotiated with the government—and these new concessions were to be limited in duration. The United States sent a Wall Street investment banker, Dwight Morrow, to Mexico as its ambassador. His quiet negotiations eventually worked out a compromise. The oil interests were allowed to continue their concessions without the duration lid.

Calles caused the presidential term to be changed from four years to six years. He then prepared to turn the government back over to Obregón in the 1928 presidential election. There was a rebellion, again, and it was again put down. The election ratified the earlier military victory. But before Obregón could take office, he was killed by a religious mystic. Calles assumed power again—ruling through puppets as the *jefe maximo* ("maximum chief") until 1934. During this period, called in Mexican history the *maximato,* Calles established Mexico's ruling party in order to institutionalize his political control, since he was not charismatic or dynamic enough to rule by power of personality. Calles shifted the Revolution to the right. Powerful leaders of labor, business, and government became immensely wealthy during the Calles *maximato.* Calles, himself, seemed to own property almost everywhere.

THE CÁRDENAS *SEXENIO*

With the end of the 1928–1934 *sexenio,* the *maximato* had run its course. Calles was the last survivor of the great revolutionary *caudillos*—Madero, Zapata, Villa, Carranza, and Obregón had all been assassinated—and he was now to lose control. But Calles did not know that that was about to happen when he chose the populist and popular governor of Michoacán and his former minister of war, Lázaro Cárdenas, as the National Revolutionary Party (PNR) presidential candidate in the elections of 1934. Elected, Cárdenas turned out to have a mind of his own. Once he had cut down the strength and influence of the military and had bolstered his own political position with labor, the peasants, and other elements in the country, he confronted Calles and exiled him from the country.

Cárdenas undertook more land reform—mostly by delivering land to *ejidos*—than all of his predecessors put together. He instituted socialist education in the schools and expanded education generally. He reorganized the national labor union into the Confederation of Mexican Workers (CTM) and made this organization a much more aggressive and representative body. The minimum wage was raised. The old hacienda system was broken. A limited peace was achieved with the Church. The railroads were nearly all nationalized. Nationalistic artists were encouraged. A cultural nationalism blossomed. The ruling party, PNR, was reorganized to make it much more broad based and more truly representative of the people to the government, rather than, as it had been, from the government to the people. The name of the party was changed to Mexican Revolutionary Party (PRM).

Then, in 1938, came the major decision of the Cárdenas *sexenio,* the confrontation with big oil. Oil workers had gone on strike. By modern standards, their demands in regard to wages, hours, and working conditions were modest. But the oil interests, chiefly based in the United States and Great Britain, were adamant in their rejection of the demands and in their intention to crush the strike. When the companies showed their arrogance toward the president himself and, thus, toward Mexican sovereignty, Cárdenas invoked Article 27 of the constitution and nationalized the oil industry. He did not turn the industry over to the workers as they wanted, but he did create a public corporation, Petróleos Mexicanos (PEMEX), to run it. He saw to it that this public company dealt generously with the *petroleros,* or oil workers, as it has done ever since.

In the United States, the powerful oil industry called upon the United States to take action—from economic sanctions to outright invasion—to protect their oil holdings and businesses. The U.S. government, and the government of Great Britain, were only too happy to back the companies. They boycotted Mexican oil and sought to isolate PEMEX from oil-production and exploration technology and technical assistance (thus, it turned out, forcing Mexico to build what is today a first-rate oil industry of its own).

Cárdenas had spent a great part of his term walking among the ordinary people of Mexico. Unannounced, he would visit small villages and, on the spot, sign orders for irrigation projects, for distribution of land, for clinics, and for other responses to local petitions that were humbly presented to him. The people of the country saw Cárdenas as one of their own. Now, with the expropriation of oil, the people—including even leaders of the Church and many conservatives—stood up with Cárdenas and with their country against the "greedy" oil companies and against foreign powers—particularly *el coloso del norte* ("the colossus of the North"), the United States. Never had there been such an outpouring of popular support for a president and his government.

Today, Cárdenas remains the greatest hero of Mexico's modern history. The anniversary of his birth and the anniversary of his expropriation of Mexico's oil are national holidays (by contrast, Calles is not considered to have been one of the "revolutionary family"). Under Cárdenas, Mexico's political system became more firmly institutionalized—in the presidency and in the official party (later renamed Institutional Revolutionary Party, PRI).

MEXICO SINCE 1940

Mexico's history since 1940 can best be capsulized by considering a series of "lasts" and "firsts" among its presidents during that period and earlier. Calles was the last presidential exemplar of *continuismo,* continued control past one term. Cárdenas (1934–1940) was the last of the openly and consistently leftist and populist presidents. After his *sexenio,* the Mexican government increasingly focused its attention and efforts on rapid economic growth—the *milagro mexicano* ("Mexican miracle")—to the detriment of economic equity.

Avila Camacho (1940–1946), chosen by Cárdenas to succeed him, was the last military man to serve as president. Interestingly, it was he who disbanded the military arm of the official party (though this action by no means eliminated the influence of the military on government and policy). Miguel Alemán Valdés (1946–1952) was the first civilian president. He allowed new parties to form (some had formed earlier, too). But the PRI's monopoly was not seriously challenged. Alemán was the first Mexican president to exchange visits with a U.S. president. Trade with the United States flourished, as did U.S. private investment in Mexico. Alemán was the last president to devote a really substantial portion of Mexican public investment to agriculture. After his term, the trends toward rapid industrialization and urbanization were accelerated, and Mexico eventually became an urban nation and a net importer of food.

Gustavo Díaz Ordáz (1964–1970) was the last Mexican president to come from outside the metropolis of Mexico City, and he was the last president to have held prior elective office. His political experience did not protect his popularity, though, when economic conditions worsened. The legitimacy of the Mexican political system was seriously strained when students at the national university and other protestors mounted huge demonstrations against government policies and were brutally attacked, with many killed and imprisoned, at Tlatelolco. Still, Díaz Ordáz was the last president under whom Mexico's foreign debt was below double-digit billions of dollars. He was the last president, too, during whose administration the rate of inflation remained at tolerable levels and the value of the peso continued to be stable.

Luís Echeverría Alvarez (1970–1976) was the first of four "insider" presidents—Echeverría, José López Portillo, Miguel de la Madrid Hurtado, and Carlos Salinas de Gortari; each came from the Federal District, had built his career in federal-government positions, and had served in the cabinet of his predecessor. Echeverría was also the first president since 1954 to devalue the peso. He was the first president to lead Mexico into an activist role in foreign affairs, particularly in regard to its own region and Third World countries, and this role increasingly diverged from U.S. policy. Echeverría was the first Mexican president to institute government-backed family planning—none too soon, since Mexico's population had gone from 16.5 million in the 1930s to around 51 million by 1970 (and over 80 million and growing by 1987).

José López Portillo (1976–1982) was the first Mexican president to expropriate Mexican private banks. He did so after hopes had soared at the beginning of his term, when new oil was discovered, only to plummet with a drop in world oil prices. This drop in prices, coupled with skyrocketing federal deficits, inflation, foreign borrowing, and two devaluations, as well as reports of widespread corruption, produced a crisis of confidence for his government.

Miguel de la Madrid Hurtado (1982–1988) and his successor, Carlos Salinas de Gortari (1988–), were two "technocrats" who had spent their adult lives in federal-government financial and budgetary posts. De la Madrid was the first president to institute a *sexenio*-long austerity program, causing increased Mexican unemployment and poverty. Pressured to follow this course by the International Monetary Fund and the foreign banks that held Mexico's mammoth $100 billion foreign debt, he was the object of increasing public criticism and opposition during his term.

Salinas de Gortari was the first modern president to take office with questioned legitimacy, his victory having been clouded by serious charges of widespread election fraud, as were previous PRI-claimed victories in certain northern state elections. He was the first president to face heavy parliamentary opposition—240 of the 500 Chamber of Deputies seats at the time of his inauguration being held by opposition parties, principally PAN and a leftist coalition headed by Cuauhtémoc Cárdenas. Cárdenas, former PRI member and Governor of Michoacán, son of the revered Lázaro Cárdenas, had been a candidate for president against Salinas de Gortari. He claimed that massive fraud had robbed him of victory. Salinas de Gortari was the first president whose inaugural ceremony in the great hall of the Chamber of Deputies was marred by a raucous demonstration and a protest walkout. Improvement in economic conditions and restoration of the legitimacy of the Mexican system— these were the fundamental challenges Salinas de Gortari had to confront.

CONCLUSION

Mexican politics and government are products of—and are to some degree constrained by—Mexican history. The role of the "great leader" is still highly important. Authority is still concentrated in the national government and, within it, in the president. Mexicans have a justified cynicism about government and a skepticism about the revolutionary rhetoric of candidates and officials. Still, candidates and officials know that they must make the obligatory obeisance toward the principles of the Revolution and the constitution. They would act in substantial and open opposition to these principles at their peril—although, obviously, they can fail to act in pursuance of these principles. And, at the beginning of each *sexenio*, there is hope anew (tinged, of course, with some skepticism). Each new president becomes the symbolic leader of the country as well as its official leader, the repository of national authority and national honor, and the focus of Mexican aspirations. For more than fifty years, the Mexican system was stable, and the country's governmental system generally was seen as legitimate by Mexicans—despite gross inequities that have existed, and still exist, and a good deal of misery. The "institutionalization" of the Revolution and the legitimacy of the "official" PRI government faced serious questioning and challenge as Carlos Salinas de Gortari began his *sexenio* in 1988.

NOTES

1. Raúl Béjar Navarro, *El Mexicano: Aspectos culturales y psicosociales* (Mexico City: Univérsidad Nacional Autónoma de México, 1979).
2. William C. McNeill, *Plagues and People* (Garden City, N.Y.: Doubleday, Anchor Press, 1976), p. 207.
3. John Duffy, "Smallpox and the Indians in the American Colonies," in Roger L. Nichols, ed., *The American Indian, Past and Present,* 2d ed. (New York: John Wiley and Sons, 1981), p. 64.

SUGGESTED READINGS

El Colegio de México. *Historia General de México*. 3d ed. 2 vols. Mexico City: Colegio de México, 1981. An authoritative and detailed Spanish-language history of Mexico from earliest times, written, under various headings, by a number of Mexican scholars.

Grayson, George W. *The United States and Mexico: Patterns of Influence*. New York: Praeger, 1984. This is an excellent history and assessment of relations between Mexico and the United States, with particular emphasis on key issues, including marketing of oil and gas, policy toward Central America and Cuba, and illegal immigration of Mexicans to the United States.

Hellman, Judith Adler. *Mexico in Crisis*. New York: Holmes and Meier, 1979. An important study of Mexican politics from a leftist perspective, this book is also very useful because of its treatment of the history of the Mexican Revolution, its institutionalization, and the formation of the ruling political party.

Levy, Daniel, and Gabriel Székely. *Mexico: Paradoxes of Stability and Change*. 2d ed. Boulder, Colo.: Westview Press, 1987. An outstanding brief text, this book discusses Mexican politics and government from precolonial days to the time of President de la Madrid.

Meyer, Michael C., and William L. Sherman. *The Course of Mexican History*. New York: Oxford University Press, 1979. This is a highly readable and well-researched history of Mexico from pre-Cortés times to the election of President José López Portillo.

Pastor, Robert A., and Jorge Castaneda. *Limits to Friendship: The United States and Mexico*. New York: Knopf, 1988. A U.S. and a Mexican authority have written alternating chapters in this illuminating book about U.S.-Mexican relations and the misperceptions that have hampered their greater cooperation.

Raat, W. Dirk, and William H. Beezley. *Twentieth Century Mexico*. Lincoln: University of Nebraska Press, 1986. This highly worthwhile anthology contains chapters that usefully explain Mexico "from Porfirio Diaz to petrodollars."

Ruíz, Ramón Eduardo. *The Great Rebellion: Mexico, 1905–1924*. New York: W. W. Norton, 1980. This is a well-researched and fully footnoted study of the events, conditions, and leaders that made the Mexican Revolution. It concludes that the Revolution was a bourgeois revolt, led by middle-class dissidents, that did not produce the social and economic justice some of its rhetoric promised.

Wilkie, James W., and Albert L. Michaels. *Revolution in Mexico: Years of Upheaval, 1910–1940*. New York: Alfred A. Knopf, 1969. This excellent source book reprints a large number of works of various authors, as well as some original documents, and contains several useful chronologies.

Wolf, Eric. *Sons of the Shaking Earth*. Chicago: University of Chicago Press, 1959. Written by an anthropologist, this history of Mexico is particularly useful in regard to the pre-Cortés and colonial periods.

Womack, John, Jr. *Zapata and the Mexican Revolution*. New York: Random House, 1970. This is a detailed, step-by-step account of the Mexican Revolution and the part played in it by the heroic fighter for agrarian reform.

17

CONTEMPORARY MEXICO

MARTIN C. NEEDLER

More U.S. political scientists consider themselves specialists on Mexico than on any other Latin American country. Of course Mexico is, together with Canada, the nearest neighbor of the United States, its third or fourth largest trading partner, the destination of millions of U.S. tourists annually, and the ancestral home of other millions of inhabitants of the United States. But there are other reasons for paying special attention to Mexico. Mexico is the largest Spanish-speaking country, with more than twice the population of Argentina or Colombia and almost twice the population of Spain herself. And Mexico is now the fourth largest world producer of that most valuable strategic commodity, petroleum, after the United States, the Soviet Union, and Saudi Arabia.

All of these factors make Mexico of interest for its own sake. But Mexico is also worth studying for what can be learned, by social scientists and statesmen of other countries, from the Mexican political and economic model. In a region of the world noted for the instability of its political life, Mexico has, for over fifty years, provided an unparalleled example of a political system that has combined stability with change as presidents succeed each other in the constitutionally prescribed fashion—avoiding the more typical Latin American extremes of continuous turmoil, revolts, and short presidencies on the one hand and the lifetime rule of harsh dictators on the other.

This political stability persisted despite periodic "crises," which every few years had alarmist commentators foreseeing all kinds of impending disasters. Moreover, for forty years, from 1940 to 1980, it went hand in hand with a sustained economic growth without parallel elsewhere—although recent events have led to major economic difficulties. Let us first review the major economic, social, and political characteristics of the country.

ECONOMIC AND SOCIAL CHARACTERISTICS

Economic Policy

Like the countries of Western Europe, Mexico has a mixed economy, with government ownership of several industries and a great deal of government regulation, direction, and intervention but with most of the economy in private hands. There is exclusive government ownership in several basic fields such as petroleum, electric power, banking, railroads, airlines, and telephone and telegraph. There are government corporations in other fields, such as steel production and agricultural marketing, but private activity is also permitted in those fields.

One of the distinctive provisions of economic legislation in Mexico is that, in principle, all companies doing business in Mexico must have Mexican majority ownership; that is, foreign ownership is limited to less than 50 percent of any company. In some fields, the quota of Mexican ownership must be two-thirds. However, as with the rest of Mexican legislation, discretion is left in the administration of the law, and it is possible to extend periods of grace before compliance with the law is enforced. There are other nationalist features of Mexico's economic legislation, such as the existence of a commission that decides the amounts that can be paid for the use of foreign patents and licenses and limits the use of foreign brand names.

Economic Structure and Performance Until 1980

The economic performance of the country was very impressive until the early 1980s. The long-term rate of growth in the gross national product between 1940 and 1980 was 7 or 8 percent annually. Industry has grown, producing both for the domestic market and, under special tariff arrangements, for export; but about 8 million Mexicans work on the land. Nevertheless, for several years prior to 1980, the demand for food had outstripped the country's ability to grow it. In that year, an all-out campaign by President López Portillo raised foodstuff production enough to cover demand, although at quite heavy cost. In addition, commercial farmers in the north of Mexico grow a great many specialty crops, such as winter vegetables, which are exported to the United States and are a valuable source of foreign exchange.

Petroleum

Since the middle of the 1970s, Mexico's major industry, and major export, has been petroleum. Early in the century, Mexico was the world's leading producer of petroleum, when demand for the product was very small. The international oil companies were active in Mexico until 1938. They played the obstreperous role they have often played elsewhere, mixing in the country's politics to try to keep down their tax payments and labor costs and making themselves generally disliked. The 1938 expropriation was thus very popular in Mexico and is looked upon as a kind of economic declaration of independence. Of course, after the expropriation, the international corporations got their crude elsewhere, and Mexican production declined to the level necessary simply to supply the domestic market. The state oil corporation, now called Petróleos Mexicanos, or PEMEX, contented itself with producing mostly from already established wells, lacking the incentive or the funds for serious exploration.

However, over the years, PEMEX built up the technical capabilities necessary for all phases of the industry—exploration, production, refining, and marketing—except for offshore drilling. With the development of an adverse balance of payments and the sharp rise in world petroleum prices in the early 1970s, PEMEX undertook explorations that established Mexico's possession of huge reserves; at the time of writing, proved and potential reserves exceeded 300 billion barrels. Yet this figure represents the exploration of only a small fraction of the sedimentary basins that could contain hydrocarbon deposits. Mexico advanced to fourth place among the world's petroleum producers and became the third largest exporter after Saudi Arabia and Venezuela.

Oil production on the scale of Mexico's is a source of great national political and economic strength, but it also carries with it dangers. Principal among these is the possibility of runaway inflation. Oil production is highly capital intensive. It employs very few people, but it generates large amounts of money. The danger is that the money will go into creating a rapid rise in the price level, thus actually worsening the standard of living of those who do not directly share in oil income. The tendency in most oil-producing states is for the new oil income, which accrues directly to government, to be used simply to expand the bureaucracy without increasing genuinely productive employment and producing goods to absorb the additional purchasing power. The new quantities of foreign exchange encourage imports, often replacing domestically produced goods and contributing to unemployment. These effects became visible in Mexico.

Some Mexicans, moreover, are afraid that the oil will make Mexico more valuable to the United States and that in the event of severe oil supply problems, the United States might be tempted to intervene in Mexico and seize the country's oil fields. Although such an occurrence may seem unlikely to most U.S. citizens, one must remember that there are precedents for this kind of action in past U.S. relations with Mexico and countries in the Caribbean. At all events, Mexico is concerned about allowing excessive U.S. dependence on Mexican oil supplies and has been endeavoring to limit the United States to 50 percent of Mexico's oil exports. In addition to diversifying markets for oil, Mexico has also been diversifying its sources of foreign investment and has been fairly successful in attracting capital from Japan, which is also a major purchaser of Mexican petroleum.

ECONOMIC PERFORMANCE SINCE 1980

The country experienced a sharp economic downturn in the early 1980s, which may have severe structural effects. During the second half of the

1970s, Mexico rode an oil boom, with export income from oil sales doubling every year. The country's spending rose to meet, and pass, its income. Corruption reached new orders of magnitude, especially in PEMEX but also in the presidential palace itself. Massive foreign debts were accumulated, as foreign banks assumed that oil revenues would always be adequate to meet repayment schedules. However, the world economy went into a slump in the late 1970s, and demand for oil, and consequently its price, dropped. In 1982, Mexico plunged into a serious financial crisis, and President José López Portillo, seeking to shift the blame and counteract the precipitous drop in his popularity, nationalized the banking system, thus ending his term in a blaze of nationalist glory. Psychic income is nonmonetizable, however.

Under the subsequent presidents, Mexico managed to compile an impressive record of meeting payments on a renegotiated debt schedule. The austerity program imposed to save money for debt repayment and reduce inflation succeeded, but only at the cost of considerable hardship, especially for poorer Mexicans.

During the 1980s, the situation of the poorest Mexicans deteriorated sharply. The distortions resulting from the oil boom, the drop in oil prices, the sacrifices so the foreign debt could be repaid, and the effects of a devastating earthquake that hit Mexico City in 1985, made the decade one of economic deterioration. Per capita income was lower in 1989 than it had been in 1980. Inflation gathered speed, passing 100 percent per year in 1987 and 1988. This situation led to a groundswell of political opposition, culminating in the presidential elections of 1988, won only with difficulty by the PRI candidate, Carlos Salinas de Gortari.

Income Distribution

In worsening the economic condition of poor Mexicans, the inflation and economic downturn of the 1980s have aggravated one of the great failings of the government since the Revolution. Although Mexico's economic growth until the 1980s was undeniable, the benefits of that growth were concentrated in the upper and middle ranges of the income distribution. The coefficient of concentration of income in 1977 was 0.496, certainly more equal than income distribution in Brazil or El Salvador but very much less equal than in Britain or the United States, not to mention Norway or Iceland.

As the data in Table 17.1 indicate, the share in national income of the bottom 10 or 20 percent of the population, which was perhaps staying the same or even improving slightly in absolute terms, was declining in relative terms, so that the gap between the very poor, or "marginals," and the rest of the population was widening. In relative terms, the share of the 50 percent of income recipients between the second and seventh deciles remained more or less the same. The share of the top 5 percent fluctuated without showing a clear trend. The share of the 25 percent below the top 5 percent, however, showed a substantial increase, from 33.9 percent of the national income in 1950 to 41.87 percent in 1963, fluctuating somewhat since but remaining at 41.6 percent in 1977. With the economic deterioration of the 1980s, the

Table 17.1
Income Distribution by Deciles, 1958–1977, Percentages of Total National
Income

	Deciles	1958	1968	1977
Lowest 10 percent of population	1	2.32	1.21	2.21
	2	3.21	2.21	1.08
	3	4.06	3.04	3.23
	4	4.98	4.23	4.42
	5	6.02	5.07	5.73
	6	7.49	6.46	7.15
	7	8.29	8.28	9.11
	8	10.73	11.39	11.98
	9	17.20	16.06	17.09
Highest 10 percent	10	35.70	42.05	37.99
(Highest 5 percent)		(25.46)	(27.15)	(25.45)

Source: Enrique Hernández Laos and Jorge Córdoba Chávez, "Estructura de la
distribución del ingreso en México," *Comercio Exterior* (May 1979), p. 507.

standard of living of almost all Mexicans worsened in absolute terms, meaning
hunger and privation for those at the bottom of the scale.

Social Structure in Urban Areas

The social structure in the urban areas could be described as consisting
of, first, a small upper middle class, approximately equivalent to the 5 percent
of the income distribution that receives 25 percent of the national income,
of owners, managers, professionals, and high-level public employees. Below
that class comes a middle-income sector—approximately the 25 percent below
the top 5 percent referred to above—consisting of the families of those
earning more than the average national income. These workers include lower-
level government and private-sector employees, unionized workers in businesses and modern factories, some skilled workers and craftsmen, and operators
of small businesses. Another one-third of the urban population consists of
people just getting by, regularly employed in unskilled or semiskilled jobs
at the minimum-wage level or slightly below or self-employed in very small-
scale businesses.

The remaining 35 percent to 40 percent of urban residents range from
those employed only occasionally, to very low-paid domestic servants, to
street vendors and various kinds of hustlers and petty criminals. This
"marginal" population (except for live-in domestic servants) lives in crowded
conditions in decaying central-city housing or, along with some members of
the unskilled, minimum-wage sector, in substandard, largely self-built shantytowns.

Despite the government programs designed to assist the poorest classes,
such as subsidized prices for food and transport and birth control clinics,

life is a continual struggle to get by for most urban Mexicans. As the population grows, people continue to move to the cities, and inflation takes its inexorable toll.

Rural Social Structure

In the countryside, the population continues to grow despite migration to the urban areas. Although some land that should be subject to redistribution under the agrarian reform laws still escapes that fate through one or another ruse, it is unlikely that enough land would ever be available to satisfy the needs of the increasing numbers of landless. While most of Mexico's agricultural exports come from modern agribusiness operations, many on irrigated lands in the north of the country, the vast majority of Mexicans working in agriculture farm tiny plots—either owned outright or the legal property of an *ejido* agricultural community—in the central portions of the country where centuries of continuous cultivation, mostly of corn and beans, have depleted the soil.

Of the 8 million Mexicans working the land, about one-third are members of *ejidos,* joint landholding units established by the agrarian reform laws, and most of these peasants individually farm small allotments of land that they cannot mortgage or sell. There are something over a million private owners of farmland, most of them farming tiny plots about the size of those of their counterparts in the *ejidos,* though generally getting somewhat higher returns. Over 4 million agricultural workers have no land of their own.

The acculturation of Mexico's Indians has reached the point at which it is possible to write of people being more Indian or less rather than simply Indian or non-Indian. Nevertheless, about 20 percent of rural Mexicans speak an Indian language by preference, especially in the southwestern state of Oaxaca and Yucatán in the southeast, and these people remain closer to Indian customs, religious practices, and dress.

Most rural residents do not live much above the subsistence level. It would be unfair, however, to overlook the efforts made by most revolutionary governments to improve conditions for the poor in both urban and rural areas. Prices of many basic items are controlled, and a government agency, CONASUPO, runs small stores that supply articles of prime necessity at rock-bottom prices in poor districts all over the republic, even in rural areas. With all its defects, the land reform program has provided about 100 million hectares (247 million acres) to about 25,000 *ejidos.* The steady improvement in conditions of life has been reflected in the gradual increase in life expectancy at birth, which indicates levels of health and nutrition, from forty-eight years in 1950 to sixty-eight years in 1986. Illiteracy, similarly, has dropped steadily over the years, to below 10 percent of the adult population in 1986, reflecting the fact that elementary schooling is now available in the most remote hamlets in the republic. As the rate of growth of Mexico's population continues to decline (it went from 3.2 percent in the 1960s, to 2.9 percent in the 1970s, to 2.4 percent in the 1980s), many remaining social problems may prove more manageable.

The Problems of Mexico City

Even if the rate of population increase should decline further, however, it will come too late to avoid the onset of some major problems. The combination of population growth and migration to the cities has already made Mexico City the largest urban agglomeration in the world. This has meant the loosing of an avalanche of problems—in the areas of housing, employment, transportation, sanitation, and so on. Government performance, while energetic and probably above the average level for Latin America or Third World cities, has fallen short of a satisfactory resolution of these problems, which were worsened by the effects of the 1985 earthquake. Unemployment and underemployment are especially acute; standards of housing are very uneven, ranging down to very poor in the satellite city of Netzahualcoyotl; and pollution has reached health-threatening proportions. Surface transportation can be a nightmare; a worker may have a miserable journey aboard an overloaded rickety bus for as much as two hours each way to get to work and back each day. Construction of the long-overdue subway system, now functioning, has alleviated the situation somewhat, however.

POLITICAL STRUCTURE

Major Political Features

The formal constitutional system of Mexico resembles that of the United States in having a separation of powers among executive, legislative, and judicial branches; a division of authority between state and federal levels; a two-house federal legislature; staggered terms for members of the Senate, two of whom represent each state; and single-member districts for the election of members of the lower house of the federal legislature. The president is elected by direct popular vote, however (there is no Mexican equivalent of the U.S. electoral college).

Still, several key differences ensure that the actual allocation of power in the Mexican system varies in important respects from that in the country's northern neighbor. The federal government in Mexico is stronger in relation to the Mexican states than in the United States; there is no question that federal preferences override those of the states in the event of conflict. The federal Senate can remove state governors and, in fact, still does so, although not so frequently now as in the 1920s and 1930s. Within the federal government, the power of the president is clearly supreme. It is all but unheard-of for the national Congress to defeat a legislative initiative supported by the president. The Supreme Court has, very rarely, ruled opposite to the president's preferences in some cases, but under somewhat obscure circumstances that do not permit clear conclusions to be drawn.

This does not mean, however, that the president is an absolute ruler whose every whim becomes law, like a traditional oriental potentate. As in every government, the bureaucracy goes its own way most of the time, with only limited control by the politicians who are its hierarchical superiors. There are powerful economic interests that must be consulted and whose preferences must sometimes be honored. Politicians with their own bases of power— regional strongmen and party leaders with important popular followings— are listened to and sometimes heeded. Governors generally have their way within their states if their conduct is not too notoriously scandalous. Nevertheless, the president remains overwhelmingly the key factor in Mexican politics.

However, the president's power is limited by one of the most distinctive features of Mexican political mores, a feature shared by Mexico with most other Latin American countries living under constitutional regimes, the prohibition of presidential reelection.[1] This provision, a commonplace of Latin American constitutions for over a century, is designed to prevent, or inhibit, the establishment of perpetual dictatorships by presidents who simply extend their mandates indefinitely. Some U.S. citizens, used to presidents who subordinate other considerations of policy to the requirements of their reelection campaigns, regard this provision as an idea that might profitably be adopted by the United States. According to the law, which was given its present form as part of the institutionalization of the system that took place in Mexico after the assassination of President-elect Alvaro Obregón in 1928, a Mexican president serves six years and may never again be reelected.

The Official Party

Perhaps the most distinctive feature of the Mexican political system is the dominance of the country's politics by a single "official" party. Founded over fifty years ago as the National Revolutionary Party, the party is now the Institutional Revolutionary Party (PRI). During the entire period of its existence, the official party has won every election for president and governor, almost all those for federal senator, and the overwhelming majority of elections for federal deputyships and mayoralties. On occasion, fraud has been involved in those victories, and forms of official influence that make the system less than perfectly fair, such as the government party's dominance of the communications media, are brought to bear. Nevertheless, the striking thing is the relatively small amount of fraud that has been necessary to produce the outcome; the plain truth is that most people have preferred the PRI to the alternatives. In part, this preference has been because the party's policies have broad popular appeal, but also because the alternatives have usually lacked plausibility. Everyone knows the PRI will win, so it makes more sense to try to work from within the party, to get what one wants by going along, rather than to waste energy in a doomed struggle.

Nevertheless, some hardy souls have led other parties in opposition to the PRI. Some of these parties, such as the Authentic Party of the Mexican Revolution (PARM) and the Popular Socialist Party (PPS), started in opposition but became drawn into the orbit of the PRI, endorsing its presidential candidates and being rewarded with subsidies and a few deputies' seats and mayoralties. Another party, the Party of National Action (PAN), has opposed the PRI from a more conservative, proclerical position, has never endorsed the PRI's candidates, and has seen its vote grow slowly over the years. Paradoxically, the PRI is delighted to have the PAN as its leading "loyal opposition." The PAN's conservative policy positions have given substance to the PRI's claim to be a revolutionary party of workers and peasants, and the PAN's dogged presentation of candidates who always lose the major offices has validated the system's claim to be democratic without presenting any real threat to the group in power.

Another basis for the PRI's claims to be both democratic and a party of workers and peasants lies in the party's internal organization. The party is structured as a federation of three "sectors"—labor, agrarian, and popular—and each of the sectors is itself a federation of organizations. The labor sector comprises most of the country's labor unions, though there are several important unions outside the PRI, and the agrarian sector consists principally of the members of *ejidos,* the joint landholding units established under the country's land reform laws. The popular sector was envisioned as a middle-class sector, beginning with white-collar unions of teachers and government workers, but it has expanded in other directions, especially in enrolling organizations of slum dwellers.

This form of organization can be considered democratic in the sense that, in principle, all of these constituent membership groups have a voice in candidate selection and policymaking, and every conceivable type of vocation or other interest is represented within the party. In fact, the constituent organizations are often simply vehicles for their leaders to work themselves into prestigious and well-paying government positions. In any case, the party as such does not make decisions on policy or on candidates, except for minor local-level positions. The president himself decides on the party's candidates for president, governor, and senator, and for most of the deputyships too. However, he takes into account the strength represented by different groups and interests within the party. Because of this, local leaders trying to promote themselves also try to increase membership in the party organizations that they head. In trying to recruit members, however, they must pay attention to the concerns of the potential recruits and thus provide a channel for the expression of desires or the posing of demands—another feature of the system that can be called "democratic."

Political Freedoms

Within the official party, there has for some time been a struggle between those who favor the maintenance of tight control of the political system by the ruling group and those willing to contemplate a loosening of the system, a "democratic opening," that would make it easier for opposition groups to win representation in the federal Congress and for dissidents within the PRI to have a greater say in policy and nominations. Critics of the system are no doubt correct in commenting that most of the supporters of "democracy" within the PRI are interested more in effective co-optation of dissidents, in pacifying opposition without actually jeopardizing control by the ruling elite,

Table 17.2
Party Representation in Chamber of Deputies, 1988–1991

	Seats Won in Single-member Districts	Seats Won by Proportional Representation	Total
Partido Revolucionario Institucional (PRI)	233	27	260
Partido de Acción Nacional (PAN)	38	63	101
Cardenistas[a]	29	110	139

[a]These supporters of the presidential candidacy of Cuauhtémoc Cárdenas were from the following parties and coalitions: Frente Democrático Nacional, 22 seats; Partido Popular Socialista, 32; Partido Socialista Mexicano, 19; Partido de la Frente Cardenista de Reconstrucción Nacional, 35; Partido Auténtico de la Revolución Mexicana, 31.

Source: Press release, Embassy of Mexico, Washington, D.C., August 31, 1988.

than in truly democratizing the system. However, the first steps involved in genuine democratization and in more effective co-optation are the same, so the question of ultimate motivations need not be all that relevant during the first stages of the process.

In any event, those first steps have been taken. President Adolfo López Mateos (1958–1964) introduced a modification to the electoral system that allows for representation of opposition parties on the basis of their percentage of the total vote, whether or not they won any individual districts. On the basis of a rather generous interpretation of those provisions, the tame "satellite" parties, the PARM and the PPS, were given a few Chamber of Deputies seats as was the larger conservative opposition party, the PAN. The law was greatly amplified under José López Portillo (1976–1982) to earmark 100 seats out of 400 in the Chamber of Deputies for parties winning under 60 percent of the vote in any of the five electoral regions into which the country is divided. The first application of this new version of the law, in 1979, resulted in parliamentary representation for several parties that previously had held no seats in the Chamber of Deputies, including the Mexican Communist Party (PCM).

THE 1988 ELECTIONS

Before the 1988 elections, another 100 proportional representation seats were added, bringing total membership in the Chamber to 500, of which no single party was allowed more than 260. In fact, the PRI's vote dropped so far in 1988 that it became entitled to share in the proportional seats, and as it had won fewer than 260 districts it was awarded proportional seats up to the 260 maximum, giving it a bare working majority of the Chamber (see Table 17.2). The PRI also accepted defeat in four Senate races, as part of the policy of gradual retreat in nonessential matters that it was hoped would take the wind out of the opposition's sails.

This was the lowest point to which the PRI's electoral fortunes had ever fallen, clearly as a result of the unprecedented economic hard times the country had suffered. The PAN reached its high point of a little over 17 percent for its presidential candidate, Manuel Clouthier, a spokesman for business interests, but the normally splintered left managed to unite and cut heavily into the PRI's base of support to win an officially reported 32 percent for its candidate. This candidate was Cuauhtémoc Cárdenas, son of the great president of the 1930s, and formerly a PRI state governor. Most observers suspected that the Cárdenas total had actually been higher than that reported, but that the PRI had added to the vote of their candidate so that he could be spared the indignity of winning less than half of the vote; as it was, Salinas was credited with a bare 50.36 percent. Cárdenas was supported not only by the successor to the old Communist party, now called the Mexican Socialist Party (PSM), and a miscellany of other left opposition splinters, but even by the formerly dependable PRI satellites, the PPS and the PARM.

It seemed unlikely that a united left could pose a permanent threat to the PRI's hegemony, however. The natural splintering tendencies of the left will no doubt be helped along by renewed inducements to cooperate with the PRI; moreover, after 1988 the economic crisis eased while oil prices tended upwards; and Salinas started off his administration with popular anticorruption measures. While new presidents, even those who steal money notoriously at the end of their terms to cushion their retirements, like José López Portillo, typically begin their terms with an anticorruption campaign, the measures taken by Salinas were directed against powerful labor and business figures previously thought to be untouchable.

The Bureaucracy

Although "the political reform," as it is known, has resulted in livelier congressional debates and has raised the level of popular political discussion, most political decisions in Mexico are still made behind closed doors, without an effective process of checks and balances or ultimate popular control. Despite intermittent campaigns by well-meaning presidents, of which the current one under President Salinas seems the most determined, it is sadly true that considerations of personal gain frequently enter into such decisions. Financial disclosure, independent auditing, and conflict-of-interest statutes are nonexistent or not enforced, and high political office in Mexico is generally an avenue to great personal wealth. Many middle- and low-level officials are more concerned with arranging for kickbacks on supply contracts, the hiring of personnel, and union agreements than with doing their jobs. But even honest officials, at the higher levels of the hierarchy, enjoy substantial incomes quite legally. Salaries are high, and supplementary payments are made in various categories, such as for service on the boards of directors of public corporations.

For these and other reasons, it is possible to see emerging in Mexico a privileged clan, or caste, composed of high public officials, often themselves the children of politicians. The occupants of the policymaking higher levels of the bureaucracy are typically recruited from among the best students at the principal university, the Autonomous National University of Mexico (UNAM) in Mexico City, especially from the law school and technical schools such as economics. This tendency has been reflected in the origins of the most recent presidents. Luis Echeverría Alvarez (1970–1976), José López Portillo (1976–1982), Miguel de la Madrid Hurtado (1982–1988), and Carlos Salinas de Gortari (1988–1994) were all products of UNAM, raised in the Federal District, and career public officials who had not run for political office before being nominated for the presidency.

These high Mexican officials are often extremely competent. Not only are they recruited from among the top students in the professional schools of the national university, but their advancement is based on merit. This may seem paradoxical. Most so-called merit systems of public personnel management are ostensibly based on promotion by merit but actually work by seniority. A bureaucrat who doesn't stick his neck out and make enemies can expect to rise gradually through the system on sheer longevity. In the Mexican system, however, in which political criteria dominate the upper echelons of the public service, actual merit is quite important. Aspiring bureaucratic politicians, with their eyes set on an ultimate position in the cabinet, if not the presidency, build up networks of contacts, on the same level and on those lower and higher, that will advance their careers. You do favors for others, expecting them to reciprocate when called on. You build up a corps of able assistants so that your own performance will stand out. You try to contribute to an outstanding performance by your superior officer so that as he moves up the ladder, he will take you along and you will move up with him. Competence is thus demanded and rewarded. One's career is not advanced on the basis of having a staff of people who cannot do their jobs.

Antidemocratic Practices

In addition to the corruption endemic in the bureaucracy, and the practice of making important decisions behind closed doors, there are other characteristics of the Mexican system antithetical to democratic practice. Although "loyal opposition" within the boundaries of the system is accepted and even encouraged, antisystem opposition is, as in all countries, prohibited and persecuted. In Mexico, however, illegal methods are sometimes used by the government to deal with opposition that is revolutionary, violent, or sometimes only impatiently direct—such as peasants' occupation of land they believe to be held in violation of the agrarian reform laws. From time to time, guerrilla movements spring up in Mexico, especially in the southern state of Guerrero. They have no serious prospect of success, but they have been met with no-holds-barred treatment from the military and political police forces, and needless deaths have resulted. From time to time, opposition peasant leaders meet death in circumstances that suggest political assassination, and there are persistent reports of interrogation centers that use torture. It should be emphasized that these cases are not numerous, and it may be that such practices take place without the consent, or even against the instructions, of presidents. It may well even be true that more crimes of this nature are committed by the various federal, state, and local law enforcement agencies in the United States than in Mexico. Nevertheless, any official violation of human rights is an abhorrent and a criminal act, which casts a shadow on the respectability of any government under which it occurs.

In Mexico, a certain amount of manipulation of the freedom of the press also occurs, taking various forms. For a long time, the government newsprint monopoly allocated paper at subsidized prices, often influenced by considerations of political favoritism. Other forms of subsidy, such as advertisements paid for by government agencies, go to cooperative newspapers. Journalists may be given government sinecures or regular pay-offs if they report as they are supposed to. While Carlos Salinas made clear that he wished to end such practices as part of a general attempt to modernize and moralize Mexican government, it remained unclear whether such practices would return once his reformist energies had spent their force.

FOREIGN POLICY

Mexico's foreign policy attitudes have grown out of national experience. Colonized by Spain and invaded by troops from France and the United States, Mexico has developed a foreign policy based on principles of national autonomy, freedom from foreign intervention, the equality of states, and the peaceful resolution of disputes. Mindful of its own Revolution, Mexico has shown sympathy for the republican cause in the Spanish civil war, to the Cuban and Nicaraguan Revolutions, to the Allende government in Chile, and to the insurgents in the Salvadoran civil war. Resentful of how the country's mineral resources were exploited with little benefit to the Mexican economy during the Porfirio Díaz administration, Mexico is economically nationalist, insisting on national economic sovereignty and quick to oppose anything that can be identified as economic imperialism or exploitation.

At the same time, Mexico's proximity to the United States has meant a heavy interdependence with its northern neighbor with respect to trade, investment, and tourism. The United States has the ability, which it has used on occasion—for example, when offended by Mexican reluctance to cooperate against the drug traffic—of inflicting serious economic damage on the Mexican economy. Thus, Mexico's foreign policy has followed a middle way between pressures to conform to the wishes of the United States on the one hand and loyalty to its revolutionary and anti-imperialist heritage on the other. Toward revolutionary Cuba, for example, Mexico has been symbolically supportive while covertly supplying U.S. intelligence agencies with information on Cuban activities. President Echeverría instructed the Mexican delegates at the United Nations to vote for an antiracism resolution, which unfortunately identified Zionism as a form of racism, but was forced to backtrack when an angry reaction on the part of U.S. citizens threatened to inflict severe damage on Mexico's tourist industry.

With the new self-confidence engendered by the country's oil wealth, Mexico moved temporarily further away from U.S. foreign policy positions, especially in Central America: There, the United States has generally opposed—as tending toward communism—popular insurrections against repressive governments, and Mexico has generally taken the opposite position. Mexico also strongly supported the Panamanians' complaints about the arrangements governing the canal and the Canal Zone, which were finally settled by the Carter-Torrijos treaties. As the economy weakened, however, Mexico became less able to withstand U.S. pressure.

In general, the relationship between the United States and Mexico is a good one. Each country realizes that the other has different interests and attitudes, but they generally try to cooperate, when possible, to each other's mutual advantage and to avoid letting differences of opinion degenerate into confrontations or conflicts. Nevertheless, divisive issues are continually being generated out of the facts of contiguity and asymmetrical trade relations. The pattern has generally been for such issues to surface, produce disagreement and sometimes tension, especially when exacerbated by U.S. arrogance or Mexican resentment, and then gradually be negotiated to some kind of mutually acceptable solution. This has been the case with issues concerning border demarcation, the assignment of commercial air routes, the exchange of prisoners, and the division of Colorado River water. Disputes that are current and have not yet been resolved concern drug trafficking, fishing rights, and migratory workers, among others.

OVERVIEW

The Mexican political system is so complex and multifaceted that it can be interpreted in a variety of ways. Partly this situation exists because the system changes somewhat with each president. Although each president represents continuity with his predecessor, who is responsible for selecting him, he also wishes to distinguish himself and make his own mark on Mexican history; he also takes care not to make the same mistakes as his predecessor. Thus, despite the elements of continuity, each presidential term represents a change, and sometimes a significant change, from the politics of the previous administration.

Most of the academic commentary on the Mexican political system today identifies it as an authoritarian system in which the democratic elements are only a façade behind which, it is usually said, the system is run in the interests of the ruling group itself or perhaps of the business classes and foreign business corporations. In this view, any progressive legislation is designed only to co-opt potential opposition, to disarm radical critics, or to disguise the true nature of the regime. That interpretation is true as far as it goes, and the protestations of government leaders that Mexico is simply a democratic state whose leaders unswervingly promote the goals of the Revolution lack plausibility. Such a view does not capture all of the relevant elements, however. In Mexico, in contrast to traditional authoritarian regimes, education is extended, and popular participation is encouraged. The country's rulers do not act simply to preserve the status quo, in the manner of a Francisco Franco; government efforts are designed to achieve progressive social and economic goals, including the alleviation of the plight of the lower classes. Mexican presidents are clearly not content simply to serve as puppets for the U.S. government or powerful multinational corporations; they seek to defend Mexico's sovereignty and extend its freedom of action.

In fact, the government is still a revolutionary one, just as its leaders claim. The Revolution is not a liberal one, to free individual entrepreneurs from traditional restrictions; nor is it a socialist revolution, to replace private profit making with state enterprise as a matter of principle. The ongoing Mexican Revolution is a social democratic revolution, true to its origins at a time prior to the Bolshevik seizure of power in Russia but after the fading of the hegemony of liberal capitalist ideology. Its objectives are economic and social development, national independence, and the use of whatever means seem effective to improve the lot of the peasants and workers. The appropriate means may vary from the promotion of state enterprise to the encouragement of private initiative, to a combination of the two, to an alternative that is neither. Corruption and privilege have set in, but they are a deformation of the system, not its essence.

After unproductive deviations to one side or the other, policy has usually reached a balance between state and private initiative, established religion and anticlericalism, national autonomy and dependence, democracy and authoritarianism. In the history of that evolution lies a wealth of lessons for the developing, and some of the so-called developed, countries of today's world.

Mexico's is a postrevolutionary regime in which the interaction between revolutionary impulse and the realities of governing has led to the evolution of the ruling group from combatants and agitators to bureaucratic politicians and technocrats. The cohesiveness and ability of that ruling group have given it the strength to withstand, to some extent, pressures from the U.S. government and from multinational corporations, pressures that are great for a country bordering the United States. In Central America and the Caribbean, governments and societies are porous. The CIA, U.S. embassy military attachés, and representatives of major corporations are everywhere with carrots and sticks, usually getting their way. Of course Mexico lives in an interdependent world economy and polity, as all countries must. As much as any country can be, however, Mexico is the master of its own fate.

NOTES

1. Except for the Dominican Republic, no Latin American democracy allows a president to be reelected to a second consecutive term. In Mexico and Costa Rica, he may never be reelected; elsewhere, he may be reelected after skipping one or more terms.

SUGGESTED READINGS

Alvarado, Arturo, ed. *Electoral Patterns and Perspectives in Mexico*. San Diego: Center for U.S.-Mexican Studies, 1987. Detailed case studies, mostly of state-level politics.

Camp, Roderic. *Mexico's Leaders: Their Education and Recruitment*. Tucson: University of Arizona Press, 1980. A detailed analysis, based on extensive archival research and interviews, of the education and career patterns of hundreds of political leaders since the Revolution. It shows clearly the tendencies toward higher education, more technical training, and Federal District origins referred to in this chapter.

Cosío Villegas, Daniel. *El sistema político mexicano: las posibilidades de cambio*. Mexico City: Cuadernos de Joaquín Mortiz, 1973. A short, well-written, ironic book, one of a series of four, based on newspaper articles written by "the dean of Mexican historians."

Gentleman, Judith, ed. *Mexican Politics in Transition*. Boulder, Colo.: Westview Press, 1987. Treatments of various aspects of Mexican politics, focusing on the possibilities of reform.

Grayson, George, ed. *Prospects for Mexico*. Washington, D.C.: Department of State, 1988. A useful collection of pieces covering economics, interest groups, and relations with the United States, as well as the usual political topics.

Hansen, Roger D. *The Politics of Mexican Development*. Baltimore: Johns Hopkins University Press, 1971. Balanced and politically sophisticated, the best treatment of Mexican economic policy.

Hellman, Judith Adler. *Mexico in Crisis*. New York: Holmes and Meier, 1978. A good critique of Mexican political practice from the left.

Informe. This annual report, delivered every year by Mexico's president, is one of the most valuable sources on Mexican politics and policies. It consists of a compendium of figures, a review of the previous year's performance (hardly an impartial one, of course), and a prognosis of what is to come. The report is reproduced in the major newspapers, and it is usually made available as a separate document by the office of the president (and sometimes in translation by the U.S. Embassy).

Needler, Martin C. *Mexican Politics: The Containment of Conflict*. New York: Praeger, 1982. This general book covers the country's history, geography, economy, and social structure— as well as politics—from the same point of view as this chapter.

———. *Politics and Society in Mexico*. Albuquerque: University of New Mexico Press, 1971. Interpretive essays, generally optimistic and favorable in tone.

Paz, Octavio. *The Labyrinth of Solitude*. Translated by Lysander Kemp. New York: Grove Press, 1961. A brilliant discussion of the national character of Mexico by one of the country's leading men of letters.

El Sistema mexicano. Special issue of *Nueva política* 1:2 (April-June 1976). An interesting collection of articles, most of them written especially for this publication, by a number of distinguished Mexican and foreign observers.

Weil, Thomas, Jan K. Black, et al. *Area Handbook for Mexico*. 2d ed. Washington, D.C.: Government Printing Office, 1975. No prizes for style, but a useful storehouse of information.

PART EIGHT
CENTRAL AMERICA AND PANAMA

18

CENTRAL AMERICA: BACKGROUND TO THE CRISIS

RICHARD MILLETT

After decades of relative obscurity, Central America emerged in the 1980s as a major focus of world attention. Long seen as the backyard of the United States, a region where North American companies raised bananas and U.S. Marines deposed and installed governments, Central America now experiences the benefits and the pains of involvement by a multitude of governments and political organizations. Even Israel and the Palestine Liberation Organization (PLO) have found in Central America a new arena for their ongoing rivalry. Reluctantly, and at an appalling cost, this traditional backwater area has been dragged into the world of late-twentieth-century power politics. Old social and political structures are collapsing, but what will succeed them is still unclear.

For most North Americans, the result of this forcible intrusion of Central America upon their public consciousness has been a series of confused impressions. Violent clashes and presidential visits, coups and elections, murdered nuns and Cuban-trained guerrillas combine to form a chaotic montage of a region apparently gone mad. Explanations of this situation frequently center on simplistic responses of "Communist subversion" or "U.S.-supported repression." An adequate analysis, however, requires an understanding of Central America's tortured past and a critical examination of its violent present.

The first step in this task is to define the area under consideration. Historians have generally defined Central America as the five nations that were originally part of the Spanish colonial Captaincy General of Guatemala: Guatemala, El Salvador, Honduras, Nicaragua, and Costa Rica. Since these same nations make up the Central American Common Market, economists also generally accept this definition. Geographers, however, usually include

Panama and the newly independent nation of Belize, formerly British Honduras. In recent years, this latter approach has gained growing support from some political scientists as the interactions between Panama and Belize and the five traditional republics have steadily increased. The focus of this chapter will be something of a middle course: Emphasis will be placed on the traditional republics, but some attention will be paid to Panama and Belize, especially in regard to their involvement in regional politics.

Compared to the United States or such Latin American nations as Brazil and Mexico, the five Central American republics are small. But on a world scale they look somewhat different. Three of them (Guatemala, Honduras, and Nicaragua) are larger than East Germany, and the combined area of the five republics exceeds that of both Germanies and Austria combined. Their combined population is also small, but it has grown rapidly in recent years. In 1916, the combined population was under 5 million; by 1960, it had passed 10 million; and by 1982, it was approximately 22 million.

The cultural and ethnic patterns of Central America are varied and quite distinct from those of Mexico. Half of Guatemala's population is Indian. Descendants of the ancient Maya, they speak a wide variety of indigenous languages, still wear traditional dress, and, where the violence of the last few years has not yet reached them, live much as they did centuries ago. The predominant ethnic element in El Salvador, Honduras, and Nicaragua is mestizo, but even among these nations there is little uniformity. Diet, work habits, even some aspects of physical appearance differ from nation to nation. In addition, the Caribbean coastal areas contain a heavy concentration of black and black-Indian peoples, especially in Nicaragua, Costa Rica, and Belize. They frequently speak English as their primary language. They enjoy strong Caribbean cultural influences, and have traditionally played a limited role in national politics. Except for this coastal area, Costa Rica's ethnic composition is largely European, especially in the central plateau area. If Belize and Panama are included in this panorama, the variety becomes even greater. Belize is English speaking, the dominant culture is that of the Commonwealth Caribbean, and its politics is based on the Westminster model. Panama (see Chapter 19) has the most complex cultural pattern of any nation in the region.

This ethnic and cultural variety has played a major role in the differing national histories of the region, and it helps explain the wide variations in literacy rates, political systems, and racial attitudes. In Guatemala and El Salvador, less than half of the adult population is literate whereas in Costa Rica, the literacy rate is nearly 90 percent. In Guatemala, the Indian majority has been victimized by the prejudice of the ruling elites for centuries. One result has been the failure to integrate the Indian into Guatemalan society; a more recent product of this situation has been the growing influence of radical-left guerrilla movements among the Indian population. In Costa Rica, the predominant European population has long felt superior to the mestizos of neighboring nations and to their own country's Caribbean black minority. Until World War II, blacks from the coast were even prohibited from settling in the central part of the country. By contrast, neighboring Nicaragua, even during the decades of the Somoza family dictatorship, has been almost a model of racial toleration and integration.

For most of its history, Central America has been a rural, overwhelmingly peasant society, dependent on one or two basic crops for foreign exchange. This pattern, though, has changed greatly in recent years. Today, over half the populations of Nicaragua and Panama live in urban areas, and Costa Rica is rapidly approaching 50 percent urbanization. Export diversification and industrial development have proceeded rapidly in the region during the last quarter of a century. In 1981, manufacturing contributed more than agriculture to the GNP of Costa Rica, and the amounts were roughly equal in Nicaragua and Panama. In these areas, as in virtually every other, Central America is a region of increasing diversity and change, an area experiencing all the trauma of attempting to leap from the mid-nineteenth to the late twentieth century in a few decades.

SPANISH CONQUEST AND COLONIZATION

The history of Central America is a depressing mixture of violence, exploitation, and neglect. That pattern extends back to pre-Columbian times. Conflict more than cooperation characterized relations among the varied indigenous groups. Most developed were the Maya of Guatemala, Honduras, and northern El Salvador. They reached a relatively high level of civilization from the fourth through the ninth centuries, but a combination of civil conflicts, natural disasters, and agricultural failures led to their decline and fragmentation. In the last centuries before the Spanish conquest, Aztec influence from Mexico became an important factor, but Central America remained divided into a host of disparate tribal groups with distinct languages and cultural patterns.

The arrival of the Spaniards had a generally disastrous effect on the peoples of Central America. Slave raiding along the Honduran coast and a smallpox epidemic spreading down from Mexico preceded the actual arrival of the conquistadores. The divided nature of the indigenous populations, the difficult terrain, and divisions among the Spaniards all combined to make the conquest period a prolonged and destructive one. Actual occupation began in 1524, but parts of highland Costa Rica and Honduras were not effectively controlled by Spain until the latter half of the century. The last Mayan city held out until 1697, and some of the Caribbean lowlands were never effectively controlled by Spain.

Long before they had completely subdued the indigenous populations, the new conquerors began fighting among themselves. Meanwhile, enslavement and diseases brought by the Spaniards decimated the indigenous population. Over 200,000 Indians were shipped from Nicaragua to Panama and Peru, and tens of thousands of others were sent from Honduras and Guatemala to the Caribbean. In the 1520s, the Spanish estimated the Indian population of Nicaragua as in excess of half a million; in 1548, a census could locate only 11,137 Indians.

Both the political situation and the population began to stabilize in the second half of the sixteenth century. At the same time, other trends emerged that were to become long-term features of Central American life. One was the development of monocultural export agriculture, beginning with the cacao industry. The collapse of this export industry after a few decades also established a boom-and-bust cycle for the region's economy, a pattern reinforced a few decades later when a similar fate overtook indigo exports and Honduran silver mining.

The seventeenth century witnessed the beginnings of international rivalry and conflict in Central America, a development that would plague the region from then until the present. English and Dutch adventurers began to attack along the Caribbean coast, and in some areas, English log cutters began to establish settlements. This disrupted commerce, contributed to the general seventeenth-century economic depression in the region, and laid the basis for British control over Belize and claims to influence over the Miskito coast of Nicaragua and Honduras. During the eighteenth century, Spain's alliance with France led to increased conflicts with the English, who began to use the coastal Miskito Indians as allies for forays into the settled highlands.

By the start of the nineteenth century, the outline of present-day Central America had begun to take shape. Although overall administration was handled from Guatemala City, provincial divisions, generally corresponding to present national boundaries, were firmly established. The British were developing their own government for Belize, Panama was administratively and economically separate from the rest of the region, and the Caribbean coast, though claimed by Spain, was developing a cultural identity tied to the British Caribbean. Guatemala's population was largely Indian while 84 percent of the people living in Nicaragua were classified as ladinos, the Central American equivalent of mestizos. In the region as a whole, 65 percent of the population was Indian, 31 percent was ladino, and 4 percent was of European descent. Blacks were still rare in Spanish Central America.

INDEPENDENCE AND THE
CENTRAL AMERICAN REPUBLIC

Independence came to Central America with a minimum of actual conflict. In 1821, following news of Mexico's independence, Guatemala declared its independence from Spain. Early the following year, all of Central America was joined with the new Mexican Empire of Agustín de Iturbide. When Iturbide fell in 1823, Central Americans moved rapidly to sever their links with Mexico. After some confusion all but the province of Chiapas, which remained under Mexican control, joined the United Provinces of Central America, a federated republic with a three-member executive. This union lasted only until 1838, but it left a lasting mark upon the Central American political consciousness. Union as a political ideal has been a continuing force in the region.

Unfortunately, the union period also left two other, equally enduring, heritages. One was a pattern of conflict and jealousy among the Central

American states; the other, a deep division between Liberal and Conservative political factions within each state and across state lines. The net result is that Central Americans have found it almost impossible to live with or without each other. Efforts at union have been constantly disrupted by war. Since 1837, the Central American nations have fought more than twice as many wars among themselves than have all other nations of Latin America combined. Except in Costa Rica, the ongoing conflicts led to a tradition of strong-man leadership and the involvement of the military as the ultimate arbiter of the political process.

COFFEE CULTURE AND FOREIGN INTRIGUE

The mid-nineteenth century witnessed two developments that would be basic to Central America's future. The first was the rise of coffee as a primary export crop. It created a new class of landowning elites, export oriented, interested in scientific agriculture, and increasingly conscious of common interests. Conversely, it meant the displacement of peasants from communal or subsistence plots (though not to the extent that occurred with the spread of cotton plantations in the mid-twentieth century). The primacy of coffee also led to foreign immigration and investment, with Germans and Britons being the most prominent. Finally, as commerce expanded, so also did government revenues.

The other major development of this period was the rise in foreign, especially U.S., interest in the region. In 1849, a group of U.S. investors, headed by Cornelius Vanderbilt, began operating a transportation system across Nicaragua. This produced a potential conflict with British interests, so in 1850 the United States and Great Britain concluded the Clayton-Bulwer Treaty, which provided that neither nation would seek to control the transit routes through Central America or "exercise any dominion" over any part of the Central American republics. In the years following the signing of the treaty, British influence in the region declined while that of the United States expanded. British presence on the Miskito coast, however, continued until the end of the century.

The increased North American presence was all too frequently violent. In 1854, U.S. Marines burned San Juan del Norte in retaliation for an alleged insult to the U.S. minister to Nicaragua. In 1856, marines landed for the first time in Panama, a process they repeated in 1860. But the most notable intervention was unofficial. Beginning in 1855, a Tennessee adventurer, William Walker, began a series of filibustering expeditions designed to establish his personal control over Nicaragua and, perhaps ultimately, much of the rest of Central America. He succeeded in making himself Nicaragua's president for a brief time, but the efforts of a combined Central American army, financed in part by Cornelius Vanderbilt, finally defeated him. A later effort in Honduras also failed. Walker surrendered to a British naval commander, who promptly turned him over to a Honduran firing squad. Walker's death ended serious filibustering efforts in Central America but left behind a heritage of suspicion of U.S. motives in the area.

In the 1860s, the Civil War diverted U.S. interest away from Central America, which entered upon a relatively stable and prosperous period. In the 1880s, Costa Rica began its tradition of one-term, elected presidents, a tradition that, despite brief interruptions in 1917 and 1948, has endured ever since. Strong, Liberal Party dictators emerged in the region, with Presidents Justo Ruffino Barrios in Guatemala (1873–1885) and José Santos Zelaya in Nicaragua (1893–1909) being the most influential.

In the late nineteenth century, bananas also became a major Central American export. Unlike coffee, this new trade was overwhelmingly concentrated in foreign hands. The United Fruit Company and, to a lesser extent, the Standard Fruit Company represented major U.S. business involvement in the area.

THE ERA OF DIRECT INTERVENTION

The Spanish American War signaled a greatly increased U.S. interest in the Caribbean and Central America. A new treaty with Great Britain (Hay-Pauncefote) abrogated the Clayton-Bulwer Treaty and cleared the way for the United States to build a transoceanic canal. After considerable debate, the Nicaraguan route was rejected and a site through Panama was selected. Panama was then part of Colombia, but it was liberated in 1903 with considerable help from the U.S. Navy.

Marines landed in Panama, Honduras, and Nicaragua several times during the early twentieth century, culminating in a major intervention in Nicaragua in 1912. A force of marines remained in Nicaragua until 1925, ensuring that no government at all unsympathetic to U.S. interests took power in that nation. During this period, Nicaragua agreed to the Bryan-Chamorro Treaty, which gave the United States exclusive rights over canal construction through the nation. In reality, the effect of this treaty was to ensure that no canal would be built through Nicaragua, thus protecting Washington's strategic and economic interests in Panama.

During the first three decades of the twentieth century, the U.S. government and North American banana companies exercised dominant influence over most of Central America. U.S. pressures played a major role in governmental changes in every nation but El Salvador. The overall thrust of U.S. policy during this period was summed up in 1927 by Under-Secretary of State Robert Olds, who wrote:

> The Central American area down to and including the Isthmus of Panama constitutes a legitimate sphere of influence for the United States if we are to have due regard for our own safety and protection. . . . Our ministers accredited to the five little republics stretching from the Mexican border to Panama . . . have been advisors whose advice has been accepted virtually as law . . . we do control the destinies of Central America. . . . There is no room for any outside influence other than ours in this region. . . .
>
> Until now Central America has always understood that those governments which we recognize and support stay in power, while those which we do not recognize and support fall.

These attitudes and actions produced a nationalistic backlash in much of Latin America. Opinion in El Salvador and Costa Rica was especially critical of U.S. policy, but the most effective protest came in Nicaragua. The marines had left that nation in 1925, but returned the following year when renewed civil conflict seemed to threaten U.S. dominance. A peace treaty—providing for general disarmament, supervised elections, and a prolonged marine occupation during which a new, supposedly nonpartisan National Guard would be created by marine officers—was imposed on the warring Liberal and Conservative factions. One Liberal general, however, refused to accept the terms and began a guerrilla war against the marines and the National Guard that would last until 1933. His name was Augusto César Sandino, and he became a heroic symbol to thousands of Latin Americans because of his resistance to North American intervention.

DEPRESSION AND DICTATORSHIP

The era of overt U.S. interventions came to an end in the 1930s, and a quartet of strong military dictators enforced stability in every Central American nation except Costa Rica. Maximiliano Hernández Martínez in El Salvador, Jorge Ubico in Guatemala, Anastasio Somoza García in Nicaragua, and Tiburcio Carías Andino in Honduras all began long terms in power in the 1930s. All but Somoza lost this power in the 1940s—the Somoza family was destined to retain its control of Nicaragua until 1979—but each left a deep imprint upon his nation.

The first to gain power was Martínez in El Salvador. After helping to unseat an elected civilian president, he moved rapidly to consolidate his control over the military and the rest of society. The economic rigors of the depression had combined with rising population pressures and the activities of Central America's strongest Communist Party to generate a major uprising by rural, largely Indian, peasants. Badly planned and executed, the uprising was quickly put down with only a few casualties. Afterward, however, the military, urged on by a frightened rural oligarchy, massacred between 10,000 and 30,000 peasants, decimating what remained of the nation's indigenous population. This slaughter, known as the *matanza,* left a heritage of class fear and hatred that has persisted up to the present. But it also solidified General Martínez in power. Despite such personal eccentricities as hanging colored lights across streets in the capital to avert a smallpox epidemic, he managed to prolong his rule until 1944.

General Jorge Ubico ruled Guatemala from 1931 until 1944. He was a strong supporter of the United States and especially of the United Fruit Company, which reached its peak of influence during this period. Indian labor was ensured by a law that made unemployment a crime. This was accompanied by another Ubico innovation, a maximum wage law for rural Indians. Other Ubico "reforms" included the abolition of independent local government, the expansion and strengthening of the armed forces, and during World War II, the confiscation of all German landholdings. The United States provided rather bizarre assistance in this last case, interning Germans from Guatemala, El Salvador, and other parts of Central America in Texas and then shipping them back to Germany, where many of them had never lived, late in the war.

In Honduras, the rule of General Tiburcio Carías Andino was less colorful than that of his Salvadoran or Guatemalan contemporaries, but it endured even longer. He took power in a relatively honest election in 1932, then through a variety of maneuvers, maintained himself in office until the end of 1948.

Nicaragua's Somoza Dynasty

By far the most enduring of these dictatorships was that established by General Anastasio Somoza García in Nicaragua. Unlike the other dictators, Somoza had begun his career as a politician, not as a military officer. He had studied in the United States and then married into a prominent political family. General Somoza learned early in life that the path to power in Nicaragua ran through Washington, and he made a career out of cultivating ties and influence with North Americans. He served as an intermediary between Nicaraguan President José María Moncada and the U.S. Marines and State Department during the 1926–1933 intervention, somehow persuading each side that his real loyalties lay with it. This role made him an acceptable candidate to most factions for the post of commander of the new National Guard when the marines left Nicaragua in 1933.

The guerrilla leader Sandino had fought against the intervention until it ended, but once the marines left Nicaragua, he rapidly agreed to a truce with the government. The following year the National Guard, with Somoza's support, murdered Sandino and scattered his remaining followers. After two more years of maneuvering, Somoza overthrew his wife's uncle and, supported by the guard, installed himself as Nicaragua's president. With one brief interruption, he retained control over the country until he was assassinated in 1956. By then, the system he had established proved so strong that his two sons, Luis and Anastasio Somoza Debayle, were able to keep the family in power until 1979.

The keys to the Somoza dynasty's success were numerous. Most basic was absolute control over the U.S.-created National Guard, a mixed military-police force that monopolized armed power within Nicaragua. This control was achieved through massive corruption, personal favoritism, ruthless purging of any officer who showed signs of personal ambition or loyalty to anything but the Somoza family, and a long tradition of always having a family member in command.

Other factors that made the family's long rule possible were a constant cultivation of U.S. support, creating the image in Nicaragua that Somoza was Washington's choice for president and that no effort to overthrow him would be tolerated, and the conversion of the traditional Liberal Party to a compliant instrument of Somoza ambitions. The Somozas were also able to co-opt much of the traditional opposition in the middle and upper classes by offering them some share in the spoils of power, usually guaranteeing their lives and property even when they tried to overthrow the family, and constantly presenting themselves as the only sure bulwark against the left. In all of this, General Somoza García combined an uncanny political skill with a blatant disregard for the real interests of the nation. The Somozas became the richest as well as the most enduring family in Central America's political history, corruption became the dominant national institution, and the military became a private guard.

The Tumultuous Aftermath of World War II

World War II accelerated the modernization process in Central America. U.S. training and equipment helped modernize the armed forces, and a massive propaganda campaign, which portrayed the war as a fight of democracies against dictators, caused some officers to begin to question their own national political systems. In 1944, massive popular uprisings, with some military support, toppled Generals Ubico in Guatemala and Martínez in El Salvador. In the latter case, reform efforts proved short-lived, and a form of institutional military rule was established. In Guatemala, however, more fundamental changes were begun.

Guatemala: Abortive Revolution and Counterrevolution

After some infighting, a group of young, reform-minded officers gained control of the revolution in Guatemala. They promptly set about writing a new, liberal constitution and holding elections for president and Congress. The presidential elections were won by Dr. Juan José Arévalo, a scholar who had been exiled for years. Under President Arévalo, numerous major reforms were initiated. Compulsory labor for the Indians was abolished, illiterates (the vast majority of the population) gained the right to vote, and education, especially in rural areas, was expanded. Even more notable was the government's encouragement of labor unions and the passage of a liberal labor code. This, combined with the establishment of a rudimentary social security system, gained considerable support for the government but, at the same time, produced growing alarm among traditional elites.

Controversy within the military over the pace of reforms and over the presidential succession led to bitter conflict, which culminated in 1949 when the leader of the more conservative faction, Colonel Francisco Arana, was assassinated. His chief rival, Colonel Jacobo Arbenz Guzmán, was then able to consolidate his own power and assure his election as Arévalo's successor.

Urged on by his wife, Arbenz was determined to accelerate the pace of change in Guatemala. In this process, he found Guatemala's Communists to be eager allies. Although relatively small, Guatemala's Communist Party had the advantages of organization, discipline, and external support, elements that the democratic left usually lacked. Party members were also hardworking, relatively honest, and anxious to take on the entrenched Guatemalan power structure. The result was a rapid polarization process. The upper classes and the Roman Catholic Church were quick to denounce reforms, such as the forced reduction of rates by the private electric company, as "Communist inspired." For their part, the Communists, aided by their increasing role in the media, were quite content to take credit for reforms in which they had actually played a limited role.

It soon became clear that the chief issue was the Agrarian Reform Law, Decree 900, of 1952. This provided for the expropriation of uncultivated landholdings in excess of 665 acres (269 hectares). Members of the rural oligarchy were furious because this law threatened their economic and political power and because compensation was to be paid on the basis of tax-assessed value, something they had long notoriously underdeclared. The giant United Fruit Company (UFCO) felt at least equally threatened. Already engaged in a bitter dispute with the government over taxes on the national railroad system, which UFCO controlled, the company now saw the Agrarian Reform Law as threatening its survival in Guatemala. Labor disputes and popular resentment over UFCO's power and arrogance all contributed to growing tension and hostility.

Unfortunately for Arbenz, the Dulles family was closely connected with UFCO, and in 1953, John Foster Dulles was the U.S. secretary of state and his brother, Alan, was head of the CIA. They were easily convinced that Guatemala was on the verge of a Communist takeover. At the Tenth Inter-American Conference of Foreign Ministers, held in Caracas in March 1954, the United States, over bitter Guatemalan opposition, pushed through a resolution declaring that communism was a threat to inter-American security.

While the diplomats were arguing in Caracas, the CIA was organizing and training Guatemalan right-wing exiles in Honduras and Nicaragua. U.S. arms shipments to both of these nations were sharply increased, and many of the arms were passed directly to the exiles. Plans for an invasion of Guatemala were accelerated in the spring of 1954 as strikes began to hit the U.S. banana plantations in Honduras and as Arbenz began seeking arms from the Soviet bloc. With CIA support, especially air support, the exiles, led by Colonel Carlos Castillo Armas, crossed the border. Actual fighting was limited, as the Guatemalan army showed little desire to defend the Arbenz government. Under strong U.S. pressure, the army ultimately forced President Arbenz to resign and go into exile; then, after some additional maneuvering, it yielded to the U.S. ambassador's demands and allowed the installation of Castillo Armas as president.

The new Guatemalan government promptly set about reversing many of the reforms of the previous decade. United Fruit and other large landowners got much of their land back, labor unions were purged of Communists and other leftist leaders and their influence was greatly reduced, and political parties on the left were brutally suppressed. For a brief period, the Eisenhower administration pumped aid into Guatemala in a demonstration of support for the new government, but as time passed and the "Communist menace" faded, this assistance was gradually reduced. Castillo Armas was assassinated by one of his own bodyguards in 1957, but after some confusion, another right-wing officer, General Miguel Ydígoras Fuentes, was installed as president, and the policy of maintaining the status quo continued.

The U.S.-sponsored overthrow of the Arbenz government represents a watershed in Central American history. The exact degree of Communist influence in that regime remains a matter of some dispute, but it now seems clear that the Communists were never in control and that the Eisenhower administration reacted in a heavy-handed, arrogant manner to an essentially nationalistic reform movement.

Costa Rica: The Rise of the National Liberation Party

Costa Rica's electoral campaign of 1948 was marred by violence, and the returns, which seemed to give victory to the opposition candidate, Otilio Ulate, were disputed. The moderately reformist administration of Teodoro Picado Michalski used its control over the Congress to annul the elections and, shortly thereafter, arrested Ulate and several of his supporters. These actions gave José ("Pepe") Figueres, leader of a new social democratic party, an opportunity to rebel against the government. Actual fighting was limited, but by Costa Rican standards, surprisingly bloody. Ultimately, former President Rafael Calderón Guardia, the government's candidate, and Picado fled to Nicaragua and a junta, headed by Pepe Figueres, was installed. In a few months, the junta held elections, won by Ulate; nationalized Costa Rica's banks; outlawed the Communist (Vanguardia Popular) Party; and dissolved the Costa Rican army. The army was replaced by a constabulary force known as the Civil Guard. What distinguished this force from constabularies in Panama and Nicaragua was the nonprofessional nature of the higher officers who were appointed by each new administration.

Figueres, who for a time had concentrated his energies on trying to bring down dictators in the Caribbean area, won the Costa Rican presidential election in 1953, representing his National Liberation Party. In 1955, Figueres's archrival, Somoza, sought to topple the Costa Rican government. Costa Rican resistance, strengthened by U.S. and OAS support, defeated this movement. Somoza was assassinated the following year, but the dictator's sons, Luis and Anastasio Somoza Debayle, succeeded their father in power and maintained the feud with Figueres.

ECONOMIC GROWTH AND POLITICAL FERMENT

The late 1950s and early 1960s saw relative calm and progress in Central America. In Costa Rica, the National Liberation Party and its more conservative opponents regularly succeeded each other in power, beginning a pattern in which the party in power has lost every subsequent presidential election but one from 1948 through 1982. In Nicaragua, after a brief wave of repression following General Somoza García's assassination, Luis Somoza, who succeeded his father as president, began a slight liberalization: He even allowed a non-Somoza to serve as president for the 1963–1967 term. Real power, however, including command of the military, remained firmly in Somoza family hands.

In El Salvador, a period of extreme corruption was ended in 1960 by a junior officers' coup, but their moderately leftist government lasted for only a few weeks before other officers, responding to pressures from the oligarchy and the United States, staged a countercoup and installed Colonel Julio Adalberto Rivera as president. Rivera initiated a series of limited reforms, mostly in urban areas, and began to allow opposition parties to function openly.

Even Honduras enjoyed a brief period of reformist, democratic government under Liberal Party President Ramón Villeda Morales (1957–1963), but this was brought to an end by yet another military coup, led by Colonel Osvaldo López Arellano. Guatemala remained the most depressing nation, at least from a political standpoint, with fraudulent elections, military coups, and an increasingly bitter conflict with left-wing guerrillas in the 1960s. One reasonably honest election was held in 1966, and the victorious civilian candidate actually managed to complete his term. But real power remained with the military, which launched a particularly brutal campaign in 1966, decimating the several hundred rural guerrillas along with several thousand uninvolved Indian peasants.

Two broader trends overshadowed domestic political developments during the 1959–1968 period. The first was the growing preoccupation of regional elites and the United States with the Communist regime in Cuba. The Cuban exiles who attacked Fidel Castro in the 1961 Bay of Pigs invasion had been trained in Guatemala and launched their invasion from Nicaragua. In 1965, Honduras, Nicaragua, and even Costa Rica contributed units to the U.S.-sponsored Inter-American Peace Force sent to the Dominican Republic. Castro, for his part, began to offer some assistance and training to left-wing guerrilla groups in Central America, most notably to the newly organized Sandinista National Liberation Front (FSLN) in Nicaragua. All these events contributed to a growing climate of repression in much of the region and to increased U.S. concern with military assistance and training. During the Kennedy administration, there was also considerable emphasis on economic and political reforms to undercut the appeal of the Cuban model, but as the Johnson administration got bogged down in Vietnam, this emphasis was replaced with an overriding concern for stability and order.

The other, more positive development was the rapid economic growth of the region, a trend spurred on by the establishment of the Central American Common Market, formalized by treaty in 1961 (Costa Rica did not join until 1963). During this same period, a Central American Development Bank was established, and several other regional organizations, including a U.S.-sponsored defense pact (Central American Defense Council, CONDECA), were created.

As the Common Market developed and prices for basic exports such as coffee and cotton rose, the economies boomed. This economic growth was partly offset by rapid population growth, which at times, especially in Costa Rica and El Salvador, was as great as anywhere in the world, but when this was taken into account and allowance also made for inflation, actual per capita income still increased by well over 40 percent during the period.

This growth produced important alterations in the region's social and economic patterns. One obvious effect was a rapid increase in urbanization, accelerating the growth of the middle class. Previously a small and weak buffer between the landed elite and the poor rural mass, the middle class by the early 1970s had become a significant force in the region, especially in Costa Rica and El Salvador. Members of this class wanted to curb the power of the military and the traditional elites, and they often sought to forge alliances with the more upwardly mobile sectors of the working poor.

Perhaps the most significant change in Central America during the 1950s and 1960s, however, was the revolution in communications. At the end of World War II, the average Central American was a peasant who could expect to spend his entire life as an isolated illiterate, never venturing more than 20 mi (30 km) from the place of his birth. By the early 1970s, the growth of the economy had produced a boom in road building, followed by the creation of a network of rural bus services. The great majority of Central Americans could now get up in the morning and be in a major city before dark.

Increased education and mobility and such technological innovations as the transistor radio led to greatly expanded access to information about the outside world. The net effect of all these factors was to greatly increase the number of individuals involved in national politics, or at least beginning to question the inevitability and justice of existing structures and to be aware of competing political and economic philosophies and the possibility of change.

There were other, less desirable results of Central America's economic development. In many rural areas, land concentration increased as large landowners began to convert plots formerly used by the poor for food production into plantations for commercial, export-oriented agriculture. Cotton, sugar (after the elimination of Cuba's quota in the U.S. market), and cattle began to rival the traditional dependence on coffee and bananas. While the GNP increased, the nutritional level of many Central Americans actually declined as food production failed to keep pace with population growth.

Two natural results of the situation in the countryside were accelerated migration to urban centers and the growth of belts of poverty within and surrounding the principal cities. This contributed to rising crime rates and greatly increased the level of class tension. As long as the economy continued to grow at a steady, relatively rapid rate, these pressures could be controlled, but beginning in 1969, the Central American economic miracle began to falter.

ECONOMIC CRISIS AND POLITICAL REPRESSION

A slowdown in the world economy contributed to the crisis of 1969, but the major issue was the brief war that summer between El Salvador and Honduras. In an effort to shore up his sagging popularity and deal with the weakened economy, Honduran dictator Osvaldo López Arellano began expelling tens of thousands of illegal Salvadoran immigrants. This led to a rapid escalation of tensions between the two nations, and in July, following a bloody clash at a soccer match, El Salvador invaded Honduras. In less than a week of fighting, El Salvador managed to seize large chunks of Honduran territory, but its air force was decimated, and a combination of U.S. and OAS pressures soon forced El Salvador to withdraw from most of the captured territory. An OAS mission was set up to control the remaining pockets of disputed territory, known as *bolsones,* and to prevent further outbreaks of fighting. Until 1981, formal diplomatic relations remained suspended, and trade was virtually shut off between Honduras and El Salvador, with disastrous consequences for both nations.

An even greater blow to the region's economy was the rapid rise in petroleum prices beginning in 1973. Guatemala would begin limited petroleum production in the late 1970s, but in 1973 all of the Central American nations were totally dependent on imported oil. This dependence had been increased by the economic growth of the preceding years, not only because of the considerable increase in automobile and truck traffic, but because of the heavy use of petroleum-based fertilizers and pesticides in the production of new export crops such as cotton. The increased energy costs not only slowed economic growth, they also led to increased government borrowing to cover current accounts deficits. By the late 1970s, service on debts and payments for imported petroleum products were consuming the bulk of Central America's export earnings.

Polarization in El Salvador

While the economy was slowing down, the apparent progress toward more-democratic structures in the region was being reversed. By the late 1970s, only Costa Rica and the British self-governing colony of Belize (formerly British Honduras) had functioning democratic governments. The worst changes had taken place in El Salvador. There, during the 1960s, the military, ruling through the National Conciliation Party (PCN) had allowed opposition parties to function and even gain a large number of congressional seats and local offices. The Christian Democratic Party (PCD) profited most from this apparent liberalization. Its leader, José Napoleon Duarte, had been elected mayor of the capital city, San Salvador; with Social Democrat Guillermo Manuel Ungo as his running mate, Duarte appeared to have a good chance of winning the 1972 presidential election. Blatant fraud, however, was used to give the victory to the army's candidate, Colonel Arturo Molina. A subsequent revolt by part of the army was crushed, Duarte was arrested and exiled, and right-wing paramilitary groups began to attack Christian Democratic and other opposition leaders throughout the country.

The fraud of 1972 damaged both the Christian Democrats and the legitimacy of the entire electoral process. Two results were the growth of mass organizations further to the left and the slow resurgence of both urban and rural guerrilla conflicts. In 1975, several labor and peasant organizations joined with the national teachers association (ANDES) to form the Popular Revolutionary Block (BPR). Other coalitions, even further to the left, also came into existence, providing a powerful set of opponents to the continued rule of the military-oligarchy alliance. By the time of the 1977 elections, violence was growing, and the government had little legitimacy left. Its international image was further eroded when the army's chief of staff was arrested and convicted in the United States for attempting to sell weapons to organized crime syndicates. The battered democratic opposition parties united again for the 1977 elections. Realizing that the military would not permit a civilian to win the presidency, this coalition nominated a retired military officer, Colonel Ernesto Claramount. But the military resorted to even more blatant fraud to secure the victory of the official candidate, Colonel Carlos Humberto Romero, then brutally crushed popular demonstrations of protest.

Guatemala's Official Terrorism

In Guatemala, too, the military strengthened its stranglehold over politics in the early and mid-1970s. Colonel Carlos Arana, chief architect of the bloody counterinsurgency campaign of the mid-1960s, was elected president in 1970 and continued his efforts to crush all opposition from the left. The guerrillas responded by turning to urban terrorism, murdering the U.S. ambassador in 1968 and the German ambassador in 1970. But guerrilla ranks were steadily decimated, and by 1973 they no longer appeared capable of offering a serious challenge to the government.

The real challenge to oligarchic rule now came from moderate reformist parties such as the Christian Democrats, the Social Democrats (led by former Foreign Minister Alberto Fuentes Mohr), and after 1974, the United Revolutionary Front (FUR) led by Guatemala City's mayor, Manuel Colom Argueta. In 1974, these parties backed the presidential candidacy of General Efrain Rios Montt. In classical Central American fashion, Rios Montt apparently won the election but lost the official count to the government's candidate, General Kjell Laugerud García.

Costa Rica: The Price of Prosperity

While elections in El Salvador and Guatemala were dominated by fraud and violence, Costa Rica managed to continue its tradition of open democracy. "Pepe" Figueres was elected to a second presidential term in 1970. Growing tourism, high coffee prices, and foreign investment fueled a steady economic growth, which gave Costa Rica a gross domestic product per capita of $1,311 in 1979, fifth highest in Latin America. Economic progress was translated into such social benefits as Latin America's fourth highest literacy rate, second longest life expectancy, and, along with Cuba, lowest infant mortality rate.

These favorable statistics, however, masked growing problems. The administration of President Daniel Oduber Quirós, who succeeded Figueres in 1974, responded to economic pressures by promoting tourism, the settlement of retired North Americans in Costa Rica, real estate sales to foreigners, and, increasingly, borrowing abroad to cover deficits in current accounts. As a result, the nation's external debt, which was only $277 million in 1970, had reached $1,869,000,000 in 1979. Debt service that year cost Costa Rica $255 million, more than the entire national debt nine years earlier.

Honduras: Corruption and Military Musical Chairs

While Costa Rica continued to develop in the 1970s, Honduras continued to stagnate. Severe hurricanes, economic mismanagement, and internal political conflict added to the devastation of the 1969 war with El Salvador. In a rigged election, marked by massive national indifference, the military had allowed the civilian leadership of the conservative National Party to return to the Presidential Palace in 1971, but the new president, Ramón Ernesto Cruz, proved inept and, after a year and a half in office, was unceremoniously removed by the armed forces and replaced by General López Arellano.

To the surprise of most outside observers, the new military government actually promoted some modest reforms, including a limited agrarian reform program. Peasant and labor unions also grew in the mid-1970s, and clashes with the entrenched landed oligarchy increased. These clashes were particularly acute on the north coast, where the military and local landowners murdered numerous peasant leaders and even killed two missionary priests. In this latter case, again in contrast to Honduran tradition, the military officer responsible for the killings was actually tried, convicted, and imprisoned.

Corruption, however, remained rampant; even President López Arellano was eventually detected taking large bribes from the United Fruit Company in order to keep Honduras from joining other banana-exporting nations in levying an export tax on bananas. This was too much even for the Honduran military, which dumped its erstwhile president and replaced him with another officer, Colonel Juan Alberto Melgar Castro. As compensation, López Arellano assumed control of both Honduran national airlines.

The new president found himself sharing power with a Superior Council of the Armed Forces, a group of twenty-five or more officers who assumed control over internal army functions and could exercise a de facto veto over most major areas of national policy. This situation inevitably led to conflicts, and in 1978 the Superior Council removed Melgar Castro from office, installing Army Commander-in-Chief General Policarpo Paz García in his place. Known neither for his personal ambition nor for his sobriety, General Paz was to prove a more compliant instrument of the wishes of the officer corps.

Nicaragua: Prelude to Revolution

On the surface, Nicaragua seemed to be experiencing little change during the first two-thirds of the 1970s. Presidents came and went in the other republics, but the Somozas remained Nicaragua's overwhelmingly dominant political force. Anastasio Somoza Debayle, the younger and less able of the two legitimate sons of the dynasty's founder, took his turn as president in 1967. He set about using the office of president to further increase his already enormous fortune and to reward his relatives and the National Guard. As long as the economy continued to grow and the traditional elite and the opposition parties were allowed to share in the profits, though not in the power, they largely accepted this situation.

This intra-elite accord, along with most of Nicaragua's capital city of Managua, collapsed in the devastating earthquake of December 1972. For a brief period, the destruction of the quake and the near-total disintegration of the National Guard in the subsequent confusion, appeared to threaten Somoza dominance, but thanks in part to the energetic support of the U.S. ambassador, the system survived. General Somoza declared martial law and began using the misery of this natural disaster to further enrich himself and his supporters. He also expressed his gratitude to the U.S. ambassador for his support by placing the latter's picture, along with his own, on Nicaragua's twenty-cordoba bill.

All of this increased popular discontent with Somoza rule and damaged what remained of the family's international image. It even alienated the business community, which found the Somozas now intruding in areas of the economy, such as banking and construction, that they had previously left to the private sector. Seeking to take advantage of this situation, the Sandinista National Liberation Front (FSLN) guerrillas increased their activities. In 1974, they staged a spectacular raid on Managua itself, seizing several cabinet ministers and Somoza relatives as hostages. This action resulted in considerable publicity for the Sandinistas and revealed the extent of popular disaffection with the regime, as crowds of loudly cheering Nicaraguans ignored government orders and demonstrated their support for the guerrillas. At the time, however, the FSLN still did not seem able to seriously threaten Somoza rule.

ESCALATING CONFLICT

By late 1977, tensions were rising throughout Central America, and with the exception of Costa Rica, existing political systems became subject to increasing strain. Several factors, in addition to growing economic and social problems, contributed to this. The Roman Catholic Church, especially in Nicaragua and El Salvador, was becoming increasingly vocal in its condemnations of existing inequalities and repression. The victory of Jimmy Carter in the 1976 U.S. presidential elections weakened right-wing influences in Washington and led to a greatly increased emphasis on human rights by the U.S. State Department. As hopes for peaceful, democratic change in the region were increasingly frustrated by electoral fraud and political violence, guerrilla groups and other organizations of the radical left began to gain influence. Alarmed by these developments, the anachronistic power structures of most of the nations turned increasingly to military force and private right-wing terrorist groups to maintain their grip on power.

Revolution in Nicaragua

El Salvador's situation appeared to be the most explosive at the start of 1978, but the collapse of the old order actually began in Nicaragua. The Sandinistas had increased their activities in 1976 and 1977, but the Somozas and their National Guard appeared up to the challenge, even managing to kill the FSLN's founder, Carlos Fonseca Amador, in a late 1976 encounter. Then, in January 1978, assassins, connected with business associates of President Somoza, killed Nicaragua's leading newspaper publisher and opposition political leader, Pedro Joaquin Chamorro. The result was an explosion of national defiance and international indignation. Mass popular demonstrations were followed by a prolonged national strike, with employers actually paying their employees not to work, and by scattered popular uprisings, most notably in the city of Masaya. A group of twelve business, political, and intellectual leaders, known as *Los Doce,* began issuing calls for Somoza's resignation and for the inclusion of the FSLN in the government of post-Somoza Nicaragua.

These developments alarmed both the Somozas and the Carter administration. The United States began pressuring Somoza to end the state of siege and open up the political system. Other nations, notably Panama and Venezuela, were much blunter in their condemnation of the Nicaraguan government. They even established contacts with the Sandinistas, which gave them much greater legitimacy than that provided by their traditional Cuban connection.

In an effort to defuse both domestic and international opposition, the Nicaraguan dictator, who had only recently recovered from a heart attack, adopted a series of somewhat contradictory actions. On the one hand, he lifted the state of siege; ended press, but not radio, censorship; allowed the members of *Los Doce* to return to Nicaragua; and pledged not to be a candidate for reelection in 1980. At the same time, he increased the use of force by the National Guard against the Sandinistas, raised his son to the rank of lieutenant colonel and placed him in charge of the military's best combat unit, and stubbornly resisted all suggestions that he step down before 1981.

By mid-summer of 1978, it appeared that the Somozas had successfully weathered another crisis. The general strike had collapsed, the Sandinistas seemed unable to seize major towns, and even the United States had modified its opposition as President Carter sent General Somoza a letter expressing his appreciation for the "improvement" in internal conditions. Then, in August, the situation underwent a dramatic change.

The immediate cause was the seizure of the National Palace by a Sandinista commando group headed by Eden Pastora (known as Comandante Cero). The Congress and several cabinet members were held hostage until Somoza agreed to free Sandinista prisoners (including Tomas Borge, the last surviving founder of the FSLN), publish and broadcast an antigovernment manifesto, and allow free passage to Panama for the commandos and the freed prisoners. This humiliation was rapidly followed by others. A plot against the dictator by moderate guard officers was discovered and crushed, but a series of popular uprisings that broke out shortly thereafter proved much more difficult to deal with. Several cities were taken over for days or even weeks by the FSLN and were returned to government control only after bloody fighting, during which National Guard tactics caused thousands of civilian casualties.

A national strike further compounded the dictator's problems, as did the rising tide of international opposition to his continued rule. Costa Rica began openly to provide a haven for the FSLN, and Venezuela and Panama began funneling arms to the anti-Somoza guerrillas. Even the Carter administration apparently decided that the longtime U.S. ally had outlived his usefulness and had to go.

The method chosen by Washington to remove Somoza, and at the same time prevent a Sandinista military victory, was international mediation under OAS auspices. Both the dictator and the traditional opposition were persuaded to agree to this process. The FSLN refused to participate directly, but was at first represented by *Los Doce*. When it became apparent, however, that Somoza hoped to use the process to hang on to at least a major share of power, *Los Doce* withdrew, as did other leftist elements. The United States and the moderate, traditional opposition continued the effort to negotiate Somoza's departure until the start of 1979 when the entire mediation process collapsed. Convinced that the United States would not use significant economic or military force to remove him and still believing that he could force the middle and upper classes to resume their support for, or at least acceptance of, his rule in order to keep the Sandinistas out of power, Somoza had used the time of the mediation to expand his armed forces for a showdown with the guerrillas.

By early 1979, Nicaragua was on the verge of collapse. The economy was in a shambles. The gross domestic product had declined 7.2 percent in 1978 and would decline an additional 25.8 percent in 1979. The international debt was soaring past the $1.4-billion mark, and the currency had to be devalued. Tens of thousands of Nicaraguans had been killed or wounded, and many had become homeless refugees within Nicaragua or had fled to neighboring countries. General Somoza seemed quite willing to destroy his own nation in order to postpone his fall from power.

Sandinista strength increased dramatically following the collapse of the mediation. With U.S. policy apparently adrift and the traditional opposition discredited by its participation in the mediation effort, the FSLN appeared to offer the only hope of bringing down the dynasty. Previously divided into three competing factions, the FSLN now forged a unified national directorate of nine individuals and undertook a coordinated military strategy. Meanwhile, *Los Doce* did an effective job of mustering international support for their cause in Europe and Latin America and in further isolating the tottering Somoza regime.

In May, the FSLN began an all-out offensive. Operating openly from Costa Rica, it soon managed to seize several major towns and even staged uprisings within the capital. OAS delegates, in an emergency meeting called to deal with the crisis, refused to go along with a U.S. proposal to send a peacekeeping force to Nicaragua to end the fighting. Instead, with only two dissenting votes, the OAS called for Somoza's replacement.

Following this meeting, the United States concentrated its efforts on removing Somoza, ending the fighting, and preserving some elements of the

National Guard. The Sandinistas established a provisional government, including many moderates and non-Sandinistas, which was quickly granted belligerent status and even recognition by many Latin American governments. As the national uprising continued to spread, the guard began to run out of fuel and supplies. Now anxious to get himself and his leading supporters out of Nicaragua, General Somoza finally agreed to resign and hand over power to an interim government, which would then turn it over to the Sandinista-appointed junta. But, in private, the dictator urged his supporters to continue the war, promising that once he had departed, the United States would join the fight against the guerrillas. When he fled to Miami on July 17, 1979, his handpicked successor, Dr. Francisco Urcuyo, therefore announced his determination to hang on to power. The United States immediately denounced this move, and the Sandinistas stepped up the military pressure. In a matter of hours the National Guard dissolved. On July 19, the Sandinistas entered Managua in triumph, bringing to an end the longest-lasting family dictatorship in Latin American history.

Spreading Hopes and Fears

With the end of the civil war, large credits were provided by other Latin American nations to the virtually bankrupt new government of Nicaragua, and President Carter requested $75 million in aid from the U.S. Congress. In addition, Washington stepped up its pressures on Honduras, El Salvador, and Guatemala to move toward more-representative government and, in the latter two cases, to cut down on widespread human rights abuses.

For a while it appeared that there was some reason for optimism in regard to Central America's future. The military rulers of Honduras scheduled elections for a civilian Constituent Assembly for April 1980. In Nicaragua, the Sandinistas had imprisoned thousands of exguardsmen and confiscated the holdings of Somoza and his supporters but had avoided the predicted bloodbath after the dictator's fall; they had included numerous prominent moderates and even several priests in their new government, and they were allowing a high degree of individual freedom. The economy was in terrible condition, but the government and the private sector appeared to be trying, with the help of massive foreign assistance, to put it back on its feet.

Guatemala and El Salvador remained the major problems. In the former case, the military had arranged the election of General Romeo Lucas García as president in 1978 but had allowed a moderate civilian reformer, Dr. Francisco Villagran Kramer, to become vice-president. The Sandinista uprising and ultimate triumph in Nicaragua, however, had led to a growing polarization within Guatemala and had drawn the army into an ever-closer alliance with the extreme right. Prominent civilian politicians, including Social Democratic leader Alberto Fuentes Mohr and FUR head Manuel Colom Argueta, were assassinated by the far right. In response, guerrilla violence began to spread in the countryside.

While options were being closed in Guatemala, they appeared to be opening up in El Salvador. In October 1979, an internal military coup ousted the corrupt and incompetent Romero government and installed a mixed military-civilian regime, including a relatively moderate young colonel, Adolfo Majano; the head of the small Social Democratic Party (MNR), Guillermo Manuel Ungo; and former Catholic University rector, Ramon Mayorga. The cabinet included representatives of almost every imaginable sector from conservative urban businessmen to the Salvadoran Communist Party (UDN). Reforms, an end to repression, and free elections were promised; U.S. aid was resumed and increased; and prospects for avoiding a Nicaraguan-style civil war seemed fairly good. The year seemed to be ending on an optimistic note.

The hopes of late 1979 soon dissolved into the tragic realities of 1980. Except for Honduras and Belize, conditions deteriorated notably throughout Central America during that year. In a surprisingly honest election, the Honduran Liberal Party managed to gain a small majority in the constituent Assembly over the promilitary National Party. Economic growth, however, slowed from 6.7 percent in 1979 to only 2 percent in 1980, and rising debt also caused concern.

In Costa Rica, the administration of President Rodrigo Carazo proved unable to cope with the mounting burdens of rising debt, regional turmoil, and stagnant exports. The GDP increased by only 3.3 percent in 1979 and 1.9 percent in 1980. Inflation climbed past 18 percent and the government's deficit rose to 12 percent of the total GDP.

Bullets, not ballots, were Guatemala's answer to political problems in 1980. The year opened with a massacre of antigovernment protestors who had seized the Spanish embassy, and conditions deteriorated steadily thereafter. Guerrilla activity grew, with large numbers of Indians joining guerrilla ranks for the first time. Church-state relations became increasingly tense; the army even exiled the president of the National Bishop's Conference. Relations with the United States also reached a nadir as the Lucas government, anticipating a Reagan victory in the fall, refused to accept the Carter administration's choice for ambassador. Despairing of any chance for political progress, Vice-President Villagren Kramer fled abroad and resigned.

In Nicaragua, the highlight of 1980 was a massive literacy campaign, which mobilized national energies in a largely successful effort to deal with the heritage of adult illiteracy left by the Somozas. Other developments, however, were less positive. As it became clear that all real power in Nicaragua lay with the nine-member, self-appointed National Directorate of the FSLN, not with the provisional Government of National Reconstruction, moderates began to leave the government. The most notable defections were those of junta members Alfonso Robelo and Violeta Barrios de Chamorro, widow of murdered opposition leader Pedro Joaquin Chamorro. *La Prensa,* the nation's leading newspaper, became increasingly critical of the regime and of what it perceived as growing Cuban influence over the government. Relations with the United States also began to deteriorate, despite final approval of the $75-million aid package, as the Carter administration charged that Nicaragua was supporting the growing insurgency in El Salvador.

The Salvadoran Tragedy

It was in El Salvador that the tragedy of 1980 was most profound. Caught between growing pressures from mass organizations on the left and the intransigence of the increasingly murderous right, the first junta collapsed because of the military's inability or unwillingness to halt repression. The Christian Democrats joined a second civilian-military junta, but it, too, proved unable to deal with the situation, and several of its members quit. Thanks, in part, to U.S. efforts, right-wing plots to overthrow the government—often linked to a former army major, Roberto D'Aubuisson—failed, but the military refused to arrest the major or his supporters. Under pressure from Washington, the government did decree a sweeping agrarian reform program, but its implementation was slow and subject to widespread official abuse. In a desperate effort to gain credibility, the military installed Christian Democratic leader José Napoleon Duarte in the junta, but gave him little real power.

The growing disarray in politics was paralleled by increasing violence throughout the country. In March, Archbishop Oscar Romero, who had supported the first civil-military junta but had become increasingly critical of the government's failure to curb right-wing violence, was assassinated by elements of the extreme right. His funeral degenerated into a bloody confrontation between the mass organizations of the left and government security forces. Civilian leaders, such as ex-junta member Guillermo Ungo, now joined an umbrella left-wing opposition group, the Democratic Revolutionary Front (FDR), while the guerrillas, openly linked to the front, formed their own united command, the Farabundo Martí National Liberation Front (FMLN). Efforts to call a national strike in the fall failed in the face of growing government resistance and the decimation of the leadership of the left's mass organizations by officially tolerated, if not supported, death squads. In November, six FDR leaders were seized in San Salvador and murdered. The following month, three U.S. nuns and a religious worker were killed by elements of the security forces, and a few weeks later, the head of the agrarian reform program and two U.S. government advisers were assassinated with the complicity of elements of the military.

This produced a major dilemma for the outgoing Carter administration, a problem compounded by the ousting of moderate Colonel Majano from the junta and the rise to real power of Defense Minister Colonel José Guillermo García. Aid was suspended briefly, until the junta was reorganized with Duarte installed as provisional president. But in January 1981, the guerrillas launched a massive offensive. Washington hurriedly resumed aid and even began shipping lethal military equipment to El Salvador, the first case of such open assistance in Central America since the mid-1970s.

THE EARLY YEARS OF
THE REAGAN ADMINISTRATION

Right-wing elements in Central America joyfully celebrated the election of Ronald Reagan as president of the United States, believing that he would abandon the country's concern about human rights and provide massive military assistance for their struggles against the guerrillas and all other elements working for meaningful changes in their societies. At first, the rhetoric, if not the deeds, from Washington seemed to measure up to right-wing expectations. Military assistance to El Salvador and Honduras was quickly increased while economic assistance to Nicaragua was suspended. Secretary of State Alexander Haig talked of "drawing a line" against Communist expansionism in Central America and of "going to the source" of subversion, a source that he identified with Cuba and Nicaragua rather than with the decades of domestic misrule and foreign exploitation.

Unfortunately for the Reagan administration, it soon became obvious that it was easier to propound slogans in Washington than it was to implement effective policies in Central America. In El Salvador, the guerrilla offensive failed, but the government could not regain control of guerrilla strongholds in rural areas, nor did it seem capable of controlling abuses by its own security forces. Investigations into the murders of the U.S. citizens dragged on without visible progress, and the economy continued to decline at an alarming rate. In Guatemala, efforts to open a dialogue with the Lucas regime, which would lead to some amelioration of the murderous internal repression in return for a resumption of U.S. assistance, succeeded only in convincing some elements of the Guatemalan right that Ronald Reagan, too, was soft on communism. As the government's slaughter of its opponents mounted, so too did support for the numerous far-left guerrilla organizations. Guatemala seemed to be heading down the road of violent civil conflict already taken by El Salvador and Nicaragua.

Efforts to intimidate Nicaragua's Sandinista rulers also backfired. At first, they had shown signs of willingness to make some compromises, reducing their support for El Salvador's guerrillas and making gestures toward an accommodation with internal opposition forces. But as the months passed and pressures from Washington continued, they began to crack down on internal dissent and to move closer to Cuba and the Soviet Union in international arenas. In 1981, Arturo Cruz left the government, and Eden Pastora left Nicaragua. Conflicts began developing along the Honduran border with ex-guardsmen and even some former Sandinistas now launching guerrilla attacks against the Sandinistas. The rising tensions served to short-circuit efforts at economic recovery and produced a growing climate of hostility between the private business sector and the government. Church-state relations also became strained, and finally, open clashes broke out on the isolated Atlantic coast over government efforts to forcibly relocate thousands of Miskito and Suma Indians. By 1982, Nicaragua seemed to be heading for another civil war, especially after Pastora announced that he would fight against the regime.

In Honduras and Costa Rica, democratic institutions managed to survive, despite the pressures of rapidly declining economies. In late 1981, presidential and congressional elections in Honduras resulted in victories for the Liberal Party and its presidential candidate, Dr. Roberto Suazo Córdova. A new constitution was also adopted, basically democratic in character but carefully drawn to ensure the autonomy of the armed forces. In Costa Rica, elections in early 1982 swept the discredited Carazo administration from power and brought the National Liberation Party, with its candidate, Luis Alberto Monge, back into office. In both cases, the new presidents inherited bankrupt treasures, monumental debt burdens, soaring inflation and unemployment, and deteriorating relations with Nicaragua.

The dreary pattern of escalating violence and collapsing economies established in 1981 continued through 1982. Despite the inauguration of new civilian administrations in Costa Rica and Honduras, the achievement of full independence for Belize (over Guatemalan threats and objections), and the apparently successful holding of Constituent Assembly elections in El Salvador, the basic problems confronting the region remained unresolved. In March, Guatemalan junior officers ousted the corrupt government of General Lucas. The Lucas regime had just staged a rigged election, which had been won by General Anibal Guevara, Lucas's handpicked successor. Seeing no hope under such conditions of reversing the growing strength of the guerrillas, curbing the rampant corruption that was weakening the army, or restoring access to badly needed U.S. assistance and military supplies, junior officers took over the government. To head their movement, united only in its dislike of Lucas and Guevara, they seized on a retired army general, Efrain Rios Montt. Now a "born-again" Christian pentecostal, Rios Montt at first had to share power with two other generals, but in June he ousted them and took control himself. He purged the most corrupt members of the government, ended right-wing terrorism in the cities, and restored some measure of fiscal integrity. He also began a rapprochement with the United States and offered some concessions to Belize, publically dropping Guatemala's traditional claim to that nation's entire territory. But he was unable or unwilling to stop the slaughter of Indians and other peasants by the military, and he tolerated little criticism from the press or from traditional political leaders. As for the guerrillas, he offered them a limited amnesty, but when that offer was rejected, he made it clear that death was the only fate they could expect at the hands of his government.

In El Salvador, the Reagan administration at first hailed the 1982 elections as a popular rejection of the guerrillas and the left, since the left had urged the population to boycott the elections and had tried to disrupt them. But the elections had produced a victory for a far-right coalition, led by Major D'Aubuisson, which undercut the agrarian reform, resisted efforts to curb human rights abuses, and even tolerated or encouraged attacks on Christian Democratic leaders in rural areas. Government infighting increased steadily, and guerrilla strength once again began to increase.

In Nicaragua, the government continued to drift to the left, and conflicts with domestic critics and armed exile factions increased. The revelation of the Reagan administration's support for armed opposition groups, mostly operating from Honduras, and of other efforts to destabilize the Sandinista government helped revive the government's sagging prestige and served to discredit its opponents. This also served to justify the Soviet- and Cuba-supported internal arms buildup and new restrictions on domestic critics.

While failing to produce any notable weakening of the Sandinistas' grip on power in Nicaragua, Washington's policies did undermine the newly installed civilian government in Honduras. The increasing involvement of that nation in the civil conflicts of both Nicaragua and El Salvador and the growing power of the Honduran military, led by General Gustavo Alvarez (a highly conservative, ambitious graduate of Argentina's military academy), fueled growing domestic dissent and international criticism. Human rights abuses, especially against resident aliens, increased, and at times, the nation seemed on the verge of war with Nicaragua.

Meanwhile, Costa Rica's declining economy, burdened by a monumental debt, produced high unemployment, declining living standards, and increased labor unrest. U.S. emergency economic assistance, much of it funneled through the new Caribbean Basin Initiative, served to avert complete national bankruptcy in Costa Rica, El Salvador, and Honduras but did nothing to cure the underlying causes of the economic crisis. By the start of 1983, Central America was caught in a vicious circle. Economic problems contributed to political instability, which, in turn, aggravated the economic situation. Moderate political solutions proved ineffective, strengthening the extremes of both left and right. Service of the enormous regional debt, rapidly approaching the $10-billion mark, combined with the cost of imported energy consumed the overwhelming bulk of the region's foreign currency earnings. The 1981 regional deficit in balance of payments exceeded $2 billion, and by late 1982, regional monetary reserves were a negative $840.7 million. Optimists believed that if the violence could be reduced and stability and trade restored, Central America could regain its 1978 standard of living by 1990; pessimists felt that a return to 1978 levels was unlikely in this century.

CAUSES OF THE CONFLICT

The transformation of Central America from a relatively quiet, stagnant backwater area of "banana republics" to an arena of violent conflicts with international involvement can be attributed to five basic, interrelated factors. The first of these is the accumulated burden of the region's history. In Central America, social and political debts were postponed, not paid. In El Salvador, Guatemala, and Somoza's Nicaragua, entrenched, inflexible oligarchies refused to give up any of their control and met pressures for change with increasingly violent repression. When the Church supported the status quo, these oligarchies were supporters of the Church, but when the Church began to criticize conditions, ruling elites unleashed their hired killers on lay workers, priests, and in El Salvador, even the archbishop. They used money, flattery, and fear of communism to enlist the military in their support, at times undertaking "dirty tasks" that the military preferred to avoid. Reform was equated with subversion; criticism, with treason; and national security, with the interests of their own small class. When threatened, the ruling elites sent their money and their families to Miami but reserved part of their wealth to finance death squads, military coups, and any other available means of postponing the inevitable death of their anachronistic social order.

The military institutions of Central America also bear a heavy responsibility in this area. Their increasing professionalization in the post–World War II era did not produce greater loyalty to the nations as a whole or a commitment to defend the rights of the majority of their citizens; rather, it produced a growing concern with the power and survival of the military institutions. In El Salvador, loyalty to classmates from the military academy frequently overrode any concept of allegiance to the government or the nation. Military careers were frequently viewed as a road to personal enrichment. Corruption became totally institutionalized in Nicaragua, where the National Guard served as the personal bodyguard of the Somoza family and functioned more as an occupying force than as a national army. But corruption also weakened military efficiency and undermined potential popular support for the governments of Honduras, Guatemala, and, especially, El Salvador. The situation in the last nation was further complicated by the division of the security forces into separate, but closely linked, organizations performing both police and military functions. The net result of all these factors was that the military in Central America was at least as much the source of violence and disorder as it was the promoter of order and stability.

A second destabilizing factor in the region is the nature of the economic structures that developed during the post–World War II era. Economic growth was rapid for much of this period, but the rewards were unevenly distributed, and the economic structures that emerged were extremely vulnerable to both internal and external pressures. The rapidly growing cities were service oriented, producing little and consuming much of the wealth from the countryside. Their biggest source of employment for newly arrived rural dwellers was in construction, but this industry was exceptionally vulnerable to downturns in the economy.

The industrial growth that did occur was largely designed to serve the Common Market. Much of it was dependent on imported raw materials and was relatively inefficient. When violence disrupted the Common Market and economic conditions made foreign exchange increasingly unobtainable, many of these industries were forced to reduce operations or to shut down entirely.

The emphasis on new and expanded export-crop production also reduced food production, accelerated rural to urban migration, and increased the economies' vulnerability to price and demand fluctuations in the world market. In summary, the economic growth of earlier years produced few lasting benefits, inflated middle-class consumer appetites, and forced governments to engage in excessive borrowing to maintain existing structures when world conditions deteriorated. Far from contributing to greater stability, the economic changes of the 1960s and 1970s actually set the stage for increased instability.

A third factor in Central America's current crisis is the failure of the moderate, reformist parties, notably the Christian Democrats and the Social Democrats. These parties were frequently believed to be the wave of the future in the 1960s and early 1970s. They remain influential political actors in many areas and continue to exercise power in Costa Rica. But they have been unable to resolve the area's basic problems and have proved ineffective in dealing with the extremes of both left and right. In Guatemala and El Salvador, moderates joined in coalitions with far-right, antidemocratic elements in the hopes of modifying conditions or gaining influence. As the cases of Francisco Villagran Kramer in Guatemala and José Napoleon Duarte in El Salvador demonstrate, the moderates were simply being used to lend legitimacy to the right while being denied any real influence over basic developments. Many moderate parties were also too dependent on foreign support, especially that emanating from the United States. In Nicaragua, they stuck with the U.S.-sponsored mediation effort until the bitter end, discrediting themselves in the process and making themselves largely irrelevant in the final struggle for power between Somoza and the Sandinistas.

Whereas the first three factors are largely domestic, the remaining two basic causes of Central America's problems relate to external influences. The most obvious of these is the impact of world economic conditions. Beginning with the 1973 rise in energy costs, these conditions have had an increasingly negative impact. In recent years, the rise in the costs of imported manufactured goods has been paralleled by declines or, at best, stagnation in the prices received for regional exports. An even greater impact was brought about by the rapid rise of interest rates in the early 1980s, which made service on the huge new debts virtually impossible. Finally, the world economic recession of the early 1980s reduced demand for Central America's exports; cut the region's sources of available foreign assistance, especially from Mexico; and contributed, along with the insecurity generated by the spreading violence, to drying up most sources of new investment capital.

As harmful as external economic influences have been, the effects of foreign political involvements have been even worse. Cuban involvement in Central America has encouraged guerrilla activities and provided right-wing forces with a convenient excuse for increased repression. But the greatest destabilizing factor has been the inconsistent policies of the United States. For decades, U.S. concern with stability served to lend support to a series of corrupt, repressive regimes. Nicaragua's civil conflict of 1978–1979 clearly had its roots in the U.S. intervention of the late 1920s and early 1930s and the subsequent U.S. support of the Somoza dynasty. Many aspects of Guatemala's current conflict can be traced to the CIA-sponsored exile invasion of 1954. Activities of both U.S. government and U.S. private businesses, especially the United Fruit Company, have contributed also to Honduras's problems. The pattern of manipulation there was continuing in early 1984 as the United States was attempting to use Honduras as a base for operations against Nicaragua. This action was threatening the tenuous civil-military balance in that nation and even raising the possibility of a regional war. In El Salvador, U.S. efforts have done more to prolong the current conflict than to resolve it. If anything, far-right intransigence has been increased by the perception, based on statements emanating from Washington, that a victory by the left would not be allowed.

Part of the basic contradiction in U.S. policy toward Central America is Washington's determination to maintain regional control coupled with an unwillingness to assume the responsibilities of or to pay the price associated with such control. While activities of the left are frequently ascribed to Cuban and Soviet influence, no responsibility is admitted for the brutality or corruption of past or present allies on the right. Rightist factions have learned how to play the Cuban card to get Washington's attention and support. They constantly strive to force the United States to choose between supporting them and accepting the armed triumph of a left violently denied any peaceful access to power. They also promise cheap stability in exchange for military assistance rather than acknowledging the high costs of dealing with the social and economic roots of Central America's problems.

Finally, U.S. policy toward the region is inconsistent and often confusing. Central American politicians have to constantly strive to keep abreast of the latest nuances from the north, embracing human rights, economic development, anti-communism, or whatever other panacea is currently being promoted by Washington. Conflicts between the U.S. Congress and the executive branch and even changes within the executive, such as those produced when George Shultz succeeded Alexander Haig as secretary of state, add to the confusion. Frequently, the United States seems to act like a petulant, fearful child with a limited attention span, a capacity for throwing occasional public tantrums, and a constant demand for attention and control. In a situation already made desperate by other factors, the ultimate impact of U.S. involvement in Central America has usually been to make things worse.

Central America is likely to remain all too frequently in that part of U.S. news coverage reserved for wars, murders, and other disasters. The region retains the economic and human potential for considerable development and progress, but it also contains the potential for conflict and destruction beyond that experienced to date. The situation was summed up by Costa Rican President Luis Alberto Monge in May 1982 when he said: "The political crisis that afflicts our region has internal roots, of old injustices and lost hopes, which are jumbled together with the intervention of foreign interests. There will be no peace in Central America and the Caribbean while the infernal game of hegemonic interests continues in our region. In the cruel conflicts of our peoples, the Central Americans provide the bodies and others gather the advantages."

SUGGESTED READINGS

There is no truly adequate history of Central America in English. The best available, although already somewhat dated, work is Ralph Lee Woodward, Jr., *Central America: A Nation Divided* (New York and London: Oxford University Press, 1976). Colonial history is covered by Murdo J. MacLeod, *Spanish Central America: A Socioeconomic History, 1520–1720* (Berkeley and Los Angeles: University of California, 1973). The subsequent century can be traced in Miles L. Wortman, *Government and Society in Central America, 1680–1840* (New York: Columbia University Press, 1982). The best survey of the modern situation is Thomas P. Anderson, *Politics in Central America* (New York: Praeger, 1982), but this study for some reason omits Costa Rica.

No scholarly history of U.S.–Central American relations is yet available. The problems for the first third of this century were covered in two volumes by Dana G. Munro in *Intervention and Dollar Diplomacy in the Caribbean, 1900–1921* (Princeton: Princeton University Press, 1964) and *The United States and the Caribbean Republics, 1921–1933* (Princeton: Princeton University Press, 1974). Varied views of the current situation are surveyed in Richard E. Feinberg, ed., *Central America: International Dimensions of the Crisis* (New York: Holmes and Meier, 1982).

Two specialized studies contribute important insights into the regional situation. The first is Patrick Cotter and George Bowdler, *Voter Participation in Central America, 1954–1981* (Washington, D.C.: University Press of America, 1982). The other is William Cline and Enrique Delgado, *Economic Integration in Central America* (Washington, D.C.: Brookings Institution, 1978).

The amount of material available on individual nations varies widely. By far the least studied nation in the region is Honduras. William Stokes, *Honduras: An Area Study in Government* (Madison: University of Wisconsin, 1950), remains the basic work in English despite its notable weaknesses and the fact that it is very badly outdated. Thomas P. Anderson, *The War of the Dispossessed: Honduras and El Salvador, 1969* (Lincoln: University of Nebraska, 1981), sheds important light on the 1969 conflict with El Salvador.

In recent years El Salvador, not surprisingly, has come in for considerable attention. Basic to any understanding of that nation's problems is Thomas P. Anderson, *Matanza* (Lincoln: University of Nebraska, 1971), a scholarly study of the 1931 peasant uprising and the subsequent government massacre. Additional background, this time on El Salvador's Christian Democratic Party, is found in Stephen Webre, *José Napoleon Duarte and the Christian Democratic Party in Salvadoran Politics, 1960–1972* (Baton Rouge: Louisiana State University Press, 1979). Among the host of studies on recent developments, the most readable and useful is probably Cynthia Arnson, *El Salvador: A Revolution Confronts the United States* (Washington, D.C.: Institute for Policy Studies, 1982).

There has also been a wave of writing on Nicaragua in recent years. Background to the Revolution can be found in Neill Macaulay, *The Sandino Affair* (Chicago: Quadrangle Books, 1967); Richard Millett, *Guardians of the Dynasty: A History of the U.S. Created Guardia Nacional de Nicaragua* (Maryknoll, N.Y.: Orbis Books, 1977); and Bernard Diedrich, *Somoza and the Legacy of U.S. Involvement in Central America* (New York: Dutton, 1981). Among the host of available volumes on the Revolution and its aftermath, the best to date is probably John A. Booth, *The End and the Beginning: The Nicaraguan Revolution* (Boulder, Colo.: Westview Press, 1982).

Guatemala has been of greater interest to anthropologists than it has been to political scientists or historians. Richard Adams, *Crucified by Power* (Austin: University of Texas, 1970), is still the best introduction to the basic realities of that nation. Important aspects of Guatemalan history are covered in Kenneth Grieb, *Guatemalan Caudillo: The Regime of Jorge Ubico, Guatemala, 1931–1944* (Athens, Ohio: Ohio University Press, 1979), and Stephen Kinzer and Stephen Schlesinger, *Bitter Fruit: The Untold Story of the American Coup in Guatemala* (New York: Doubleday, 1982).

Belize has been the subject of a surprising number of studies, the most up to date of which is William D. Stetzkorn, *Formerly British Honduras: A Profile of the New Nation of Belize* (Athens, Ohio: Ohio University Press, 1981). Costa Rica has long been a favored topic of research by North Americans, probably because of its tradition of peace and democracy. Among the most useful books in English on that nation are Charles Ameringer, *Don Pepe: A Political Biography of José Figueres of Costa Rica* (Albuquerque: University of New Mexico, 1977), and Mitchell Seligson, *Peasants of Costa Rica and the Development of Agrarian Capitalism* (Madison: University of Wisconsin, 1980).

19

CENTRAL AMERICA'S
LOST DECADE

ELDON KENWORTHY

As time ran out for the Reagan administration, Assistant Secretary of State for Inter-American Affairs Elliott Abrams offered this assessment of what the administration had achieved. "As historians look back over the 1980s, I believe they will view it as the decade of democracy. . . . For Central America, it has been a period of democratic transformation."[1] According to Abrams, the region also recovered its capacity for economic growth: "Now [December 1988], only five years after the passage of the Caribbean Basin Economies Recovery Act, CBI countries have turned their economies around. They are growing again. Last year, the growth rate was 3 percent. This year, expansion continues."[2] Inasmuch as the five Central American nations constitute only one-third of the Caribbean Basin group, Abrams's figures may be correct; he made no effort to distinguish the larger isthmian countries from the more numerous but smaller island republics.[3]

However one measures it, economic expansion was not the Reagan legacy in Central America, not even in the year in which Abrams spoke. In 1988, not one of the five Central American economies generated so much as one percent growth in real per capita national product, or Gross Domestic Product (GDP).[4] The 1980s were a lost decade economically. Table 19.1 shows national variations on this pattern, understating the free fall of the Nicaraguan economy after 1981.[5] More accurate than Abrams's assessment, then, was that of *New York Times* reporter James LeMoyne who in 1987 noted that "six straight years of recession, devaluation and political instability have forced the vast majority of Salvadorans, Hondurans, Guatemalans, Nicaraguans, and even some Costa Ricans, traditionally the most affluent of Central Americans, to accept living conditions and wage levels that are equivalent to those of a decade ago."[6]

But what of democracy? "In Central America ten years ago," Abrams told a University of Kansas audience in 1987, "Costa Rica was the only

346

Table 19.1
Change in Real Per Capita Gross Domestic Product in Percentages

	1970–1979	*1980–1988*
Costa Rica	34	− 9
El Salvador	15	−15
Guatemala	33	−20
Honduras	15	−14
Nicaragua[a]	−28	−27

[a]From 1970 to 1975, Nicaragua registered a 9 percent gain. The negative number for the seventies reflects the costs of a revolution fought in 1977–1979.

Sources: María Eugenia Gallardo and José Roberto López, *Centroamérica: la Crisis en Cifras* (San José, Costa Rica: IICA-FLASCO, 1986), p. 48; U.N. Economic Commission for Latin America and the Caribbean, *Statistical Yearbook for Latin America and the Caribbean,* 1988 edition (Santiago, Chile: CEPAL, 1989), annex, table 1.

democracy. Today, new civilian-led democracies have emerged in Guatemala, El Salvador, and Honduras. Nicaragua's communist dictatorship is the exception."[7] Virtually every member of the Reagan administration who dealt with Central America made a similar pronouncement. In 1986, Secretary of State George Shultz noted, "Just a few years ago Costa Rica was a democratic island in a sea of dictatorship. Today, Costa Rica has been joined by democratic governments in Honduras, El Salvador, and Guatemala."[8] In addition to islands in the sea, during Reagan's second term "winds," "tides," and "waves" of democracy swept Central America.*

Could the democratization be real, however, in the midst of slumping economies, displaced populations, and civil war? This chapter explores that question by delving beneath elections to examine the conditions that make elections meaningful. From this perspective, the democratization of Central America remains problematic. Throughout the chapter, trends in the politics of Central America will be linked to movements in economy and in foreign relations, inasmuch as all these factors impinge upon fragile democracies.

The chapter ends by taking seriously Abrams's and Shultz's characterizations of Costa Rica as a deeper democracy than the others. If one Central American nation is "making it," the obstacles to vibrant democracy are either not universally present (as cultural explanations suggest) or not insuperable (as some dependency theorists imply). Thus Costa Rica holds implications for the theoretical choices outlined in the introduction to this book. More importantly, it may point to strategies other countries could adopt to strengthen democracy and equity without sacrificing economic growth.

---

*Elections that took place in Costa Rica and Nicaragua in February 1990, after this chapter was prepared, resulted in victories for opposition candidates supported by the U.S. government (see Chapters 11 and 14).

Table 19.2
Unemployment, Underemployment, and Marginality, 1980: Percentage of the
Economically Active Population by Category

	Officially unemployed	Underemployed	Informal sector[a]	Unionized
Costa Rica	6.0	26	19	15
El Salvador	16.1	55	40	15
Guatemala	3.2	43	40	8
Honduras	15.2	64	82[b]	8
Nicaragua	18.3	49	69[b]	55[c]

[a]Workers in quasi-legal operations, typically working for themselves or for family
members, with little security or access to credit.
[b]1970; no 1980 data.
[c]a majority of these in unions controlled by the ruling party.

Sources: María Eugenia Gallardo and José Roberto López, *Centroamérica: la
Crisis en Cifras* (San José, Costa Rica: IICA-FLASCO, 1986), pp. 188–189;
James Wilkie and Enrique Ochoa, eds., *Statistical Abstract of Latin America*
(Los Angeles: UCLA Latin American Center Publications, 1989), vol. 27, table
1339; "In Long-Suffering Central America," *New York Times,* September 8,
1979, p. A14.

ECONOMIES IN REVERSE

Although the recession of 1981–1983, which set back per capita income
one to two decades depending on the country, eased somewhat by the
decade's end, there was no assurance that El Salvador and Nicaragua would
soon pull out of their nosedives or that the other three nations would resume
the vigorous growth they enjoyed in 1950–1975. Quite the contrary, now
the region was saddled with unprecedented foreign debt on top of a drop
in world prices for its traditional exports. Servicing the foreign debt had
taken 12 percent of export earnings in 1980, but eight years later that figure
was 40 percent and climbing.[9] By 1988 trade within the region had fallen
to half its 1980 level while compensating gains in the U.S. market were
few, Washington's promises in the Caribbean Basin Initiative notwithstanding.[10]

All this occurred against the backdrop of one of the highest population
growth rates in the world, which contributed to the massive un- and
underemployment illustrated in Table 19.2. North Americans who feel
threatened by a growing urban underclass might reflect on Central America
where (Costa Rica excepted) up to half the population are marginals making
a living through quasi-legal informal activities that lie beyond the reach (and
the protection) of laws, taxes, and organized markets. Added to the landlessness
and unemployment that have accumulated for decades, recent civil wars
generated 1.8 to 2.8 million refugees and displaced persons and 160,000
fatalities. These long- and short-term trends combined to place more Central
Americans in poverty than at any time since World War II. Such are the

somber statistics amassed by the International Commission for Central American Recovery and Development, whose 1989 report estimated that merely to meet the survival needs of its poor and displaced populations Central America needed transfusions from abroad of $850 million annually over three years. To restart economic growth would require another $2 billion annually for five years.[11]

But more than money, ideas are needed. Long absent has been a strategy of development that could address Central American conditions (including those exhibited in Table 19.2) yet not be vetoed by powerful elites. *New York Times* reporter LeMoyne again pinpoints the problem, "No official study of the region in recent years has offered a solution that will allow bankrupt local economies to even begin to absorb the hundreds of thousands of new job-seekers each year."[12] LeMoyne wrote before the International Commission released its report. Reactivating Central America's common market and speeding up the diversification of exports are among that group's less controversial recommendations. But in a sharp departure from Central America's decades-old pattern of mechanizing agriculture and trying to attract high-tech industries, the report also gives priority to investment in human resources.

One recommendation, for instance, is investment in *microempresas,* those minifirms employing fewer than ten people and capitalized at less than $10,000 that constitute nine-tenths of the businesses in several Central American countries and employ half the workforce. The report also advocates new legal rights for the women who produce between 30 and 40 percent of the region's food. Establishing clear property titles for small farmers also is recommended as part of a multifaceted effort to return the region to feeding itself, as it did prior to 1950. (Currently 40 percent of Central America's food is imported. Purchased at world market prices, these imports drive up the debt and sap the income of the poor. Donated food imports undercut peasant producers and confirm large landowners in their decision to concentrate on nonfood crops.[13])

Behind these specific recommendations stands an overall strategy of investing in grassroots health and education, recognizing that this means less investment in mechanization. "In the long run," states the commission's report, "a strong human resource development strategy is a prerequisite for increased productivity; and in both the short and long run, it is a means of sharing benefits more widely."[14] Such an approach turns unemployment on its head by viewing people as Central America's main asset, arguing that what is missing are the health, skills-based education, access to markets, and minimal capital needed for the region's poor to put their God-given entrepreneurial drives to productive use. This view squares with recent studies of the "informal sector" that document its remarkable productivity within the constraints it must work under.[15]

Investments in human resources have the advantage of addressing several targets at once: human survival needs in the short term; productivity, equity, and democracy in the long. (Stable democracy requires a literate populace that can form organizations and articulate goals and a public predisposed to support a state that offers it opportunity and respect.) Such a strategy also takes pressure off the environment, inasmuch as decent jobs on already cleared land alleviate "the necessity for poor people to establish small farms on hilltops, forest land, or other marginal areas."[16]

The paradigm that permeates not only the International Commission's report but also the statements of the Central American presidents to whom it was delivered is holistic and synergistic. Everything is seen as connected to everything else, with the whole system poised between upward and downward spirals. As the 1984 Kissinger Report referred to a "seamless web" tying security issues to political and social issues, so the International Commission took as its "fundamental premise . . . that lasting peace, genuine democracy, and equitable development are inextricable. These three objectives are mutually reinforcing. None is sufficient by itself; all are necessary."[17] This might seem another instance of the classic ploy of tying ignored problems to publicized ones, as when a U.S. politician links inadequate schools in the ghetto to drugs and crime. Costa Rica, however, provides empirical evidence that investments in human resources do indeed generate a resilient economy and a democratic polity. The final section of this chapter will examine that evidence.

However sound, the human investment strategy runs counter to powerful interests and cultural norms. Democratic governments might overcome both, for this is a strategy that should attract majority support. But there must be democratic executives strong enough to withstand the vetoes of powerful elites and the pressures of international leaders, especially when both coincide in viewing investments in people as "nonproductive" and premature leaps into social democracy. Even in deeply democratic and ostensibly socially democratic Costa Rica, commercial banks currently make only 1 percent of their loans to *microempresas,* while in El Salvador, conservatives seem poised to use their elevation to the presidency in 1989 to unravel the land entitlements and rural cooperatives instituted (ironically) by a military government. Indeed, everything is connected to everything else. The future of Central American economies as well as the well being of the people who inhabit them are hostages to political change. We must turn, then, to the other transformation that Elliott Abrams saw in the 1980s: democratization.

LIMITS OF DEMOCRATIZATION

U.S. news media echoed Washington in celebrating the democratization of Central America in the 1980s. According to the *Los Angeles Times,* democracy returned to El Salvador in 1980, to Honduras in 1981, and to Guatemala in 1986, an assessment that found its way into the authoritative *Statistical Abstract of Latin America.*[18] Yet, all that happened in El Salvador in 1980 was that a military-civilian junta, which had evolved out of a coup, drafted the politician José Napoleon Duarte into its ranks after other civilians resigned in frustration over being used as windowdressing. To enhance its standing with Washington, by year's end the officers elevated Duarte to a

Table 19.3
Selection of Presidents and Civilian and Military Domination of Governments, 1980s

	1980	1981	1982	1983	1984	1985	1986	1987	1988	1989
Costa Rica	· · · · · · · · · · · EC · · · · · · · · · · · · · · · · · · EC · · · · · · · · · · · · · ·
El Salvador	NC + + + + + LC + + .. + + EC ... + ... + ... + ... + ... + ... + EC
Guatemala	+ + + + + + +GM + GM + + + + + + + + +EC .. + + .. + + .. + + .. +
Honduras	+ + + + + + + EC .. + + .. + + ... + ... + ... + EC ... + ... + ... + ... +
Nicaragua	> > > > > > > > > > > > > > > > EP > > > > > > > > > > > >

E, chosen by general election.
G, came to office by military coup.
N, named by a junta that originated in a coup.
L, chosen by a legislature that was elected by the public.
C, president is a civilian.
M, president is a military officer.
P, president is head of a party that controls the military.

+ + + +	military dominates the government.
+ + .. + +	military exercises strong veto power over the civilian president.
+ ... + ... +	military exercises a less strong veto over the president.
....	civilian politicians dominate the government.
> > > > >	government dominated by party that controls the military; military's loyalty is to party rather than to the constitution.

post they created called the presidency. It is examples like this that lead us to ask if the democratization of Central America was any more consequential than its economic recovery.

Table 19.3 summarizes the indisputable facts, sidestepping nuances and controversies over the freedom and representativeness of individual elections. Here we see civilians *elected* to the presidency by the voters at large—unlike Duarte in 1980—in Honduras (1982, 1986), El Salvador (1984, 1989), and Guatemala (1986). An election as free and representative as El Salvador's (i.e., far from fully) was also held in Nicaragua in 1984, while Costa Rica continued its well-established pattern of electing a new president every four years. All five nations either have had or are preparing for a second election as this is written, Honduras a third.

Even though important political forces were excluded or muted by official intimidation, by and large these elections represent an important step toward more representative government. That "by and large" is prompted by the realization that superficial democracies may disguise ongoing authoritarian regimes, shielding them from scrutiny and hence from change. Such "democracies" may legitimate, thereby solidify, undemocratic practices by incorporating them into the constitutional structure. In Guatemala, two scholars note that under the constitution that accompanied the return to "democracy" in 1985–1986,

> the power of the military has been increased, not reduced, over the situation created by the military in the constitution of 1965. In effect, "exceptional" states of seige and emergency have become normal, and institutionalized, and national security, not democracy or human rights, is the key concept.[19]

Before we pronounce the changes Central American governments underwent in the 1980s, then, we need answers to three questions that recur in democratic theory.

The first is: Did the electorate that went to the polls represent all classes and regions as well as a goodly proportion of citizens of voting age? Further, when they entered the voting booth, did these citizens find on the ballot choices that reflect major currents of opinion within that country? Second, was the atmosphere surrounding the campaign and election such that all parties could organize their followers and publicize their views free of intimidation and censorship? Third, were those who were elected able to exercise their constitutional powers? That is, once in the presidential chair, could the new civilian leaders *act* as presidents? Could they transform into policy their understanding of the national interest or of the voters' mandate?

Such questions lie at the heart of most definitions of liberal democracy. A distinguished group of U.S. and Latin American leaders, drawn from public and private sectors, endorsed just such a definition as appropriate for Central America. According to the Inter-American Dialogue, "democracies are characterized by political freedom, broad participation, regular and free elections, constitutional guarantees, and the effective control of government by elected civilians."[20] We shall refer to this definition as we evaluate Central America's progress toward democracy.

Having begun with El Salvador in 1980, let us return to its performance over the decade. The Salvadoran military conceded to elections primarily to maintain the flow of U.S. aid—nearly $4 billion during the Reagan years—since this was the *quid pro quo* demanded by the U.S. Congress. The officers struck the following deal with those elected:

> the civilian government would not try to control either the military's prosecution of the war or the absolute independence of the military as an institution. In effect, this has meant that elected governments could have no control over how the war was fought, financed, or might possibly be settled—arguably the most important issues shaping El Salvador's economic, social, and political life.[21]

These prohibitions may have been relaxed following the 1989 election of wealthy businessman Alfredo Cristiani of the right-wing ARENA party.

Cristiani was chosen by 53 percent of the voters in an election in which "an unprecedented 50 percent of the eligible electorate did not cast ballots, despite compulsory voting laws."[22] In elections held in 1982 and 1984, 75 to 80 percent of those eligible voted. One can never be certain why people do not vote. In this instance, the leftist guerrilla movement fighting the Salvadoran government asked its supporters not to vote after that movement's request for negotiations was rejected by the army and the government. The guerrillas sought a postponement of the election while the terms for their inclusion in it could be negotiated. It is fair to say, then, that participation in the 1989 election fell short on the criteria found in question one, while up until Cristiani at least, elected civilians were not allowed to rule, disqualifying El Salvador on question three. There were problems with question two as well.

While the staggering human rights abuses of the early 1980s diminished in the middle years of the decade, they accelerated at the end. In the middle years, exiled dissidents returned to test the political opening. Labor unions did likewise, staging strikes and demonstrations to protest the halving of real wages since 1979. The response to this testing of the political waters was a rise in arbitrary arrests by the military and a renewal of death-squad activities. The number of political killings increased after 1987. In early 1988, the government's own human rights commission noted the return of "the violence of the past," which threatened "to plunge us into a bloodbath."[23]

Similar problems appeared in Guatemala, where the new civilian president, Vinicio Cerezo, "has given the military a free hand in setting security policies" and where his attempt to open a dialogue with that country's leftist guerrillas (and to raise taxes in a country where the rich pay little) drew a shot across the bow in the form of two attempted coups.[24] Concluding an analysis of Guatemala in these years, Robert Trudeau stated, "it is clear that no elected civilian government has the power seriously to affect the institutional, economic, and political influence of the military and of some sectors of the civilian elite," and military influence is second to none in that society.[25]

Here too, a brief political opening quickly faded once exiles, center-left politicians, union and peasant leaders, and university critics began to make use of it. Following the second failed coup, and as the country moved toward elections, politically motivated killings and bombings rose in Guatemala, suggesting that right-wing officers and civilians were not prepared to let the limited democratic opening broaden. Among those targeted were the editorial staff of a liberal newsweekly, a support group for families of disappeared persons, union organizers, and university student leaders. From January to July 1989, this violence claimed 1,600 lives with another 800 kidnapped or "disappeared." President Cerezo's response consisted of excuses that reflected his impotence.[26]

Thus, it is clear that human rights violations have a political goal. That goal is to keep democracy superficial. Assassination and intimidation are employed to reduce both the actors in the democratic game and the options under discussion. While the number of human rights abuses in 1988 and 1989 may not have reached those of the early 1980s, numbers are beside the point. What counts is that the mechanisms of repression remained in place over the decade and that the new civilian presidents were unable to touch those mechanisms. The chill the mere presence of death squads and military torture houses cast over a society compromises democracy.

With regard to all three conditions for democracy, then, little overall progress could be discerned in El Salvador and Guatemala; gains in one department were offset by losses in another. Honduras, which was largely free of death-squad activity as the decade opened and had a history of organizing by rural workers, came to resemble its neighbors more with each passing year. Honduras is the one country where it can be said that civil liberties suffered an uninterrupted decline over the decade. Costa Rica remained largely, though not completely, free of citizen abuse by authorities and, along with Nicaragua, experienced high turnouts in elections that offered as full a spectrum of parties as that found in any North Atlantic democracy.[27]

Afflicted by more war and graver economic problems than the other four countries—both factors traceable to U.S. actions—the Nicaraguan government curbed free expression and channeled workers and peasants into organizations it dominated. The Sandinistas' record on various dimensions of democracy remained a bone of contention among scholars who claim to measure such things systematically. For 1985, the Fitzgibbon-Johnson index of political democracy (which includes free speech, independent judiciary, and the right to organize, alongside fair elections) placed Nicaragua ahead of Honduras, El Salvador, and Guatemala, in that order.[28] Freedom House, on the other hand, saw Nicaragua as the weakest of the four countries on both "political rights" and "civil liberties" in the same year.[29] The only clear agreement concerned Costa Rica, which everyone singled out as the only fully established, genuine democracy in the region. It placed first on the Fitzgibbon-Johnson ranking of twenty Latin American nations, while the other four countries were found in the third quadrant.

The third aspect of democracy, "effective control of government by elected civilians," is probably the most difficult to measure. More than the other two, however, it was directly—and negatively—influenced by the United States in the 1980s. Before exploring Washington's interference in Central America's governments once they were elected, we should note in passing that Washington also interferes in elections. The CIA is said to have spent $1.4 million bolstering two of the four parties competing in El Salvador's 1984 election, while in the same year U.S. officials cajoled and probably bribed Sandinista opponents not to participate in Nicaragua's presidential election, so as to discredit an anticipated Sandinista victory. In 1989, the Bush White House was again overtly and covertly pouring millions into the presidential campaign of Nicaraguan opposition candidate Violeta Barrios de Chamorro.[30]

KEEPING CIVILIAN PRESIDENTS IN LINE

In Central American politics, the ever-present threat of a coup acts as a no-confidence vote does in a multiparty parliamentary system. The leader knows that his or her tenure may be terminated at any moment. Thus, most Central American presidents play it safe, sacrificing reform for tenure. This was the choice made by Duarte and Cerezo. Pledges they had made as candidates to negotiate with guerrilla forces were shelved once the military high command vetoed serious negotiations. No reforms and no peace meant little progress on the economic front, especially in El Salvador where guerrillas engage in economic sabotage. This pattern fails democracy's third test. When presidents elected on popular platforms shelve those goals in response to small, unelected elites, the correct term for the ensuing regime is oligarchy, not democracy.

Honduras replicates the pattern seen in Guatemala and El Salvador. General Gustavo Alvarez headed the Honduran armed forces when the first elected president in a decade, Roberto Suazo Córdoba, took office. Alvarez continued to exercise "control in all matters pertaining to the military and its role, major foreign policy issues, internal security through his control of the police, and any major political or economic question before the government."[31] This situation survived Alvarez's ouster by fellow officers in 1984. In 1988 the Washington Office on Latin America noted that "the large amount of military aid the U.S. has provided in exchange for Honduras' cooperation has helped tip the internal political balance in favor of the already powerful armed forces."[32] Thus a triangle emerges: the president, the army, and Washington.

"The objective of [U.S.] military assistance is to create a shield to protect democratization and growth," according to the U.S. State Department.[33] One effect of that military assistance, however, is to enhance the veto power over elected presidents exercised by military officers and by other elites close to them. Limits on elected leaders arise not just through the military, moreover, but directly from Washington, as may be seen in the case of armyless Costa Rica. Costa Rica was as hard hit by the worldwide recession of the early 1980s as any of the five countries. Its gross domestic product fell 2.3 percent in 1981, then 7.3 percent the following year. Trying to keep afloat, Costa Rica acquired one of the largest external debts, per capita, in the world. Rising interest rates in the United States and the disruption of trade with Nicaragua caused by U.S. policies are among the blows the Costa Rican economy received in quick succession. President Luis Alberto Monge turned to Washington for assistance. Assistance came; U.S. foreign aid to Costa Rica, most of it economic, rose from $16 million in fiscal year (FY) 1981 to over $200 million per year in FYs 1984–1986.

The Reagan White House's insistence on channeling a portion of this aid directly to the private sector forced Costa Rica to change laws that had been on its books for three decades, creating an uproar in the sovereignty-conscious congress and a cash-flow crisis in the treasury.[34] It could be argued that Washington has a right to set conditions on the use of its money, that conditions and money are a single package that the receiving government is free to take or leave. What seems a clear infringement of Costa Rica's "effective control of government" was the pressure Washington applied to Costa Rica regarding a matter completely unrelated to the economy—a matter having more to do with U.S. policy toward Nicaragua than with Costa Rica.

Just prior to taking office in 1982, President Monge turned down a CIA scheme to promote a southern front for the Contras (Nicaraguan exiles attempting to overthrow their country's Sandinista leaders) that involved creating Contra facilities on Costa Rican soil. The following year, Monge publicly and strongly reasserted Costa Rica's traditional neutrality, a policy supported by 79 percent of the public, according to polls. But as the economy deteriorated and other options dried up, Monge realized that he needed Washington's help and, as a Costa Rican official put it at the time, "Monge can only say no to a generous friend so many times."[35] So, in secret, Monge reversed course, eventually "looking the other way" while his security minister helped the CIA construct Contra facilities, including an airstrip, on Costa Rican soil. Monge also allowed the United States to begin converting Costa Rica's civil guard into a modern army, another violation of a longstanding, publicly supported Costa Rican policy.[36]

Ironically, a dictatorial regime might have found it easier to withstand Washington's pressure. Ruled by the military harshly and undemocratically from the 1970s into the early 1980s, Guatemala told Washington to keep its money when the conditions attached to that aid included reforming Guatemala's egregious human rights abuses. The Costa Rican government was caught between its need for U.S. economic assistance, a need fueled by public expectations of a high level of government services, and its well-formed sense of Costan Rican national interests, which included the neutrality and demilitarization also supported by the public. At the time, two U.S. scholars noted that "U.S. offers of aid are first criticized, and then cautiously accepted," suggesting the pressure Monge was under.[37]

When Oscar Arias replaced Monge as president, the Costa Rican economy was on the mend. Among Arias's first moves was a return to those established policies of neutrality and demilitarization. This elicited renewed pressures from Washington. CIA director William Casey flew down and demanded a secret meeting with Arias. When Arias said he would only meet Casey openly, the CIA director left in a huff, to be followed by the Assistant Secretary of State for the region Elliott Abrams, the head of the U.S. Army's Southern Command, General John Galvin, and National Security Adviser Frank Carlucci, among others.[38] As Arias stuck to his defense of Costa Rican national interests, U.S. economic assistance fell. From the more than $200 million typical of the middle years of the decade, it descended to $83 million in the last Reagan administration request (FY 1990).[39]

Similar cases could be cited for the other countries, with Honduras and El Salvador the recipients of both the greatest pressure and the largest amounts of foreign aid, much of it covering the current accounts deficits of those governments. The 1984 Kissinger Report, which the Reagan administration claimed as its guide to Central American policy, states that "there is no self-determination when there is foreign compulsion or when nations make themselves tools of a strategy designed in other countries."[40] Like many statements aimed at Sandinista Nicaragua, this one boomerangs into a commentary on U.S. actions elsewhere.

In some instances the strategy designed in Washington and foisted on a Central American president was part of an effort by one branch of the U.S. government to influence another branch. One is hard put to argue that the national interests of the Central American country caught in such a maneuver were being served. Again, one example stands for many. In March 1986, Sandinista troops crossed into Honduran territory to attack Contra camps. In order to persuade the U.S. House of Representatives to vote military aid to the Contras, the Reagan administration wanted to portray this Sandinista incursion as an all-out offensive to wipe the Contras out.

> The White House wanted maximum publicity and to this end decided to make available $20 million in emergency military aid to Honduras. But the law required a formal request from the recipient. Honduras refused to admit there was an incursion because that would confirm the presence of contra camps [complicating Honduran relations with Nicaragua to the detriment of Honduran national interests]. The Honduran army refused even to call a state of alert.[41]

Honduran civilian and military leaders correctly read the incursion for what it was—limited—and went on holiday.

To bring the Honduran government around, U.S. Ambassador John Ferch was dispatched to President José Azcona's bungalow, telling him, "You don't have a choice now." Azcona thought it over and replied, "Okay, let's draft something." Azcona duly consulted the Honduran military command then sent the White House the request it wanted.[42]

Descriptively, no summary of Central American domestic politics can avoid Washington's role. Analytically, no treatment of democracy can stop with citizens casting ballots on election day, the government counting those ballots, and a civilian ending up in the president's chair—even if all this is done freely and fairly. To have meaning, democracy must include not just a leader freely chosen by a broad electorate that has real options before it, but a leader who then is able to make policy with that country's interests foremost in mind. Presidents act within limits set up by each country's constitution, congress, and courts, to be sure, but those limits are distinguishable from limits imposed by nonelected military officers and by foreign officials.

Since the foreign officials most deeply involved in Central American governments in the 1980s were from the United States, and since the independent power of the Central American military is underwritten by Washington, it is small wonder that U.S. officials frequently link democracy in Central America to elections rather than to what happens in between them. The one time when U.S. officials can be counted on to give a more complete definition of democracy is when the government in question is Marxist, nationalist, or both, as was true of the Sandinista regime in Nicaragua. Speaking to the U.N. General Assembly in 1987, President Reagan said, "We will not, and the world community will not, accept phony 'democratization' designed to mask the perpetuation of dictatorship." Reagan went on to enumerate a set of conditions that a government must meet to be worthy of the name democracy, including the right of exiles to return and to organize, free media, no political prisoners, and "the people's rights to choose their own destiny."[43] This is a test that Guatemala, El Salvador, and Honduras would have failed along with Nicaragua.

Can Central America's newly elected presidents wrest power from their guardians at home, the military, or from their guardians abroad, primarily Washington? This question will be decided in a complex game played with the economic elites that traditionally have turned to the military to stave off "communism"—by which they mean income taxes higher than 10 percent and anyone to the left of Ronald Reagan. Time has eroded the dominance that the oligarchy had over both the military and the *oficialista* political parties to win staged or stolen elections. First in Guatemala, later in El Salvador and Honduras, army officers have asserted their autonomy from traditional economic elites while stopping short of a complete divorce. (In Nicaragua, the Somozas went down relying on the National Guard and a small circle of cronies, having alienated business as a class.)

In this shifting but still synergistic relationship, business elites have come to rely on the military for protection in the broadest sense, including the nullification of economic reforms, while officers have turned to private sector leaders both to provide the economic motor of military regimes and to cut individual officers into lucrative business opportunities. Shared concern for stability in the social order, aided by an ideology of virulent anti-communism, has kept this alliance intact even while the balance of dominance and subordination within it has shifted.

Washington's recipe for empowering civilian regimes led by middle-class politicians has been the "professionalization" of the military through advanced training and equipment, supposedly to induce officers to respect civilian supremacy. To date, however, no amount of U.S. training has produced a Central American officer corps willing to subordinate itself to elected civilian leaders it did not like, although large amounts of U.S. aid do buy compliance for awhile. Over the past half century, civilian supremacy has been achieved only by abolishing the established military elite, never by reforming it. Following its 1948 revolution, Costa Rica disbanded its army, substituting a small civil guard led by officers appointed by the president. Costa Rica turned to international organizations and civilian volunteers to defend it from external invasion. The Sandinistas replaced Somoza's army with one loyal to themselves, its leadership drawn from their own guerrilla ranks.

But a solution can originate in the other partner as well. Economic elites may discover better ways to defend their interests than by violence and polarization. As the Somozas learned, repression may mean never having to compromise, but it carries the risk of losing it all. Some observers see such a transformation just beginning in Guatemala where the traditional oligarchy is losing ground to pragmatic businessmen in this the Central American economy with the greatest industrial output.[44] Much further along is Costa Rica, where over decades economic elites have learned how to defend their interests through wings of both political parties, through peak interest groups, and through what might be called the "mobilization of economic realities." When international donors insist upon "structural adjustments" to make the

Costa Rican economy more "efficient" (i.e., more privatized, export-oriented, and austere), business executives echo such advice as being rational and in the national interest. Even popular social democratic presidents have accepted that argument. During difficult economic times, the World Bank and the International Monetary Fund may be all the allies a modern economic elite needs.

Another variation on this process of incorporating economic elites into civic politics was visible in August 1989, when Nicaragua's internal, civilian opposition joined their opponents, the Sandinistas, in calling for the demobilization of the U.S.-backed Contras, despite efforts by the White House to keep the Contras alive. This internal Nicaraguan opposition includes the peak business association COSEP (Superior Council of Private Enterprise). Disassociating themselves from the armed strategy of the Contras not only won the *quid pro quo* of Sandinista guarantees of a freer election in 1990, but enhanced the legitimacy of the opposition within the country. Whatever the outcome in 1990, by choosing the electoral over the violent path, Nicaraguan businessmen and ranchers will have more influence with future governments.

The 1989 election in El Salvador saw the far-right Republican Nationalist Alliance (ARENA) capture the presidency following previous successes at the municipal and congressional levels. ARENA is a modern political party along the U.S. model, combining media skills with large financial resources, capable of projecting a simple message to the average Salvadoran. ARENA's movement from previous leader Roberto D'Aubuisson, linked to death squads and hardliners within the military, to a leader linked to the business community may signal an evolution of the Salvadoran elite or merely reflect its divisions. Both Washington and the Salvadoran military have accepted electoral outcomes in El Salvador that were not their first choice, another sign of modest movement in a democratic direction.

In all these countries economic elites are divided on the question of democratization, while the political leadership still contains politicians who, having "come up" under the old system that encouraged wheeling and dealing for personal gains, are ambivalent about genuine democracy (e.g., Suazo's behavior in Honduras in 1985). Stiffening the resolve of civilian presidents in recent years has been a highly publicized regional forum created by Contadora diplomacy and sustained by the Esquipulas process. By bringing to a regional forum previously domestic issues, such as the relationship of a government to its armed opposition, progressive civilian leaders may have found a way to strengthen their power vis-à-vis undemocratic elements at home. In yet another example of reality confounding categories, the line between domestic politics and international relations has been blurred in Central America.

REGIONAL DIPLOMACY: SIGNS OF HOPE

Local militaries failed to stamp out the armed opposition and thereby deliver the much sought-after peace on military terms. The Reagan administration failed to rally regional governments to its solutions, due in part to its incapacitation following the Iran-Contra scandal, and in part to the intrusiveness and hypocrisy that characterized Reagan policy all along (including the double standard of democracy discussed in the preceding section). Into this vacuum moved the presidents of the five republics, led by Costa Rica's Oscar Arias. In a wavering trajectory stretching from Esquipulas II (August 1987) through El Tesoro (February 1989) to Tela (August 1989), the presidents advanced to a point where they no longer could turn back. Alternatively bolstering and hectoring each other, the five leaders accepted the link between peace and democracy that Washington asserted, but turned this logic against the White House by demanding the demobilization of the Contras, claiming that the political space reopened inside of Nicaragua no longer justified an externally mounted military opposition.

In theory Nicaragua was not singled out; negotiations aimed at incorporating leftist guerrillas into the political processes of El Salvador and Guatemala also were to go forward. Ironically, but hardly surprising, advances appeared only in "nondemocratic" Nicaragua, for only there did the president control the military. In Guatemala and El Salvador, as we have seen, the army vetoed efforts by Cerezo and Duarte to negotiate solutions to long-standing civil wars, sensing perhaps that their power and purse would diminish as a result, or merely not accepting home-grown Marxists as a legitimate domestic opposition.

Cerezo's proposal of creating a Central American parliament was yet another part of the peace plan, a feature that could expand the visibility, and eventually the clout, of civilian politicians by keeping a regional forum alive. Such a parliament is also important in attracting European support. As of late 1989, this parliament awaited only the approval of a Costa Rican congress diverted by a national election campaign.

One way to diversify and thereby lessen the external pressures on Central American democracies is to interest Japan and the European Economic Community (EEC) in supporting the region's peace process and economic recovery. While recognizing the economic significance of Central America's location and potential markets, these "trading states" are less interested than Washington in monitoring who rules Central American governments. Costa Rica's Arias toured European capitals in mid-1987. By mid-1989, European foreign ministers had met with the Central American leaders twice and promised to finance the revival of the isthmus' intraregional trade and to open European markets to Central American goods. Europe's 1989 economic assistance to Central America tripled that of 1988.[45] While that left Europe still contributing less than the United States, European aid was less likely to vanish down the rathole of government deficits or to be used as tourniquets on the wounds of war.

The most hopeful scenario for the 1990s, then, starts with the completion of the peace and reconciliation processes set in motion by the Esquipulas II Accords. Success here will release local and external resources currently locked up in war and refugees as well as attract long-term aid from Europe and Japan. Success not only would bring the new democracies greater bargaining power in dealings with Washington, due to the "diversification of dependency" created by adding Europe and Japan to the mix of major foreign supporters; success also would demonstrate to Central American publics that democracies can work. Effective performance strengthens democratic institutions more than do showcase elections.

These new foreign donors have *their* conditions for assisting Central America, to be sure, but unlike the Reagan agenda, theirs are aligned with goals the Central American presidents have chosen: peace through reconciliation of warring factions (with ideology no barrier), respect for sitting governments (again with ideology not a consideration), democracy broadly defined and tailored to each country's circumstances, and greater unification of the region, especially in economic matters.

Tenuous and reversible as these trends remain, at decade's end they could be seen falling into place. Reports such as that of the International Commission for Central American Recovery and Development lent this movement both intellectual underpinning and international visibility. Nurtured, these beginnings could generate the synergies of peace, democracy, and equitable development that so eluded the region in the 1980s.

A LOCAL MODEL?

While it is foolish to idealize Costa Rica, as some do with talk of a "Switzerland of Central America," it is equally important not to lose sight of the implications Costa Rica holds for theories outlined in the introduction to this book and for choices open to other Central American countries today. How can we "blame the Iberians" by attributing the authoritarianism of Central America to longstanding cultural traits if Costa Rica has an effective, functioning democracy with less militarism than many Anglo-Saxon countries? Costa Rica may have been a backwater of the Spanish empire but Spain provided its roots.

Costa Rica also raises problems for *dependencia* fundamentalists who suggest that the game is over—all options lost except that of a breakaway socialist revolution—in a peripheral country dependent on the industrialized world to buy its produce and finance its debt. At least some Costa Rican governments have carved from the conditions of dependency significant room for maneuver. Finally, while there is much about Costa Rica that seems to vindicate modernization theory, practitioners of that theory rarely give politics the determining role it deserves. Modern values did not simply wash into Costa Rica through its contacts with the industrialized world. Costa Ricans took charge of their destiny at specific political moments.

Earlier in this chapter investments in human resources were singled out as one way to promote democracy and production while meeting the immediate needs of Central America's poor. One of the political choices Costa Rican leaders made in the postwar era was to adopt such a strategy. The success of that strategy explains, as well as any single factor can, Costa Rica's being today both more democratic politically and more resilient economically than its neighbors. Notice that this explanation owes little to the "history is destiny" view of those who would note Costa Rica's success only to dismiss its relevance. On several indicators of public welfare, Costa Rica was scarcely different from its neighbors in the 1950s and 1960s. If it is different in 1990, that is due to decisions Costa Rican governments took that other governments also can take—including Washington as it decides how best to support democracy and development in this region. This is not to suggest that a priority on human resource investment would come easily or cheaply elsewhere—especially where militaries drain government budgets—only that it is not as difficult as other solutions, such as dismantling those military establishments.

Through something as obvious as bringing safe drinking water to most of the population (79 percent by 1982), the Costa Rican government removed the leading cause of death and debilitation among Central American children— diarrheal diseases—and with it a major contributor to malnutrition. An aggressive immunization program accompanied by a network of free local clinics completed this task of eliminating many chronic diseases. As a consequence Costa Rica not only has a healthy population but a declining birth rate, since parents who have confidence in the survival of their first-born feel less need to have more children. Costa Rica's population growth dropped from 3.7 percent per year in 1960–1965 (one of the world's highest) to 2.7 in 1980–1985, while Honduras's only moved from 3.5 to 3.4. The life expectancy of Costa Ricans is just one year shorter than that of U.S. citizens but thirteen to fourteen years longer than that of Guatemalans, Hondurans, and Nicaraguans.[46] Malnutrition in children, which stood at 14 percent in 1966, was just 2 percent in 1988.[47]

Investment also was made in schools, roads, and electrification throughout the countryside. The results of these complementary investments are visible in various "quality of life" scales. One scale concocted by the Overseas Development Council, using data from the early 1980s, placed Costa Rica at 91 on a scale of 100. Japan and Sweden were 99. The other four Central American republics ranged from 60 to 71.[48] A high quality of life reduces "brain drain"; a country does not educate people to see them emigrate. (How much talent lies among that quarter of the Salvadoran population now estimated to reside in the United States?) Healthy children are easier to educate. Educated, healthy workers adapt more readily to new economic conditions, including new markets and technologies. Thus Costa Rica can do a better job than its neighbors of diffusing information, utilizing the cooperatives to which many producers belong.

It is not surprising, then, that Table 19.1 shows Costa Rica gaining more ground economically in the 1970s and losing less ground in the 1980s than the other countries. It is the only one of the five to have gotten much benefit from the Caribbean Basin Initiative, which it did by rapidly developing nontraditional exports and expanding its niche in the U.S. apparel market.[49] World Bank studies claim that the economic returns on investment in education exceed those from any other sector.[50] Costa Rica would seem to substantiate that.

The Costa Rican political system also is resilient, owing to the legitimacy it derives from a public that feels decently treated; owing also to the flexibility generated by two national political parties alternating in the presidency. In a study of Costa Rican voting and public opinion, Seligson and Goméz found a reservoir of public support for the system that was not shaken in times of economic crisis, even though the public was critical of specific leaders.[51] This generalized support gives democratic institutions and leaders room to make mistakes and to recover. Earlier we saw Monge's administration drawn into Washington's machinations; we also saw the next president, Oscar Arias, reassert Costa Rica's priorities. Within two years, Arias had outflanked Reagan in regional diplomacy and positioned his country to take advantage of new debt reduction measures. Thus, mistakes made under previous administrations, such as the excessive borrowing from abroad under Oduber or Monge's failure to defend Costa Rican neutrality, were rectified.

In the preceding chapter, Richard Millett accurately portrays most Central American elites as postponing payments on their country's social and political debts until their options dwindle. While not always on time, Costa Rica's elite has made those payments, thus avoiding a buildup of unresolved issues. As a result Costa Rica has been able to process new issues as they arose, including ecological viability, regional unification, drug trafficking, and women's roles. Costa Rica is at the forefront of efforts to redefine national security in Central America away from unilateral military capability toward regional agreements backed by international organizations and is at the forefront of environmental policies for the tropics.

There are many explanations for Costa Rica's ability to work through problems that have trapped sister republics in vicious cycles of class conflict, political instability, and stop-go economies. One difference is difficult to duplicate: the absence in Costa Rica of that autonomous military elite Washington has strengthened in the name (yes) of democracy. Another difference, however, could be put in place throughout the region without so major a change, assuming international funding and the support of modern elements within local economic elites. This change is the strategy of investing in human resources that has so clearly paid off for Costa Rica.

NOTES

1. Address to the Twelfth Annual Conference on the Caribbean Basin, Miami, December 2, 1988, reprinted as *Current Policy* 1137 (Washington, D.C.: U.S. Department of State, January 1989).

2. Ibid.

3. In this chapter Central America includes Guatemala, Honduras, El Salvador, Nicaragua, and Costa Rica, following a common usage explained in the preceding chapter by Richard Millett. The Caribbean Basin embraces these countries plus Belize and Panama on the isthmus and ten island states in the Caribbean.

4. These are preliminary data from CEPAL's year-end *Balance Preliminar de la Economía Latinoamericana*. See the Economist Intelligence Unit's quarterly country reports *Guatemala, El Salvador, Honduras* and *Nicaragua, Costa Rica, Panama,* 1989.

5. A team of international economists, invited by the Sandinista leaders to analyze Nicaragua's economy and given unusual access to that country's records, discovered a 70

percent decline in consumption since 1979. The prognosis in 1989 was for further contraction. "Nicaragua Study Reports Economy in Drastic Decline," *New York Times,* June 26, 1989, p. A1; "For Sandinistas, Newest Enemy is Hard Times," *New York Times,* July 6, 1989, p. A6.

6. "In Long-Suffering Central America, the Workers Suffer Most," *New York Times,* September 8, 1987, p. A14.

7. Speech reprinted in *Current Policy* 944 (Washington, D.C.: U.S. Department of State, April 1987).

8. Letter of transmittal opening "The U.S. and Central America: Implementing the National Bipartisan Commission Report," U.S. Department of State Special Report 148 (Washington, D.C.: U.S. Department of State, August 1986).

9. Different sources cite different debt-to-export earning ratios, owing to the variety of short- and long-term, public and private, debt. The sharply rising trend appears in all calculations, however. This figure is from "La cooperación internacional para Centroamérica," *Esta Semana* (San José, Costa Rica), April 14, 1989, p. 6.

10. Compromising the publicized policy of opening U.S. markets to Central American and Caribbean goods were a series of measures taken on behalf of U.S. producers of sugar, citrus juice, textiles, flowers, etc. The net effect, according to a GAO study, is that "the resulting trade and investment have not been sufficient to generate broadly based economic growth, alleviate debt-servicing problems, or create lasting employment." The General Accounting Office is the research arm of the U.S. Congress. See its July 1988 report "Caribbean Basin Initiative: Impact on Selected Countries" (GAO/NSIAD-88-177).

11. *The Report of the International Commission for Central American Recovery and Development* (Durham, N.C.: Duke University Press, 1989), pp. 5, 21–23. Hereafter referred to as *The Report.* This international body, also known as the "Sanford Commission" after its instigator, U.S. Senator Terry Sanford, consisted of forty-seven experts drawn from twenty countries. One of the co-chairs and twenty of the members were Central Americans. The Commission's recommendations were widely published in Central America in the early months of 1989. See, for example, March and April issues of the Costa Rican weekly *Esta Semana.*

12. "In Long-Suffering Central America," p. A14.

13. *The Report,* pp. 40–50. On food imports, see "Para Xabier Gorostiaga la Comisión Sanford ofrece una alternative regional," *Esta Semana,* April 7, 1989.

14. *The Report,* p. 40.

15. Hernando de Soto, *The Other Path: The Invisible Revolution in the Third World* (New York: Harper and Row, 1989).

16. *The Report,* p. 54–55.

17. *The Report,* p. 1.

18. James Wilkie and Enrique Ochoa, eds., *Statistical Abstract of Latin America,* vol. 27 (Los Angeles: UCLA Latin American Center Publications, 1989), table 1002. Hereafter referred to as SALA-27.

19. Jennifer Schirmer's forthcoming work cited by Robert Trudeau. "The Guatemalan Elections of 1985," *Elections and Democracy in Central America,* ed. John Booth and Mitchell Seligson (Chapel Hill: University of North Carolina Press, 1989), p. 118.

20. The Inter-American Dialogue, *The Americas in 1989: Consensus for Action* (Queenstown, Md.: Aspen Institute, 1989), p. 50.

21. Morris Blachman and Kenneth Sharpe, "Things Fall Apart: Trouble Ahead in El Salvador," *World Policy Journal* 6:1 (Winter 1988–1989), pp. 124–125.

22. Terry Karl, "Negotiations or Total War," *World Policy Journal* 6:2 (Spring 1989), p. 321.

23. "Plummeting Into the Abyss," *Newsweek,* May 23, 1988.

24. "Unlikely Allies in Guatemala: Army and Civilian Chief," *New York Times,* July 6, 1988, p. A2.

25. Trudeau, "The Guatemalan Election of 1985," p. 106.

26. "Crean frente contra la violencia en Guatemala," *Esta Semana,* September 22, 1989, p. 10; Amnesty International, *Guatemala: Human Rights Under the Civilian Government* (New York: Amnesty International U.S.A., 1989).

27. As a percentage of the population twenty years or older, voters in presidential elections reached 87 in Costa Rica (1982) and 91 in Nicaragua (1984). The other three countries fell in the 60 to 80 range. SALA-27, table 1008.

28. SALA-27, table 1005.

29. Raymond Gastil, *Freedom in the World: Political Rights and Civil Liberties 1987–88* (New York: Freedom House, 1988), table 6.

30. José García, "El Salvador: Recent Elections in Historical Perspective," in *Elections and Democracy in Central America,* p. 75; Latin American Studies Association Delegation, *The Electoral Process in Nicaragua: Domestic and International Influences* (Austin, Tex.: LASA Secretariat, 1984), p. 31. On Nicaragua, also see Roy Gutman, *Banana Diplomacy: The Making of American Policy in Nicaragua, 1981–1987* (New York: Simon and Schuster, 1988), chap. 11.

31. Philip Shepherd, "Honduras," in *Confronting Revolution,* ed. Morris Blachman et al. (New York: Pantheon Books, 1986), p. 135. As its Contra card lost value with the peace agreements of 1988–1989, Honduras positioned itself to retain U.S. largesse by becoming a host for U.S. military installations being phased out of the Canal Zone.

32. *Latin America Update* 13:5 (September–October 1988), p. 1.

33. U.S. Department of State, "The U.S. and Central America," p. 2.

34. Economic data on Costa Rica are from SALA-27, tables 1306, 2800, 2808, and 2837.

35. Morris Blachman and Ronald Hellman, "Costa Rica," in *Confronting Revolution,* ed. Morris Blachman et al. (New York: Pantheon Books, 1986), pp. 175–176, 180.

36. On the militarization of Costa Rica's civil guard, see ibid. Costa Rica's collaboration with the CIA and the Contras is one of the "admitted facts" provided disputants in the Oliver North trial by the Justice Department in lieu of declassifying federal documents. My source: "Costa Rica en el affaire Irán-Contras," *Esta Semana,* May 5, 1989.

37. Blachman and Hellman, "Costa Rica," p. 179.

38. James Morrell, "The Nine Lives of the Central American Peace Process," an International Policy Report (Washington, D.C.: Center for International Policy, 1989), p. 3.

39. It could be argued, of course, that Costa Rica needed less aid as its economy recovered. While not all the data are in, per capita production in Guatemala at the end of the 1980s would not seem that much different from Costa Rica's, yet the Reagan administration requested $149 million in economic aid for Guatemala in FY 1990 but only $83 million for Costa Rica. SALA-27, table 2837; "EE.UU daría al país $83 millones," *La Nación* (San José, Costa Rica), January 10, 1989, p. A4.

40. National Bipartisan Commission on Central America, *Report of the National Bipartisan Commission on Central America* (Washington, D.C.: U.S. Government Printing Office, 1984), p. 12.

41. Gutman, *Banana Diplomacy,* pp. 324–325.

42. Ibid. Several CIA actions that damaged Nicaragua were similarly staged with Congress in mind. "Fucking Casey wants something that makes news," said the exasperated CIA operative in charge of contra operations, meaning news *in the United States* that the Contras are effective in taking their war to Nicaraguan cities. CIA Director William Casey got his "news" with the shelling of a Nicaragua port, the bombing of the airport serving the capital, and the mining of Nicaraguan harbors. Bob Woodward, *Veil* (New York: Pocket Books, 1988), p. 293, passim.

43. U.S. Department of State, "America's Vision of the Future," *Current Policy* 1001 (Washington, D.C.: U.S. Department of State, 1987).

44. Mario Solórzano Martínez, "Surge un arco iris político en Guatemala," *Esta Semana,* August 11, 1989. The author is a leading Guatemalan social scientist and social democratic politician.

45. Economist Intelligence Unit's country report *Guatemala, El Salvador, Honduras,* 1989, no. 3, p. 8. "CEE considerá ayuda al istmo tras la cumbre," *La República* (San José, Costa Rica), February 22, 1989.

46. María Eugenia Gallardo and José Roberto López, *Centroamérica: la Crisis en Cifras* (San José, Costa Rica: IICA and FLACSO, 1986), pp. 35 and 191 (Tables 1.2 and 4.1).

Other data from Dr. Howard Hiatt, "Costa Rica: Success in a Tough Neighborhood," *International Herald Tribune,* December 10, 1986.

47. "Malnutrition in Kids Down," *Tico Times* (San José, Costa Rica), February 17, 1989, p. 30.

48. A composite index of infant mortality, life expectancy, and literacy. Council on Hemispheric Affairs, "Quality of Life in the Americas," *Washington Report on the Hemisphere,* April 2, 1985.

49. Stuart Tucker, "Trade Unshackled: Assessing the Value of the Caribbean Basin Initiative," *Central American Recovery and Development,* ed. William Ascher and Ann Hubbard (Durham, N.C.: Duke University Press, 1989).

50. "Investing in People," *The Newsletter from the International Center for Economic Growth,* 3:1 (July 1989). Paraphrasing Gerald Meier, this article suggests that "capital stock should be interpreted as including the body of knowledge possessed by the population and its capacity to use that knowledge."

51. Mitchell Seligson and Miguel Goméz B., "Ordinary Elections in Extraordinary Times," *Elections and Democracy in Central America.* A generalized trust in the system can be read in a declining rate of abstention in elections and in the inability of leftist candidates to attract more than 8 percent of the vote. It also appears in public opinion polls.

SUGGESTED READINGS

Ameringer, Charles. *Democracy in Costa Rica.* New York: Praeger, 1982. Analyzes the one Central American country to successfully bring democracy and development to most of its population. Ameringer's analysis stops as the recession of the early 1980s hit; for a description of what followed, see the chapter on Costa Rica in Blachman et al.

Anderson, Thomas P. *Politics in Central America: Guatemala, El Salvador, Honduras and Nicaragua.* Second edition. New York: Praeger, 1988. A solid introduction to the history and politics of four of the five nations treated in this chapter. (For the fifth, see Ameringer above.) Contains helpful bibliography.

Barry, Tom, and Deb Preusch. *The Central American Fact Book.* New York: Grove Press, 1986. Data-laden introduction to all the countries of the region, including Belize and Panama, emphasizing the role of U.S. corporations and government. Written from a critical perspective familiar to readers of the NACLA reports.

Blachman, Morris, William LeoGrande, and Kenneth Sharpe, eds. *Confronting Revolution: Security Through Diplomacy in Central America.* New York: Pantheon Books, 1986. A collection of individually authored essays on the nations of Central America as well as countries that interacted with them in the 1980s (Soviet Union, Cuba, Mexico, the United States, etc.). Domestic trends are related to international relations.

Booth, John, and Mitchell Seligson, eds. *Elections and Democracy in Central America.* Chapel Hill: University of North Carolina Press, 1989. Individually authored essays analyzing recent elections in the five republics accompanied by chapters by the two editors that provide helpful definitions and hypotheses.

Booth, John, and Thomas A. Walker. *Understanding Central America.* Boulder, Colo.: Westview Press, 1989. An up-to-date overview and interpretation of Central America's situation by two U.S. political scientists who have written frequently on the region, especially on Nicaragua.

Current History. A monthly periodical that usually devotes one issue each year to Central America with articles written by scholars that summarize recent developments in selected countries as well as U.S. policy.

Gilbert, Dennis. *Sandinistas: The Party and the Revolution.* New York: Basil Blackwell, 1988. An analysis of this "odd man out" in Central America that focuses on the Sandinistas' ideology and organization—and thus helps one understand their conceptions of democracy and elections.

Gutman, Roy. *Banana Diplomacy: The Making of American Policy in Nicaragua, 1981–1987.* New York: Simon and Schuster, 1988. A thorough and critical history of Reagan policy toward the region, exposing the contradictions and infighting of a divided administration. By a *Newsday* reporter.

Hamilton, Nora, Jeffrey Frieden, Linda Fuller, and Manuel Pastor, Jr., eds. *Crisis in Central America: Regional Dynamics and U.S. Policy in the 1980s.* Boulder, Colo.: Westview Press, 1988. Individually authored chapters on a broad range of topics from perspectives critical of Washington. Includes chapters analyzing economic trends and refugees as well as diplomatic and military strategies.

International Commission for Central American Recovery and Development. *The Report of the International Commission for Central American Recovery and Development: Poverty, Conflict and Hope.* Durham, N.C.: Duke University Press, 1989. Analysis and recommendations of the "Sanford Commission" of international experts, half of them Latin American. Includes the Esquipulas II Accords and a wealth of data. Stresses the interaction of political, economic, and security issues—as have most such reports including the Kissinger Commission's—with a strong emphasis on investment in human resources.

Irvin, George, and Xabier Gorostiaga. *Towards an Alternative for Central America and the Caribbean.* London: George Allen & Unwin, 1985. Perspectives from Europe and Latin America. Includes essays by Xabier Gorostiaga and Edelberto Torres Rivas, two Central Americans who write frequently and well on the region's current crisis and future prospects.

Mexico & Central America Report. Newsletter published every five weeks by Latin American Newsletters (London), providing objective updates on political and economic trends for English readers. Alternative sources include the quarterly "country reports" of the Economist Intelligence Unit, one on Nicaragua, Costa Rica, and Panama, another covering Guatemala, El Salvador, and Honduras.

Torres-Rivas, Edelberto. *Repression and Resistance: The Struggle for Democracy in Central America.* Boulder, Colo.: Westview Press, 1989. A cogent interpretation of Central America today, stressing political and economic factors, by a prominent Guatemalan-born social scientist living in Costa Rica, where he heads FLACSO (Facultad Latinoamericana de Ciencias Sociales). Some of this material first appeared in *Centroamérica: La Democracia Posible* (San José, Costa Rica: Editorial Universitaria Centroamericana, 1987).

20
PANAMA AND THE CANAL

STEVE C. ROPP

Panama is a country that should be well known to every citizen of the United States, because we were literally present at the creation. Panama gained its independence in 1903 largely because the United States, under President Theodore Roosevelt, was interested in constructing a canal across the isthmus. After independence, U.S. citizens in large numbers journeyed to Panama to dig "the big ditch." Upon completion of the canal in 1914, many chose to stay, becoming permanent residents of the Canal Zone. During subsequent decades, the U.S. political and economic presence on the isthmus was massive, and it was not until the 1978 signing of the Carter-Torrijos treaties that the United States recognized Panama's sovereign rights in the Canal Zone area. During recent years, Panama has remained in the public eye due to the confrontation between the U.S. government and General Manuel Antonio Noriega. The administration of President Ronald Reagan at first supported Noriega and the Panamanian Defense Forces (PDF) in exchange for help he provided in dealing with the crisis in Central America. But a policy shift began to occur in 1986 for a number of reasons, including increasing national concern about the drug problem. Beginning in 1987, both the Reagan and Bush administrations used economic sanctions and other means in an attempt to unseat Noriega. When these policies failed to remove him, President Bush launched a military invasion in December 1989 that resulted in Noriega's capture and transport to the United States to face drug trafficking charges.

And yet, in spite of our historical and contemporary involvement in isthmian affairs, there is little understanding in the United States of Panama and its people. Ironically, the very presence of the canal and the associated zone enclave seem to have led to a general belief that the canal is all (or most) of what there is to Panama. Scholarly studies have concentrated more on relations between the United States and Panama than on Panama as an independent country with a political and social system worthy of study on its own terms. With these thoughts in mind, we turn to a consideration of some of the major historical and contemporary characteristics of Panamanian politics and society.

HISTORICAL SETTING

Although geography is not always destiny, Panama has been influenced more than most countries by its location. Panama is an isthmus, a narrow strip of land 420 mi (676 km) long, which joins Central and South America. As both the narrowest and the lowest point in the Southern Hemisphere, the isthmus has historically served as a transit route from the Atlantic Ocean to the Pacific. The first Europeans to take advantage of Panama's location were the Spaniards, who occupied the isthmus soon after Vasco Nuñez de Balboa discovered in 1513 that it linked the Atlantic to the great "south sea." With the Spanish discovery and conquest of the Incan Empire after 1532, Panama became a major transit route for treasure shipped back to Spain and for slaves and foodstuffs flowing to Peru.

The social and economic system that emerged on the isthmus during colonial times reflected Panama's importance as a strategic "bridge." A small urban elite developed that derived its influence from the ability to control isthmian trade. The political and economic position of this urban elite was quite strong until the middle of the eighteenth century because the Spanish crown had made Panama City one of only three ports in all of Latin America through which trade with the mother country could be conducted. However, Panama City (and hence the urban elite) lost its favored position in the Spanish Empire during the seventeenth and eighteenth centuries when the Spanish trade monopoly in Latin America began to erode. By 1655, the British had established a military and trading base in Jamaica from which they began rapidly to expand their reach. The final blow to Panama's favored economic position came in 1739 when the British destroyed the forts protecting the isthmian trade route.

Termination of Panama's port monopoly had the effect of seriously undermining the economic base of the urban commercial and bureaucratic elite. Some members of this elite managed to maintain their power positions, but on greatly reduced sources of income. Although no longer controlling the port monopoly, they were able to turn to contraband trade with the British or to provisioning the military garrisons that continued to occupy the isthmus under Spanish, and later Colombian, rule. Most important, termination of Panama's port monopoly led to diversification within the social and economic system. While many of the high-ranking, Spanish-born administrators returned to the mother country or found bureaucratic posts elsewhere in Latin America, the locally born Creoles were forced to find other local sources of income, particularly in the countryside. There they could invest in cheap rural land. Because there was no large indigenous labor force like that found in the Andes, the major rural activity became cattle raising. Termination of the port monopoly and the attendant decline in trade thus led to the creation of a new economic class of small property owners in the interior.[1]

During the nineteenth century, those who remained on the isthmus had to adjust to a new set of relationships with outside powers. On November 28, 1821, Panama declared its independence from Spain. After considerable debate, a decision was made to affiliate with the former viceroyalty of New Granada. This led, in turn, to Panama's becoming a province of Colombia when Colombia went its separate way.

As a small but strategically important province of a weak Latin American country, Panama was tugged in a number of directions. Lacking any strong historical allegiance to Colombia, Panamanians made numerous attempts to achieve either outright independence or increased autonomy within the Colombian political system. Both Great Britain and the United States were interested in the isthmus because of its central importance to the existing and potential hemispheric transportation network. As the United States expanded across the North American continent, the isthmus came to be viewed as a major component of the "domestic" transportation system, linking the industrialized cities of the East Coast to the rapidly expanding settlements in the West.[2] In 1851, U.S. financiers underwrote the construction of a railroad across the isthmus. To forestall any possible conflict over future canal rights, the United States and Great Britain had signed the Clayton-Bulwer Treaty in 1850. This treaty guaranteed that any canal constructed by either country anywhere in Central America would not be exclusively fortified or controlled.

The social and economic consequences of Panama's new relationship with these outside powers during the nineteenth century cannot be overestimated. Renewed attention to the transit function restored the economic vitality of the urban transit area and even led to the creation of an entirely new city, called Colón, on the Atlantic side of the isthmus. Panama City once again became an economic magnet, drawing workers from the interior to construct the railroad and later to work on the canal project undertaken by the French in 1878. A second major effect of these new external relationships was to change the composition of Panama's urban lower class. Until the middle of the nineteenth century, the urban lower class consisted largely of Hispanicized blacks who had come to Panama as slaves during the colonial period to work in the transit area. Beginning with construction of the railroad, English-speaking black workers were imported in great numbers from the Caribbean islands. At the height of the U.S. canal-building effort in 1910, the Panama Canal Company employed over 35,000 such workers. Many remained in urban Panama after the canal was completed in 1914. Their English language and Protestant religion set them apart from preexisting Panamanian culture and society.

Growing U.S. interest in constructing a canal across the isthmus led to Panama's independence from Colombia in 1903. President Theodore Roosevelt gave tacit encouragement to Panamanian nationalists intent on liberating the isthmus from Colombian rule. The result was an uprising on November 3, 1903, that led to the creation of the Republic of Panama.

Not surprisingly, U.S. influence in early Panamanian politics was extensive. Article 136 of the new constitution granted the United States the right to "intervene in any part of Panama, to reestablish peace and constitutional order if it has been disturbed."[3] Panamanian politicians frequently called upon U.S. officials in the Canal Zone for help in restoring order when it suited their purposes. Additionally, many high-level positions in the Panamanian bureaucracy were held by U.S. citizens. The United States also exercised overwhelming economic influence in the new republic. The primary source of such influence was the Canal Zone, the 10-mi-wide (16-km) strip of U.S.-controlled land that cut the isthmus in half. Employing a large number of U.S. and Panamanian workers, it was both a major source of jobs and a market for Panamanian products. Furthermore, large banana plantations established by the U.S.-owned United Fruit Company in the interior employed many Panamanians and served as a primary source of export income for the new nation.

As in a number of other Latin American nations, the highly visible U.S. political and economic presence eventually caused a strong nationalist reaction, particularly in the 1920s and 1930s. During this period, a number of factors worked to seriously undermine the economy. There was a massive reduction of the canal work force after completion of the locks in 1914, and heavy debts were incurred by the national government, leading to a cutback in public sector employment after 1916.

On August 19, 1923, a semisecret nationalist group was formed that embodied much of the resentment felt by Panamanians toward the United States as well as toward the Antillean blacks who held many of the jobs in the Canal Zone. Called Community Action, it espoused Hispanic nationalism.

Although not the founder of Community Action, Arnulfo Arias soon became its natural leader. Born on a small cattle ranch in the interior in 1901, Arias graduated from Harvard Medical School and returned to Panama where he practiced medicine and began to dabble in politics. Elected president on three separate occasions (1940, 1949, and 1968), he was never allowed to complete a full term.

The political movement led by Arnulfo Arias was partially displaced by another emerging political force beginning in the 1950s. After Panama achieved independence in 1903, the army was disbanded due to the threat it posed to the political elite and to the United States. Only a small police force was retained. However, during the 1930s, the National Police gradually began to gain political influence under the guidance of José Antonio Remón. By the late 1940s, Colonel Remón and his police organization had become important arbiters in the feuds among leaders of the traditional political parties. Using the police as a springboard, Remón won the presidential election in 1952. Several years later, the National Police was converted into a National Guard and given a new, expanded military role.

With the rise in the power and influence of the National Guard in the 1950s, the base was laid for the contemporary structure of Panamanian politics. Although the government returned to civilian hands after Remón's assassination in 1955, the National Guard retained much of its political influence. During this period, the guard became increasingly professionalized as more officers with academy training entered it. Because of the Cold War, the United States greatly expanded its military assistance programs during the 1950s, and many Panamanian soldiers were trained at U.S. installations.

On October 11, 1968, the civilian government of President Arnulfo Arias was overthrown by a military coup. The young lieutenant colonel who soon emerged as the central figure in the National Guard was Omar Torrijos. He quickly moved Panamanian policy in a symbolically anti-U.S. direction and restored diplomatic relations with Castro's Cuba. Although Torrijos and the National Guard never displayed the same degree of anti-U.S. sentiment that existed in the early days of Community Action, the restoration of the armed forces to a central position in Panamanian politics created an important new institutional base from which nationalist sentiments could be voiced.

SOCIOECONOMIC STRUCTURES AND THEIR IMPACT ON POLITICS

Panama's contemporary social and economic structures are the product of its unique development as a transit area that continues to attract the attention of major world powers. From 1903 until the 1970s, the factor that most directly affected the nature of the economy was the existence of a foreign-controlled enclave (the Canal Zone) in the heart of urban Panama. Although foreign-controlled enclaves have been common elsewhere in Latin America, the economic importance and geographic centrality of the Canal Zone were such that they largely determined not only the rate and direction of national economic growth but also the nature of the domestic class structure. Urban commercial groups and rural cattlemen depended heavily on the Canal Zone as a market for their products. Perhaps most important, the existence of the zone played a determining role in the evolution of Panama's urban working class.

In many Latin American countries, the urban working class has served as an important base of support for political leaders intent on restructuring internal relations between elites and masses or relations between the nation and outside powers. In the case of Panama, the working class has remained relatively dormant. This dormancy is due to the fact that since 1903, workers have operated within the context of an alliance between Canal Zone and Panamanian elites that actively worked to limit the workers' influence. During the early years of the republic, repression of working-class interests was often brutal and exercised through the direct use of military force. For example, when canal workers living in Panama City went on strike in 1925 to keep rents from being raised, Panamanian slumlords called on U.S. troops from the zone to quell the rioting.

The ease with which working-class demands were historically repressed was due to two rather unique features that affected labor's bargaining power. First, Canal Zone workers were organized into unions that had their primary ties to the United States rather than to Panama. Second, the Canal Zone work force was largely composed of English-speaking blacks who enjoyed little sympathy among the Spanish-speaking Panamanian population. The fact that Canal Zone workers historically received higher wages by national standards led to the general perception that they were a "labor elite," privileged and culturally distinct from Panamanians elsewhere in the republic.

During the 1960s and 1970s, the rapid movement of people from the interior provinces to Panama City and the canal area served to reduce somewhat the cultural distance between the national population as a whole and the working class. As in many other Latin American countries, Panama's urban population grew very rapidly, increasing from 36 percent of the national total in 1950 to 48 percent by 1970.[4] The result of this massive internal migration was the creation of a large, culturally and economically heterogenous class of urban poor living in numerous squatter settlements around Panama City.

A secondary effect of the massive migration of the 1960s and 1970s was to reinforce the historic marginality of the countryside. The interior provinces continued to be neglected by urban politicians representing the interests of commercial elites, so that neither the rural cattlemen nor the peasants really prospered. However, the structure of the rural economy was significantly altered during these two decades. Historically, the Panamanian peasant engaged in subsistence farming on small plots of land that were owned by the government. The expansion of commercial cattle-raising activities greatly reduced the amount of land available to peasants. In addition to forcing many of them off the land and into the cities, this development had the effect of increasing tension between cattlemen and peasants.

Panamanian politics stands on the foundation of these specific social and economic structures. The economic centrality of the canal enclave gave the urban commercial elite the economic resources with which to govern but, at the same time, undermined its political legitimacy. The commercial elite was viewed by many Panamians (particularly those in the interior) as acting not so much in the national interest as in its own class interest and in the interest of the United States. The divisions that existed within the urban working class (because this class was partially composed of black Antilleans) also had a major impact on the nature of Panamanian politics. Politicians who wished to alter class relations had difficulty constructing broadly based mass coalitions in the urban areas.

The military regime that controlled politics following the 1968 coup came to power partly because of changes that occurred in Panama's basic social and economic structures. Power was taken from the hands of the urban economic elite that had held sway since 1903. In contrast to members of this elite, General Torrijos was born and raised in the interior. And although his anti-urban biases were not as strong as the smoldering antagonism of the marginalized cattlemen who supported Arnulfo Arias, his concern for the culture and economy of rural Panama was just as real. This concern was reflected in the facts that Torrijos spent a great deal of time traveling in the countryside and that the government moved rapidly after 1968 to address some of the economic problems of Panamanian peasants.

The Torrijos years (1968–1981) were transitional ones with the National Guard's leadership attempting to reconcile the historically antagonistic interests of urban Panama and the interior provinces.[5] With the mass migration to the cities, urban and rural Panama drew closer together. Changes in the racial composition of the labor movement and the process of industrialization began to bring this movement into the political mainstream. Although not a central component of the military regime's coalition, labor played a more important political role after 1968.

Paradoxically, while Torrijos devoted considerable attention to the economic problems of the long-neglected countryside, changes in the structure of the national economy during the 1970s further reinforced the interior's economic marginality.

Industrial growth since World War II had created an economy that consisted by the 1960s of three major parts. Supplementing the traditional service and agricultural activities was an expanded industrial manufacturing sector, which led to growth of the industrial working class. The most important economic development of the 1970s was the dramatic change in the overall importance to the Panamanian economy of these three sectors. While the service economy continued to expand at a rapid rate, industrial manufacturing activities began to level off. The same was true for the agricultural sector, which experienced a number of problems related to international competitiveness, marketing, and farm technology.

The continued rapid expansion of the service sector is important in qualitative as well as quantitative terms. Growth of this sector during the 1970s was largely the result of Panama's emergence as a "service center" for multinational corporations. Panama played a key role in the expansion of the "Latindollar" market. Traditionally, the U.S. dollar was the official Panamanian currency, and Panama could thus service the financial transactions of U.S. banks and multinationals with a minimum of red tape. During the 1970s, banks and multinational corporations located in other developed industrial nations, such as Japan, began to follow the U.S. example. Panama became a center not only for multinational banking activity but for other services that the major multinational corporations needed, such as transportation, communication, and warehousing.

The importance of this continued rapid growth of the service sector for Panamanian social and political development is difficult to assess. However, it may result in a reduction of the political influence of urban laborers engaged in manufacturing activities. Not only has the growth of the industrial labor force slowed, but the nature of the "new" service sector (with its close ties to the multinational corporations) would seem to suggest impediments to the further organization of the urban work force. One of the attractive features of service-sector workers, as perceived by multinational corporations, is their current lack of organization.[6]

A more general effect of the expansion of the service sector has been to reduce Panama's economic dependency on the United States and the U.S. government. Until the 1970s, Panama's economy relied heavily on income derived from the Canal Zone and from the banana plantations of the United Fruit Company. Service-sector expansion has reduced this direct dependency on the United States and substituted a more amorphous dependency on the international capitalist system. Given the rapidity with which major changes in the economy have taken place, it is still too early to determine precisely their political and social significance.

GOVERNMENT AND POLITICAL DYNAMICS

Although there was some modification of the Panamanian government structure after the National Guard seized power in 1968, most of its fundamental characteristics can be traced back to the isthmus's Iberian political heritage. When Panama declared its independence from Colombia in 1903, a new constitution was drafted that was based on Colombian law. Provision was made for a centralized unitary government composed of three branches—executive, legislative, and judicial. The president was to be elected for a four-year term and to be ineligible for immediate reelection.

The legislative branch centered around a unicameral National Assembly, whose members were elected for four-year terms at the same time as the president. Assembly representatives were elected from circuits corresponding to the nine provinces into which the country was divided. This traditional political system was eminently "presidential" as the chief executive normally dominated both the legislative and judicial branches. Through his power to appoint provincial governors, the president's authority extended into the countryside and influenced administration on the local level. Although the municipalities theoretically possessed more autonomy than the provinces, this autonomy was seldom manifest in practice.

After the military coup in 1968, the dominance of the executive branch became even more pronounced, but power was concentrated in military rather than in civilian hands. A new constitution was promulgated in 1972, which made General Omar Torrijos Maximum Leader of the Panamanian Revolution. As for the legislative branch, this constitution substituted a system of representation based on the nation's 505 municipal subdistricts for the National Assembly. Members of the new Assembly of Corregimientos (as the subdistricts are called) were elected for six-year terms in a process that was tightly controlled by the executive branch; the traditional political parties were allowed no role. Assembly members met only one month a year and served on local municipal councils during the remaining months. In effect, the 1972 Constitution converted the legislative branch into part of the central government's administrative apparatus.

Of central importance to understanding the changes that have occurred since 1968 has been the expanded role of the military (now called the Defense Forces). Prior to the military coup, the president of the republic was commander-in-chief of the guard as specified in the 1946 Constitution. As such, he had the right—if not always the power—to appoint and remove military personnel. Under provisions of the 1972 Constitution, the president (appointed, in fact, by Torrijos) had no such powers. Furthermore, Article 2 stated that government agencies were to act in "harmonic collaboration" with the armed forces.

General Torrijos maintained control of the military (and hence, of the political system) through a highly centralized administrative apparatus. Lines of authority ran directly from the commander-in-chief to all military units without being channeled through the General Staff. Torrijos maintained direct control over all seven of Panama's infantry companies, and no officer assignments were made, even at the lieutenant level, without his express approval.

One reason for the major political role played by the military after 1968 was that the traditional parties had been banned, largely because they were perceived as representing the interests of the traditional elites. The exception was the Communist Party, to which Torrijos turned in 1968 when he faced the possibility of a countercoup by military officers tied to the traditional elites.

From 1972 until 1978, Torrijos governed by exercising tight control over the restructured legislative branch and by relying on the Communist Party and marginalized economic groups for support. However, these tactics became increasingly untenable during the mid-1970s. The exclusion of other parties from even minimal political participation and the inability to manage the economy successfully increasingly exposed Torrijos and the General Staff to charges of administrative incompetence. Within this context, a political solution was required that would simultaneously distance the armed forces from day-to-day government affairs, preserve their influence over policy formulation, and increase the regime's support among members of the traditional commercial elite.

Torrijos's solution was to relinquish the special constitutional powers he had been granted in 1972 by promulgating a new constitution in 1978. He then "returned to the barracks" and appointed a civilian president. The traditional parties were to be allowed to participate once again in the political process through direct presidential elections held in 1984.

In 1978, the Democratic Revolutionary Party (PRD) was formed to incorporate and guide the various political groups that had historically supported the military regime. According to its declaration of principles, the PRD was to be democratic, multiclass, unitary, nationalistic, revolutionary, popular, and independent.[7] In many respects, it resembled other Latin American political parties established by military leaders to give civilian institutional form to their ideas. As with Mexico's Institutional Revolutionary Party (PRI), the Democratic Revolutionary Party attempted to ensure, through close collaboration between military, government, and party leaders, that participation of opposition groups would be carefully channeled.

Panama's gradual transition to democracy came to an abrupt end during the early 1980s for a variety of reasons. First, General Torrijos was killed in a plane crash in 1981. Although it is by no means certain that Torrijos could have successfully guided the transition process, there can be little doubt that his eventual successor as chief of the Defense Forces had no intention of doing so. By 1984, General Noriega had consolidated his domestic power base and was able to engineer the fraudulent election that resulted in a victory for presidential candidate Nicolas Ardito Barletta.

A second reason for the failure of democracy in the early 1980s was that the Reagan administration looked the other way when electoral fraud was perpetrated in 1984. The administration had proposed to Noriega that Barletta be selected as the official government candidate because of his close ties to Secretary of State George Shultz and the international banking community. Since Panama had become an important strategic ally within the context of the growing crisis in Central America, the Reagan administration was willing to settle for the construction of a democratic facade in Panama.

The U.S. invasion of December 1989 destroyed the military institution that had governed Panama for twenty years and thus appeared to enhance prospects for the creation of a true democracy. Guillermo Endara, winner of the aborted May 1989 elections, was appointed president for a five-year term and the traditional National Assembly once again assumed legislative functions.

COOPERATION AND CONFLICT
WITH FOREIGN POWERS

Because of its small size and unique geographical position, Panama's foreign relations and domestic development have been heavily influenced by outside powers.[8] By 1903, the United States had emerged as the dominant outside power with multiple sources of influence over Panama's foreign initiatives. The fact that the United States maintained a large troop presence in the Canal Zone and considered the isthmus of great strategic importance limited the contacts the Panamanian government was allowed to develop with global adversaries of the United States, such as the Soviet Union. In addition to this military presence, U.S. dominance of the economy meant that independent foreign-policy initiatives had to be cautiously pursued. During the post–World War II decades, Panama's economic reliance on the U.S. government and private companies was probably greater than that of any other country in the world.[9]

Because of the dominant position of the United States throughout most of the twentieth century, Panama's foreign policy was largely bilateral in nature. The commercial elites who controlled the foreign ministry were primarily interested in extracting the maximum economic benefit from their relationship with the United States. A secondary concern was to modify the colonial aspects of the U.S.-Panamanian relationship, particularly as it related to the Canal Zone. According to the terms of the 1903 treaty, the United States could act "in perpetuity" in the Canal Zone "as if it were the sovereign of the territory . . . to the entire exclusion of the exercise by the Republic of Panama of any such sovereign rights, power, and authority."[10] Because this broad grant of authority antagonized most Panamanians, members of the elite realized that letting it stand unchallenged risked undermining their political legitimacy. Numerous attempts were made to renegotiate the 1903 treaty in a manner that would at least symbolically satisfy Panama's nationalistic aspirations.

In spite of these attempts, the major provisions of the 1903 treaty remained unchanged until 1978. In that year, the U.S. Congress ratified two completely new treaties, the Panama Canal Treaty and the Treaty of Neutrality. The former recognizes Panamanian sovereignty over the Canal Zone and specifies that U.S. troops will be withdrawn from this area by the year 2000. This treaty was of additional importance to Panama because it conferred major economic benefits. Panama was to receive $10 million annually in the form of a fixed annuity and an additional $10 million for the performance of certain basic services for the newly formed Panama Canal Commission. In addition, Panama received $0.30 for every ton of cargo transiting the canal for an annual estimated total of between $50 million and $60 million.[11]

Ratification of the canal treaties led to a period of greater cooperation between Panama and the United States. And yet, there were storm clouds on the horizon. The fact that the Carter administration had placed so much faith in one man (and a military dictator at that) meant that it was difficult thereafter for the U.S. government to distance itself from the regime that General Torrijos left as his legacy. The Reagan administration inherited this relationship to Panama's civil-military regime and built upon it to serve its own strategic purposes.

The long "honeymoon period" in U.S.-Panamanian relations that had been created by the new canal treaties and by General Noriega's cooperation in Central America ended abruptly in 1986 when Seymour Hersh published several scathing accounts of Noriega's activities in the New York Times. Quoting high U.S. government officials, he accused the General of involvement in the torture-killing of Panamanian dissident Hugo Spadafora, lending support to left-wing guerrilla movements, and drug trafficking.[12]

Following several attempts by Noriega in late 1986 to patch up his relations with the Reagan administration, tensions increased. In June 1987, a high-ranking officer who had been forcibly retired by Noriega confirmed many of the charges that had been made earlier in the Hersh articles. Domestic opposition groups came together under the banner of the National Civic Crusade and demanded that the Defense Forces return to the barracks.

The growing conflict between the United States and the leadership of Panama's longstanding military regime was partially the product of changing definitions of national security. During the early 1980s, the United States defined national security strictly in military terms, praising Noriega for the aid he provided in preventing the spread of communism in Central America. By 1987, however, drug trafficking had also come to be considered a major security threat. The Senate Subcommittee on Terrorism and Narcotics held a series of hearings that documented Noriega's involvement in money laundering operations for the Medellin Cartel. By late 1987, Congress was leading the charge against Noriega and the White House was hurrying to catch up.

In February 1988, Noriega was indicted by two Florida grand juries on charges of drug money laundering. Its hand having been forced by these indictments, the Reagan administration moved quickly to oust him. A series of economic sanctions were implemented between March and April that succeeded in devastating the Panamanian economy but not in removing the General. For the remainder of the year and on into 1989, the United States and Panama hurled invectives at each other. Noriega claimed that the efforts to undermine his authority were intended to assure U.S. control of the canal after the year 2000.

PANAMA AFTER NORIEGA

The U.S. invasion and the rapid approach of the year 2000 make it imperative that we better understand Panama and its people. According to the terms of the 1978 treaties, the United States will turn over the canal to the Panamanian government and all U.S. troops will leave Panamanian soil at the end of the millennium. Unless a stable government can be constructed in Panama and friendly relations maintained between our two countries, the path to the future will be fraught with danger.

One key to such understanding lies in the observation that General Noriega was merely symptomatic of Panama's longstanding political and social problems. The military came to power in 1968 not because of General Noriega but because of major flaws in Panama's civilian-dominated political system. Although formally a democracy, the country had often been governed by members of the commercial elite who were largely insensitive to the needs and aspirations of the lower classes.

The military regime that came to power in 1968 represented a strain of populism and nationalism that had been repressed during previous decades by both the commercial elite and the United States. During the 1970s and early 1980s, this regime received support from various U.S. presidential administrations for many different reasons. The Carter administration considered General Torrijos a "friendly tyrant" because of his progressive social policies and a desire to negotiate new canal treaties. The Reagan administration supported General Noriega because he was both an intelligence "asset" and an ally in Central America.

Establishment of a stable democracy in Panama following Noriega's departure is in the interest of the United States because it would ensure support from the Panamanian people for the long-term security of the canal. However, the establishment of such a democracy is unlikely unless there is a historical reconciliation between the political representatives of Panama's feuding social classes. If a stable democracy is to be established, the United States must encourage such a reconciliation. The U.S. government cannot conveniently look the other way, as it has at times in the past, when fraudulent elections are held.

Although Panama's prospects for democracy are not particularly bright following twenty years of military rule, there are a few hopeful signs. Prior to implementation of U.S. economic sanctions, Panamanians enjoyed one of the highest standards of living in all of Latin America. Thus, it is well above the economic and educational thresholds that determine whether democratic government is possible at all. Furthermore, the U.S. invasion destroyed a military-police institution that had shown no inclination to facilitate a democratic transition.

Paradoxically, the long duration of Panama's military regime has created conditions that for the first time at least make possible the establishment of a true democracy. The fact that it endured for more than twenty years suggests that the preceding civilian regimes failed to fully satisfy popular aspirations. The fact that the regime decayed into a corrupt and brutal dictatorship suggests that military government is not the answer. Thus, twenty years of military rule may have at last convinced those who support democracy that there can be no return to the civilian *or* military politics of the past.

NOTES

1. Omar Jaén Suárez, *La Población del Istmo de Panamá del siglo XVI al siglo XX* (Panama City: Impresora de la Nación, 1978), pp. 187–190, 301.

2. Walter LaFeber, *The Panama Canal: The Crisis in Historical Perspective* (New York: Oxford University Press, 1979), p. 8.

3. Juan Materno Vásquez, *Teoría del estado panameño* (Panama City: Ediciones Olga Elena, 1980), p. 122.

4. Panama, Dirección de Estadística y Censo, Contraloría General, *Panamá en cifras: 1973–1977* (Panama City, n.d.), p. 38.

5. Steve C. Ropp, *Panamanian Politics: From Guarded Nation to National Guard* (New York: Praeger, 1982), pp. 60–61.

6. Ibid., p. 60.

7. Partido Revolucionario Democratico, Documentos fundamentales (Panama City: September 22, 1979), pp. 16–17.

8. Jan Black, "The Canal and the Caribbean," in Richard Millett and W. Marvin Will, eds., *The Restless Caribbean: Changing Patterns of International Relations* (New York: Praeger, 1979), pp. 90–91.

9. Neil R. Richardson, *Foreign Policy and Economic Dependence* (Austin: University of Texas Press, 1978), pp. 103–106.

10. U.S. Congress, Senate, Committee on Foreign Relations, *Hearings on the Panama Canal Treaties,* 95th Cong., 1st sess., September 1977, pt. 1, p. 588.

11. Steve C. Ropp, "Ratification of the Panama Canal Treaties: The Muted Debate," *World Affairs* 141:4 (Spring 1979), p. 284.

12. *New York Times,* June 12, 13, and 22, 1986.

SUGGESTED READINGS

Biesanz, John, and Mavis Biesanz. *The People in Panama.* New York: Columbia University Press, 1955. This is a classic book on Panamanian politics and society. It offers insights that are still valuable.

Bunau-Varilla, Philippe. *Panama: The Creation, Destruction, and Resurrection.* New York: McBride, Nast, and Company, 1920. A fascinating account of French involvement in the construction of the Panama Canal and the subsequent involvement of Mr. Philippe Bunau-Varilla in the revolution of 1903.

Jaén Suárez, Omar. *La Población del Istmo de Panamá del siglo XVI al siglo XX.* Panama City: Impresora de la Nación, 1978. A detailed, scholarly examination of population and settlement patterns on the Isthmus of Panama from the colonial period to independence in 1903.

Jorden, William J. *Panama Odyssey.* Austin: University of Texas Press, 1984. A former ambassador to Panama, Jorden presents a fascinating and detailed description of the behind-the-scenes negotiations leading to passage of the 1978 canal treaties.

LaFeber, Walter. *The Panama Canal: The Crisis in Historical Perspective.* New York: Oxford University Press, 1979. Historian Walter LaFeber deals with U.S.-Panamanian relations during the nineteenth and twentieth centuries as a background to discussion of the Carter-Torrijos treaties. This is a highly readable book.

McCullough, David. *The Path Between the Seas: The Creation of the Panama Canal, 1870–1914.* New York: Simon and Schuster, 1977. An epic book dealing with the French and U.S. efforts to construct the Panama Canal.

Meditz, Sandra W., and Dennis M. Hanratty, eds. *Panama: A Country Study.* Washington, D.C.: Library of Congress, 1989. Written under contract for the U.S. government, this volume contains a great deal of useful information about Panamanian society.

Pippin, Larry Larae. *The Remón Era: An Analysis of a Decade of Events in Panama (1947–1957).* Stanford, Calif.: Institute of Hispanic American and Luso-Brazilian Studies, 1964. One of the few books on Panamanian politics in English that offers an in-depth view of a major historical figure—Remón was the founding father of the National Guard.

Ropp, Steve C. *Panamanian Politics: From Guarded Nation to National Guard.* New York: Praeger, 1982. A short introductory examination of Panamanian politics from the nineteenth century to the present.

PART NINE
CUBA AND THE CARIBBEAN

21

THE CUBAN REVOLUTION

NELSON P. VALDÉS

A social revolution is a radical, abrupt, thorough, and systematic alteration of the social relations, the patterns of behavior, and the institutional structures that exist in the economic, political, cultural, and social life of a country. By definition, a social revolution touches every facet of interaction in society. It often attempts a total break with tradition. But even revolutionaries cannot escape their material and historical contexts.

The agendas of social revolutions have changed through time. From the seventeenth century on, Western Europe dealt with a series of critical problems, ranging from nation building (the creation of national institutions, a central system of authority, and a national economy) to the creation of representative political institutions and industrialization. This process of becoming modern capitalist nation states took centuries to unfold and was often plagued with social conflict at home and war abroad. During this century, the countries of the Third World (including most of those in Latin America) have confronted some of the same difficulties (nation building, economic development, the problems of citizenship) as well as new ones (national self-determination and ending foreign control and neocolonial institutions and practices).

In general, revolutionaries have defined their tasks in such a manner that their aims are, to say the least, awesome. Social revolutions are supposed to bring about the full blossoming of national sovereignty, fight foreign influence, develop national resources, distribute the economic benefits of growth, centralize political power while increasing the sense of citizenship and the degree of political participation, and carry out a total transformation in the major institutions of the country. And all of these tasks are to be done in a short period of time with the few resources the country may have at its command.

The Cuban Revolution is worthy of study because it presents us with an example of what a revolutionary state has tried to do, how it has gone about it, and what has resulted from the effort. Also, this Revolution, although multifaceted and complex, has been a unique phenomenon that a number of countries have attempted to emulate. Finally, the very fact of the Revolution has placed this small island in the center of the struggle between the superpowers. The impact of the Cuban Revolution, in other words, has been felt not only within its own borders but beyond its shores as well.

THE HISTORICAL CONTEXT

Social revolutions occur in particular places and times. They cannot escape either of the two. The fact that Cuba is an island in a very strategic location has made it a crossroads of trade and cultures. And the fact that it lies only 90 mi (145 km) from the U.S. mainland has preoccupied U.S. as well as Cuban authorities, particularly since 1959.

Yet the islanders have been somewhat isolated from most of Latin America. There is a certain attitude of self-containment and self-sufficiency in the culture. Moreover, Cubans are not sufficiently aware of the dramatic differences between a country that developed a plantation economy very early in its history and the agrarian, peasant, and other traditional forms of social interaction found elsewhere in the hemisphere. This has led some Cubans to consider their experience a model that could be emulated elsewhere—a vanguard rather than an exception.

Social revolutions do not occur in a historical vacuum; they are shaped and bound by history. History, as such, is a dynamic, ever-changing process. How that process unfolds and how it is interpreted do not have to coincide. Yet the interpretation that a society or a portion of a population gives to that process may have a power all its own. Historical interpretation may be a tool for understanding as well as a call to action. Revolutionaries know this well.

Spanish Colonial Period

The history of Cuba has been quite different in its basic pattern from that of most of Latin America. From the onset of the Spanish conquest, the island became a springboard for the conquest of Mexico, Central America, and even portions of South America. Lacking mineral wealth and a large native labor force, Cuba offered little incentive for settlement. The population was fairly small, and the economy was geared toward servicing the fleet system that visited the port of Havana once or twice a year. Most of the population tended to concentrate in the small towns. Colonial institutions were not as strong as in Peru or Mexico, and the Catholic Church held sway only in the urban milieu.

From the 1760s on, Cuba experienced dramatic changes in its economic, social, and political organization. These changes were initiated by the development of the sugar plantation economy and, with it, of a cohesive class of sugar planters (referred to in Cuba as the *sucarocracia*). As sugar production rose, the demand for labor also increased. Since this shift in production occurred just as the British began their industrial revolution, the steam engine was soon introduced into the refining of sugar. This generated a greater demand for sugarcane and thus for the labor force that cut it. Hence, with the sugar plantation and the modernization of production, black slaves arrived in ever-larger numbers. Sugar production was essentially for profit, although dependent on slave-master relations. The sugar economy dominated the western part of the island, particularly around Havana. In the eastern region, however, a small farming class, mainly white, produced coffee, tobacco, and cattle—a significant portion for barter or direct use.

The sugar areas were held by people born in Spain (*peninsulares*), and the rest of the land was essentially in the hands of poor farmers who had little contact with the Spanish colonial system. The latter were, in a sense, the early *criollos*; the first indications of a Cuban national identity would be found in the eastern part of the island. The differences between the two economic regions, with their distinct modes of production, gave rise to tensions between the Spaniards and the Cubans. The latter, of course, were barred from political power.

The early nineteenth century witnessed independence struggles throughout most of Latin America. Cuba, however, remained under Spanish control. This was due to three factors. First, economic prosperity brought about by sugar cultivation kept much of the population contented. Second, the defeats suffered by the Spanish military forces throughout the hemisphere meant that a large proportion of the defeated personnel ended up in Cuba—thus fortifying colonial rule there. Finally, the sugar planters, as well as many other whites who were not directly connected to the sugar economy, were afraid that a war of independence would be transformed into a slave revolt, as had been the case in Haiti after 1791.

In 1868, Cuba began a war of independence led by the independent, small, white farming class of eastern Cuba. The war went on for ten years but ended in defeat for the rebels as well as in the total destruction of the nonsugar economy. The plantation became ever more powerful and began to expand to the east. The class system, at the same time, was simplified: A basic tension surfaced between the slaveowners and the slaves. In this confrontation, the Catholic Church sided with the plantation and the colonial system. Thus, sugar-plantation-slaves and colonial rule became one side of the equation, while the emancipation of the slaves, the reduction of the dominance exerted by the plantation, and Cuban independence became united themes. It is in this period that one begins to find the antisugar mentality that has dominated the thinking of Cuban revolutionists ever since.

In 1895, the war of independence broke out again, this time led by the Cuban Revolutionary Party (PRC) under the guidance of Cuba's most important poet, national hero, and thinker: José Martí. The PRC was a unique development. No other independence war in Latin America was organized by a political party. The party had political and military control of the entire struggle. This was new as well. But the PRC went even further. José Martí had studied the conditions of Latin America and concluded that even though many countries had attained political independence, the laws, traditions, practices, and institutions of colonialism had survived. The PRC therefore had a decolonization program. In that respect, the party foretold a process that would take root throughout the Third World in the second half of the twentieth century.

The American Protectorate

But the war of independence did not achieve its goal. The international situation was far different from what it had been when the rest of Latin America became free of Spain. Late in the nineteenth century, the United States was emerging as a major power in the hemisphere. Manifest Destiny had numerous adherents in Washington, D.C., and the Caribbean was considered an American lake. The Cuban war of independence was lost when the United States and Spain went to war in 1898. U.S. military intervention in the island brought to an end Spanish colonial rule, but only to initiate a new period of U.S. hegemony.

The island became an integral part of the U.S. economy. The culture and education of the Cubans became ever more Americanized. The United States imposed a new economic arrangement, new trade partners, and a new political system. The U.S. dollar became the main currency. From 1899 to 1902, the U.S. military ruled over Cuba, restructuring its socioeconomic system so as to meet U.S. needs. U.S. investors began to control the strategic sectors of the Cuban economy (sugar, transportation, utilities, trade). All communal lands were lost, passing into U.S. ownership.

An amendment to the Cuban Constitution, dictated by U.S. military authorities, allowed the U.S. government to pass judgment on the acceptability of Cuban public policy. And should that judgment be negative, the United States asserted, through the Platt Amendment, the right to intervene militarily to ensure that its dictates were honored.

A new regime in Cuba, ushered in by the so-called sergeants revolt, unilaterally repudiated the Platt Amendment in 1933. Other progressive and nationalistic reforms that had followed the sergeants revolt were soon undermined as the leader of that revolt, Fulgencio Batista, assumed dictatorial powers and curried favor with the United States. But that revolt, which elevated noncommissioned officers of lower-class background to command positions, had severed the tie between the traditional Cuban elite and the officer corps, a factor that later worked to the disadvantage of the military.

The Cuban Revolutionary Party, which had spearheaded the struggle for independence from Spain, had disintegrated after the death of its leader, Martí. But in 1944, a new populist party, of the same name and inspiration, was elected and allowed to rule until 1952, when Batista displaced it and again established a dictatorship.

From 1953 to 1958, the opposition to Batista clustered around the 26th of July Revolutionary Movement. This was a movement formed by ex-members of the Cuban People's Party (PPC), a splinter of the PRC, many of whom remained committed to populism, nationalism, and general concepts of social justice. Under the leadership of a young lawyer, Fidel Castro, they successfully carried out a guerrilla war that managed, for the first time in

Latin America, to overthrow a military regime. The United States apparently misunderstood the degree to which these revolutionaries were committed to thorough and rapid social change. But it soon became obvious.

From Nationalism to Socialism

The young revolutionaries sought control over the major economic decisions affecting their country in order to redistribute wealth and promote development. There is no evidence that they had envisioned either a complete break with the United States or a thorough socialization of the economy. But the U.S. government and business community equated the nationalist policies of the Revolution in regard to foreign investments and the reformist policies, beginning with land reform, with communism. U.S. countermeasures, including the slashing of Cuba's sugar quota and, later, the economic embargo, pushed the Cubans to further expropriations.

By late 1960, the state owned a significant portion of the means of production in Cuba. No one had planned this. Through a process of confrontation and nationalist actions and reactions, the capitalist economy of Cuba had been socialized, even though the Cuban state did not have the personnel to run all the enterprises. At issue had been the right of Cuba to make decisions within its own borders, and failure to reply to the U.S. challenge would have amounted to forfeiting sovereignty.

It was the identification with, and the defense of, nationalism that led the Cuban revolutionaries, in practice, to socialism. The United States had come to represent capitalism as well as imperial power, and Cuban nationalism and socialized property were integrated into the new revolutionary ideology. The Bay of Pigs invasion, organized and financed by the CIA, captured the dichotomy well.

On April 15, 1961, airplanes piloted by Cubans hired by the CIA bombarded the airports at Santiago de Cuba and Havana. This was the softening-up period prior to a Cuban-exile invasion. Seven persons died. Speaking at the burial ceremony the next day, Fidel Castro said that a counterrevolutionary invasion, seeking to return capitalism, was imminent. And on that day, he characterized the Cuban Revolution as socialist. The invasion began on April 17, but within two days, it had been defeated. Again, just as the cutting of the sugar quota led to the socialization of the basic means of production, the Bay of Pigs invasion made Cuba's identification with socialism the only possible reaction that a radical nationalist movement could take.

This turn of the Revolution surprised the United States as well as the USSR. In fact, the Cuban experience defied some basic tenets of orthodox Marxist theory. Communists, following the views of Lenin, had believed for quite some time that without a revolutionary theory (i.e., Marxism-Leninism), there could be no revolutionary party or movement. And without the party, there could be no revolutionary practice—seizing political power and socializing the means of production. In Cuba, the formula was reversed. Power was seized without a revolutionary theory or party. The state took over a significant part of the economy and months later called the outcome socialism. Only much later, on December 2, 1961, was there a formal adoption of Marxism-Leninism. It was only in early 1962 that a revolutionary party began to be formed, and it held its first party Congress thirteen years later. Thus, the Cuban experience has been unique in many ways.

THE POLITICAL SYSTEM

During the first sixteen years of revolutionary rule, Cuba's leaders successfully merged charisma with patrimonialism and a high degree of mass mobilization. The Communist Party did not play an important role during that first phase of the Revolution because the very nature of a political party runs counter to charismatic authority. Until 1970, political and organizational work was concentrated on the growth and development of mass organizations (Cuba has six mass organizations: Cuban Confederation of Labor, Federation of Cuban Women, National Association of Small Farmers, Federation of Secondary School Students, the Union of Young Pioneers, and the Committees for the Defense of the Revolution).

The institutionalization of the Revolution, after 1975, redefined the role of the Communist Party. It was to coordinate, control, lead, and supervise the tasks of the state and the mass organizations, without administering. But to assume such roles, the party had to grow, train its cadres, develop efficient methods of leadership, establish internal discipline, and improve its political training as well as the educational level of its members.

In 1965, the Communist Party had just 45,000 members; ten years later, the number had increased to 211,642, and in 1980, the membership numbered 434,143. The educational level has changed as well. In 1970, 33.6 percent of the members did not have a sixth-grade education; nine years later, that proportion had declined to 11.4 percent. The proportion of members with higher education has also been rapidly increasing, from 2.8 percent in 1970 to 6.2 percent in 1979. Party cadres have shown an even greater improvement, with 16 percent having had a high school education in 1975 and 75.5 percent five years later. Meanwhile, membership in the mass organizations has ceased to grow. Since the 1970s, the revolutionary leadership has been preparing the party to play the "leading role" that Marxist-Leninist theory had claimed for it.

Communist Party Organs

The present system of government is characterized by a complex web of interlocking power relations. The Communist Party, the state, and the government are functionally differentiated, although some individuals occupy more than one post in each of these three centers of power. The Communist Party, at present the locus of political power, is highly structured. At the base, the party membership is organized in cells, or *nucleos,* 26,500 of them in 1980. The party is organized on a territorial basis (local, municipal, provincial, and national).

On the national level, the party Congress is the highest authority, but only in a formal sense since it meets only once every five years. Delegates to the party Congress, elected from subordinate territorial levels, in turn elect (really ratify) from among themselves the members of the Central Committee (CC). Because of its size, and the fact that its members have other responsibilities, the CC has only about two one-day plenums annually. At these meetings, the CC selects the members of the Political Bureau (PB) and the Secretariat.

The PB makes policy between congresses and plenums on behalf of the CC and the party. Its task consists of translating general principles and aims into more-precise policy, and its decisions are binding.

The Secretariat is also a powerful institution. To some it has appeared that the PB is much more powerful than the Secretariat because the latter has to answer to the former (just like the PB answers to the CC, and it, in turn, responds to the party Congress). However, it would be more useful to see the PB and the Secretariat as functioning in different arenas.

The Secretariat is responsible for the maintenance of the party apparatus. It decides who may join or who is expelled. It also takes care of internal political education and promotion within party ranks. The Secretariat also transmits to the institutions of the state, government, and mass organizations the guidelines of the PB.

The internal organization of the Communist Party parallels that of the administrative and political divisions of the island, with fourteen committees representing the provinces and 179 representing municipalities. Below the municipal committees are the party cells, organized at work centers, schools, and military barracks. At the base, then, the party is organized by function rather than by territory (which discriminates against people who are not employed, do not study, or are not in the military).

The functions and hierarchical lines of the CC, the PB, and the Secretariat are clearly demarcated, but in practice, the demarcations seem to be insignificant. Many of the same individuals can be found in all three bodies. The Secretariat has nine members—five are full members of the PB, and two are alternates. Political power is interlocked for the simple reason that the same person can have two entirely different statuses and roles. On the basis of that web, it can be stated that in 1982, thirty men and one woman comprised the core of revolutionary power in Cuba (what in Mexico has been called "the revolutionary family").

The Communist Party makes decisions but does not execute them, guides but does not administer. The implementation of policy—that is, practical day-to-day decision making and policy formulation—is carried out by a different set of institutions. From 1959 to 1975, the people who had political power and those who held key government posts were the same; there was no distinction of roles. In 1976, however, a constitution was issued proclaiming the socialist nature of the Cuban state and establishing the rules of government. Executive, legislative, and judicial powers were separated. Granted, the executive still had some legislative prerogatives, but nothing similar to those of the 1959–1975 period.

In the 1980s a number of changes took place within the Communist Party. Some of these were due to the internal dynamics of the revolution itself. The party grew from just 50,000 persons in 1965 to 523,639 members in 1986. There was some fluctuation in the growth; however as a whole party recruitment increased faster than population increase. In the period 1975–1980, it grew almost 21 percent; in the 1980s it dropped to 4.1 percent (1980–1986). After 1986 there was a greater effort to gain members again, particularly young ones. Tied to the reduction in membership age was an improvement in educational level. In 1975, 19.6 percent of the members had a ninth grade education or more; in 1986 the figure was 72.4 percent. This shift reflects the overall improvement in the educational level of the population at large.

There have been some changes in the internal organization of the party over the years. The Central Committee membership can be divided into full members (who actually participate in decision making) and alternates (who may take the place of full members due to death, promotion, etc.). There were 100 full members in the CC in 1965. As the PCC membership grew, new members were incorporated into leadership positions. The PCC avoided demoting CC full members, however, by inventing the concept of alternates. By 1986 the Central Committee had 146 members and seventy-nine alternates.

The Political Bureau had also expanded. Whereas it had eight members when the party was organized in 1965, it had thirteen full members and fourteen alternates in early 1990. Eleven of the fourteen alternates had assumed their positions since 1986.

At the 1986 Party Congress, Fidel Castro noted that "we had to renew or die." Thus, he went on, "we must trust our youth." Indeed a policy of affirmative action that targeted women, the young, and blacks began from the 1986 Congress on. At previous Congresses the party stressed the recruitment of workers and peasants. In other words, class had priority. By 1980 special attention was being given to having more women in the PCC. The same theme was repeated at the Third Congress, but the PCC went further this time, enunciating a policy of affirmative action for women, blacks, and the young. The Main Report read by Fidel Castro stated, "The mechanisms that ensure the correct selection, permanence and promotion of cadre must be improved constantly on the basis of thorough, critical, objective and systematic evaluations and with appropriate attention to development and training. Women's representation in keeping with their participation and their important contribution to the building of socialism in our country must be ensured, along with the existence of a growing reserve of promising young people born and tempered in the forge of the Revolution."

In 1986 women accounted for 21.5 percent of party membership. (The number of women in the CC had increased to 18.8 percent of the combined CC membership.) Ethnicity has become an important issue in the party, perhaps related to the growing influence, education, and expectations of the black population. A Communist Party document stated that, "In order for the Party's leadership to duly reflect the ethnic composition of our people, it must include those compatriots of proven revolutionary merit and talents who in the past had been discriminated against because of their skin color."

Fidel Castro has noted that the "rectification of historical injustices" such as racial discrimination "cannot be left to spontaneity." By 1986, only 28.4 percent of the CC membership was black or mulatto. But the affirmative action policies adopted by the revolutionary leadership suggested that the failures in this area were acknowledged and steps were to be taken to address them.

The Communist Party internal organization was also confronted by the changes begun in 1985 in the Soviet Union, and then taken up by Eastern Europe in the late 1980s, as well as by Communist Parties throughout the rest of the world. Thus, in mid-February 1990, the Communist Party leadership announced new plans to transform itself. The promised changes, however, did not imply the abolition of the one-party state. A party document stated, "What we are talking about is the perfecting of a single, Leninist party based on the principles of democratic centralism." (This happened precisely as the Soviets abandoned a constitutional monopoly on power.)

In 1990 the ten-member Secretariat was reduced to six persons. No explanations were given. As a consequence of the changes, the labor movement no longer had a representative (the peasant/farmer sector had no direct voice either). The representative of the labor movement (former head of the Cuban Confederation of Labor) was also dropped from the Political Bureau at that time.

In summary, while the permanent full-time membership of the Political Bureau remained fairly constant throughout the 1980s, the alternate membership experienced drastic change. However, the alternates have little power as long as they remain in that position. In a sense, the increasing number of alternates suggests that rising stars within the revolutionary ranks have been promised power and authority, but they have not been given enough of it to shape decisions within the Political Bureau and the Secretariat. True, the alternates have power vis-à-vis the society at large. They participate in controlling key social, economic, and governmental institutions; but since the core of power resides within the party, they merely implement the significant decisions made elsewhere.

In 1991 the Communist Party should hold its Congress. It is expected that major new policies will be announced at the time, including the possibility of joining the party if one is not an atheist. In mid-1990 there was a major debate underway on such matters as degree of freedom to be given to the mass media, the role of foreign investment, and the best way of integrating the larger number of party members and the general population into the work of the revolution.

The National Assembly

In 1977, a National Assembly (NA) with formal legislative powers was established for the first time. The NA is a representative institution whose members are elected for five-year periods. Election is indirect, delegates being chosen by provincial assemblies. (Provincial elections are popular and direct.) The NA has 481 delegates and meets twice a year, usually for less than a week. It can generate legislation as well as approve it, but laws must be consonant with the general guidelines of the Communist Party. How much real power the NA possesses is debatable. Sessions are so short that there is little time to study, analyze, and debate. Recently, some delegates have tried to represent their respective local constituencies, but the NA is not receptive to that idea. In general, the NA serves to legitimize decisions made elsewhere.

The real work of the NA is done by standing work committees and the Council of State (CS). Committee members are appointed. Chosen for their specialized knowledge rather than for their political credentials, they need not be delegates to any legislative body. The NA has fifteen committees, fourteen commissions, and nine departments. It should be noted that the persons elected to the assemblies, whether on the national, provincial, or municipal level, do not run on a particular political platform. They have no individual set of policy proposals; instead, they are chosen for their personal characteristics. It is a given that a candidate's political platform will be that of the Communist Party.

The National Assembly has come under criticism by the general population, its members, and members of the Communist Party. The population, at meetings with their elected representatives, have expressed dismay at the institution's lack of power and its incapacity to deal with substantive issues. The members of the municipal and provincial assemblies, on the other hand, have begun to lobby their own constituencies as well as the National Assembly, in order to acquire a greater role in making policy decisions, particularly in the area of economic and social policy. Finally, National Assembly members have complained that they ought to be able to work for a longer period of time, taking for themselves the powers enjoyed by the executive committees. They also have demanded a say in determining budgetary priorities, the size of the budget, and real control over matters of foreign policy. It is assumed that at the Communist Party Congress in 1991 these matters will be addressed. However, they could not be acted upon unless the constitution is revised.

When the NA is not meeting, its functions and prerogatives are assumed by its executive committee, the Council of State, which is selected by the NA from its own ranks. The CS carries out the decisions of the NA as well as tasks outlined in the 1976 Constitution. The CS, in 1982, had forty members. Its most important power is that of issuing laws when the NA is not functioning (in a sense, the CS is the country's real legislature). The CS also interprets the law, exercises legislative initiative, declares war or makes peace, removes or appoints members of the Council of Ministers, gives instructions of a general nature to the office of the attorney general and to the judiciary, supervises the diplomatic corps, vetoes ministerial decisions as well as those made at any other level, and exercises any other power that the NA may give it.

The president of the CS is expected to control and supervise the activities of all government ministries and administrative agencies. He could take over any ministry or government post and propose to the NA the members of the Council of Ministers. He is also commander-in-chief of the armed forces. The president, first vice-president, and five vice-presidents of the CS are all in the Political Bureau. The president and the first vice-president also head the Secretariat. The other thirty-three members of the CS are either in the PB, the CC, or the Secretariat.

The Council of Ministers

The government proper is the Council of Ministers (CM), whose members are appointed by the president of the Council of State and ratified by the NA. The CM has one president, one first vice-president, twelve vice-presidents, thirty ministers, forty-eight commission members, eight advisers, one deputy-secretary, and one minister-secretary. The CM administers the state apparatus, executes the laws, issues decrees in accordance with existing laws, develops ✓ and administers the national budget, carries out foreign policy, and organizes and directs social, economic, cultural, scientific, and military matters. The CM's Executive Committee (comprising the president, first vice-president, and the twelve vice-presidents) is the real power in government. In 1982, of the fourteen persons on the Executive Committee, nine were in the PB, two were in the Secretariat, five were full members of the CS, and six others were alternates.

Before 1976, the same individuals performed numerous functions although they had one role: They were revolutionaries with power—revolutionary leaders assumed both political and administrative functions. Political leadership and administration are now separate. Charismatic authority is being transformed into a legal-rational system of authority, but during that transition, which may take years, the rules and regulations of the new political structure are elaborated, defined, and given content as well as life by the charismatic authority.

Fidel and Raúl Castro have a tremendous amount of power and control over the key institutions of Cuban society. But this is to be expected. A charismatic system of authority transfers legitimacy to a legal-rational type of authority by placing the representatives of the previous system in key positions. As time goes on and the charismatic leaders play by the new rules, the institutions themselves gain legitimacy. Of course, it remains to be seen whether such a process will continue to unfold in the future. In 1982, Fidel Castro held the following posts: first secretary of the Political Bureau and the Secretariat; member of the Central Committee; deputy to the National Assembly; president of the Council of State, the Council of Ministers, and the Executive Committee of the Council of Ministers; and commander-in-chief of the armed forces. Raúl Castro was the second secretary of the Political Bureau and the Secretariat; member of the Central Committee; deputy to the National Assembly; first vice-president of the Council of State, the Council of Ministers, and the Executive Committee of the Council of Ministers; and minister of the Armed Forces. Thus, the answer to the perennial question, What will happen when Fidel Castro dies?, has to be—

on the basis of the institutionalization of authority and the resources that Raúl Castro commands—that Raúl would succeed his brother.

The succession question, a problem confronted by any political system based on charismatic authority, has become more acute as the revolution and its leaders have gotten older. To the concerns with a gerontocracy should be added the international situation as of late. The Communist movement is in disarray. In the Soviet Union as well as Eastern Europe the one-party state monopoly has disappeared; electoral politics are now accepted as a matter of political necessity, and Communists everywhere no longer claim to have all the answers. Elections in Nicaragua, the dissolution of Communist parties in Eastern Europe, the revamping of NATO, and the rediscovery of western political "democracy" have imposed tremendous pressure on the Cuban political system.

The European Parliament, as well as traditional leftist friends of the Cuban Revolution, are demanding the establishment of a more open political system in the island. To these pressures should be added the very success of the revolution: It has created a more sophisticated political culture, a more educated population, and a more generalized belief that the people can rule themselves. The period of charismatic rule, in other words, confronts its major crisis. It has one option: to transfer authority from the charismatic leader to representative institutions that enjoy legitimacy.

How this will be accomplished has not yet been resolved. Nor is there a consensus within Cuba that this should be done. Many people still identify solely with Fidel Castro, the charismatic leader ("el original," the man who conceived, organized, made, consolidated, and maintained the revolution for over 38 years). In fact, those who wish to preserve the charismatic type of political regime note that "in the face of the crisis of socialism and the aggressive euphoria of North American imperialism" it is impossible to play with western political models. Their reasoning suggests that the United States is now ready to attack Cuba, as the revolution becomes one of the few surviving socialist/revolutionary regimes in the world. In their view the only possibility for survival is to be in a permanent state of readiness, which only the mass mobilization qualities of charismatic authority can assure. Perhaps this reasoning would be easily dismissed if the revolutionaries thought that the United States had no intention of attacking the revolution, but U.S. policymakers, in a sense, have contributed to the fear of attack. (See "U.S.-Cuban Relations" below).

At present the Cuban revolutionaries have returned to the methods of earlier years. Mass mobilization and calls to nationalism have become a daily occurrence. The revolutionary leadership asserts that Cuba's independence and the very future of socialism depend on the survival and durability of the revolution. Thus, political reforms have been defined as concessions that could lead to revolutionary defeat. According to Fidel Castro, in a number of speeches given in late 1989 and early 1990, Cuba's independence, national sovereignty, and the defense of "socialism" are inexorably linked. The battle cry "Fatherland or Death" of earlier years has been transformed into "Socialism or Death."

Calls to emulate the experience of Eastern Europe are dismissed by Cuban revolutionaries as another form of "intellectual and political colonialism." Cuba's realities, they say, are different from those of Europe. Cuba, and the rest of Latin America, must find their own answers on the basis of their own material and cultural conditions.

REDISTRIBUTION AND ECONOMIC EXPERIMENTATION

Cuba is a poor and underdeveloped country. When the Cuban revolutionaries attained power, the country confronted serious economic problems. Foremost among these was dependence on one crop—sugar—and one buyer—the United States. How much sugar the United States bought was determined by the U.S. Congress and the Agriculture Department. The sugar harvest lasted, at best, four months; thus, Cuba also faced serious unemployment and underemployment.

Prior to the Revolution, the unemployment rate averaged 16.4 percent of the available work force. However, when the sugar harvest ended, it could climb to 20–21 percent. In 1957, only 37.2 percent of the labor force worked the entire year. Social inequality was also a problem. According to a Labor Ministry report issued in 1957, 62.2 percent of the employed received an average monthly salary of less than 75 pesos (peso value was then equal to the dollar). Only 38 percent of the male workers earned more than $75 per month. In 1956, 34 percent of the total population of Cuba received 10 percent of the national income, and only 7.2 percent of the employees earned more than $1,000 a year. A family of six, on the average, had a yearly income of $548.75 and could spend about $0.17 per person for food on a daily basis. In the first year of the Revolution, 73 percent of all families had an average income of $715 per year. Poverty was widespread, particularly in the rural areas.

Land was unequally distributed. A small portion of the landowners owned most of it. In 1959, 8.5 percent of all farms comprised 71.6 percent of the land area in farms; on the other hand, 80 percent of all farms comprised 13.8 percent of the farmland. At the time, 94.6 percent of the land was privately owned; the state controlled just 5.4 percent. Only 32.2 percent of the landowners worked their own land; 25.5 percent of the farmland was administered on behalf of the landowners, and 42.3 percent was rented out or sharecropped. One-quarter of the best agricultural land was owned by U.S. companies, while 63.7 percent of the agricultural work force had no land of its own. Most of those who owned their land were usually engaged in production for family use since their parcels were very small. Altogether, U.S. corporate interests controlled 2 million acres (810,000 hectares) of land in the island, out of a total surface of 23 million acres (9.3 million hectares)—that is, 8.7 percent of the national territory. In Camagüey Province, six companies controlled 20.7 percent of the land.

U.S. interests could be found elsewhere as well. Total U.S. investments had reached a little over $1 billion when the revolutionaries took power; this was the equivalent of 40 percent of the GNP. U.S. capital dominated

90 percent of the utilities, 50 percent of the railways, 40 percent of the production of raw sugar, 25 percent of all bank deposits. U.S. interests controlled more than 80 percent of mining, oil production, hotels, pharmaceuticals, detergents, fertilizers, auto dealerships, tires, imports, and exports. Of 161 sugar mills, U.S. companies owned 36. U.S. capital was shifting away from traditional investments (sugar, utilities, mining) and moving toward new areas (loans, imports, exports, light industry). The reported rate of return on U.S. investments was 9 percent, but Cuban revolutionary authorities have estimated that the real rate was about 23 percent. From 1952 to 1958, U.S. companies repatriated an average of $50 million yearly (new investment during the period was $40 million yearly).

In 1958, the United States supplied 72 percent of Cuban imports and bought 69 percent of Cuban exports. Cuba's balance of trade from 1948 to 1958 was positive with most of the world, except the United States. It has been estimated that the rate of economic growth from 1945 to 1958 averaged 4.3 percent per year while the per capita income growth was 1.8 percent.

When the revolutionaries seized power, they found an economy that relied on sugar production, primarily controlled in its numerous facets by U.S. capital, as well as an economy that was unable to generate sufficient jobs in the primary or secondary sectors to absorb the surplus labor. The Cuban economy was essentially capitalist in nature, with a large proletarian labor force in the countryside (over 64 percent of the rural laborers were wage earners).

In the first two years of the Revolution two major trends developed. On the one hand, a progressive redistribution of income took place.

- February 2, 1959: all debts owed to the Cuban state were suspended
- March 10, 1959: house rents lowered 50 percent
- May 17, 1959: Agrarian Reform Law began redistribution of land
- December 23, 1959: social security made available to all workers
- October 14, 1960: Urban Reform Law established procedure by which renter will use rent payments as amortization in order to purchase home
- June 7, 1961: free universal education established
- August 1, 1961: transportation costs lowered
- September 21, 1961: child care centers subsidized by the state
- March 12, 1962: rationing introduced, price of all food items frozen (remained frozen until the early 1980s)

The second trend was a radical change in prevailing property relations. By the end of 1960, the critical areas of the Cuban economy had been taken over by the state: All of banking, export-import operations, energy, and utilities were owned by the state. More than three-quarters of industry, construction, and transportation was also in the hands of the government. Only the bulk of agriculture was in the hands of the private sector, and that was primarily the result of the redistribution of land.

During the period 1959–1960, there was no talk of socialism on the part of the authorities. Economic thinking revolved around the ideas of rapid industrialization, import substitution, and reducing the role of sugar while diversifying agriculture. There were no real controls of an economic nature. The capitalist market was not replaced; it disappeared, and nothing took its place. No one seemed to pay attention to capital accumulation. The central idea was simply to establish greater equality by increasing the income and resources of the lower classes. This was the distributionist phase of the Revolution. As the state moved into the private economy, it found that it lacked the personnel to run the new enterprises; often those who were considered loyal were put in command. They had to learn their jobs while performing them. Consumption improved altogether, but it led to shortages because no effort was made to increase stocks.

In 1961, after the revolutionaries discovered that they had socialism, they began looking for a model to emulate. The Czechoslovakian model was copied, and industrialization was stressed; sugar was set aside. From 1961 to 1963, some problems developed with the emerging rural middle class. Since the revolutionary regime had little use for sugar and industry seemed more appealing, a second agrarian reform was issued that abolished the remaining medium-sized landholdings. During this period, the state further socialized the means of production so that it controlled 70 percent of the agricultural sector and more than 95 percent of industry, transportation, and construction. The private sector could sell only to the state. The Cuban economy had the highest index of state control in the world. A generalized process of centralization of economic decision making took root, led by Ché Guevara from the Ministry of Industries.

It should be noted that this is the period when Cuba and the United States had reached the equivalent of a state of war (in 1961, the Bay of Pigs; in 1962, the October missile crisis). Within Cuba, the revolutionaries continued their distributionist policies. Health care, for example, became free in this period. Unemployment disappeared—primarily because the productivity of labor declined and more people were hired to do a job that in the past had been performed by one person. Also, many of the previously unemployed were absorbed by the service sector. From 1961 to 1962, sugar output dropped from 6.8 million tons to 3.8 million. Yet, few sectors were growing or generating the necessary foreign exchange. This led to a rectification of the economic policy.

In 1963, the revolutionary authorities abandoned their stress on industrialization; sugar was to be the pivot of Cuba's economic development. The new economic strategy was to be based on modernizing Cuban agriculture, introducing more up-to-date forces of production, while improving the skills of the workers. The effort would be centered on the state farms. At the time, two entirely different economic models for constructing the future socialist society were being discussed.

Meanwhile, the United States had imposed an economic blockade on the island in 1962, and except for Mexico, no country in the hemisphere traded with the Cubans. Moreover, Cuba's terms of trade deteriorated from 1964 to 1966 due primarily to the drop in the price of sugar (in 1963, the price was 8.3 cents per pound; by 1966, it had dropped to 1.8 cents). So the cost of imports increased greatly.

In 1966, Cuba's most original phase began. It lasted until 1970. The goal was to produce ever-larger amounts of sugar, regardless of the world market situation. Moreover, since the country did not have the material resources to reward effort, moral (i.e., political) incentives were to be used to motivate the workers. The highly centralized economic plans of the previous period were replaced by sectoral, independent, decentralized plans. The plans (and enterprises) received money allocated through a central budget. Enterprises did not engage in mercantile relations with one another, and they did not have to show a profit. Cost accounting was disregarded altogether. Efficiency depended merely on meeting output goals, regardless of cost. During the period, a concentrated effort was made to avoid bureaucratic rigidity and to discourage criticism of the approach. Revolutionary consciousness and commitment, it was believed, would do the trick.

At the same time, the state took over complete control of industry, all of construction, 98 percent of transportation, and every single retail business. The labor force involved in harvesting sugar was militarized in 1969. Sugar output went through cycles. From 1966 to 1967, it went up from 4.5 million tons to 6.2 million; then it dropped to 5.1 million in 1968 and to 4.4 million in 1969. The 1970 harvest was the largest in the history of the country, but it had a tremendous negative impact on the larger economy since most of the national resources were concentrated on meeting the goal of producing 10 million tons of sugar.

There was an abrupt drop in economic efficiency during this period. Economic growth averaged just 0.4 percent. The revolutionary authorities had ended the connection between output and salaries; that is, workers got paid regardless of production. Moreover, during this period, the state distributed, free of charge, water, public phone service, and child care, among other things. Gratuities were on the increase, and labor productivity declined. An excess of money in circulation ensued; purchasing power exceeded goods available, contributing to labor absenteeism. During the period, the country invested up to 30 percent of its material product on economic growth, which forced it to rely more than ever on imports. The economy did not fare as poorly as one might have expected because the price of sugar consistently climbed during these years (in 1966, the price was 1.8 cents per pound; 1967, 1.9; 1968, 1.9; 1969, 3.2; 1970, 3.68).

In 1970, the revolutionary authorities reconsidered their strategy and revised it, shifting from the budgetary system of finance to what is called *calculo economico,* or self-finance system. The new system stressed centralized economic planning, cost accounting and enterprise profitability, material rewards, mercantile relations among enterprises, and contracts between enterprises and labor unions. Productivity and efficiency came to be measured on the basis of the rate of return (connected to the cost of production).

Managerial expertise on the administrative level began to take precedence over revolutionary zeal. The role of sugar was deemphasized somewhat, as more attention was paid to the diversification of agriculture and the development of mineral resources. The *calculo economico* had become nationwide in its application by 1977. Thus, 1971 to 1976 were years of transition. It should be noted that the shift away from the budgetary system coincided with the move toward institutionalization. This was not coincidental. Cuba's economic and political organizations are highly interrelated. Charismatic authority went hand in hand with moral incentives and mass mobilization to achieve economic goals; rational-legal authority now permeates the political as well as the economic spheres.

The new economic and political organization seemed to pay off very well. The gross material product (GMP)—that is, the gross value of production from agriculture, industry, and construction—has shown some remarkable developments; for example, the GMP growth rates for the 1970s were as follows.

1971:	4.2%
1972:	9.7
1973:	13.1
1974:	7.8
1975:	12.3
1976:	3.5
1977:	3.1
1978:	8.2
1979:	2.4

The improvement and subsequent deterioration of the economy in the 1970s, however, was not due to internal conditions. Rather, the price of sugar in the world market affects the general performance of the Cuban economy. Sugar prices rose from 4.5 cents per pound in 1970 to 29.6 in 1974 and 20.3 in 1975 before they began to drop, reaching 7.4 cents in 1982. The cycle was reflected in the Cuban economy because, more than twenty years after the Revolution, the export of sugar has remained crucial to the overall functioning of the economy. Sugar accounts for 80 percent of foreign earnings.

It should be stressed, however, that the revolutionary government has worked out an arrangement with the Soviet Union that has allowed the island to escape, to some extent, the cycles of the capitalist economy as far as sugar is concerned. Since the 1960s, the Soviets have paid a much higher price for Cuban sugar than the price in the open world market. Only on three occasions (1963, 1972, 1974) were world market prices higher than those paid by the Soviets. By 1979, when the world price had reached a low point of 9.6 cents, the Soviets were paying 44 cents. The treatment that the revolutionary government has received from the Soviet Union has been positive and extraordinary. In 1972, the USSR agreed to postpone until 1986 the payment of Cuba's debt. The debt covered a period of twenty-five years during which Cuba has paid no interest.

Table 21.1
Annual Growth Rates of Latin American and Cuban Per Capita Gross Domestic
Product, 1982–1988

	Latin America	*Cuba*
1982	−3.5	3.3
1983	−4.7	4.3
1984	1.4	6.5
1985	1.4	3.9
1986	1.6	0.3
1987	0.3	−4.7
1988	−1.5	1.0

Source: Economic Commission for Latin America and the Caribbean, *Preliminary Overview of the Latin American Economy,* Document LG/G. 1536, Santiago, Chile, 1988, p. 18.

Approximately 20 percent of Cuba's trade in the early 1980s was with the capitalist market economies. The terms of trade are such, however, that while the price of sugar has declined, the prices of the products Cuba must buy to process the sugarcane and produce sugar have gone up. (A metric ton of urea in 1972 sold for $76, but by 1980, the price was $303. The same situation occurred with ammonia nitrate: its price changed from $206 to $506.) Thus, while the price of sugar declines, the cost of producing it rises. In constant 1970 prices, a pound of sugar in 1982 sold for 2.8 cents. Thus, in order to import the same amount of goods, Cuba has to export much more.

Cuba's economic performance in the first five years of the 1980s was significantly better than that of the rest of Latin America (see Table 21.1). But the Cuban situation started to change in 1986. That is precisely the year that Fidel Castro announced the initiation of the "rectification" campaign in the economy. The campaign denounced and took steps against private enterprise (the free peasants' market created in 1980, the appearance of private urban businesses, and the reliance on protifability as indicator for the allocation of resources). The rectification campaign, in other words, put political decisions rather than "economic logic" in command. The overall performance of the economy has suffered as a result.

Moreover, recent events in Eastern Europe and the Soviet Union have damaged external trade. The Eastern European countries have shifted toward convertible currency transactions, and the democratization of the Soviet political system has led to a greater demand for consumer goods just as the Soviet economic system is going through its own major restructuring. This situation has produced tremendous uncertainty in the supply of goods from abroad. Cuban economic planning and performance, hence, have suffered. The revolutionary government, with little foreign exchange on hand, has adopted a policy of more import substitution. The strategy has been accompanied by greater stress on export diversification.

In early 1990 Fidel Castro told the Cuban people that very difficult years could be expected and that rationing may be extended to new products. At the same time, the Cuban authorities have contacted Mexican, Brazilian, and Japanese investors; and new offers have been made to transnational corporations in the hope that the shortage of capital could be overcome. Cuban foreign reserves in 1988 and 1989 have been less than $100 million. And it is expected that within the next five years Soviet assistance will drop. Opening up to foreign tourists and the Cuban exile community might be one of the few options that could afford some leeway to Cuban economic planners. Future prospects do not look very promising.

Table 21.2 shows the major changes that have taken place in the economy since 1958. Despite Cuba's limited economic resources, the revolutionary government has been able to distribute social services in a manner that has produced profound positive results. The population of Cuba is about 10 million. The country is highly urban (in 1958, 58.7 percent of the people lived in cities; by 1983 the figure was 64.5 percent). The mortality rate is 5.6 per 1,000 inhabitants, and life expectancy has increased from 58 years in 1959 to 73.5 years in 1981. The infant mortality rate, a major index of how much poverty and inequality a society has, has been radically changed—from a high of 33 it dropped to 19 in 1983. The age distribution of the population has changed as well. Before the Revolution, 36.2 percent of the population was younger than fifteen; in the early 1980s the figure was 32 percent. At the same time, the percentage of people over sixty-five increased from 4.2 percent in 1958 to 7.3 percent in 1980.

Illiteracy has been reduced to less than 4 percent, and almost the entire population has received a primary education. At present, 96–97 percent of all the children of primary school age go to school. More than a million people have received a secondary education since 1959. One out of every 2.83 Cubans studies today. Full employment was achieved, although in the last few years unemployment has begun to grow (it is estimated that it was 2–4 percent of the male labor force in 1982). The social benefits that the population receives in the form of old-age pensions; workers' compensation; and maternity, illness, and social security allowances place Cuba at the forefront of all Latin American countries. It is by this means that the popularity and legitimacy of the Revolution have been maintained. The distributionist policies of Cuba's revolutionary government have been far more successful than its economic policies. It remains to be seen whether the tremendous investment in human capital will pay off in the foreseeable future. The next few years, however, will be difficult ones for Cuba.

U.S.-CUBAN RELATIONS

From 1959 to 1961, relations between the United States and Cuba progressively deteriorated. From 1961 to 1965, the two countries were in a state of semiwar. After 1965, the situation relaxed somewhat, but the two had no contact with one another. This situation continued until the last years of the Nixon administration, when some unofficial talks began. Finally,

Table 21.2
Cuban Economic Indicators, 1958–1980

	1958	*1980*
Gross social product (1965 current pesos)	6,013 [a]	22,358 [b]
Exports (f.o.b.) (million pesos)	733	3,967
Imports (c.i.f.) (million pesos)	771	4,509
Trade balance (million pesos)	−37	−542
Per capita income (pesos)	365	2,016 [c]
Sugar output (million metric tons)	5.8	8.2 [b]
Tobacco (thousand metric tons)	51	51 [d]
Citrus fruits (thousand metric tons)	7	250
Rice (thousand metric tons)	253	384
Eggs (thousand metric tons)	315	2,018
Coffee (thousand metric tons)	30	19
Bread (thousand metric tons)	na	417
Fish (thousand metric tons)	21	193
Nickel (thousand metric tons)	18	37
Cement (thousand metric tons)	748	2,645
Electricity (million kw)	2,550	9,391
Oil refining (thousand metric tons)	3,600	6,371
Fertilizers (thousand metric tons)	159	872
Steel (thousand metric tons)	24	327

[a]1962
[b]1982
[c]1981
[d]1976
na = not available

when Carter was elected president of the United States, relations began to thaw. Diplomatic relations were renewed on the section level (as opposed to the embassy level), but no steps were taken toward restoring trade relations. The U.S. economic embargo was relaxed somewhat, as well as travel restrictions between the two countries. When Reagan arrived at the White House, however, every major social upheaval in Latin America was interpreted as the work of Cuban subversion. Consequently, the United States returned to policies reminiscent of the Eisenhower administration. There were even claims from the Cubans that the Reagan administration attempted to assassinate the leaders of the Revolution.

After eight years of the Reagan administration, the Cuban government assumed that President George Bush would improve bilateral relations. But relations, in fact, have deteriorated. The dramatic changes in world communism led the White House to conclude that Cuba would be one more "domino" and that there was no need to take any initiatives that would change the island's isolation. Rather, the White House began to broadcast television programs to the island and tightened the economic embargo, while attempting to link improvement in the relations between the United States and Eastern Europe with the severance of their ties with the Revolution.

Such a policy has reinforced the "besieged fortress" mentality in Havana. The Soviets, however, continue to assist Cuba with military and economic resources. And the revolutionary authorities have initiated a worldwide campaign to break away from their isolation. At present, however, there is little prospect of improvement in the relations between the United States and Cuba.

Regardless of what anyone may think, the Cuban Revolution is there to stay. It has radically affected every facet of Cuban life as well as of the country's international relations. What will happen as the population becomes better educated and the political system further institutionalized, no one knows. It is clear, nonetheless, that internal developments—as is the case with other social revolutions—will be affected by the international context.

SUGGESTED READINGS

Periodical Literature

Following are a number of very useful periodical sources that can help the student of Cuba to keep up with events.

Bohemia. This major Havana weekly covers social, economic, cultural, and political events.
Cuba internacional. A glossy monthly portraying achievements of the Revolution.
Cuba Resource Center Newsletter. The main English-language publication presenting a friendly view of revolutionary Cuba. Published in New York City.
Cuban Studies. The best scholarly journal published on Cuba. Published in Pittsburgh, it concentrates on the post-1959 period. Each issue contains the best bibliography available on publications dealing with Cuba.
Foreign Broadcast Information Service. Daily translations of Cuban radio and television broadcasts monitored by U.S. intelligence agencies. Available on microfiche.

Translations on Latin America. Translations of the documents and articles that are considered most important by the U.S. intelligence community. Deals with all of Latin America and has a section on Cuba. Is published at least twice a week.

Books

Dominguez, Jorge I. *Cuba: Order and Revolution.* Cambridge: Harvard University Press, 1978. This is a massive, thorough, and encompassing book covering the period 1902–1978. Functionalist in approach, it concentrates on politics.

MacEwan, Arthur. *Revolution and Economic Development in Cuba.* New York: St. Martin's Press, 1981. A friendly Marxist presentation dealing with the problems of building socialism.

Mesa-Lago, Carmelo. *The Economy of Socialist Cuba: A Two-Decade Appraisal.* Albuquerque: University of New Mexico Press, 1981. A most important work tracing the different stages of the Revolution, its accomplishments, and its failures. Essentially an institutional-economist approach.

United Nations, Economic Commission for Latin America. *Cuba: Estilo de desarrollo y politicas sociales.* Mexico City, 1980. Provides an overview of the Cuban economy and the Revolution's social accomplishments.

22
THE CARIBBEAN:
THE STRUCTURE OF
MODERN-CONSERVATIVE
SOCIETIES

ANTHONY P. MAINGOT

In a geopolitical sense, it is best to define the Caribbean in terms of all the countries that border on that sea. This includes the islands as well as the countries of the mainland whose eastern coasts form the western perimeter of the Caribbean. Together, they form a "basin" of which the sea is the crucial geopolitical feature.

Geographical definitions, however, are ultimately arbitrary things: Their validity depends on the purpose or ends pursued, i.e., on their utility. So El Salvador, which has no border on the Caribbean Sea, is regarded by some as a Caribbean Basin country, whereas Mexico, Colombia, and most Central American countries are two-ocean countries yet look more toward the Caribbean than toward the Pacific. A simple explanation lies in the fact that colonization and subsequent trade and cultural contacts developed as part of the Atlantic expansion, first of Spain and later the rest of Europe.

For the purpose of this chapter, "the Caribbean" is considered to be the islands plus those mainland territories that, until recently, were part of the British, Dutch, and French colonial empires. Clearly, it is difficult to generalize on any level about countries as varied as these. Haiti has almost six times more land and five times the population of Trinidad and Tobago but only one-fifth the gross domestic product (GDP). Haitians speak Creole, and 80 percent of them are illiterate; Trinidadians speak English, and 95 percent are literate. The former has been governed by dictators throughout its 180 years of independence; the latter had a functioning parliamentary system even before it became independent in 1962.

As with any other geographical region or expression ("Africa," "Latin America," "Asia"), each unit in the region deserves to be studied individually.

And yet, there is also value in an understanding of the broader continuities and similarities that make any region a culture area. In the Caribbean, these continuities and similarities result from a blending of modern and conservative features in the composition of major institutions as well as in social and behavioral dynamics. It is useful to call Caribbean societies modern-conservative systems.

THE CONCEPT OF MODERN-CONSERVATIVE SOCIETIES

Like all concepts or heuristic devices in the social sciences, the concept of modern-conservative societies is used to explain complex social structures and social processes. This is especially important in a region as varied as the Caribbean. The point is that the concept appears to describe Caribbean social structure well, and we conclude therefore that it will also help explain the political manifestations of that social structure.

It is important to note that we are not talking about traditional societies: those relatively static, passive, and acquiescent societies generally resistant to change. The modern-conservative society is not only capable of social change, it is often prone to dramatic calls or movements for change. Two cases from the English-speaking Caribbean will illustrate the latent explosive character of the modern-conservative society.

In 1970, the island state of Trinidad and Tobago was suffering both from a decline in oil production and from low world prices for oil. OPEC had not yet managed to control the market; it would do this in 1972. The economy had been radically changed by oil. The production of sugar, cacao, and other agricultural commodities was now subsidized; the state became the largest employer. By 1970, there was 22 percent open unemployment and 23 percent hidden unemployment while the unemployment among moderately educated youth (more than eight years of schooling) was 40 percent higher than the average. Additionally, since 80 percent of the women indicated no desire to work, the problem was squarely centered on the young males. These youth were integrated into the modern sector: urban, educated, organized, and in close contact with the outside world.

With the Black Power Movement in full bloom in the United States and Canada, two events outside Trinidad lit the spark of Trinidad's own Black Power uprising. One occurred in Jamaica, where authorities prohibited a Guyanese university lecturer, Walter Rodney, from reentering Jamaica from Canada. The so-called Rodney affair stirred the university students in Trinidad as did the "riot" of a dozen Trinidadian students in Canada claiming racial discrimination. Racial grievances, unemployment, unrest among the professional military men, and accusations of graft and corruption against certain government ministers all came to a head in a massive movement against "the system." And yet, the motor, the driving force, was not class conflict but a deep sense of righteous indignation. The target of the movement, Prime Minister Eric Williams, was repeatedly invited to join the moral crusade for black identity and ownership. Clearly, he had lost his moral authority, but not his political legitimacy.

In 1970 in Trinidad, righteous indignation took on psychological and cultural dimensions: a return to history, to a purer and more integral past as a means of collective and individual cleansing and redemption. African names and apparel were adopted and modern European ways rejected to such an extent that the movement's leadership soon began to alienate large sectors of the Indian and colored populations as well as the black middle class. A reorganized police force put an end to the movement; ten years later, the same leaders competed in a free election and were soundly defeated. Had the problems of the society been solved by the massive influx of oil revenues since 1973? Not at all. Fully 83 percent of those who in 1981 felt that life was getting worse on the island attributed that deterioration to corruption.

Although the incumbent party won a sizable electoral victory in 1981, race again showed its strength: The victorious People's National Movement (PNM) won the safe "black" seats; the opposition United Labour Force (ULF), the safe "Indian" seats. As in 1970, a deterioration in the economy could again spark unrest, but it will have to play on certain moral cords and generate a sense of indignation among both leaders and followers, with totally unpredictable outcomes. The case of St. Lucia in early 1982 illustrates this aspect of political behavior in modern-conservative societies.

On January 16, 1982, the prime minister of St. Lucia resigned under pressure. This forced the dismissal of Parliament and mandated the calling of elections within a few months. The caretaker government was led by a member of a radical party, the smallest of St. Lucia's three main parties. It was not this party, however, that had led the antigovernment movement, nor were the issues in the movement ideological ones in the political sense. That movement was headed by the chamber of commerce and other middle sectors, protesting what they regarded as official corruption and abuse of government authority.

The upheaval in St. Lucia was very similar to that which had occurred in Grenada three years earlier: Incompetence, corruption, and abuse of authority had engendered a massive sense of indignation among a multiplicity of sectors. In Grenada, the opposition movement was called the Committee of 21, indicating the number of groups involved in the opposition to Prime Minister Eric Gairy. The difference between Grenada in 1979 and St. Lucia in 1982 was that a small clique managed to wrest power by force of arms in the former, teaching a lesson to the middle classes in the latter. Although all groups participated in the 1982 elections in St. Lucia, the moderates won every seat in the House of Assembly. Similar defeats of radical parties had already occurred in Dominica, St. Vincent, St. Kitts, Jamaica, Barbados, and Trinidad. Elections in the Dominican Republic in mid-1982 also indicated a tendency toward the center in political-ideological terms; it appears to be a Caribbean-wide phenomenon.

These illustrations allow us to identify some of the characteristics of the modern-conservative society. It should at the outset be understood that to speak of "structures" does not imply anything static: It merely means that

certain underlying factors or interrelationships are more durable, more te-
nacious and retentive, than many of the immediate and observable manifestations of those relationships suggest. Such ideas or concepts as history,
life, being, and essence are central to this conservative view of life and are
logical products of ex-colonial, multiethnic, and deeply religious societies,
as we shall see. As Karl Mannheim has noted, these patterns of thought,
far from becoming superfluous through modernization, tend to survive and
adapt themselves to each new stage of social development.[1] Because it has
a real social basis, conservative thought is functional and useful as a guide
to action.

The modern conservative society, then, tends to mobilize politically around
issues that strike chords of a conservative type, issues that engender a collective
sense of moral indignation. Mobilization occurs, however, through modern
mechanisms and institutional arrangements. The most conservative of values,
if widely shared and if the spokesmen have access to modern institutions
and mechanisms, can have impacts that have revolutionary manifestations
though something less than revolutionary goals—if "revolutionary" implies
a complete overthrow of the existing sociopolitical structure, not merely the
regime.

The myth of the modern, revolutionary nature of Caribbean societies
stems from a misunderstanding of the nature of many of the movements
that brought revolutionary elites to power. Even in modern-conservative
societies (as Lenin theorized and demonstrated), a determined elite can bring
about a designed outcome. This is so because after the initial mobilization,
the movement tends to enter into a qualitatively new phase. This phase has
dynamics of its own, dynamics that tend to represent a combination of the
unpredictability and complexity of all mass actions and the more predictable—
or at least understandable—actions of revolutionary cadres and elites. The
latter can turn the movement in a revolutionary direction even in modern-
conservative societies; they are less capable, however, of initially generating
a revolutionary mobilization in such societies.

This explains why the Surinam Revolution (1980) and the Grenadian
Revolution (1979), like the Nicaraguan Revolution, had to coexist with
strong private sectors, established churches, and other aroused but hardly
revolutionary sectors. These regimes were confronted with the complexity
of the modern-conservative society. (They were also confronted, of course,
by the hostility of the U.S. government, which in 1983 took advantage of
internal strife in Grenada to invade and to dismantle the revolutionary
government.)

Understanding the nature of political change in these societies, then,
requires an analysis not only of the immediate political happenings in the
area—the political landscape—but also of what might be called the structural
or enduring aspects of Caribbean political dynamics: the political substructure.
What is required, thus, is a political economy approach to the area in which
demographics and economics are central, though not exclusive, topics of
analysis.

CARIBBEAN POLITICAL ECONOMY

In part because it involves modern societies with relatively skilled labor and a high degree of unionization, and thus high wages, the development process in the Caribbean has tended to be industrial and capital intensive. The overflow of available labor (because of reduced migration) has tended to be absorbed by the public sector. The financial and economic retrenchments made necessary by the energy crisis (and consequent balance-of-payments difficulties) have forced a slowing down of this public employment. The result is not merely unemployment but, rather, a process that is creating a whole generation of "never employed." The vast majority of this group has attained at least some high school education and has aspirations and some skills. Alas, they tend not to be the skills that are in demand nor the aspirations that would encourage needed activities such as agricultural enterprises. Only the latter, with its labor intensity, could in fact absorb the large numbers of people who annually enter the labor market.

Such an agricultural orientation and direction is to be found nowhere in the Caribbean except Haiti, which is still 80 percent rural. The decline of the agricultural sector is a fundamental fact of Caribbean political economy. The movement is toward the urban areas and, critically, migration abroad. In the English-speaking Caribbean, migration accounted for a 46,000-person decrease in the labor force during the 1960s. Because of a slowdown in migration, this labor force is calculated to have increased by about 400,000 during the 1970s, two-thirds of the increase being among young adults.

On every one of the Caribbean islands, youthful adults make up an ever-increasing percentage of the total population, and everywhere they share the restlessness of youth the world over. But the "complexity" approach cautions that it would be a terrible mistake to associate, a priori, all this modern political ferment and activity with a state of social revolution. Such an association might preempt a closer look at the substratum—the political economy—of Caribbean society. Although the configurations and expressions of this conservatism vary, the following aspects of Caribbean society show great similarities from one country to another.

Throughout the area there is a deep and dynamic religiosity, even though the intensity and pervasiveness of religion—as doctrine and as institutions—do vary. One situation is that of the dominant church in the central plaza being attended by women and children once a week; such was the case in Cuba before the Revolution and is the case in Puerto Rico today.[2]

Another situation is that of the English-speaking West Indies, where one finds multiple denominations and many churches scattered throughout neighborhoods, urban and rural. This case illustrates a living presence of religion rather than a ceremonial one and is typical also of countries such as Haiti, where Christianity combined with West African religions to create a syncretism called Voodoo (also called *santería* in Cuba and *Shango* in Trinidad). This religiosity impinges on other spheres of life.

One attitudinal spin-off from the doctrines of the major religions in the area is the belief in private property, especially land. There is an intense love and respect for the land and a desire to own a piece of it. The popular Haitian saying *se vagabon qui loue kay* ("only vagabonds rent their homes") expresses the desire for ownership, for full possession. On Nevis, 80 percent of the home owners own their house lot; on St. Vincent, the figure is 75 percent. Although the figure is only 46.8 percent on Barbados, travel around that island reveals that even the smallest house has a name; the name represents the emotional dimension of property ownership. The little picket fence around the house is the physical expression of the emotional dimension. That picket fence (or cactus fence in the Netherlands Antilles) also expresses another characteristic of Caribbean peoples. In the midst of their gregariousness, they like their privacy, an expression of their intrinsic independence. This characteristic, usually identified as a rural phenomenon, is pervasive even in urban areas. This explains the living presence in West Indian language of old English sayings such as "a man's home is his castle" or, as used with an additional meaning in Creole, "two man rat can't live in same hole."

This latter saying expresses the idea that in any house, only one of the partners can wear the pants. It is taken for granted that the male partner does. And yet, these societies are fundamentally matriarchal and matrilocal: Because of the very high illegitimacy rate among the working class, it is the mother who raises the child, and the child lives where the mother (as well as the maternal grandmother) lives. As the 1981 study by Gary and Rosemary Brana-Shute demonstrates, there is a deep underlying conservatism in the socialization processes and aspirations of even the hard-core—and angry— unemployed youth in the area.

And yet, as Caribbean history has repeatedly shown, these generally moderate and family-oriented societies, and especially the youths, are capable of sudden, quite unpredictable political and social outbursts. This was very evident in Curaçao, in the Netherlands Antilles, in 1969 when a minor industrial strike exploded into a class and race attack on the system. Half of the buildings in the main commercial sector of the island were burned to the ground.

The basically conservative substrata of Caribbean societies also sustain very modern and highly mobilized societies and their corresponding agencies. Note, for instance, the following dimensions and configurations of that modernity—with certain exceptions, such as Haiti, the populations are literate and schooled. On island after island, from 90 to 100 percent of the children of primary school age are in school, and literacy rates everywhere are above 85 percent. Although there is some evidence that conservative attitudes are positively correlated with greater degrees of education,[3] the fact is that a population that participates in the articulation of grievances and wishes and that can utilize the modern techniques of communication is one that has an increased capability for mobilization. Throughout the Caribbean, people are politically mobilized. There are everywhere political parties and interest groups with capacities for extensive articulation of interests and aggregation of these into policy demands. No government today, of the left, middle, or right, can ignore the demands of the groups. Literacy and education also make the labor union system more effective. In the West Indies, from 30 to 50 percent of the work force is unionized, and historic ties with political parties give unions additional leverage in the bargaining processes.

Another of the modern agencies that a literate and schooled population makes possible is the state bureaucracy, which, according to Max Weber, is the most "rational" of all forms of organization. Such state bureaucracies are found throughout the Caribbean in the form of a relatively skilled public or civil service. In Trinidad, there are three and a half times more people with diplomas or degrees in public service than in the private sector, and in Jamaica, the institutionalization and legitimacy of the public service is evident in its capacity to survive dramatic shifts in political party fortunes. The top echelons of these bureaucracies are now being educated in the area. The University of the West Indies (UWI), with campuses in Jamaica, Trinidad, and Barbados, now makes university education accessible to a much broader sector, as do the universities in Guyana, Martinique, Surinam, Curaçao, and elsewhere. Whereas in 1957 there were 2,632 West Indians studying at universities abroad compared to only 566 at UWI, by 1982 the number abroad had doubled, but the number of students at UWI had increased twelvefold.

Caribbean modernity is reflected also in other areas. The fact that Caribbean working people have largely developed both the habits and the skills required of labor in modern societies has made them very desirable as immigrant workers. This explains the long tradition of migration, and return, of Caribbean workers; they are and always have been a mobile population. Whether building the Panama Canal and Central America's railroads and ports or running the London public transportation system, Caribbean workers have had the attitudes and skills of urban workers. They return with new skills, but also with the hope of buying that house or piece of land for which they have saved. In Haiti, the "Bahamas" house was built with remittances from Haitians working in the Bahamas.

While abroad, Caribbean workers are able to communicate with their countrymen. Note, for instance, the mailboxes along every road, the widespread use of radio and newspapers, direct-dialing telephones from the United States to many islands, and in the French West Indies, Netherlands Antilles, Jamaica, Trinidad, and Barbados, the widespread use of television. Modern communications assist both in modernizing the Caribbean and in preserving ethnic attachments. Literacy in one or more of the major languages of the world (English, Spanish, and French) gives Caribbeans access to the major currents of ideas and technology, while their native variations on those languages (Creole in Haiti, papiamento in Curaçao, taki-taki in Surinam) strengthen the sense of *volk,* or nation, of *gemeinschaft,* or community.

If one adds the fact that any particular sector of the islands is within, at most, a two-hour bus ride of some urban center, one understands something of the modernity of the society as well as its continued proximity to rural village life. Ties to the land and to tradition are not broken by a move to the city; rather, those links provide something of the underpinnings of the conservative values and orientations of the urban residents even as the diversification of memberships and involvements (churches, sport clubs, unions, political parties, service clubs) contributes to and expresses the society's modern dimensions. The glue that holds all together is the Caribbean family, both the nuclear and the extended family with its *compadres* ("god-fathers"), *comadres* ("godmothers"), "cousins," and "aunties."

These, then, are some of the native aspects of these modern-conservative societies. Yet, an analysis of the substrata also has to take into account the external factors affecting change. Although, on balance, internal factors tend to carry more weight in any causal analysis of social change, the small size of the Caribbean states makes external factors somewhat more important than they would be for most states.

There can be no question that smallness makes them vulnerable to a host of problems. One of these is national insecurity, as was illustrated by the extraordinary 1981 attempted invasion and subversion of the Dominica government by U.S. mercenaries in league with local politicians. Furthermore, securing a degree of national representation abroad is costly. But such representation is important not only to facilitate contact with foreign nations through traditional diplomatic ties but also to attract attention from the ever-increasing number of international and multilateral banking or lending agencies.[4]

Also contributing to the vulnerability are the cleavages created by the race and ethnic divisions that characterize the politics of nations such as Trinidad and Tobago, Guyana, and Surinam. In each of these countries, Indians (originally from British India) comprise half or more of the population. Predominantly Hindu in religion (some 20 percent are Muslim), these sectors are in themselves prototypical modern-conservative groups. Reconciling Hinduism with secular ideologies such as Marxism is a difficult task in itself; to do so in a context in which major elements of that Indian population are capitalists, landowners, and merchants (as in the case of Guyana and Surinam) is an even more complex proposition. Whether the cleavage is black vs. white, Indian vs. black, or black vs. mulatto, race and race conflict contribute to social division and to the vulnerability of Caribbean societies.

Understanding and awareness of the vulnerabilities resulting from smallness have led to many attempts at regional or subregional integration. Dreams of a united Caribbean are not new. They were expressed in José Martí's theme that Cuba and Puerto Rico were wings of the same dove; in Haitian President Jean Pierre Boyer's dream of liberating all the slaves, first of neighboring Santo Domingo (which his armies occupied from 1822 to 1844), then of other islands; and in the West Indies Federation, which lasted from 1958 to 1961. The repeated failures of such attempts, however, created skepticism about the viability and, indeed, the desirability of such union.

The mini-nation state is now a reality of the Caribbean scene. Today, the area limits itself to attempts at economic integration through such instruments as the Caribbean Common Market (CARICOM) and the Caribbean Development Bank. Even the Association of Eastern Caribbean Community[5] emphasizes the economic aspects of association, leaving politics, including foreign policy, to each individual member.

Unfortunately, while insularity gathers strength on each island, international politics and transnational forces (including multinational corporations) press for a reduction in state sovereignty. And today, as in the past, size and isolation make these territories targets for international expansion. In the late twentieth century, escalating ideological competition among international forces has made the Caribbean a cockpit, the modern-day equivalent of the European battlegrounds of the seventeenth and eighteenth centuries. Today, the Marxist-Leninist Movement, the Socialist International, the Christian Democrats, and international labor organizations as well as new regional actors such as Cuba, Venezuela, and Mexico have all joined the battle for the minds of Caribbean peoples. The United States has long been engaged in the competition. To these may be added many proselytizing religious and semireligious groups, from Islam to the Seventh Day Adventists to the Rastafarian Movement (now of Pan-Caribbean character). Since the foreign offices and intelligence services of the major states never left the area, the present ideational scene in the Caribbean is a bewildering panorama of competing radio broadcasts; roaming sports, cultural, and scientific missions; state visits; and sojourning consultants from international aid agencies—and these activities are only the overt ones. While insularity strengthens the barriers to movements of labor, governments pursuing development put out red carpets to entice foreign capital as it moves from one nation to the other.

The structural elements revealed in this bare-boned sketch of external factors tend to contribute to the generalized idea that these societies are potentially revolutionary. To be sure—as the many cases of dramatic political change illustrate—Caribbean societies are not static; they have the capacity and propensity to react with apparent abruptness and even violence against targets of popular grievances and resentments. This capacity is one structural characteristic of political participation in the area. The central questions, however, remain. Who reacts, why, and over what? What do the answers tell us about the ongoing, and therefore relatively predictable, aspects of Caribbean political culture and dynamics? Crucially, what has been the nature of leadership in the area?

POLITICAL-IDEOLOGICAL LEADERSHIP

The career of Trinidad's Prime Minister Eric Williams, who governed from 1956 until his death in 1981, illustrates the complexity of style and orientation of the region's leadership. Much has changed in the Caribbean since 1956, when Williams first came to power as a celebrated scholar-administrator. His Ph.D. thesis at Oxford, "Capitalism and Slavery," had become the standard radical interpretation of European industrialization (made possible by the triangular slave trade) and emancipation (made necessary by the very success of that industrialization). He was living proof that a man of color was indeed capable of great achievements in a mother country's highest centers of learning.

This success and his later "telling off" of the English, Americans, French, and Dutch in the Caribbean Commission—an agency set up by the colonial powers to assist in Caribbean development—were proof sufficient to make him the man to lead the island's decolonization movement. "Massa day done" became William's battle cry, a welcome prospect to the black and colored middle and working classes who followed his charismatic leadership. The psychic scars of colonialism had found their soothing balm. But where to turn for models?

Asia and Africa were also going through the pains and pleasures of decolonization, and those continents—more than neighboring Latin America—provided some, but not all, of the models. It was in the paths of Nehru, Nkrumah, Sukarno, and Kenyatta that Dr. Williams saw represented the post–World War II, nonwhite decolonization process. Like those leaders, Williams understood very early that decolonization had both racial and political connotations. The very concept of empire had been based on ideas of racial superiority and inferiority. These men had to give living rebuttals to the imperial myths that people of color could not govern themselves and that non-Western societies could never be viable nations. Not only did they have to prove their people's capacity by leading the political struggle, they also had to prove their personal worth through exceptional achievement. In colonial situations, the burden of proof is always with the colonized.

It is no surprise therefore that more often than not, these decolonizers began to perceive themselves as the very—if not the sole—embodiment of their countries. This perhaps was the genesis of their eventual sense of indispensability. Williams acted for twenty-five years on that belief. Repeated victories at the polls did little to dispel the illusion.

But Trinidad, like the rest of the English-speaking West Indies, was in the Western Hemisphere where the majority of the independent countries were Spanish speaking, and most were far from being democratic models. Surrounded by dictators who enjoyed warm relations with Washington and London, Williams understood that the decolonization of the English-speaking Caribbean was to be a lonely process in the Latin American setting. The parliamentary system adopted by the West Indies differed from the executive system of Latin America, and Williams always felt that the former suited the West Indies better.

This belief was shared by an array of truly exceptional West Indian leaders: Alexander Bustamante and Norman Manley in Jamaica, Grantly Adams and Errol Barrow in Barbados, and Cheddi Jagan in Guyana (a true constitutionalist despite his Marxist rhetoric). By the mid-1960s, these leaders had laid the foundations of West Indian constitutional democracy, thereby giving the lie to colonial racists and modern ideologists who argued that only authoritarian one-party states fit the Caribbean reality.

Williams governed long enough to deal with two elected Manleys, father and son, two elected Adamses, father and son, to see the OPEC-created explosion in revenues from gas and oil, to see the collapse of the West Indian Federation and the rise of the Caribbean Common Market, and to see the decline of Britain and the rise of Cuba and Venezuela as regional powers. He lived long enough to see the rise and fall of Michael Manley's "democratic socialism" in Jamaica (1972–1980), and he appeared ready to deal with Jamaica's new leader, Edward Seaga, who emphasized the role of the private sector.

By the time of Williams's death in 1981, the Caribbean had witnessed many a social and economic experiment and was quite a different area. Although there were some governments "for life" (Cuba, Haiti, and probably also Guyana), there were now democratic governments in virtually all the other Caribbean island states, making the Caribbean the largest area governed by democratically elected regimes in the hemisphere. The parliamentary system was working in the West Indies.

The first generation of postindependence leaders in the English-speaking Caribbean had sown well and, in so doing, left their marks on the immediate postcolonial era. In the 1980s, there is some indication that the passing of that era has meant not only generational change but also the passing of the charismatic, "indispensable" man as a part of the political culture. This change is demonstrated by a recent trend in the region's politics: the emergence in the 1980s of the less-than-charismatic "manager" political type. Edward Seaga of Jamaica, Mary Eugenia Charles of Dominica, Tom Adams of Barbados, George Chambers in Trinidad, and Antonio Guzmán and Jorge Blanco in the Dominican Republic all fit this mold.

What explains this shift in leadership? Certainly there is some truth to the view that the trend is partly reactive: a response to the dismal administrative performance of some of the area's most celebrated charismatic leaders of the 1960s and 1970s, Fidel Castro of Cuba, Michael Manley of Jamaica, and Forbes Burnham of Guyana, for example. But a fuller explanation would bring us closer to the issue of complexity that was posited earlier, that dual process involving enduring, underlying relationships, values, and interests (substrata) and the changing political landscape. The careers of Caribbean leaders of Marxist or non-Marxist socialist persuasion, i.e., the secular modernizers, are illustrative.

One such case is Aimé Césaire, mayor of Fort-de-France, Martinique, and Communist *député* to the National Assembly in Paris for over thirty-five years. When Césaire resigned from the French Communist Party in 1956, it was a sensational event. "Thinking of Martinique," he wrote, "I see that communism has managed to encyst us, isolate us in the Caribbean Basin." To Césaire, there was an alternative path: "Black Africa, the dam of our civilization and source of our culture." Only through race, culture, and the richness of ethnic particulars, he continued, could Caribbean people avoid the alienation wrought by what he called the "fleshless universalism" of European communism.[6]

This return to history, to culture, and ultimately, to race has been a fairly consistent response to many Caribbean socialist modernizers—who never stop referring to themselves as Socialists—who are faced with the difficulties of attempting secular revolutionary change in largely nonrevolutionary and conservative societies. The counterpoint between a rational and secular universalism and a particularism of "being" has resulted in some original and dynamic West Indian ideological modifications to Marxism and non-Marxist socialist thought. In Césaire's case, it led to his fundamental contributions to negritude, a literary-political movement highlighting African contributions to contemporary society, as well as to an accommodation with continued French-Caribbean integration (though not assimilation) into the French system.

Trinidad's first major socialist activist in the 1920s, Andrew Cirpriani, yearly paid his homages to Fabian thought and the British Labour Party, but after decades of militancy, he withdrew in the face of two challenges to his basic conservative view of the world: the divorce bill, which he saw as a threat to the family, and the use of violence in strike action. Those who used violence (such as Uriah Butler, the leader in Trinidad's 1937 labor movement and uprising) themselves ended up turning to religion (quoting biblical passages) and to history (studying the rule of Henry VIII). The "pull" on the leadership of the conservative values and norms of the masses has been powerful. Even Eric Williams, whose early historical writings were gems of Marxist thought and careful documentation, would eventually abandon what one admirer called "the infinite, barren track of documents, dates and texts" to write "gossip . . . which experience had established as the truth."

A review of Trinidadian C.L.R. James's five decades of thought on socialism and revolution indicates that he never resolved the universalism-particularism counterpoint. In his *The Black Jacobins* (1938), perhaps the most influential West Indian work of the twentieth century, James vacillates and hedges but ends up on the side of the Dessalinean Black Revolution as distinct from the universalist experiment of Toussaint.

It is not at all evident that there can be in practice a working and productive relationship between racial or ethnic populism and a program based on premises of secular modernism, whether socialist or not. Even in theory, the reconciliation appears improbable. A case in point is the work of the Martinican, Frantz Fanon. Like Césaire—whom he knew and greatly admired—Fanon wished to be liberated from the "fleshless shackles" of European thought; thus he searched for a key to what he called the "psycho-affective equilibrium" of the angry Third World intellectual. This search is central to an understanding of the dynamics of modern-conservative societies. Fanon felt compelled to describe and explain what he perceived as the relentless determination of revolutionary elites to return to history: to "renew contact once more with the oldest and most pre-colonial springs of life of their people." Fanon understood the enduring consequences of the racial hurts and angst inflicted during colonialism. "This state belief in national culture," he wrote, "is in fact an ardent despairing turning toward anything that will afford him anchorage."[7] Even such a lifelong and dedicated Marxist as Guyana's Cheddi Jagan finds a practical, and perhaps even psychological, need to blend his Marxism with an ongoing devotion to Hinduism. Clearly then, race and a desire for a return to history have been powerful forces blocking a universalist and secular approach to politics.

The rational and secular view of the world that is necessary for modern (especially socialist) revolution is not easily sustained in these societies. In the cases of Césaire, Williams, Norman Manley, Forbes Burnham, and others, Marxist or socialist thought was mediated by pressures from the multiethnic, religious, and conservative societies they led—and which eventually forced them to succumb to the particularistic note in the particularism-universalism counterpoint. It is a fundamental characteristic of a conservative society that views of the world and of social change resist any notions of dealing with problems in any way other than in terms of their historically perceived uniqueness. This characteristic has been, more often than not, part of the Caribbean experience.[8]

This experience explains how a Dr. François Duvalier ("Papa Doc") could come into power in Haiti in 1957 advocating a radical Black Power revolution but revert to a very traditional form of political barbarism. He played the most retrograde cords of a deeply conservative society to entrench himself—and then his son, Jean Claude—in power.

OPTIONS AND OBSTACLES

In 1956, the only independent countries in the Caribbean were Cuba, the Dominican Republic, and Haiti. On the mainland, Venezuela was ruled by a dictator, Pérez Jiménez, and Colombia was ruled by another dictator, Rojas Pinilla. By the end of the 1950s, many such dictators were dead or out of office, and a new movement had gained power in Cuba, with Fidel Castro at its head. Although initially espousing the electoral path and a reformist economic program, the Cuban Revolution speedily moved toward a centralized, single-party model accompanied by a rapid socialization of virtually all productive sectors. This was a new model for the Caribbean, though it contained elements that had long been part of the Caribbean political milieu: fear of U.S. intentions, intense nationalism, and a desire to mobilize all the people in a heroic movement of national reconstruction and liberation. The anticolonial movements of the area had a potentially powerful model in Cuba.

The example of the Cuban Revolution, however, has not proved to be as attractive as originally thought. Certainly part of the explanation lies in the perception that the Revolution has been something less than an economic success. But there is also the fact that language, cultural orientation, and the political realities of decolonization have tended to keep the attention of Caribbean societies focused elsewhere.

In the English-speaking Caribbean, attempts to create a federation of island states—the West Indies Federation—lasted three years (1958–1961). Subsequently, in the early 1960s, Jamaica, Trinidad and Tobago, and Barbados each moved toward independent status within the British Commonwealth.

British Guiana, which had refused to join the federation, became independent in 1966. Virtually all the other British colonies gained independence in the late 1970s and early 1980s: Dominica, 1978; St. Lucia, 1979; St. Vincent and the Grenadines, 1979; Antigua and Barbuda, 1981; and St. Kitts-Nevis, 1983. The Netherlands Antilles were content to decolonize by expanding the autonomy of their political and administrative systems within the Kingdom of the Netherlands. Aruba, however, opted for a separate status (*Status Aparte*) within the Kingdom of the Netherlands. The French West Indies and Cayenne (French Guiana), made integral parts of France as overseas departments in 1946, appear satisfied with that status. They participate in every aspect of the French social welfare system, but at the same time, retain their cultural identity and autochthonous political culture.

During the 1980s, the Caribbean island-states were drawn ever more closely into the affairs of the Western Hemisphere, increasingly sharing the forums and the problems of the Latin American mainland. Like the rest of Latin America, the Caribbean suffered serious economic setbacks in the 1980s. The decline in the traditional sectors of the economy (sugar, bauxite, oil) increased unemployment and further aggravated what was already a bad trade and balance of payments situation. This at a time when payments on a substantial international debt were creating serious financial strains on virtually every nation in the region.

While the Caribbean Basin Initiative launched by the administration of Ronald Reagan in 1983 created considerable growth in nontraditional exports in selected countries (in garment and electronic manufacturing especially), it hardly made up for the losses suffered during the 1980s. Additionally, like other Latin American states, in the 1980s the Caribbean islands saw a dramatic increase in narcotrafficking and drug money laundering. Their geographical location between the producers (especially Colombia) and the United States, the world's largest consumer of drugs, made them natural transshipment centers. The corrupting influence of this trade was increased since several Caribbean countries started to compete for one of the most lucrative businesses in the area: offshore services, especially those associated with tax havens. A British colony, the Cayman Islands, became the world's largest tax haven by 1990, while the British Virgin Islands and the Bahamas were running a close race for second place.

The 1980s saw riots, gang violence, insurgencies, coups, and other forms of political turmoil in several Caribbean states. In Surinam, a pseudo-populist, authoritarian regime that had seized power in 1980 and carried on a sporadic campaign against "Bush Black" insurgents, retreated a few steps in 1987. In a constitutional referendum that year, the electorate opted for a return to democracy. The opposition won the elections that took place later that year, but the former strongman, Daysi Bouterse, continued to cast a shadow across the official scene.

A popular uprising in Haiti in 1985–1986 deposed the government of Jean-Claude ("Baby Doc") Duvalier, but left intact the corrupt military and protected thugs (tonton macoutes) that had supported it. Elections in 1987 were aborted as troops and thugs attacked voters at the polls, killing at least 30 of them. Anarchy alternated with tyranny through the end of the decade. After another uprising in early 1990, the military stepped aside, leaving government in the hands of Supreme Court Justice Ertha Pascal-Trouillot until elections could be scheduled. Violence, however, did not abate.

The Dominican Republic also faced elections in 1990; and despite the rioting that had punctuated the late 1980s, the campaign season, featuring the two grand old men of Dominican politics, incumbent President Joaquin Balaguer and challenger Juan Bosch, had been remarkably tranquil.

By the end of the 1980s some interesting political and ideological changes revealed themselves. Michael Manley, whose first two terms in office (1972–1980) were characterized by pro-socialist and pro-Cuban rhetoric, won a landslide victory from his conservative opponent in 1988, Edward Seaga, promising moderation and pragmatism in his new government. A similar transformation was evident in candidate Bosch, leader of the Dominican left. Ideology and programs had been tempered by the collapse of world socialism as well as the harsh realities of debt and the power exercised by creditor institutions.

Finally, as had been true of other Latin American, and particularly Central American, countries in the 1980s, emigration from the Caribbean accelerated. For most emigrants, the final destination was the United States, particularly New York, New Jersey, or Miami. Puerto Rico, however, long a way station, was also becoming a Caribbean melting pot.

It is fair to say that within the past decade the majority of countries in the area had moved rapidly to consolidate their own political systems. In all the ex-European possessions (with the exceptions in the early 1990s of Guyana and Surinam), political parties and groups operated freely, and human rights appeared protected by a range of independent government and private institutions and organizations.

By the end of the 1980s, then, the Caribbean was subjected to various pressures and exposed to several models or sources of attraction and interest:

1. The continued and increasing presence of the United States, which moved to replace the European powers as the major economic partner and strong cultural influence.
2. The Cuban Revolution, which epitomized heroic, popular mobilization.
3. The Puerto Rican model, which appeared to have brought economic development with political freedom.
4. Africa, where a decolonization process had produced charismatic leaders such as Kwame Nkrumah, Jomo Kenyatta, and Julius Nyerere.

Clearly, these models were not always in harmony either in theory or in practice. The attraction of Africa resulted from a heavy dose of racial identification as well as personal associations between leaders who had shared the anti-European sentiments and ideas of preindependence days. This did not harmonize with the appeal of Cuba, which responded to a Spanish

American variant of anti-Americanism. The Puerto Rican attraction was a pragmatic one based on what was regarded as a realistic assessment of the region's political economy. Above and among all these attractions was a strong love-hate relationship with the United States. In a region with a predominantly black population, how does one admire the United States with its recent history of Jim Crow laws, and yet how does one ignore not only its power but also its sincere, albeit grudging, struggle for civil rights for all?

The "U.S. dilemma" has its own Caribbean counterpart. The desire of Caribbeans for modernity draws their attention to the United States, yet their yearning for liberation and economic justice for themselves (and their African brothers) turns their eyes occasionally toward Cuba. Both sentiments have as context societies with deep attachments to organized religions, private property, and highly diversified and plural social structures. The result is ambivalence and unpredictability. And yet, in many ways, the ebb and flow of Caribbean politics and social change can be illustrated through the metaphor of the counterpoint between the desire and capacity for modernization and change and the strength of conservatism. Each tendency has well-developed idea systems, as well as institutional and organizational representation. Not surprisingly, both tendencies can be found in the vast majority of Caribbean peoples. Thus, it is useful to characterize Caribbean societies as modern-conservative societies, an ideal-type construct that helps us understand what otherwise might appear to be contradictory, or even unintelligible, in the behavior of this multilingual, multiracial, and multistate area.

NOTES

1. Karl Mannheim, "Conservative Thought," in Paul Kecskemeti, ed., *Essays on Sociology and Social Psychology* (New York: Oxford University Press, 1953), pp. 77–164.

2. Cuba and Puerto Rico were perhaps the least structurally conservative of the Caribbean societies, in large measure because of the considerable influence of secular North American values and interests.

3. See Selwyn Ryan, Eddie Greene, and Jack Harewood, *The Confused Electorate* (St. Augustine and Trinidad, 1979); and Anthony P. Maingot, "The Difficult Path to Socialism in the English-Speaking Caribbean," in Richard R. Fagen, ed., *Capitalism and the State in U.S.-Latin American Relations* (Stanford: Stanford University Press, 1979).

4. This is not only a question of the asymmetry of power but also a question of commanding respect and dignity.

5. Antigua, St. Vincent, Dominica, St. Lucia, and Grenada.

6. Aimé Césaire, "Lettre à Maurice Thorez," *Présence Africaine* (Paris) (1956), p. 15.

7. Frantz Fanon, *The Wretched of the Earth* (New York: Grove Press, 1968), p. 217.

8. One interesting exception is the New Jewel Movement, which came to power in Grenada in 1979, attempting to portray that experience as an extension of a Caribbean decolonization process begun in Cuba. It was deposed through U.S. military intervention in 1983.

SUGGESTED READINGS

A good general treatment of the Caribbean as a whole is Franklin W. Knight, *The Caribbean: The Genesis of a Fragmented Nationalism* (New York: Oxford University Press,

1970). Knight also edited, with Margaret E. Crahan, *Africa and the Caribbean: The Legacies of a Link* (Baltimore: Johns Hopkins University Press, 1979). On the English-speaking Caribbean, Gordon K. Lewis, *The Growth of the Modern West Indies* (New York: Monthly Review Press, 1968), is somewhat outdated but contains excellent insights and analysis. David Lowenthal's *West Indian Societies* (New York: Oxford University Press, 1972) is especially strong on race relations and the analysis of the "plural society." On the development of socialist politics, see Anthony P. Maingot, "The Difficult Path to Socialism in the English-Speaking Caribbean," in Richard R. Fagen, ed., *Capitalism and the State in U.S.–Latin American Relations* (Stanford: Stanford University Press, 1979).

Contemporary affairs are best followed through journals such as *Caribbean Studies* (Puerto Rico), *Caribbean Review,* and the newsletter from London, *Caribbean Insight.* The best geographical treatment of the area is Helmut Blume, *The Caribbean Islands* (London: Longman, 1974).

PART TEN
THE ANDES

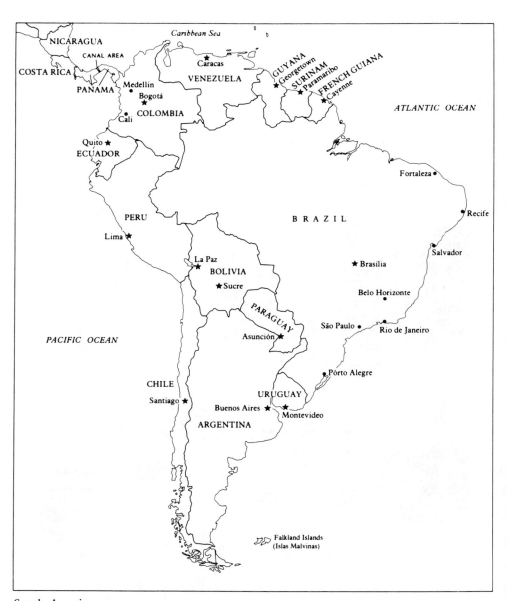

South America

Reprinted, with permission, from Howard J. Wiarda and Harvey F. Kline, eds., *Latin American Politics and Development,* Second Edition (Boulder, Colo.: Westview Press, 1985).

23

VENEZUELA, COLOMBIA, AND ECUADOR

JOHN D. MARTZ

"America is ungovernable. Those who have served the revolution have plowed the sea." Such was the embittered disillusionment of Simón Bolívar by the time of his death on December 17, 1830. Not the least of his disappointments was the dissolution earlier that year of his cherished Gran Colombia, a political union of today's Venezuela, Colombia, Ecuador, and Panama. From 1819 until 1830, this fragile creation had survived periodic insubordination to the central authorities in Bogotá. Resentment in both Venezuela and Ecuador mounted until the former withdrew in April and the latter in May of 1830. The Bolívar-enforced union had been unnatural, destined for inexorable failure. Yet there were commonalities that went well beyond sheer geographic contiguity, and even today the tradition of the Bolivarian ethos lends justification to collective consideration of the three republics.

In recent and contemporary times, these countries have collaborated with Peru and Bolivia in the Andean Pact. In 1990 all three enjoyed elected civilian governments and were outspoken hemispheric champions of democracy, freedom, and human rights. Within the Latin American context, each constitutes a multiracial society in which enlarging middle sectors are breaking down historic class rigidities. And to varying degrees, each possesses sufficiently diverse natural resources to provide a basis for economic growth and modernization. In the course of the past quarter century, both Venezuela and Colombia have significantly strengthened their political institutions, while in Ecuador, the process has been introduced more recently.

Venezuela in 1958 ousted the dictatorship of General Marcos Pérez Jiménez and inaugurated a constitutional, party-based regime, which stands today as the most vigorously open and competitive system in all Latin America. Seven successive presidents have abided by the rules of the game while guiding economic modernization fueled by vast petroleum and other natural resources. A shaky multiparty system has evolved into one dominated by the social democratic Democratic Action Party (AD) and the social christian party (Committee for Independent Political and Electoral Organization, COPEI). Political legitimacy has thrived as four of the last five governments have been defeated at the polls and have yielded power to the victorious opposition. Social mobility is substantial, notwithstanding major inequities and injustices. Internationally, the country has assumed an increasingly active and vigorous role, both regionally and in the inner circles of the Organization of Petroleum Exporting Countries (OPEC).

The year 1958 also marked the ouster of military authoritarianism in Colombia, with General Gustavo Rojas Pinilla being replaced by a carefully engineered alliance between the Conservatives and Liberals. The two historic rival parties agreed upon a constitutional pact whereby for sixteen years they shared political power equally. An informal variation since 1974 has allowed traditional elites to maintain control over the pace and character of change and modernization. Although far less representative or responsive than that of Venezuela, the Colombian leadership has nonetheless been able to draw on varied economic resources to meet the more pressing priorities of society. It has also shown a willingness to employ a variety of controlling mechanisms as a further check against domestic upheaval or a recasting of social relationships.

Ecuador, by all indices the least progressive or modern of the three countries, falls less neatly into a chronological category. The unparalleled succession of three elected governments from 1948 to 1960 then gave way to more typical instability. During the next twelve years, Ecuador was ruled by two elected presidents, two provisional presidents, one military junta, and a vice-president who ousted his erstwhile superior. In a sense, the contemporary experience parallels the advent of Ecuador's petroleum era, which began in 1972. Seven years of military rule yielded to an elected government in 1979 under the reformist leadership of Jaime Roldós Aguilera. A new generation of political leaders also came to power and has undertaken to implement socioeconomic change supported primarily by income from oil. Social distance and hierarchical rigidities remain far greater in Ecuador than in the other two countries and will prove far less susceptible to modernization.

By the decade of the 1980s, then, both similarities and differences among the three countries were pronounced. To understand them more fully, we will undertake a brief excursion into the Spanish colonial legacy and the evolution of political and socioeconomic patterns during the following century and a half.

HISTORICAL SETTING

With the arrival of the conquistadores early in the sixteenth century, Spain moved to implant its colonial system of control and domination. Personifying the king in the New World was the viceroy, whose role as spokesman of the distant monarch enhanced his powers. The primary viceroyalties were New Spain and Peru until the creation of New Granada in 1717. Although dismantled seven years later, the last was reinstituted in 1740. With the capital in Bogotá, it bore responsibility for today's Venezuela, Colombia, and Ecuador. New Granada received relatively low priority during the first two colonial centuries and was largely isolated from the major imperial centers of power. With creation of the viceroyalty, it gradually received more attention, yet by the final years of Spanish rule, it was still of only marginal concern to Madrid. It was not coincidental that early cries for freedom came from such backwaters of the empire.

Among the greatest precursors of independence was Francisco de Miranda, born in Caracas in 1750. By the turn of the century, he was renowned throughout Europe as an advocate of freedom, and in 1810, he had returned home as dictator of the newly independent junta. Defeated and captured by royalist forces two years later, he was imprisoned and transported to Spain, while leadership fell to another Caracas-born figure, Bolívar. It was the Liberator who brought about the ultimate victory over royalist forces in Venezuela, Colombia, and Ecuador. After 1810, there was periodic collaboration and communication among rebel leaders in the three future countries, and in December 1819, Gran Colombian unity was proclaimed by the Congress of Angostura. Francisco de Paula Santander, as vice-president, directed the affairs of government while Bolívar continued to lead the armed struggle.

As time passed, differences between Bolívar and Santander were aggravated while in Venezuela, the illiterate *llanero* ("plainsman") José Antonio Páez, a brilliant military leader, plotted secession from Gran Colombia. There was similar restiveness in Ecuador, far removed from the government in Bogotá. So it was that with the ailing Bolívar's final retirement in May 1830, Gran Colombia disintegrated, giving way to three separate countries. In Caracas, Páez became Venezuela's first president; he was to rule with the support of Caracas's conservative oligarchy until 1848. Colombia began its independent existence under Santander, who ruled until 1837. In Ecuador, Venezuelan-born General Juan José Flores was proclaimed president, and he succeeded in perpetuating his power until 1845.

The nineteenth century was a period of civil strife, turbulence, and sporadic anarchy in all three countries. In Venezuela, which had an eminently rural population dominated by merchants and coffee growers, the relative prosperity and peace of the Conservative oligarchy under Páez eventually yielded to heightened conflict between Conservatives and Liberals. Intermittent civil war and governmental instability in 1870 led to the rule of the Liberal Antonio Guzmán Blanco. Until 1888, he ruled either from the presidency or through puppets while bringing efficiency to government, suppressing opposition, and glorifying his own image. Following his overthrow, renewed Conservative-Liberal conflict raged until a band of revolutionaries descended upon Caracas from the Andes in 1899. This introduced authoritarian rule under a succession of Andean military figures, which, with one brief interruption, would endure until 1958.

The central figure of Andean hegemony was Juan Vicente Gómez, "the tyrant of the Andes," who exercised despotic rule from 1908 until his death in 1935. It was during the Gómez era that pastoral Venezuela underwent its transformation to an industrial, petroleum-based society. The first major oil strike came in 1922, and Gómez capitalized upon the discovery to strengthen the economy, develop a basic infrastructure, centralize governmental authority, and preserve his personal hegemony. The oil multinationals arrived with a vengeance, while foreign investment acquired central importance to the economy. Yet it was also under Gómez that student rebellion planted the seeds of the contemporary party-based system.

During the decade following Gómez's death, a youthful Rómulo Betancourt created and built the Democratic Action Party (AD), Venezuela's first modern, mass-based party. Its initial exercise of power, from 1945 to 1948, saw the party undertake massive and far-reaching changes throughout the polity and society. The AD introduced major reforms that were radical within the context of the times, meanwhile enhancing its organizational base and national popularity. Impatient, arrogant, determined to remake Venezuela overnight, the AD eventually overreached itself and was deposed by the military. Beginning in 1948, the country experienced a bleak decade of harsh repression, political persecution, and profligate corruption under Pérez Jiménez and his collaborators. With his flight from power in the face of massive protests in January 1958, the stage was set for the return of political leaders and creation of the system that has endured to the present.

To the west, in Colombia, regional rivalries and strife emerged soon after Santander's departure from power. The Conservative-Liberal conflict was more profound in Colombia than in Venezuela. Divided over the character of government authority, the role of the Church, and economic policies, the combatants alternated in power throughout the first century of independence and beyond. The 1860–1862 Federal War resulted in a Liberal victory, enhancing that party's advocacy of states' rights and anticlericalism. The pendulum later swung back to the Conservatives under Rafael Núñez, president in 1880–1882 and 1884–1894. The 1886 Constitution enshrined centralized authority and restored the preeminence of the Church through an 1887 concordat with the Vatican. The bloody War of a Thousand Days (1899–1902) left Colombia under Conservative domination as it entered the twentieth century, and a year later, the loss of Panama further shattered both the economy and national morale.

From 1904 to 1909, Rafael Reyes presided over a period of authoritarian reconstruction. While Conservative elites reestablished unchallenged dominion, the rise of coffee production stimulated the economy. Not until 1930 were the Liberals to regain power, aided by the repercussions of the world depression and a division of the Conservative elites. In time, the Liberals themselves split between reformist and traditionalist forces, ultimately permitting the election of a minority Conservative government in 1946. Increasing bitterness between both elitist and rank-and-file Conservatives and Liberals introduced a rising wave of rural violence. When the charismatic and controversial Liberal leader Jorge Eliécer Gaitán was assassinated in the streets of Bogotá on April 9, 1948, an unprecedented wave of lawlessness and urban destruction—the infamous *bogotazo*—spread across the country. For more than a decade, the *violencia* ("violence") raged at a high pitch of intensity and intemperance. By conservative estimates, some 250,000 lives were lost.

Increasingly repressive Conservative rule eventually led to the first military regime in decades, but General Gustavo Rojas Pinilla failed to end the *violencia* while assuming increasingly dictatorial authority. Toppled from power in May 1957, he was succeeded by an interim military junta, which led in August 1958 to the so-called National Front. Negotiated by Conservative and Liberal leaders, the front sought to minimize partisan conflict and revive the stagnant economy while assuring continuation of rule by national socio-economic and political elites. *Paridad* ("parity") divided legislative seats and cabinet posts equally between Conservatives and Liberals, while *alternación* ("alternation") provided for the rotation of four-year presidencies between the two parties. Thus, it was the National Front that introduced the arrangement that has explicitly or implicitly characterized the political dynamics of contemporary Colombia.

The nineteenth-century Ecuadoran experience with independence was also marked by instability, civil unrest, and periods of hegemony under either Conservatives or Liberals. By the time of Juan José Flores's departure in 1845, the familiar issues between the two groups had become well established. During the 1850s, the Liberals restricted the Church, expelled the Jesuits, and abolished slavery. Their replacement by the Conservatives in 1860 was accompanied by perhaps the most theocratic regime known to Latin America. While establishing civilian control, promoting public works, and achieving fiscal soundness, President Gabrial García Moreno (1861–1865 and 1869–1875) directed a regime of fanatical religious absolutism. The Jesuits were readmitted, a concordat with the Vatican negotiated, and education virtually handed over to the Church. In 1873, the republic was officially dedicated to "the Sacred Heart of Jesus," while Liberal opponents were ruthlessly persecuted.

Successful beyond all his predecessors in fostering a spirit of national identity, García Morena created a system that survived his 1875 assassination by some two decades. Only in 1895 did the Liberals, under Eloy Alfaro, regain power. With minor interruptions, their control was to endure a full half century. While a number of both military and civilian governments were ousted by unconstitutional means, the country was ruled by the banking and commercial oligarchy that grew up in Guayaquil. The booming cacao market generated economic wealth until its collapse in the 1920s, but the subsequent decline in agricultural productivity left political power largely unchanged. Only military defeat and humiliating capitulation to Peru in the 1941 border war created the conditions necessary for the ouster of the Liberals. This defeat also contributed to the prominence of the erratic, charismatic, and demagogic José María Velasco Ibarra, whose figure cast the dominant shadow across national politics for over four decades.

A self-styled populist of great oratorial skill, Velasco governed on five different occasions, only once completing his constitutional term. Waging war against both Conservatives and Liberals, vacillating between rhetorical radicalism and opportunistic collaboration with the oligarchy, he lacked a well-defined program. Elected to his fourth term in 1960 with an unparalleled popular mandate, he was replaced by his vice-president only fifteen months later. After a succession of provisional civilian and military governments, he again won election in 1968. Two years later, he suspended the constitution and assumed dictatorial powers, which were maintained until military intervention in 1972. Only with Velasco's death in 1979 at the age of eighty-six was Ecuador to pursue its political evolution free from his extraordinary omnipresence. And it was in that same year that the military turned over power to a new generation of civilian leaders, whose responsibility it was to capitalize upon the petroleum era, which had been initiated in 1972.

SOCIAL AND ECONOMIC STRUCTURES

Despite geographic proximity and historical similarities, the socioeconomic characters of the three Gran Colombian republics are markedly varied. Venezuela's multiracial society enjoys an openness of attitude and class mobility encouraged by its contemporary political system and supported by oil income and its rich resource base. In Colombia, mestizo ethnic diversity overlies social rigidities and class distinctions, which took root in colonial days. The social aristocracy retains its preeminence in politics, as illustrated in 1974 by the presidential competition of three offspring of former presidents. An increasingly diversified economy continues to benefit largely the wealthy and a portion of the urban middle sector. Unlike its two sisters, Ecuador continues to have a large Indian population—40 percent at the very least. This includes the Andean descendants of the Incas, primitive Amazonian tribes, and the distinctive coastal *montuvios*. No more than 15 percent are of European ancestry, although this group remains the dominant one in national life. Traditional social and economic structures are resistant to modernization, and the impact of petroleum on deep-seated rigidities cannot yet be assessed.

Turning first to Venezuela, we encounter an estimated population of 18 million, to which at least 2 million illegal immigrants from Colombia should be added. Society is increasingly youthful, mobile, and urbanized. Over half the population is too young to vote (under eighteen); some 40 percent no longer live in or near their birthplace; the urban population has risen from 30 percent in the 1940s to 80 percent today; literacy has doubled during the same period of time. Ethnically, Venezuela is at least 70 percent mestizo, with its Indian component largely in the southwestern Andean region and the people of African ancestry scattered along the Caribbean coast. Racial discrimination, although not unknown, is not a serious barrier to advancement. During the contemporary era, mestizos and mulattoes have been among those to achieve prominence in politics, business, and commerce. Mobility between social classes and subgroupings is also common, and Venezuela has little of the white Hispanic aristocracy that survives in Colombia and Ecuador.

While social opportunity therefore exists, the number of marginals remains large. The influx to the cities has aggravated the condition of those living in the slum barrios, and easily one-third of the population lives in abject poverty, many of whom are at least underemployed if not unemployed. In rural areas, small farmers, who initially benefited from the 1960 agrarian reform, have often been pushed aside by large, mechanized agribusiness interests, ultimately seeking refuge by flight to the cities. An enlarging middle sector has been more conservative than social minded in its determination to reap the benefits of an affluent society, further its own interests, and discount the needs of the dispossessed. Despite the powerful reformist currents of the post-1958 political system, social inequalities remain a major challenge to Venezuela's leadership.

The modernization and diversification of economic structures have been predicated upon the application of petroleum earnings to other sectors of activity. To "sow the oil" (*sembrar el petróleo*) has been an unchallenged slogan since the 1940s, while the potential for growth has been dramatically expanded as the result of rich deposits of iron ore, nickel, coal, aluminum, and bauxite, further enhanced by the availability of massive hydroelectric power. During the 1960s, Venezuelan governments stressed import substitution within a context of protective tariffs and government subsidies. This policy was to be followed by the expansion of new export-oriented activities, and in the decade of the 1970s, government emphasis was placed upon a massive expansion of economic infrastructure and public works, accompanied by the promotion of heavy industry. President Carlos Andrés Pérez (1974–1979) in particular followed this developmental strategy, with high priority being accorded to an integrated iron and steel industry, to petrochemicals, and to modernized transportation and communications facilities.

Although the effectiveness of this strategy cannot yet by adequately judged, there is little debate about the country's inability to modernize the agricultural sector after years of effort and a massive infusion of government funds. The 1960 agrarian reform directed attention to a peasant-oriented strategy with land redistribution at the core. Relative success with this phase did not, however, lead to broader sectoral productivity. By the 1970s, both COPEI and AD had turned toward the promotion of mechanized agriculture in response to periodic shortages of basic foodstuffs and expensively subsidized imports. The consequence has been a strengthening of the rural entrepreneurial sector at the cost of implicit abandonment of small farmers and marginal producers. By the early 1980s, the country was importing some $1 billion of food supplies annually, nearly 20 percent of its total imports. The decline of international petroleum prices, which had set in by 1982, also forced a reduction in government programs and expenditures. Economic conditions also suffered as the foreign debt grew, reaching some $35 billion by 1989, when major demonstrations protested the austerity program of a new government.

Notwithstanding such problems, the long-range outlook for the Venezuelan economy remains bright. Although traditional reserves of petroleum stand at some 18 billion barrels, exploration by the state-owned Petróleos de Venezuela is identifying additional subsoil deposits. More important, the vast Orinoco Tar Belt is in the early stage of exploitation. Although modern technology can presently recover only some 10 percent of this oil, advances can be expected to render a higher yield, and estimates of these deposits run from 700 billion to a staggering 2 trillion barrels. Given the impressive performance of the industry since nationalization in 1976, income from petroleum should remain substantial well into the twenty-first century. In the meantime, the wealth of other minerals and the fertility of the land provide further potential for the country. Thus, the long-range obstacles are constituted not by natural resources but by the underdevelopment of human capabilities.

Venezuela is not lacking in technicians and experts of great skill and sophistication, but the quantity of such personnel is wanting. Despite progress in recent years, the country still lacks sufficient managerial ability, technological competence, and labor productivity. Education, traditionally humanistic, has only belatedly turned toward scientific and technical fields. In a characteristic effort to ameliorate conditions through lavish government funding, the Pérez administration in 1974 created the Gran Mariscal de Ayacucho fellowships, whereby thousands were sent abroad for training in areas of critical need.

In neighboring Colombia, the predominant ethnic character is also mestizo. With the population approaching 30 million, an estimated 20 percent is of European ancestry, with Indians and blacks together numbering no more than 5 percent. Over 60 percent of Colombians are now urban, and the urban growth rate is more than double that of the rural. Unlike many Latin American countries, the urban population is dispersed. Although metropolitan Bogotá is over 4 million, there are ten cities with more than 200,000 inhabitants. The ruggedly mountainous topography, with three Andean chains dividing Colombia into sometimes isolated valleys, has limited somewhat the physical mobility of the population. Regionalism has consequently been an enduring national phenomenon, one that until contemporary times retarded the growth of national consciousness and of socioeconomic integration. It has also slowed the modernization of class structures and the unifying of social attitudes and values.

Unlike Venezuela, Colombia retains a social structure heavily dependent upon Hispanic cultural traditions. Attitudes toward authority and religion are largely inflexible, and the improvement of transportation and communications has opened society only marginally. At the pinnacle stands an upper class erected on generations of intermarriage, economic cohesion, and shared values of political elitism. Kinship in the Hispanic Catholic tradition is deeply embedded in socioeconomic and political life, the upper class grudingly permitting only those mild reforms necessary to maintain its hegemony. Such is the social-rank distinction between elites and masses that only limited mobility is available to the middle and lower sectors. Education and urgan migration provide the more favorable avenues to self-advancement, yet the infrastructure is insufficient to respond to more than a small number.

One-third of the children of primary school age never see the inside of a classroom. As migration from country to city has grown, unemployment has exceeded the growth of the urban labor sector, and increasing numbers live amid devastating slum conditions.

Since the early 1970s, industry has outstripped agriculture as the major sectoral contributor to the economy, although much of Colombia's wealth remains agricultural. Coffee has long stood as the foundation of the export trade, in recent years earning over half the country's legal foreign exchange. Much of the crop is produced by small independent farmers, although the owners of large plantations largely control its production and export. Most rural Colombians follow the traditional pattern of subsistence farming of food staples for local markets. Land distribution is still dominated by the large hacienda, while nearly one-third of the rural parcels are too small to be economically viable. Recent governments have achieved relative success in developing a variety of commodities for export, with the diversification reducing somewhat the past dependence on the international price of coffee. This trend has been accompanied by greater emphasis upon industrialization as a key to economic growth and modernization.

Manufacturing of consumer goods, notably food products and textiles, has strengthened the economic base. To this has been added the expansion of heavy industry, iron and steel in particular. Known deposits of minerals have increased, including largely untapped supplies of coal, the Cerro Matoso nickel reserves, and newly developed fields of petroleum and natural gas. Both the state-owned Empresa Colombiana de Petróleos and multinational corporations are increasing their explorations, suggesting the possibility that Colombia may become an exporter on a small scale. Not appearing in many official reports, but increasingly crucial to the economy, is the illicit trade in drugs, which has helped to swell Colombia's foreign exchange reserves to record highs.

In recent years, the major economic difficulties have been inflation and unemployment. The former has been running above 20 percent, and the flourishing drug traffic has now magnified the problem. The spiral of prices presses on the middle class, and many basic staples have been priced beyond the means of the poor. As capital-intensive industrialization continues to receive high priority from both public and private sectors, the work force cannot fully absorb the swollen urban population. Rising foreign investment, encouraged by recent governments, contributes to overall economic growth but does not respond to the needs of the unemployed and underemployed. The contemporary Colombian profile therefore reveals a growing economy, increased fiscal reserves, expanding industry, and agricultural diversification— yet little of this progress benefits the bulk of the people or encourages social justice and individual mobility.

Ecuadoran society, as already noted, presents a sharp contrast to its neighbors because of its Indian component. Its population of over 10 million is divided almost equally between the coast and the highlands (*costa* and *sierra*). The regional contrasts are central to an understanding of Ecuador and are epitomized by the rivalry between the port city of Guayaquil and Quito, the highland capital. Its population having now reached 1 million, Guayaquil has been the center for banking, commercial, and export-import interests since the early 1900s. Despite massive unemployment, economic opportunities do exist for the poor, who can rise from the lower to the middle class. Elites have acquired their wealth in recent generations, and the basic outlook is sympathetic to modernization. There are linkages to the international system, and the cultural outlook on the coast is Western rather than Indian. There is a spirit of independence and individual freedom, which encourages social mobility, economic activity, and political volatility.

In the sierra, in contrast, the Indians live in accord with attitudes dating from colonial times. Indentured, at least until 1964, to the *hacendado,* many now divide their time between farming tiny, almost vertical plots and doing seasonal wage labor on coastal plantations. Others have joined the migration to crowded city slums and an urban subsistence existence. Unable to achieve mobility or improve their economic lot, the impoverished of the highlands remain tied to ancient values, dominated by traditional elites as deeply entrenched as those in Colombia, yet less enlightened socially. The expansion of highland industry has touched only lightly the lives of the masses, while conservatism and an affinity for the status quo endure. In the wake of expanded petroleum production since 1972, job opportunities have gradually expanded, but far too slowly to accommodate those flocking to the cities in the vain hope of an oil bonanza and its rewards. Although urbanization has come later and less dramatically than in Venezuela and Colombia, it has transformed Ecuadoran society from two-thirds rural in 1960 to roughly 50 percent urban today.

Ecuadoran economic structures have been predominantly agricultural. Cacao provided the first important export commodity late in the nineteenth century and continued to be an important export until being ravaged by witchbroom disease in the 1920s. Bananas, long a staple of the coastal economy, received a major government impetus after World War II. Acreage grew tenfold between 1948 and 1954, making Ecuador the world's leading banana exporter. This boom also was to ebb, and by the 1970s, the banana trade was characterized by the stagnation that existed for cacao, coffee, and sugar. Agricultural productivity has been slumping for years, and such basic commodities as milk, barley, and corn are periodically imported in order to compensate for inadequate domestic supplies. As the agricultural growth rate barely held even with population increase in the 1970s, the economy has rested primarily on increased earnings from petroleum.

After four decades of modest oil production, Ecuador contracted with a Texaco-Gulf consortium in 1964 to explore in the northeastern Amazonian area. Resultant discoveries led to the initiation in 1972 of what many anticipated would be an oil-induced "dance of the millions." A refinery was constructed, a pipeline laid across the Andes to the Pacific, and production facilities increased. In 1973, the government created the state-operated Corporación Estatal Petrolera Ecuatoriana (CEPE) and initiated its own participation in the industry. Joining OPEC the same year, Ecuador eventually raised production to over 350,000 barrels per day. By way of comparison, Venezuelan production is running slightly below 2 million barrels per day. Moreover, Ecuador's known reserves have been drawn down to slightly over 1 billion barrels.

Several years of nationalistic policies induced Gulf to withdraw, and Texaco has been reluctant to undertake any major exploration. With CEPE lacking much of the necessary technical expertise, the oil industry has therefore been stagnating. Earnings continued to rise in the 1970s but as a result of higher prices on the international market rather than increased productivity. In the meantime, inflation has exceeded 20 percent, the price of foodstuffs has increased sharply, and the civilian government inaugurated in 1979 has been forced to adopt unpopular austerity measures. Massive expenditures by the military rulers between 1972 and 1979 created additional burdens on the economy, generating the highest foreign debt in the country's history. As Ecuador passed through the 1980s, it was confronted by dwindling oil reserves, an expanded but inefficient industry, fiscal imbalances, an agricultural sector stubbornly resistant to stimulation and growth, and the same weakened petroleum market that was plaguing Venezuela.

GOVERNMENTAL AND POLITICAL DYNAMICS

The institutional profiles of the three governments bear much in common: a highly centralized system under which local and regional power is limited; a dominant executive with extensive constitutional and ad hoc authority; a vocal, even vociferous, legislature, which nonetheless is more often obstructive than constructive; a judiciary that exercises limited influence on national politics; and a vast array of state-related organs and agencies with responsibility extending into many areas of social and economic activity. From a less formal perspective, the political parties are central to the operation of the system, while ever sensitive to the views and interests of a politicized military. Major economic and commercial interests enjoy well-established access to the political leadership, generally espousing policies opposed by organized labor and by student activists. The role of the Church varies considerably in the region, as do the form and extent of popular participation in politics. In this latter regard, Venezuela stands out among the three.

Perhaps no other nation in Latin America enjoys the level of popular participation and the political centrality of organized mass-based parties that distinguish Venezuela. Beginning with the storied student uprising against the despotic Gómez by the generation of '28, young activists undertook a lengthy task of organization, from which came the Democratic Action Party under Rómulo Betancourt in 1941. It was during the AD-dominated *trienio* that the social christian COPEI emerged under the guidance of Rafael Caldera. With the return to Venezuela of long-exiled party leaders in the wake of Pérez Jiménez's 1958 ouster, a concerted effort was concentrated upon the building of democracy and creation of a fully competitive party system. In the 1958 Pact of Punto Fijo, AD and COPEI were joined by the Democratic Republican Union (URD) of Jóvito Villalba in pledging civic collaboration as the means of nurturing the fledgling democratic system. The electoral victory of Betancourt and the AD led to a coalition government for five years. Although the URD withdrew in 1960, COPEI remained a staunch partner throughout Betancourt's term.

Despite episodic assaults by recalcitrant right-wing officers, an assassination attempt on Betancourt directed by the Dominican dictatorship, and both rural and urban terrorism from Cuban-inspired revolutionary leftists, the administration completed its term and transferred power to the AD's Raúl Leoni in 1964. Five years later, a division of AD opened the door to electoral victory for COPEI and Rafael Caldera. For the first time in Venezuelan history, a government party accepted defeat and transferred the reins of power to the opposition. As democratic practices and values grew more commonplace, the opposition party was to win elections in 1973, 1978, and 1983. Thus the AD under Carlos Andrés Pérez replaced Caldera, only to give way once again to COPEI when the latter won the presidency with Luis Herrera Campins in 1978. The AD regained the presidency in the elections of December 1983 with the victory of Jaime Lusinchi over former-President Caldera. It retained office when Pérez won a second term in December 1988.

The Venezuelan party system underwent marked change during these years. In 1958, there were only four organizations—AD, COPEI, URD, and the Communist Party of Venezuela (PCV). A proliferation of parties soon dotted the political landscape, however, reaching a zenith when twelve candidates contested the presidency in 1973. In popular reaction, the electorate that year cast 85 percent of the vote for the AD and COPEI candidates. Five years later, the percentage was 89, leaving the two parties virtually unchallenged. Given their organizational strength, wealth of leadership, rank-and-file support, and access to financial resources, the two parties appear likely to maintain their hegemony over the party system. The greatest threat would come from internal disunity or division, which only COPEI has successfully avoided through the years. At the same time, the Venezuelan system is more than a pure two-party one.

In addition to several small, personalistic, ad hoc organizations—"microparties" in the Venezuelan political vernacular—the country has seen the rise and fall of numerous organizations centered about popular independent leaders. None has won the presidency, but several have polled a large number of votes. Perhaps more important, the return to constitutionality of once-proscribed Marxist parties has produced a vigorous sector on the left of the political spectrum. Although the left consistently suffers from a lack of unity and incessant factional squabbling, the Movement to Socialism (MAS) appeared to be the major Marxist organization by the 1980s. Not yet capable of amassing 10 percent of the presidential vote, it has nonetheless won congressional seats, and it participates vigorously in congressional debate, where its votes are sometimes necessary to achieve a majority. Initially created by young Communists who split from the PCV following the Soviet invasion of Czechoslovakia, the MAS has built a following among university students and certain labor unions.

Organizational activity has been the hallmark of success for both AD and COPEI. Ceaselessly active on the local and regional levels, and deeply involved in the governing of the country, the parties have vigorously championed popular participation. Electoral turnout is consistently over 90 percent of the electorate, and survey data amply document the commitment of the people to democratic politics. At the same time, there is also evidence of disillusionment with party politicians and with government performance. The realization of economic democracy and social justice is a goal far more difficult to achieve than political democracy, and party leaders themselves recognize the increasing urgency of the challenge.

The potential for military intervention is ever present, notwithstanding over twenty years of judiciously sympathetic and cautious treatment by civilian leaders. The Herrera government, less skillful than its predecessors in this regard, was seriously threatened by military rebellion in mid-1979 and again in late 1980. Only the personal persuasiveness and moral authority of the two principal founders of the democratic system—Betancourt and Caldera—discouraged a military seizure of power; thus, the attitudes of the armed forces cannot be discounted. An increasingly professionalized officer corps, well educated and knowledgeable about socioeconomic policy matters, also expresses the popular disenchantment with a rise in corruption and public immorality. Betancourt himself, who died in September 1981, spoke out forthrightly on the subject. As a consequence, the survival of the present democracy cannot be assumed, notwithstanding its accomplishments since 1958 and the strength of civic approval. For the younger generation of political leaders, who experienced neither the struggle against Gómez nor the decade of *perezjimenista* persecution, the easy affluence of oil-generated riches exercises a corrupting influence.

Colombia's democracy is qualitatively different from that of its neighbor. Characterized by Alexander Wilde as an oligarchical conversation among gentlemen, it is a system built upon a tradition of political compromise devoted to maintenance of elitist control. Resurrected by Conservative and Liberal leaders in response to *la violencia* and to the military incursion under Rojas Pinilla, the system sought to restore oligarchical hegemony through a collaborative sharing of power. The Liberal Alberto Lleras Camargo, an architect of the system and the first of its presidents (1958–1962), viewed Colombia as insufficiently mature to enjoy truly competitive democracy. Thus, a sixteen-year period would be required to reunify the republic, modernize the economy, and consolidate the attitudes and practices requisite for constructive partisan competition. For critics, the National Front also provided the vehicle for a solidification of control by the upper bourgeoisie while clouding the lack of meaningful difference between Conservative and Liberal leaders.

Unlike Venezuela's, the Colombian system more closely approaches the two-party model. Although third parties have appeared periodically, none has survived, and the Marxist left is severely divided among its several contending groups. More important has been a tendency toward factionalism within the two major parties since the introduction of the National Front. With interparty competition effectively stifled from 1958–1974 by the front arrangement, competition turned inward for both Conservatives and Liberals. More often reflecting rival personal ambitions than genuine policy disagreements, it has continued to be waged among members and/or representatives of the traditional Colombian elites. Rare indeed have been popular leaders of the masses, such as Gaitán during an earlier era.

Contrary to early predictions, the National Front ran its entire course. The Conservatives' Guillermo León Valencia served as president from 1962 to 1966, the Liberals' Carlos Lleras Restrepo from 1966 to 1970, and Misael Pastrana for the Conservatives from 1970 to 1974. Legislative bodies remained equally divided between the parties, as were the cabinet and other high administrative posts. The front officially ended with the August 1974 inauguration of the Liberal Alfonso López Michelsen, who polled 56 percent of the vote in the first competitive elections in more than a quarter century. Yet López maintained virtual parity between the two parties throughout his term, as did Liberal Julio César Turbay Ayala, who was elected in 1978. The same pattern was also followed by Conservative Belisario Betancur after his electoral victory in May 1981 over former-President López. Only with the August 1986 inauguration of the Liberals' Virgilio Barco did the nation have a one-party government.

The party system nonetheless seems likely to continue the emphasis on compromise and collaboration. Internal disunity still plagues both parties, as former presidents, ex-candidates, and would-be aspirants divide into personalistic cabals linked by family, business, and social ties. At the same time, neither Conservatives nor Liberals are mass based in organizational dimensions comparable to those of the Venezuelan system. On the other hand, family allegiances to one or the other party are often permanent, dating back for generations. Yet the constant recruitment and proselytizing found in Venezuela are more the exception than the rule in Colombia. Policy differences are now modest at best, as the historic issues that divided Conservatives and Liberals in the nineteenth and early twentieth centuries have dissipated.

A by-product of the party system and its performance is a profound dissatisfaction on the part of the citizenry. Voter abstention during the years of the National Front was usually more than 50 percent of the eligible population, prompting the explanation that the lack of meaningful competition discouraged the voter from casting a ballot. Since 1974, the figure has not increased markedly, however, suggesting that the negativism reported in public opinion surveys has not been mitigated by recent events. With grassroots preferences frequently ignored by the party elites, decisions about candidates and presidential aspirants reflect the inner dynamics of leadership circles rather than mass support. Thus, the system remains faithful to the intentions and interests of the oligarchy.

Developments in the late 1970s further diminished the extent of popular support. The congenital lawlessness in urban areas, combined with sporadic if small-scale guerrilla activity in the countryside, has enforced a climate in which civil liberties and freedoms do not engender a sense of personal security. Wealthy businessmen live behind high walls, travel to work with bodyguards, and fear for their safety; for the masses, crime is an everyday peril. Underworld activity linked to the drug traffic has aggravated the situation, and state security forces are increasingly active. Provisions of an official state of siege until mid-1982 and prevailing security practices have left much of the implementation of justice in military hands. Although the armed forces have shown little present inclination to seize power, they have exerted strong pressure for repressive powers while frequently violating individual freedoms in the pursuit of guerrillas and leftists, most notably the FARC and M-19 movements.

President Betancur sought, with some success, to reverse the trend toward polarization and to interrupt the cycle of escalating insurgency and repression. After ending the state of siege in 1982, he granted amnesty to political prisoners and to the active guerrillas who would lay down their arms. To the surprise of most observers, many accepted the offer. Unlike its predecessors, the Betancur government stressed respect for human rights. It also launched investigations into the fate of the "disappeared" and into the activities of right-wing death squads. The progress achieved by Betancur, however, proved temporary, and under Barco the level of violence again escalated. In 1989 the drug lords assassinated the Liberal Party's presidential candidate, who had pledged a campaign against them. The government responded with an all-out assault on narcotraffic. The drug cartels escalated by declaring open season on justice ministry personnel, judges, lawyers, and journalists, along with their more frequent targets: intellectuals, human rights monitors, labor leaders, and politicians on the left.

If Colombian democracy is portrayed as a structured manifestation of oligarchical control, that of Ecuador is still more artificial. Jaime Roldós Aguilera, the first elected president in a decade, said that his country has never experienced true popular democracy. Rather, it has been merely for-malistic at best, honoring appearances rather than substance. Such had been the case when three consecutive elected governments held office from 1948 to 1960. The facade of democracy was stripped away by the events of succeeding years. Only Velasco won national elections (1960 and 1968)—failing to complete either term—until the restoration of constitutional gov-ernment under Roldós in 1979. The armed forces remained the ultimate political authority, twice assuming direct government responsibility (1963–1966 and 1972–1979). And whether the regime was military or civilian, traditional socioeconomic elites continued to wield decisive influence on policymaking.

While the clash for power between the coastal oligarchy and dominant highland interests continued unabated, the armed forces departed from its usual role as constitutional arbiter to undertake a remolding of development policies. The effectiveness of military rule, however, was severely constrained by a lack of internal unity and by disagreement over procedures and objectives. The 1963–1966 military junta adopted certain moderate reformist policies, including Ecuador's first agrarian reform. At the same time, it was incapable of resisting the pressures from traditional economic elites and exhibited virtual paranoia over alleged threats from the left. Repression of opposition and extreme sensitivity to criticism created a climate of popular resentment, which ultimately led the junta to despair of its task and to resign in frustration.

When the military terminated the fifth Velasco government in 1972 and resumed power, General Guillermo Rodríguez Lara characterized the new regime as "revolutionary and nationalist." For two years, the so-called *peruanista* reformist elements held the upper hand, and although there was more rhetoric than substance to the government, nationalistic interests were sometimes promoted. With petroleum becoming the prime source of economic strength, the minister of natural resources, Vice-admiral Gustavo Jarrín Ampudia, devised a vigorously independent policy. Contracts were renegotiated with multinational corporations on relatively more favorable terms; the state petroleum agency, CEPE, was created; and Ecuador became a member of OPEC. Official decrees pledged more favorable treatment to the agricultural worker, and commitments to amelioration of social injustices were extended. Organized labor for a time supported the regime, and even the Communist Party offered guarded approval.

The military had never reached consensus on the nationalistic approach, however, and hard-line *brasileño* officers stiffened their resistance. By 1974, the balance of power within the leadership had shifted. General Rodríguez deftly responded to the pressures, policy emphases were revised, and such figures as Jarrín were forced out of government. As popular sympathies waned and official repression became more pronounced, traditionalist officers secured the resignation of Rodríguez in January 1976, established a three-man Council of Government, and announced the intention of restoring constitutional government and withdrawing to the barracks. The agonizingly slow and complex process took a total of forty-three months, during which the military remained divided over the desirability of yielding power. It was the continuing disunity within the armed forces that ultimately permitted the inauguration of Roldós, whose candidacy had been at best unpopular with the military.

As civilian forces reorganized for electoral competition beginning in 1976, the party system remained disorganized and fragmented. The single party with significant popular support was the Confederation of Popular Forces (CFP), led by its irascible, autocratic, and impetuously demagogic *caudillo* Asaad Bucaram. Atypical of Ecuadoran political leaders, he was a largely self-educated man of modest origins whose parents had immigrated from Lebanon. Mistrusted for his unpredictability and scorned for his humble background, Bucaram was anathema to both civilian and military leaders. When his presidential candidacy was barred on a specious legal technicality, Bucaram chose the party's leading thinker and political tactician—and also the husband of his niece—Roldós. Following a national plebiscite to choose a new constitution, Roldós unexpectedly won a six-candidate race by polling 29 percent of the vote. In the subsequent runoff against the rightist Sixto Durán Ballén, he won by 69 percent, while the CFP also led the congressional race.

Representing a new generation of political leadership, the thirty-seven-year-old Roldós worked closely with his electoral allies, Popular Democracy. This christian democratic force under Vice-President Osvaldo Hurtado provided effective support in seeking to realize campaign promises of economic progress and social reform. However, the new president immediately found himself challenged by his former mentor Bucaram, who controlled the *cefepista* (CFP) congressmen and secured his own selection as president of the new unicameral National Chamber of Representatives. During its first year, the Roldós administration was stalemated by the executive-legislative competition personified by Roldós and Bucaram. Only after the president's threat of a constitutional plebiscite was Roldós able to secure a slender congressional majority for the session opening in August 1980. With Bucaram at least temporarily diminished in power, Roldós nonetheless faced determined opposition to his pursuit of moderate change.

The outbreak of border conflict with Peru in early 1981 was followed in May by the death of Roldós in a plane crash. His christian democratic vice-president succeeded to power and attempted to maintain legitimacy while pursuing Roldós's reformist objectives. In the meantime, it is significant that in the 1980s, past leaders and parties were displaced by a younger generation. The historic Conservative and Liberal parties fragmented and lost force; *velasquismo* without its *caudillo* became meaningless; a handful of former presidents either retired or lost popularity and influence; and in November 1981, Asaad Bucaram died.

The presidential elections of January 1984 saw two candidates emerge from the pack and pull ahead in a close and indecisive race. They were Rodrigo Borja of the Democratic Left (ID), a relatively new but rapidly growing party having philosophical and organizational links to European socialists and social democrats, and León Febres Cordero, a leader of populistic style and liberal, laissez-faire economic persuasion whose vehicle is the conservative Social Christian Party. As neither candidate won an absolute majority of the vote, the two front-runners competed in a runoff election in May. The winner was Febres Cordero.

The next four years proved hectic as the fiery Febres undertook free-market policies in vigorous but erratic fashion. Despite early successes, the economy soon worsened. Official corruption and ineffective policymaking combined with declining oil prices and a costly earthquake to wreck government plans. The atmosphere was worsened by presidential scorn for the rights of the opposition, while meddling with the military provoked both an attempted *golpe de estado* and, in 1987, a brief kidnapping of Febres by Air Force commandos. Leaving office on a wave of unpopularity, he also assured a weak showing by conservative forces in the 1988 elections. The victor was Rodrigo Borja of the *Izquierda Democrática,* or Democratic Left. Borja's social democratic government was confronted by a large foreign debt, an ailing economy, and the unenviable necessity of applying stringent austerity measures.

FOREIGN RELATIONS

The three republics have not historically been hemispheric leaders, although Colombian diplomats have long enjoyed a reputation for professionalism. In more recent years, however, their presence in inter-American circles has been increasingly noticeable. The prestige of democratic regimes, the collective ambitions of the Andean Pact, and a greater concern about international relationships have all encouraged heightened activity in foreign affairs. This situation is particularly true in Venezuela, with its wealth of petrodollars providing economic legitimacy to its energetic initiatives. During the earlier years of its democratic period, Venezuela under Betancourt and Leoni established its credentials as a staunch bastion of liberty in the conflict with authoritarianism of both right and left. By the beginning of the 1970s, the internationally minded Caldera had extended Venezuelan influence through his own hemispheric stature as guided by christian democratic principles. When Pérez took office at the time of soaring oil prices, the nation's role was even further enhanced.

In conjunction with Mexican president Luis Echeverría, Pérez championed creation of the Latin American Economic System (SELA), with its seat located in Caracas. The windfall of profits from petroleum permitted contributions of $500 million each to the World Bank, the Inter-American Development Bank, and the International Monetary Fund; $60 million to the Andean Development Corporation; and $25 million to the Caribbean Development Bank. There was a flurry of activity in the Caribbean, including major impetus in the elaboration of trade and economic agreements with newly independent English-speaking countries. As private interests followed increased government investment, some people even charged Venezuela with launching a new imperialist campaign toward the islands—most notably Trinidad and Tobago's Prime Minister Eric Williams.

Luis Herrera Campins maintained Venezuela's high profile. His christian democratic government did not continue the uncritical Pérez approval of Nicaragua's Sandinistas; it provided instead strong encouragement to the much criticized junta in embattled El Salvador. Despite the deterioration of the Salvadoran situation and charges that Venezuela was acting in part as surrogate for the United States, the Herrera government continued with both moral and material support. It worked sympathetically with the quasi-christian democratic Costa Rican government and in 1980, joined with Mexico in a plan to supply oil at less than market price to Central American and selected Caribbean countries. Venezuelan anger at the United States over the latter's position toward the Malvinas/Falklands conflict in 1982, however, stimulated a rethinking of policy in Caracas. Since then, on Central American and other issues, Venezuela has been disinclined to follow the lead of the United States. With the 1989 return to power of Carlos Andrés Pérez, moreover, Venezuela swiftly assumed a position of leadership among the Latin American democracies.

Notwithstanding its hemispheric visibility, Venezuela has yet to resolve basic disputes with its neighbors. To the east, the border disagreement with Guyana, reopened by Betancourt in 1962, continues to resist resolution despite periodic negotiation. The relationship with Colombia is also still marred by multiple disputes. The estimated annual toll of 200,000–300,000 head of cattle smuggled into Venezuela has continued. More seriously, the migration of illegal Colombians in search of Venezuelan employment and wages unavailable at home had become a growing problem to the Caracas government by the 1980s. Reliable figures do not exist, but 2 million to 3 million *indocumentados* ("undocumented workers") are estimated to be living in Venezuela. Equally grave is the contested Gulf of Venezuela boundary, lying as it does in an area of offshore oil deposits. Fears of drug-related violence from Colombia also worry the Caracas government.

Colombia in part has shared recent Venezuelan efforts to promote and encourage democracy and civilian government, although at a reduced level of commitment. The government concurred with Pérez's efforts on behalf of the canal treaty negotiations between Panama and the United States and also favored the overthrow of the Somoza dictatorship in Nicaragua. Through the Andean Pact, it expressed opposition to the military disruption of the electoral process in Bolivia in mid-1980. Greater attention, however, centered on continued haggling with the United States over the drug traffic. North American charges that the Colombian government was unconcerned were met with the retort that the thriving demand in the United States bore primary responsibility.

When Ecuador returned to democratic rule in 1979, Jaime Roldós stressed the importance of hemispheric freedom and elected government. His championing of such principles as a manifestation of national sovereignty was overshadowed in early 1981 by the unexpected renewal of border hostilities between Ecuador and Peru. Vice-President Osvaldo Hurtado followed the same patterns during his portion of the constitutional term, but León Febres Cordero shifted emphases through his pronounced friendship with Ronald Reagan. Ecuador remained a virtual handmaiden of Washington's hemispheric policies until the inauguration of Rodrigo Borja, who recognized the importance of good relations with the United States while asserting national independence through renewed relations with Nicaragua.

By the close of the decade, with fellow social democrats Borja and Pérez maintaining a longtime friendship while Virgilio Barco shared many of their views, prospects for envigorated hemispheric activism were evident. Their collective and individual commitment to democratic principles is unquestionable, and the roots of representative constitutional government are apparent in all three countries. Despite severe economic dislocations, varying degrees of public alienation, and the still-unresolved problem of the foreign debt, these three Gran Colombian nations are among the more solid democracies on the continent.

The democratic order in the Andes is increasingly threatened by the trade in narcotic drugs. Nevertheless, the Bush administration's so-called War on Drugs comes as a mixed blessing. The new security assistance for anti-drug efforts, amounting to $261 million in 1989 for Colombia, Peru, and Bolivia, was likely to strengthen military and paramilitary forces whose roles in the drug war were sometimes murky and whose loyalty to civilian leaders was less than fully reliable. Furthermore, some U.S. gestures, such as stationing naval vessels off the Colombian coast, have been seen as an affront to national sovereignty.

In Venezuela, a vibrantly competitive party-based system still searches for solutions to problems of modernization. Colombian elites, historically adept in designing policies to ensure their hegemony, face increasing obstacles in manipulating a discontented and alienated citizenry. And in Ecuador, the emergent younger generation of civilian leaders must co-opt, outmaneuver, or otherwise counter a rigidly traditionalist oligarchy determined to resist reforms and defend its perquisites. For each of these countries, government performance in shaping and implementing development policies to assure both economic growth and social justice is central to the survival of democratic government.

SUGGESTED READINGS

Baloyra, Enrique A., and John D. Martz. *Political Attitudes in Venezuela: Societal Cleavages & Political Opinion.* Austin: University of Texas Press, 1979. The second of two volumes on Venezuelan mobilization and political attitudes; based on extensive survey data.

Berry, R. Albert; Ronald G. Hellman; and Mauricio Solaún, eds. *Politics of Compromise: Coalition Government in Colombia.* New Brunswick, N.J.: Transaction Books, for the Center for Inter-American Relations, 1980. A multi-authored review based on a conference discussing recent and contemporary events in Colombia.

Blank, David Eugene. *Politics in Venezuela.* Boston: Little, Brown and Company, 1973. A thoughtful overview of Venezuelan society and politics into the early 1970s.

Conaghan, Catherine A. *Restructuring Domination: Industrialists and the State in Ecuador.* Pittsburgh: University of Pittsburgh Press, 1988. Examines Ecuador's industrialists within the context of national development.

Dix, Robert H. *Colombia: The Political Dimensions of Change.* New Haven: Yale University Press, 1967. Although dated, this analysis is still rich in historicopolitical patterns.

———. *The Politics of Colombia.* New York: Praeger, 1987. An insightful reinterpretation twenty years after his earlier book, again stressing political factors.

Fitch, John Samuel. *The Military Coup d'Etat as a Political Process: Ecuador, 1948–1966.* Baltimore: Johns Hopkins University Press, 1977. An excellent and well-documented study of the armed forces that ties their role to the evolution of contemporary Ecuadoran politics.

Gil Yepes, José Antonio. *The Challenge of Venezuelan Democracy.* Trans. by Evelyn Harrison I., Lolo Gil de Yanes, and Danielle Salti. New Brunswick, N.J.: Transaction Books, 1981. The work of a Venezuelan sociologist that builds on the literature of administrative decision making in studying the Venezuelan business sector and its impact on national politics.

Hartlyn, Jonathan. *The Politics of Coalition Rule in Colombia.* Cambridge: Cambridge University Press, 1988. A careful study that stresses both formal and informal aspects of two-party collaboration.

Herman, Donald L. *Christian Democracy in Venezuela.* Chapel Hill: University of North Carolina Press, 1980. A detailed treatment of COPEI through the Caldera administration and including the 1978 election of Luis Herrera Campins.

————, ed. *Democracy in Latin America: Colombia and Venezuela.* New York: Praeger, 1988. Well-known authorities on both countries collaborate for this comparative study.

Hurtado, Osvaldo. *Political Power in Ecuador.* Trans. by Nick D. Mills, Jr. Albuquerque: University of New Mexico Press, 1980. Historical and sociological analysis of Ecuadoran politics by the subsequent president of the republic. The book includes a brief epilogue discussing the withdrawal of the military and the 1979 Roldós-Hurtado victory.

Martz, John D. *Acción Democrática: Evolution of a Modern Political Party in Venezuela.* Princeton: Princeton University Press, 1966. A detailed study of Venezuela's original mass-based party; includes attention to the genesis and emergence of the party system.

————. *Ecuador: Conflicting Political Cultures and the Quest for Progress.* Boston: Allyn and Bacon, 1972. Now dated, but the first political overview of Ecuador in over two decades.

————. *The Politics of Petroleum in Ecuador.* New Brunswick: Transaction Press, 1987. Contrasts in policymaking characteristics of respective military and civilian regimes over the past two decades, especially as regards petroleum. Also incorporates extensive treatment of parties and elections.

Martz, John D., and David J. Myers, eds. *Venezuela: The Democratic Experience.* New York: Praeger Publishers, 2d ed., 1986. A multi-authored work examining major aspects of Venezuelan politics and economy.

Osterling, Jorge Pablo. *Democracy in Colombia: Clientelist Politics and Guerrilla Warfare.* New Brunswick: Transaction Press, 1989. A perceptive overview that includes a wealth of information on governmental structures and institutions.

Schodt, David W. *Ecuador: An Andean Enigma.* Boulder, Colo.: Westview Press, 1987. A succinct review by a knowledgeable political economist.

24

PERU AND BOLIVIA

JOSÉ Z. GARCÍA

The widest, most massive chunk of the great Andean Cordillera straddles the boundary line between what is today southeastern Peru and northwestern Bolivia. Nestled between high mountains and volcanoes on both sides of the border at an altitude of well over 12,000 ft (3,658 m) lies a huge plain the size of the U.S. state of Colorado, punctuated by steep valleys and known simply as the Altiplano. On it, some of the most advanced civilizations in the Western Hemisphere—the Tiahuanaco, the Aymara, and finally, the Inca—forged empires over the disparate tribes that populated the area. To this day, in spite of many centuries of many kinds of change, the Altiplano and its surrounding highland area, the sierra, continues to be home for a majority of the people of Bolivia and Peru. It forms the cultural core of both countries. Cuzco, the ancient capital of the Incas on the edge of the Altiplano is referred to by the Indians in respectful terms as *El* Cuzco (*the* Cuzco). The Spaniards placed their capital in Lima, on the coast, even before the conquest was complete.

The ruggedness of the high Andean terrain, always more densely populated than the surrounding coastal or jungle lowlands, made communication and transportation difficult, giving rise to powerful regional jealousies. This is as true today as it was 2,000 years ago and accounts, in part, for the relative difficulty rulers have had over the centuries in governing the peoples of the area. Only extremely well-organized societies have been able to rule over the people of the Altiplano.

The Spaniards captured the Incan Empire by destroying the royal family and its power in a process that took four decades to complete. By then, diseases imported from Europe and psychological damage associated with defeat and enslavement began to take their toll on the native population, which was reduced, as in Mexico, by 90 percent. Having conquered the Incan homeland, the Spaniards proceeded to assault the culture of the people and created a complex, multilayered caste system—which lasted for four centuries—in which Indians provided what amounted to slave labor for white masters. The cultural destruction occurred at an extremely rapid pace: A magnificent tradition of artistic pottery production, some of it (Nazca, Chavin, Chimu, Mochica) among the most aesthetically pleasing ever produced, was reduced within half a century after conquest to a pitiful, shriveled parody of what it had once been. Such are the consequences of conquest.

Today, in spite of great economic and social strides made during the past three decades, Indians, comprising a large proportion of the populations of both Peru and Bolivia, have not yet successfully been integrated into the mainstream of modern Latin American life. The sad music of the peasants of the Andes—one step forward, two steps back in dance and recognizable instantly today, even by first-time visitors from far away, as the sounds of people who have endured hardship and oppression for centuries—still serves as a vivid reminder that much remains to be done. In Mexico, a brilliant resurgence of painting, literature, and archaeology, focusing on the Aztec and Mayan past, occurred just prior to major policy changes favoring the Indian population. Mexican national identity was profoundly influenced by this new awareness of the country's pre-Columbian roots. In Peru and Bolivia, national identification with the Indian cultural heritage has not yet permeated the collective psyche to the extent found in Mexico, even though all of the ingredients are there: archaeological remnants of several civilizations of great accomplishment stretching over an area now comprising three countries, among the most inspiring of which are the massive fortress at Sacsahuaman, the temple of the sun in Cuzco, and the haunting ruins of Machu Picchu high on a promontory bathed by swiftly moving clouds with a raging river cutting through the granite a thousand feet below. The awe-inspiring remnants of these great civilizations have provoked some of the best minds and artists in the world to learn more about them and to express this interest in art. The descendants of these great stone masons of the past are likely someday to incorporate these identities into a national heritage.

HISTORICAL SKETCH OF BOLIVIA: CONQUEST TO 1884

Almost from the beginning, the Spaniards distinguished between what they called Upper Peru, or Charcas, roughly the area now comprising Bolivia, and Lower Peru, where modern Peru lies. Upper Peru was made administratively subordinate to governments in Lower Peru throughout the colonial period. In 1545, a phenomenal silver deposit was discovered at Potosí in Upper Peru, the development of which made Chuquisaca, the capital of Charcas, and Potosí, where the mines were located, among the richest cities in the world. These cities were famous for an excellent school of painting and two superb universities during the sixteenth and seventeenth centuries. Gradually, silver production declined, due to rising costs of imports (especially mercury) essential to mining operations, and periodic weaknesses in the international silver market. This decline, combined with a long period of relative geographic isolation from the rest of the world, made Bolivia one of the poorest areas in Latin America by the nineteenth century. The status of the Indian population, comprising a large majority, remained abysmal throughout the entire colonial period.

When independence came to the area in 1825, Bolivia was separated from both Peru and Argentina as a buffer between what were thought to be two emerging powers. The mining industry, already in decline, nearly collapsed in the early part of the century due to a severing of traditional trade routes during the independence period. Economic stagnation persisted between 1825 and 1880 and was marked by a shift in power away from the silver producers, who had dominated the political life of Bolivia for centuries, toward a landed aristocracy. With the increased importance of land, a new assault against the Indians, many of whom lived on legally recognized communal lands, took place. The government first confiscated Church-owned lands, to be rented or sold for state revenues, and then began to confiscate communal lands, some of which predated the Spanish conquest. This forced the Indian residents to purchase individual plots from the same government that had taken their common land away. Many peasants were thus reduced to semiserf status. It is estimated, for example, that Mariano Melgarejo, a *caudillo* who ruled from 1862 to 1871, abrogated the land titles of more than 100,000 peasants, about 10 percent of the entire population of Bolivia.

Melgarejo is also known in Bolivian history as the ruler who sold the country to the highest bidder. Within a few decades after independence, Bolivia had lost one-half of its territory to its neighbors: Brazil, Argentina, Chile, Peru, and, later, Paraguay. Territory was ceded to Brazil in 1867 by Melgarejo for questionable commercial advantages; a war with Brazil resulted in the loss of more land in 1903. In 1879, Chile occupied Bolivia's small coastal strip on the Pacific Ocean between Peru and Chile. Bolivia, with the support of Peru, declared war. In 1884, a truce was declared; Bolivia lost its coastland and has been a landlocked nation ever since.

Bolivia's economy was revived with the discovery during the 1870s of huge tin deposits very near the old silver mines. Tin prices remained high on world markets for several decades thereafter. The wealth generated by large-scale tin mining paid for the repair of the silver mines and for the modernization of the country as a whole. Three new railroad lines were built, connecting Bolivia with the rest of the world for the first time. Highways integrated larger areas of the country. A new era of prosperity set in.

Politically, the tin boom meant that the landed aristocracy would once again have to share power with mineral entrepreneurs. Three families emerged to monopolize all of the booming tin-mining industry. But unlike previous elite groups, these families did not seek directly to control the government; rather, they encouraged the development of a professional army and a middle class to rationalize the government bureaucracy after decades of neglect. University students, anxious to join these rising groups, began to organize themselves for the first time as a political force. The traditional silver mining interests also organized themselves, forming a conservative political party. The landed aristocracy maintained its position throughout the period. In short, the economic bonanza meant that a new mixture of powerful economic elites was emerging while, at the same time, several soon-to-be powerful middle-sector groups were being expanded and strengthened. Although competition for the presidency remained intense and sometimes violent during this period, there was widespread agreement on economic policy, which remained remarkably consistent. A serious structural problem in the political system, however, began to emerge; it was not resolved until the Revolution of 1952.

During this period, the middle class prospered as a result of the wealth generated by tin, which paid for the building of railroads, highways, and other infrastructural projects that required an increase in the national stock of middle-class skills. Two factors in this growth and prosperity made the emergence of powerful middle classes extremely dangerous to the upper classes. First, during periods of economic collapse, not enough revenues would be available to satisfy the growing demands of the middle-class professionals. These had tasted power, though, in military, financial, and bureaucratic organizations and were highly likely to raise serious distributional questions with the upper-class elites during a bust rather than to accept high rates of unemployment or lowered status. To them, maintaining social and economic position during a depression could be accomplished only by creating a middle-class government powerful enough to control the private mining-sector revenues, through confiscation of or tight control over the wealth of the somewhat insecure upper classes. Thus, when the tin barons delegated political power to the middle classes, they were helping their logical future enemies.

Second, when the poor began to organize—with middle-class assistance after the depression and the Chaco War—the instrument for middle-class acquisition of the major economic enterprises of the country for the state was created. Both economic and political roles for the middle class were possible for the first time in Bolivian history. If the tin-mining enterprises provided a potential economic base for the middle classes, the organization of the lower classes gave them the potential power to acquire it. The alliance forged between certain sectors of the working and middle classes, consummated in 1952, would produce one of the few revolutions in Latin American history.

PERUVIAN COLONIAL AND NATIONAL HISTORY TO 1968

Peru's colonial and early national history was quite different from that of Bolivia. The Spaniards located the viceregal capital city, Lima, on the coast. Lima's port, Callao, in turn, became one of the two primary ports in the Americas—the other being Veracruz in Mexico—to which trade to and from Spain was directed. The relative frequency of contact with the outside world, the relative wealth of the area (some of which was generated in the administratively subordinate region of Upper Peru), and the opportunities provided by the strategic and administrative importance of the city all combined to make Lima and its neighboring valleys and mountains an attractive and prestigious area for permanent settlement by large numbers of Spaniards. The Upper Peruvian economy, on the other hand—based on the extraction of a single mineral at extremely high altitudes through the forced labor of Indians—caused the Bolivian area to become an exploitation colony. Relatively few Spaniards considered Bolivia a permanent place of residence. Little attention was paid by Spain to the development there of autonomous and resilient civil institutions. In Peru, on the other hand, a settlement colony appeared, based on land ownership. Black slaves were imported to work the land on coastal and sierra estates, and Spain endeavored to create a diversified economy with adaptable institutions and endless bureaucratic controls to ensure a multilayered caste system roughly based on skin color. Peru's institutions were therefore more long lasting and resilient, with a conservative strain that persists into the late twentieth century. By the seventeenth century, Peru had a thriving economy, producing wine, olives, sugar, rice, wheat, livestock, cotton, and wool and had simple manufacturing, some mining, and a brisk trade with Spain. The aristocracy was cosmopolitan in outlook and extremely self-assured. Bolivia remained tied to mineral production, its inhabitants subject to the vagaries of boom and bust.

By the end of the eighteenth century, settlement patterns in Peru had reduced the Indian proportion to less than 60 percent of the total population of around 1 million, with whites, blacks, and "half-castes" accounting for the remainder. Since nearly half of the white population lived in three main cities (Cuzco, Lima, and Arequipa), Indians vastly outnumbered whites in rural areas, where treatment of the Indians varied considerably from place to place and from time to time. A major Indian rebellion led by Tupac Amaru, a descendant of the Inca royal family, was able to last for nearly two years, with much bloodshed, before it was put down. Thereafter, in spite of halfhearted reforms designed to reduce the threat of further violence, the imperial hold over the Peruvian population began to weaken, due to a gradual decline in Spain itself. Peru's internal institutional fabric, however, was so strong and conservative that Peruvians rather reluctantly accepted independence after José de San Martín, an Argentinian, wrested control from Spanish royalists with the aid of Simón Bolívar and Gen. Antonio José de Sucre, both Venezuelans. For the next two decades, Peru was wracked by bloody civil wars and power struggles, the sorry legacy of an independence movement with few internal roots.

The chaos produced by the sudden amputation of centuries of economic, social, and political relations betweeen Peru and Spain was halted with the growth of the guano trade at mid-century. Bird deposits discovered in large quantities on islands off the coast were found to be superior as fertilizer. Guano was shipped throughout the world from these islands. The Peruvian government handled these shipments as a state monopoly, the revenues of which were used to modernize the state bureaucracy and, especially, to make infrastructural improvements in the city of Lima.

The Rise of APRA

Later in the nineteenth century, a handful of families began acquiring large tracts of land in the northern coastal valleys of Peru and converting them into sugar plantations with refining mills. Very quickly, these families, in alliance with older, more traditional sierra hacienda owners, began to dominate the political, social, and economic life of the country. The way in which the sugar plantation owners acquired their land had profound consequences for the Peruvian political system.

The sugar interests bought out a large number of middle-class landowners, often using deceptive means and questionable legal tactics. Their aggressiveness and often ruthless style caused considerable disgruntlement among the middle-class owners who suddenly found their power and status fading. By 1923, a young north coast intellectual named Victor Raúl Haya de la Torre began to channel the discontent that had been festering in the north, forging an alliance between the frustrated northerners and a youthful left-wing university movement. The fact that the American Popular Revolutionary Alliance (APRA) grew into the single-largest political party in Peruvian history is testimony to the growing power of the proportionately minuscule middle class during this period. The anti-imperialist ideology of APRA responded to a frustration felt by many middle-class members that foreign concerns were too dominant in Peru. After all, most of the mining interests in Peru were foreign. Guano prices had for many years been dictated by a take-it-or-leave-it attitude on the part of foreign firms contracting to buy it. Foreign capital had assisted in the consolidation of sugar plantations on the north coast. Resentment against foreigners was high. APRA's success was due not only to the channeling of middle-class discontent but also to the organizational genius of Haya, who built the first mass political party in Latin American history.

As APRA, a clear threat to traditional upper-class rule in Peru, became increasingly popular, steps were taken to prevent its leaders from gaining power. Accused of being communistic, the party was outlawed, its leaders exiled. But it continued to organize the masses. Thereafter, both the upper classes and APRA tried to resolve the impasse by conspiring within the military (an increasingly middle-class institution and, hence, potentially susceptible to APRA appeals) for access to power. The military became the key institution in the country, with pro-APRA officers and anti-APRA officers contending for power within the armed forces. Given the new importance of the role of the military, it is hardly surprising that the institution tended to side with the oligarchy against APRA; after all, if APRA gained power, it would certainly act to reduce the political importance of the armed forces, the only other political organization in the country that could compete with it. Peruvian politics for more than three decades was determined by this power struggle for access to the military by pro- and anti-Aprista groups, with the military usually taking an anti-Aprista stance, although at the cost of considerable internal dissent. By the time a group of officers ideologically committed to the original APRA program came to power in Peru in 1968, the APRA party had lost much of its ideological dynamism; it had become committed more to governing Peru for the rich than to fighting without power for the poor. It is one of the great ironies of twentieth-century Peru that officers who for decades had prevented APRA from taking power implemented the original APRA program. One of the first major steps the officers took was to nationalize the sugar haciendas of the north coast, resolving a long-festering problem that had stimulated the creation of APRA in the first place. The APRA leader, Haya de la Torre, died a very old man during the military regime that implemented his policies.

RECENT MAJOR POLITICAL MOVEMENTS: THE BOLIVIAN MNR AND THE PERUVIAN MILITARY REGIME OF 1968

Origins of the MNR

Most countries of Latin America suffered severely throughout the Great Depression. Bolivia was no exception. The added factor of the Chaco War (1932–1935), lost by Bolivia, culminated in the temporary rise to power of a civil-military movement that would dominate Bolivian politics intermittently for decades to come.

Partly as a means of deflecting attention from the government's failure in domestic matters, conservative President Daniel Salamanca began building a powerful army during the depression, while, at the same time, drastically cutting other government services. During a border skirmish in the disputed Chaco border region, Salamanca ordered his army to invade Paraguayan territory—even though his military advisers warned that such a move would have disastrous consequences. Paraguay responded with full mobilization and eventually entered Bolivian territory in a rout of the Bolivian army. A peace treaty was signed in July of 1935.

Several groups were embittered by this experience. In the first place, the officer corps was outraged that a civilian president could have forced an unwinnable war on an unwilling military. For the next two decades, military officers ruled the country. Second, the war effort had mobilized over 10 percent of the population of Bolivia, at that time one of the least-mobilized countries in Latin America. Groups that were mobilized, especially the Indian and mestizo peasants and labor union members, would play major political roles in the country's politics thereafter. The organization of the Chaco War army into three castes—white officers, mestizo subofficers, and Indian front-line soldiers—would further create class and caste consciousness. Finally, a hitherto largely ineffectual left-wing intellectual group was able to galvanize the general outrage against the political system that had produced the war. Its goal was to undo the power relations of the previous half century.

From the end of the Chaco War in 1935 to 1939, young military officers destroyed the conservative political system that had been created in response to the tin boom of 1880. Standard Oil Company was nationalized without compensation, the first such confiscation in Latin American history. An interventionist constitutional convention created an activist state for the first time. Large mining concerns were required to turn over their foreign exchange to the national bank, which could then tax corporations more effectively. The mines were not, however, nationalized. A far-reaching labor code, favorable to the laboring classes, was written.

The Rise and Fall of the MNR

As a result of the social ferment following the Chaco War, several new political parties were formed, including three socialist parties and two profascist parties, all responding to middle-class interests. The most talented leadership came from the National Revolutionary Movement (MNR), organized with fascist tendencies. The leader of the MNR, Victor Paz Estenssoro, was also highly pragmatic. Under his leadership, the MNR dropped its pro-Nazi stance when convenient and was able to co-opt the leader of the Trotskyist party, Juan Lechín, who had organized the mine workers into a powerful force. The MNR did not come to power until after several successive presidents had tried in vain to gather enough power to initiate and consolidate reform. The party thus had time to learn from the mistakes of others and to mature. Further, the party had a period of co-government with a young military officer, Major Gualberto Villarroel, who took over in a coup in 1943 and who combined reformism with brutal repression. Villarroel was murdered, burned, and then hanged from a lamp post by an angry mob in 1946. The MNR then faced six years of conservative government, during which the party leadership focused less on fascism and ideology and more on the question of gaining power. In 1952, after years of repression against the middle class from right-wing rulers, a revolt against the regime was organized by the MNR. Peasants and labor union members were armed. The military was divided, and its conservative leaders were defeated. The MNR was in power.

The MNR accomplished several major changes in Bolivian society. First, Indians, for the first time since the conquest, were given full citizenship rights plus the material and physical means to defend their citizenship. In reality, these rights were not so much granted to the Indians by the MNR as they were seized by the Indians during the revolt and ratified by the MNR. Indians had overtaken many haciendas and distributed the land among themselves. Tin miners had occupied the mines. The peasants who had been armed during the Revolution were reluctant to put down their arms. The MNR legalized these changes by nationalizing the tin mines, formalizing an agrarian reform, and limiting the size and power of the military. The middle-class bureaucrats, created by the tin barons in the boom of the 1880s, finally had power.

The MNR had succeeded only because it had unified several of the major political forces of the country: the miners, who had been a force since their organization in the early 1930s; the armed forces; and large sectors of the emerging middle classes. After the Revolution, a fourth group emerged, the peasants, who rapidly organized themselves once the land was available for redistribution. The MNR ultimately failed because it was unable to maintain this coalition of forces; within a few years the miners withdrew, and the armed forces contended with the MNR for power.

At the time of the Revolution four of the top leaders, each of whom started out with different power bases, forged a pact by which they would rotate the presidential candidacy among themselves every four years until 1964. The Revolution at the time was so popular it was reasonable to assume the men who led it would be able to withstand electoral challenges to their rule until then. Victor Paz Estenssoro would be the presidential candidate for the MNR from 1952 until 1956; he would be followed by Hernán Siles Suazo from 1956 to 1960, who in turn would be followed by Walter Guevara Arce until 1964, when labor leader Juan Lechín would become the candidate. Much of Bolivian political history from 1952 to 1989 was the byproduct of the intrigues and betrayals of these four men.

Siles Suazo indeed followed Paz as the presidential candidate in 1956, as called for in the pact. He was elected and served out his term as president. But in 1960 former president Victor Paz intervened in MNR party affairs to block the agreed-upon candidacy of Walter Guevara in favor of his own. Paz became president once again, but the ruling MNR party split as a result. As a means of protecting himself against potential reprisals by Guevara and his followers, Paz acted to fortify and woo the armed forces, badly weakened as a fighting force under President Siles. Then, as the 1964 presidential elections approached, Paz used his influence in the legislature to amend the constitution to permit him to run for yet another term in office, this time betraying his agreement to back Trotskyist labor leader Juan Lechín for president. In this effort he was supported by elements of the U.S. government and by large portions of the armed forces, both concerned about the potential implications of a government headed by an avowed Marxist.

The armed forces accepted the ploy by Paz but only after insisting that the MNR candidate for vice-president should be a member of the armed forces. Paz was duly elected under these circumstances. But a few months later the armed forces overthrew Paz, and, respecting the constitutional succession of the vice-president, allowed Vice-President (General) René Barrientos to become president. Barrientos, a truly popular leader who tried to create a power base of his own, independent of that of the MNR, was killed three years later in a helicopter incident that many attribute to jealousies within the armed forces. A succession of military governments followed. The most bizarre was the regime of General Juan José Torres, who allowed peasants, students, labor unions, and left-wing ideologues to form a Popular Assembly—sidestepping traditional institutional powers—but did not permit them to arm themselves against the inevitable right-wing reaction. General Hugo Banzer, who represented conservative wealthy interests in the Santa Cruz area, was able to oust Torres from office in less than one year. Banzer remained in office for several years, in which time he was able to form a power base and take advantage of an economic boom to favor the interests of the Santa Cruz oligarchy.

By the late 1970s international pressures—especially the foreign-policy orientation of U.S. President Jimmy Carter, favoring elections to dissolve military dictatorships in Latin America—forced Banzer to hold elections. Elections were held in 1978, pitting former President Siles Suazo against General Juan Pereda Asbún, a candidate publicly favored by President Banzer. Several other candidates also ran. Siles denounced electoral fraud on behalf of Pereda during the vote count, and the tally eventually indicated neither had received enough votes (the minimum requirement is 50 percent plus one of valid votes cast) to be elected outright, throwing the whole election into the legislature, where Siles clearly had enough votes to be elected. Pereda then staged a coup d'etat and assumed dictatorial powers. He in turn was deposed a few months later by General David Padilla, who held elections in 1979.

This time the major candidates were former presidents Siles and Paz Estenssoro; again, neither candidate received an outright majority of the vote and again the election was handed to the legislature, which gridlocked over the issue for days. It finally resolved the presidency in favor of none other than Walter Guevara Arce, who had been betrayed by Paz Estenssoro as presidential candidate in 1960 and who was now president of the Senate. Guevara had not been a candidate in the 1979 elections and the constitutionality of his election is still disputed. He did, however, become president in an act that was widely seen as correcting a wrong committed twenty years earlier. He was overthrown a few months later, however, in a military coup headed by General Alberto Natusch Busch, known to be connected with international cocaine trafficking. Facing widespread and intense opposition, Natusch stepped down after accepting a formula whereby the legislature would reconvene to elect a new president. Lydia Gueiler, the first woman to serve as president of Bolivia, was selected as interim president until new elections could be held in 1980, once again pitting former presidents Siles and Paz against each other. These were held on schedule. Siles won a plurality of votes, but again not a majority. Before the legislature convened to settle the issue the government was toppled by General Luis García Meza. Two years later a coup interrupted García's rule, the legislature (elected in 1980) was reconvened, and they chose Siles as president in 1982 for a term of four years. His competence as president began to be challenged as Bolivia plunged into a free-falling economic collapse after a period of solid economic growth. Siles retired from the presidency voluntarily in 1985, one year before the expiration of his four-year term. Victor Paz Estenssoro, president then for the third time, supervised a successful economic recovery. His nephew, Jaime Paz Zamora, was elected president in 1989 by the legislature after he failed to receive a majority of votes in the general election, which he contested with General Hugo Banzer.

Thus, of the four men who had agreed in 1952 to alternate their candidacies, three eventually became president, all were deposed at one time or another, and all remained active politically until the 1980s. The fourth, Juan Lechín, remained an outsider; but as undisputed leader of the labor movement, he remained a political force to be reckoned with by all governments throughout the period. Today the four, though still alive at the time of writing, are in their ninth decade. The election of Jaime Paz signaled the beginning of a new generation of political leadership in Bolivia, the first in four decades.

Bolivia now stands at a crossroads in its political development. A strategic error of the first magnitude made by the minuscule upper class in Bolivia at the turn of the century resulted in the destruction of that class and the power structures supporting it. But the middle-class leaders who presided over the loss of power of the tin barons and *hacendados* were unable to forge a permanent base for stable rule as several sectors within that middle class, including military officers, public servants, labor union leaders, and landed peasants fought among themselves for access to the limited resources of the state. The relative weakness of this middle-class coalition of forces created to govern the nation has enabled new political actors—the dynamic Santa Cruz business community, financial intermediaries surrounding the petrochemical and cocaine industries, and others well connected to transnational capital flows—to circumvent many of the distributional postulates of the Bolivian Revolution. A governing coalition capable of subsuming the activities of these new groups has not yet emerged, although President Jaime Paz Zamora appears to be trying to strike a balance between Bolivian nationalism, deeply rooted in history, and the economic realities facing his country.

The Peruvian Military Regime of 1968–1980 and the Collapse of Traditional Power Structures

By 1968 the aging leadership of APRA had mellowed to the point of bland advocacy of the status quo. Years of struggle had taken the fight out of Haya, but he refused to step down gracefully. Younger members of the party in the 1960s had even joined Marxist guerrilla groups fighting in the highlands, convinced that legal institutional changes were unlikely. Although the armed forces snuffed out these efforts with ease, some military officers sensed in the general mood of the public a desire for long-overdue changes, especially in the direction of reducing the political power of foreign investors and wealthy landowners, long allied with each other and virtually untouchable. Taking advantage of a corruption scandal within the constitutionally elected government of Fernando Belaunde Terry, a small group of officers led by General Juan Velasco Alvarado overthrew the president, replacing him with a governing junta and cabinet composed entirely of active-duty generals in the three branches of the armed forces. Their first official act was to expropriate the holdings of the U.S.-owned International Petroleum Company, accused of collaborating with government officials to lower the price paid by them for Peruvian oil. This act was extremely popular, enabling the progressive officers who had organized the coup to consolidate their position within the armed forces. Six months later they announced the expropriation of the sugar haciendas in the north (long a political power base for the wealthy), a comprehensive redistribution plan for agricultural land in the highlands, a scheme to initiate profit sharing for industrial workers, and a series of stiff regulations to control the activities of foreign investors.

Internal dissension within the armed forces made full implementation of these policies impossible, and eventually conservative forces within the military were able to wrest power away from the original group of reformist officers. But the officers who replaced them soon found themselves mired in economic problems, corruption, and political opposition from both right and left. Following the trend in Latin America at the time, the military retired from power in 1980. As if to spite the military, the public again elected as president Fernando Belaunde, overthrown by the armed forces twelve years earlier.

Twelve years of military rule, however, had changed the face of Peruvian politics forever. Most important, the spine of the nation's capricious right-wing oligarchy had been broken through the expropriation of some of their holdings. While these did not lessen their overall economic strength, it was clear after 1969 for the first time that the actions of the wealthy could be regulated through government policy. The rather effete reaction of the oligarchy to assaults on their perquisites further undermined their aura of invincibility. By the time Belaunde was elected in 1980 the right wing as a political force was discombobulated and would remain so for a decade. Only the organized center and left of the political spectrum retained electoral vitality.

In addition, the populist rhetoric of military rule during the Velasco years awakened the long-dormant expectations of the masses of peasants and *cholos,* who had for centuries known military might as an unpleasant if intermittent reminder that Peruvian society was controlled exclusively by the upper classes. For several years important members of the armed forces openly advocated and in some cases facilitated political organization by the nation's poorer sectors. And by the time reformist impetus in the armed forces waned, it was clear that the upper class was in no position to control the destinies of the nation. Making matters worse, Peru entered into a period of economic decline, with only two years of positive growth between 1975 and 1990. The centrist governments of Belaunde (1980–1985) and APRA leader Alan García (1985–1990) grappled without much success against economic and political problems. García's economic policies especially caused the wealthy to disinvest in Peru's economy. As this deterioration in the capacity of the traditional oligarchy to rule became evident during the 1980s and reverberated throughout the political system, leftist organizations of all kinds began to sense that history had handed them a golden opportunity. One of these, a small group of Marxist guerrillas known as the Sendero Luminoso (Shining Path) began to challenge through force of arms all of the conventional notions of what was needed for Peru.

The Rise of the Sendero Luminoso

In the ancient Inca stronghold of Ayacucho, today the poorest region of Peru, during the early 1960s a small group of Marxist university professors and students began a series of experimental political activities among the peasants of neighboring villages. This initiative would culminate during the 1980s with their launching of a full-fledged revolutionary movement—national in scope, tailored carefully to fit Peruvian realities, and dangerous enough to threaten the very survival of the regime. Their methods were sometimes bizarre, often astonishingly successful. Before moving to control a village they would sometimes hang dead dogs from nearby trees or posts—as a warning sign to villagers against resistance. Once on the birthday of their leader, Abimael Guzmán Reynoso, they blew out the night lights of the entire city of Lima, a city of nine million inhabitants, leaving only one huge torchlight symbol, a hammer and sickle glowing in the dark on the side of a hill.

Sendero's growth as a fighting force was dramatic. Starting out in the early 1980s with only around 100 warriors, it numbered by the end of the decade perhaps 10,000. Violence had caused over 15,000 deaths and well over $12 billion in property damage. Sendero efforts to intimidate those who would participate in the regime's administration caused nearly one-quarter of the municipalities to hold mayoral elections in 1989 with no candidate willing to risk running for the job. In 1990 Sendero violence caused the government to declare nearly one-half of the provinces of Peru to be in a state of emergency. In 1988 the armed forces swept Sendero out of the Huallaga Valley, where most of Peru's coca plants are grown, only to see the area fall back under Sendero control over the next two years. Some observers went so far as to suggest that by 1990 Sendero could, if it wanted to, cut the nation's supply lines to Lima, isolating the capital city from the rest of the country.

Sendero derives most of its ideological principles from the thoughts and experiences of Mao Zedung in China. It envisions an expanding alliance of peasants, workers, and small-scale business persons that will establish "liberated" areas in the countryside that will eventually encircle the large cities, causing the government to collapse. This process, Senderistas believe, could take as long as fifty years. They also believe that Peruvian governments as presently constituted are fascist dictatorships, with whom no dialogue or compromise is possible. They believe they must accomplish their revolution with a minimum of outside support, since there are no governments in the world today that share their goals. While there is a good deal of disagreement among specialists about the exact nature of the obvious appeal the movement has among its adherents, it seems clear that support for Sendero derives in part from fear of reprisals—terrorism, in part from centuries of alienation of *cholos* from the system (in this sense the movement is redemptive or millinarian), and in part from its characterization of Peru's governmental system as thoroughly corrupted. There can be no doubt that Sendero's period of maximum growth took place during a time when Peru's government was being mismanaged to an extraordinary degree and during a period of nearly unprecedented economic decline. Sendero probably appeals to different types of persons for different reasons. While its eventual victory is by no means certain, neither should it be discounted.

As political violence, economic decline, and administrative mismanagement continued during the 1980s, yet another guerrilla group, calling itself the Tupac Amaru Movement (in honor of an eighteenth century descendant of the Incas who revolted unsuccessfully against Spanish rule) began to acquire a following. Toward the end of the decade the wealthy finally began to regroup, this time around what is rapidly becoming conservative doctrine throughout Latin America, the neoconservative movement to "privatize" state enterprises and to encourage foreign investment and other transnational capital flows.

As the elections of 1990 approached, the democratic left seemed increasingly fragmented over fundamental issues (what to do about Sendero, drugs, economic policy, etc.). Thus it appeared that the resurgent right, having presented as its candidate a world-class novelist, Mario Vargas Llosa, would win the presidency. A political novice, however, Alberto Fujimori, an agricultural engineer, former university rector, and television personality, running as an independent, forced Vargas Llosa into a run-off. In the run-off election on June 10, with the support of the left, Fujimori scored an upset victory. In contrast to the economic shock therapy proposed by Vargas Llosa, Fujimori, the son of Japanese emigrants, called initially for price controls and food subsidies. Unless he can act decisively, however, against the many ills affecting Peru, the regime is unlikely to last in its present form through the 1990s.

CONTEMPORARY SOCIAL AND ECONOMIC STRUCTURES

Peru

Peru, with a population of 20 million, is socially and economically more complex than Bolivia, due to the greater geographic, economic, and historical diversity of its people. Thirty-five to 40 percent of the population can be classified as Indian, this proportion having dropped slightly, from around 50 percent, during the past few decades. Precise data on Indians are difficult to obtain, since the definition of an Indian in Peru is more cultural than racial. When an Indian sheds Indian clothing, eating habits, or in general indicates a desire no longer to be an Indian, he or she becomes a *cholo,* on the way to integrating with "white" Peruvian society. The vast majority of Indians live in the sierra and are employed as farm workers, peasants, or small merchants.

A dwindling proportion—less than one-half—of the population lives in the sierra, one-third on the coast, and one-sixth in the Amazon jungle region on the eastern slopes of the Andes. Economic and social opportunities for upward mobility exist almost exclusively in the coastal regions, causing a massive migration of persons toward these areas. Huge congregations of *cholos* in slum areas in and around Lima have outstripped the ability of the city to provide them with government services. As the metropolitan population of Lima has tripled in two decades, crime rates have soared, alcoholism is rampant, and social and family decomposition leave millions in an anomic state, vulnerable to all kinds of "true believer" social cults and sects that replace lost value systems, including terrorism as a way of life.

Indians or *cholos* provide most of the country's manual labor. The middle classes, who provide most of the management for both public and private sectors, identify almost exclusively with their employers, having only an inchoately separate identity. The upper-class landowners of the sierra and agroindustrial and financial entrepreneurs on the coast have over several centuries assiduously avoided contact with the rest of Peruvian society. An exclusive Creole culture, complete with its own musical tradition (the most popular genre being the "marinera"), literature (such as the *Tradiciones* of Ricardo Palma), and food (for example, *papas a la Huancaina*) has developed, and the long-standing habit of importing European cultural traditions—bullfights, classical music and drama, literary fashions, modern dress and design—persists. Legislative efforts were made during the early part of the Velasco regime (1968–1975) to diminish the foreign content of radio and television music programming and advertising, but they were not enforced. Popular Peruvian literary and visual artists today respond more to Western norms than to native traditions: It is in part against these trends that Sendero Luminoso is rebelling.

In spite of extraordinary mismanagement during the 1980s, Peru's diversified economy is potentially quite strong. It has a huge fish-meal industry, and large-scale production of cotton, sugar, petroleum, copper, iron, and silver. Illegal coca leaf production accounts for as much as 25 to 40 percent of foreign exports. The government sector has grown to account for about 15 percent of gross national product (GNP). Peru was one of the first countries in Latin America to find itself unable to pay back the enormous foreign debt incurred during the 1970s. In fact, President Alan García tried, right after he was elected in 1985, to lead a Third World movement to limit repayment of the debt to transnational lending institutions. In this effort, however, as in others, he failed. In Peru, as in many other Latin American nations in the 1980s, a conservative movement advocating "privatization" of state-owned enterprises—considered to be inefficient and corrupt—is gaining widespread support, and these measures are likely to be implemented during the 1990s. Whether they can mobilize the potential resources of Peru and stimulate the investment needed to turn the economy around—while at the same time finding a set of distributional policies to thwart the social support base of Sendero Luminoso—remains to be seen.

Bolivia

Between 60 and 65 percent of Bolivia's population of 7 million is Indian, the proportion having slowly declined throughout the century. Two out of three Bolivians live on the Altiplano in the western part of the country; the rest live at lower altitudes in the south or east to which recent economic development has drawn many new settlers. Migration to the Santa Cruz area and the region of Cochabamba, where coca leaves are grown, has been especially rapid.

Indians are far less subservient in status and demeanor than their counterparts in Ecuador or Peru. For more than two generations Bolivian Indians have been aware of the value of organization and have participated in most of the major political events of the nation. This awareness began with mass conscription during the Chaco War and grew with unionization of the tin mines during the 1940s and Indian armed participation in the Revolution of 1952 and the agrarian reform that followed. Indians have voted since 1954.

The traditional upper class in Bolivia has lost its former perquisites of power. This does not mean that the class has disappeared but rather that the economic stranglehold it once had has been broken. Like the upper classes in more developed societies, it must compete with powerful labor groups, government bureaucracies, the military, and middle-class organizations—certainly to a greater extent than in Peru or Ecuador. If the middle groups have not yet unified into a coherent class they have at least periodically shared power with other power contenders, including the lower classes. In this respect Bolivia is well ahead of other Andean countries, where little political mingling has taken place between middle and lower classes.

Economically, Bolivia in the past twenty years has undergone one of the biggest booms in its history. This time the growth has been not only export led, but also quite diversified. The effect has been dramatic. From the turn of the century through the 1960s, Bolivia's exports of unrefined tin and silver accounted for an average of over 90 percent of total export value. Today these minerals account for less than one-half of the value of exports, even though the price of tin has more than doubled since 1973. Natural gas and legal agricultural products (principally cotton and sugar) account for nearly 20 percent of exports; petroleum exports account for over 15 percent of the total; and refined minerals and other manufactures account for most of the rest. These new sources of income have greatly undermined the economic base—tin mining—toward which the precepts of the Bolivian Revolution were directed. Nevertheless, a truly national consensus about the political rules of the game for the twenty-first century has not yet emerged. Critical issues include the role of the armed forces, the size and scope of the state, and distributional goals.

The Cocaine Trade in Peru and Bolivia

Over 90 percent of the world's supply of coca leaves is grown on the Altiplano of Peru and Bolivia. Until the 1970s most coca leaves were grown for local consumption by peasant farmers for other peasants. A minuscule narcotic effect (it numbs the gums and stomach nerves) is activated when one inserts a small sandy stone containing lye (known as a *llucta*) into the mouth while chewing or sucking on the leaves. Virtually all peasants on the Altiplano have been chewing coca legally for centuries. As the demand for the more powerful coca-derived chemical cocaine grew in the United States to staggering proportions in the 1970s and 1980s, peasants accommodated by vastly increasing acreages planted in coca. The Upper Huallaga Valley in

Peru now produces one-half of the world's supply of cocaine. Most of the rest comes from Bolivia.

It is difficult to calculate the effects of coca production on the national economies of Peru and Bolivia, but they are large. In Peru estimates range from $750 million to $1.2 billion in foreign exchange; in Bolivia up to $600 million, in each case easily over 25 percent of legal exports. Secondary effects are also important, since the revenues from the coca trade are used at least to some degree to purchase in internal markets and to invest and reinvest in legal enterprises, hence contributing to long-term economic development. Since the truly deleterious effects of cocaine consumption are visible principally in the slums of northern cities far away from the Andes, it is sometimes difficult for Andean people to understand why U.S. policy-makers seem so intent on destroying such a lucrative source of hard currency. Nevertheless, the U.S. government has tried to offer incentives for peasants to grow alternative crops, for police and military forces to destroy excess crops of coca, to smash laboratories set up to process coca leaves into paste, and to interdict drug shipments out of these countries. In fact, President Bush in 1989 and 1990 encouraged the U.S. military to involve itself in these efforts. Whether these and other measures in the "War on Drugs" will overcome hard economic realities remains to be seen. That Sendero Luminoso has at times acted to protect the interests of coca growers in the Upper Huallaga Valley is a strong indicator that it believes a nationalist policy favoring the grower against the wishes of the U.S. government will win adherents in the battle over hearts and minds. In general terms the drug traffic has created new and strange political cleavages and alliances within Peru and Bolivia since it pits the interests of those benefiting from an enormous and dynamic source of national wealth against the medium-sized and only partially effective governments struggling to cooperate with the United States against a truly transnational cartel. The cartel has the financial capability to corrupt or punish virtually all sectors of law enforcement. Hence the "War on Drugs" will have a powerful impact on the political future of both countries.

POLITICAL DYNAMICS

In both countries a long and sometimes deadly "dance" between the armed forces and a middle-class political party has dominated national political life for many years. In Bolivia elements of the military joined forces with the MNR only to see the military institution curtailed drastically by the party. Taking advantage of splits within the ruling party, the armed forces were able to overthrow the MNR in 1964 and remain in power for nearly twenty years. Thereafter internal divisions forced them to accede to inter-national pressures for civilian government. A continuation of civilian rule seems assured for the moment, but a tense relationship between the armed forces and the government persists, and civilian political power is divided between a number of parties more narrowly based than the older MNR. A number of civil-military coalitions (such as those surrounding the drug issue) could catapult the military to power under certain circumstances.

In Peru the military acts with more institutional unity and with fewer ties to other political groups. The armed forces on three occasions prevented the APRA party from coming to power; nevertheless, a reformist group of officers, once in power, was able to institute the original APRA reform program with a few innovations of their own. During the late 1980s the armed forces allowed the coming to power of an APRA president—under extraordinarily difficult circumstances—but they cooperated with him as president only with great reluctance. Alan García was able to finish his term in office in 1990 only because the overall economic and political situation was so disastrous the armed forces apparently dared not tackle it.

In recent times it has become clear that in both Peru and Bolivia the military institutions and the dominant middle-class parties that shaped the political agenda during the post–World War II period have been in decline. The ideological dynamism of the MNR and APRA a quarter of a century ago gave way to pragmatic and often cynical concern for the perpetuation of the old leadership. Although the torch in both countries has been passed to a new generation of leaders in recent years, neither party has been able to articulate an agenda for the future that is meaningful to the children and grandchildren of their founders. Similarly, in both countries the armed forces have proven incapable either of containing the very real threats to their nations' security—in the form of drug trafficking or guerrilla movements—or of articulating coherent visions of new strategies for national security. In both countries smaller, more sophisticated groups linked to transnational networks have been able to establish the political agenda. Nevertheless, the long history of military involvement in the politics of both countries makes it highly likely that the armed forces will develop a coherent political vision in each country and influence the national agenda accordingly. Should the governments of Jaime Paz or Alberto Fujimori run into trouble in the early to mid-1990s, military coups are likely.

EXTERNAL RELATIONS

Since independence both Peru and Bolivia have faced periods of extreme tension with their neighbors. Bolivia has lost territory to all of its neighbors (Brazil, Paraguay, Chile, Peru, and Argentina)—most painfully during the War of the Pacific (1879–1883), when Chile seized Bolivia's only coastal territories, and during the Chaco War (1936–1939), which Bolivia lost to Paraguay. Peru, too, lost territory to Chile during the War of the Pacific. In the twentieth century Peru has engaged in numerous border skirmishes with its northern neighbors, Ecuador and Colombia. In 1932 a border flare-up in the Amazon region near Leticia led to hostilities with Colombia. During a border conflict in 1941, Peru forcibly seized a large portion of lightly populated and unused Amazonian territory claimed by Ecuador. A team of mediators, including a delegation from the United States, fixed the present boundaries largely in accordance with the status quo after the seizure.

Ecuador remained dissatisfied with the terms of the protocol signed at the time, and this has given rise to several decades of tension along the border between the two countries. A border crisis in 1981 led to open hostilities and mobilization of troops on both sides of the border. Tensions are likely to persist.

In Latin American geopolitical terms neither Peru nor Bolivia can compare, as international powers, with Mexico or with Brazil or Argentina, the two superpowers of South America. Peru, however, has the potential to become one of the most important of the secondary powers in Latin America—on a par, perhaps, with Venezuela. Both countries have participated in regional efforts to stimulate trade and industrial investment, such as the Latin American Free Trade Association of the 1960s and the more recent Andean Common Market. In 1990 Bolivia began to open river ports connecting to the Amazon River near Manaus, Brazil, a development quite likely to pull Bolivia geopolitically into the Amazon Basin orbit; traditionally Bolivia has been viewed as an Andean nation with some ties to Argentina.

CONCLUSIONS

In both countries, after centuries of rule by agricultural and mining elites, in a relatively short period of time middle-class groups would rise to challenge their almost absolute and capricious control. In the case of Bolivia the relative newness of the tin-mining elite, combined with the vulnerabilities inherent in their small size and relatively enormous economic importance, caused the collapse to be sudden, early, and with little prolonged violence. In Peru a more complicated undermining of traditional elites came about with the prolonged challenge to upper-class rule by the middle-class APRA party, followed by a coup de grace delivered by the armed forces.

In both cases the vacuum left by the demise of upper-class rule was filled intermittently and incompletely by middle-class parties and the armed forces, in each case with only partial success. With global trends favoring conservative democratic rule during the early 1990s, it appeared as though deliberate efforts might be made in both countries to relegitimize, at least partially, the right wing of the political spectrum.

Thus as the 1990s begin, relatively young and conservative leaders will attempt to redefine the national agenda in ways that can accommodate the economic and political imperatives of the wealthy, consolidate the real gains made by the middle classes in what are now predominantly middle-class countries, and fight off the challenges to democratic rule posed by the international drug cartels or terrorist, semimessianic organizations like Sendero Luminoso. Should they fail, military intervention is likely, particularly in Peru, a nation fighting problems of a magnitude rarely encountered in recent Latin American history.

SUGGESTED READINGS

Pre-Columbian history on the Altiplano and throughout the Andean region has been studied carefully, if intermittently, for several centuries, and at the present time such study is flourishing. A comprehensive, if somewhat dated, summary of this literature can be found in Luis G. Lumbreras, *The Peoples and Cultures of Ancient Peru* (Washington, D.C.: Smithsonian Institution, 1974). A more recent brief summary is found in Richard Keatinge, *Peruvian Prehistory* (London: Cambridge University Press, 1988). The conquest of the Inca empire is also well recorded, with English works beginning with William H. Prescott's classic *Conquest of Peru* (New York: Merrill and Baker, 1874), and continuing with many more modern versions including John Hemming, *Conquest of the Incas* (New York: Harcourt Brace Jovanovich, 1970).

Recent surveys of the entire range of Bolivian and Peruvian history abound. Herbert S. Klein's *Bolivia: The Evolution of a Multiethnic Society* (New York: Oxford University Press, 1982) is excellent; for lighter fare Eric Lawlor's *In Bolivia* (New York: Vintage Departures of Random House, 1989) is interesting and quite contemporary. For Peru a good place to start is D. Scott Palmer, *Peru: The Authoritarian Tradition* (New York: Praeger, 1981). Also superb is Raul Saba's *Political Development and Democracy in Peru: Continuity in Change and Crisis* (Boulder, Colo.: Westview Press, 1987).

In a more specialized vein, Peter F. Klaren's *Modernization, Dislocation, and Aprismo: Origins of the Peruvian Aprista Party, 1870–1932* (Austin: University of Texas Press, 1973) offers an imaginative interpretation of the origins of APRA. Hernando de Soto's *The Other Path,* translated by June Abbot (New York: Harper and Row, 1989), discusses contemporary economic issues from a neoconservative perspective. "Terrorism as a Revolutionary Strategy: Peru's Sendero Luminoso," a chapter in Barry Rubin, ed., *The Politics of Terrorism* (Washington, D.C.: Foreign Policy Institute, 1989) is an outstanding introduction to this subject. The Bolivian Revolution is chronicled in Robert J. Alexander, *The Bolivian National Revolution* (New Brunswick: Rutgers University Press, 1958); and the decline of the MNR is covered in Christopher Mitchell's *The Legacy of Populism in Bolivia: From the MNR to Military Rule* (New York: Praeger, 1977).

PART ELEVEN
THE SOUTHERN CONE

25

CHILE: THE DEVELOPMENT, BREAKDOWN, AND RECOVERY OF DEMOCRACY

J. SAMUEL VALENZUELA AND
ARTURO VALENZUELA

Chile, a country of 12 million people isolated by the formidable Andes mountains on a narrow and elongated strip of land running 2,650 miles into the far southern reaches of the earth, developed early on a distinctive political system that set it apart from its Latin American neighbors. Soon after independence from Spain, conservative leaders were able to establish a national government that successfully resisted armed challenges to its authority, thereby avoiding the instability that plagued most of Spanish America. Through successive reforms in a pattern reminiscent of British history, Chile toward the end of the nineteenth century had built a democratic regime, although suffrage in national elections was limited to literate males until 1949. The regularity of electoral contests led to the rise of strong parties that have dominated political life during the twentieth century. Running the full range of the ideological spectrum from a communist and socialist left to a conservative right, the Chilean party system has more in common with those of Latin Europe than of Latin America.

This unusual history and party system permitted the election in 1970 of President Salvador Allende, whose leftist government tried to lead the nation to socialism within its constitutional and democratic framework. Allende's experiment attracted world attention and was observed with particular interest in Italy and in France where the left was attempting to follow the same political path. It ended on September 11, 1973, when General Augusto

---

This chapter is a revised and expanded version of the authors' chapter, "Chile and the Breakdown of Democracy," in Howard J. Wiarda and Harvey F. Kline, eds., *Latin American Politics and Development*, Second Edition (Boulder, Colo.: Westview Press, 1985).

Pinochet staged a bloody military coup that destroyed Chile's democracy and inaugurated a sixteen-and-a-half-year eternity of harsh authoritarian government. Within the context of Chilean history, such military rule was highly exceptional. Prior to Pinochet's regime, Chile had only once before, for less than five months in 1924, been governed by a strictly military junta. The crisis years of 1891 and 1932 produced juntas with military and civilian figures that lasted only a few weeks. The great majority of Chilean presidents had been regularly replaced by their successors following constitutional procedures. The national Congress, an institution that played a crucial role in Chilean political history, was also closed by the military for the first time since independence.

With the inauguration of President Patricio Aylwin on March 11, 1990, in highly emotional ceremonies attended by delegates from sixty-seven countries, including sixteen heads of state, Chile began the recovery of its more than centennial democratic tradition. A new phase in the nation's history has opened, full of possibilities as well as great and difficult challenges.

This chapter examines the origins, evolution, characteristics, and breakdown of Chile's democratic system. It also reviews the main features of the recently terminated military regime and analyzes the difficulties faced in the reestablishment of the nation's democracy.

AN OVERVIEW OF CHILEAN POLITICAL HISTORY, 1818–1970

Phase 1: The Founding of an Oligarchical Proto-Democracy (1818–1850)

As elsewhere on the continent, the defeat of Spanish and Chilean royalist forces after the wars of independence (1810–1818) did not lead to an easy transition toward autonomous rule. The break with Spain did not alter the socioeconomic order. The predominantly rural population, located mainly between Valparaíso and Concepción, continued to live on large estates without sharing the fruits of a weak economy based on exports of animal products, grain, and copper. The break, however, clearly disrupted the political system. Gone was the omnipresent and complex colonial administration as well as the legitimating power of the Crown, the final arbiter of all conflicts. The nation became engulfed in political anarchy as different family, regional, and ideological groups fought each other only to produce unsuccessful dictatorial governments and a series of paper constitutions.

Political anarchy ended in the early 1830s, but it is a mistake, often made in Chilean historiography, to look to those years for an explanation of the subsequent stability of government. Surely the defeat of what were viewed later in the nineteenth century as the liberal factions in the Battle of Lircay (1830), the skillful political and financial maneuvers of ministers Diego Portales and Manuel Rengifo in the administrations of President Joaquín Prieto (1831–1836; 1836–1841), and the adoption of a centralizing constitution in 1833 were important steps in establishing new authority structures.

But there is a difference between *establishment* of such structures and their *consolidation*. Consolidation involves the acceptance of the viability and legitimacy of new institutions by the political elites. It is a lengthy process, subject to continuous challenges and reversals. It took many years and was aided by several factors.

The first was the victory of Chilean forces over those of the Peru-Bolivia Confederation. Though the confederation led by General Andrés Santa Cruz had sought to extend its dominion southward, the real spark that ignited the Chilean war effort was the assassination of Portales in 1837. Portales's policies, repressive measures, and advocacy of the war had made him the target of great enmity in Chile. Ironically, because it was rumored that he had been assassinated by agents of Santa Cruz, his death stirred a wave of patriotic emotions that were channeled to military preparations. For the first time Chilean elites mounted a joint endeavor to fight a common enemy, since the war of independence had been as much a civil war as a struggle against colonialism. Plots against the government were forgotten, and victory led to internal amnesty and to a restitution of pensions and ranks for the defeated forces of the 1829–1830 civil war. It also led to the election of the first truly national hero, Manuel Bulnes, to the presidency in 1841. A Chilean defeat in the war would have magnified factional disputes and threatened the stability of fragile institutions. The clear-cut victory, with no parallel in Latin America, created common symbols and a new sense of unity and led to the inauguration of an elected government with unprecedented support.

The second factor was the decisive control of the military by civilian authorities. As leader of the victorious army, Bulnes did not experience much opposition from the military in his first years in office. However, under his leadership the government deliberately reduced support for the regular army, so that by the end of Bulnes's term there were fewer soldiers than at the beginning and the budget for the regular military was severely curtailed. In place of a regular army, the executive encouraged the development of a highly politicized National Guard. Led by loyal government supporters (leadership positions became patronage devices for the president), the part-time guard was composed mainly of lower-middle-class civilians such as artisans, shopkeepers, and small proprietors. It numbered ten to twenty-five times the size of the peacetime army. The outbreak of a revolt against the government in 1851 was partly the reflection of the discontent of regular army officers, based in Concepción, with military policy. Bulnes himself led National Guard forces to suppress the uprising aimed at preventing his elected successor from taking office, even though his cousin was the rival leader. A similar revolt in 1859 was put down by mobilizing loyal army and National Guard forces.

As illustrated by Bulnes's decisive 1851 action, the third factor in the consolidation of the regime was the deliberate support he gave to the fledgling institutional system during his two five-year terms in office (1841–1851). Indeed, Bulnes's role in the consolidation process was, contrary to assertions in Chilean historiography, much greater than that of Portales, whose actual ministerial tenure was short. A written constitution, fixed terms of office, and impersonal authority based on suffrage, however limited, were revolutionary precepts at the time. Bulnes was certainly in a position to ignore those precepts and draw on his prestige and military strength to impose personal rule as did his counterparts in Argentina, Mexico, and Venezuela. Instead, under his leadership the broad outlines of the formal rules of the Republican Constitution of 1833, with its separation of powers between the executive, the Congress, and the courts, became a reality.

The most important single element contributing to this process was the president's refusal to rule autocratically. Following the example of his predecessor, he relied on a strong collegial body, the cabinet, to carry out the main tasks of government. But, unlike those of his predecessor, Bulnes's cabinets drew from different sectors of public opinion, and its members were periodically changed to reflect new pressures and interests.

Though the executive took the initiative, Congress had to approve all legislation. The legislature gradually became more assertive and a platform for dissenting views. As early as the 1840s the Congress resorted to delaying approval of the budget law in order to extract government concessions. Rather than defying this challenge to his authority, Bulnes sought compromise with the legislature. The legitimacy of Congress was therefore not questioned, even if cabinet officials manipulated the electoral process in favor of the official list of congressional candidates. This set the rudiments of the political game for the rest of the century.

Throughout the nineteenth century all relevant factions gained representation in the cabinet or in the legislature, and diverse opposition groups had to learn to collaborate within the shared institutional base to further their interests. It is noteworthy that every nineteenth-century head of state, with the exception of Jorge Montt, who became president after the 1891 civil war, had extensive prior experience as an elected representative in Congress. And the five presidents who succeeded Bulnes until 1886 began government service as young men in his administration.

The fourth factor contributing to regime consolidation was economic prosperity. The break with the colonial trade limitations opened the country to the international market, and Chilean exports thrived. Mining, primarily of silver and copper, expanded with the opening of new mines, and the new markets of California (after the gold rush), Europe, and Australia led to a boom in agricultural sales, mainly of wheat. The state played an important role in encouraging economic development based on external markets: It obtained foreign credit, improved dock facilities, opened new ports, began railway lines, and established a merchant marine. From 1844 to 1864 Chilean exports increased five times, and foreign creditors were quick to take note as Chilean issues brought higher prices on the London market than those of any other Latin American country.

Underlying the success of the government in promoting economic growth, and indirectly the success of the consolidation process itself, was the broad elite consensus on the merits of an "outward-oriented" development policy. Landowners in the central valley, miners in the north, and merchants in Santiago and in port cities all benefited from and promoted an economy based on the export of primary goods in the production of which the country had a decisive advantage. Most manufactured products were imported. There was no protectionism for domestic industry and no effective political force to press for it. The potential internal market for Chilean industry was small, and many obstacles, including the long distances from Europe and the United States and the latter's tariff barriers, discouraged manufacturing for export. However, an incipient industrialization did begin around textiles and iron works in the 1850s and 1860s. It supplied the military and produced materials used in mining, construction, and railways. Chilean artisans also built most of the boats that made their way up and down the long coast.

In sum, by midcentury Chile had laid the foundations for constitutional republican rule based on the separation of powers. Victory in an international war, the control of the military by the constitutionally established authorities, political leadership respectful of the formal rules, and economic growth had contributed to this result that set Chile on a unique course in Latin America. The Congress had, in particular, taken its place as a basic arena for political accommodation, compromise, overview of the executive, and opposition. And although the franchise was limited and subject to intervention, it became the only mechanism for selecting political office holders.

Phase 2: State Expansion and Elite Reaction (1850–1890)

Sharp political differences developed among nineteenth-century elites. The differences stemmed from the reaction of local and national notables, particularly those close to the Church, to the expansion of the state. When state institutions began to expand into the local level, rationalize taxes and duties, invest in public-works projects, and reduce church influence over national life, they generated bitter opposition. Our perspective is different from that of many historians, who have interpreted nineteenth-century controversies as a struggle between a Conservative rural aristocracy with a firm grip on the state and a rising group of miners, bankers, merchants, and professionals seeking political control. That view presupposes that political differences were the product of a fundamental, economically based cleavage among the elite. In fact, as already suggested, there was broad consensus on the merits of free-trade policies and on the pursuit of a development model based on primary goods exports. Moreover, socioeconomic divisions among the dominant sectors were not so clear-cut: The wealthiest families often had cross-investments in all areas of the economy. It is also clear that the Conservatives, whose political bases were largely among landed elites (although not all landed elites were Conservative), were far from controlling the government. Quite to the contrary, they were driven into opposition at an early date and remained so for most of the century.

Moreover, by midcentury the state was not simply a tool of economic elites but had a considerable degree of autonomy. An entirely new profession of urban-based government officials and politicians had appeared on the political scene. Like President Manuel Montt (1851–1856; 1856–1861) himself, they relied on the state for their positions and had a real stake in the expansion of governmental authority. By 1860 over twenty-five hundred persons worked for the state, not counting thousands of workers hired by municipalities and government-financed public-works projects or the many individuals associated with the National Guard and the armed forces.

State autonomy was in part a function of growing governmental institutionalization and of the ability of state officials to manipulate the verdict of the electorate. But it was also the product of a system of revenue collection tied to an export economy. Reliance on customs revenues in a time of export expansion meant an incremental and automatic infusion of larger sums of money into state coffers without imposing large-scale domestic taxation. From 1830 to 1860 government revenues from customs duties, representing about 60 percent of all revenue, increased seven times. State revenues enabled the construction of numerous public-works projects, including the second railroad system of Latin America and the first to be operated by a government. In the fifteen-year period 1845–1860, expenditures on education alone quadrupled.

Given the encroachment of the state on the localities, it is not surprising that control of the state and its expenditures became the most important political issue of the time. Were urban or rural areas to be favored by state resources? Which port facilities should be improved? Where were the railroad lines to be built? Should local officials remain subordinated to the national government's decisions and largess, or should they be autonomous from it? And most importantly, should the state or the Church control the expanding educational system, civil registry, cemeteries, and hospitals?

The Conservative party became the foremost expression of elite discontent over the decreasing autonomy of rural areas and the challenge to the Church's monopoly over educational, cultural, and family life, the maintenance of which it viewed as essential to the preservation of the traditional social order and thus of elite privilege. The party was originally formed by a group that split away from the Montt government as Manuel Montt pressed further to enhance the role of the state. In opposition, the Conservatives soon made alliances of convenience with some ideological Liberals who, while supporting the concept of a secular state, wanted more decentralization of political authority and an expansion of electoral participation. The unsuccessful 1859 uprising reflected the seriousness of the political controversies as a few Liberal, Conservative, and regional elements attempted to prevent Manuel Montt's closest associate from succeeding him to the presidency. Though the government forces, known as the Nationals, controlled the rebellion, Montt's associate wisely withdrew his candidacy. The new National president, José Joaquín Pérez (1861–1866; 1866–1871), saw the political wisdom of granting amnesty to the rebels and, following the Bulnes precedents, of incorporating both Conservatives and Liberals into cabinets of national unity in what became known as the Liberal-Conservative Fusion.

A few measures were adopted during the Pérez administrations to curb the power of executive authority. The president was restricted to one term, armed personnel were barred from voting booths, and other electoral reforms were made. However, the basic character of the state remained unchanged. With Pérez's support, the Liberals outmaneuvered their Conservative allies and continued the basic policies of the preceding National governments. State power transformed the Liberals, not vice versa. State authority expanded further, state-sponsored projects increased, and the secularization of public institutions continued.

By the midpoint of the administration of Liberal president Federico Errázuriz (1871–1876), the Conservatives had had enough. They left the government determined to oppose the drift toward a secular society and the continued encroachment of the state over national life. Ironically, the Conservatives once again made an alliance of convenience with another opposition group, the anticlerical Radical party, which upheld the Liberal principles its government colleagues had seemingly abandoned. This unlikely alliance held a majority in Congress, since the Conservatives had formed part of the official candidate lists in the 1872 election. The Conservatives took advantage of this majority to press for a dramatic liberalization of the electoral system in 1874. As a result the electorate tripled from 50,000 to 150,000 by 1878, as suffrage was extended to all literate males.

The 1874 reforms were not sufficient to counteract the strong intervention of local agents of the executive in the electoral process, an intervention that became more blatant and violent as the government's control over the electorate diminished. Hence, the Conservatives demanded genuine local autonomy, in which full control of elections (going beyond certain 1874 provisions) would be given to elected local governments independent of the executive. To electoral reforms they added the cry for municipal reform.

The Conservatives stood to gain from these reforms. Given the failure of armed conspiracies, their only hope of curbing state authority and of gaining control of government resources lay in the expansion of suffrage and in the reduction of government manipulation of the voting process. Like their counterparts in northern European countries, the Conservatives knew that their dominant position in small towns and in rural areas gave them the upper hand in capturing the ballot box. The more urban-based Liberals and Radicals stood to lose, since only 12 percent of the population lived in cities over twenty thousand and 26 percent in towns over two thousand. The key role played by the Conservatives in suffrage expansion (which, surprisingly, has been attributed to the Liberals and Radicals by most historians) meant that the principal party of the Chilean right became committed to expressing its power capabilities *through the electoral system,* not, as in other countries, through conspiracies within the armed forces or by gaining the allegiance of the central bureaucracy. It also meant that Church opposition to republican electoral democracy, typical of Latin Europe until at least the 1890s, would not develop in Chile. The use of the electoral system as a mechanism for national leadership selection was reinforced by these circumstances.

The stakes involved in the control of the executive increased dramatically with the Chilean victory in the War of the Pacific (1879–1883), again against

Peru and Bolivia. In the 1860s and 1870s customs duties as a percentage of government revenue had declined to as low as 40 percent. After the war, with the incorporation of Peruvian and Bolivian land with enormous nitrate wealth into Chilean territory, customs duties once again climbed to over 70 percent of government income, eventually eliminating the need for internal property taxes. Though a majority of nitrate fields fell into the hands of foreign interests, the Chilean state was able to retain close to 50 percent of all profits through taxation. From 1870 to 1890 government revenues climbed over 150 percent, leading to a new wave of public-works projects and other government expenditures.

The struggle over the role of the state in society finally resulted in the civil war of 1891, during the closing months of José Manuel Balmaceda's government (1886–1891). With burgeoning nitrate wealth, his administration embarked on the most ambitious effort yet to channel governmental resources into massive public-works projects. Though some of his detractors objected to his hostile attitude toward British nitrate interests, opposition to Balmaceda crystallized over the perennial issue of the nineteenth century: control over state resources. The anti-Balmaceda forces included a wide spectrum of political opinion ranging from dissident Liberals to Conservatives and Radicals, not to mention the British nitrate entrepreneurs. The defeat of Balmaceda led to the long-awaited liberalization of electoral registration and counting processes and to a significant change in the character of the political system.

Phase 3: The Party System and Incipient Participation (1890–1925)

After 1891 the center of gravity of the Chilean political system shifted dramatically from the center to the locality. Municipal autonomy and electoral reform finally gave local notables control over suffrage and, therefore, over congressmen and senators. Acting as agents of their local sponsors, the legislators sharply reduced the role of the executive and of the cabinet through constitutional reforms. Politics in the so-called Parliamentary Republic (1891–1925) became an elaborate logrolling game in which legislative factions jockeyed for influence. Budget laws were carved up to please local supporters, and public employment became a primary source for congressional and party patronage. Central government employees increased from 3,048 in 1880 to 13,119 in 1900 and 27,479 in 1919, and the monolithic character of the state changed as its structures were permeated by different political elites. The incredible ministerial instability of the period, with its constant coalition shifts and complex electoral pacts, must be seen in this light.

A key organization of twentieth-century politics, the political party with extensive local bases, developed principally during the Parliamentary Republic. An unanticipated consequence of the liberalization of suffrage was the transformation of elite factions and protoparties into largescale party organizations and networks. Buying of votes and the manipulation of the electorate became a complex and demanding job, and much of the day-to-day party activities shifted from the hands of notables to those of professional politicians and brokers of lesser status. A new political class began to take shape.

The Conservative rural notables gained influence with local suffrage control. But other forces were not left out of the political game. This resulted partly from the profound socioeconomic transformations set in motion by nitrate production, which gave political groups new potential electoral clienteles. Nitrate fields soon employed 10 to 15 percent of the active population and by expanding the internal market generated a host of other activities, including metallurgical works, clothing industries, and transportation. Rural areas and their commercial networks also experienced changes, as agriculture sought to meet the demand for food in the arid north. The urban population increased dramatically from 26 percent of the total in 1875 to close to 45 percent by the early 1900s, and the Radicals as well as a new group of Social Democrats assured themselves an increased role in politics with their skillful organizational efforts in changing cities, towns, and nitrate areas.

Political parties with direct access to the legislative process developed simultaneously with the establishment of a large-scale government bureaucracy. The growth of the public sector in this period was thus shaped by organizations whose primary goal was electoral success and accountability, organizations that continued to exert a major influence over state institutions and the policy process until the military coup of 1973. Where, as in Brazil or Argentina, the bureaucracy emerged before the structuring of strong party networks, the latter could not become, as they did in Chile, a fundamental linkage mechanism between society and the state.

Parties were not the only important organizations with local bases to appear in this period. Labor unions mushroomed, as nitrate, dock, railway, and industrial workers and artisans sought to improve their lot. However, labor unions were restricted and repressed. Dominant government and business elites thought labor militancy threatened the viability of the whole system. Since nitrate revenues were the lifeline of the state and of the economy, any cut in export revenues because of strikes would have devastating repercussions. The army was repeatedly used to put down strikes, often with great brutality, as in the Iquique massacre of 1907 when (depending on the account) between five hundred and two thousand workers were killed. Repression of labor union activities created a radical union leadership, since radical workers were more likely to assume the great personal risks involved.

Ironically, the openness of the political system, a product of the intense conflict among established elites, meant that industrial repression was not accompanied systematically by political repression. Working-class leaders were allowed to publish newspapers, create cultural associations, lobby Congress, and create political parties. Despite their intensely radical outlooks, they soon realized that their cause could best be advanced politically through alliances of convenience with traditional parties eager to maximize their fortunes. Thus in 1921 the founding father of the labor movement and of the Communist party, Luis Emilio Recabarren, and one of his comrades were elected to Congress through an electoral pact with the Radical party. This repeated earlier successes in local elections in which pacts had been forged with either Radicals or Democrats. The repression of the working class therefore contributed to the formation of a Marxist labor union and party leadership, and the relatively open and representative character of the political system meant that the Marxist parties soon turned to traditional political strategies to advance their positions.

The freewheeling and free-spending Parliamentary Republic could not survive the decline in nitrate exports with the discovery of synthetic nitrate during World War I and the inability of the complex logrolling process to come up with solutions to many of the social pressures spawned by a changing society. The challenge from reform sectors was matched by a challenge from more traditional groups, which resented excessive democratization. President Arturo Alessandri's (1920–1924) populist politics violated many of the norms of political accommodation and led to demands to do away with politics and to obtain order. Though young army officers had reformist objectives in mind, their intervention in politics in late 1924 marked the end of the Parliamentary Republic and opened the way for the election of a "nonpolitical" figure, Col. Carlos Ibáñez. During his government (1927–1931), Congress lost influence and the president resorted to heavy-handed tactics in an attempt to reduce the role of parties and the strength of the Communist-controlled labor federations, which represented a majority of organized workers.

Ibáñez expanded the bureaucracy, revised the budgetary system, and "purified" the civil service. Liberal parliamentary politics were to be replaced by a more corporatist conception of the state. Interpreting the comprehensive labor laws approved in 1924 to suit his own end, Ibáñez established legal unionism only where his agents could find leaders who agreed to support his government. But the military president failed. Party politics were too entrenched to be easily purged or manipulated from above. His use of the 1924 labor laws only delayed their full and correct implementation until the late 1930s. With the catastrophic effects of the Great Depression (in which Chilean exports dropped to less than a fifth of their value by 1931), a political crisis erupted, forcing Ibáñez to resign. And after a short interval of unrest, Arturo Alessandri was reelected president by a large margin.

Phase 4: Polarization and
Mass Participation (1925–1970)

The collapse of the Parliamentary Republic produced constitutional reforms that strengthened the presidency and established the separation of Church and state. However, the so-called 1925 Constitution does not represent the most important political change of the 1920s, which is surely the rise of the left. The Communist party was officially founded when the Socialist Workers' party convention of December 1921 voted to adhere to the Third International. By the end of the decade, a Trotskyite splinter had been expelled from the party, and various Socialist groups had been created. After Ibáñez's resignation, all these organizations emerged from their underground work to produce a confusing array of political groups on the left. However, in April 1933 a core of highly popular leaders formed the Socialist party of Chile by bringing together some of the preexisting Socialist and Trotskyite organizations. The new Socialist party quickly gained significant working-class bases by attracting the support of the country's legal unions, with which the Communists had refused to collaborate because of their origins. Thus by the early 1930s two major parties claiming to represent the workers had emerged on the political landscape, leading to a complex relationship of competition and/or cooperation between them that continues to this day. And with the rise of the Marxist left, the party system became highly polarized, covering the full range of the ideological spectrum.

Following the Popular Front strategy adopted in late 1934 by the Third International, the Communist party agreed to a previous Socialist initiative designed to unite the labor movement and to coordinate political strategies. With an eye on the next presidential elections, the by then historical Radical party decided to withdraw its support of the conservative second Alessandri administration (1932–1938) and to join the left's discussions. These resulted in the merger of the labor movement into a single federation in 1936 and in the creation of a Popular Front coalition that elected the Radical Pedro Aguirre Cerda to the presidency in December 1938. This electoral victory over the candidates of Liberals and Conservatives marked the success, for the first time, of a center-to-Marxist left coalition, which would govern the country until 1947. The coalition government expanded state social services in areas such as health, education, and social security. It also encouraged the rise of legal unionism, including Communist-led unions, within the framework of the 1924 labor laws that shaped Chile's elaborate industrial-relations system. And the Popular Front government created a State Development Corporation (CORFO) in order to plan and direct an industrialization process aimed at substituting imported consumer goods with locally produced articles.

The creation of CORFO was symptomatic of a change of direction in the Chilean economy and economic policy. The depression had dealt the final blow to the crippled nitrate industry, and by the late 1930s copper had become Chile's principal export, representing roughly 55 percent of export earnings in the 1940s and 80 percent by 1970. With the drastic decline of the capacity to import in the early 1930s, policymakers became convinced that the nation should not rely on imported consumer goods to satisfy most of its needs. They sought to encourage industrial growth by establishing new lines of credit, protectionism, direct and indirect subsidies, price controls, and state investments in key areas such as steel and energy, which required large capital outlays. As a result, by the late 1960s Chile's industrial sector produced a broad range of consumer goods, if not always at internationally competitive levels of efficiency.

One of the Popular Front government's objectives in fostering industrialization was the creation of jobs in urban areas, which were urgently required because of the decline of the labor-intensive nitrate industry and of the influx of new migrants into the cities. By 1940, 53 percent of the population lived

Table 25.1
Distribution of the Labor Force and Gross Domestic Product (at Market Prices),
1940, 1955, and 1970 (Rounded to Nearest Percentage)

	1940		1955		1970	
	Labor Force	GDP	Labor Force	GDP	Labor Force	GDP
Primary sector	35	15	29	14	24	7
Secondary sector	30	38	33	39	33	48
Service sector	35	47	38	47	43	45

Source: Estimated from Instituto de Economía de la Universidad de Chile, La
Economía de Chile en el Período 1950–1963, and ODEPLAN figures.

in urban areas, a figure that increased to 76 percent by 1970. The population
in cities with more than twenty thousand people increased at an even faster
rate. The new industrialization, however, in the long run did not generate
employment at a faster rate than the increase in urban population. The
secondary sector (including for present purposes mining, construction, transport, and particularly manufacturing) absorbed roughly the same proportion
of the economically active population in 1970 as it had in 1940, even though
its proportion of the gross domestic product increased from 38 percent in
1940 to 48 percent in 1970. As illustrated in Table 25.1, it was the service
sector that absorbed increasing shares of total employment while contributing
a smaller share of the GDP, while the primary sector (agriculture, forestry,
and fishing) declined on both counts.

The Popular Front coalition broke down in part because of bitter internecine
squabbles among Socialists and between Socialists and Communists and in
part because of the fear of both Socialists and Radicals (particularly after
the 1947 municipal election) that the Communists were making too much
electoral progress. The onset of the cold war and U.S. pressures also played
a role in the Radicals' decision not only to expel the Communists from the
cabinet but also to declare the party illegal in 1948. The disarray of the
left and the unpopularity of the Radicals after so many years of opportunistic
bargaining with both the left and the right finally led the electorate (including
women for the first time in a presidential election) to turn to an old stalwart
of Chilean politics, who once again promised progress at the margin of party
politics. Gen. Carlos Ibáñez (1952–1958) was easily elected to the presidency
by a surge movement ranging from the far right to the Socialist left.

Ibáñez's heterogeneous movement did not become a durable political
force. As he began his term, the economy entered a recession and inflation
increased sharply, finally reaching a high of 86 percent in 1955. Ibáñez
abandoned the populist appeal of his campaign and early programs and
attempted to apply an austerity economic program. One of Ibáñez's last
measures, however, was the legalization, once again, of the Communist party.

The disintegration of the Ibáñez movement might have allowed the Radicals
to move once again to fill the center of Chilean politics. However, they were
challenged in that role by the emerging Christian Democratic (DC) party,
whose candidate, Eduardo Frei, outpolled the Radicals in the 1958 presidential

contest. But the real surprise of that election was the showing of Salvador Allende, the candidate of the Communist and Socialist parties. With 28.9 percent of the vote in the sharply divided contest, he failed by a fraction (2.7 percent) to defeat the winner, Jorge Alessandri.

In office, Alessandri (1958–1964), a businessman supported by the right and occasionally by the peripatetic Radicals, applied a new set of austerity measures and obtained increased foreign aid to attempt economic stabilization. In the wake of the Cuban Revolution, the United States became determined to prevent a growth of leftist influence in the rest of the hemisphere. Chile, with its large Marxist parties, became a priority of the Kennedy and Johnson administrations' foreign-aid programs and covert intelligence operations.

During the 1964 presidential election, the Chilean center and right as well as the U.S. government sought to prevent what almost occurred in 1958—an Allende victory. As a result the right decided to support the centrist Frei candidacy, which promised a "Revolution in Liberty," and the CIA contributed $1.20 per Chilean voter to the antileft propaganda effort, over twice as much as the $.54 per U.S. voter that Lyndon Johnson and Barry Goldwater jointly spent in their own presidential campaigns that year. Frei was elected with an absolute majority of the votes. His government, that of his successor, and the breakdown of democracy will be discussed after reviewing the principal aspects and actors of the political game of twentieth-century Chilean politics.

POLITICAL GROUPS AND THE STATE: THE POLITICAL SYSTEM AT MIDCENTURY

By midcentury the Chilean state had evolved into a large and complex set of institutions. Even before the election of Salvador Allende to the presidency in 1970, total state expenditures represented about 24 percent of the GDP. The state also generated over 55 percent of gross investment and roughly 50 percent of all available credit. About 13 percent of the active population worked for the state, not counting the employees of the thirty-nine key corporations in which CORFO owned majority shares or the forty-one other enterprises where its participation was substantial. Government agencies were responsible for health care and social-security benefits, for the regulation of prices and wages, and for the settlement of labor disputes. Indeed, the dominant role of government in regulatory, distributive, and redistributive policies meant that private groups were constantly turning to state agencies and to the legislature, at times through elected local government officials, to gain favorable rulings and dispensations.

Over the years, myriad interest groups developed, closely paralleling the expansion of the state. They ranged from professional societies and business organizations to student unions, trade and pensioners' associations, youth and church groups, mothers' clubs, and neighborhood councils. Workers were represented by industrial, craft, and peasant unions (the latter legalized only in 1967), which were subjected to a series of state regulations and restrictions, although their leadership was democratically chosen by the rank and file. Civil servants were organized into a series of associations that, though acting as unions, were never officially recognized as such. Most groups sought to maximize their political clout before the state by organizing national associations with national headquarters. Large industrial, agricultural, and commercial interests were, for example, respectively organized into the Society for Industrial Advancement (SOFOFA), the National Agricultural Society (SNA), and the Central Chamber of Commerce. Professional societies were grouped in the Confederation of Professional Associations. Roughly 60 percent of all unionists were affiliated directly or indirectly with the Central Labor Federation (CUT). Some categories of specialized workers, small industrialists and retail merchants, truck owners, and so on also had national confederation offices.

Following the 1925 Constitution, the president—elected for a six-year term—was the source of major initiatives in the political process. Yet the president was far from an all-powerful figure. The most important checks on executive authority came from the competitive party system, which will be described in the next section. But presidential authority was also checked by the differentiation of governmental institutions and the marked autonomy of agencies even within the executive chain of command.

The legislature was no longer the focal point of the system, as it had been in the Parliamentary Republic. Nevertheless, the Chilean Congress remained the most powerful in Latin America, with the ability to modify and reject executive proposals. The Congress was the main arena for discussion and approval of budgetary matters as well as for the all-important issue of wage readjustments for public and even private employees.

In the final analysis, legislative politics was party politics, and presidents could cajole and bargain with allied as well as with adversary political groups for mutual advantage. By contrast the two other branches of government, the court system and the comptroller general (Contraloría), were well insulated from both presidential and legislative scrutiny. Judicial promotions were determined by seniority and merit, and though the president retained some power of appointment, his candidates had to come from lists prepared by the judges themselves. Equally independent was the comptroller general, who, like the Supreme Court judges, was appointed for life. His agency was charged with auditing public accounts and ruling on the legality of executive decrees. The comptroller's rulings on financial matters were final; on other matters, the president could, with the concurrence of his cabinet, overrule the comptroller. However, because of the prestige of the latter's office, this could be done only at the risk of considerable controversy, and until the Allende years presidents rarely overruled the comptroller.

Even within the executive branch presidential authority was circumscribed. Forty percent of public employees worked for over fifty semiautonomous agencies that, though nominally under government ministries, enjoyed significant managerial and even budgetary autonomy. As elsewhere, the web of private interests affected by a particular agency soon learned to develop more or less workable relationships of mutual benefits with it. Vested interests often made it difficult for a new administration to abolish old programs and bureaus, and innovations often required the creation of new agencies to administer the new projects, thus contributing to the progressive expansion of the state apparatus. Civil-service organizations and professional associations anxious to place their members in the expanding state sector further complicated the picture. Some state agencies became virtual fiefdoms of architects, civil engineers, lawyers, or doctors.

Though many agencies actually had formal interest-group representation on managing councils, such representation never became as important as the more informal and fluid constituency ties. Chilean politics never became corporative politics. Most private groups did obtain legal recognition. But that was a routine procedure and hardly meant that the government was officially sanctioning particular associations with exclusive rights to represent functional segments of society before the state. Indeed, most claims on the state were made by highly competitive groups, often representing interests drawn from the same horizontal or class lines.

If Chilean politics was not corporative, neither was it praetorian. Despite the vast and disarticulated state apparatus and the claims of a multiplicity of interests jockeying for advantage, Chilean politics did not involve the naked confrontation of political forces each seeking to maximize its interests through direct action in the face of weak or transitory authority structures. The key to the Chilean system, which discouraged both corporatist and praetorian tendencies, was the continuing importance of political parties and a party system tied to the legislature, the principal arena for political give-and-take. From the turn of the century on, the norm in Chile was not the direct link between government agencies and interest associations or the unmediated clash of organized social forces. Rather, party structures, permeating all levels of society, served as crucial linkage mechanisms binding organizations, institutions, groups, and individuals to the political center. Local units of competing parties were active within each level of the bureaucracy, each labor union, each student federation. Parties often succeeded in capturing particular organizations or in setting up rival ones. Once an issue affecting the organization arose, party structures were instrumental in conveying the organization's demands to the nucleus of the policymaking process or in acting as brokers before the ubiquitous bureaucracy.

As the historical discussion noted, the Chilean party system was fragmented and very competitive. With the exception of the Christian Democrats in the mid-1960s, no single party received more than 30 percent of the votes in congressional or municipal elections from 1925 to 1973. The party system was also highly polarized. During the 1937–1973 period, the vote for the left (Socialists and Communists) averaged 21.5 percent (or 25.7 percent if one excludes the 1949, 1953, and 1957 elections in which the Communists were banned from participation), and the vote for the right averaged 30.1 percent. Since neither the right nor the left could obtain an effective majority on its own, center groups, especially the Radical party, played a very important if little-appreciated role in the polarized system: By dealing with both extremes, they were essential elements in most legislative majorities or in winning presidential coalitions—all of which permitted the political system to muddle through despite the sharp ideological divergences. And yet the center movements could not succeed in establishing themselves as a majority force, although they occasionally eroded the strength of either the left or the right. For example, supported by voters on the right, the Christian Democrats scored a dramatic gain in the 1965 congressional election, obtaining 42.3 percent of the vote. But the Liberals and Conservatives, having merged to form the National party in 1966, regained much of their historical strength by 1969, and their candidate outpolled the Christian Democratic nominee in the 1970 presidential election. Table 25.2 summarizes the electoral strength of the three tendencies in the 1937–1973 period.

Given the fact that no single party or tendency could capture the presidency alone, coalitions were necessary. These were either formed before the election and resulted in winning an absolute majority, as was the case in 1964, or they had to be put together after the election in order to obtain the constitutionally mandated congressional approval of a candidate receiving only a plurality of the vote, as occurred in most cases. But, invariably, coalitions tended to disintegrate shortly after the election. The president could not succeed himself, and party leaders scrambled to disassociate themselves from the difficulties of incumbency in order to maximize electoral fortunes in succeeding contests. This meant that presidents had to compromise often with new supporters in the legislature, to salvage part of their programs and to govern.

Despite the polarization of the party system, politics did not revolve around only ideological and programmatic discussions. Obtaining benefits for groups and even favors for individuals, the essence of politics during the Parliamentary Republic, continued to be an important part of party activities. In fact, officials from all parties spent most of their time acting as political brokers—processing pensions for widows, helping Protestant ministers qualify for the white-collar social-security fund, interviewing the labor minister on behalf of a union leadership, seeking a job for a young schoolteacher, obtaining bridges and sewer systems for communities, and so forth. Legislators had particular access to state agencies because of congressional influence over purse strings, promotions, and programs affecting the bureaucracy.

An important political issue that led to extended bargaining in the legislature and to a flurry of demands and pressures from organized groups was the yearly discussion of the wage readjustment law. The law was intimately related to the budgetary approval process and gave the legislators (and therefore the parties) an input into the economic policy planning process. The state-controlled wage scales in the public sector were used as guidelines for the private sector, and therefore the readjustment laws, which also regulated social-security benefits, were of direct concern to the various party constituencies. In an economy averaging over 25 percent inflation with sharp yearly variations, a fundamental demand would be readjustments that would exceed, or at least match, the rate of inflation. Occasionally, amendments favoring

Table 25.2
Percentage of the Vote Received by Parties on the Right, Center, and Left in Chilean Congressional Elections, 1937–1973

	1937	1941	1945	1949	1953	1957	1961	1965	1969	1973	Mean
Right[a]	42.0	31.2	43.7	42.0	25.3	33.0	30.4	12.5	20.0	21.3	30.1
Center[b]	28.1	32.1	27.9	46.7	43.0	44.3	43.7	55.6	42.8	32.8	39.7
Left[c]	15.4	33.9	23.1	9.4	14.2	10.7	22.1	22.7	28.1	34.9	21.5
Other	14.5	2.8	5.3	1.9	17.5	12.0	3.8	9.2	9.1	11.0	8.7

[a]Conservative and Liberal parties, and National party after 1965
[b]Radical, Falangist, Christian Democratic, and Agrarian Laborist parties
[c]Socialist and Communist parties

Source: Dirección del Registro Electoral, Santiago, Chile.

specific groups or unions, but not all in the same category, would be approved as the legislators in the majority group sought to pay off political debts or favor their party comrades in positions of leadership. And yet the political ramifications of class cleavages in the society would become apparent as the left would, in the middle of dense and legalistic discussions over specifics, normally press for higher wages and benefits for working-class sectors, and the right would generally favor the restrictive readjustments tied to fiscal and economic austerity policies.

There were no giants in the Chilean political system. No single group could win a complete majority or totally impose its will on the others. In fact, since there was no ideological or programmatic consensus among the polarized political forces, the Chilean polity was in many respects a stalemated one, in which each decision led to extensive debates and long processes of political accommodation—or to lengthy protests by the dissatisfied groups. In such a setting, change could only be incremental, not revolutionary. Though upper-class sectors were favored by existing arrangements, the intricate stalemate reflected a situation in which each group derived benefits from participating in the system and thus had real stakes in its preservation. It is therefore not surprising that there was such a strong consensus over procedure, over the expression of power capabilities through elections. But as the left gained positions through the commonly shared political process, the right and the sectors it represented began to question the validity of the process itself.

THE BREAKDOWN OF DEMOCRACY

Chile Under Eduardo Frei

The election of Eduardo Frei to the presidency in 1964 marked a significant shift in the center of Chilean politics. Unlike the Radical party or the Ibáñez movement, the Christian Democrats (DC) claimed to be a new and cohesive ideological center, intent on breaking the political stalemate. They argued that their reformist strategy would lead to genuine economic and social progress and that it represented a viable third way between the right and the Marxist left. The Christian Democrats therefore ignored the fact that they had achieved the presidency with official endorsement from the rightist parties and that their unprecedented 1965 majority in the Chamber of Deputies was obtained with the support of traditionally right-wing portions of the electorate. They tried to govern as if they had become a majority party that would monopolize the presidency without coalition support for decades to come. Thus they refused to "lower themselves" to share in the distribution of patronage to satisfy electoral clienteles. The Radicals, rather than being cultivated as a potential ally in the political center, were maligned as pragmatic opportunists and were forced to relinquish some of their hold over the state bureaucracy. With the exercise of rigid party discipline in the Chamber of Deputies, which prevented the legislature from overruling presidential initiatives, the lower house became more and more a rubber stamp and the Senate a negative force.

The animosities created by the DC's disdain for coalition politics were compounded by the reforms it set in motion. These were ostensibly designed to raise the living standards and political participation of lower-class sectors as well as to modernize the social and economic systems. Two new groups, in particular, were mobilized as never before: the urban shantytown dwellers and the peasants. The first were encouraged to set up neighborhood councils and a variety of self-help organizations with cultural and community-development ends. The second rapidly became unionized once the peasant unionization law was approved in 1967 or were included in the peasant cooperatives that were set up in the lands expropriated under the government's new agrarian-reform program. Small landholding peasants were also encouraged to form cooperatives. As a result, roughly half the peasant labor force had become organized one way or another by 1970. Many new (particularly craft) unions were also formed among urban workers. Training programs were begun for both workers and peasants to increase their skills, and an educational reform increased the minimum number of mandatory schooling years.

The reforms, especially those in the countryside, engendered great opposition on the right, which traditionally had a strong political base among the landowners, who were threatened with expropriations and peasant unionization. The reforms also caused resentment and bitterness on the left. As the many young Christian Democrats in charge of the new programs spread throughout the country using modern techniques and displaying new equipment, it became clear that the DC was attempting to build a strong political base among popular sectors, precisely those sectors that Communists and Socialists considered their own natural base of support. This led to an intense effort by the left to compete with the DC in the creation of the new popular organizations. As a result sharp party conflicts were extended to broader sections of the population, creating sectarian divisions and feelings at the grass roots as never before. The threat to the left and the overall party competition for popular support were enhanced by the rise of an extreme left movement that also sought to organize its following.

The popular mobilization of the 1960s should therefore be seen as the result of party competition, with primarily political consequences. It cannot be said that the process got out of hand, either in terms of the capacity of party elites to control it or in terms of its having overburdened the nation's economy. In fact, during the Frei administration the general economic situation improved and state income increased, thereby generating greater economic capacity to increase the income of the newly mobilized popular sectors as well as a larger government capability to finance new programs. Though state income rose with better tax collection, the economic and fiscal improvements of the period were largely due to a rise in the price of copper during the Vietnam War and to foreign credit, mainly from U.S. government and private sources. The latter caused an increase in Chilean external debt to US$3 billion by the end of Frei's term and debt-service payments equivalent to roughly a third of export earnings.

Despite all its efforts, the DC vote in the 1969 congressional elections was reduced to 29.8 percent. And given the events of the previous six years, it proved impossible to have anything but a three-way race in the 1970 presidential elections. The right would have nothing to do with the Christian Democrats and decided to rally behind the candidacy of former president Jorge Alessandri. The Radicals and other small centrist and leftist groups joined the Socialists and Communists in forming the Popular Unity (UP) coalition, which presented Salvador Allende as candidate. Allende obtained 36.2 percent of the vote, Alessandri came in a close second with 34.9 percent, and the Christian Democratic nominee trailed with 27.8 percent. It must be noted that the result was not the expression of heightened electoral radicalism. Allende, in fact, received a smaller percentage of the vote than in 1964, when he was supported by only Socialists and Communists, and fewer new voters than his conservative adversary. Moreover, although the Christian Democratic candidate ran on a leftist platform, it is clear from survey and electoral data that his voters would have gone to the right rather than the left.

Following constitutional procedure, the Congress had to elect the president from the two front runners, since none of the candidates received an absolute majority of the vote. In the most flagrant foreign intervention in Chilean history, U.S. President Richard Nixon ordered the CIA to do everything necessary to prevent Allende from coming to power, including economic sabotage and provoking a military coup. The Christian Democrats, unable to vote for their own candidate, held the key swing votes in the legislature, and President Frei and his colleagues were subjected to numerous internal and external pressures to get them to vote for Alessandri. When it appeared that they would reluctantly honor tradition by selecting the front runner, the CIA helped to organize an attempt to kidnap the chief of staff of the armed forces to provoke a military coup. Gen. René Schneider was killed and the coup attempt backfired. It was the first assassination of a major Chilean leader since that of Portales in 1837.

The Allende Years

Allende's inauguration as president represented the first time that a coalition dominated by the Marxist parties took control of the executive. The coalition had campaigned on a program designed to initiate a transition to socialism while preserving Chile's traditional democratic freedoms and constitutional procedures, and the new administration moved swiftly to implement it. With the unanimous consent of the Congress, U.S. interests in the copper mines were nationalized. Resorting to executive powers, some of which were based on admittedly obscure though never repealed legal statutes, the government purchased or took over a broad range of industries as well as the private banking sector and, using Frei's agrarian-reform law, accelerated expropriations of farmland. Some industry and land takeovers were instigated by their workers or peasants, led in most cases by leftist or extreme leftist militants, who began sit-in strikes demanding the expropriations. This phenomenon was aided by the overall political climate created by the Allende inauguration, one that favored rather than repressed working-class actions, even when they contradicted government policies.

The government also quickly set in motion a plan to raise wages, salaries, and benefits, particularly for the lowest-paid workers, and to increase the social services in poor communities. These measures were taken in part to stimulate the economy by increasing demand and in part as an attempt to strengthen the government's electoral support as well as to satisfy the expectations of the left's working-class bases, for whom socialism principally meant a better standard of living. The policies were apparently successful, as the economic growth rate during 1971 was the best in decades, and the Popular Unity obtained roughly 50 percent of the vote in the 1971 municipal elections.

The initially favorable economic trends were, however, quickly reversed. Reflecting the poor's needs, the rising demand was disproportionately channeled to a greater consumption of basic consumer items such as food and clothing, areas of the economy that were least able to respond with rapid production increases. Inflationary pressures were therefore strengthened, particularly since government spending increased without a proportional rise in tax receipts, partly as a result of greater tax evasion. By the end of 1972 inflation had reached 164 percent and currency emissions accounted for over 40 percent of the fiscal budget. Moreover, the economy was clearly hurt by politically motivated cutbacks in credits and spare parts from the usual U.S. private or governmental sources. Foreign-exchange reserves dwindled rapidly as Chile imported more food and equipment with less recourse to credit and as it sought to meet payments, though partly rescheduled, on the foreign debt. The price of copper dropped to record lows, adding to the difficulties.

Early political success also proved short-lived. In 1972 the UP suffered reverses in key by-elections as well as in important institutional elections, such as those of the University of Chile or of labor federations. The courts, Contraloría, and Congress also objected increasingly to government initiatives. And most importantly, the early tacit support of the Christian Democrats turned into active opposition, leading to congressional censorship of ministers and to attempts to limit presidential authority.

The process that led to the brutal 1973 military coup that ended the Allende experiment is a highly complex, multidimensional, and dialectical one. It cannot be reduced to a simple set of causes that are easily construed with the benefits of hindsight. Surely the government made many unwise decisions or proved indecisive at important turning points; the sabotage and conspiracies of foreign and domestic interests seeking to preserve privilege at all costs helped to create an acute economic and political crisis; the actions of revolutionary groups both within and without the government coalition contributed to the exacerbation of an atmosphere of extreme confrontation that strengthened the disloyal and reactionary opposition; elements in the armed forces proved to be less than totally committed to the constitution and the democratic system; the capacity of the state to control and direct civil society disintegrated; taking a longer view, the dependency of the economy made the Allende experiment excessively vulnerable. All these are important factors, but they are not sufficient to explain the final result if viewed apart from a historical process in which contingent events played an important role. The breakdown of the regime was not preordained. It is a mistake to view the middle sectors as hopelessly reactionary, the workers as so radicalized that they would not stop short of total revolution, the army so antidemocratic that it was only waiting for its opportunity, the economy so dependent and the United States so single-handedly powerful and intransigent that the only possible denouement was full-fledged authoritarianism. There was room for choice, but with each unfolding event in the historical process that choice was markedly reduced.

If a single factor must be highlighted, the breakdown of Chilean democracy should be viewed as the result of the inability and unwillingness of moderate forces on both sides of the political dividing line to forge center agreements on programs and policies as well as on regime-saving compromises. The UP could not obtain a workable majority on its own, and the option of arming the workers as demanded by revolutionary groups was not a realistic alternative. The Chilean left was organized to compete in elections, not fight in battles; to change strategy would not have been easy, and any attempt to do so would have provoked an even earlier coup d'état. Without support from centrist forces, principally from the Christian Democrats who had made Allende's election possible in the first place, the UP government would remain a minority government without sufficient power to carry out programs, given the vast and unwieldy character of the Chilean institutional system.

The failure of center agreements resulted from political pressures originating in the extremes of both sides of the polarized party system. The government coalition was in fact sharply divided, the basic disagreements being those separating the Communists from the majority faction in the Socialist party. The latter wanted to press as fast as possible to institute the UP program and felt that support for the government would increase only insofar as it took decisive action to implement a socialist system. Compromise with the DC would, in the Socialists' view, only divert revolutionary objectives and confuse the working class. They therefore sought to undermine UP-DC collaboration and agreements. The Communists were much more willing to moderate the course of government policies in order to consolidate a narrower range of changes and to broaden the government's legislative base by resolving differences with the Christian Democrats. Both Socialists and Communists were pressured by the non-UP extreme left, which sought to accelerate changes through direct action outside constitutional procedures. Their influence in the UP coalition was magnified by the proximity of their positions with those of elements in the Socialist party majority; therefore, the extreme left was not marginalized at the fringe of the political process.

Allende shared the Communists' position but did not wish to cause a break with his own Socialist party. He therefore projected an ambivalent image and at times failed to take decisive action—for fear of alienating his party—without the certainty of receiving consistent support from the center forces in exchange. These political differences affected the daily operations of government agencies; employees, for example, often would not take orders from superiors belonging to other parties. The president and the ministers were so often involved in tending to these daily crises that they had little time to structure long-term policies, analyze the consequences of short-term ones, or develop a coherent strategy to deal with the moderate opposition.

The Christian Democrats were also torn by internal differences: The party was divided into left- and right-leaning factions of approximately equal strength. The 1971 party leadership came from the left-leaning group, and it sought to maintain a working relationship with the government, while the right-wing faction pressed for the adoption of a tougher opposition stand. However, the party leadership was at first rebuffed by an overly confident UP government exhibiting the same arrogance the DC had shown previously, a situation that only strengthened the position of the right-wing sector within the party. Ironically, constitutional reforms adopted in 1970 by the DC and the right had diminished the role of the legislature, thus reducing the executive's need to reach agreements with the opposition. The right-wing faction was also strengthened by the vehement attacks on prominent DC leaders in the leftist media and by the assassination of a former Frei cabinet minister. Though this killing was the action of a small leftist fringe, the DC blamed the government for tolerating a climate of violence that, it argued, led to such incidents.

As a centrist opposition force, the DC was also extremely vulnerable to pressures from the right of the party system. If the DC leadership could not show that its tacit support for the government had resulted in moderating UP policies, the party stood to lose the anti-UP vote to the right without gaining greater support from the left. Therefore, the DC was soon forced to work with the right in opposition. The turning point came in mid-1971 with the first special by-election to fill a vacant congressional seat in which, given the winner-take-all nature of the contest, a UP victory was certain if the opposition fielded separate candidates. Consequently, the DC approached the government suggesting an agreement that would have led to a joint UP-DC candidacy, an offer that Allende accepted but the Socialist party vetoed. In view of this rejection, the DC turned to the right, and the joint opposition candidate won decisively. As a result of this experience, a leftover splinter group decided to leave the Christian Democratic party, which strengthened further the right wing within it. The DC alliance with the right-wing National party continued in future elections, adding to the polarization of forces.

In February 1972 the DC obtained congressional approval of legislation severely limiting the president's ability to intervene in the economy, thereby challenging the essence of the government's program and marking the beginning of a fundamental constitutional confrontation between the president and the Congress. Interpreting 1970 constitutional amendments differently from the president, the opposition argued that Congress required only a simple majority to override a presidential veto of the new legislation, while the UP maintained, in fact more correctly, that a two-thirds majority was needed. It then became clear to moderates on both sides that accommodation was essential. On two separate occasions government and DC representatives met in an attempt to reach a compromise that would have allowed the government to keep a substantial public sector of the economy while giving the private sector certain guarantees. But the talks collapsed. The Nationals suggested a DC sellout, while the Socialists and other leftist groups stepped up factory expropriations in order to present the DC with a *fait accompli.* They thus undermined the negotiating position of the moderate Radical splinter group entrusted by Allende with conducting the discussion, and as a result this group left the UP coalition to join the opposition. Again, this only polarized the political forces further, reducing the potential success of a center agreement.

By mid-1972, the critical situation of the economy and the growing aggressiveness of the opposition led the government to try once again to hold talks with the Christian Democrats. This time Allende was strongly committed to reaching a compromise, and the UP made substantial concessions leading to agreement on a broad range of issues. However, the more conservative faction within the Christian Democratic party maneuvered successfully to prevent the negotiators from finishing their work. By that point, most sectors within the DC felt that the government was clearly on the defensive and thought that by concluding an agreement with it the party would surely lose support among the increasingly discontented middle sectors, thereby running the risk of being routed by the Nationals in the March 1973 congressional elections. Considerations of short-term party interest thus carried the day.

Toward the end of 1972, qualitative changes had begun to take place in Chilean politics. The parties had repeatedly called the mass rallies that characterized the Allende years not only to increase their bargaining stakes but also to prove actual power capabilities. Nonetheless, the nature of this mobilization soon changed. Business and professional associations increasingly took matters into their own hands, and before long the DC and the Nationals were falling over each other not to direct but to pledge support for the independent action of a whole range of groups. These demonstrations culminated in the massive October 1972 strike and lockout by hundreds of truck owners, merchants, industrialists, and professionals. The government parties countered by mobilizing their own supporters, also engendering a significant organizational infrastructure that could operate at the margin of party leadership directives. These demonstrations and counterdemonstrations by a vast array of groups, the numbers of which had continued to increase during the Allende years, were partly stimulated by a vitriolic mass media giving at least two totally different interpretations of every event, generating a dynamic in which the symbolic became the real, falsehoods turned into hysterically believed truths, and perceived threats were taken as imminent. The climate of agitation was also increased by the CIA funds that flowed to opposition groups, strengthening them significantly as political actors independent of party control. For government leaders the decreased capacity of party elites to control group mobilization and confrontation was more serious than for the opposition. It meant that the government lost an important measure of authority over the society, that the state itself would be bypassed as the central arena for political confrontation, and that the legitimacy of the regular processes of bargaining was undermined. In this crisis atmosphere, Allende turned to a presumably neutral referee who would ensure institutional order until the March 1973 congressional elections could clear the political air. Military men were brought into the cabinet, and the chief of staff was made the minister of the interior.

The incorporation of the military into the government ended the strikes of October 1972 and freed the political forces to concentrate on the congressional elections, which party leaders saw as the decisive confrontation. But in serving as a buffer between contending forces, the military itself became the object of intense political pressures. The left within the UP criticized it for slowing down government programs and initiatives, while the more strident elements on the right accused it of helping a government that would otherwise fall. Other sectors went out of their way to praise the military, a tacit recognition that they were the only force with real power. These pressures politicized an institution that had largely remained at the margin of political events. Though it was hardly perceived at the time, a cleavage began to appear within the military between officers supporting the government because they saw it as the constitutional government and those more receptive to the increasingly louder voices of opposition elements calling for the government's downfall.

The March 1973 elections symbolized the final polarization of Chilean politics as the government and the opposition faced each other as two electoral blocs. Not surprisingly, the elections did not help resolve the political crisis. The opposition failed to gain the two-thirds majority it needed to impeach Allende, and the government failed to obtain majority control in either house of Congress. Given the massive inflation and serious shortages of basic goods as well as the climate of political uncertainty, the government's showing was commendable since it managed to win seats at the expense of the opposition. And yet the final results were not dramatically different from those that the two blocs had obtained as separate parties in the previous congressional contest. The electorate did not provide the magic solution. Their task done, the military left the cabinet.

Soon after, a decisive event initiated the final stage in the breakdown of the regime. On June 29, 1973, a military garrison revolted. Though the uprising was quickly put down, President Allende and his advisers realized that it was only a matter of time before the *golpista* (pro-coup) faction of the armed forces consolidated its strength. They again dismissed the far left's counsel to arm the workers, arguing that the creation of a parallel army would only accelerate the coup. Ironically, military officers were quicker to believe, or to make believe, not only that the workers could be a potent force but that sectors of the left had already structured a viable military force. But the well-publicized efforts of military commanders to find secret arms caches uncovered nothing of importance, although they attempted to convey the impression that they had.

To the consternation of the leadership of his own Socialist party, Allende once again called for talks with the Christian Democrats. And despite the vocal opposition of many of their followers, the Christian Democratic leaders, urged to do so by the cardinal, agreed to the new negotiations. However, an agreement at that point was unlikely. The hard-line faction of the Christian Democrats had replaced the more moderate leadership, and Allende was thus obliged to deal with the group most hostile to his government and policies. Moreover, the country was once again in the throes of massive lockouts, strikes, and civil disobedience campaigns led by business and professional associations (with considerable CIA funding), all demanding the president's resignation. By that time significant working-class groups, such as the copper miners, had also staged strikes to express their discontent with specific government policies, which only reinforced the confidence of the opposition. Any form of support for the government by the Christian Democrats would therefore have been seen as a sellout by the opposition. The political arena had been reduced to a few men attempting to negotiate a settlement. Even though these men no longer had the kind of control over social forces they once had, a dramatic announcement from the talks would still have placed the nation's largest parties and most respected leaders on the side of a peaceful solution and would have seriously undermined the subversive plans of military officers.

But agreement was not forthcoming. The Christian Democrats did not trust Allende's word that he really wanted a settlement, believing instead that he merely sought to buy time in order to force an armed confrontation. However, it is clear from the president's actions that he sought an agreement. He kept moderate leaders in his cabinets, even though they were severely attacked by the left within and outside the UP, and he virtually broke with his own party. Furthermore, Allende finally did agree to the Christian Democratic demand of bringing the military back into the government. In combating to the end the dubious prospect of "Marxist totalitarianism" and in constantly increasing bargaining demands, the DC leaders failed to realize how much stake they had in the political order they thought they were defending. By not moving forcefully to structure a political solution, they undermined the fragile position of the president and his advisers, who were seeking accommodation. Instead the DC supported a Chamber of Deputies declaration calling on the military to safeguard the constitution and declaring that the government had lost its legitimacy.

Two weeks later, prominently displaying the chamber's resolution as evidence of the legality and broad-based support for their action, the top military leadership led the brutal revolt against the government. Air force jets bombed and strafed the presidential palace, in which Allende himself, after offering resistance, committed suicide. Thousands of government supporters, or presumed government supporters, were arrested, mistreated, tortured, or killed in the months that followed.

Some prominent Christian Democrats condemned the coup in the initial moments. But others, including the leadership, welcomed it as inevitable and blamed the government for all that had transpired. Little did they realize what the "saving" action of the military would mean for the country's and their own future.

THE MILITARY IN GOVERNMENT

The September 11, 1973, coup marked the most dramatic political change in Chilean history. A military junta headed by the commanders of each of the services and the national police took power and argued at first that they had overthrown the Allende government in order to protect democracy and restore constitutional government. But the new authorities soon defined the Chilean crisis as one of regime rather than of government. They placed the blame for the breakdown of Chile's institutions not only on the Popular Unity government but also on liberal democracy itself. Democracy had permitted divisive party competition and the rise of Marxist political leaders intent on defining the nation's politics in class terms. It had also generated demagogic politicians who contributed to economic mismanagement. Government was best left, in their view, in the hands of "technicians" who could formulate the "best" policy choices with administrative efficiency until the people had the necessary "maturity" to exercise better judgment.

The goal of the new junta thus became one of transforming the Chilean system, creating a "new" democracy and a "new" citizen, devoid of the "vices" of the past. The Congress was closed, local governments disbanded, and elections banned. Newspapers, radio stations, and magazines were shut down, and those allowed to publish were subjected to varying degrees of censorship. Officials and leaders of the Popular Unity government and parties were arrested, exiled, and, in some cases, killed. Within months of the coup, Christian Democratic leaders, unwilling to accept an indefinite military regime, saw their activities severely curbed as well.

The military authorities sharply restricted the activities of traditional political parties and ignored the strong pressure of right-wing supporters to create a massive progovernment party or "civic-military movement." For this reason it is inappropriate to label the Chilean regime as fascist. The military regime sought political demobilization.

Neither is it appropriate to view the regime as corporatist. Despite early pronouncements that the junta intended to draw on Catholic integralist doctrine to structure corporative institutions, all of the country's major interest groups, including employers and professional associations and trade organizations (many of which had supported the coup with enthusiasm), saw their influence markedly diminished. The new authorities were simply not interested in bringing into the decision-making process any expression of societal interests. They were convinced that through disciplined administrative management and the advice of qualified experts they would be able to govern and modernize the country without the advice of "interested" or "partisan" groups. They thus sought to replace party politics and interest-group politics with technoadministrative solutions imposed by fiat. The governing style for the country as a whole paralleled the internal governing style of the military institution itself.

The Chilean military regime was extraordinary in the extent to which General Pinochet succeeded in concentrating power in himself. Since he commanded the largest and most important service, his fellow officers named him the first president of the junta, but early suggestions called for the rotation of this position among its four members. Both executive and legislative power rested in the junta. Within a year, Pinochet had acquired greater power than his colleagues. With the adoption of a "Statute of the Military Junta," a protoconstitutional document, together with declaring himself "Supreme Chief of the Nation," Pinochet assumed control of executive power, although it still formally remained in the junta, which had to approve all cabinet and ambassadorial nominations. Half a year later a new constitutional decree named him "President of the Republic of Chile," the traditional designation of Chilean presidents, in addition to preserving the prior titles of "President of the Governmental Junta" and "Supreme Chief of the Nation" and stated unambiguously that he exercised executive power. General Pinochet's position as "President of the Republic," and the junta's as the "legislative power," was reaffirmed in the so-called "transitory articles" of the constitution adopted in 1980. Pinochet also changed his military title in order to emphasize a position of preeminence over his colleagues in the other services, who then became his subordinates in rank. In 1979 he adopted the designation of "Generalissimo of the Armed Forces" and later that of "Captain General." He effectively positioned himself to control all military promotions and retirements, carefully overseeing in particular those in his own service, the army.

This concentration of power had no parallel in other military regimes in Latin America. Pinochet was not a retired military officer, like most of his Argentine counterparts, nor did he serve at the behest of the corps of generals, like Brazilian military presidents. Policy decisions never originated among high-ranking officers and were never reviewed by them. Pinochet stressed repeatedly that the armed forces were not to deliberate political matters. In this sense, their relation to the executive power was one of subordination just as it had been, in the past, to the Chilean presidents. Military officers occupied a majority of all positions in the government, but they reported to their superiors, be they military or civilian, within the government. General Pinochet led a military regime, but it was not, strictly speaking, of the military. It is best described as a dictatorship of the commander-in-chief. As such, it was a curious, personalized regime in which power derived from occupancy of the top office of a military bureaucracy.

This type of dictatorship was made possible by the highly professional, obedient, and hierarchical nature of the Chilean military. Paradoxically, these were qualities that stemmed from Chile's democratic past. The military was not involved in politics, and Chilean politicians did not expect it to be the source of political instability or coups. It is highly symptomatic that the coup against President Allende did not break the military line of command: The president had appointed General Pinochet to the top position in the army shortly before.

Policy Initiatives of the Military Government

The Pinochet government undertook more far-reaching changes than any of those that preceded it over the last fifty years. The repressive apparatus of the state increased enormously, as did the jurisdiction of military courts over offenses by civilians. But in other respects the size of the state and its role in national life were drastically reduced.

The government pursued an aggressive policy of privatization. All land held under the agrarian reform program was turned over to individual property holders. Only a handful of industries remained in the public sector (aside from the railways and utilities, the most important of these is the copper company controlling the principal established mines; new investments in copper have come from the private sector, mainly in the form of foreign/Chilean joint ventures). The rest of the industries were sold to national and foreign private investors, often at bargain prices. As part of debt-for-equity swaps to reduce an external debt that increased to $20 billion by 1986, many formerly Chilean firms have been denationalized.

The authorities put in place a radical program of privatizing state services in social security and health, which meant dismantling long-standing publicly funded institutions. The public housing development program was also turned over to the private sector. Labor legislation was extensively revamped, making it more difficult for workers to unionize and to pressure employers through collective action. The size of the unionized work force declined by about 60 percent compared to its highest membership point in the last two years of the Allende government. Wages and salaries declined in real terms by as much as 50 percent with respect to their levels in 1970, and did not recover fully—even during the years of strong growth—during the whole period of military government. The combination of the incomes and welfare policies led to a significant regression in the distribution of income.

The government also undertook educational reforms. Public, primary, and secondary schools were turned over to municipal administrations (led by mayors appointed by the government), and new legislation encouraged the formation of private schools and even universities.

The economy was opened up to external competition by drastic cuts in import duties, resulting in numerous bankruptcies as industries were unable to adjust to the shock. Except for a few years in the late 1970s and early 1980s in which the government's economic team greatly overvalued the national currency with catastrophic results, economic policies generally sought to stimulate growth through the development of new exports. These policies have generally been successful and have reduced the reliance on copper exports from about 85 percent of export earnings in the early 1970s to about 45 percent in the late 1980s.

Economic growth rates were very spotty during the sixteen years of military government. There were severe recessions in 1975 and in 1982 (in each of those years the economy declined by about 14 percent) and periods of significant growth (or recovery) with positive rates of between 5 and 9 percent in the late 1970s and late 1980s. Given this zig-zag pattern of growth, the per capita income of Chile by the end of the 1980s was roughly equivalent to its 1970 level measured in constant dollars. And yet the military government prided itself on its economic management, given the fact that the economy registered strong growth in the last three years of authoritarian rule; moreover, inflation was low, the external debt shrunk by $3 billion, and unemployment dropped significantly. Chilean businessmen also developed a new confidence in their abilities and in the economic future of the country, which they associated with the free-market and open-economy policies of the regime. This sense of success has been magnified by the disastrous recent economic performance of neighboring countries, with the exception of Uruguay.

During much of the military government, economic and social policy initiatives were in the hands of a team of young economists who came to be known as the Chicago Boys due to their free-market and monetarist approaches. They appealed to Pinochet because of their lack of identification with Chilean parties and their technical competence. Their belief that Chilean underdevelopment could be attributed to an overbloated state that restricted private initiative corresponded well with the effort to drastically restrict state institutions for political reasons, given the association of those institutions with party-sponsored clientelistic politics in the democratic past.

Opposition to the Military Regime

Many authoritarian rulers think that they can drastically reduce support for their oppositions through a combination of repression and political, social, and economic changes. This goal invariably proves to be elusive. Citizens by and large retain their political predilections, and these are passed on from one generation to the next supported by family and community ties creating a collective political memory. Party militants are also able to retain at least the rudiments of their organizations, and they often remain active as leaders in social groups and associations whose activities are allowed by the regime.

Chile was no exception to this rule. The parties retained their organizations despite the severe repression directed especially at those of the left. Many party militants remained in positions of leadership in the same social groups where they found an audience before, be it the labor movement, student federations, or community associations. Supporters of the military government rarely won the internal elections of these groups when they were held freely. The Catholic Church assumed a very important role in the overall opposition to the regime. It continually called for national reconciliation and for a return to liberal democracy and refused to lend any credence to the attempts by the authorities to use Catholic social doctrine—in its most conservative interpretation—as a formula to legitimize the regime. The Church also took decisive steps to challenge the regime for its many abuses of human rights and protected the lawyers and other professionals who actively documented such abuses and defended their victims in court. Moreover, the Church gave legal cover and other forms of support to many groups, such as social science researchers, journalists, unions, and popular community associations through which opposition views were expressed and organizing took place. It was through such Church-sponsored activities that the Christian Democrats and the left gradually came together in the first years of the military regime, leaving behind their bitter divisions from the Allende period.

Through a combination of social mobilization, calls for negotiations, and international pressures, the opposition continually tried to force the military to abdicate and accept a transition to democracy. Elements on the extreme left, some associated with the Communist party, also attempted to organize armed resistance to the regime. All actions undertaken by such groups, including a failed assassination attempt against Pinochet himself, were sharply criticized by the rest of the opposition, on grounds of both morality and expediency. The bulk of the opposition condemned all forms of violence, and such incidents—some of which were of very dubious origins—seemed to play into the hands of the regime by lending credence to its claims that the country, suffering terrorist threats, was not ready for democracy.

The opposition's attempts to mobilize people against the regime were at times enormously successful in the major cities. There was a series of massive "protests" for several years beginning in May of 1983. The movement, called by labor leaders initially, consisted of banging pots at a certain hour in the evening, boycotting classes, staging work slow-downs, and refraining from using public transportation and from shopping. The military regime eventually met such protests, which were initially held monthly, with massive displays of force and random, brutal repression by the army and police. The protests increasingly led to violence, which the government tried, with characteristic aplomb, to blame entirely on the opposition. Labor and political leaders were arrested and tried under security laws, some in military courts.

The moderate opposition eventually called the protest movement off in order to break the increasing cycle of violence. And yet, the movement served an important function. It demonstrated both to the government and to the opposition itself that after ten years of military rule, in which the government, controlling television and most of the rest of the mass media, relentlessly diffused a single interpretation of all events, the opposition could still generate a massive demonstration against the authorities. This emboldened the parties to seek new forms of exercising political leadership, and it convinced many civilian politicians on the right that the military government's long-term project was not entirely viable. Such politicians, whose concerns were dismissed high-handedly by Pinochet after he initially turned to them for help in resolving the political crisis generated by the first protests, began to organize a new political party of the right, taking some distance from the military regime. This eventually generated a new and quite bitter split on the right of the Chilean party spectrum between those who identified closely with the military regime and those who did not.

While the moderate opposition continually expressed its willingness to negotiate with the military regime over forms of transition to democracy, Pinochet himself steadfastly refused to entertain any such discussions. The personalized Chilean military regime had a very narrow and tight inner circle of power, allowing no space for the development of moderate but influential segments of political leadership within the ruling circles. If such segments had existed, it is conceivable that the opposition could have found a willing partner in the regime to search for a suitable transition formula. But all dissenters from Pinochet's leadership who emerged within the regime were simply excluded from it, and the opposition's attempts to press the government and the armed forces to negotiate came to nothing.

Throughout the military regime, the opposition enjoyed many expressions of international solidarity. The international community repeatedly condemned the government's violations of human rights. When the AFL-CIO threatened to boycott the unloading of Chilean exports in the United States in 1978, the government prepared labor legislation that allowed a significant reactivation of Chile's unions. And arms sales to the Chilean military from major American and European manufacturers were significantly curtailed. Given the orthodoxy of its economic management and commitment to its debt obligations, the Chilean government was well received only in international financial circles.

The Transition to Democratic Government

The opposition was finally able to force the military government into a transition to democracy by using the procedures Pinochet himself had put into the 1980 Constitution.

The origins of this document go back to the immediate post-coup period. The new military authorities were in a juridically untenable position. They justified their seizure of power in part by noting that the Allende coalition had violated the 1925 Constitution, but they themselves were violating it daily through their de facto exercise of power and by not reverting—as many early supporters of the coup expected—to constitutional procedures in order to reconstitute the government. The junta therefore argued that the existing constitution was inadequate to "protect" democracy and announced that a new one would be written. A committee of civilians identified with the right and the extreme right was charged in 1974 with the task of preparing the draft of a new charter.

After writing the "Statute of the Military Junta" to establish some formal procedures, the committee ran into disagreements between its extremist and more moderate members. Eventually, as head of a "Council of State," former President Jorge Alessandri took a leading role in drafting the constitution, which he presented to General Pinochet in 1978 for his approval. The document adhered to a very large extent to Chilean constitutional traditions. It also called for a transition period of five years in which General Pinochet would continue to govern as president, but would share legislative responsibilities with a Congress whose members would initially be designated.

Pinochet changed the draft in significant ways, strengthening the power of nonelected and military officials and extending the presidential term of office to eight years. Moreover he added twenty-nine "transitory articles" that suspended the application of the bulk of the constitutional provisions until the beginning of a second presidential term after the enactment of the constitution. One of these articles named Pinochet to the presidency for a first term, which was to begin on March 11, 1981, and others assigned the legislative power to the junta. The transitory articles therefore permitted Pinochet to extend his personalistic regime for another eight years.

What was to prove decisive for the transition to democratic government were the stipulations Pinochet added to the transitory articles for the presidential succession at the end of the first term. At that point the commanders in chief of the armed services (including Pinochet himself) would select a new presidential candidate, whose name would be submitted to the voters in a plebiscite. If that individual won the plebiscite, congressional elections would be held within a year, and the constitution would be fully applied. If the candidate lost the plebiscite, within a year there would be open presidential as well as congressional elections. It is safe to assume that Pinochet had every intention of running for a second term, and he had no difficulty, when the time came, in obtaining the nomination from his colleagues. Pinochet felt confident of his ability to win plebiscites. He did so by a large margin in 1978, and he obtained what was announced as 65 percent approval in the plebiscite held on September 11, 1980, to approve the 1980 Constitution and his own "first presidential term" along with it.

But both of these plebiscites were held in highly irregular manners, and the opposition had little difficulty in contesting their validity. This rejection of the plebiscites' legitimacy, especially of the one that presumably had approved the constitution and Pinochet's own "presidential term" along with it, struck a raw nerve in ruling circles. Hence, Pinochet and his supporters took pains continually to stress the "constitutionality" of the government. Moreover, adherence to the 1980 Constitution became the centerpiece of the government's political program, replacing the earlier emphasis on building a new Chile that became untenable in the context of the severe economic crisis of 1982–1983 and the rise of the protest movement. The authorities also turned the defense of the "institutionality" enshrined in the constitution into one of the principal missions of the armed forces.

Since by late 1986 the opposition had exhausted all its efforts to force the government into a transition through social mobilization and other forms of pressure, it began to look forward to the 1988 plebiscite as a possible mechanism to defeat the government. Recalling its criticisms of the prior plebiscites, the opposition stipulated a series of conditions that would have to be met for the new plebiscite to be considered a valid expression of the voters' will. These included the reestablishment of a proper electoral registry (the previous one had been burned by the military), a sufficient amount of time for the registration process to ensure that large numbers of citizens actually registered, television access for advocates of the "no" ("no" to another term for Pinochet), the necessary voting procedures to ensure secrecy, and assurances that opposition delegates would be able to observe the balloting and vote-counting processes. The American ambassador in Santiago, Harry Barnes, made it very clear to the members of the military junta that the United States agreed with all these conditions and that it would not consider the plebiscite valid unless they were all met. Given its sensitivity to charges of illegitimacy, the government explicitly or tacitly agreed to all of them.

As the campaign preparations began, the opposition organized a broad coalition for the "no" that included all groups except the Communist party, whose leaders only very belatedly saw any value in the process. The opposition used the half-hour segment the authorities gave it on television very cleverly, with a message focused on future happiness and reconciliation that was developed by social science researchers using political marketing techniques. It also organized poll watchers in every single locality of the country and an alternative vote-counting system that would give it the possibility of checking the veracity of official figures. Citizens were to vote "yes" or "no" to Pinochet's continuing in the presidency, and when the votes were counted on the night of October 5, 1988, 54.7 percent had voted "no," and 43 percent "yes." Over 90 percent of registered voters cast ballots, and over 90 percent of those eligible to register had done so.

Pinochet was shocked by this result and brooded for months over it. Yet there was little he could do to set it aside. The plebiscite was a procedure that he introduced into the constitution himself, and he could not easily turn against the "institutionality" he had for years urged the armed forces as well as his civilian supporters to uphold. The opposition also gave the regime no excuses to suspend the plebiscite or the vote count. From beginning to end, the opposition conducted an orderly campaign, refraining from staging demonstrations that might be construed as provocations, especially on the day of the plebiscite. The night of the vote count some government officials did seek to tamper with the results. But while this effort was underway, the commander-in-chief of the air force freely admitted to a journalist that the figures released by the opposition were correct, thereby revealing his opposition to any tinkering with the results.

The outcome of the plebiscite meant that within a year open presidential and congressional elections were to be held. After some difficult negotiations, the opposition parties agreed to support a single presidential candidate, Christian Democrat Patricio Aylwin, and to present basically a single list (a parallel list with some Communist and other leftist candidates running in a few districts) for the Senate and the Lower House. The opposition also demanded that the constitution be revised, and the government agreed to some minimal changes. These revisions had the advantage from the government's point of view of limiting the next presidential term, which the opposition would almost certainly win, to four years. More importantly, since the amendments were submitted to a new plebiscite, which the opposition was bound to approve, the government could claim that the constitution had been backed by the voters and thereby had received indisputable democratic legitimation.

The presidential and congressional elections were held on December 14, 1989. Aylwin won 55.2 percent of the validly cast vote, defeating two candidates of the right, and his democratic coalition obtained 56.5 percent of the vote for seats in the Lower House of Congress, despite the difficulties it encountered with the electoral system.

CHALLENGES IN REBUILDING THE CHILEAN DEMOCRATIC REGIME

The inauguration of an elected government is only a first step in the process of building or, as in Chile, rebuilding the democratic regime. For such a regime, it is not enough simply to have elections, a reasonable separation of powers, and protections for universally recognized human and political rights. The electoral system has to permit, in addition, the selection of national and local government officials and legislators who reflect, by and large, voter choice, and the parties should be able to present candidates to the electorate free from untoward interferences, threats, or menaces to the democratic system if they win. Moreover, elected authorities should be free to make decisions in all policy areas they feel are important to their governmental roles, and their overall actions should not be overseen by nonelected elites whose positions of power are buttressed by overt or veiled threats of a reversion to authoritarian rule.

From this perspective, the Chilean transition faces many challenges in re-creating a fully democratic regime. The problems stem partly from the fact that the 1980 Constitution has many features that are incompatible with a democratic regime; hence, while its rules permitted the change to an elected government, it must now be modified to allow a complete restoration of democracy. Moreover, Pinochet and the junta had one full year between the plebiscite and the inauguration of Patricio Aylwin to create additional institutional parameters and to appoint new officials who may obstruct newly elected authorities.

To modify the constitution, the new government would need two-thirds majorities—which it lacks—in both the Senate and the House. The congressional representation of the democratic coalition was severely reduced by the peculiarities of the electoral system devised for this purpose by the military government. This system limited the number of candidates the left was able to run, grossly underrepresented urban districts where the democratic coalition is stronger, and established rules, unique in the world, that greatly favor the second-placed list of candidates by granting it one of two seats that are to be elected per district whenever the first winning list does not have twice the votes of the second one. The military authorities correctly estimated that the lists of the right would take second place. The unusual vote-counting feature allowed the right to elect a net number of seven senators and fourteen representatives who won fewer *individual* votes than candidates who took second place in the democratic coalition's list. Moreover, the Senate includes eight senators who were designated by Pinochet, his National Security Council, or the Supreme Court—which itself was previously packed by Pinochet through the appointment of nine new justices for life. Hence, these procedures do not permit a fully democratic representation in the Congress, and unless agreements are reached with at least some of the right's representatives (all of whom were generally supportive of the military government), it will be impossible to dismantle the constitutional and legal limitations set in place by the military to prevent the new democratic government from exercising full authority.

The consequences of these limitations are far from insignificant. The military apparatus itself escapes completely from control by the democratically elected government. Following the constitution, General Pinochet himself cannot be removed from his post as commander-in-chief of the army. President Aylwin gently asked him to resign anyway, but he refused. Pinochet's legislation for the armed forces leaves him with full authority over officer promotions and retirements and prevents the treasury from having any say over the military budget, which has its own sources of financing derived from the sales of copper. By naming all military attachés, Pinochet can also conduct his own diplomacy. The new rules also prohibit the democratic government from having any input into national security doctrine or the curricula of military academies. Pinochet also continues to have exclusive control over army intelligence, thereby retaining what remains of the military regime's secret police. With these provisions, military autonomy has become absolute, whereas in Chile's previous democratic regime the president and the Senate had final control over promotions and retirements, over the size of the military budget, and over major expenditures.

A major difficulty is that this autonomous military apparatus is not an enclave, but has considerable influence outside its own domain. The armed forces, according to the constitution, are supposed to protect and guarantee the stability of the nation's political framework. The constitution also establishes a National Security Council, half military and police commanders with two other members indirectly appointed by Pinochet, to exercise authority over all national security matters. Pinochet has already created what amounts to a virtual "shadow cabinet" of over thirty expert advisors to follow all the actions of the newly elected government. This constitutes an attempt to create a virtual "oversight" or "tutelary" power over the new democratic government. Similarly, the military court system is allowed to continue to judge all crimes having to do with national security, even by civilians, and to initiate judicial proceedings against elected representatives in Congress. All of this has been backed with repeated assertions by the military command that the armed forces stand ready to resume their "responsibilities," if necessary, as they did in 1973. Pinochet has interpreted any attempt to prosecute military officers for human rights violations, a matter contrary to amnesty laws he enacted, as a break with "institutionality" and as such a cause for renewed military intervention. Such laws also prohibit Congress from judging any actions by former ministers and other officials, including Pinochet himself. The threats of a new coup and the tutelary power pretensions serve to retain the military apparatus as a domain removed from control by democratic authorities.

Legal norms left in place by Pinochet also prohibit the new government from replacing any public servants except for top officials. This system is in stark contrast to the actions taken by the military junta itself, which revamped the state administration at will and fired thousands of public servants. President Aylwin also inherited an undemocratic local government system. Mayors are no longer elected by the voters, and of about 360 mayoralities the new government will only be able to name fifteen. All the others were appointed for four years by Pinochet. Given the importance of local governments in delivering services to voters, this constitutes a great political asset for the right.

The new system also creates an autonomous Central Bank that controls all monetary and exchange rate policy, thereby reducing the capacity of elected government officials to address major aspects of economic policy. Pinochet named the Central Bank board members, although he did reach a compromise with Aylwin's economic advisors over the nominations.

The democratic government also faces challenges in other areas. There are many unresolved problems in Chilean society that are bound to manifest themselves through pressures exerted by a wide variety of groups on the new authorities. Although the country has grown economically in the last few years, there is now less access to public health services, low income housing, and public education; a much more regressive distribution of income; a drop in retirement benefits and coverage; lower real wages and salaries in the public and private sectors; a virtual absence of labor organization in new export growth areas of the economy, which pay very little despite high profits; and a backlog of judicial problems related to human rights violations and politically motivated crimes. It will be extremely difficult to find the proper means to address these problems through negotiations and compromises, while at the same time taking action to lift the institutional constraints that prevent a full recovery of democracy. Despite the significant achievement of a return to a democratically elected government, the road ahead will not be easy.

SUGGESTED READINGS

Angell, Alan. *Politics and the Labour Movement in Chile.* Oxford University Press, London, 1972.

Arriagada, Genaro. *Pinochet: The Politics of Power.* Unwin Hyman, Winchester, Mass., 1988.

Bauer, Robert J. *Chilean Rural Society from the Spanish Conquest to 1930.* Cambridge University Press, London, 1975.

Blakemore, Harold. *British Nitrates and Chilean Politics, 1886–1896: Balmaceda and North.* Athlone Press, London, 1974.

Boorstein, Edward. *Allende's Chile: An Inside View.* International Publishers, New York, 1977.

DeShazo, Peter. *Urban Workers and Labor Unions in Chile, 1902–1927.* University of Wisconsin Press, Madison, 1983.

De Vylder, Stefan. *Allende's Chile: The Political Economy of the Rise and Fall of the Unidad Popular.* Cambridge University Press, Cambridge, 1974.

Drake, Paul W. *Socialism and Populism in Chile, 1932–52.* University of Illinois, Urbana, 1978.

Foxley, Alejandro. *Latin American Experiments in Neoconservative Economics.* University of California, Berkeley, 1983.

Galdames, Luis. *A History of Chile.* Translated and edited by Issac J. Cox. University of North Carolina Press, Chapel Hill, 1941.

Garretón, Manuel Antonio. *The Chilean Political Process.* Unwin Hyman, Winchester, Mass., 1989.

Gil, Federico. *The Political System of Chile.* Houghton Mifflin, Boston, 1966.

Gil, Federico, Ricardo Lagos E., and H. A. Landsberger, eds. *Chile at the Turning Point: Lessons of the Socialist Years, 1970–73.* Institute for the Study of Human Issues (ISHI), Philadelphia, 1979.

Kaufman, Robert R. *The Politics of Land Reform in Chile 1950–1970: Public Policy, Political Institutions, and Social Change.* Harvard University Press, Cambridge, 1972.

Loveman, Brian. *Chile: The Legacy of Hispanic Capitalism.* Oxford University Press, New York, 1979.

Mamalakis, Markos J. *The Growth and Structure of the Chilean Economy: From Independence to Allende.* Yale University Press, New Haven, Conn., 1976.

Moran, Theodore. *Multinational Corporations and the Politics of Dependence: Copper in Chile.* Princeton University Press, Princeton, N.J., 1974.

Petras, James, and Morris Morley. *The United States and Chile: Imperialism and the Overthrow of the Allende Government.* Monthly Review Press, New York, 1975.

Pike, Fredrick. *Chile and the United States.* University of Notre Dame Press, Notre Dame, Ind., 1963.

Roxborough, Ian, Philip O'Brien, and Jackie Roddick. *Chile: The State and Revolution.* Holmes & Meier Publishers, New York, 1977.

Sigmund, Paul E. *The Overthrow of Allende and the Politics of Chile, 1964–76.* University of Pittsburgh, Pittsburgh, 1977.

Smith, Brian H. *The Church and Politics in Chile: Challenges to Modern Catholicism.* Princeton University Press, Princeton, N.J., 1982.

Stallings, Barbara. *Class Conflict and Economic Development in Chile, 1958–1973.* Stanford University Press, Stanford, Calif., 1978.

Valenzuela, Arturo, *Political Brokers in Chile: Local Politics in a Centralized Polity.* Duke University Press, Durham, N.C., 1977.

———. *The Breakdown of Democratic Regimes: Chile.* Johns Hopkins University Press, Baltimore, 1978.

Valenzuela, Arturo, and J. Samuel Valenzuela, eds. *Chile: Politics and Society.* Transaction Books, New Brunswick, N.J., 1976.

Valenzuela, J. Samuel, and Arturo Valenzuela, eds. *Military Rule in Chile: Dictatorship and Oppositions.* Johns Hopkins University Press, Baltimore, 1986.

Winn, Peter. *Weavers of Revolution: The Yarur Workers and Chile's Road to Socialism.* Oxford University Press, New York, 1986.

Zeitlin, Maurice, and Richard Earl Ratcliff. *Landlords and Capitalists: The Dominant Class of Chile.* Princeton University Press, Princeton, N.J., 1988.

26
ARGENTINA: DEVELOPMENT AND DECAY

PETER G. SNOW

In many respects Argentina is the Latin American nation furthest removed from the stereotypical notions held by people in the United States. In Argentina, there are 28 million highly literate, reasonably well-fed people, almost uniformly of European ancestry, who inhabit the world's eighth-largest nation, virtually all of which lies in the Temperate Zone. Almost a third of these people live in metropolitan Buenos Aires, one of the world's largest and most cosmopolitan cities. Even those living outside Buenos Aires fail to conform to the stereotypical image—poverty-stricken peasants working someone else's land. Almost three-fourths of the non-Buenos Aires population lives in urban centers, a fourth in cities of more than 100,000 people.

For many years now Argentina has been an almost completely "white" nation. The Indian population has steadily decreased, not just in percentage terms, but also in absolute numbers. Today there are probably fewer than 100,000 Indians in the nation, and these are concentrated near the north-western frontier. While most Indians were killed in the nineteenth century in order to push the frontier to the south, the mestizos were absorbed by waves of European immigration. Today perhaps 10 percent of the population is classified as mestizo, and these appear to be concentrated near the northern and western borders. There are virtually no blacks in Argentina. Although numerically significant at the time of independence, they have rapidly been assimilated into the general population until their number has declined to about 5,000.

Argentina is blessed with much of the world's best farmland, the Pampa, an incredibly fertile plain stretching out from Buenos Aires to cover an area the size of Iowa, Kansas, and Nebraska put together. Yet, in spite of being one of the very few cereal-exporting nations in the world, Argentina is not totally dedicated to agriculture. In fact, agriculture provides the livelihood for less than a fifth of the economically active population. Another third is engaged in the industrial sector of the economy, with the largest number working in food processing, construction, textile, and metallurgical industries. The remainder of the economically active population is engaged in commerce and services. The largest groups within this sector are the business people and their employees, public officials, and domestic servants. It is the tertiary sector that is growing in relative size, while the percentage of the population engaged in agriculture is declining and the size of the industrial sector remains relatively constant. A major part of the growth of the tertiary sector is a result of the seemingly endless increase in the size of the bureaucracy, which now employs one out of every ten economically active citizens.

The often repeated bromide about the lack of a middle class in Latin America simply is not true of Argentina, where almost half of the population can be so classified (at least in terms of being neither upper class nor working class). However, this middle class—or, more appropriately, middle sector—is in almost no way a cohesive group. Business people, members of the liberal professions, and clerks in government offices have relatively little in common and certainly lack a single coherent world view that could be translated into political action.

Unfortunately, these assets have led neither to economic nor to political stability. In these realms, Argentine reality closely approximates stereotypical notions. Since 1928, thirteen presidents have been removed from office by force, and not a single civilian president has served a full term of office. The Congress met in only three of the years between 1966 and 1983, and in spite of a constitutional guarantee of life tenure for justices, the entire Supreme Court was purged in 1955, 1966, and 1976. During the 1970s, the level of political violence was as great as in any nation in the world, as both left- and right-wing terrorists murdered with virtual impunity.

Virtually all economists agree that Argentina has all the ingredients for a sound and stable economy. Nevertheless, the nation has accumulated a foreign debt that, in per capita terms, is among the largest in the world. In every year since 1974, inflation has exceeded 100 percent; a cup of coffee, which in 1973 could be purchased for a single peso, cost about 30,000 pesos in 1983. Although these extraordinary levels of inflation and foreign indebtedness are relatively new, the nation's economc problems were not born with the 1976 military coup. During the previous civilian administration, the government of the nation's largest province spent over 90 percent of its revenue on salaries; the preceding civilian government had devoted almost 20 percent of national expenditures to cover the deficit of the national railroad.

How did Argentina, which in 1930 had levels of social, economic, and political development comparable to those of Canada, Australia, and much of southern Europe, reach such a chaotic situation? That is the subject of this chapter, which describes the nation's development and decay, offers some tentative explanations, and suggests that the prospect for the immediate future is something other than rosy.

THE AGE OF DEVELOPMENT

Argentina was originally settled by two separate streams of colonizers. The first group came from Peru and settled the northwestern region during the last half of the sixteenth century; the second came directly from Spain and founded Buenos Aires. Throughout the colonial period, these two groups led quite separate existences. The Northwest was developed primarily to provide food, livestock, and textiles for the mining areas of Peru while Buenos Aires remained oriented toward Europe. This separateness, both geographical and psychological, made it quite difficult later to create a nation.

The struggle for independence began in 1810, and for the next decade, Argentinians fought not only Spaniards but also Paraguayans, Uruguayans, Brazilians, and, most frequently, each other. De facto independence had been attained by 1819, but it took almost half a century more for Argentina to become a nation. A series of juntas, triumvirates, and supreme directors came and went without any success in the quest for national unification. During this period, there existed only an amalgamation of autonomous provinces. Seldom was there even a semblance of a national government, and if political order existed in the provinces, it was forcibly imposed by a local *caudillo*.

The inability to create a single nation was largely a result of conflict between the people of Buenos Aires on the one hand and those of the interior on the other. The former, who referred to themselves as Unitarians, demanded a strong national government run by and for the people of Buenos Aires; the leaders of the interior provinces were equally insistent upon a weak federal system, although to many of them, federalism meant only the right of the local *caudillo* to exploit his province as he saw fit.

In 1853, the provincial leaders wrote a federal constitution patterned upon that of the United States. Buenos Aires, however, boycotted the constitutional convention and maintained a separate existence. The conflict increased in intensity until it came to civil war in 1858 and again in 1861, when the forces of Buenos Aires, under the leadership of Bartolomé Mitre, gained a decisive victory. After the adoption of relatively minor constitutional amendments, Buenos Aires agreed to join the union, and in 1862, Mitre became Argentina's first truly national president.

The inauguration of Mitre marked the beginning of a new era in Argentina. For half a century, the country had known only anarchy and dictatorship; the next seven decades were characterized by peace and stability and by rapid economic and political development. Mitre and the two presidents who followed him concentrated most of their efforts on pacification and the creation of the institutions of government. The Congress was moved from the interior to Buenos Aires and began to meet regularly. A national judiciary was created and staffed by extremely competent people, including several provincial politicians. The city of Buenos Aires was separated from the province of that name and converted into a federal district, much like Washington, D.C. And, most important, general acceptance was gained for the existence of a single national government.

Beginning in 1880, emphasis shifted from politics to economics. The next several administrations set out to increase production by importing Europeans and European capital. At that time, there were barely 1.5 million Argentinians occupying 1 million sq mi (2.6 million sq km). The vast majority of these people were rural, and most were engaged in subsistence agriculture. Infrastructural development was accomplished primarily through British financing; the rail system, for example, was British owned until the end of World War II. When Mitre took office in 1862, there were perhaps 2,000 mi (3,200 km) of track; fifty years later there were 20,000 (32,200 km). During the same period, the amount of cultivated land was increased from less than 1.5 million acres (607,500 hectares) to more than 60 million (24.3 million hectares), and the amount of land devoted to grazing was increased almost as dramatically. These and similar factors meant that Argentina changed from having a subsistence agricultural system to being a major exporter of primary products, and the transformation took place with amazing rapidity. By World War I, Argentina was exporting 350,000 tons of beef and 5 million tons of cereals annually.

During this same period, there were important changes in the nature of Argentine society, changes that were largely a result of massive immigration. Beginning almost immediately after the creation of a national government, a concerted effort was made to attract Europeans to Argentina, an effort that was enormously successful. In 1870, 40,000 immigrants arrived; in 1885, 110,000; and in 1890, 200,000. From the time of Mitre's inauguration in 1862 until the first military coup in 1930, at least half of Argentina's population growth resulted from immigration.

Although a great many Argentinians attained some degree of economic well being between 1862 and 1916, the average citizen remained almost completely removed from the political process. Government machinery revolved around the person of the president. In the provinces, the legislatures were subservient to the governors, to whom most members owed their election. Each governor was also quite influential in the selection of congressional representatives from his province. The provincial legislatures chose the members of the upper house of Congress, while the governor had control over the electoral machinery so that "safe" representatives were returned to the lower house. The governors, in turn, were virtually the personal agents of the president, who could keep them in line with the use, or just the threat, of his power to remove them from office. A number of political parties were active during this period, but until almost the turn of the century, all were essentially conservative organizations representing different sectors of the aristocracy—primarily the large landowners of the interior and the commercial and livestock interests in the city and province of Buenos Aires.

This political system was perhaps appropriate for Argentina as long as its society was composed almost exclusively of a small landowning elite and a large, politically inarticulate mass; however, it ceased to be appropriate when the nation's social structure underwent fundamental alteration. The most important of the societal changes was the rapid formation of a middle class, a middle class composed largely of immigrants and their offspring.

It was this newly emerging middle class that formed the original base for Argentina's first nonaristocratic political party, the Radical Civic Union (UCR), founded in 1890. During the first four decades of its existence, this party was dominated by an enigmatic politician named Hipólito Irigoyen. Convinced that UCR participation in elections supervised by the Conservatives would serve only to place the party's stamp of approval on inevitable electoral fraud, Irigoyen saw to it that the Radicals boycotted all elections prior to 1912. Instead, they attempted to come to power by force, instigating rebellions in 1890, 1893, and 1905. When these revolts proved unsuccessful, the Radicals still did not nominate candidates for office or write specific programs; rather, they contented themselves with denunciations of the oligarchic nature of the government and insisted that it be replaced by an undefined "national renovation" led by the UCR.

In an effort to bring more people to the polls and thus increase the legitimacy of the regime, the Conservatives wrote a new election law in 1911. This law provided for universal and compulsory male suffrage, a secret ballot, permanent voter registration, and minority representation in the Congress. Within five years, the honest administration of this law cost the Conservatives their monopoly on political office.

In 1916, Hipólito Irigoyen became Argentina's first non-Conservative president. Unfortunately, the Radicals, still lacking a concrete program, had no clear idea of how to put into effect the national renovation they had promised. The UCR held power for fourteen years, but no fundamental changes were even attempted. It appears that many Radicals had lost their revolutionary zeal and that their goal had become simply recognition of the right of the middle class to participate fully in the economic, social, and political life of the nation—or at least recognition of its right to a share of the spoils of office.

In September 1930, an economic crisis, the ever-increasing corruption in the government, President Irigoyen's senility (at the age of seventy-two he was serving a second term), recognition by the elite that the rules of the game had to be changed if they were to return to power, and widespread popular disillusionment with the Radicals led to their overthrow and the establishment of Argentina's first military government.

By 1930, the institutions of liberal democracy that had served the elite so well in the past had been called into question. In 1912, the elite had been willing to share power with the Radicals, although certainly not on the basis of equality. They apparently saw the provision in the new election law guaranteeing minority representation in Congress as a means of co-opting their middle-class opponents. (The congressional debate on the law makes it clear that the Conservatives had not envisioned the possibility of their becoming the minority party.) What the elite had been unwilling to do was to relinquish power to the Radicals, yet that is exactly what happened. Voter participation increased dramatically (from 190,000 in 1910 to 640,000 in 1912 and 1,460,000 in 1928), and as it grew, so did the percentage of the vote obtained by the Radicals. By 1930, it was clear that Conservatives were quite unlikely to win any national elections in the foreseeable future, and given Irigoyen's adamant opposition to electoral alliances or coalition governments, in fact to any form of accommodation with the old regime, it was also clear that the Conservatives were to have no real voice in the determination of public policy. Although the policies adopted by the Radicals between 1916 and 1930 had not been particularly disadvantageous to the old elite, the large and growing Radical electorate meant that disadvantageous policies were a definite future possibility.

THE AGE OF DECAY

The 1930 military coup marked the beginning of a new era in Argentina. The preceding seventy years had been characterized by a degree of political stability and economic development almost unknown in Latin America. The years since 1930, on the other hand, have been characterized by exactly the opposite: economic stagnation and an incredible degree of political instability.

Following the overthrow of Irigoyen, the armed forces retained power for less than two years before returning control of the government to the Conservatives by means of elections in which the Radicals were denied participation. It was not until 1946 that open and honest elections were held once again. In fact, the period between 1932 and 1943 is often referred to as "the era of patriotic fraud." According to the Conservatives, it was their patriotic duty to engage in electoral fraud, for otherwise the Radicals would hoodwink the immature voters, return to power, and once again lead the nation down the road to ruin.

Although the elite that had governed Argentina prior to 1916 had been dedicated to national development, such was certainly not true of the elite that governed after 1930. That government did lead the nation out of the depression and restore a degree of economic prosperity; however, it also saw to it that this prosperity was distributed even more inequitably than before. Argentina was run almost exclusively for the benefit of the landed aristocracy.

At about the same time the Conservatives were returning to power, a profound change was occurring in the character of the urban working class. During World War I, the majority of the urban workers were immigrants, almost none of whom became naturalized citizens; but by World War II, they were primarily recent migrants from the countryside or, to a lesser extent, the children of immigrants. During the 1930s and early 1940s, there was a wave of migration to the cities of truly incredible proportions. In one four-year period, almost 20 percent of the rural population moved into an urban center, most into greater Buenos Aires. Politically, this new urban working class differed from its earlier counterpart in at least one important way: Its members were citizens and, hence, potential voters.

Unfortunately, the nation's political institutions were not equipped to handle large new groups of political participants. Neither the structures, nor the programs, nor the leaders of the existing political parties were able (or willing, perhaps) to offer anything of value to this working class. Until 1940, the Congress was dominated by Conservatives who seemed totally uninterested in the plight of the workers; for the next three years, the Radicals used their congressional majority only to harass the Conservative president and to prevent the enactment of any sort of program.

Such was the scene in 1943 when the leaders of the armed forces again assumed the role of keepers of the national conscience and deposed the Conservative government. In the military administration that followed the coup, power gradually came to be concentrated more and more in the hands of a colonel who was to dominate the course of Argentine politics for the next thirty years: Juan Domingo Perón.

Perón appears to have been the one army officer who saw the political potential of urban labor. Content with a secondary position in the revolutionary government, that of secretary of labor (a position without cabinet rank), he almost immediately began an active campaign for working-class support. He saw to it that wages were increased substantially and that ameliorative labor legislation was enforced for the first time. He presided over the formation of new trade unions and the enormous expansion of existing unions that were friendly to him. By 1945, his Labor Secretariat was the nation's sole collective bargaining agency, and unions utilizing its auspices were virtually certain to receive whatever they sought.

In the presidential election of February 1946, Perón was the candidate of the hastily formed Argentine Labor Party. Although opposed by a single candidate representing all the nation's traditional parties, Perón won. In 1916, it had been the newly emerging middle class that was largely responsible for the election of Irigoyen; thirty years later, it was the new urban working class that could claim most of the credit for the election of Juan Perón.

As president, Perón continued to do a great deal for the working class, both materially and psychologically. The process of unionization was continued, wages and fringe benefits were dramatically increased, and a modern social security system was created. At least as important in the long run was the thorough politicization of the working class, which came to realize its potential political strength.

Although honestly elected in 1946 and again in 1951, Perón moved steadily in the direction of authoritarian rule. Freedom of the press was virtually destroyed, the judiciary was purged as were the universities, and opposition politicians were harassed, exiled, or imprisoned. Perón had originally come to power with the support of the Catholic Church and the armed forces, in addition to urban labor. By 1955, his labor support had declined slightly, and the Church had moved completely into the opposition. Most important, an appreciable sector of the armed forces had decided that Perón must go.

In September 1955, Perón was deposed; he went into exile from which he did not return for eighteen years. It was relatively simple to get rid of Perón, but it was much more difficult to rid the country of Peronism. For two and a half years, General Pedro Aramburu presided over a provisional regime dedicated to destroying Peronism and to returning the country to civilian constitutional rule. With regard to the former, there was a near-total lack of success; in fact, the extreme anti-Peronism of the military government seems to have served only to convince Perón's followers that they must remain united in their support of their exiled leader or see the clock turned back to pre-1946. The latter goal met with only limited success, for although elections were held, as far as the military was concerned, the wrong man won.

The 1958 elections were swept by a faction of the old UCR calling itself the Intransigent Radical Civic Union (UCRI). Its leader, Arturo Frondizi, attained the presidency due largely to a deal with Perón, who traded the votes of his followers for a promise of legality for the Peronist Party. This bargain gave Frondizi the presidency, but it cost him the ability to govern effectively. The anti-Peronist sector of the population, and especially the armed forces, considered his election tainted and his administration illegitimate.

For four years, Frondizi made a concerted effort to accelerate the nation's rate of economic development and to integrate the Peronists back into political life. By 1962, his economic policies appeared to be on the verge of success, but his political maneuvers by then had cost him his job. Restored to legality, the Peronist Party emerged victorious in the congressional and gubernatorial elections held in March 1962. This was the last straw as far as the anti-Peronist military leaders were concerned, and Frondizi was deposed.

After a year of near-total chaos and virtual civil war within the armed forces, elections were held once again, and once again the Peronists were not allowed to nominate candidates for executive offices. This time, the elections were won by the People's Radical Civic Union (UCRP), the faction of the old UCR that had lost to Frondizi and the UCRI in 1958. Elected to the presidency was Arturo Illia, a mild-mannered country doctor who received only a fourth of the total vote. The three years of the Illia administration were characterized by a lack of action. In 1962, Frondizi had been overthrown because the leaders of the armed forces disapproved of his actions; in 1966, Illia was deposed because he did not act.

By 1966, the military had witnessed what it considered the failure of two civilian administrations to resolve the Peronist "problem" and to bring about an acceptable rate of economic growth—and these administrations had been led by the only two political parties that had popular support even approaching that of the Peronists. Rather than creating another provisional military government, as had been done in 1930, 1943, and 1955, the leaders of the armed forces removed from office all elected officials and many high-ranking appointees, dissolved all the nation's political parties, and then granted almost complete authority to a retired general, Juan Carlos Onganía.

General Onganía was put in power to bring about a fundamental restructuring of the nation's political system. Attempts were made to exclude the working class from the political process, and to depoliticize groups such as the trade unions and student organizations, but to no avail. Student organizations were banned by law, yet students engaged in political violence to a greater extent than ever before. The labor movement was not depoliticized, and the working class refused to accept passively a reduction in its standard of living.

By 1970, it was clear that Onganía was accomplishing very little, that the public support, or at least acquiescence, he originally had enjoyed had almost vanished, and that the nation was experiencing a completely intolerable level of political violence. The leaders of the armed forces appear to have decided that they had no choice but to hold elections and return to constitutional government. When Onganía refused to go along with this plan, he was deposed, as was his successor a few months later when he too showed no signs of moving toward elections. Finally, the army commander-in-chief, General Alejandro Lanusse, assumed the presidency and announced that he would hold office only long enough to stop the violence and hold elections.

It was obvious to all that if a newly elected government was to have any claim to legitimacy, the Peronist movement would have to be given complete electoral equality. Yet, since many military leaders were still opposed to the prospect of a Peronist government, changes were made in the election law to require a runoff election if no presidential candidate received an absolute majority of the popular vote. (It was assumed that the Peronist candidate, whoever that might be, would win a plurality of the vote but would be defeated in the runoff by a coalition of non-Peronist parties.) Moreover, a number of complicated maneuvers effectively prevented Perón himself from being a candidate.

When the elections were held in March 1973, the Peronist candidate, Héctor Cámpora (whose campaign slogan was Cámpora to the presidency, Perón to power) received 49.6 percent of the vote, more than double that of his nearest competitor. In violation of his own regulations, Lanusse decided that the results were close enough to the required absolute majority to cancel the runoff. Immediately following Cámpora's inauguration, all political prisoners—including many terrorists convicted of murder—received amnesty, and the national universities were turned over to the far left. However, after only fifty days in office, Cámpora and his vice-president resigned, necessitating new elections—this time with Juan Perón himself a candidate.

The presidential election of September 1973 was almost a carbon copy of the one held twenty-two years earlier; in each case Perón received 62 percent of the vote, and in each case he defeated Ricardo Balbín, the candidate of the Radicals. In 1951, Perón had tried, unsuccessfully, to obtain the vice-presidential nomination for his second wife, Evita; in 1973, his running mate was his third wife, Isabel.

Eighteen years after he had been rather ignominiously forced into exile, Perón triumphantly returned to the presidency. Even his most bitter opponents admitted that if anyone could begin to solve the nation's multitudinous problems, it was probably Perón. Whether or not that would have been the case will never be known, for on July 1, 1974, less than nine months after his inauguration, Juan Domingo Perón died. He was succeeded by his widow, María Estela (Isabel) Martínez de Perón.

Political violence, which had abated while Perón was president, reached an extraordinary level shortly after his death. Inflation, which was already high, increased until it approached 1 percent per day. Corruption became rampant. And, quite predictably, the armed forces once again assumed power. In April 1976, Isabel was arrested, and the army commander-in-chief, General Jorge Videla, was inaugurated as president.

Unlike 1966, when the armed forces placed all authority in the hands of a single retired general, in 1976 an institutionalized military regime was established. The major goals of this military government were the elimination of leftist terrorism and the restoration of economic stability. The former goal was largely accomplished within three years; since 1979 very little has been heard from the Peronist and Trotskyite terrorists who were so active in the early 1970s. However, this goal was accomplished primarily through the utilization of government terrorism. Thousands of people were subjected to arbitrary arrest, imprisonment, and torture, and a great many more simply disappeared. The latter goal proved more intractable. Some short-term economic policies were successful, but by 1981 the economy was not in appreciably better shape than it had been in in 1976.

By early 1982, the leaders of the armed forces appeared to be moving in the direction of elections and a restoration of civilian constitutional government. Then, on April 2, came the move to "recuperate" the Malvinas/Falkland Islands. The success of the invasion, and the relative ease with which it was accomplished, were greeted with enormous enthusiasm by all Argentinians. Unfortunately for all, the Argentine military leaders had drastically miscalculated the forcefulness of the British response. When Argentina lost the war, and so ignominiously, the government was dead. General Leopoldo Galtieri was quickly removed from the presidency and from his post as commander-in-chief of the army, and a provisional government, headed by retired general Reynaldo Bignone, was established. Soon after his inauguration, Bignone promised that general elections would be held during 1983 and that the new government would be inaugurated by March 1984.

The total failure of the military government was a bitter disappointment to many Argentinians. The military administrations that followed the coups of 1930, 1943, and 1955 were relatively brief transitions from one constitutional regime to another. Following the 1962 coup, the military did not assume the presidency but allowed the president of the Senate to preside over new elections, and the regime that followed the 1966 coup was that of a single retired general and not of the armed forces as an institution. In all these, and other, crisis situations, the prevailing attitude of Argentinians seemed to be "if this doesn't work, we can call on the military." In 1982, with the complete failure of an institutionalized military regime, there was no external force left to call upon.

WHAT WENT WRONG?

Although it is tempting to assign responsibility for the nation's political instability exclusively to the military, which has staged so many coups during the last half century, to do so would be a gross oversimplification. Certainly, there is enough blame to go around, and a large part of it must be shouldered by civilian politicians, who not only have failed to legitimate the constitutional system but also have actively conspired against it.

The failure of Argentine political parties to legitimate government action has been largely a result of two factors: (1) a lack of independence on the part of the government party, due primarily to its reliance upon the president, and (2) the lack of "loyal" opposition parties. It must be remembered that the entire political system in Argentina is centered around the president. This affects not only the legislative and judicial branches but also the political parties. In this system, the political party has become largely a means of attaining executive power, and thus has been left without meaningful functions once this has been accomplished. Only rarely has a government party played an important role in the formulation of policy. Instead, congressmen and provincial legislators who are members of the government party have been reduced to the position of enacting into law bills that originate in the executive branch.

While the government parties have been unable to act as legitimating agents because of their subservience to the president, their opponents have chosen not to perform this function; that is, they have refused to form a loyal "opposition." Whereas success in a presidential election has left a party virtually without meaningful functions to perform, defeat has simply meant a change in tactics; the goal has remained the same: control of the executive branch.

Seldom in Argentina has electoral defeat been accepted as definitive—by the losers. The opposition parties traditionally have turned to other means of attaining power. This most often has meant an attempt to provoke a military coup. If the leaders of the armed forces could be persuaded to overthrow the government, the opposition parties might be able to gain power in the revolutionary government; or, failing in this, they might fare better in new elections—especially if the former government party were denied participation at the polls.

In 1930, the Conservatives, unable to win honest elections, supported the coup of General José Félix Uriburu and soon inherited the government. Denied the presidency by means of electoral fraud, the Radicals applauded the 1943 coup; they moved into the opposition only after they realized that the revolutionary administration was not going to install them in power. Both Conservatives and Radicals were involved in the 1954–1955 plots to remove Perón, and each party supported the original revolutionary government. After the Peronist election victories in 1962, the People's Radicals might have been able to save the Frondizi administration by agreeing to serve in a coalition government. Instead, they refused and joined the chorus of people demanding that the president resign. *Frondicistas* reciprocated four years later when they were influential in persuading the armed forces to remove the Illia administration. The single important exception to this rule came in 1974 and 1975 when the Radicals, and especially their leader,

Ricardo Balbín, played a quite responsible opposition role, thus helping to forestall, temporarily, the overthrow of Isabel Perón.

It is not just professional politicians who have encouraged military intervention; to some extent at least, the general public has also done so. All the presidents deposed by the armed forces—with the possible exception of Illia—have faced very broad-based civilian opposition, and at the same time, only Perón had any appreciable popular support.

In the absence of reliable public opinion polls, it is impossible to state with exactness the level of opposition to any of the deposed presidents; however, what is most important is the military's perception of this opposition. It seems likely that this perception has been exaggerated by the fact that opposition leaders have been unwilling to wait for this opposition to be manifested at the polls, but instead have gone to friends in the armed forces in an effort to convince them of the "necessity" of a coup. As a prominent Argentine sociologist put it:

> The armed forces have been looked upon by all political groups as a potentially useful instrument for the satisfaction of their own objectives. Thus, in spite of all arguments to the contrary, recourse to the armed forces as a source of legitimation has become a tacit rule of the Argentine political game, a rule which no one openly invokes, but one which has benefited all political groups at least once. Although they must all deny it publicly, Argentine politicians cannot ignore the fact that at one time or another during the past quarter-century they have gone to knock at the doors of the barracks.[1]

If there is no simple solution to Argentina's political instability, this is even more true of the nation's economic problems. Not only is there no agreement as to a potential solution, there is not even anything approaching a consensus as to the nature of the problem. The one area in which there is some agreement is that at least part of the problem is a result of frequent, dramatic shifts from laissez-faire economic policies to extremely nationalistic policies.

For a long time, many Argentine economists have blamed inflation and other economic problems on two factors: a lack of labor discipline and the turnover of economic ministers and economic plans with such rapidity that only the most short-term policies could possibly be implemented. In 1976, in an attempt to alter this situation, the leaders of the armed forces appear to have made the decision to place responsibility and authority for economic policymaking in the hands of a single individual, and to leave that person in control for a substantial period of time. The man chosen was José Alfredo Martínez de Hoz, who, as one of the nation's most visible representatives of laissez-faire liberalism, almost automatically antagonized most nationalists. During his term, the two alleged causes of economic problems were eliminated. Labor discipline was imposed, strikes were outlawed, and Martínez de Hoz enjoyed five years of virtually unwavering support from the armed forces.

In spite of some early successes, such as the rapid accumulation of hard currency, the long-term application of a single set of economic policies was anything but a panacea. When Martínez de Hoz took office, there were 80 pesos to the dollar; when he left office five years later, there were 2,300. During this same period, the cost of living increased approximately 18,000 percent, and by 1981, the once proudly hailed foreign reserves were rapidly dwindling. By the time the armed forces relinquished power in December of 1983, there were 260,000 pesos to the dollar, inflation was running at about 500 percent, and the nation's foreign debt was in excess of $40 billion.

A TENTATIVE REDEMOCRATIZATION

On December 10, 1983, Raúl Alfonsín was inaugurated as Argentina's forty-fifth president, the first civilian to hold that office in seven and a half years. Just six weeks earlier, Alfonsín, the candidate of the Radical Civic Union, had amazed most political commentators by easily defeating his Peronist opponent, Italo Luder. In a field of twelve presidential candidates, Alfonsín received 52 percent of the popular vote. For the first time since the creation of the Peronist Party thirty-seven years earlier, the party lost a national election.

The Alfonsín presidency appeared to launch a new era of civic peace and reconciliation. The generals, however, were not to escape retribution. Every officer who had served on the junta since 1976 was indicted; most were charged with such major crimes as kidnapping, torture, and murder. In a trial that ended in late 1985, five of them were convicted and given sentences ranging from four and a half years to life.

Meanwhile, the new democracy was reaping the harvest of modern military market economics; the generals had deliberately dismantled industry, borrowed massively, and spent wastefully. Inflation continued to climb, soaring in 1985 to more than 1,000 percent, and the foreign debt became unmanageable. Difficulties in meeting the conditions of the International Monetary Fund (IMF) and creditor banks had left the country in a chronic credit crisis.

By 1986, Alfonsín's government had brought inflation down to double digit levels, and GNP growth for the year was a very respectable 5.5 percent. In order to boost trade and counter shortages in a variety of capital goods, Alfonsín, in July 1986, joined Brazilian President José Sarney in launching an ambitious integration scheme. The accords called for increasing the value of trade in capital goods between the two countries to $2 billion over the next four years.

While economic trends showed promise, however, the Alfonsín government's fortune in dealing with unrepentent militarists was wearing thin. In May 1986, Alfonsín narrowly escaped an assassination attempt while visiting a military base. In December, the army chief of staff, who had been supportive of the new government, and several other top army generals threatened to resign over the widening human rights trials. Therefore, in late December, Alfonsín pushed through the parliament a new law known as *Punto Final* (final, or cutoff, point), granting amnesty to military officers who had not been indicted for human rights offenses within sixty days of the law's enactment.

The *Punto Final* law, however, did not resolve the crisis. In mid-April an army major wanted for questioning about human rights abuses was given refuge in a military camp outside Cordoba, provoking a major civil-military confrontation. The rebellion was soon joined by some six hundred officers at an infantry school at Campo de Mayo, in the suburbs of Buenos Aires, the country's largest army base, and by a few hundred more officers and men at bases in Salta and Tucumán.

The confrontation ended four days after it began. Alfonsín, backed by hundreds of thousands of civilians who had taken to the streets, went to the Campo de Mayo base and demanded that the rebels surrender. Alfonsín bowed to the rebel demand that he replace the army commander, General Hector Ríos Erenu, however; he also fired or retired some two dozen more senior officers and retreated further on the issue of human rights trials.

The weakening of Alfonsín's grip on the slippery ship of state was further demonstrated when his party was roundly defeated by the Peronists in the elections of September 1987 for provincial governors and national deputies. Meanwhile, relations between his government and the Reagan administration, always somewhat uneasy, were further strained by reverberations of the debt crisis. Alfonsín had railed against the "ridiculous prescriptions" of the International Monetary Fund and had attempted to place the plight of debtor nations on the agendas of international gatherings.

Alfonsín increasingly acceded, nevertheless, to the demands of foreign debtors, drawing the necessary surplus from those least able to pay. Both the economy and his own popularity declined so sharply that he was persuaded to vacate the presidency in early 1989, leaving it to Peronist president-elect Carlos Saul Menem, several months before the scheduled inauguration date.

If the working class had imagined, however, that electing a Peronist would bring them a measure of relief, they were soon to be disappointed. Menem's policies were even more "internationalist," or attuned to the interests of foreign investors and creditors, and less protective of working-class Argentines, than had been those of his predecessor.

The new president's economic program was designed to reduce the size of the state, to balance the finances of the public sector, to eliminate government regulations, to make the economy more competitive, and to integrate it fully into the world economy. The program was launched with the "shock treatment" of a set of massive devaluations, a 600 percent increase in public transportation fares, and the elimination of various subsidies. These measures were followed by the negotiation of accords to limit wage and price increases. The Law for the Reform of the State authorized liquidation or privatization of public enterprises and the sale of other government assets. A follow-up plan facilitates international bidding on various concession areas, including petroleum exploration and production. An international tender was also expected for the privatization of the state telephone company, ENTEL, and Citibank of New York had expressed interest in acquiring the national railway through a debt-equity swap.

The Economic Emergency Law promotes other far-reaching changes. It liberates the Central Bank, for example, from the executive branch and strictly limits its financing of the public sector. It also expedites approval of direct foreign investments. A new tax law reduced the rate on corporate profits from 33 percent to 20 percent, placed a ceiling of 35 percent on personal incomes, and extended the base of the value-added tax to all goods and services at a uniform rate of 13 percent.[2]

The program achieved one of its short-term objectives: IMF approval of a standby loan of $1.4 billion. That action, taken in late October, was to be followed by negotiations with commercial banks, to which the country was some $4 billion in arrears. But Menem's policies failed to enhance economic security for Argentines; they also failed to attract foreign capital. By the end of 1989, inflation had climbed to some 4,300 percent, and almost all of the liquid assets of Argentines was banked or invested abroad. Meanwhile the armed forces had become more assertive, their plain-clothed thugs had become more active, and Argentine civilians had become more anxious.

NOTES

1. José Luis de Imaz, "Los que mandan: las fuerzas armadas en Argentina," *América Latina* 7:4 (October-December 1964), p. 68.
2. Adalbert Krieger Vasena, "Can Menem Maintain the Momentum?" *Hemisfile* (January 1990), pp. 6–7.

SUGGESTED READINGS

DiTella, Guido. *Argentina Under Peron: 1973–76.* New York: St. Martin's Press, 1983. An analysis of economic policies and policymaking during the second Peronist period; the author was one of the policymakers during part of this period.

Ferns, H. S. *Argentina.* New York: Frederick A. Praeger, 1969. An exceptionally well-written history of Argentina from the time of independence through 1968; a carefully reasoned interpretation of the past and its effects upon the present.

Fraser, Nicholas, and Marysa Navarro. *Eva Peron.* New York: W. W. Norton, 1980. The best of many recent biographies of Evita.

Imaz, José Luis de. *Los que mandan (Those Who Rule).* Albany: State University of New York Press, 1970. This study, by an Argentine sociologist, attempts to identify and analyze the leadership groups in Argentine society.

Kennedy, John J. *Catholicism, Nationalism, and Democracy in Argentina.* Notre Dame: University of Notre Dame Press, 1958. An analysis of the considerable body of Argentine social and political thought that can be called Catholic.

Kirkpatrick, Jeane. *Leader and Vanguard in Mass Society: A Study of Peronist Argentina.* Cambridge: M.I.T. Press, 1971. A description of Peronism based upon a 1965 sample survey; data analysis is limited largely to the presentation of marginal distributions.

Mallon, R. D., and J. V. Sourrouille. *Economic Policy Making in a Conflict Society: The Argentine Case.* Cambridge: Harvard University Press, 1975. A description of the Argentine economy and an analysis of the process of economic policymaking in that nation in the post–World War II period.

Page, Joseph. *Peron, A Biography.* New York: Random House, 1983. An exceptionally good biography of the most important political figure in twentieth-century Argentina.

Potash, Robert A. *The Army and Politics in Argentina: 1928–1945—Yrigoyen to Peron.* Stanford: Stanford University Press, 1969.

———. *The Army and Politics in Argentina: 1945–1962—Peron to Frondizi.* Stanford: Stanford University Press, 1980. A detailed exploration of the role of the army in the political life of Argentina. (A third volume, covering the period between 1962 and 1973—Frondizi to Perón—is in preparation.)

Scobie, James R. *Buenos Aires: Plaza to Suburb, 1870–1910.* New York: Oxford University Press, 1974. A beautifully written history of one of the world's most fascinating cities.

Smith, Peter H. *Argentina and the Failure of Democracy: Conflict Among Political Elites, 1904–1955.* Madison: University of Wisconsin Press, 1974. Argentine democracy is said to have broken down because of the kind of socioeconomic development that took place and the sequence between socioeconomic and political change.

Snow, Peter G. *Political Forces in Argentina.* New York: Praeger Publishers, 1979. An analysis of the role played by political parties, the armed forces, the Church and Catholic lay groups, organized labor, and university students in the Argentine political system.

Timerman, Jacobo. *Prisoner Without a Name: Cell Without a Number.* New York: Alfred A. Knopf, 1981. The horrifying story of the arrest, imprisonment, interrogation, and torture of a prominent Argentine newspaper editor in 1977; a quite controversial book.

Wynia, Gary W. *Argentina in the Postwar Era: Politics and Economic Policy Making in a Divided Society.* Albuquerque: University of New Mexico Press, 1978. A study of economic development policy, governmental processes, and the behavior of public officials charged with the formidable task of governing a conflict-ridden industrializing society.

27

URUGUAY AND PARAGUAY

DIEGO ABENTE

Uruguay and Paraguay, two of the smallest nations of South America, are often confused one with another because their names are so similar. However, their differences are probably among the greatest between any two single countries in Latin America and can be traced back as far as the beginning of the Spanish conquest in 1536.

Both countries developed around a city; Asunción in the case of Paraguay, Montevideo in the case of Uruguay. The former, established in 1537, is the oldest city in the Rio de la Plata Basin. It remained the center of the Spanish domain in the area until the end of the seventeenth century, when it lost its supremacy to the port city of Buenos Aires due to the administrative partition of the province of Paraguay. Yet it was not until 1680 that the Portuguese established the first settlement, the Colonia del Santísimo Sacramento, in what is now Uruguayan territory. Some forty-five years later, the Spaniards expelled the Portuguese and in 1726, established the city of Montevideo.

Asunción was for several reasons a suitable center for the Spanish domain. It was located on a bay overlooked by the hills of Lambare and therefore easy to defend from nearby Indian populations. Furthermore, the Spaniards were able to work out a political alliance with the Indians living in that particular area, a factor that in time contributed to some of the unique features of the Paraguayan nation. As an aspect of the alliance, the Indians gave to the Spaniards some of their women, whose brothers, in turn, were because of that very link obliged to work certain days a week for the *cuñados* ("brothers-in-law"). This hastened the process of racial integration, or *mestizaje,* and made Paraguay one of the most homogeneous mestizo countries in Latin America. The practice also contributed to the preservation of the Indian language, Guaraní, because the mestizos learned the Indian tongue from their mothers and Spanish from their fathers. Although with heavy racial overtones this bilingual situation persists to the present.

In the area surrounding Montevideo, by contrast, there were but a few Indians; they did not enter into close contact with the Spanish settlers, who were mostly cattle ranchers. As a result, the country was populated basically by *criollos* (Hispanic Creoles), and *mestizaje* was almost unknown. In addition, the waves of European, especially Italian and Spanish, immigrants in the second half of the nineteenth century and the first decades of the twentieth ultimately made of Uruguay a country racially European.

Paraguay, having acquired through the colonial years some sort of cultural, linguistic, and economic identity, proclaimed its independence from Spain in 1811, but at the same time rejected the domination of Buenos Aires, the city to which it had been administratively linked before the breakdown of the Spanish Empire in the Americas. Soon after independence, José Gaspar Rodríguez de Francia was appointed dictator in 1814 in a truly Roman fashion—first for a two-year term and then for life. Ruling until his death in 1840, he succeeded in completely isolating the country and in defeating the pro–Buenos Aires tendencies. He tolerated no political activity at all and instituted an all-embracing repressive state. Few similarities, however, can be found between Francia and the typical Latin American *caudillo* of the nineteenth century. Moreover, Francia was the only Paraguayan dictator who took no personal or economic advantage from his long and absolute rule.

Uruguay, meanwhile, was invaded and annexed by the Portuguese-Brazilian Empire in 1816 and became the Cisplatine Province until 1828. In 1830, it became an independent republic, probably the first buffer state in Latin America, created after long negotiations between Brazilians (Portuguese) and Argentinians with the important intermediation of the British envoy, Lord Ponsonby.

In Paraguay, Francia was succeeded by Carlos Antonio López, who followed some of Francia's policies but opened the door to greater commerce and allowed some very limited political liberalization. Nevertheless, he secured total power for himself and his family, particularly for his son Francisco Solano, who was made brigadier general of the Paraguayan army at the age of eighteen. In quasi-monarchic fashion, Francisco Solano López succeeded his father, who died in 1862. Solano López had been in Europe in 1852–1853 and was heavily influenced by the France of Napoleon III as well as by European geopolitical doctrines. Thus, in 1864, arguing that a partial invasion of Uruguayan territory by Brazilian troops constituted a threat to the equilibrium of the nations of the Rio de la Plata, he declared war on Brazil. Later he declared war against Argentina because of its refusal to let Paraguayan troops cross Argentine territory to engage the Brazilian army. Finally, Uruguay itself declared war on Paraguay, although its participation was minor. The war ended five years later with the almost total destruction of Paraguay and the death of Marshal López, who, true to his previous statements, heroically accepted death but not surrender.

URUGUAY

DEMOCRACY: PRACTICE AND TRADITION OF COPARTICIPATION

Until 1973 Uruguay was considered one of the most stable democracies of Latin America, a model of freedom and progress. Although such enthusiastic claims were somewhat exaggerated, it is certainly true that until the late 1960s Uruguay had a relatively stable polity and ranked among the most democratic regimes in Latin America. Let us therefore examine how this situation came into being.[1]

Early in the nineteenth century, the Uruguayan *caudillos* (later the political elites) came to a conclusion that was to be of foremost importance in the future: that institutionalized compromises were necessary. Thus, since 1830, the history of Uruguay is one of compromises among *caudillos*—broken from time to time but replaced soon thereafter by other compromises reflecting the characteristics of the new situation and the relative forces of the contending parties. This process led to the institutionalization of a practice known as coparticipation, a constant in Uruguayan history and the ideological and practical framework within which Uruguayan politics evolved until the late 1960s. Hence, regardless of which of the two traditional parties, the Blancos (Whites, conservatives) or the Colorados (Reds, liberals), was in power, there was always room, a coparticipative role, for the opposition.

The first half of the twentieth century was dominated by the figure of the Colorado populist leader José Batlle y Ordóñez. Batlle, president during the 1903–1907 and 1911–1915 periods, represented the most advanced and progressive wing of the Colorado Party, and his influence in Uruguayan politics had far-reaching consequences. Under his leadership, Uruguay underwent a rapid process of modernization financed, in part, by rising export revenues. However, it is in the fields of economic and social reforms that his influence was paramount and most lasting. Among other things, he nationalized foreign banks and the public service companies, enacted a law concerning pensions and retirements, established provisions for rest days and workmen's compensation for industrial accidents, and legalized the eight-hour working day. His policies also opened the door for the newly mobilized social and political forces of Montevideo, most of them immigrants or sons of immigrants, to enter the political arena. These new forces, representing the middle and working classes, in turn generated support for the party and faction that implemented such reforms. If one considers that by the turn of the century the population of the capital city of Montevideo already represented 30 percent of the population of the country and that 47 percent of that population was composed of immigrants, one can understand how deeply Batlle's policies changed the map of the country. In electoral terms, his reforms meant that the total number of voters jumped from 31,262 in 1910 to 299,017 in 1928.[2]

As a result of Batlle's influence, the situation in Uruguay changed drastically in the 1920s and 1930s. Two elements were of particular importance. First, the power and role of the state were greatly enhanced through state intervention in the economy. Public and semipublic corporations (*entes autónomos*) were created, necessitating a tremendous expansion of the state bureaucracy. By the 1930s, the budget of the state *entes* represented 62 percent of total national expenses, and the total number of public employees had reached 52,000—approximately 5 percent of the national population.[3] Second, through the reforms promulgated by Batlle, the middle and working classes of Montevideo gained a position as participants in the political system. This gain was also facilitated by the expansion of the industrial sector. For example, the number of industrial establishments increased from 714 to 7,403 between 1901 and 1930.[4]

This new situation did not supersede coparticipation, the old and resilient political tradition; coparticipation continued and became the backbone of Uruguay's democracy and stability. However, it changed its locus and its formula. The locus shifted from merely territorial lines (which had generated a virtual geographic fragmentation into party fiefdoms) to bureaucratic-patronage lines, implying the splitting of spoils and clientele sources among the traditional parties. The formula changed in two respects. First, the arsenal of political weapons to which the contending parties were legitimately allowed to resort was limited to the electoral arena; second, a new collegial system (*colegiado*) was introduced for the exercise of executive power.

The first *colegiado* (1917–1933), a personal triumph for Batlle, consisted of a dual executive power. On the one hand, the president was in charge of foreign affairs, defense, political, and police matters while on the other, the National Council of Administration, composed of six members representing the majority party and three the largest minority party, was in charge of all other administrative matters. The second *colegiado* (1952–1966) went further and eliminated the figure of the president. It vested all powers in the council, which, like previous ones, had one-third of its seats reserved for the first minority party.[5]

Two factors are of particular importance in explaining the long-lasting success of coparticipation. The first is the country's steady rate of economic growth in the first half of the twentieth century. That growth allowed the political system to respond quite successfully to increasing political and economic demands from different social sectors and to foot the bill for a semiwelfare state. The 1900–1930 period, considered the period of *crecimiento hacia afuera* ("outward-looking growth"), was characterized by an export boom based on meat, wool, and hides. The total value of exports increased from 29.4 million pesos in 1900 to 73.3 million pesos in 1915 and 100.9 million pesos in 1930. By the 1930s, that model of growth had been gradually replaced by a model of *crecimiento hacia adentro* ("inward-looking growth"), though exports, particularly wool, continued to provide the hard currency that ultimately financed the model. The internal dynamic of growth, however, was provided by an industrial process of import substitution. The number of industrial establishments increased from 6,750 in 1930 to 23,080 in 1952, and the number of jobs provided by them jumped from 54,000 to 141,000 in the same period.[6] The proportion contributed by industrial production to the GDP grew from 12.5 percent in 1930 to 20.3 percent in 1950.[7] The fact is that, either through exports or through import substitution, the rate of growth increased steadily, thus providing the government with the necessary resources to accommodate social, economic, and political demands and therefore maintain its political efficacy.

A second important factor in explaining Uruguay's democratic stability until the late 1960s is its peculiar legal-constitutional framework. That framework, by accepting the political reality of a highly fragmented political scene and a machine-type political party system, institutionalized a stable and mutually accepted formula for resolving political disputes. An important part of this framework of practical and legalized coparticipation was the electoral law, passed in 1910, whereby parties were able to withstand fractionalization without losing electoral strength. The law, known as the *ley de lemas* (law of party designations) established a system in which the voter, in national elections, chose, simultaneously, the party of his preference and, within that party, the candidate of his preference. In U.S. terms, that would be tantamount to having the primaries and the national elections held on the same day, the winner being the most popular candidate of the most popular party.

BREAKDOWN OF DEMOCRACY AND EMERGENCE OF THE MILITARY DICTATORSHIP

The decade of the 1950s signaled the beginning of the end of the economic bonanza and of the political model that this bonanza helped to sustain. The excessive dependence on exports, particularly on a few products, and the nature of an industrialization process that relied too heavily on protectionist measures and on foreign currencies generated by a depressed export sector brought about a series of crises of increasing gravity. Total exports dropped from US $254.3 million in 1950 to US $129.4 million in 1960. Recurrent balance-of-payments problems forced the continuing devaluation of the peso, from 1.90 to the dollar in 1950 to 11.30 to the dollar in 1960 to 250 to the dollar in 1971.[8] The average annual rate of growth declined from 4.8 percent in the 1945–1955 period to 0.9 percent in the 1955–1970 period while the per capita rate of growth for the last period was −0.3 percent.

The industrial sector lost the dynamism of the earlier period. The number of people employed by industries dropped from 200,642 in 1960 to 197,400 in 1968. The annual rate of growth of the industrial sector decreased from 6 percent for the 1945–1954 period to 1.6 percent for the 1960–1970 period.[9] The inflation rate, which had been 9.8 percent in 1955 and had never before surpassed the 15 percent mark, reached a record high of 125.4 percent in 1968.[10] There was also a dramatic decline in the real wages of workers and employees, especially after 1970. The index of real wages dropped from a base of 100 in 1957 to 76.5 in 1967[11] and from an index of base

100 in 1968 to 66.2 in 1979.[12] This last figure means that workers in 1979 earned an average of 33.8 percent less than in 1968.

This economic panorama of stagnation combined with high rates of inflation and continued balance-of-payments deficits provoked strong reactions from all economic sectors, but particularly from the landed upper classes. In the 1958 elections, the landowning elites threw their most active support to the conservative Blanco Party, which won its first national election in the twentieth century. In order to reverse what the landed elites considered a virtual confiscation of their export earnings through the mechanism of multiple exchange rates, the Blanco government passed in 1959 the Exchange Reform Law, which heavily favored the landowning class. The government was also forced to enter into a number of agreements with the International Monetary Fund (IMF) to regularize the constant balance-of-payments deficits. The crisis, however, continued to deepen. The *colegiado* system of government, implanted by the 1952 Constitution, was blamed for many of the difficulties, and in 1966, concurrent with the national election, a new constitution that restored the presidential system was approved.

The elections were won by retired General Oscar Gestido of the Colorado Party, but he died less than a year after taking office and was replaced by his vice-president, Jorge Pacheco Areco. By the time Pacheco replaced Gestido, the Tupamaro National Liberation Movement, an urban guerrilla group, had become very active. The Tupamaros, who aimed to overthrow the capitalist regime, were mainly young members of the petite bourgeoisie—intellectuals, students, and salaried members of the middle class. They established a highly efficient organization and were able to carry out some spectacular coups de main, including the kidnapping of the British ambassador, the Brazilian consul, and the U.S. police adviser, Dan Mitrione. Mitrione was later killed when the government refused to accept the Tupamaros' conditions for his release. Pacheco was thus forced to employ increasingly greater violence, and the general level of repression gradually rose.

Hence, the 1971 elections took place in a tense climate. The Uruguayan left coalesced in the Frente Amplio (Broad Front), composed of Christian Democrats, Socialists, Communists, and independent leftists. Its presidential candidate was retired General Liber Seregni, a prestigious and widely respected military man. The Broad Front, as expected, did well in Montevideo, where it captured 30 percent of the votes, but it fared poorly in the countryside. Colorado candidate Juan M. Bordaberry, with the support of his party's conservative *pachequista* faction, became the new president. Whereas Pacheco was from the upper classes of Montevideo, Bordaberry was closely associated with the even more conservative landowning classes.

The truce declared by the Tupamaros during the preelectoral and electoral periods, designed to help the Broad Front, was soon over, and a dialectic of increasing repression and rising guerrilla activities began to escalate. The army, which had been called in in September 1971 to lead the antisubversive campaign, prepared a full-scale offensive. The killings of a frigate captain and an army colonel (the brother of General Gregorio Alvarez, who became president in 1981) enraged the military, and by September 1972 they had almost completely wiped out the Tupamaro Movement. Simultaneously, a whole array of right-wing terrorist, counterguerrilla movements—death squad-type organizations—succeeded in generalizing an antileftist persecution. The army's success was based not only on its military superiority but also on the extensive and undiscriminating use of torture against anybody suspected of having any type of connection with the Tupamaros.

Once the process of overt military intervention in the political life of the country was set in motion, it became increasingly difficult, and ultimately impossible, for civilian political leaders to reverse it. Thus, although the antiguerrilla campaign was almost completely successful by the end of 1972, the military gradually assumed a larger role in the decision-making process. With documents seized from the Tupamaros, the military launched a campaign against "corruption" and demanded a greater role in the management of state corporations and other state agencies. President Bordaberry caved in to virtually every demand, and by early 1973 he was a puppet of the military.

The first stage of the final crisis began in February 1973 when the army and the air force resisted Bordaberry's designation of a new defense minister. The navy initially supported the government but later assumed a neutral position, and its head, Rear-admiral Juan J. Zorrilla, had to resign because his own officers supported the army and the air force. Once again, Bordaberry gave up, and his newly designated minister of defense resigned. But the armed forces decided to take advantage of the situation. After releasing two communiques proposing nationalistic economic reforms and a *revolución a la uruguaya,* they demanded the establishment of a National Security Council (COSENA), composed of officers and civilians, to deal with security and economic matters.

Parliament, in trying to stop the military from completely taking over the government, conducted a series of investigations into the extensive use of torture in army detention centers. On June 27, 1973, the generals retaliated by closing Parliament and replacing it with a Council of State, composed of forty-six members handpicked by the military. Political parties and activities were banned, the National University closed, workers' organizations outlawed, and the most terrible political persecution in Uruguayan history unleashed. From that time on, the only significant changes were in the degree and scope of repression. In 1976, Bordaberry was forced to resign and was replaced by a civilian handpicked by the military, Aparicio Méndez, who was never more than a figurehead.

Early in the 1980s, the military started essaying some kind of political institutionalization of the dictatorship. Following the Brazilian model of changing presidents without changing the regime, the National Security Council elected a new president, General Gregorio Alvarez, in 1981. Soon after assuming power, Alvarez called a national referendum to approve a new constitution greatly restricting political activities—particularly those of the nontraditional parties—and perpetuating a growing role for the military. The plebiscite was a crushing defeat for the military as 54 percent of the voters, ignoring official intimidation, rejected the constitution. The process of controlled liberalization continued, however, and the military promised to hold free presidential and congressional elections in November 1984. Late in 1982, the Colorado and Blanco parties were allowed to organize internal elections, and the antigovernment factions scored a major victory, winning over 70 percent of the votes. In mid-1983, the government-opposition talks regarding the transition collapsed, due to the intransigence of the military in its attempt to secure control over the decision-making process even after the elections. The government responded by increasing the levels of political repression and press censorship, but the result was a series of mass rallies (the first public gatherings in Montevideo in years) demanding the immediate return to democracy.[13]

Finally, after a prolonged period of negotiations, the military retreated to the barracks in 1984 and Colorado candidate Julio Maria Sanguinetti was elected president. Sanguinetti led the first postmilitary government through rough waters, particularly because of the adamant refusal of the military to allow officers to stand trial for human rights violations and political crimes. Sanguinetti, however, managed to consolidate the restored democratic system. In the elections of November 1989, Luis A. Lacale Herrera of the Blanco Party won the presidency.

Meanwhile, the economic situation improved in some respects in the late 1970s. Inflation was relatively controlled at the tremendous social cost of a drastic reduction in the living standards of wage earners, especially industrial workers. International prices for some traditional Uruguayan exports rose, with a consequent improvement of the balance of payments. The most significant change, however, was in the composition of Uruguayan exports. The nontraditional exports share of total exports increased from 25 percent in 1972–1973 to 64 percent in 1978, thanks to increasing tax rebates for these items. In the early 1980s, however, Uruguay plummeted into one of its worst recessions with negative rates of growth of −1.3 percent in 1981, −10.0 percent in 1982, and −8.5 percent in 1983. Inflation, on the other hand, returned to a high of 57.5 percent in 1983, and remained hovering around 60 percent thereafter.

The sectors that benefited most from the policies of the military dictatorship were precisely those linked to the export of nontraditional goods, along with bankers. The landowning classes benefited too, especially to the extent that they provided the raw materials for most of the nontraditional export industries, such as tanning and leather goods. The sectors that suffered most were industrialists producing for domestic consumption, because of the contraction of the market, and salaried workers and employees, because real wages and salaries declined 35 percent in the 1972–1979 period. Labor unions were all but destroyed, and workers were left absolutely defenseless against the military dictatorship.

THE U.S. ROLE

U.S. private investment in Uruguay has never been substantial. In 1960, it totaled only $47 million.[14] By 1980, total U.S. investment in Latin America was more than $38 billion, but Uruguay, Paraguay, and Bolivia shared less than 2 percent of that amount. Nor has U.S. economic aid been significant. U.S. loans and grants (excluding military programs) grew from $10.1 million in 1972 to $13 million in 1975 but declined sharply thereafter to $0.2 million in 1978, reflecting the general deterioration of U.S.-Uruguayan relations in the 1977–1980 period. This deterioration was due to the Carter administration's human rights policy and the failure of the Uruguayan dictatorship to take positive steps toward stopping the systematic violation of human rights and civil liberties.

U.S. military aid, however, has been a different matter. The total extended to Uruguay during the 1950–1966 period was $33.2 million. The figure for 1969 was $1.6 million, increasing to $5.2 million in 1971. Thereafter, it decreased somewhat until 1973 and then jumped to a high of $8.2 million in 1975.[15] In 1977, Secretary of State Cyrus Vance announced that because of the pattern of gross violations of human rights by the Uruguayan government, the United States was suspending all military aid to that country. That policy was reversed by President Reagan in 1981.

It is clear that regardless of the specific amount of money appropriated for military aid to Uruguay each year, there was some sort of U.S. involvement during the heyday of the repression, i.e., the 1970–1975 period. The role of U.S. police adviser Dan Mitrione, for example, killed by the Tupamaros on charges of training Uruguayan policemen in torture methods, has never been adequately explained.

FROM DEMOCRACY TO DICTATORSHIP: A REASSESSMENT

The history of the rise and fall of democracy in Uruguay permits us to draw some interesting conclusions. The uninterrupted economic growth from 1900 to 1950 allowed the political process to become relatively autonomous from the pressures of the dominant classes. The extent to which these classes were able to function normally and make a satisfactory profit was related to their willingness to maintain a low profile in the political arena and to give a free rein to the politicians. The landowning elites, for example, may have considered that their earnings were being confiscated by exchange laws, but the continuing rise in the price of products they sold allowed them to prosper anyway. In fact, it was not until almost a decade after the crisis in the export sector began that they became directly involved in purely political matters.

The relative autonomy of the political process from economic pressure by the dominant classes was also favored by the development of a system of political machines that promoted the "welfarization" of the country. Hence, whereas the economically active population represented some 39 percent of the total population, the number of people on the government payroll plus the passive groups (i.e., retirees and pensioners) represented, in 1969, almost 20 percent of the total population.[16] The state thus became a tremendous source of patronage for whose control parties developed increasingly larger political machines. The machines, in turn, restricted the ability of party leaders to implement sound policies because the parties were virtually mortgaged to the interests of the clientele that had helped them to gain power.

When the crisis emerged in the late 1950s, due to depression of the export sector and decline in the growth rate of the domestic industrial sector, it became increasingly difficult for any government to respond to the contradictory demands of various classes and economic sectors. The emergence of an armed challenge to the regime, the Tupamaros, aggravated the situation. Both the dominant classes—particularly the landowning elite—and the military felt that their interests were threatened. The process that followed the military defeat of the Tupamaros, however, suggested that the army had plans of its own—plans that presupposed the maintenance of a capitalist system but that were not necessarily inspired by the economic elite.

An external factor that may have heavily influenced the Uruguayan process is the involvement of more powerful neighboring states in internal power struggles. One should not forget that the three most powerful countries in the area—Brazil, Argentina, and Chile—were also suffering military dictatorships (except for the 1973–1976 Peronist parenthesis in Argentina) at the time of the militaristic drive in Uruguay. The influence of Brazil, especially, appears to have been quite strong. Likewise, when the winds of liberalization began to blow in Southern Cone countries, it became increasingly difficult for the military to continue refusing the domestic demand for democratization.

PARAGUAY

A SOCIETY IN CONFLICT: 1870–1940

The War of the Triple Alliance (1864–1870) left Paraguay reduced to ruins, the economy in bankruptcy, the physical infrastructure destroyed, the population decimated, the national territory reduced by some 60,000 sq mi. In 1870, a liberal constitution was approved, but it was a dead letter. The two traditional parties, the Conservative, or Colorado (Red), and the Liberal, or Azul (Blue), were founded in 1887, but the former remained in power until 1904, not precisely through democratic means. Widespread corruption among government officials made things even worse. The enactment in 1883 and 1885 of the Laws of Sale of Public Land and *Yerbales* (maté plantations) brought about not only the beginnings of the great latifundio but also the eviction of poor peasants who had occupied those lands for generations. One Spanish-Argentine capitalist alone bought 14 million acres (5.7 million hectares) of land in the Chaco. In general, most of the 74.1 million acres (30 million hectares) of public lands were absorbed by private claimants.[17]

At the end of the nineteenth century, the situation could not have been worse. A few *estancieros* ("ranchers") owned most of the land. A few foreign enterprises had a quasi-monopoly of tannin and yerba maté, two of the main export products. Poverty and backwardness were widespread. The violation of political and civil rights was routine, and the political elite was unresponsive.

With public indignation aroused by this situation, the Liberal Party organized a successful revolt that quickly won widespread popular support.

The 1904 Revolution, however, promised much but accomplished little. The main sources of wealth, including the newly developed *frigoríficos* (meat packing and processing plants), continued to be in foreign hands. The two most important export products, quebracho extract (tannin) and meat, were controlled by foreign enterprises and accounted, in the 1927–1939 period, for between 40 and 50 percent of the total value of exports.[18] The polity continued to be characterized by unstable coalitions incapable of achieving lasting legitimacy.

By the 1920s, tensions with Bolivia regarding the territory of the Chaco quickly escalated to a point of no return, and in 1932 war broke out. The Paraguayan victory proved to have lasting effects. It enhanced national confidence and heightened social and economic mobilization. It also generated demands that existing institutions could not meet. On February 17, 1936, President Eusebio Ayala was overthrown and replaced by Colonel Rafael Franco, a Chaco War hero. Although the *febrerista* (after the month of the revolution) movement was quite heterogeneous, its ranks filled by Nazi-fascists, social democrats, and Marxists alike, it set in motion some of the major social and economic reforms in Paraguayan history.

In August 1937, a military uprising toppled the *febreristas*. The provisional government held elections in 1939 and the candidate of the Liberal Party, another Chaco War hero, General José F. Estigarribia, ran unopposed. In 1940, Estigarribia assumed dictatorial powers. He then replaced the 1870 Constitution with one that greatly enhanced the power of the president and legalized greater state involvement in the economy. But Estigarribia died in an airplane crash less than two months after the constitution had been approved by a plebiscite.

THE RISE OF MILITARISM

The army, which between 1936 and 1939 had been playing the role of arbiter, slowly moved toward assuming permanent and direct control of power. The fact that the Liberals were forced to choose a military man as their presidential candidate in 1939 was highly symptomatic, for the only precedent for a military candidate was that of the victorious commander of the 1904 Revolution, who had replaced the civilian president in 1906. In reality, what the Liberals did was accommodate themselves to the growing influence of the military.

When Estigarribia died in 1940, his successor, General Higinio Morínigo, was selected by the military with little—if any—civilian influence. Morínigo was elected as provisional president, with the obligation of organizing elections within three months. In November 1940, however, Morínigo assumed dictatorial powers and became the first strictly military dictator in Paraguayan history.

Morínigo found his military support in a Nazi-fascist lodge known as the *Frente de Guerra* (War Front) and, among civilians, in a group known as the *tiempistas* (after their newspaper *El Tiempo*), which had an ambiguous, conservative Christian-corporatist ideology. Fortunately for him, World War II helped to keep exports at high levels and to increase foreign exchange reserves. Besides, although Morínigo's sympathies for the Axis powers were never a secret, he astutely managed to "sell" his hemispheric loyalty to the United States, thus securing a U.S. offer of some $11 million in lend-lease military aid as well as $3 million in economic aid.[19]

Morínigo's economic policies were characterized by the increasing intervention of the state—a trend that started in the early 1930s leading to the creation of public corporations. Among them were COPAL (now APAL) in the field of alcohol production and sale, COPACAR in meat commercialization, and FLOMERES, the state merchant fleet. The cost of living increased dramatically from an index of 110 in 1940 (base: 1938 = 100) to 432 in 1948, an average annual increase of 41.5 percent.[20]

Morínigo's regime was far more repressive than had been any of its predecessors. His corporatist and authoritarian views were well expressed in the motto of his "revolution": Discipline, Hierarchy, Order. In 1942, he decreed the dissolution of the Liberal Party. In 1944, under pressure from the War Front, he dismissed the *tiempistas* from his cabinet. In June 1946, he repeated the move, but now against the front, and worked out a coalition with *febreristas* and Colorados, a formula that brought about a brief democratic interlude. Soon afterward, however, the *febreristas* were outmaneuvered by the Colorados, and the experiment collapsed. With a Colorado-military coalition, Morínigo returned to harshly repressive policies, which prompted the rebellion of the Concepción military garrison in March 1947 and, with it, the outbreak of a bloody five-month civil war. With the majority of the army and the officer corps against the dictator, the Colorados turned for help to the United States. They needed it—the petition said—"to protect hemispheric security from the bloody designs of Stalinist imperialism," but the U.S. State Department, after sending a CIA man to check on that claim, concluded that the rebellion was "far from being communist-dominated," and the request of the Colorados was turned down.[21] The Argentinian President, Juan D. Perón, though, viewed a similar petition sympathetically and secretly provided the weaponry that permitted the Paraguayan government finally to defeat the rebels in the outskirts of Asunción. Morínigo's victory, however, was a Pyrrhic one, for the Colorados grew stronger and, fearing that Morínigo would not turn over power to their presidential candidate, Natalicio González, overthrew him in February 1948.

THE ERA OF STROESSNER

The period that followed the 1947 government victory was marked by the increasing "coloradization" of the country. Civil service positions and access to and promotion within the army were contingent upon having a proven Colorado background. Meanwhile, the Korean War helped keep exports at high levels from 1949 to 1953. Monetary reserves, which had dropped from $11 million in 1946 to $3.1 million in 1949, jumped to $17.7 million at the end of 1953. In spite of that, the internal economic situation deteriorated rapidly. Inflation grew at an annual average rate of 67 percent in the 1947–1953 period and reached a record high of 157 percent in 1952. The value of the local currency, the guaraní, decreased by more than 700 percent in the 1946–1954 period.[22]

The worsening internal economic situation coupled with the intense conspiratorial activities of almost every *presidenciable* politician submerged the country into one of the most unstable periods of its history. There was, indeed, a brief but full-scale return to praetorianism, for the Colorados themselves were bitterly divided by factional struggles, each faction seeking the support of some key army officers to advance its particular goals. As a result, the public mood—which in 1936 had favored change—in 1954 called for peace and order.

On May 4, 1954, taking advantage of that situation, forty-two-year-old General Alfredo Stroessner staged a coup that overthrew the Colorado president, Federico Chávez. Another Colorado leader, Tomás Romero Pereira, was installed as provisional president. Three months later, Stroessner assumed power as the victorious candidate in a one-man presidential election. Although he was believed to be a transitional figure, Stroessner quickly proved that all forecasts were wrong. He skillfully played military and civilian sectors against each other, and in 1959, after almost a year of increasing labor and student unrest, he consolidated his position by closing the Colorado Parliament and expelling from the country almost one-half of its members. He carefully constructed, destroyed, and reconstructed the politico-military alliances that allowed him to remain in power. He successfully coped with an unknown number of conspiracies, paramilitary invasions, rural guerrillas, and all types of attempts to overthrow him and made of his very success a powerful deterrent against further attempts. By the beginning of the 1960s, he had become the unquestionable leader; few *políticos* ("politicians") or military men dared to challenge him.

THE SOCIOECONOMIC STRUCTURE

Between 1954 and the early 1970s, the Paraguayan economy was characterized by very low rates of growth within the framework of a traditional social structure with widespread precapitalist forms of production in the countryside. Vast sectors of the peasantry were virtually excluded from the monetary economy and were devoted to subsistence crops on lands that most frequently they did not own. By the end of the 1950s, for example, 1,549 landowners controlled some 85 percent of the land, and only 0.9 percent of the territory was dedicated to agriculture.[23] In addition, Paraguay did not undertake import substitution, like most other Latin American countries; the industrial sector, therefore, was quite underdeveloped. By 1963, for example, out of a population of some 1.9 million, only 35,000 were employed by industrial establishments, and more than half of them, 17,482, worked in plants employing fewer than ten workers; there were only thirty-one industrial firms that employed more than 100 persons each.[24] Foreign investment, mostly British and Argentine, was concentrated in a few relatively dynamic sectors, particularly the meat packing and processing industry, lumber, banking, and, more recently, cottonseed-oil manufacturing.

The economic situation in general was one of quasi-stagnation. The GDP increased between 1954 and 1969 at an annual rate of 3.7 percent, while the GDP per capita increased at an annual rate of only 1.3 percent.[25] The government, nevertheless, was successful in regard to two goals: controlling inflation and developing infrastructure. The former was achieved through an extremely tight monetary policy; the latter, through foreign loans and grants. The government also achieved some equilibrium in the balance of payments thanks to standby agreements signed with the IMF and to U.S. economic aid, especially the U.S. PL-480 program that allowed Paraguay to import wheat with credit granted on favorable terms.

Economic stagnation was accompanied by highly unequal income distribution. Although there are no reliable studies for that period, economist Henry D. Ceuppens estimated that 5 percent of the population had an income share of 50 percent of GNP; 15 percent, an income share of 20 percent of GNP; and 80 percent of the population shared the remaining 30 percent of GNP.[26]

The 1970s witnessed the most rapid and thorough process of modernization in recent Paraguayan history. Two basic factors account for the dynamics and characteristics of this process. First is the Itaipú hydroelectric dam, a project jointly undertaken by Paraguay and Brazil at a cost of $15 billion— almost five times the GNP of Paraguay in 1980. When in full operation, the dam will be the greatest in the world, producing 12.6 million kilowatts per hour.

The second factor was an agricultural boom associated with a shift to commercial export agriculture, particularly soybeans. The construction of the Itaipú dam and the agribusiness boom brought about a massive influx of foreign capital. As a result, foreign exchange reserves increased dramatically from $18 million in 1970 (the same level as 1953) to $781 million at the end of 1981. The process was also marked by a decline in the importance of Anglo-Argentine investments in relation to Brazilian, U.S., European, and Japanese investments. Meanwhile, there emerged a powerful commercial agricultural sector, dominated by multinational companies, which dramatically transformed the countryside.

The rate of GNP growth increased from an average of 6.4 percent for the 1970–1975 period to an average of 10.2 percent for the 1976–1978 period. In 1979, the rate was 10.7 percent and in 1980, it reached a record high of 11.4 percent. In 1981, it dropped to a more modest 8.5 percent,[27] and 1982 and 1983 witnessed a deep recession and negative growth rates. Furthermore, the commercial deficit increased dangerously and reached a record high of $545 million. Moreover, the factor allowing substantial balance-of-payments surpluses in spite of increasing commercial deficits over the last five years—the influx of foreign capital, mostly related to the Itaipú project— started to decline in 1981 and is likely to continue to do so. The foreign debt, on the other hand, increased from $98 million (16.7 percent of the GNP) in 1970 to $2.2 billion (52 percent of the GNP) in 1988.[28]

The modernization process has had other negative consequences, too. Inflation reached a high of 28.1 percent in 1979; it decreased to 22.4 percent in 1980 and to 13 percent in 1981, but the real rate may have been much higher than these official figures. The government reacted with tough monetary restrictions, so tight that the country was thrown into one of its worst recessions. The real minimum wage fell by some 17 percent between 1964 and 1980. Although the GNP per capita in 1980 was $1,131, 62 percent of the urban population had an income of between $150 and $440.[29] In Asunción, the capital city, 13 percent of the population, or 68,000 people, live in eighty-nine *villas miserias* ("shantytowns") scattered around the city.[30]

The most important consequence of the rapid process of economic modernization, however, is the parallel process of social mobilization that is, in turn, greatly increasing social and economic demands on the political system. The facts that the Itaipú project is nearing completion and that the influx of capital associated with it is decreasing are placing a considerable strain on the government. Moreover, the approximately 12,000 Paraguayan workers employed in the Itaipú project are being gradually laid off, and there is no new project in sight big enough to absorb them. The Yacyreta hydroelectric dam, a joint Paraguayan-Argentinian project, seen by the government as the needed safety valve for providing jobs, attracting foreign capital to offset the commercial deficit, and stimulating the economy, has been delayed again and again due to the grave Argentine economic crisis. An agreement was signed in September 1983, but with the election of the new democratic government in Argentina, there were further delays. Hence, with the exhaustion of the modernization process nearing, the government will probably face very difficult economic and social problems in the years to come.

THE POLITICAL PROCESS

By the early 1960s, Stroessner was able to consolidate a power structure based on three pillars: Stroessner himself, the army, and the Colorado Party. He was able to erect and sustain this structure first by demonstrating his ability to remain in power against all odds, second, by harshly repressing people opposed to him, and third, by co-opting the rest, particularly army officers and members of the Colorado Party. Corruption and contraband for the benefit of a small clique became widespread and were part of the arsenal of payoffs at the regime's disposal. Officially, it was considered *el precio de la paz* ("the price of peace").

The dominant economic classes readily and happily "exchanged the right to rule for the right to make money," to borrow Barrington Moore's phrase. In actuality, they had never quite governed, and therefore the transaction was most favorable. Their pressure groups, chronically weak, have been satisfied with the "peace" that few other rulers had been able to deliver over such an extended period of time. Important sectors of the population, discouraged by the high level of political repression from any type of political activity, also accepted the situation as an unchallengeable fait accompli.

During a first period (broadly 1954–1962), the regime relied heavily on massive repression and coercion. That approach gradually gave way to an authoritarian model that, without renouncing repression as an occasional necessity, placed increasing emphasis on limited co-optation. Co-optation in Paraguay, however, did not involve access to public offices. Because of the very rigid structure of power, it implies only the absence of politically motivated harassment or repression of individuals as long as they stay away from the political arena. However, the regime continued to unleash periodic waves of repression to remind the real and potential opposition, as well as its own followers, that should they opt for a change in the status quo, they would have to pay a very heavy price. The elements of psychological terror and latent threat therefore remained very effective.

The turning point in the transition from a naked dictatorship to an authoritarian regime was the legal recognition, in 1962, of a splinter Liberal group. In exchange for recognition, the group participated in the 1963 presidential "elections," thus providing a token opposition. Soon afterward, the participationist groups within the opposition prevailed over those proposing an insurrectionary strategy. In 1964, the Febrerista Party was legally recognized, and most of the exiled Liberal leaders were allowed to return. The municipal elections of 1965 witnessed the participation of a Lista Abierta (Open List) registered by the Febreristas but headed by a distinguished independent physician and supported by the mainstream of the Liberals. The "elections," as usual, were plagued by widespread official fraud, but they demonstrated that the majority of the Liberals did not support the Liberal minority splinter group recognized in 1962. That helped the leaders of the majority to win legal recognition as the Liberal Radical Party, the word "radical" being added to distinguish the group from the one legalized in 1962. In 1962 and again in 1967, as well as in the 1964 recognition of the Febrerista Party, U.S. pressure for liberalization played a significant role.

In 1967, with the participation of four opposition parties, a national convention was held to amend the 1940 Constitution. In reality, the only important issue was the addition of an article allowing Stroessner to run for reelection two more times. He did so, in 1968 and 1973, winning easily in elections characterized by widespread fraud.

Participation, however, proved to be a one-way street: All the benefits accrued to the government. Legal opposition parties, though not openly repressed, had their activities restricted to such an extent that they gained very little political ground. An office-seeking elite within those parties remained satisfied to the extent that they had access to some thirty seats in the Senate and Chamber of Deputies, with the corresponding salaries and benefits. Soon, however, it became clear that there were too many politicians and too few sinecures. Politicians began to fight fiercely for the spoils that the regime put at their disposal. Such party infighting further debilitated the legal opposition, already perceived by the public as a highly ineffectual ornamental device.

It was in this context of the debilitation of the legal opposition that student and peasant movements rose to prominence in the late 1960s and early and middle 1970s. Both groups had become disenchanted with the legal opposition, not only because of its chronic inefficacy but also because it failed to provide a real ideological alternative to the right-wing regime. In a few years, they succeeded in organizing some of the largest mass movements in recent Paraguayan history. As a result, peasants and students were harshly repressed. The persecutions unleashed in the 1975–1980 period were of such magnitude that the mass movements were badly crippled.

Other sources of opposition to the regime were the Catholic Church and Church-related groups. Since the late 1960s, the Catholic hierarchy has steadfastly opposed and denounced abuses of the regime as a matter of public posture. The Church, however, does not perceive itself as being an opposition force and therefore does not have a clear political strategy.

Hence, the decade of the 1970s was characterized by the increasing strength of the government vis-à-vis the opposition. The general improvement in economic conditions and the Itaipú-related boom of the late 1970s further reduced the ability of the opposition to draw support from wide sectors of the population. In 1977, the government succeeded in further dividing the legal opposition by isolating those sectors that refused to go along with a 1977 constitutional amendment devised to allow Stroessner to run for reelection indefinitely. Splinter groups of the Liberal Party took advantage of the government search for potential "opposition" parties. At one moment, there were five Liberal parties, four of them bidding for recognition from the government to participate in the 1978 elections. Two of them were finally selected, thus assuring for themselves the highly contested parliamentary seats and for the government the continuation of the democratic facade.

Strengthened by its political and economic success, the regime continued to harass the nonparticipationist opposition. In the late 1970s, these sectors succeeded in articulating a joint opposition front, the Acuerdo Nacional (National Accord), uniting the Liberal Radical Authentic Party, the Febrerista Party, the Christian Democratic Party, and the Popular Colorado Movement (MOPOCO), a Colorado group expelled from the country by Stroessner in 1959. The Acuerdo was born under and encouraged by international, and particularly U.S., pressures against the Stroessner regime for its violation of human rights. It grew stronger as this pressure grew stronger during the Carter administration years. But as international pressure decreased, particularly after the election of Ronald Reagan in November 1980, the importance of the Acuerdo gradually diminished. Its activities, in any case, had been confined to public condemnation of the regime, but it did attain high visibility and have significant public impact.

For the government, nevertheless, there were problems. The international criticisms of its human rights violations were translated into actual sanctions when the U.S. government almost terminated its military assistance program and greatly reduced its economic aid. Moreover, the country was unable to obtain some loans from international institutions on the preferential terms it was accustomed to because of the U.S. refusal to vote favorably on those credits. Internally, the government faced some of its most severe domestic problems since the late 1950s. Within the Colorado Party, there were numerous confrontations among sectors competing for control of the party organization, particularly local branches or sections (*seccionales*) and student organizations. Furthermore, discontent among the youth whose potential role was being postponed while the ruling old guard refused to leave them room for upward mobility increased significantly. Moreover, growing politicization of student and labor sectors resulted in mounting pressures for liberalization. The transition to democracy in neighboring Argentina and Brazil further undermined the Stroessner regime.[31]

But the final blow to the thirty-five-year-old Stroessner dictatorship came as a result of the military ramifications of a major split in the ruling Colorado Party. In August 1987, an aging Stroessner moved virtually to expel from the party a sizable part of its leadership. That group became known as the traditionalists and was believed to be considering ending the automatic endorsement of the Stroessner candidacy for president. The attack on the traditionalists was led by a group of extreme right-wing zealots and die-hard Stroessner loyalists known as militants.

Upon seizing control of the party, the militants moved to secure their positions in the state apparatus and the military. When Stroessner underwent major surgery in late August 1988, and his health became increasingly worrisome, the militants sped up their moves and sought to position Stroessner's eldest son, a just-promoted Air Force colonel, next in the line of military succession. To do so, a large number of generals and colonels had to be retired or reassigned, a move that began in early January 1989. But when, on February 2, Stroessner sought to retire General Andres Rodriguez, his major military rival and First Army Corps Commander, Rodriguez struck back and with widespread support from all units overthrew Stroessner on the morning of February 3, 1989, after ten hours of bloody battles.

General Rodriguez became provisional president and called for elections within ninety days as the first step in a process of transition to democracy. He ran as the candidate of the Colorado Party. Adopting a strong pro-democracy message, Rodriguez won the elections of May 1 by a landslide; he captured slightly more than 70 percent of the votes, against 20 percent for his closest competitor, PLRA leader Domingo Laino. Opposition parties complained that they could not organize for elections in such a short period of time after three decades of repression. While the pre-electoral campaign allowed parties full political freedoms, and although General Rodriguez became a very popular candidate who would have won anyway, the elections were marred by many irregularities and systematic and widespread, although not massive, fraud.[32] This fraud was committed at the local level, but was not stopped or condemned by the remnants of the Stroessner dictatorship entrenched in the Colorado Party.

Upon assuming the presidency, General Rodriguez began to move decisively in the direction of greater liberalization and the incorporation of opposition or independent leaders into positions of leadership, including the Supreme Court and some ambassadorships. Nevertheless, much remains to be done before a true democratic system emerges. Fundamental political and constitutional reforms need to be adopted and fraud eliminated from future contests, chiefly the 1990 municipal elections and the presidential and congressional races of 1993. From a broader perspective, the needs of low-income groups, especially landless peasants and workers, have to be adequately addressed. Yet, in general, and although the process of transition has experienced some setbacks, the prospects for continued liberalization and eventual democratization look better now than at any time in recent Paraguayan history.

NOTES

1. For an elaboration on the theme of coparticipation as a framework to study Uruguayan politics see Martin Weinstein, *Uruguay: The Politics of Failure* (Westport, Conn.: Greenwood Press, 1975), whose general approach this section follows.

2. Juan E. Pivel Devoto, "Uruguay independiente," in Antonio Ballesteros, ed., *Historia de America y de los Pueblos Americanos,* vol. 21 (Barcelona: Salvat Editores, 1949), pp. 628–632, and Martin H.J. Fynch, *A Political Economy of Uruguay Since 1970* (New York: St. Martin's Press, 1981), pp. 11–13.

3. Martin Weinstein, *Uruguay: The Politics of Failure,* p. 69.

4. Luis Macadar, Nicolas Reig, and Jose E. Santias, "Una Economía Latinoamericana," in Luis Benvenuto et al., *Uruguay Hoy* (Buenos Aires: Siglo 21, 1971), pp. 50–52.

5. Victor Pastorino, *Itinerario del colegiado* (Montevideo: Agencia Periodstica Interamericana, 1956).

6. Walter Luisiardo, *Reflexiones sobre aspectos de la historia económica del Uruguay: Periodo 1900–1979* (Montevideo: COMCORDE, Comisión Coordinadora para el Desarrollo Económico, 1979), pp. 12–24.

7. Fynch, *Political Economy of Uruguay,* p. 171.

8. Luisiardo, *Reflexiones,* pp. 44–48, 69.

9. Fynch, *Political Economy of Uruguay,* pp. 220–223; Luisiardo, *Reflexiones,* p. 68.

10. James W. Wilkie and Peter Reich, *Statistical Abstract of Latin America* (Los Angeles: University of California Press, 1979), p. 332.

11. Weinstein, *Uruguay,* p. 119.

12. Luisiardo, *Reflexiones,* p. 95.

13. For an excellent analysis of this complex process, see Charles G. Gillespie's "Uruguay Transition from Collegial-Technocratic Rule," in *Transitions From Authoritarian Rule,* edited by Guillermo O'Donnell, Philippe Schmitter, and Laurence Whitehead (Baltimore: Johns Hopkins University Press, 1986), II, pp. 173–195.

14. Fynch, *Political Economy of Uruguay,* pp. 183–184, 264.

15. Wilkie and Reich, *Statistical Abstract,* pp. 144, 518.

16. Macadar, Reig, and Santias, "Una Economía Latinoamericana," p. 102. The estimation goes as follows: 213,000 public employees + 346,000 pensioners = 559,000, which of a population of around 2.8 million is 19.96 percent.

17. Domingo Laino, *Paraguay: De la Independencia a la Dependencia* (Asunción: Ediciones Cerro Corá, 1976), p. 171, and Harris G. Warren, *Paraguay and the Triple Alliance: The Post-War Decade 1869–1878* (Austin: Institute of Latin American Studies, University of Texas Press, 1978), p. 286.

18. U.S. Department of Commerce, *Commerce Yearbook* (Washington, D.C.: Government Printing Office, 1928–1932), and *Foreign Commerce Yearbook* (Washington, D.C.: Government Printing Office, 1932–1950).

19. Michael Grow, *The Good Neighbor Policy and Authoritarianism in Paraguay* (Lawrence: Regents Press of Kansas, 1981), p. 115.

20. U.S. Department of Commerce, *Investment in Paraguay: Conditions and Outlook for United States Investors* (Washington, D.C.: Government Printing Office, 1954), pp. 15–17, 84.

21. Grow, *Good Neighbor Policy,* pp. 63, 118, 146–147, n 27.

22. U.S. Department of Commerce, *Investment in Paraguay,* pp. 84–85.

23. Carlos Pastore, *La Lucha por la tierra en el Paraguay* (Montevideo: Editorial Antequera, 1972), p. 422.

24. Censo Industrial 1963, cited in Henry D. Ceuppens, *Paraguay Año 2,000* (Asunción: Editorial Gráfica Zamphirópolos, 1971), p. 61.

25. Wilkie and Reich, *Statistical Abstract,* p. 262.

26. Ceuppens, *Paraguay Año 2,000,* pp. 37, 124–126.

27. Banco Interamericano de Desarrollo (BID), *Progresso económico social en America Latina: Informe 1980–1981* (Washington, D.C., 1981), pp. 358–360. *ABC Color,* "Suplemento económico," July 25, 1982, pp. 4–5.

28. Ricardo Rodriguez Silvero, "Paraguay: El Endeudamiento externo," *Revista Paraguaya de sociología* 17:50 (January-May 1980), p. 81. *Ultima Hora* (26 February 1989), p. 12.

29. Fernando L. Masi, "Paraguay: Analysis of the Socio-Economic Evolution" (Manuscript prepared in Washington, D.C., at the American University, 1982), p. 21.

30. Study done by the *Comité de Iglesias,* cited in *ABC Color,* "Actualidad profesional," March 5, 1982, pp. 2–3.

31. An extended discussion of these issues can be found in Diego Abente, *Stronismo, Post-Stronismo and the Prospects for Democratization in Paraguay,* Working Paper No. 119, Kellogg Institute, University of Notre Dame, 1989, and "Constraints and Opportunities: External Factors, Authoritarianism, and the Prospects for Democratization in Paraguay," *Journal of Interamerican Studies and World Affairs* 30:1 (Spring 1988), pp. 73–104.

32. For a discussion of the elections see the Report of the Latin American Studies Association International Commission to Observe the Paraguayan Elections "The May 1, 1989, Elections in Paraguay: Toward a New Era of Democracy?" *LASA FORUM* XX, 3 (Fall 1989), 39–48.

SUGGESTED READINGS

Uruguay

Benvenuto, Luis, et al. *Uruguay Hoy.* Buenos Aires: Siglo 21, 1971. Uruguay as seen by the Uruguayans; interesting perspectives.

Fynch, Martin H.J. *A Political Economy of Uruguay Since 1970.* New York: St. Martin's Press, 1981. An excellent analysis of the Uruguayan economic process until the late 1970s; a must.

Handelman, Howard. *Military Authoritarianism and Political Change in Uruguay.* AUFS Report. Hanover, N.H.: American Universities Field Staff, 1978. A good short analysis of contemporary trends and events.

———. *Economic Policy and Elite Pressures in Uruguay.* AUFS Report, Hanover, N.H.: American Universities Field Staff, 1979. A good short study on recent changes regarding the decision-making process.

Kaufman, Edy. *Uruguay in Transition.* New Brunswick, N.J.: Transaction Books, 1979. An interesting up-to-date work on Uruguayan politics.

Pivel Devoto, Juan E. "Uruguay independiente." In Antonio Ballesteros, ed., *Historia de America y de los Pueblos Americanos,* Vol. 21:405–638. Barcelona: Salvat Editores, 1949. One of the many good and short historical introductions to Uruguay.

Quijana, José M., and Guillermo Waksman. "Las Relaciones Uruguay–Estados Unidos en 1977–1979." In *Cuadernos semestrales* 6 (2⁰ semestre, 1979), pp. 310–343. A good study on recent trends in U.S.-Uruguayan relations with a useful statistical appendix.

Weinstein, Martin. *Uruguay: The Politics of Failure.* Westport, Conn.: Greenwood Press, 1975. A comprehensive analysis of Uruguayan politics; especially good for the study of the 1900–1960s period.

Paraguay

Abente, Diego. *Stronismo, Post-Stronismo, and the Prospects for Democratization in Paraguay.* Working Paper No. 119, Kellogg Institute, University of Notre Dame, 1989.

Bouvier, Virginia M. *Decline of the Dictator: Paraguay at a Crossroads* (Washington, D.C.: WOLA, 1988).

Cardozo, Efraim. *Breve historia del Paraguay.* Buenos Aires: EUDEBA, 1965. A good and short introduction to Paraguayan history.

Grow, Michael. *The Good Neighbor Policy and Authoritarianism in Paraguay.* Lawrence: Regents Press of Kansas, 1981. A very well-documented study of the 1939–1949 period.

Hicks, Frederick. "Interpersonal Relationships and Caudillismo in Paraguay." *Journal of Inter-American Studies and World Affairs* 13 (January 1971), pp. 89–111. A very interesting, although somewhat outdated, study of Paraguayan politics.

Lewis, Paul H. *The Politics of Exile: Paraguay's Febrerista Party.* Chapel Hill: University of North Carolina Press, 1968. An in-depth study of the Febrerista Party.

———. *Paraguay Under Stroessner.* Chapel Hill: University of North Carolina Press, 1980.

Pastore, Carlos. *La Lucha por la tierra en el Paraguay.* Montevideo: Editorial Antequera, 1972. A very good social history of Paraguay with special emphasis on an analysis of the agrarian process.

Warren, Harris G. *Paraguay and the Triple Alliance: The Post-War Decade 1869–1878.* Austin: Institute of Latin American Studies, University of Texas Press, 1978. The best analysis of the first postwar decade.

PART TWELVE
BRAZIL

28

BRAZIL: FROM INDEPENDENCE TO 1964

MICHAEL L. CONNIFF

Brazil's independence in 1822 was unusual among the anticolonial movements in the Western Hemisphere, and it launched the new country on a trajectory different from the rest of Latin America. Throughout much of the nineteenth century, Brazil enjoyed a stable and prosperous monarchy envied in neighboring countries. Much of the stability, however, was due to the avoidance of major decisions affecting the society and economy, decisions that by the 1880s became urgent and indeed overwhelmed the government's capacity to act. The monarchy was swept away in 1889 and replaced by a transitional military regime, whose leaders created a republican system that lasted for forty years. This era, known as the First Republic, saw Brazil gradually modernize along the lines of Western Europe and North America.

Brazil established closer relations with the rest of the American republics, especially the United States, during these years. The sui generis political system, however, broke down in 1930 during a presidential succession crisis. The man who emerged victorious from the crisis (known as the Revolution of 1930) was Getúlio Vargas, Brazil's leading political figure of the twentieth century. Until his suicide twenty-four years later, Vargas dominated national politics in various roles, both in power and out. Afterward, other politicians, following directions charted during the Vargas era, attempted to preserve democratic and constitutional government in the face of growing military interest in power and increasingly difficult international and economic circumstances. In 1964, the army, joined by some civilian forces, ended the country's brief "experiment in democracy" and inaugurated what became one of the most resilient military governments in Latin American history.

THE FIRST AND SECOND EMPIRES

Brazilian independence came at the hands of Prince Pedro of Alcantara, who governed the prosperous colony on behalf of his father, King João VI of Portugal. João and the entire Portuguese court had resided in Brazil's capital city, Rio de Janeiro, from 1808 until 1821 in order to elude Napoleon's hostile armies and then to manage the burgeoning economy of their giant tropical possession. By long tradition, the British had played a role in protecting the Portuguese Empire, in exchange for which England was granted free access to Brazilian resources and trade. João had more to fear than foreign threats to his colony, however: Independence wars were raging across the continent, and similar movements had erupted in Brazil as well. Thus, when João returned to Portugal, he instructed his son Pedro, who remained as prince regent, to assume the leadership should independence become inevitable. Thereby a dynastic, if not a colonial, relationship would continue between Portugal and Brazil.

Pedro—brash, impetuous, ambitious, and advised by persons sympathetic to independence—was all too ready to take command of the colony. On September 7, 1822, in response to insults from the Portuguese Parliament (temporarily in the ascendancy), Pedro declared Brazil independent and soon received the crown of the newly created empire. With the help of the British, he quelled several pro-Portuguese rebellions and received recognition from the United States, England, Portugal, and finally, the Vatican. True to the spirit of the Enlightenment, which inspired many of his supporters, Pedro gave the country a quasi-parliamentary government in the Constitution of 1824. He retained and exercised an overriding authority, however, the so-called moderating power.

Pedro's reign, known as the First Empire (1822–1831), proved turbulent and ill starred. The great prosperity of the preceding decades broke in the mid-1820s as a hemispherewide depression set in. Even coffee, rapidly becoming Brazil's leading export, experienced a slump. Pedro's authoritarian style, deemed necessary during the independence period, now irritated Brazilians, as did a scandalous extramarital affair. The decline in his popularity was also due to prolonged meddling in the Portuguese succession struggles (João VI died in 1826) and to a costly and unsuccessful war against Argentina over the Banda Oriental (to become Uruguay in 1828). In 1831, confronted with financial insolvency, street demonstrations, and a hostile Brazilian elite, Pedro abdicated.

The end of the First Empire contributed to a prolonged period of internal conflict, because the emperor's son (also named Pedro) was only five years old and could not ascend to the throne until he was eighteen. Brazilian political leaders quickly formed a regency triumvirate to rule in the prince's name. They lacked the legitimacy a true monarch would have enjoyed, however, and the country drifted toward dissolution. Nearly every region experienced an uprising of some sort, and two—the Cabanagem in Amazonas (1835–1840) and the Farroupilha in Rio Grande do Sul (1835–1845)— were outright civil wars. Ineffectual central rule permitted considerable authority to shift into the hands of officers, typically *coronéis* ("colonels"), of the newly created National Guard. Most *coronéis* were in fact prominent planters or cattlemen who used their commissions to legitimate armed control over their rural dominions.

Pedro II, it is generally agreed, symbolically and personally brought peace to the country in the 1840s and made it a true nation in the 1850s. In 1840, he was approached by leading politicians who proposed that Parliament declare him of age immediately in order to stem the provincial warfare and aimlessness of government. Young Pedro agreed, and the following year he was duly crowned Pedro II, ushering in the Second Empire (1841–1889).

In the 1840s, two principal parties became consolidated, the Liberals and the Conservatives, and Pedro II relied on each in alternation to staff high executive posts in the government. Within several years, a workable, albeit authoritarian, version of the British parliamentary system was in operation, allowing Pedro to exercise the moderating power while more experienced men ran the affairs of state on a daily basis. From 1853 to 1868, in fact, Pedro managed a bipartisan government of some sophistication during the conciliation era. Powers that had been ceded to the provinces during the 1830s were reconcentrated in the imperial court, and in several major cases (notably the Queiros Law of 1850, which ended the African slave trade), Pedro displayed considerable statesmanship.

The Brazilian economy recovered its dynamism during the 1840s, aided by the growth of coffee exports from the Paraiba Valley northwest of Rio de Janeiro. Since the time of independence, landowners in the region had secured their hold on huge tracts, which were planted in coffee. By mid-century, Brazil had become the world's leading supplier of coffee, and the new planter elite dominated imperial government. The general prosperity kept government solvent, spurred infrastructure development and ancillary industries, and financed a major war in the south against the Paraguayan dictator Francisco Solano López (War of the Triple Alliance, 1864–1870). Yet the Paraiba Valley coffee boom was relatively short-lived because planting methods caused great erosion and relied heavily on slave labor, which was becoming scarce.

Labor shortages were chronic throughout Brazilian history, due in part to poor treatment of Amerindians, blacks, and racially mixed persons over the centuries. After the end of the African slave trade, planters faced an apparently insoluble dilemma: The slave population was growing older and less productive, and no new laborers could be attracted as long as slavery existed. Since the 1820s, the government had attempted to attract European immigrants, but with few exceptions, these attempts had not relieved the general shortage of plantation labor.

The decline of the Second Empire began during the War of the Triple Alliance and gathered momentum in the following decades. Pedro's obstinacy in eliminating Solano López prolonged the war, nearly destroying Paraguay and severely taxing the Brazilians. The war became unpopular, and Pedro's esteem fell correspondingly. Inflation, indebtedness, financial crises, food shortages, and disruption of the labor supply were among the more serious consequences of the war. Politically, the costs were also high. The bipartisan conciliation arrangement failed, and Pedro was obliged to exercise far more than moderating powers. Moreover, army officers, having fought loyally for five years under trying circumstances, resented demobilization and inattention from the court after 1870.

Some officers began openly to criticize the government and to advocate republicanism, to which the government responded with an order requiring prior clearance from the minister of war for any political statements. The ranking general, Marshal Deodoro de Fonseca, objected to these restrictions and launched a campaign to defend officers' prerogatives and to further the cause of republicanism, which he personally embraced. A critical juncture in this campaign was the formation of the Military Club in 1887 to protest orders that the army pursue slaves who ran away from their owners. Indeed, the causes of republicanism and of the abolition of slavery had become closely intertwined by this time.

The antislavery movement of the 1880s ranks as a major *tomada de conciencia,* or moral crusade, in Brazilian history. Based in the cities and drawing upon new professional groups, the movement enlisted thousands of supporters from all walks of life and carried on an unprecedented propaganda effort. The issue split the two parties and caused great administrative instability. Emancipation advocates penetrated the coffee zones and encouraged slaves to revolt or run away, which many did. By 1887, the level of tension and violence was so high that many planters manumitted slaves voluntarily, so the end was clearly in sight. Pedro, however, was in Europe for treatment of his diabetes, and the final emancipation decree, known as the Golden Law, was promulgated by Princess Regent Isabel on May 13, 1888, amid great rejoicing.

The euphoria that accompanied emancipation lasted for several months but did not save the monarchy. Isabel was recognized as talented, but by now, too many people believed that a basic change of government was necessary. Meanwhile, the planters, dominant throughout the two empires, no longer defended the monarchy. In these circumstances, the army became the critical arbiter, and Deodoro became the reluctant agent of Pedro's overthrow on November 15, 1889.

THE OLD REPUBLIC

The beginnings of civilian-military rivalry in Brazilian government are rooted in the five-year transition period during which Deodoro (1889–1891) and army Marshal Floriano Peixoto (1891–1894) ruled the country more or less dictatorially. To be sure, Deodoro declared Brazil a federal republic, but once in power, he and his successor found it difficult to step down, for political as well as circumstantial reasons. For one thing, the country had very few persons experienced in representative government and quite a few who desired restoration of the monarchy. Civil uprisings of various sorts punctuated the 1890s and made strong rule necessary. For another, the country was plunged into a depression following a crisis in the London capital market, the economic effects of which were extremely harmful for Brazil.

The United States quickly recognized Deodoro's government and initiated trade overtures designed to end the long-standing advantages enjoyed by the British. The same depression that assailed Brazil impeded freer imports into the United States, but in 1896, President Cleveland made a permanent friend of the baron of Rio Branco by favoring the latter's case over the Argentinians' in arbitration of the Missiones Territory. When Rio Branco became foreign minister in 1901, he replaced Brazil's traditional orientation toward London with one favoring Washington, in what came to be known as the unwritten alliance.

Ruy Barbosa, a firebrand republican appointed minister of government in 1890, held a constitutional convention and orchestrated the adoption of a charter like that of the United States. The Constitution of 1891 provided for a federal republic, a broad bill of rights, a president elected for a nonrenewable four-year term, a bicameral legislature, a separate judiciary, and important powers vested in the states. Among the last were supervision of all elections, collection of export taxes (important for the coffee states), maintenance of militias, financial autonomy, and state-enacted constitutions. Although for several years the constitution was unenforced, due to army control, depression, and civil wars, it did last until 1930 and gave shape to the country's modern administration.

A republican leader from São Paulo, Prudente de Moraes, skillfully maneuvered himself into the presidency in 1894 and ended Brazil's first period of military rule. During his four years of turbulent administration, he did little to institute formal democracy but he did lay solid claim to the presidency on behalf of his state, whose exports of coffee were all that stood between Brazil and financial ruin. São Paulo gradually pulled ahead of the rest of the states, driven by coffee exports but also drawing on the dynamic leadership of its elite families. Immigrants now flowed into São Paulo to work on plantations and eventually to settle in cities and towns throughout the temperate south. The rail system, installed during the last quarter of the nineteenth century by British companies, made possible an integrated regional economy in which the transition from export agriculture to manufacturing was not only easy but natural. For these reasons, São Paulo emerged as the leading state in the federation during the Old Republic and exercised great influence over the national administration in Rio.

During and after the administration of Manuel Ferrax de Campos Sales (1898–1902), politics settled into predictable patterns, albeit not those the constitution prescribed. The main reason for the renewed stability was the return of coffee prosperity and, with it, respite from the difficult economic problems of the 1890s. Campos Sales rescheduled the debt held by Brazil's international creditors, the English branch of the Rothschilds, and arranged with the governors of leading states to have a free hand in meeting conditions imposed by the bankers: return to a convertible hard currency and balanced budgets. In exchange for federal autonomy in financial policies, Campos Sales conceded substantial prerogatives to the governors of the leading states, in what came to be known as "the politics of the governors."

During the first three decades of this century (and in some respects longer), Brazil's governments operated according to two unwritten codes, "the politics of the governors," covering relations between presidents and governors of leading states, and *coronelismo,* which regulated relations between most governors and regional bosses (called *coronéis* because, at first, many were colonels in the National Guard). The politics of the governors gave to the heads of major states the right to choose presidential successors and to rule their states with no federal interference. In practice, this meant that the governors of São Paulo (the economic power) and Minas Gerais (the most populous and best-organized state) aspired to and often won the presidency in rigged, coordinated elections. Their candidates usually ran unopposed, and in the 1920s, a gentlemen's agreement (called *café com leite* ["coffee with cream"]) stipulated that the presidency alternate between the two states.

Rio Grande do Sul, a quasi-garrison state with a disciplined single-party regime, also played an important role in the politics of the governors, although it never captured the presidency. By judiciously opposing the São Paulo–Minas alliance, Rio Grande could represent the interests of the smaller states in the Northeast, much like a broker. This occasionally gave Rio Grande the chance to veto official candidates and to play a spoiler role in federal politics.

Military power definitely enhanced the states' influence during the Old Republic, so that during crises a kind of military federalism prevailed. Police forces maintained by the larger states were veritable armies, capable of offering a good fight to the national armed forces should the occasion arise. State police also made it possible for governors to rule their own territories more effectively.

Each governor had to manage local politics in order to guarantee his influence in national affairs. Most did so through the Republican parties, formal networks of politicians who kept their subordinates in line and carried out their governors' commands. On the informal level, however, governors made deals with regional bosses, the famous *coronéis,* by which the latter supplied votes (usually fraudulent) and military backing on request. The governors in turn provided the *coronéis* with jobs, public works moneys, important positions in the state assemblies and executives, armed support when needed, and almost total freedom in local affairs. The *coronéis,* then, were potentates in their regions; most were already powerful by virtue of owning ranches, plantations, or businesses.

Coronelismo existed in most states (all had to elect congressmen and governors), but the politics of the governors was limited to a few. The rest of the states had to adjust their actions in accordance with what the big three did. The possibilities for alliances were enormous, and many strange combinations emerged during presidential contests. In all, it was an effective, quasi-federal oligarchical system for rotating the presidency among the most powerful states.

The army's part in republican politics made it the functional equivalent of a "big state." In a sense, the army inherited the moderating power of the emperor, and even after Floriano stepped down in favor of a civilian, the army kept watch as guarantor of the republican system it had spawned.

Military intervention brought side effects not contemplated by commanders. In the 1920s, hundreds of younger officers and cadets joined the revolutionary movements of *tenentes,* so-named because many were lieutenants. They objected to using the army to control the smaller northeastern states (from which many came). They protested rural poverty, illiteracy, violence against labor, imperialism, and undemocratic government. The *tenente* movements were insufficient in themselves to overthrow the government, but they bolstered reformist sentiments in the urban middle classes. The *tenentes* also expanded the army's political mission from guarantor of democracy to socioeconomic reformer. The most famous *tenente* exploits were their capture of São Paulo city for nearly a month in 1924 and their subsequent "long march" of 15,000 mi (24,135 km) through the backlands to publicize rural poverty and backwardness.

Just as the *tenente* movements broke down the army's internal unity, dissident political groups in the major states also gummed up the politics of the governors and *coronelismo.* As cities grew and industrialization proceeded, the political system seemed outmoded and archaic. Too many groups, especially in the cities, found themselves virtually disfranchised in national elections. In addition, the so-called social questions—poverty, illiteracy, poor health, and alienation among the lower classes—demanded the attention of presidents and governors whose priorities lay elsewhere. Thus the 1920s, although quite prosperous, saw a new kind of political unrest: middle-class reformism and demands for more-representative government. This was the scenario for the Revolution of 1930.

The politics of the governors worked well when Minas Gerais and São Paulo could agree on a presidential candidate; if they couldn't, Rio Grande gained considerable leverage by breaking the impasse. In 1928, incumbent Paulista president Washington Luis broke the *café com leite* pattern and chose a Paulista candidate for the 1930 election. The governor of Minas, Antônio Carlos de Andrada, convinced he was being cheated out of the presidency, made a deal to support Getúlio Vargas of Rio Grande, with the implicit understanding that four years hence *he* would be the official candidate. Vargas accepted and created the Liberal Alliance coalition to conduct his campaign. The Revolution of 1930, then, began as a succession crisis and contested presidential election. What made this election different was the heavy voter recruitment conducted by both sides, especially among middle- and working-class voters in the cities. Vargas posed as a reformer, despite the fact that he was a conventional politician with a record of working within the system. He was, above all, an extremely versatile mediator, and he nearly won the election with his daring campaign: He polled over 48 percent of the record turnout of 1.9 million.

THE 1930 REVOLUTION AND THE SECOND REPUBLIC

Vargas and the older politicians were prepared to live with defeat, but a number of younger men in Rio Grande and Minas Gerais decided to overthrow the government, on the grounds that Vargas had been fraudulently denied the presidency. The onset of the depression heightened their resolve to take the government by force.

These younger leaders recruited a number of *tenente* officers to staff the revolt, and they convinced Vargas and Antônio Carlos de Andrada to go along with the plot. Two outstanding figures emerged at this point: Oswaldo Aranha, coordinator of the revolution, and Colonel Pedro Aurélio Góes Monteiro, chief of staff of its armed forces. Already counting on the state police of Rio Grande and Minas, they won over enough army officers in the south to make their revolt militarily feasible. After several false starts in mid-1930, they launched their revolt on October 3. Troops from Minas secured that state and awaited the drive north by the main body of revolutionaries from Rio Grande. As the final showdown neared in late October, the army high command in Rio de Janeiro decided to intervene to prevent massive bloodshed. It deposed the incumbent president and negotiated an agreement whereby Vargas would become provisional president. He was sworn in on November 3.

The Revolution of 1930 brought about many changes in the political system of the country and is held to have initiated a Second Republic. Moreover, the concurrent depression altered the economy deeply, a process that interacted with politics. Finally, large-scale migration to cities commenced at this time, so that by the end of the first Vargas presidency, Brazil would be ripe for mass politics. Most of these changes occurred in unplanned fashion, however, because the Revolution of 1930 had no clear blueprint or mandate for such sweeping changes.

Vargas's principal challenge after taking office was to stabilize the country and secure his hold on power. For nearly a year, he experimented unsuccessfully with various coalitions until he decided to create a dictatorship while relying heavily on *tenente* leaders who had fought with him in 1930. This course alienated civilian politicians and provoked a civil war in São Paulo in mid-1932. Always conciliatory, Vargas agreed to restore civilian representative government once his control was secure, and in 1933 he oversaw elections for a constitutional convention. Many of the reforms attributed to Vargas and the Revolution of 1930 were actually portions of the *tenente* program adopted during the dictatorial interlude of 1931–1932.

The constitution promulgated in 1934 ended the provisional government and confirmed Vargas in the presidency for four years. The Liberal-progressive regime of the mid-1930s was not at all to Vargas's liking, so he began to rely on the federal police, the army, and conservative political groups to help contain what he believed were threatening leftist movements. Thus, politics became increasingly polarized. Symptomatic were extremist clashes and uprisings. Yet perhaps more important in the long run was the emergence of a populist movement in Rio de Janeiro, led by former *tenente* Pedro Ernesto Baptista.

Pedro Ernesto, a wealthy surgeon who had aided the *tenentes* in the late 1920s, had become their leader during the period of dictatorship, at which time he was appointed mayor of Rio. He became Brazil's first genuine populist leader by forming a multiclass reform movement in the country's largest city. Vargas quashed the populist experiment in mid-1936. Nevertheless, Pedro Ernesto proved that urban voters could be recruited for coalition politics in large numbers, a lesson to be demonstrated amply following World War II.

By 1936, Vargas had decided to stay in power as long as possible, so he gradually assembled a plan to abort the presidential elections scheduled for 1938 and impose another dictatorship, this time inspired by European fascism. Briefly, Vargas's associates helped create a climate of political crisis that justified suspension of democratic procedures. The army was especially interested in such a policy, for most high-ranking generals regarded normal political byplay as a temptation for Communist agents to subvert Brazil. On November 10, less than two months before the election date, Vargas and the army carried out a *continuismo* coup, which gave him a new term and near-dictatorial powers under a fascist constitution. The new regime, called the Estado Novo (New State) after Salazar's in Portugal, lasted until late 1945; it has also been termed the Third Republic.

Vargas's New State was milder than most European fascist regimes, though it was harsher than anything Brazilians had experienced for several generations. Until 1942, Vargas assumed a posture of strict neutrality in the war and allowed fascist sympathizers to operate freely. The police and army seemed to be the warmest supporters of the Axis.

In early 1942, however, Vargas broke relations with the Axis and began supporting the United States. Brazil sent 25,000 men to participate in the Italian campaign of 1944, the Brazilian Expeditionary Force (FEB). This qualified Brazil to receive lend-lease military and other aid from the United States and established a cooperative relationship between the two military forces that lasted into the 1970s. In 1949, the Pentagon aided Brazil in establishing the Superior War College (ESG), which developed a full-scale plan for Brazilian development and national security.

In internal politics after 1942, Vargas tried to assuage critics and to appear a man of the people. Indeed, an elaborate publicity campaign proclaimed Vargas to be "the protector of the working class" because of the favorable decrees he had signed during his administration. These benefits had multiplied during the New State, albeit in exchange for putting the union movement under the control of the Ministry of Labor.

In 1945, Vargas tried to make a risky transition from dictator to democrat and failed. The mood of the country would no longer tolerate censorship, police spying, political prisoners, and totalitarian powers invested in the executive. Even the army, fighting for democracy in Europe, favored a return to constitutional representative government. Vargas, a wise politician with friends throughout the country, recognized the public mood and announced that elections would be held in December. He created two parties, one made up of traditional politicians from leading states, called the Social Democratic Party (PSD), and another called the Brazilian Labor Party (PTB). The latter was based exclusively in the Ministry of Labor and sought to tap the support of workers in Rio, São Paulo, and Rio Grande do Sul. The PSD nominated General Eurico Dutra for the presidency, apparently with Vargas's blessing.

Opposition to Vargas grew during the year. He tried to change his image, removing some of the worst autocrats and courting leftist support, and it seemed the country would return to democracy. However, the opposition (which coalesced into the Brazilian Democratic Union, UDN) continued to attack him energetically. Indeed, such was Vargas's influence that politicians took stances for or against him rather than for programs or ideologies. This overwhelming presence convinced many, including Dutra, that Vargas would again execute a *continuismo* coup to stay in power, as he had in 1937.

The army high command, led by Dutra and Góes Monteiro, ushered Vargas out of office in late October and held the elections on schedule. Dutra won, but he was hardly a popular choice. Short, pudgy, reclusive, Dutra won only because of support from parties Vargas had created. Elections in 1946 and 1947 showed that the Communists enjoyed the support of about 10 percent of the voters and that populists like Adhemar de Barros in São Paulo could attract great multiclass support in urban areas.

Dutra presided over what amounted to a caretaker government. His undertakings included a new constitution in 1946, a return to free market economics, establishment of the Superior War College, and a ban on the Communists in 1947. Dutra followed U.S. wishes in foreign policy and was rewarded with credits under the Point Four Program and from the World Bank. Yet he provided little leadership and even lost control of his own party, the PSD. By 1950, the voters were ready for a change, and Vargas offered them one.

Vargas had begun rebuilding his career soon after his overthrow in 1945. He was elected to Congress from several states, cultivated the image of "father of the poor," and campaigned on his labor record. (Government inattention to falling real wages in the postwar years inadvertently helped him.) He proclaimed the need for greater economic independence and industrial expansion, together with wage increases to broaden the internal market. His new program is sometimes referred to as "developmentalist nationalism." As the 1950 election approached, Vargas pulled ahead and even made a deal to receive the São Paulo votes of Adhemar de Barros.

Vargas won 49 percent of the votes in the hotly contested three-man race, a relative landslide. Brazil enjoyed a year and a half of prosperity due to high commodity prices, and Vargas made good his promise to raise real wages. He also asked Congress to nationalize the petroleum and electric power industries. In support of the draft laws, Vargas pointed out that these sectors were crucial for industrial development, but because they were foreign owned, national planners could not influence management decisions. Apparently Vargas had, during the preceding fifteen years, completely changed his ideas about the role of the state.

Vargas's new economic nationalism and prolabor policies were increasingly formulated by younger, aggressive men around the aging president. João Goulart, PTB leader from Rio Grande and minister of labor from 1953 to

1954, was prominent among these new forces pushing Vargas to the left. Vargas, in fact, was losing control over the government, unable in his late sixties to manage the bureaucracy that he had done so much to inflate.

Economic and political crises mounted in 1954, and Vargas grew more desperate. The end of the Korean War brought reduced prices for the country's exports. On Labor Day, Vargas decreed a 100 percent wage increase, but other sectors—including military officers whose pay was in arrears—protested and nearly brought the government down. Corruption had become endemic in the higher echelons of the regime, though Vargas himself was honest. Finally, one of his bodyguards, apparently acting alone, made an attempt on the life of Carlos Lacerda, UDN leader and Vargas's most outspoken foe. Vargas said, "I feel like I am standing in a sea of mud." His days were clearly numbered.

In August 1954, an air force uprising brought the army back into politics— and gave Vargas his second ouster in less than ten years. At this point, however, the president decided on a different course. Rather than face an ignominious retirement and continued vilification by his enemies, Vargas took his own life. His dramatic suicide note spoke of covert forces that jeopardized the very sovereignty of the nation. Only he had defended the people against subjugation by international companies like the great oil monopolies, and now that he was gone, the people would need to redouble their vigilance. The suicide note wrought a political miracle, resurrecting Vargas's reputation and casting him as a martyr for the nation.

Vargas's fame as a populist comes largely from the early 1950s, yet paradoxically, he accomplished little during his second term in office. The national petroleum monopoly, Petrobras, stands as a sole monument. By comparison, his first term (1930–1945) virtually remade the Brazilian state and ushered in major socioeconomic changes. The early Vargas years will remain controversial, but they were unquestionably the most dynamic in this century.

Vice-President Café Filho took over the executive branch in 1954, but he was little more than a weak stand-in assailed by powerful pressures. To his credit, he managed honest elections in 1955, in which Juscelino Kubitschek of the Minas PSD won a narrow plurality. Army units almost blocked the succession, objecting to the vice-president elect, João Goulart, but a countercoup restored constitutional rule. Kubitschek took office in early 1956.

The new administration promised "fifty years of progress in five" and indeed accomplished a great deal. Kubitschek followed the economics of the "structuralists," who argued that daring and unorthodox measures were required to break through obstacles to progress. Brazil gave lucrative concessions to U.S. and European firms to start up the now-booming automobile industry. It built hydroelectric dams and highways in the rural areas. It set up regional development agencies such as the famous SUDENE for the depressed Northeast. And finally, Brasilia, the twenty-first century capital, was built at the geographical center of the country, more as a symbol of economic independence than a contributor to it. Much of this rapid expansion, however, was financed through enormous budget deficits, which, after a lag, caused high inflation. Moreover, many of the new industries enjoyed subsidies and tax credits that shielded them from competition and protected inefficiency. Unquestionably, Kubitschek, for better or worse, followed Vargas's lead in pursuing an end to dependence on imported manufactures and capital.

Politically, Kubitschek managed quite well by balancing wage increases with bigger profits for business. Lucrative construction contracts kept political cronies happy and party coffers full. Meanwhile, Goulart, chastened by the abortive military coup against him, kept a low profile and tried to live down his reputation as a labor radical. In a sense, Kubitschek managed to "export" dissidence by drawing on international resources to prime the pump and keep everyone happy. When the borrowing became excessive, the International Monetary Fund cut him off, leading to Brazil's angry withdrawal from the agency. Kubitschek then made a memorable proposal to the United States for a vast developmental effort to be called Operation Pan-America. Several years later, the idea germinated and became the Alliance for Progress.

Elections held in 1960 saw voters bolt the old parties and images to support a newcomer, Janio Quadros, for the presidency. Having enjoyed a meteoric rise from schoolteacher to governor of São Paulo in the 1950s, Quadros had a fresh quality untainted by the old parties and alliances. His campaign symbol was a broom, with which he promised to sweep the rascals out of office. He eschewed party affiliation and accepted the UDN nomination only because it was traditionally the party of the "outs." Quadros was eccentric, a loner, appealing but aloof, a savior who appeared out of nowhere.

Two other factors helped Quadros's victory in 1960. Center-of-the-road politics had begun to fade away, leaving the field increasingly to radicals of the left and right, who attacked one another indecorously to win voters in the big cities. During the 1950s, a subtle but important change had occurred. Urban voters no longer reacted en masse to whatever was served up on the political platter; rather, they had become more discriminating and interest oriented. According to one analyst, class politics replaced mass politics in the big cities, raising the level of competitiveness and complexity. In this perspective, Quadros was the last of the consensual populists who could appeal to the masses and middle class without a program. Unfortunately for those who placed their trust in him, Quadros's presidential career lasted a scant seven months.

Quadros's victory, backed by the disorganized UDN, seemed to give him unusual freedom of action, but his inexperience made it hard to work with Congress. He instituted budget retrenchment to check inflation yet kept the economy moving with Alliance for Progress and IMF funds. He promised a bold new foreign policy in keeping with a changed world situation. Brazil would pursue its interests in the international arena regardless of old sympathies (e.g., with the United States). He envisioned Brazil leading the Third World nations, especially those of Africa, with which Brazil shared historic ties.

Finally, Quadros dispatched Vice-President Goulart (reelected in 1960) on a goodwill and trade mission to Russia and Communist China.

Quadros lacked patience and staying power, however, and he soon wilted in the hothouse political environment of Brasília. Frustrated with slow congressional deliberations over many of his programs, he decided in August 1961 to force the issue by resigning. Congress would not (he assumed) allow him to leave, for Goulart was in China and the new administration had barely been set up. A more cooperative Congress would beg him to stay. Yet Quadros mishandled the ploy and made it impossible for Congress to call him back even had the will existed, which was doubtful. Quadros's departure was accepted, and congressional and military leaders debated whether to allow Goulart to assume the presidency. A compromise agreement stipulated that Goulart could become president if Congress amended the constitution to create a parliamentary system with limited executive powers.

With hindsight, it is clear that the Quadros resignation and Goulart succession were critical events in the chain that led to the military coup of 1964. Quadros symbolized the failure of consensus and moderate politics. Goulart—notwithstanding years of "good behavior"—was still considered a dangerous radical and the alter ego of Vargas. The interaction between Goulart, Congress, the army, and the United States was extremely complex, and ultimately disastrous for the Goulart presidency and for Brazilian democracy.

CONCLUSION

Looking back over nearly a century and a half of Brazilian history since independence, we can discern several major themes or continuities. The political elite, whether Pedro II's nobility or Vargas's cronies, distrusted representative government because the masses were too backward and uneducated. The elite gradually remedied the situation with schools, hospitals, and literacy campaigns, but never quickly enough. The masses were expected to—and did—follow unquestioningly. Even the architects of the great populist expansion of the 1930–1964 period assumed that the masses were not fully capable of participatory democracy. Second, the coercive powers of the army were always posed to prevent civil disturbances, whether slave uprisings or Communist revolts. By this century, the army had assumed the role of "moderating power" from the 1824 Constitution, whereby it could save the country should the politicians lose their way. The army has continually intervened in politics since the 1880s. Third, Brazil moved rapidly through several economic phases—from sugar and coffee production in the nineteenth century to light manufacturing in the early twentieth to heavy or basic industry by mid-century. This progression concentrated more people and resources in the major coastal cities. Finally, constitutions have been only imperfect guides to the operation of politics, which, instead, was based upon old traditions as well as shifting balances of power. All these trends were evident in the events leading to the 1964 coup.

SUGGESTED READINGS

Burns, E. Bradford. *A History of Brazil*. New York: Columbia University Press, 1970. A fine, well-written synthesis from colonial to modern times.

Conniff, Michael L. *Urban Politics in Brazil*. Pittsburgh: University of Pittsburgh Press, 1981.

Conrad, Robert. *The Destruction of Brazilian Slavery, 1850–1888*. Berkeley: University of California Press, 1972. Portrays the events leading to emancipation, the burning issue of the day that helped bring down the monarchy.

Dean, Warren. *The Industrialization of São Paulo, 1880–1945*. Austin: University of Texas Press, 1969. An essential account of the rise of São Paulo to economic preeminence by shifting from coffee to manufacturing.

Dulles, John W.F. *Vargas of Brazil*. Austin: University of Texas Press, 1967. Still one of the best political biographies covering this century.

Flynn, Peter. *Brazil: A Political Analysis*. Boulder, Colo.: Westview Press, 1978. An excellent survey from independence on, emphasizing trends that culminated in the 1964 coup.

Graham, Richard. *Britain and the Onset of Modernization in Brazil*. New York: Cambridge University Press, 1968. A broad and sympathetic portrayal of development under Pedro II, especially as influenced by the British.

Haring, Clarence H. *Empire in Brazil*. Cambridge: Harvard University Press, 1958. Traditional account of politics during the First and Second Empires.

Levine, Robert M. *The Vargas Regime*. New York: Columbia University Press, 1970. Monographic study of the period 1934–1938, during which Vargas moved from democrat to dictator.

Love, Joseph L. *Rio Grande do Sul and Brazilian Regionalism*. Stanford: Stanford University Press, 1970. One of the first detailed studies of state-level politics during a time when a few major states dominated the nation.

McCann, Frank D., Jr. *The Brazilian-American Alliance*. Princeton: Princeton University Press, 1973. Diplomatic and military focus that highlights the Washington-Rio axis during World War II.

Poppino, Rollie. *Brazil: The Land and the People*. New York: Oxford University Press, 1973. Fine survey from colonial times to the present, with emphasis on socioeconomic themes.

Skidmore, Thomas E. *Politics in Brazil*. New York: Oxford University Press, 1967. Standard work on the later Vargas years and the period that culminated in the 1964 coup.

Stein, Stanley J. *Vassouras*. Cambridge: Harvard University Press, 1957. Classic study of coffee in the Paraiba Valley before São Paulo dominated the industry.

Stephan, Alfred. *The Military in Politics*. Princeton: Princeton University Press, 1970. Major study of the military after World War II tracing the military's involvement in politics up to and after the 1964 coup.

Wirth, John D. *The Politics of Brazilian Development*. Stanford: Stanford University Press, 1970. Fine study of Vargas's policymaking style based on three case studies spanning his first and second terms.

29

BRAZIL TODAY: A STUDY IN FRUSTRATED DEMOCRATIZATION

BRADY TYSON

Brazil has always been best understood and characterized as a nation existing on two levels—the "two Brazils,"[1] one the rich, developed, educated minority (dominated by less than 10 percent of the population, owning 50 percent of the national wealth[2]) and the other Brazil of the poor majority, many living on a subsistence level, passive, semi-educated, unorganized, leaderless.[3] The best and most well-known model of the two Brazils today is of "Belindia":[4] one Brazil, maybe 10 to 15 million people, that is like Belgium—European, consumer oriented, developed, modern. Of course in a changing, complex society, there is the middle sector, comprising perhaps 20 to 30 million (of the about 150 million total population of Brazil), struggling to maintain its economic and social foothold in modern society in the midst of permanent inflation and perhaps hyperinflation. The other Brazil, about 100 to 110 million people, is like India, an underdeveloped nation, under-educated, neglected, unorganized, and leaderless, with a great mass living in poverty. "Belindia" summarizes the dilemmas or the "hard choices"[5] that Brazil confronts; the uneasy coexistence creates tensions and a challenge that Brazil has attempted to meet since perhaps 1930. The growing gap between the rich and the poor, pressures seeking both national modernization and social change, and the inadequate and weak formal political institutions lead to an impasse, such as that of 1962–1964, with a consequent demand for stability that led to the military coup of 1964 and twenty-one years of military dictatorship.

It is easy to visit Brazil today and see the bustling, prosperous upper and middle sectors of society in their great modern cities with large shopping centers and luxurious, extensive residential areas and to imagine that this top 10 percent of the population is a symbol of hope for the "other Brazil," hope that with time the whole nation will be pulled upwards toward a minimal standard of living. But in fact, the skewing of income distribution in Brazil is among the world's worst. Brazil is the fifth largest country by population, tenth in gross national product, but fifty-second in terms of *per capita* gross national product. In educational national achievement, Brazil ranks seventy-fourth—lower than Madagascar, Ghana, Indonesia, Zimbabwe, Tunisia, Zaire, and Egypt.[6]

THE MILITARY COUP OF 1964: MODERNIZATION AND STABILITY WITHOUT SOCIAL CHANGE OR DEMOCRACY

The "Revolution" of 1964, when the army seized power in a coup, marked an abrupt change of direction in Brazilian political life: The army generals, profoundly disturbed by the often tumultuous political life as civilian leaders struggled to cope with the growth of population, the uneven impact of modernization of the nation, and the rising tide of expectations and discontent, toppled constitutional president João Goulart in 1964. Leaders of political, academic, labor, and other sectors identified with basic reforms (including members of the congress and former presidents) were summarily stripped of their offices; several thousand prominent persons had to flee, and hundreds were arrested by the army as the generals assumed total control of the state apparatus.

The Army's Plan for the Modernization of Brazil

But the "Revolution" of 1964, under the direction of the High Command of the army, composed of the top eleven generals, was not a traditional Latin American military coup, designed to restore an old, tottering elite system. From the beginning, the generals had a master plan, a set of very specific projects as well as a general theory or philosophy of modernization. The national plan had been developed in the Escola Superior de Guerra (the Advanced War School), directed for many years by General Humberto Castelo Branco, who became the first president-general.

Castelo Branco announced that he intended to return power to the civilians within eighteen months, assuming that the problems defined by the generals as "corruption, chaos, and communism" could be destroyed by taking out of political life the leaders of agitation and that other civilian leaders would readily accept the rational national project developed by army officers over the previous decade. But the generals soon discovered there were three problems they had not anticipated.

First, not even conservative civilian political leaders and normally apathetic citizens would be easily persuaded to accept the leadership of the generals; criticism and resistance continued and increased in spite of repression and censorship. Repression and torture began the day of the coup, but they were sporadic initially. Several police, vigilante groups, and parts of the navy and air force began to develop their own, autonomous repressive teams (that practiced torture), and the generals finally had to assume responsibility and develop a plan for suppressing opposition. Castelo Branco had believed it would be possible to live with a relatively sanitized congress, purged of its most assertive critics. But as repression continued some members of congress reacted, and the High Command dictated a comprehensive "Institutional Act Number 5" (a decree known as "AI-5," promulgated in December 1968) that closed the congress, extended the cancellation of civil rights to many other political leaders, and centralized power in the president-general.

Second, the challenges of modernizing, integrating, and disciplining the economy and society were much more complex than the generals had imagined, and they became aware that any serious national project of modernization would take more time. Traditional conservative politicians, linked with the modernizing entrepreneurs and technobureaucrats, were up to the task—but they resisted the national plan of the generals. Furthermore, soon the original model of Castelo Branco, which intended to make an Americanized Brazil, encountered resistance from his successor, President General Arturo Costa e Silva. He was concerned with nationalistic themes, and he discovered a base in the nationalist entrepreneurs.

Third, President-General Castelo Branco had signed a basic law on agrarian reform—still considered a model for such programs. Everyone knew that it was necessary to stem the flow of poor and untrained peasants to the cities and make them more productive, content, and secure in the heartland. However, the generals soon discovered that the implementation of such a land reform would have led them to direct confrontation with the pugnacious landowners, always allied with the state governments, judiciary, police, and militia. As a result, very little was done and the problem festered.

The triple failure of nerve of the president-generals—to create a popular movement that would support the military and maintain a dialogue with the civilian politicians, to develop sufficient bureaucratic leadership and efficiency, and to implement an agrarian reform—finally demoralized the generals; their overview and national plan had been undercut. Learning from observation of the ruthless apparatus of repression mounted by the Argentine army while it was in power, the Brazilian army began to have second thoughts and to contemplate returning government to the civilians before losing all their own popular support and respect.

The Economic "Miracle" and the High Tide of Repression

In August of 1969 General Emílio Garrastazu Médici became president on the incapacity of President-General Costa e Silva, victim of a stroke. Médici had been director of the National Information Service (the SNI—combined FBI and CIA), which had directed the repressive apparatus, and the level of repression that had appeared in December 1968 was maintained throughout his five-year term. Only with the next president, General Ernesto Geisel, did the repression abate.[7]

A heated debate continues even today as to whether the economic "miracle" (1968–1973, averaging 11 percent per year growth in that period) was caused by military policies or whether it was just part of a regular cycle in which a significant accumulation of investment power had reached a ready market.[8] The economic policies of the military regime, believing devoutly that the free market would create a new dynamic system, led to an unexpected reconcentration of economic power, and the economy boomed suddenly; "growth euphoria"[9] stimulated national planners, bankers both in Brazil and in the creditor nations, industrialists, and commercial leaders in Brazil. Economic growth marched ahead while the foreign debt ballooned, and the rich became even richer, more satisfied, and less sensitive (if possible!). The "miracle" process developed some strong choking-down tendencies as the wealth it generated dribbled down to the poor. Finally, many of the trade unions had succumbed to government and management pressure, under the pressure of unlimited, unorganized, cheap labor; there was no other balancing political sector to restrain the distributional skewing of the "miracle."

The External Debt and the End of the "Miracle"

From 1967 until 1982 Brazil, like many other Third World countries, contracted large foreign debts in the expectation that the country's production could grow rapidly and thus overcome the development gap.[10] By 1990 Brazil had a foreign debt of more than $120 billion, and, more seriously, economic growth had plummeted since the end of the "miracle" in 1973. Many of the loans were contracted to build major works—highways, bridges, dams, great hydroelectric plants, etc.—that were intended to stimulate the economy. The generals and their advisors believed that industrial development would dribble down to the poor, but they failed to understand that post-industrial technology did *not* generate nearly enough new jobs. They were still stuck with the vision of industrial—not post-industrial—technology and its consequences.

TRANSITION TO "DEMOCRACY"

The "economic miracle" gave a free ride for several years to the military leadership even though it did not address the deep social and structural imbalances and injustices. By 1974 the worldwide oil crisis had profoundly rocked the vulnerable Brazilian economy. By that time the generals had had enough of growing opposition in the middle class, restlessness among industrial workers, and general loss of respect for the army. In 1977 President-General Ernest Geisel introduced the "April package"; it launched a deliberate process of relaxing political constraints and stretching political freedom, leading finally towards a civilian government.[11]

In 1979 the last of the president-generals, João Figueiredo, assumed the presidency and continued the deliberate process of return to the rule of law. In that year an amnesty bill was signed that served both to shield members of the armed forces from charges of "excesses" (torture and other similar acts) and to relieve some of the repressed resentment on the part of the opposition. Also that year, the artificial two-party system, imposed in 1965, was scrapped, allowing more space for political groups in a multiparty system.

Labor Strikes and the "New Union Movement"

In 1974 the metalworkers union (essentially, the automobile workers union), protesting the steady decline of labor's earning power, began to pressure the government. The metalworkers union has always had a privileged position among unions, with higher skills and higher wages, thus more power, and a history of struggle for more equitable contracts. It was in that period of ferment and conflict, in the union's stronghold, the triangle of the three industrial cities known as "ABC,"[12] that Luis (Lula) Inácio da Silva, a rank-and-file toolmaker, emerged as a leader. In 1978 the first illegal strikes began, giving birth to "new Unionism,"[13] and to the PT, or Labor Party, led by Lula.

The Emergence of the Progressive Church

Soon after the coup of April 1, 1964, the military and the police embarked on a campaign to "sanitize" Brazilian society, and torture was sometimes used even against progressive clergy and nuns. The bishops were stung by the indifference to their pleas to the military, who had become involved in torture and other forms of repression of some priests, nuns, and lay leaders involved in the Basic Reform movement during the Goulart period. For a time the most significant actions of opposition were led by bishops, protesting against torture and deaths under torture.[14] But bishops and their allies, concerned about the plight of the dispossessed majority of the nation, began to develop some plans for the future that would "empower" the poor. Soon, encouraged by the "opening" initiated by Pope John XXIII, the bishops began to take seriously their precarious situation, and the result was the "progressive church" or "the Church of the People."

The Roman Catholic Church had been, until 1965 or 1966, an ally of the establishment in Brazil, but the Catholic Action movement, brought to the nation by young Brazilian priests who had been studying in France and Belgium, introduced a new style and mentality that had become a major factor in the Basic Reform movement during the presidency of João Goulart. Soon scattered by Episcopal opposition, allied with the military at the time of the "Revolution" of 1964, many radical young Catholics sowed the seeds of a broader, grass-roots movement through the human rights movements in the early phase of the dictatorship, and then in the flowering of the Basic Ecclesiastical Communities (CEBs).[15] For a time the CEBs tried to be a political force, but under pressure from conservative forces they became again oriented towards local, human rights issues.

The Campaign for Direct Elections

The slow-paced return to civilian rule, planned by the generals themselves, appeared too slow to the impatient middle class. The military government announced elections in 1982 for governors, members of congress, and local officials—the presidency being excluded from direct election. The system of indirect elections, which included some senators and governors named by the government, was an election only of the congress, a congress always dominated by the generals and under threat of another intervention.

In spite of a broadly based middle- and upper-class mobilization to pressure the military government, the generals stuck with their own plan and maintained the slow pace of democratization. For the presidency, the congress finally chose Tancredo Neves, a skilled, traditional, but mildly progressive, politician whose reputation as a stalwart opponent of the worst excesses of the military regime stood him in good stead, and as vice-president, José Sarney, a very traditional, conservative politician who had always supported the military regime. This congressional compromise gave the army a way to retreat from open political power without being subjected to post-dictatorship purges and indictments of the military involved in torture and repression.

The Death of Tancredo Neves

Tancredo Neves had earned the respect of millions of Brazilians during the difficult years of the dictatorship. He had been a leader of the opposition in the senate, patiently seeking openings and developing programs that would ameliorate the sufferings of the poor. He himself was socially and religiously conservative; nevertheless, he was deeply committed to democratic procedures and to a government that would be paternalistic (as opposed to authoritarian and insensitive). Furthermore, he was able to maintain communication with the military and the conservatives without sacrificing his essential convictions. Thus, he became almost a savior to many Brazilians, to guide the state and the nation in the times of transition—the first civilian president. He was elected indirectly by the senate, but he received a resounding mandate from the Brazilian people in spite of their reservations about indirect elections. And then, after a short illness, he died on the eve of the day he was scheduled to be inaugurated as president. The nation was badly shaken.

The Sarney Administration

José Sarney assumed the presidency under this tragic situation, and he apparently benefitted from the goodwill of most Brazilians. It was a situation similar to those in the United States in which Harry Truman and Lyndon Johnson assumed their presidencies. It was a time of great hope, in spite of the death of Tancredo Neves, a moment of transition to democracy that the Brazilians felt they had earned through struggle. The administration of José Sarney (1985–1990) assumed the mandate of Tancredo Neves: the re-institutionalization of a democratic political system that had been set aside by the army for twenty-one years. But he had two other challenges: first, to stabilize the economy, make growth possible again, and negotiate some tolerable arrangement with foreign creditors; and second, to begin to address the "social debt," to move towards reform and the integration of the poor majority into modern society. Unfortunately, Sarney was unable to meet either.

Under his administration, the formal legal and political system was re-established, and a new constitution was drafted and adopted, but without meeting the problem of inflation-stagnation and lack of stronger human services, the political system was destined to be impotent. Moreover, Sarney was unable during his administration to develop a sound and organized political base, either in the congress or in the general population.

The Failure of the Movement for Agrarian Reform

The Catholic bishops and some of the unions began in 1982 to plan a national movement to promote agrarian reform, anticipating the civilian government and a full and extended debate before the Brazilian people. It was believed that the essential bottleneck was the landowners and the denial of participation to peasants and poor farmers. Furthermore, it was thought that there must be a way to stem the surge of poor towards the *favelas*. But it was discovered, after a full campaign with even the passive support of the Pope, President Sarney, and the military, that the Agrarian Reform movement did not have enough political power to be effective in the key states where integrated and entrenched opposition to land reform was based in the big landowners. After four or five years of high tension and at a high cost (500 to 600 assassinations per year in that period, mostly of peasant leaders but including some priests, labor lawyers, and union and church organizers), the campaign led by the National Council of Brazilian Bishops retreated from active support for new peasant movements.

THE NEW CONSTITUTION AND THE POST-DICTATORSHIP BRAZILIAN POLITICAL SYSTEM

After living under several successive versions of a military-imposed constitution, Brazilians agreed that the nation needed an updated constitution. Following Brazilian precedents, a Constituent Assembly was formed—with military acquiescence—under leadership partially appointed by the military government, partially by newly elected congressional leaders. The new constitution reflects many big and little compromises. The biggest compromise was between the presidential and the parliamentary systems, an issue that long deadlocked the Constituent Assembly. Through the compromise the president would be weakened but the congress would lack the power to really dominate the national political system. Further, the issue was soon to be resolved through a national plebiscite.

The problem is that in the absence of a strong system of popular participation and responsibility and grassroots-based political parties, it really does not make much difference whether the system is parliamentary or presidential. The political system is a "moderating system" between the existing articulated and represented political, social, and economic powers. Politics is made by politicians who wheel and deal among themselves, beholden only to elite clients or limited constituencies. This system, of course, leaves out some 80 to 90 percent of the Brazilian people. The constitution offers many hopes but few means to effective realization of popular participation. After twenty-one years of military dictatorship, it was a great advance simply to have a national constitution, the result of democratic debate and discussion. Tragically, the Constituent Assembly was not able to enlarge the consensus machinery: It is still locked in a small minority—called in Brazil "the political class." Obviously, with some exceptions, the elected political officials—federal, state, and local, and especially the congress—are dominated by the "system" (what Americans call the "establishment") and the constitution did not change the basic structures or create the means of effecting such changes.

The Bitter Fruits of Twenty-one
Years of Military Tutelage

As it has been said that peace conferences at the end of a war are the worst preparation for peace, it could also be argued that a prolonged dictatorship is the worst preparation for democracy. Its legacy is hidden hate, resentment, revanchism, fears, and unbridled exploitation by national and foreign corporations without safety rules and labor union protection of the two-thirds of the population that is poor.

Twenty-one years of military rule has left a growing gap between the rich and the poor—a fruit of the "economic miracle," product of the master plan of the generals and their advisors in their conscious neglect of social investment and the accumulation of the "social debt," with interest. Twenty-one years of military dictatorship yielded bitter fruits, not only those immediately obvious. There are the obvious political costs: the political party system left even weaker, without traditional, grass-roots organization or skills. The destruction of what was the left (after the dictatorship of Getulio's Novo Estado) created a vacuum; the lack of a dynamic opposition left the society lacking ferment and democratic, mobilizational skills.

Then there is what the Brazilians call "The Social Debt," the national and social costs imposed by intentional neglect, the lack of human development programs, the lack of leadership development. The master plan of the generals assumed the social and human cost to build the very expensive economic and technical infrastructure, but no one tried to measure the human cost. These costs included the growing *favelization* (building of squatter shanty-towns by the poor in and around Brazilian cities), the increasing infant mortality rate, and the deterioration of health, educational, and other services.

And then there are the deep and imponderable cultural costs: the deterioration of morale and national values; the repressed and supressed traumas and fears and resentments of violations and violence; the nurturing of contempt for law, because the army and police themselves were often lawless; and insensitivity to basic human rights and freedoms. The imposed culture of fear created a climate in which the social skills of dialogue, of cooperative effort (except in a bureaucratic context), of critical analysis, of building a consensus, of building a community were inhibited. How then could a democracy appear suddenly and flourish, especially when there was never a broad cultural base for a grass-roots, responsible, accountable participatory democracy? Rather than nurturing the very tender shoots of democracy in

Brazil, the army leadership smothered the feeble skills that were being nurtured. Two classic cases in point would be the way in which the peasant leagues in the northeast (1960–1964) and Catholic Action (1962–1965) were smashed by the military and the police. The peasant leagues were destroyed through a connivance of the landowners and the bishops; and Catholic Action, destroyed by a cooperative effort among the army, police, university administrators, and bishops—the same bishops who had nurtured the movement a few years before! Both movements were developing democratic cadres with team skills, consensus builders, and organizers in a society characterized by passivity, unorganized and helpless before a wanton power elite. Though it cannot be blamed entirely on the military governments, perhaps the most negative impact on the future was the concentration of political and economic power in Brazil, and the policies of the government became an added factor to the "growing gap."[16]

THE END OF THE TRANSITION: CIVILIAN GOVERNMENT AND DIRECT ELECTIONS

The Brazilian people were excited about the prospect of a national campaign and the election(s)—more than one if there were need to have a run-off; but the electorate really did not become involved. In spite of twenty-eight political parties and twenty-six candidates for the presidency, with available national television time for all candidates (prorated according to their popular support), the majority remained perplexed. (Some polls showed that about half of the electorate would have some interest in returning to the nonrepressive military government of Figueiredo.) Conservative groups were sometimes panicked about the possibility of either Luis Inacio (Lula) da Silva (the candidate of the Worker's Party, the PT) or Leonel Brizola (a traditional populist who considers himself as a nationalist social-democrat); they cast around almost frantically for an electable candidate who would be amenable to their interests and who would not encourage popular demands for basic political and social reform.

The winner of the presidential run-off on November 15, 1989, Fernando Collor de Mello, the former governor of the state of Alagoas, is an attractive and young new face, with a reputation of being a "maharaja" buster.[17] He was chosen to be the candidate of the conservatives virtually by default, and his personality and youth along with the money of his backers, made him the president. In the campaigns, there was no attempt to address the growing gap between the rich and the poor or to deal with other profound national problems. The nation expected the unknown as Collor was inaugurated.

A preliminary analysis of the election showed that the old guard politicians were pretty well shelved; old parties were ignored, but the electorate maintained its naive faith in elections without a real political party system—in spite of the well-known Brazilian skepticism about everything in politics. Collor was elected as something different without interrupting traditional public values, a new face with the same old rhetoric. He really has little organized political base, and he entered the presidency without any well-designed political program or ideology.

Prospects for Democracy

Given the weak and fragile Brazilian political system, the very poorly distributed national wealth, and the entrenched informal and semi-visible power structure in Brazil, the prospects for true democracy are not very bright. The first obstacle is the traditional, patronage-oriented congress, which will block any significant reforms. Then, there are the powerful lobbies, including the bureaucracy and the state systems. And there are the traditional political parties—more markets for exchanges of interests and favors than a peoples' forum or a mobilizational and educational national process.

There is, however, an emerging political movement in Brazil that could offer a new chance. What is new is the mere possibility of the beginning of a clearer definition of a political agenda and a clear alignment in two multiparty blocs. The conservatives have rallied behind Collor for fear of both Lula and Brizola, and these two are showing some signs of working together to produce a broad alliance of progressive, popular, and leftist groups. Such a two-bloc system could offer clearer options than did traditional Brazilian political parties and coalitions.

Overwhelming Problems

Brazil, like many other Third World nations, confronts formidable national problems. The emerging post–Cold War world environment appears to be even more indifferent to painful dilemmas than was the Cold War period, with its possibilities of playing the superpowers off against each other. The foreign debt would make even the most competent and socially committed government impotent. Brazil faces the choice of continuing to try to borrow a little more than required for minimal payments on the foreign debt interest in the hope that some day, some way, the foreign debt will be negotiated down to a level where repayment could be undertaken, or declaring a moratorium on servicing or repudiation of the foreign debt with its consequent probable freezing of subsequent loans.

Meanwhile, the "rural drift"—peasants attracted by the illusions of economic opportunity in the cities and driven away by the agrobusiness and mechanization of rural areas—exacerbates "urban blight," the growth of shantytowns, or *favelas,* not only in the great cities of Brazil but also increasingly in its middle-sized cities with the consequent overburdening of social service infrastructure. The major cities of Brazil are sinking into a permanent division between the rich and the poor, accentuated by gross inequity of social services between the classes.

Perhaps the major problem of Brazil is the unyielding and greedy elite, staunchly opposed to real power-sharing and determined not to pay taxes. The Brazilian elite—that 10 percent who possess 50 percent of the national wealth—will continue to equate "democracy" with the "free market" or capitalist system.[18] Obviously, such a system will be run by and for the upper class, mocking all democratic values and processes.

Collor has promised that his administration will prosecute tax-evaders and has named a respected law-enforcer to seek and punish the many evaders. He has promised to streamline and make more efficient the unproductive, often corrupt, and grossly overpaid bureaucracy. One of his major challenges is to redress the gross inadequacy of social services. To make the civil service more effective and humane would indeed be revolutionary.

It is difficult for a population that is unorganized and untrained in the skills of political participation and mobilization for political and social action to effectively discipline the greedy rich and the indulgent bureaucracy. The Brazilian electorate is overwhelmingly poor, malleable, and aimless, lacking leadership, skills, and education, increasingly aware of public issues but dependent upon television for political opinions.

THE BRAZILIAN CHALLENGE TODAY

One of the dominant aims of the world's modernizing elites is to move rapidly towards the "internationalization and privatization" of the world economy. For Brazil that would mean to be integrated into the "free-market economy," led by the U.S. and Japanese economic pacesetters. This, of course, was the original model of President-General Castelo Branco and the U.S. investors and bankers who backed the counterrevolution of 1964. Brazil can become dynamic and productive again, it is argued, only if it accepts its role as a junior member of the emerging global economy. With the emerging configuration of political and economic world power, Brazil and other Third World nations have come to realize that they may become even more marginal to the world metropolitan centers. They may be not only neglected, but also further exploited by the richest, technically most developed nations. Many fear that "internationalization and privatization" will exacerbate the already great gap between the rich and poor and even less will dribble down to the poor.

There is a broad consensus in Brazil among conservatives as well as progressives that four basic changes are urgently needed:

- First, the foreign debt must be canceled; that can only be done by the industrial capitalist nations, especially the United States.
- Second, the government bureaucracy must be disciplined and reoriented so that it will be productive of human services rather than parasitic.
- Third, the private sector and the economic elite must be required to pay their taxes and to invest in Brazil rather than to exploit its people and export flight or risk capital.[19]
- Fourth, Latin American and other Third World governments must learn to consult and cooperate for their own sake—to demand, for example, a new "Bretton Woods" process.

With Brazilian "democracy" enshrined in the public rhetoric of a system of multiparty free elections, honest and universal suffrage, and a free press, the Brazilian political system is embedded comfortably in a pyramidal social structure that tolerates no real challenge to existing elites and their political and economic system. The informal structure of real power has four hundred years of experience in demobilizing, intimidating, and co-opting potential popular leaders and denying challengers access to the media. Given this reality, it is well to look twice at the nature of this "democracy" and these elections. Elections must offer some real options, with a meaningful set of competitive leaders who are capable of executing their programs if elected, and who can administer, under law and as the result of a democratic process, an efficient and effective government apparatus.

The new president of Brazil, Fernando Collor de Mello, has inherited the burden of history in Brazil, and like Vinicio Cerezo, Alan García, Raul Alfonsin, Carlos Menem, and other Latin American leaders, he is trying various "shock treatments," calling for freezing prices and wages to stop inflation and trying to discipline the state bureaucracy as well as the rich and middle class to assume their responsibility. Democracy will become operative only when the party system becomes effective and participatory and able to restrain the runaway rich and when there is a dynamic that will narrow the gap between the rich and the poor. Unless there can be a serious breakthrough, the "system" will finally find it necessary to reimpose repression and to safeguard the traditional system of passivity, disorganization, and ignorance of the poor. It is necessary to understand that under these circumstances anyone elected president is very likely to be condemned to frustrations and political impotence.

The U.S. government and the North American economic network will continue to support the elitist system until it begins to totter or blow up. The Bush-Baker foreign policy, designed to replace the rhetoric of the Cold War, has adopted "democracy and free market" rhetoric. The "mission" is to protect and promote "democracy," and to stabilize the world system. (The new red button is "chaos"—and that often means popular unrest and demand for change.) "Democracy" in the language of the Bush-Baker administration assumes the old "trickle down" theory, which worked more effectively with industrial technology, with some labor union and government protection for workers. Now, with the globalization of the economy, multinational corporations have become global mega-conglomerates, beyond much control or regulation by nation-states because they can play off one labor market against another.

It was, finally, the middle class that grew restless under military tutelage and expected to benefit the most from an open society—more consumption, more freedom, free market, and so on. But the middle class, being squeezed by inflation (40 percent per month in October 1989, 73 percent in February 1990), including periodic crises of "hyperinflation," grows disillusioned.

It would be comforting to many to believe that the Brazilian system will maintain itself, with the appearances of democracy and participation, and that the massive problems of poverty, lack of social services, lack of real participation, corruption, and the irresponsibility of the dominant classes can be addressed by piecemeal and partial programs. Unfortunately, there is little evidence that Brazil is creating conditions in which the majority of its people can achieve a life of dignity and security.

NOTES

1. To see some of the classic statements (from different viewpoints) on the "two Brazils," see:

Bastide, Roger. *Brasil: Terra de Contrastes* (Second edition). São Paulo: Difusao Européia do Livro, 1964. 261 pages.
Freyre, Gilberto. *Brasis, Brasil e Brasília.* Rio de Janeiro: Gráfica Record Editôra, 1968. 270 pages.
Machado, Germano. *Os Dois Brasis.* Salvador: Imprensa Oficial de Bahia, 1963. 85 pages.

For an extensive discussion of the "basic dualism of Brazilian society," see Chapter 2, Jaguaribe, Helio. *Alternativas do Brasil.* Rio de Janeiro: José Olympia Editora, 1989.
2. To compare the concentration of wealth in the top 10 percent of the population of other nations:

Brazil:	50.6 percent
Mauritius:	46.7 percent
Zambia:	46.4 percent
Kenya:	45.8 percent

To compare the low level of wealth of the poorest 20 percent:

Peru:	1.9 percent
Brazil:	2 percent
Kenya:	2 percent
Malaysia:	2 percent

Jaguaribe, *Alternativas do Brasil,* page 27.
3. The image of "two Brazils" is, of course, simplified to make a point. Brazil's social structure has become more complex with the introduction of the industrialization process and, later, the mechanization of great segments of the agricultural sector, the post-industrial modernization process, and the expansion and diversification of the middle class. A more sophisticated profile of Brazil by class is as follows:

1 percent of the rich have 13 percent of the national income.
10 percent of the richest population have 50.6 percent of the national income.
50 percent of the poorest population have also 13 percent of the national income.
20 percent of the poorest population have 2 percent of the national income.

Jaguaribe, *Alternativas do Brasil,* page 27.
4. This term was created by Edmar Bacha.
5. Professor Sylvia Ann Hewlett in her book *The Cruel Dilemmas of Development: Twentieth Century Brazil* (New York: Basic Books, 1980) has described both the "two Brazils" and the "cruel choices."
6. Jaguaribe, *Alternativas do Brasil,* page 27.
7. It is necessary to note that the repression in Brazil was brutal and vicious, but it never affected as great a proportion of the population as the repression and torture in Uruguay, Argentina, and Chile.

8. See Bacha and Malan in *Democratizing Brazil,* ed. Alfred Stepan, page 123. The "miracle" was fueled by the "peace" between labor and management imposed by the army: Strikes were declared illegal and the army broke any attempts to strike.

9. Bacha and Malan, page 136.

10. The expanding foreign debt of Brazil was caused by a series of factors: (1) the OPEC cartel that imposed a great increase in petroleum prices (Brazil has few domestic sources of petroleum); (2) the great jump in the international interest rate for borrowers from the Third World; (3) the military's master plan to develop the "Pharonic works" (as the opposition came to call them) that were planned to give a jump-start to the economy; (4) the inevitable bleeding of the national economy through bad planning and management and sometimes through corruption.

11. For a more detailed discussion, see Thomas Skidmore, "Brazil's Slow Road to Democratization: 1974–1985," in *Democratizing Brazil,* ed. Alfred Stepan, pages 5–42.

12. São Andre, São Bernardo, São Caetano—three industrial cities that are part of greater São Paulo.

13. "New Unionism" is a movement that intends to be free of the old inherited "corporatist" system, instituted by Getulio Vargas. The "old unionism" or corporatist system makes the union movement almost a branch of the government, regulated by the Minister of Labor.

14. There were six famous funerals over a period of five years, led by bishops, of young men who had been killed by torture. These funerals became the focus of rallying and public repudiation of the military government's methods and programs.

15. The Basic Ecclesiastical Communities began in the 1965–1966 period as a way to give more vitality to the Catholic Church among the poor, given the need for supportive communities, the scarcity of priests, and the lack of social programs. The CEBs (using the Portuguese acronym) blossomed by 1985 or 1986, with 100,000 to 110,000 basic communities. Due to opposition from the conservative Church leaders and the Vatican, and the perception by some among the poor that the CEBs were not necessary once there was an elected civilian government, the movement has not grown much since then.

16. There ought to be a lesson in these consequences for future "internationalization and privatization" policies, even though the administrations of President George Bush and Prime Minister Margaret Thatcher still believe that these approaches can respond positively to the Third World necessities.

17. In Brazilian terms, a "maharajah" (coming from India, a rich potentate who lives in luxury and ease while many toil for little) means a government high-level bureaucrat with a very high salary who hardly works at all.

18. There are many gradations and types of capitalism: "Savage capitalism," or the devil for last and whoever wins, is most characteristic of Brazilian capitalism. "Free enterprise" means, to most Brazilian industrialists and bankers, complete lack of regulation and of social responsibility and a cozy relationship with the government.

19. A very well-known Brazilian moderate said in despair immediately after the national presidential elections that it is absolutely necessary to jail four or five of the wealthiest persons for tax evasion to send the message to the Brazilian elite. No one believes that this will happen.

SUGGESTED READINGS

Bernard, Rui, and Huberto Kirchheim (coordinators). *The Roots of Poverty and Hunger in Brazil.* São Leopoldo, RS: Editora Sinodal, 1990.

Chacel, Julian M., Pamel S. Falk, and David V. Fleischer, eds. *Brazil's Economic and Political Future.* Boulder: Westview Press, 1988.

Dassin, Joan (Edited and with an Introduction). *Torture in Brazil: A Report by the Archdiocese of São Paulo.* Translated by Jaime Wright. New York: Random House, 1986.

Hagopian, Frances, and Scott Mainwaring. "Democracy in Brazil: Problems and Prospects." *World Policy Journal,* IV:3 (Summer 1987), pp. 485–514.

Harrison, Lawrence E. "Brazil: Scapegoating Debt." *Washington Post,* February 9, 1989.

Helder Camara, Archbishop. *Spiral of Violence.* Translated by Della Couling. Denville, N.J.: Dimension Books, 1971.

Kucinski, Bernardo. *Brazil: State and Struggle.* London: Latin American Bureau, 1982.

Mainwaring, Scott. *The Catholic Church and Politics in Brazil, 1916–1985.* Stanford, Calif.: Stanford University Press, 1986.

Marques Moreira, Marcilio. *The Brazilian Quandary.* A Twentieth Century Fund Paper. New York: Priority Press Publications, 1986.

Nyrop, Richard F. (ed.). *Brazil: A Country Study.* Foreign Area Studies, American University (Sponsored by the Department of the Army). Washington, D.C.: Government Publications Office, 1983.

O'Donnell, Guillermo. "Challenges to Democratization in Brazil: The Threat of a Slow Death." *World Policy Journal,* Spring 1988, pp. 281–300.

Skidmore, Thomas. *The Politics of Military Rule in Brazil, 1964–85.* New York: Oxford University Press, 1988.

Stepan, Alfred (ed.). *Democratizing Brazil: Problems of Transition and Consolidation.* New York: Oxford University Press, 1989.

————. *Rethinking Military Politics: Brazil and the Southern Cone.* Princeton, N.J.: Princeton University Press, 1988.

Wesson, Robert. *The United States and Brazil: Limits of Influence.* New York: Praeger, 1981.

Wirth, John D., Edson de Oliveira Nunes, and Thomas E. Gobenschild. *State and Society in Brazil: Continuity and Change.* Boulder: Westview Press, 1987.

Summary Bibliography in Portuguese

Almeida, Maria Herminia T. de., e Bernando Sorj (eds.). *Sociedade e Politica no Brasil Pos-64.* Editora Brasiliense, 1984.

Bacha, Edmar, and Herbert S. Klein (eds.). *A Transicao Incompleta: Brasil desde 1945.* Rio de Janeiro: Paz e Terra, 1986.
> Volume I—Populacao/Emprego/Agricultura/Urbanizacao
> Volume II—Desigualdade Social/Educacao/Saude Previdencia

Bresser Pereira, Luiz. *Pactos Politicos: Do Populismo a redemocratizacao.* Editors Brasiliense, 1985.

————. (Ed.). *Divida Externa: Crise e Solucoes.* São Paulo: Editora Brasiliense, 1989.

Chaui, Marilena. *Conformismo e Resistencia: Aspectos da Cultura Popular no Brasil.* Editora Brasiliense, 1986.

DaMatta, Roberto. *O Que Fax O brasil, Brasil?* Rocco, 1986.

D'Alva Gil Kinzo, Maria. "O Quadro partidário e a Constituinte." *Revista Brasileira de Ciência Política,* Vol 1, No. 1 (marco de 1989), pp. 91–124.

Faoro, Raymundo. *Os Donos do Poder: Formacao do Patronato Politico Brasileiro.* Editora Globo, 1958.

Jaguaribe, Helio. *Alternativas do Brasil.* Rio de Janeiro: José Olympio Editora, 1989.

Jaguaribe, Helio, Nelson do Valle e Silva, Marcelo de Paiva Abreu, Fernando Bastos de Avila, and Winston Fritsch. *Brasil: Reforma our Caos* (Third Edition). Rio de Janeiro, 1988, 1989.

Jaguaribe, Helio, Francisco Iglésias, Wanderley Guilherme dos Santos, Vamireh Chacon, and Fábio Comparato. *Brasil, Sociedade Democrática* (Second Edition). Rio de Janeiro: José Olympio Editora, 1986.

Machado, Ivan G. Pinheiro (ed.). *Nova Republica: Um Balanco.* L&PM Editores, 1986.

Rattner, Henrique (ed.). *Brasil 1990: Caminhos alternativos do Desenvolvimento.* Editora Brasiliense, 1979.

Valle, Alvaro. *As Novas Estruturas Politicas Brasileiras* (2a edicao). Nordica, 1978.

30
CONCLUSION

JAN KNIPPERS BLACK

GETTING TO KNOW THE NEIGHBORS

There can be no doubt that Latin America has undergone dramatic change in the last three decades. Nevertheless, much of what Anglo-Americans are inclined to see as change in Latin America may actually be change in our perceptions of Latin America, as well as in our perceptions of our own society.

Latin America is more familiar to us now. That is due only in part to the enormously increased volume of academic studies inspired by the birth of a multidisciplinary field. It is also due to increased travel and investment by U.S. citizens and to expanded U.S. public and private programs of exchange, propaganda, proselytizing, relief, and development. The perspectives of diplomats and others, whose writings provided our images in decades past, derived almost exclusively from contacts with the political and economic elites. But thousands of Peace Corps volunteers and other young Americans coming of age in the sixties and seventies have come to know Latin America's peasants and workers and marginalized would-be workers as real people—friends.

Can it be that Latin America's poor, stereotyped in the not-so-distant past as ignorant and passive, have only recently become clever, energetic, and enterprising? Or is it that we are only beginning to learn of the courage required to overcome official intimidation and of the ingenuity required to survive on the edge? Is it possible that Latin America's middle classes, traditionally hedonistic and lackadaisical, have only recently been energized? Or can it be that we have only recently realized that the professional who seems never to be in his office actually juggles three offices: his bureaucratic post, his chair at the university, and his private practice?

A student of mine once commented that "Brazilian women don't work; they have maids." No doubt there are still women throughout the Americas who are pampered and cloistered. But now that we know the maids as well as the mistresses, we know that the issue "to work or not to work" is even phonier for most Latin American women than for their Anglo-American counterparts. In fact, we have now seen that the greater the economic or political threat to survival, the more central will be the role of women in combating that threat. Women have long been the economic and organizational mainstays of the poorest urban shantytowns. More recently, the large-scale involvement of women in danger-fraught human rights networks and in revolutionary movements has been particularly striking. To declare that Latin Americans, for reasons of work roles or sex roles, intellect or temperament, are unequal to the task of their own development on their own terms is to declare our ignorance of them.

While Latin America has been overrun in the past three decades with U.S. slogans, products, and advisers, there has also been movement in the other direction. Latin American scholars have set the tone for studies by U.S. academic specialists in Latin American affairs. Some of the best U.S. novelists have experimented with literary styles pioneered by Latin American novelists. Latin American graphic arts, music, and cinematography have gained in popularity with U.S audiences. U.S. churches have been influenced by the "liberation theology" that swept first, like a fire storm, through Latin America's religious communities. Some of Latin America's "best and brightest," driven from their own countries by dictatorial regimes supported by the U.S. government, have settled in the United States and have deepened our own national debates about domestic and foreign policy.

Of course, Anglo-America and Latin America share the shame of past and present mistreatment of native American and Afro-American populations. Furthermore, much of what is now the United States shares with much of Latin America the heritage of Spanish conquest and settlement and 300 years of Spanish colonialism. Indian and Spanish cultures, never quite suppressed in the United States, are now being revitalized by the influx of Mexican workers, estimated to be in the millions, seeking employment that eludes them at home and of hundreds of thousands of Salvadorans and Guatemalans fleeing the savagery of their governments. Miami, of course, has been Cubanized, and the northeastern part of the United States has absorbed great numbers of Caribbeans. As these workers, refugees, and immigrants, documented or otherwise, move from state to state and city to city in search of work, no part of the United States is wholly immune from the process of Latinoization.

It is estimated that by the turn of the twenty-first century, Hispanics will surpass blacks in numbers to become the largest ethnic minority in the United States. Although some people lament the trend, I lament only its causes. There is no reason to doubt that Latin Americans will enrich our culture and our national life as have past waves of immigrants.

Finally, we are getting to know Latin Americans as a consequence of our government's incessant meddling in their affairs. Despite the wonders of technology and the imaginative means of intimidating whistleblowers, government secrets have become ever harder to keep. The media sooner or later catches up with our boys in camouflage. Their exploits, along with the images of peasants' fighting and dying and of leaders' pleading, in flawless English, for arms or for reason, are brought into our homes nightly in living color.

A question raised urgently and often in the United States in the 1980s was, Will Central America become another Vietnam? There are many arguments as to why it has not, but the most important may be that the Central Americans are our neighbors. The Vietnamese were to North Americans a most exotic people. While we opposed U.S. involvement in that distant war for a myriad of reasons, we were not prepared to understand the problems and aspirations of the people of Indochina. Latin Americans, by contrast, are now a familiar people. In underwriting the oppressors of the people of Central America, the authors of U.S. policy run the risk that the people of the United States will begin to understand the problems of Latin Americans and, in so doing, gain insight into the problems of our own country.

AMERICA IS ONE

U.S. presidents always begin their Columbus Day speeches before the assembled dignitaries of the Organization of American States with the assertion that America is one. Such assertion is followed by rhetorical fluff about individualism, democracy, godliness, private enterprise, and the Communist threat. But there is a growing unacknowledged reality to the oneness of America. Latin America is increasingly sharing not only the blessings of U.S.-style modernization but its demons as well. And many of the problems that have long plagued Latin America are more and more apparent and bedeviling in the United States itself. The clearest trend in the Americas is a trend toward convergence—if not of interests, at least of problems.

Latin America, now predominantly urban, boasts or frets of several of the world's largest cities. To Latin America, as to the United States, urbanization has brought both advantages and disadvantages. It has led to new, more effective forms of political organization and has facilitated the extension of services—electricity, running water, health care, public schools—to a greater proportion of the population. It has extended the reach of the communications media, enhancing their ability to disseminate information, misinformation, and disinformation. In Latin America, as in the United States, urbanization has weakened the constraints, but also the socialization and the security, that flowed from extended family systems. To Latin America, more recently than to the United States, it has also meant traffic congestion, pollution, and anonymous, impersonal street crime.

Latin American economies have long suffered from fluctuations in world prices for a limited number of minerals or agricultural products and from deterioration in the terms of trade for such primary products. Before World War II, agriculture contributed twice as much to regional gross product as manufacturing did. Although most Latin American countries are still highly dependent upon the export of one or two primary products, manufacturing's share of gross regional product, by the late 1960s, was well above that of agriculture. In the 1970s, Brazil began to earn more from the export of manufactures than from that of primary products. By the early 1980s, more than half of Latin America's exports were at least processed. At the same time, however, the importation of capital goods and, in the case of most countries, of energy to fuel the industrialization process led to soaring debts and other problems.

While Latin America has been industrializing, the United States has been moving in the other direction. Spurred by incentives, offered by both U.S. and foreign governments, and lured by cheap labor, U.S.-based corporations have shifted capital—and jobs—to the Third World, including Latin America. Thus, the United States, for several decades the virtually unchallenged provider of manufactured goods to Latin America, has itself become increasingly dependent upon foreign investment, the importation of manufactured goods, and the export of primary products, particularly wheat.

In most Latin American countries, as in the United States, the idea of stimulating the economy from the bottom up—of expansion of the domestic market and production to meet effective mass demand—has been abandoned in favor of production for export and/or for the relatively affluent. Modernization, in Latin America as in the United States, has meant increasingly capital-intensive—as opposed to labor-intensive—industry, resulting in chronic unemployment. In the absence of stunningly innovative policy, the unemployment problem in both Americas promises to get worse.

Since the Iberian conquest of the New World, the concentration of land ownership has been among Latin America's most obstinate problems. Conquistadores and others favored by the Iberian monarchs carved out for themselves enormous estates complete with the previous native American claimants or imported African slaves to do the work. But the land grabs of the colonial period pale by comparison to those inspired since the mid-nineteenth century by the growth of export markets for primary products. Effective and enduring land reform has been rare in the twentieth century, and in some countries—Guatemala and El Salvador, for example—the ongoing process of seizure of peasant lands leaves an ever-increasing proportion of the rural population dependent upon seasonal work for the large landholders. As semi-feudal estates are transformed into agribusinesses and machines replace workers, displaced peasants will be left with neither land nor wages.

In the 1970s, many Latin American governments, recognizing that their agricultural sectors had been neglected or milked while import-substitution industrialization was being promoted, turned their attention to the modernization of agricultural production and offered new incentives for the exportation of agricultural products. One consequence was that lands that had been used to produce staples for domestic consumption were converted into production for export. Export earnings, not usually redistributed in any form to the general population, have risen, but increasingly, basic foodstuffs must be imported, resulting in higher prices for the consumer.

As is often pointed out in comparisons of Anglo-America and Latin America, Anglo-America was early blessed with a land tenure pattern of small holdings, or family farms. However, while the U.S. government, in the 1960s, spoke of the need for land reform in Latin America, the process of concentration of landholdings, favoring agribusiness conglomerates, assumed a dizzying pace in the United States. By the early 1980s, the family farm was clearly an endangered species.

Denationalization, the process whereby the ownership or control of resources passes from national to foreign hands, has long been a major problem for Latin America. For the first century or so of independence, it was primarily the land and mineral resources that attracted foreign investors, with the diplomatic—and sometimes military—backing of their governments. Transportation, public utilities, and other infrastructural projects also were often undertaken and controlled by foreigners. By the mid-twentieth century, foreign firms and multinational corporations had begun to capture, or recapture, domestic markets for durable consumer goods and to buy out or squeeze out local industries. More recently, foreign firms have competed successfully for control of distribution and services as well.

For most of the century in Meso-America and for several decades in South America, the denationalizers have been predominantly U.S.-based corporations. Since the 1970s, however, firms based in Western Europe and Japan have been gaining rapidly in the competition for Latin American markets and for the fruits of Latin American land and labor. The same European and Japanese companies, along with those of Middle Eastern oil potentates, have also been increasing their shares of U.S. consumer markets, at the expense of U.S.-based companies, and their shares of ownership of U.S. farmland and urban real estate, banks, and industries.

A kindred and more insidious problem in the United States, which has received less attention even though it is far more serious, is that of "delocalization." The same multinational banks, conglomerates, and chains that have displaced Latin American businesses and rendered Latin American economies dependent have also bought out or squeezed out local businesses in Tennessee and Michigan and New Mexico. Such companies, which pay campaign debts in Washington and taxes in the Bahamas, have no national or local allegiances. When they see greater profits to be made in São Paulo or Seoul, they leave Nashville or Albuquerque jobless with no regrets; they were never a part of the community.

Several Latin American countries made headway in the 1960s and 1970s toward gaining control over their resources and their economies. Expropriation of mineral resources was particularly common, and was so popular that even the most *entreguista* right-wing military dictators rarely dared to try to reverse it. The assumption that subsoil resources are national domain was inherited by most of the Latin American countries from the Spanish crown. Mexico, in 1917, declared its petroleum and other subsoil resources social property, to be owned and exploited by and for the people as a whole; it made the claim an economic reality in 1938. Most other Latin American countries have since established public corporations to manage the production, importation, or distribution of petroleum and other energy products. Meanwhile, in the United States, an ever-smaller number of companies make ever-larger profits, while consumers undergo a price-gouging energy crisis every fifteen to twenty years.

Attempts by Latin American nationalists to regain control of their economies have often been undertaken at great cost. Such attempts generally have the effect of adding the great weight of the multinational corporate community and the U.S. government to the ever-present schemes against popular governments. And foreign creditors and multilateral financial institutions weighed in heavily in the 1980s with pressure for "privatization" and debt-for-equity swaps. But the extension of national control over the economy is central to the agenda of popular movements in Latin America; no political leader who aspires to popularity can afford to ignore the issue. In the United States, the ideas of nationalization and localization and, in general, of placing public interest over private profit are still in the category of heresy.

Even orthodox First World economists, pleased with the export promotion, privatization, deregulation, and austerity that have characterized recent economic policy in the region, speak of the 1980s as a "lost decade" for Latin America. The foreign debt, for the region as a whole, exceeded $426 billion in 1988 and claimed about half of the area's export earnings for interest payments alone. The debts of Brazil and Mexico, $114 billion and $94 billion respectively, at the end of the decade, though dwarfed now in absolute terms by the U.S. debt, were the highest in the Third World; and those of several other Latin American states were higher still in per capita terms.

Latin American economies were also being wrenched by inflation rates averaging 437 percent in 1988. As if to spite those economists who had posed a choice between inflation and unemployment, the latter was also rising. Official figures on urban unemployment showed a regional average of 11.2 percent for 1986 and 1987; but most Latin Americans assumed that official figures were artificially low. Underemployment, furthermore, was far higher.[1]

These problems, along with declining rates of investment, of production, and of productivity, and declining real wages and salaries, were exacerbated by the sharp rise in energy costs and the global recession of the early 1980s, but they were in large part also a consequence of the modern international version of debt peonage and of the punishment creditors and their collection agency, the International Monetary Fund, were able to inflict on delinquents. That punishment had generally included currency devaluation, higher interest rates, lower wages and longer working hours, a slashing of government services, subsidies, and welfare programs, and a veritable fire sale of government assets. As the rich made the usual choice of whether or not to accept sacrifice, the additional load of sacrifice was being borne mainly by those who had no choice.

Moreover, Latin American debts, like Third World debts in general, are increasingly owed to private banks. To many of the same banks, the United States now owes much of its national debt of some $3 trillion. The U.S. debt tripled in the 1980s, and both the debt itself and its proportional claim on the budget are expected to increase over the next decade. To an even greater extent than is true of most Latin American countries, the rising U.S. debt may be attributed to increases in unproductive military spending.

Indices of health, education, services, and infrastructure suggest that the quality-of-life gap between the United States and Latin America has been narrowing steadily in the period since World War II. Even discounting the limitations of statistics and of index-making, this indicates very promising long-term progress for Latin America. In the shorter term, however—the 1970s and 1980s, for example—it also suggests slowed progress or even retrogression on the part of the United States. The U.S. National Commission on Excellence in Education reported in 1983 that functionally illiterate U.S. citizens numbered some 23 million, more than the entire population of most Latin American countries. At the beginning of the 1990s, Americans were spending more per capita on health care than any other people in the world; yet 37 million lacked any kind of medical insurance. Immunization programs for children had been among the casualties of budget cuts in the 1980s, and cases of measles had multiplied ten-fold in ten years. After a decade in which the number of pregnant women receiving no prenatal care climbed by 50 percent, the United States ranked twenty-second in the world in infant mortality prevention, placing it squarely in a Third World category. Life expectancy for white Anglo-Saxons continued to rise, but for minorities it had begun to drop.

More than 5 million Americans who needed housing assistance in 1990 were not getting it, up from 3.5 million in the mid-1970s. The census bureau reported in 1989 that one-fifth of American children (under age 18) and more than one-third of American Blacks were living in poverty. Among the policy decisions reflected in these trends were changes in tax laws since the late 1970s that, according to the Congressional Budget Office, had left 90 percent of Americans paying more while the richest 10 percent payed up to a third less. Meanwhile, the richest 5 percent of the population enjoyed a real increase in their income of 46 percent. The income of the richest 400 Americans alone grew by $50 billion in the 1980s. While the gap between Latin America and the United States has been narrowing, the gap between the United States and the more prosperous and egalitarian states of Western Europe has been widening. As Latin America, in aggregate, becomes more nearly a part of the "developed" world, the United States becomes more nearly a part of America.

In 1982, for the first time in the postwar period, Latin America's overall gross national product registered negative growth. Average per capita gross domestic product (GDP) for the region dropped more than 7 percent in the 1980s.[2] Since mid-century, Latin American economies had been growing, on average, at rates of 4 to 6 percent annually. Meanwhile, within most Latin American countries, as within the United States, especially during the last fifteen years, the gap between rich and poor has been widening—generally the outcome not of policy failures, but of policy decisions. Whether or not Latin America is perceived to have been developing during this period depends upon which countries, which years, and which indices one chooses to emphasize. What is more readily apparent, however, is that the United States, since the late 1960s, has been underdeveloping.

Even if Latin America and Anglo-America increasingly share the blessings and the curses of modernization—along with such problems as competition from stronger economies, excessive dependence on the export of primary products, concentration of land ownership, the undermining of local businesses by multinational corporations, staggering debts, chronic unemployment, and a growing gap between rich and poor—is it not obvious that the two Americas are centuries apart in matters of government and politics? Perhaps. But there, too, similarities and convergences can be found.

In the 1960s and 1970s, much of Latin America experienced the rise of a new and very modern kind of military dictatorship—institutional, technocratic, self-confident, and ruthless. In demobilizing civilian political organizations and imposing their new order, these military establishments were assisted by paramilitary, intelligence, and police networks with expertise in surveillance, torture, and assassination. This development is not unrelated to the economic problems mentioned above. Those who are left on the margins by modernization, who are needed neither as workers nor as consumers, and who are written off by the economic planners, cannot simply be ignored. They are the ill-fed, ill-clothed, ill-housed masses who are presumed to constitute a spawning ground for communism. The greater their numbers and the greater their sophistication and potential for political organization, the more elaborate will be the apparatus of repression required to contain them. But there are limits to the efficacy of rule by brute force, and the wielders of economic power—domestic and foreign—rediscovered the fact that a civilian government that is uninterested in acting upon or unable to act upon a popular mandate, and unwilling or unable to control military and paramilitary forces, is often a better hedge against social change than a repressive military government.

The 1980s witnessed the withdrawal of the generals from Latin America's presidential palaces and a process of "redemocratization." But the withdrawal has been only partial—not to a safe enough distance to allow democracy a free rein. And the new democracies, to a large extent, represent the victory of form over substance. Redemocratization has been accompanied by increasing indebtedness and surrender of economic sovereignty, the discrediting of reformist leaders and programs, and a return to economic elitism buffered by parties and parliaments and the ritual of elections. Civilian leaders have sometimes appeared to be virtual prisoners in their own presidential palaces, and violence, particularly against the poor, continues unabated.

Politics in Latin America has often been associated, in the minds of Anglo-Americans, with violence and petty corruption. But political assassination has also become common in the United States, and in the aftermath of Watergate, Koreagate, the Iran-Contra affair, and so many other recent scandals in the heart of the U.S. government, Anglo-Americans are perhaps learning humility and empathy, if not tolerance for free-lance corruption. Meanwhile, Latin American politicians—democrats and demogogues alike—are drawing upon U.S. expertise in a more sophisticated, institutionalized form of corruption. Consultants, pollsters, and fund raisers, accredited with political miracles in the United States, are being hired by Latin American candidates to pass on the art of taking money from the rich and votes from the poor on the pretext of protecting each from the other. Media campaigns and media advisers may be expected to replace political organizations and machines, and campaign contributions, legal and more substantial, may replace under-the-table bribes. Where elections in Latin America retain any representational meaning at all, we are likely to see the increasing capitalization and frivolization of the process.

It should not go unnoticed in the United States that it has been the most highly developed politically of the Latin American states that have suffered the cruelest fates since the early 1970s. Many of the same anti-egalitarian economic policies that were imposed on Brazil in the 1960s and the Southern Cone countries in the 1970s by counterrevolutionary military regimes have recently been adopted in the United States without a rupture in democratic processes. Perhaps the majority in the United States has been saved—by the myth of a classless society, the alienation of almost half of the eligible electorate, and the lack of effective political organization—from a fate worse than economic deprivation.

But not all U.S. citizens are spared the kind of official violence that is commonly employed in Latin America and elsewhere to contain a growing sector of marginalized, would-be workers. Such containment in the politically decentralized United States is carried out by increasingly autonomous local police forces. Police brutality, particularly against minority groups, is common from coast to coast; the United States federal prison population doubled in the 1980s to some 700,000, the highest per capita prison population of any industrialized Western nation with the possible exception of South Africa. In 1990, one in every four Black American men in their twenties was in jail or on probation.

Except for such brief skirmishes as those in response to the inner-city riots following the assassination of Dr. Martin Luther King and to Vietnam War protests, the United States has been spared the spectacle of troops on the streets. But it has not been spared the general trend toward militarism. The enhanced power of the U.S. military establishment has thus far been expressed primarily in the increasing militarization, since World War II, of the U.S. foreign policymaking apparatus and in the military's ever-increasing peacetime share of the national budget.

The role expansion of military establishments in the two Americas has proceeded in tandem. The incorporation of Central America and the Caribbean into the U.S. sphere of influence in the early twentieth century, through military intervention and, in some cases, direct military occupation, left a more modern form of militarism firmly entrenched. In the 1950s and 1960s, the U.S. military, on the premise of the need for a global strategy in the face of a permanent global war, undertook the organizational and technological modernization of the South American military establishments as well. An aspect of the Cold War world view, inculcated or reinforced through U.S. training, was the idea that the political arena is the battleground of the Cold War, and, as such, too important to be left to the politicians.

The increased involvement of the U.S. military in the making and implementation of policy toward Latin America and other areas has given it a greater claim on the national budget and, in general, a status in policymaking circles that a generation ago would have been unthinkable in peacetime. Likewise, the U.S. intelligence technicians and techniques that have been employed to ferret out "subversives" in Latin America have increasingly been unleashed on U.S. citizens as well. The people of the United States are reaping at home what they have allowed the U.S. government to sow abroad. As U.S. Senator Hubert H. Humphrey commented in 1973:

> With Watergate we have seen officials of our government commit criminal acts that strongly resemble the practices and methods directed against foreign governments and other peoples. Counterespionage, coverups, infiltration, wiretapping, political surveillance, all done in the name of national security in faraway places, have come home to haunt us. The spirit and the purpose of domestic policy is said to condition our foreign policy. The reverse is also true.[3]

Like Watergate, the more effectively suppressed Iran-Contra scandal of the 1980s proved once again that a democracy cannot maintain an empire without detriment to the essentials of its democratic character.

The end of the 1980s also marked the end of the Cold War. Soviet leader Mikhail Gorbachev had simply opted out. But as the Christmas season 1989 U.S. invasion of Panama demonstrated with great clarity, the end of the Cold War did not mean the end of U.S. intervention. The Cold War was never the reason for such intervention; it was only the rationale, and a new rationale, in the form of the "War on Drugs," has already been adopted.

Meanwhile, many Latin American patriots remain locked in a desperate struggle for freedom. They seek freedom from abuse and fear, from disease and hunger. They seek the freedom to choose their own leaders and fashion their own policies. They seek freedom, in particular, from the suffocating embrace of the United States.

How such freedom is to be pursued is a choice that must be made by the Latin Americans themselves. But the context within which that struggle will take place—the degree of violence and of scarcity, for example—will be determined in large measure by the stance of the U.S. government. U.S. citizens must be aware, furthermore, that the manner in which the U.S. government confronts Latin America's contemporary struggle for independence will affect not only the outcome in Latin America; it will also affect the level of freedom to be savored in the United States.

NOTES

1. Inter-American Development Bank, *Economic and Social Progress in Latin America, Annual Report 1988* (Washington, D.C.), pp. 9–14.

2. *The IDB* (Washington, D.C.), Vol. 16, No. 9–10, September–October 1989, pp. 6–9.

3. Hubert H. Humphrey, "The Threat to the Presidency," *Washington Post,* May 6, 1973.

APPENDIX:
PROFESSIONAL ETHICS
IN THE STUDY OF
LATIN AMERICA

The authors of these chapters hope that some of the students who use this textbook will decide to become professional scholarly specialists in some aspect of the study of Latin America. Thus, we deem it appropriate that those students be invited to consider the challenges that have been encountered and the affirmations collectively sealed by the contemporary generation of specialists organized in the Latin American Studies Association (LASA).

This document, a set of ethical guidelines, was drawn up by a subcommittee chaired by the editor of this textbook. It was adopted by unanimous vote at LASA's ninth national meeting in 1980, an adoption subsequently confirmed by a secret ballot vote by mail of the entire membership of the organization. The need for such guidelines has been underlined by the course of events in the 1980s.

SUGGESTED GUIDELINES FOR THE RELATIONS BETWEEN U.S. SCHOLARS AND UNIVERSITIES AND LATIN AMERICAN SCHOLARS AND UNIVERSITIES UNDER REPRESSIVE REGIMES

As scholars, we seek to understand our world and to make the great struggles and achievements of civilization more comprehensible to others. But our scholarly pursuits have a larger underlying purpose: to make the world a more hospitable place.

As beneficiaries of a heritage of democratic ideals, we advocate the blessings of liberty for all peoples, not only for ourselves. The denial of these blessings in the area of special academic interest to us is a tragedy that must be addressed by each of us in our own ways. But it also poses a myriad of problems and challenges that should be addressed collectively through the Latin American Studies Association.

The guidelines proposed here are not meant to serve as a general code of ethics for the members of LASA. It is assumed that all members adhere to the professional principles of scholarship in general. It has become apparent, however, that the interest we share in the welfare of the people of Latin America obliges us to address ourselves to the particular problems of conducting research in countries governed by repressive regimes and in an area the United States has long regarded as lying within its sphere of influence.

Our responsibility ultimately is to ourselves, but we also have a responsibility to each other and to the integrity of our profession. The reputation, credibility, and effectiveness of American social scientists have been damaged by the few who have engaged in covert collaboration with intelligence agencies or who have acted unwisely in relation to autocratic host-country regimes.

For more than a decade after the ill-conceived Operation Camelot of 1965, Latin Americanists, through various ad hoc communities, have attempted to dissociate themselves from unwholesome practices on the part of the U.S. government. We were availed a glimpse of the much larger scope of the problem in early 1976 when the U.S. Senate Select Committee on Intelligence Activities reported that the CIA was at that time using several hundred administrators, faculty members, and graduate students at more than 100 colleges and universities for intelligence purposes. Such collaboration makes a mockery of professional responsibility and ethics and casts an intolerable shadow of doubt across our dealings with each other, not to mention those with our Latin American colleagues.

Given the severity of abuses in the recent past, we should take advantage of the current official interest in human rights to make known to our government and society, as to the governments and peoples of Latin America, the principles on which we stand.

Members of the Latin American Studies Association affirm that we accept and will adhere to the following principles:

1. Covert operations and covert sponsorship of open operations have no place in scholarly pursuits. For the sake of the integrity and effectiveness of the profession as a whole, LASA members must shun all projects the purposes and sponsorship of which cannot be openly acknowledged.

2. LASA members must struggle against censorship in all its forms, including the most subtle, most pervasive, and most threatening form of all: self-censorship. We must guard against distortion of our own work and against the suppression by any public or private entity of information that should be in the public domain. And we must guard against giving credence to "disinformation."

3. To the extent that LASA members participate in international exchange programs, or accept funding from U.S. or host-country organizations for research or teaching in Latin America, we must insist that it be made clear to all parties to such agreements, including host governments, that we do so only on condition that our own freedom of expression and of association

be in no way impaired. Furthermore, if we are to participate in or lend our support to such programs, we must insist that applicants be judged on their professional merits, with no discrimination against U.S. or Latin American scholars who have been critical of their own or other governments.

And we should make a special effort to strengthen independent scholars, centers of research, and educational institutions wherever we find them.

4. Where there is any danger of reprisal by host governments, our collaborators and sources of information must remain anonymous unless they choose to assume the risk of being identified. When, in spite of our precautions, reprisals are taken, we are under obligation, individuallly and collectively, to report such actions immediately to international bodies entrusted with the investigation of human rights violations.

5. Honesty—not neutrality—is the guiding principle of scholarship. In Dante's vivid imagination, "the hottest place in hell is reserved for the man who in time of great moral crisis remains neutral." We must continue, therefore, to raise our voices against abuses of human rights throughout the Americas.

ABOUT THE BOOK
AND EDITOR

This textbook, extensively revised and updated in this new second edition, introduces the student to what is most basic and most interesting about Latin America. The authors—each widely recognized in his or her own discipline, as well as among Latin Americanists—analyze both the enduring features of the area and the pace and direction of change. The book conveys the unifying aspects of Latin American culture and society, together with the distinct characteristics of major subregions and countries.

Highlights of the second edition include discussions of a decade of conflict in Central America, the tenuous trend to redemocratization in South America, and the traumatic impact of drugs and debt throughout the hemisphere. Contributors also carefully examine new developments in the second half of the 1980s, such as the emphasis on the export sector, a trend to privatization, general retrenchment with regard to social welfare programs, and the recognition that distinctive ecological zones are threatened. The expanding influence of Latin American intellectual, literary, and artistic contributions is also given special attention.

Jan Knippers Black teaches at the Monterey Institute of International Studies and is research professor of sociology at the University of the Pacific in Stockton, California. Previously, she has served as research professor of Public Administration at the University of New Mexico and as senior research scientist and chair of the Latin American Research Team in the Foreign Area Studies Division of American University.

ABOUT THE CONTRIBUTORS

Diego Abente is associate professor of political science at Miami University, Ohio. He is the author of several articles on the politics of Paraguay, Uruguay, and Venezuela that have appeared in scholarly journals, including *Comparative Politics, Latin American Research Review, Journal of Latin American Studies, Journal of Interamerican Studies,* and *The Americas.* He is currently working on a book on the politics of Paraguay.

Peter Bakewell is professor of history at Emory University in Atlanta. He has taught previously at Cambridge University and at the University of New Mexico, where he also served as associate editor of the *Hispanic American Historical Review.* Among his many publications are definitive studies of colonial-era silver mining in Mexico and Bolivia.

Jan Knippers Black teaches at the Monterey Institute of International Studies and is research professor of sociology at the University of the Pacific. Previously she was research professor of public administration at the University of New Mexico and senior research scientist and chairman of the Latin American Research Team in the Foreign Area Studies Division of American University. A former Peace Corps volunteer in Chile, she holds a Ph.D. in international studies from American University in Washington, D.C. Her publications include *United States Penetration of Brazil* (1977); *Sentinels of Empire: The United States and Latin American Militarism* (1986); *The Dominican Republic: Politics and Development in an Unsovereign State* (1986); and *Development in Theory and Practice: Bridging the Gap* and *Development on a Human Scale* (both forthcoming, Westview Press). She has also edited and coauthored several books and published dozens of chapters and articles in reference books and anthologies, journals, magazines, and newspapers.

E. Bradford Burns is professor of history at the University of California, Los Angeles. Since receiving his Ph.D. from Columbia University, he has spent thirty years studying Latin America, particularly Brazil. He has traveled extensively in the area and occasionally lived there. The author of numerous essays on Latin America, he also has written and edited twelve books about the area. His first, *The Unwritten Alliance: Rio Branco and Brazilian-American Relations,* won the Bolton Prize (1967). Professor Burns has two popular texts, *A History of Brazil* (2d ed., 1980) and *Latin America: A Concise Interpretive History* (5th ed., 1990). His latest book is *At War in Nicaragua* (1987).

Michael L. Conniff, professor of history at Auburn University, specializes in modern Latin American history, particularly that of Brazil and Panama. He lived many years in the region, working with the Peace Corps, USAID, Ford Foundation, and on various research and teaching projects. His books include *Urban Politics in Brazil* (1981), *Latin American Populism in Comparative Perspective* (1982), *Black Labor on a White Canal* (1985), *Modern Brazil* (1989) with Frank McCann, and *The U.S.-Panamanian Alliance* (1991). He is presently working on a monograph about the populists of Brazil in the 1945–1964 period and on a textbook on African-American history.

José Z. García is professor of political science and director of the Latin American Institute at New Mexico State University in Las Cruces. He has lived in Ecuador and Peru and has done extensive research on military factionalism in Peru. More recently, he has been researching the military in Central America; he is currently working on a book on the Salvadoran military. Professor García is experienced also in practical politics; he served for several years as chairman of the Democratic Party of New Mexico's Doña Ana County.

William P. Glade is professor of economics and former director of the Institute of Latin American Studies at the University of Texas, Austin. Before assuming those positions in 1971, he taught at the University of Maryland and at the University of Wisconsin, Madison. For eight years, Professor Glade was involved with the Council for International Exchange of Scholars. He has also been active in the Latin American Studies Association (Executive Council, vice-president, and president). In 1982, he was designated chairman of the Academic Council of the Wilson Center's Latin American Program at the Smithsonian Institution, a post he held until September 1987, when he became senior program associate in the Wilson Center. From January to August 1989, he served as acting secretary of the program, leaving to accept a presidential appointment as Associate Director for Educational and Cultural Affairs in the United States Information Agency.

Alfonso Gonzalez is professor of geography at the University of Calgary (Alberta, Canada). Since receiving his Ph.D. from the University of Texas, Austin, he has been on the faculty at San Diego State College, Northeast Louisiana State College, Southern Illinois University, and the University of South Florida, where he served as chairman of the Department of Geography. Professor Gonzales has specialized in Latin American geography with particular attention to population, settlement, and socioeconomic development.

He has performed field and archival research in several areas of Hispanic America, particularly the coastal region of southwestern Mexico, and has presented and published numerous professional papers.

Mary Grizzard received a B.A. in European history from Rice University and a Ph.D. in history of art from the University of Michigan. She has been teaching Spanish colonial and modern Latin American art history at the University of New Mexico since 1979. She is the author of three books and numerous articles on Spanish, Spanish colonial, and modern Latin American art in a variety of publications, including the *Art Bulletin* and *Revue du Louvre*. She was a visiting professor at the Universidad Nacional Autónoma de México, Mexico City, in 1987 and 1990.

Fred R. Harris, a former member of the U.S. Senate (D-Oklahoma, 1964–1972), is a professor of political science at the University of New Mexico, teaching U.S. politics and U.S.-Mexico relations. He has been a Fulbright Scholar in Mexico (1981), a visiting professor at the Universidad Nacional Autónoma de México (1982), a Distinguished Fulbright Lecturer in Uruguay (1989), and has taught and lectured extensively in Mexico and Latin America. He is the author of twelve books, including an introductory university text, *America's Government* (with Gary Wasserman), now in its fourth edition, and *Estudios sobre Estados Unidos y su Relación Bilateral con México,* with David Cooper.

Tamara Holzapfel is professor emeritus of Spanish and former chairman of the Department of Modern and Classical Languages at the University of New Mexico. Her numerous publications on Spanish American literature have appeared in *Hispania, Revista Iberoamericana, Latin American Theatre Review, Modern Drama,* and other scholarly journals. She has collaborated as book editor and has contributed chapters to anthologies of literary criticism. She is past associate editor of the *Latin American Research Review* and continues to serve on the editorial boards of the *Latin American Theatre Review* and *Studies in Twentieth Century Literature.*

Eldon Kenworthy is associate professor of government at Cornell University and a member of the Latin American Program there. His early writing concerned Argentina and the processes of coalition building under Latin American conditions. In recent years, he has published articles on U.S. policy toward Central America, including one in *Reagan Versus the Sandinistas,* a 1987 collection edited by Thomas Walker (Westview Press). Kenworthy's writings on this topic also have appeared in *World Policy Journal, Current History, Bulletin of the Atomic Scientists,* and *Democracy.* During the 1980s Kenworthy visited both Costa Rica and Nicaragua. He holds a B.A. from Oberlin College and a Ph.D. from Yale University.

Anthony P. Maingot is professor of sociology and editor of *Hemisphere* at Florida International University (Miami). He has previously taught at Yale University and at the University of the West Indies in Trinidad and served as acting dean of International Affairs at Florida International. A citizen of Trinidad, Professor Maingot studied at the University of Puerto Rico and the University of California, Los Angeles, before receiving his Ph.D. from the University of Florida. He was a member of the Constitutional Reform Commission of Trinidad and Tobago from 1971 to 1974 and president of the Caribbean Studies Association, 1982–1983.

John D. Martz has written or edited sixteen books plus numerous articles, many of which deal with the Andean republics. His most recent book is *United States Policy in Latin America* (1988). Since 1988 he has served as editor of *Studies in Comparative International Development*. He was editor of *Latin American Research Review* from 1975 to 1980. He is presently professor of political science at Pennsylvania State University and was previously on the faculty of the University of North Carolina, where he earned his Ph.D.

Gilbert W. Merkx is professor of sociology and director of the Latin American Institute at the University of New Mexico. He is also currently serving as editor of the *Latin American Research Review*. Born in Venezuela, Professor Merkx did his undergraduate work at Harvard and received his Ph.D. from Yale. His research has included a study of economic trends and the incidence of coups d'état in Argentina.

Richard Millett is professor of history and chairman of the Latin American Studies Committee at Southern Illinois University, Edwardsville. Professor Millett, who earned his Ph.D. at the University of New Mexico, is author of *Guardians of the Dynasty* (1977) and coeditor of *The Restless Caribbean: Changing Patterns of International Relations* (1979). A regular visitor to Central America, he has made frequent appearances on national television interview programs and before congressional committees to testify on the crisis in that area.

Martin C. Needler is dean of the School of International Studies at the University of the Pacific and senior associate member, St. Antony's College, Oxford. He has previously held teaching positions at Dartmouth College, the University of Michigan, and the University of New Mexico and postdoctoral fellowships or research positions at UCLA, Harvard, and the University of Southampton. He has published thirteen books, principally on Latin American politics and U.S. foreign policy, including *Political Development in Latin America* (1968), *Politics and Society in Mexico* (1971), *The Problem of Democracy in Latin America* (1987), and *Mexican Politics: The Containment of Conflict* (2d ed., 1990). Professor Needler holds a Ph.D. in political science from Harvard.

Jorge Nef is associate professor of political studies at the University of Guelph (Ontario, Canada), where he also chairs the International Development Program. He served as president of the Canadian Association of Latin American and Caribbean Studies from 1981 to 1983. Born in Chile, he studied at the University of Chile, Vanderbilt University, and at the Facultad Latinoamericano de Ciencias Sociales before receiving his Ph.D. from the University of California, Santa Barbara. Among his publications in English are many articles in books and journals including *Latin American Research Review, Administration and Development, International Perspectives,* and the *Indian Journal of Public Administration.* He also edited *Canada and the Latin American Challenge* (1978) and *Repression and Liberation in Latin America* (1981).

James Lee Ray accepted a position as professor of political science at Florida State University (Tallahassee) in the fall of 1984. Previously, he had spent almost a decade on the faculty of the University of New Mexico, where he served as chairman of the Department of Political Science from 1982 to 1984. Professor Ray is author of *Global Politics* (1990) and has published articles in a number of journals, including *International Interactions, International Organizations, International Studies Quarterly,* and *Journal of Conflict Resolution.* Recently he contributed chapters to *Prisoners of War?* (1990) and *The Long Postwar Peace* (1990).

Steve C. Ropp is professor of political science at the University of Wyoming. He holds a B.A. in history from Allegheny College and a Ph.D. in political science from the University of California, Riverside. Professor Ropp is author of *Panamanian Politics: From Guarded Nation to National Guard* (1982) and coeditor with James A. Morris of *Central America: Crisis and Adaptation.* He has testified before both houses of Congress concerning the crisis in Panama.

Karl H. Schwerin is professor of anthropology at the University of New Mexico. Since receiving his Ph.D. from the University of California, Los Angeles, he has conducted fieldwork in several Latin American countries, with particular emphasis on economic and subsistence patterns, adaptive strategies, and processes of culture change. Professor Schwerin has served as president of the American Society for Ethnohistory and the University of New Mexico chapter of Sigma Xi—the scientific research society. Currently he is chair of the Department of Anthropology at the University of New Mexico. He has published four books and numerous papers on a broad range of topics relating to Latin America and tropical societies worldwide. At present he is writing a comparative analysis of Carib social organization and continuing a long-term study on the ethnographic researches of the French explorer Alcide d'Orbigny.

Jerome Slater teaches political science at the State University of New York at Buffalo. He has written widely on U.S. policy in Latin America and other aspects of U.S. foreign policy and international politics, both for academic and general audiences. Among his published works are *The OAS and United States Foreign Policy* and *Intervention and Negotiation: The United States and the Dominican Revolution* (1970). Professor Slater earned his Ph.D. at Princeton University.

Peter G. Snow is professor of political science at the University of Iowa. He has been a student of Argentine politics for more than two decades, during which time he has written two books—*Argentine Radicalism* (1965) and *Political Forces in Argentina* (1979)—and several articles and book chapters on various aspects of the political system of that nation. During the last eighteen years, he has visited Argentina with some regularity, most recently in 1982, when he held a Senior Research Grant from the Fulbright Commission, and in 1983, when he witnessed the elections that returned the nation to civilian, constitutional government.

Fred Gillette Sturm is professor of philosophy at the University of New Mexico. He holds a Ph.D. from Columbia University and has done research at the Institute for Brasilian Studies of Vanderbilt University, the Universidade de São Paulo (Fulbright 1965, 1988), the Centro de Estudios Filosoficos of the Universidad Nacional Autónoma de México (Social Science Research Council fellow, 1966), and the Universidade de Coimbra (Calouste Gulbenkian fellow, 1982, 1983). He is past-president of the Society for Iberian and Latin American Thought (SILAT), an honorary member of the Instituto Brasileiro de Filosofia, a fellow of the Centro de Estudos de Pensamento Luso-Brasileiro, and an "effective member in perpetuity" of the Academia Brasileira de Filosofia.

Brady Tyson is professor of international relations at the American University's School of International Service and the initiator of that school's International Development Semester program. During the Carter administration, he served as a special assistant to Andrew Young, U.S. ambassador to the United Nations. Professor Tyson, whose Ph.D. is from American University, has studied and taught in Brazil, visits that country regularly, and has published numerous articles about its political processes.

Nelson P. Valdés is associate professor of sociology at the University of New Mexico. Born in Cuba, he came to the United States in 1961. Professor Valdés has published five books on Cuba and numerous articles. He is presently working on a manuscript dealing with the ideological roots of the Cuban revolutionary movement. Since 1977, he has traveled to Cuba on more than a dozen occasions. He is also the Latin American analyst for the Pacific News Service. Professor Valdés holds a Ph.D. in history from the University of New Mexico. In 1986 he became the director of the Latin America Data Base, a computerized data base producing two electronic newsletters: the *Central America Update* and the *Latin American Debt*

Chronicle. Professor Valdés is a board member of the Center for Cuban Studies (NY) and the Instituto de Estudios Cubanos (Miami).

Arturo Valenzuela is professor of political science and director of the Latin American studies program at Georgetown University. He is the author of *Political Brokers in Chile: Local Politics in a Centralized Polity* and *The Breakdown of Democratic Regimes: Chile.* With J. Samuel Valenzuela he is coauthor of *The Origins of Democracy: Theoretical Reflections on the Chilean Case* and coeditor and coauthor of *Chile: Politics and Society* and *Military Rule in Chile: Dictatorship and Oppositions.* He taught previously at Duke University and has been a visiting fellow at the University of Sussex and the Woodrow Wilson International Center for Scholars.

J. Samuel Valenzuela is professor and chair of the Department of Sociology and Senior Fellow of the Kellogg Institute at the University of Notre Dame. He was formerly on the faculty at Yale and Harvard universities. He is the author of *Democratización vía Reforma: La Expansión del Sufragio en Chile,* and coeditor of *Military Rule in Chile: Dictatorship and Oppositions,* and of *Chile: Politics and Society.* He has also written numerous articles on the intersection between labor and politics and on social and political change.

Larman C. Wilson, professor of international relations and former associate dean at the School of International Service, the American University, specializes in international law and organization and in inter-American relations. He has been a fellow of the Hague Academy of International Law in Holland and of the OAS's Inter-American Juridical Committee in Brazil. He has done research in the Dominican Republic, Mexico, and Spain. His publications include articles, book chapters, and monographs on inter-American relations; he is coauthor of two books, the more recent being (with Harold E. Davis) *Latin American Foreign Policies: An Analysis* (1975).

INDEX